TALENT IDENTIFICATION AND DEVELOPMENT IN YOUTH SOCCER

Talent development pathways in youth soccer provide opportunities for young players to realise their potential. Such programmes have become increasingly popular throughout governing bodies, professional clubs, and independent organisations. This has coincided with a rapid rise in sport science literature focused specifically on optimising player development towards expertise. However, the decreasing age of recruitment, biases in selection, inconsistencies in the language used, underrepresented populations, and large dropout rates from pathways have magnified the potential flaws of existing organisational structures and settings. Moreover, despite both the professionalisation of talent development pathways and growing research attention, we still know little about the characteristics that facilitate accurate recruitment strategies into pathways and long-term development outcomes.

Talent Identification and Development in Youth Soccer provides an all-encompassing guide for both researchers and practitioners by gathering the existing literature to help better understand the current context of this discipline. Chapters are contributed by a team of leading and emerging international experts, examining topics such as technical, tactical, physical, psychological, social, activities and trajectories, career transitions, relative age effects, creativity, and genetics, with each chapter offering important considerations for both researchers and practitioners. With a dual emphasis on both theory and practice, this book is an important text for any student, researcher, coach, or practitioner with an interest in talent identification, talent development, youth soccer, soccer coaching, or expertise and skill acquisition.

Adam L. Kelly, PhD, is Senior Lecturer and Course Leader for Sports Coaching and Physical Education at Birmingham City University, United Kingdom. Alongside attaining his PhD at the University of Exeter, United Kingdom, Adam is Senior Fellow of the HEA, BASES Sport and Exercise Scientist, and FA UEFA A and AYA Licenced Coach. Broadly, his research interests explore organisational structures in youth sport to better understand the athlete development process and to create more appropriate settings. He is currently collaborating with a number of regional, national, and international organisations across a range of sports, including cricket, rugby, soccer, squash, and swimming.

TALENT IDENTIFICATION AND DEVELOPMENT IN YOUTH SOCCER

A Guide for Researchers and Practitioners

Edited by Adam L. Kelly

NEW YORK AND LONDON

Designed cover image: Getty Images

First published 2024
by Routledge
605 Third Avenue, New York, NY 10158

and by Routledge
4 Park Square, Milton Park, Abingdon, Oxon, OX14 4RN

Routledge is an imprint of the Taylor & Francis Group, an informa business

© 2024 selection and editorial matter, Adam L. Kelly; individual chapters, the contributors

The right of Adam L. Kelly to be identified as the author of the editorial material, and of the authors for their individual chapters, has been asserted in accordance with sections 77 and 78 of the Copyright, Designs and Patents Act 1988.

All rights reserved. No part of this book may be reprinted or reproduced or utilised in any form or by any electronic, mechanical, or other means, now known or hereafter invented, including photocopying and recording, or in any information storage or retrieval system, without permission in writing from the publishers.

Trademark notice: Product or corporate names may be trademarks or registered trademarks, and are used only for identification and explanation without intent to infringe.

ISBN: 978-1-032-23277-5 (hbk)
ISBN: 978-1-032-23275-1 (pbk)
ISBN: 978-1-032-23279-9 (ebk)

DOI: 10.4324/9781032232799

Typeset in Bembo
by Apex CoVantage, LLC

CONTENTS

List of Figures   *viii*
List of Tables   *x*
Contributors   *xii*
Foreword   *xxiv*
Acknowledgements   *xxv*
Testimonials   *xxvi*

1   Disciplinary Approaches and Chapter Summaries:
Introducing Talent Identification and Development in Youth Soccer   1
Adam L. Kelly

2   Technical:
Examining Subjective and Objective Performance Parameters That
Contribute Towards Developmental Outcomes and Career Progression   17
*Adam L. Kelly, Jan Verbeek, James H. Dugdale,
and Matthew J. Reeves*

3   Tactical:
Measuring and Developing Tactical Knowledge and Performance in
Youth Soccer Players   34
Adam L. Kelly, Mark R. Wilson, and Greg Wood

4   Physical:
Considering the Influence of Maturity Status on Physical Performance   47
*John M. Radnor, Adam L. Kelly, Craig A. Williams,
and Jon L. Oliver*

5 Psychological:
   Supporting Psychosocial Growth, Development, and Potential
   Challenges Experienced in Youth Soccer 67
   *James H. Dugdale, Alban C. S. Dickson, Alex Murata, Adam L. Kelly,
   and Kacey C. Neely*

6 Social:
   Investigating Social Influences on Talent and Development in Soccer 84
   *Colin D. McLaren, Mark W. Bruner, Luc J. Martin, Adam L. Kelly,
   Achuthan Shanmugaratnam, and Mathieu Simard*

7 Sociocultural:
   Reflecting on the Social and Cultural Influences on Talent in Soccer 97
   Matthew J. Reeves, Simon J. Roberts, and Adam L. Kelly

8 Activities and Trajectories:
   Exploring Pathways of Athlete Development in Youth Soccer 109
   *Alex Murata, Alexander B. T. McAuley, Matthew P. Ferguson, Martin
   R. Toms, and Adam L. Kelly*

9 Career Transitions:
   Navigating Players from Youth Team to First Team 121
   Sofie Kent, Robert Morris, and Adam L. Kelly

10 Relative Age Effects:
   Looking Back and Moving Forward 132
   Adam L. Kelly, Laura Finnegan, Kevin Till, and Kristy L. Smith

11 Playing-Up and Playing-Down:
   Conceptualising a 'Flexible Chronological Approach' 152
   Adam L. Kelly, Daniel E. Goldman, Jean Côté, and Jennifer Turnnidge

12 Creativity:
   Creating Supportive and Enriching Environments 167
   *Sara Santos, Diogo Coutinho, Adam L. Kelly, Sergio L. Jiménez Sáiz,
   Alberto Lorenzo Calvo, and Jaime Sampaio*

13 Transformational Coaching:
   Developing a Global Rating Scale to Observe Coach Leadership Behaviours 183
   Jordan S. Lefebvre, Adam L. Kelly, Jean Côté, and Jennifer Turnnidge

14 Genetics:
   Understanding the Influence and Application of Genetics in Soccer 197
   Alexander B. T. McAuley, Joseph Baker, Bruce Suraci, and Adam L. Kelly

15	Nutrition: Optimising Development and Performance Through Nutrition *Matthew North, Adam L. Kelly, Jennie Carter, Lewis Gough, and Matthew Cole*	212
16	International Perspectives: Evaluating Male Talent Pathways from Across the Globe *Adam L. Kelly, Chris Eveleigh, Fynn Bergmann, Oliver Höner, Kevin Braybrook, Durva Vahia, Laura Finnegan, Stephen Finn, Jan Verbeek, Laura Jonker, Matthew P. Ferguson, and James H. Dugdale*	228
17	Gender: Disentangling Talent Identification and Development in Women's and Girls' Soccer *Stacey Emmonds, Adam Gledhill, Adam L. Kelly, and Matthew Wright*	263
18	Para-Soccer: Emphasising the Complex and Multidimensional Factors When Identifying and Developing Players with Disabilities *John W. Francis, Dave Sims, Adam Bendall, Adam L. Kelly, and Andrew Wood*	276
19	The Goalkeeper: Highlighting the Position Data Gap in Talent Identification and Development *Durva Vahia and Adam L. Kelly*	294
20	Language Games: Improving the Words We Use in Soccer Research and Practice *Joseph Baker, Adam L. Kelly, Alexander B. T. McAuley, and Nick Wattie*	316
21	The COVID-19 Pandemic: Rethinking Directions for Talent Development in Youth Soccer *Alysha D. Matthews, Meredith M. Wekesser, Karl Erickson, Scott Pierce, and Adam L. Kelly*	327
22	From Knowledge to Action: Bridging the Gap Between Research and Practice in Youth Soccer *Adam L. Kelly and Jennifer Turnnidge*	339

Index   *348*

FIGURES

1.1	Key elements of the identification, selection, and development process in soccer.	2
1.2	Disciplinary approaches that can be applied to talent identification and development in youth soccer.	4
3.1	Occlusion displays for PCE tests.	36
3.2	Representative examples of the virtual environments used in the study.	39
3.3	A visual representation of VR drills taken from the VR environment: (a) rondo scan, (b) colour combo, (c) shoulder sums, and (d) pressure pass.	40
4.1a	The Youth Physical Development model for males.	53
4.1b	The Youth Physical Development model for females.	54
4.2	Responses to six specific questions by players of contrasting maturity status to participation in the bio-banded tournament.	57
5.1	An overview of concepts, sub-categories, and categories pertaining to psychosocial competencies associated with soccer success during adolescence.	68
5.2	Examples of how to promote the development of psychosocial skills in youth soccer using the '5Cs'.	70
6.1	Relationships between task cohesion, psychological need satisfaction, and positive youth development outcomes in youth soccer.	88
6.2	Comparing task and social cohesion among recreational soccer athletes of coaches trained to promote a task-related motivational climate (MAC) and controls (AC and Control).	90
7.1	A map of Italy's regions.	103
8.1	Soccer trajectories within the Developmental Model of Sport Participation.	112
9.1	The individual, external, culture model of the youth-to-senior transition.	126
9.2	The DRIVE model illustrating loan demands, loan resources, individual differences, personal resources and demands, and transition outcomes.	127
10.1a	The percentage of players selected onto a male youth soccer development programme within each BQ, compared to the expected national BQ distribution.	134

Figures ix

10.1b	The birth month distribution of U14 players selected into a male youth soccer development programme in Ireland.	134
10.2a	Birth quartile distribution for competitive female soccer players in Ontario, Canada, aged 10–16 years (longitudinal, 1-year cohort).	136
10.2b	Birth quartile distribution for recreational female soccer players in Ontario, Canada, aged 10–16 years (longitudinal, 1-year cohort).	137
10.3	The percentage of professional contracts awarded based on the total number of academy players within each BQ, compared with the expected BQ distribution based on national norms.	139
10.4	Birth quartile distribution of the ten best male European professional soccer leagues.	141
10.5	Optimum age profile (mean + range) during ATA competitions.	142
11.1	Considerations for coaches and practitioners to reflect upon when selecting players to play-up within the context of the Four Corner Model.	156
12.1	Representation of the Creativity Developmental Framework structure.	169
12.2	Messi, using the referee to create space and dribble past his opponent during a game between Barcelona and Celta from the 2016/17 season.	170
12.3	Main results from the effects of varying the number of creative players in the creative components performed by a control team during a 4 vs. 4 plus goalkeepers small-sided game.	172
12.4	Examples of boundary conditions that coaches can manipulate to emphasise different creative components.	173
12.5	Representation of the Skills4Genius practice design.	176
12.6	Representation of the Skills4Genius practice design applied in soccer.	177
13.1	Full-Range Leadership Model.	184
13.2	Coach Leadership Assessment System—Global Rating Scale (CLAS-GRS).	190
14.1	Progress of genetic research in soccer.	201
14.2	Prominent characteristics of genetic research in soccer.	204
15.1	The key practical considerations for sports nutritionists and soccer clubs to consider when developing nutrition support for soccer players.	222
17.1	Example of Olympic-style weightlifting activities in players before the growth spurt. In this example, coaching used analogies to animal shapes at different points in the lift.	267
17.2	Schematic representation of decision-making process practitioners can employ in the field to help focus training for girls across maturation groups and based upon fundamental movement skill competence.	268
18.1	A comparison of sprint fatigue index, based on talent development pathway and timing of visual impairment.	284
21.1	Key strategies for stakeholders to incorporate while supporting youth soccer players' development.	332
22.1	Applying the KTA framework to youth soccer.	344

TABLES

2.1	Technical test results, including z-scores and t-tests based on age phase (i.e., FDP and YDP) and non-standardised means based on age group (i.e., U9–U16)	19
2.2	Match analysis statistics, including z-scores and t-tests based on age phase (i.e., FDP and YDP) and non-standardised means based on age group (i.e., U9–U16)	22
2.3	Final list of agreed player attributes resulting from an e-Delphi poll	23
2.4	Final list of agreed position-specific attributes resulting from an e-Delphi poll	24
2.5	Comparison between 'reselected' and 'deselected' players for coach subjective ratings of 'skill' attributes	25
2.6	Players per Dutch national youth soccer team from the 2010–2011 to 2014–2015 competitive seasons based on footedness	26
3.1	Age group mean values and z-scores across PCE 'during' and 'post' tests	36
4.1	Maturation classifications for bio-banding pre-, circa-, and post-PHV youth players	56
4.2	Technical performance measures of an U14 chronological age group competition compared to 85–90% bio-banded competition	58
4.3	Benchmarking data from a male English Football League academy for a range of physical tests in youth soccer players of different maturity status	59
5.1	High- and low-order themes describing coach perceptions of the deselection process in girls' competitive youth sport	75
6.1	Relationships between motivation, social identity, and mental health among adolescent male athletes	86
7.1	Age group mean scores for socioeconomic markers	100
8.1	Degree of soccer specialisation and risk of injury	110
8.2	Ingredients of the early sampling pathway	111
8.3	Pros and cons of early specialisation and early sampling	115
9.1	Summary of non-zero coefficients for the likelihood of signing a professional contract	123

10.1	Birth quartile distribution based on gender, age group, and qualification status in European U17, U19, and senior tournaments	138
12.1	Description of the TCSP assumptions applied in youth soccer teams	178
12.2	Description of the six design principles derived from applied in youth soccer teams	178
13.1	Leadership dimensions of the Coach Leadership Assessment System (CLAS)	187
15.1	Overview of studies examining EI and/or EE in HPYS players	216
16.1	An evaluation of male talent pathways based on country	239
16.2	Contextual and methodological considerations for researchers and practitioners based on country	249
17.1	Physiological and motor determinants of future playing success in elite female youth soccer players	265
18.1	Summary of para-soccer impairment-specific squads	277
18.2	The Blind Soccer Technical and Tactical Instrument (B1TTI)	281
19.1	Summary of talent identification literature for GKs	299
19.2	Summary of talent development literature for GKs	304
19.3	Summary of performance tracking literature for GKs	309
21.1	Sample quotes from each stakeholder when reflecting on the aspects of the PAF	334
22.1	Considerations for researchers and practitioners when using the KTA framework	345

CONTRIBUTORS

Joseph Baker, PhD, is a professor and head of the Lifespan Performance Lab at York University in Toronto, Canada. His research considers the varying influences on optimal human development, ranging from issues affecting athlete development and skill acquisition to barriers and facilitators of optimal aging. He works with high performance sports teams and organisations around the world in their quest for international success. He is the author of hundreds of scientific articles as well as 12 books, including the forthcoming *The Tyranny of Talent: How It Compels and Limits Athlete Achievement . . . and Why You Should Ignore It.*

Adam Bendall has been coaching blind sport for over 12 years and has worked for the Football Association, acting as the Assistant Coach and Guide to the Senior Squad for over six years, bringing a wealth of experience and knowledge within the international blind game. He is a UEFA B licensed coach and worked with others to create the first coaching manual for Blind Football on behalf of the International Blind Sports Association. Adam has designed and created a small-sided version of blind football to aid the development of the game and help with player recruitment, acting as the lead for a VI Participation and Engagement Project. In September 2022, Adam was appointed as the Head Coach for the England Men's Blind Football Coach and is helping to develop players to perform at a high level in major competitions.

Fynn Bergmann, MSc, is a research assistant and PhD student in the Department of Sport Psychology and Research Methods at the Institute of Sports Science of the Eberhard Karls University, Tübingen, Germany. His research focuses on sports coaching, skill acquisition, and talent development with a special emphasis on team sports. Within his PhD project, Fynn investigates the contribution of different practice and coaching approaches to facilitate football talents' competence development. Alongside his academic career, Fynn is a youth football coach within the German Football Association's (DFB) talent development program. He holds a UEFA-A License and is certified as a goalkeeping coach for Performance Football by the DFB.

Kevin Braybrook, MSc, is Course Leader for the BSc football studies course at Solent University, Southampton, United Kingdom. Alongside this position, he is a doctoral candidate studying at

Birmingham City University, United Kingdom, where he specialises in elite football coaching and the journey of female coaches within football. Kevin has leading industry knowledge within professional football, which has enabled him to achieve the highest coaching award in football, the UEFA Pro licence Diploma. Additional industry awards have also been achieved, 2 x UEFA A licence qualifications across two nations within UEFA. These achievements align industry to academia and support research interests around female coaching barriers, female coaching opportunities ("lone girl"), and talent identification towards players and coaches. These areas of research have been presented across a range of conferences, events, and media within the UK, Egypt, China, and South Africa and have been used within consultancy support towards National Football Associations.

Mark W. Bruner, PhD, is Canada Research Chair in Youth Development through Sport and Physical Activity and a professor in the School of Physical and Health Education at Nipissing University. He earned a PhD at the University of Saskatchewan and completed his postdoctoral training at Queen's University. His research programme, which is funded by Social Sciences and Humanities Research Council of Canada (SSHRC), investigates group dynamics and psychosocial development in youth sport and physical activity settings. Dr. Bruner has published over 80 academic journal articles, nine chapters, and co-edited a book, *The Power of Groups in Youth Sport*. Dr. Bruner has been a mental performance consultant for over 20 years and worked with elite youth and university sport teams, the Canadian Armed Forces, and business corporations. Dr. Bruner enjoys coaching his two daughters in competitive youth soccer.

Alberto Lorenzo Calvo, PhD, is Senior Lecturer at Universidad Politécnica in Madrid, Spain, and a professional basketball coach in Spain (ACB League, Leb Gold) and Great Britain (Head Coach of GB basketball). His research interests explore talent identification and long-term talent development, usually in team-sports, in different areas of sports science, such as monitoring training load and psychosocial factors. He is currently working with high performance sports teams and athletes around the world to help achieve the goals they have set for themselves.

Jennie Carter, MSc, is Senior Lecturer and Course Leader for Sport and Exercise Nutrition at Birmingham City University, United Kingdom. Jennie is a registered practitioner on the Sport and Exercise Nutrition Register (SENr) and has over 12 years' experience of working as an applied performance nutritionist within professional football. Jennie is also studying for a PhD, researching nutrition intake and requirements of professional football players.

Matthew Cole, PhD, is Associate Professor in Sport and Exercise Nutrition at Birmingham City University and has extensive leadership, teaching, and research experience within academia over the last 15 years. His main research interests lie in endurance sport, having initially earned an MSc in sport and exercise nutrition at Loughborough University before subsequently completing his PhD via the University of Kent, investigating the influence of different nutrition interventions on cycling efficiency. Matt currently supervises several PhD students and continues to provide nutrition support to a variety of elite athletes and sports teams.

Jean Côté, PhD, is Professor in the School of Kinesiology and Health Studies at Queen's University in Canada where he served as the Director of the School from 2006 to 2019. He is a fellow of the Canadian Society for Psychomotor Learning and Sport Psychology (SCAPPS) and the International Society of Sport Psychology (ISSP). Dr. Côté's research interests include the examination of (a) the interaction between youth, their social dynamics (coaches, parents, peers), and the environment for the development of personal assets and excellence in sport, and (b) the factors that affect personal development, participation, and performance in sport.

Diogo Coutinho, PhD, is currently Assistant Professor at the University of Maia (UMAIA) and at the University of Trás-os-Montes and Alto Douro (UTAD), Portugal. He is an integrated member of the Research Centre in Sports Sciences, Health Sciences and Human Development (CIDESD)—CreativeLab Research Community. His main research interests include football training interventions grounded on variability and exploring the effects of different rules on players' behaviour during game-based situations. He holds the UEFA A License and has been working as assistant and head coach at different levels of performance (from semi-professional to professional).

Alban C. S. Dickson, MSc, is a sport and exercise psychologist presently completing a PhD at Edinburgh Napier University. Alban's current research explores psychosocial development in youth football. His industry-funded studentship is directed towards establishing an innovative approach to promoting sport psychology. In applied practice, he presently works in professional football and across governing bodies of sport.

James H. Dugdale, PhD, is Lecturer in Sport Science and Coaching on the Football Coaching, Performance, and Development degree at Edinburgh Napier University in Scotland. Prior to joining Edinburgh Napier, James completed a postdoctoral research fellowship at the University of Stirling, working on an Innovate UK and industry-funded Knowledge Transfer Partnership, developing a talent identification and development platform for youth soccer players. James also completed a PhD studentship match-funded by the University of Stirling and Soccer PDP in the same discipline. James' research includes talent identification and development systems, selection and deselection processes and decisions, and performance assessment with a particular focus on youth soccer athletes.

Stacey Emmonds, PhD, is Reader in Sports Performance at Leeds Beckett University, United Kingdom. Stacey currently supervises a number of PhD projects across both men's and women's professional football. Alongside her role at the university, she is the physical performance coach for England women U19s and holds consultancy roles with both FIFA and UEFA. Stacey's research interests include long-term athletic development, talent identification and development, and match and training characteristics in football.

Karl Erickson, PhD, is an assistant professor in the School of Kinesiology and Health Science at York University, Canada. Karl's research focuses on athlete development and coaching in sport, with a particular emphasis on understanding youth sport as a context for personal development. He is interested in the integration of performance, health, and psychosocial outcomes and how interpersonal processes associated with participation in sport influence these developmental outcomes. His work examines the influence of coach-athlete interactions, the learning and development of sport coaches, and the influence of different contexts in which youth sport takes place.

Chris Eveleigh, MEd, is currently Grassroots Manager with Richmond Hill Soccer Club based in Ontario, Canada. Chris was born and raised in England, where he coached with Exeter City Football Club before moving to Canada in 2013. Over the past 9 years, Chris has held a number of senior management positions at soccer clubs within Ontario as well as coaching in the Ontario College Athletics Association with St Lawrence College (Kingston) men and women's team, as well as the University of Toronto, Mississauga, Canada. Furthermore, Chris is a learning facilitator with Ontario Soccer and holds a number of qualifications, including his Canada Soccer A Licence, the FA Youth Award, and a master's degree in adult education. Chris has experience in coach development, program development, partnership development, and player development.

Matthew P. Ferguson, MSc, is a third-year doctorate in sport and exercise science candidate at the University of Birmingham. His main area of research revolves around early specialisation and sport sampling, regarding its determination in sport participation and expertise, along with the use of long-term athletic development models in talent development, primarily in soccer. Matthew earned an MSc in sport coaching at the University of Birmingham and resides in Houma, Louisiana, where he works as Director of Coaching for Houma-Terrebonne Soccer Association and Technical Department Coordinator for Louisiana Soccer Association. Matthew is a UEFA and Concacaf licensed soccer coach who works with players and coaches from club to Olympic Development Program levels.

Stephen Finn, BA, is a UEFA A Licensed Coach and has been a member of South East Technological University (formerly Waterford I.T.) Football Research Group since 2020. He earned a BA Humanities (psychology major) at Dublin City University. He is currently head coach of Longford Town FC's U19s in the League of Ireland and is completing the UEFA Elite Youth A Licence with the Football Association of Ireland this year. A former sports journalist, Stephen has also been a coach and analyst with the Republic of Ireland U18s national team and an assistant manager of the Republic of Ireland's national futsal team. His research into football can be found at https://futsalfinn.wordpress.com/.

Laura Finnegan, PhD, is a lecturer in talent development at the South East Technological University (formerly Waterford I.T.), Waterford, Ireland. She earned an MA in sport psychology and a PhD in organisational structure and practice in relation to talent development in youth football. She has delivered on UEFA Pro licences and US Soccer Talent Scout licences. She has several research interests which span across a range of talent development areas, including relative age effect, place of birth, and football developmental environments, for which she recently received a UEFA research grant to study club environments for 6- to 12-year-olds across seven European countries. She founded the Football Research Group in 2020.

John W. Francis, PhD, is Senior Lecturer in Performance Analysis at the University of Worcester, United Kingdom, and is Course Leader for the Applied Sports Performance Analysis MSc. John is a fellow of the HEA and accredited as an applied (Level 4) and scientific (Level 3) performance analyst by the International Society of Performance Analysis in Sport. His research explores the use of performance analysis within disability/para-sport, having completed his PhD in wheelchair basketball. Alongside his academic work, he oversees the para-football performance analysis provision for the English Football Association, leading the support for the blind and powerchair teams.

Adam Gledhill, PhD, is Course Director for Sport, Exercise, and Health Sciences at Leeds Beckett University, Chair of the British Association of Sport and Exercise Sciences (BASES) Division of Psychology, a BASES Accredited Sport and Exercise Scientist, and a fellow of BASES. He is Editor of *The Sport and Exercise Scientist*, Associate Editor with *British Journal of Sports Medicine*, and sits on the editorial board of *Case Studies in Sport and Exercise Psychology*. He has almost 20 years' applied experience working in a range of sports, including female youth and senior women's football, supporting athletes and teams with needs ranging from talent development to performance enhancement to injury prevention and rehabilitation.

Daniel E. Goldman, MSc, earned an MSc in sport psychology at Queen's University, Canada. His research explored youth soccer players' perceptions of playing-up at higher age levels. He currently works as a high school science teacher in Toronto, Canada. He enjoys facilitating positive youth development in his work as a teacher and a soccer referee.

Lewis Gough, PhD, is Senior Lecturer at Birmingham City University. He is also Course Leader for the Master's by Research course. Lewis has published over 40 internationally peer-reviewed articles in the field of sports nutrition within athletic populations and holds editorial roles with multiple journals. He collaborates primarily in football, swimming, and cycling, supporting professional athletes and the sport science support teams through his research.

Oliver Höner, PhD, is Full Professor for Sport Science, Director of the Institute of Sports Science, and Head of the Department of Sport Psychology and Research Methods at the Eberhard Karls University Tübingen, Germany. His football-related research addresses topics such as talent identification and development, perceptual cognitive and decision-making skills, coach development, and coaching. Oliver's dissertation on decision-making in football was awarded with the research award presented by the German Sport Federation in 2005, and since then, he led several applied sport science projects that were funded, for example, by the German FA (DFB), DFB-Academy or VfB Stuttgart 1893 AG. Oliver is a UEFA A Licensed Coach and Vice-President for science and methodology of the German Association of Football Coaches (BDFL).

Sergio L. Jiménez Sáiz, PhD, is Senior Lecturer at Universidad Rey Juan Carlos in Madrid, Spain, and professional basketball coach in ACB League (1st Spanish League). His research considers the long-term talent development in sports and physical activity in different areas of sports science, such as strength training, monitoring training load, nutrition, sleep, supplementation, and psychosocial factors. He works with high-performance sports teams and athletes around the world to help achieve the goals they have set for themselves.

Laura Jonker, PhD, is an entrepreneur at XOET, which focuses on producing innovative solutions for sports organizations, coaches, and athletes in order to create the optimal learning and performance climate in sports. The theory of self-regulation (i.e., how to foster the use of self-regulated learning skills in sports and education) is the main focal point of her work. Based on her experiences as a researcher at the University of Groningen and as an employee at the Royal Netherlands Football Association and the Netherlands Olympic Committee, Netherlands Sports Federation, she uses scientific methods and insights in all the projects for XOET's clients.

Contributors   **xvii**

Adam L. Kelly, PhD, is Senior Lecturer and Course Leader for Sports Coaching and Physical Education at Birmingham City University, United Kingdom. Alongside earning a PhD at the University of Exeter, United Kingdom, Adam is Senior Fellow of the HEA, BASES Sport and Exercise Scientist, and FA UEFA A and AYA Licenced Coach. Broadly, his research interests explore organisational structures in youth sport to better understand the athlete development process and create more appropriate settings. He is currently collaborating with a number of regional, national, and international organisations across a range of sports, including cricket, rugby, soccer, squash, and swimming.

Sofie Kent, PhD, is Senior Lecturer in Sport and Exercise Psychology at Leeds Beckett University. Sofie has a number of published articles that aim to explore stress, well-being, and high performance across a variety of contexts. She also has a specific interest within the design, delivery, and evaluation of psychological interventions that aim to facilitate high-performance and well-being. Sofie is a British Association Sport and Exercise Psychologist who has provided and continues to provide extensive mental performance and lifestyle support with team and individual athletes across varied demographics, such as junior and senior athletes, professional performing at elite (e.g., international), and sub-elite levels.

Jordan S. Lefebvre, PhD, is a postdoctoral researcher at the University of Queensland in Brisbane, Australia. He earned a PhD at McGill University in Montreal, Canada. Dr Lefebvre publishes in the areas of leadership (e.g., transformational leadership), mentoring (e.g., developmental networks), and mental health sport. More recently, he has been examining factors related to mental performance for coaches in high-pressure situations. In addition, Dr Lefebvre works as a mental performance consultant with elite athletes along with performers in other industries.

Luc J. Martin, PhD, is Associate Professor and Associate Director at the School of Kinesiology and Health Studies, Queen's University. Dr Martin's research interests lie in the general area of team dynamics, with a specific focus on topics such as cohesion, social identity, team building, and subgroups/cliques. Although much of his research resides in the context of sport, he is also interested in other high-performance groups, such as military and surgical teams. He serves as a section editor and on the editorial board for top sport psychology journals (e.g., *International Journal of Sport and Exercise Psychology*, *Journal of Applied Sport Psychology*) and has consulting experience with athletes and teams ranging from developmental to elite levels of competition.

Alysha D. Matthews, MSc, is a doctoral candidate studying at Michigan State University (MSU) in East Lansing, Michigan, USA. Alysha earned a master's degree in kinesiology at MSU, after earning a bachelor's degree at Laurentian University in sport psychology. Her research interests surround the context of youth sport and range from organisational processes, stakeholder education, coaching, and athlete development. She hopes to pursue further research opportunities after graduation and work alongside youth sport organisations. Outside of academics, Alysha enjoys coaching young children through their initial experiences with hockey and tee-ball.

Alexander B. T. McAuley, MSc, is a PhD Researcher in Sport Genomics and Assistant Lecturer in the Sport & Exercise and Life Science departments within the Faculty of Health, Education, and Life Sciences (HELS) at Birmingham City University, United Kingdom. He is the primary investigator of the Football Gene Project, a multi-disciplinary investigation that aims to identify novel genotype/phenotype associations in football, to enhance understanding of the biological mechanisms underpinning performance and ultimately facilitate greater individualised athlete development.

Colin D. McLaren, PhD, is Assistant Professor in the Department of Experiential Studies in Community and Sport at Cape Breton University, Canada. His research examines the social psychological processes of sport groups and the influence on individual and group outcomes. A primary focus of this research is positive youth development through sport. His work is published in leading journals in the areas of sport psychology and group dynamics, and his research is currently funded by the Social Science and Humanities Research Council of Canada.

Robert Morris, PhD, is Senior Lecturer in Sport Psychology and Deputy Head of Sport at the University of Stirling, UK. He is an HCPC Registered Sport and Exercise Psychologist and a senior fellow of the Higher Education Academy. He has several research interests, which span across a range of talent development and transitions in sport topic areas, including dual careers, transitions, and mental health in sport. He is also an applied practitioner in sport psychology, providing support to a range of athletes in sports, including football, rugby union, canoe, swimming, and golf.

Alex Murata, MSc, is a doctoral student studying at Queen's University in Kingston, Ontario, Canada. Alex earned a master's degree in kinesiology at Queen's following time spent at the University of British Columbia (BA psychology) and the University of Ottawa (Hons BA communications). Broadly, Alex's research interests lie in the examination of how adult stakeholder behaviour (i.e., sport parents, sport coaches, sport administrators) can affect athlete experiences, athlete development, and the youth sport environment overall. Outside of his studies, Alex coaches youth ice hockey at a variety of levels and tries to sample as many different sports as possible.

Kacey C. Neely, PhD, is Lecturer in Sport Psychology in the Faculty of Health Sciences and Sport at the University of Stirling in Scotland. Prior to moving to Stirling, Kacey earned a PhD in sport psychology at the University of Alberta, Edmonton, where she was awarded the Governor General's Gold Medal. She is a BPS Chartered Psychologist and Fellow of the Higher Education Academy. Kacey's research broadly examines psychosocial aspects of youth sport, with a specific focus on stress, coping, and emotion in high performance youth sport. Kacey has a particular interest in examining issues related to selection and deselection processes in sport and the impact of deselection on athlete well-being. Kacey is also interested in positive youth development through sport and how positive youth development can be integrated into grassroot sport programs. Kacey is also an applied sport psychology consultant with the Canadian Women's Para Hockey Team and works with various sport organisations in the UK and Canada.

Matthew North, MSc, is a third-year doctoral student in sports nutrition at Birmingham City University, whilst also working as a performance nutrition practitioner in a category 1 football academy, after earning a master's in sports nutrition at Liverpool John Moores University. Matthew is also a member of the registered practitioner on the Sport and Exercise Nutrition Register

(SENr). His main area of research is investigating the current nutritional intakes and energy requirements of academy football players and its interaction on growth and development.

Jon L. Oliver, PhD, is Professor of Applied Paediatric Exercise Science at Cardiff Metropolitan University, where he co-founded the Youth Physical Development Centre. His interests focus on three interlinking themes of long-term athlete development: physical performance, injury risk, and health and well-being of young athletes. Jon has published over 150 international peer-review articles and has contributed to numerous consensus and position statements on youth resistance training and athletic development. Jon has worked with a host of national governing bodies and professional organisations on collaborative research projects and in the development of education materials for coaches and practitioners.

Scott Pierce, PhD, CMPC, is Associate Professor in the School of Kinesiology and Recreation at Illinois State University. He is from New Zealand and earned a PhD in sport psychology at Michigan State University. His research interests focus on the development of psychological skills for sport performance and the development and transfer of life skills from sport. As a mental performance consultant, Scott works at the high school and collegiate level and is involved in the development, implementation, and evaluation of education programs focused on leadership, resilience, and psychological skill development for athletes in sport and life.

John M. Radnor, PhD, is Senior Lecturer in Strength and Conditioning at Cardiff Metropolitan University. His research interests broadly surround long-term athletic development, investigating physical performance enhancement in youth. John is an accredited strength and conditioning coach (ASCC) with the United Kingdom Strength and Conditioning Association (UKSCA) and has worked with youth athletes from a range of sports for over 10 years, predominantly in the Youth Physical Development Centre at Cardiff Met. John has also collaborated with a number of professional organisations and national governing bodies delivering coach education.

Matthew J. Reeves, PhD, is Reader in Sport and Performance at the University of Central Lancashire (UCLan), UK. He leads the Football Innovation Hub at UCLan that encompasses a number of areas of specialism from equipment design and manufacture to injury prevention. Matthew's broad research interest is in the identification and development of footballers, with a particular interest in systems and process within talent development systems. He undertaken funded research activities for the Premier League, Nike, and, most recently, the Saudi Arabian Ministry of Sport.

Simon J. Roberts, PhD, is an associate professor and programme leader for the Professional Doctorate in Applied Sport and Exercise Sciences at Liverpool John Moores University. Simon has a number of peer-reviewed publications surrounding the complexities of conducting talent identification and development research in professional football environments. Simon is currently supervising doctoral talent related projects with practitioners working in the English Premier League and United States Soccer Federation (USSF).

Jaime Sampaio, PhD, holds a position of professor with tenure at the University of Trás-os-Montes and Alto Douro in Portugal. He was the director for the Research Centre for Sports, Health and Human Development (CIDESD, 2013–2021). In the university, he heads the CreativeLab research community and two labs—CreativeLab and SporTech—dealing, respectively, with performance analysis in team sports and technological applications in sports. His current research activity is focused on performance analysis in team sports using complex systems frameworks, having produced several publications in international peer-review journals (h-index 52) and textbooks supported by granted projects.

Sara Santos, PhD, holds a position as a researcher at the University of Trás-os-Montes and Alto Douro (UTAD), Portugal. She is an integrated member of the Research Centre in Sports Sciences, Health Sciences and Human Development (CIDESD)—CreativeLab Research Community. Her main research interests are focused on exploring the influence of enrichment environments to nurture the creative behaviour in youths. Also, she is the mentor of the Skills4Genius program, which was awarded by the Calouste Gulbenkian Foundation and the Olympic Committee of Portugal. Finally, she is the 2018 recipient of the Ruth B. Noller Award. This award supports paradigm shifting research with high potential for impact communities of practice and was offered by the Creative Education Foundation, USA.

Achuthan Shanmugaratnam is a Master of Science in kinesiology candidate at Nipissing University in North Bay, Ontario, Canada. He works with the Groups 4 Youth Development Lab at Nipissing University, where his research interests broadly explore group dynamics and psychosocial development in youth sports. Alongside being a Canadian soccer licensed coach, he has transitioned from a player into an assistant coach for the Nipissing University's men's and women's soccer programmes.

Mathieu Simard is a Master of Education candidate, currently in his second year of his program at Nipissing University in North Bay, Ontario, Canada. He works with the Groups 4 Youth Development Lab at Nipissing University with Mark W. Bruner, where his research interests broadly explore group dynamics and psychosocial development in youth sports. Alongside being a Canadian soccer licensed coach at the U15–18 level, he has transitioned into his new teaching role at the Louis-Riel soccer academy in Ottawa, Ontario, Canada.

Dave Sims, PhD, is Physical Performance and Strategic Lead: Para England Teams and Talent. Dave currently works across all of the Football Association's six impairments and all levels of the para football programme supporting players through physical preparation for training camps and major tournaments. This includes daily monitoring of player activity, nutritional guidance and support, strength and conditioning support, and key physical performance indicator measures. He earned a PhD at Manchester Metropolitan in 2018 and is currently working to uncover and describe the physical parameters of an international para footballer through the use of global positioning system, performance analysis, bio markers, and fatigue analysis as well as understanding and developing strategies to better prepare para football players leading into major tournaments through achieving and understanding the physical characteristics of competitive play.

Kristy L. Smith, PhD, is Lecturer at the University of Windsor, Canada. Her previous work has examined the impact of relative age and community size on female sport participation across the developmental spectrum. She completed a systematic review and meta-analysis of RAEs across and within female sport, which was presented at the 14th World Congress of Sport Psychology.

Kristy's current research interests include athlete development, physical activity participation across the lifespan, and factors that contribute to positive sport experiences for youth. Outside of work, she enjoys spending time with her family, travelling, and sport.

Bruce Suraci, MSc, is a professional doctorate student at the University of Portsmouth, Portsmouth, UK, where he also completed an undergraduate degree in sport and exercise science and a master's in research, which explored different training programmes designed based on genetic profiling. Bruce is currently Academy Head of Coaching and Development at AFC Bournemouth and is specialising his doctoral thesis in mental health literacy of Elite Academy Coaches in the UK, where Bruce's main area of research is investigating the mental health and well-being of elite coaches and elite coaching within soccer.

Kevin Till, PhD, ASCC, is Professor of Athletic Development within the Carnegie School of Sport at Leeds Beckett University. Kevin is the co-director of the Carnegie Applied Rugby Research (CARR) centre. Kevin has published over 180 international scientific peer-review publications over the last decade related to youth athletes, talent identification and development, sport science, and coaching. His research and applied work have led to policy and practice changes within youth sports. He is also a strength and conditioning coach at Leeds Rhinos RLFC within their academy programs.

Martin R. Toms, PhD, is an associate professor and head of global engagement in the School of Sport, Exercise and Rehabilitation Sciences at the University of Birmingham, UK. With a PhD in youth sport and talent/participation from Loughborough University, Martin has been involved in multiple funded projects across sport, talent, and international contexts and is currently involved in international TNE. His interests lie in the socio-cultural contexts of youth sport participation, and he currently works across multiple national and international TNE projects across the world (most notably in India) and with governing bodies and federations supporting the development of grass roots children's sport, talent strategies, and sports policy. His latest edited work is the *Routledge Handbook of Coaching Children in Sport*.

Jennifer Turnnidge, PhD, is Health Education Research Associate with the Office of Professional Development and Educational Scholarship in the Faculty of Health Sciences at Queen's University. She completed her master's and doctoral degrees in kinesiology and health studies. Using both quantitative and qualitative methods, her work focuses on developing, implementing, and evaluating evidence-informed resources to promote high-quality interpersonal relationships and positive developmental outcomes.

Durva Vahia, MSc, earned a MSc in sports and health science at the University of Exeter, where she graduated with distinction. Her research focused on training load in youth football and resulted in published research. An Asian Football Confederation Licensed football coach, she has been the assistant coach for the Indian Women's youth teams and is currently Head of Performance at Reliance Foundation Young Champs, India's leading youth boy's academy. Through her work in India, she aims to improve the youth development structure in the country and hopes to shift the conversation from performance to development.

Jan Verbeek, MSc, is a part-time second-year doctoral candidate in the Department of Developmental Psychology at the University of Groningen specialising in talent development in football. Jan currently also works across the Dutch Football Association's technical department as a researcher supporting player development at all levels, from national youth teams to grassroots football. His doctoral research project includes applying a dynamic bioecological model to better understand the development of players, especially during junior-to-senior transitions.

Nick Wattie, PhD, is Associate Professor and Head of the Expertise and Skill Acquisition Lab at Ontario Tech University in Oshawa Canada. His research examines how complex systems and constraints interact to influence talent identification and development, and expertise development, in sport. His work also explores how functional states and practice structure influence skill acquisition in sport and medicine. He is the editor and author of the *Routledge Handbook of Talent Identification and Development in Sport* and *Sport Officiating: Recruitment, Development, and Retention*.

Meredith M. Wekesser, MS, is a fourth-year doctoral candidate in the Department of Kinesiology at Michigan State University specialising in psychosocial aspects of sport and physical activity. Meredith earned an MS in kinesiology with a concentration in sport and exercise psychology at Georgia Southern University. Her research interests include coaching in youth sport, positive youth development through sport, and measurement in sport and exercise psychology. Upon graduation, Meredith plans to pursue a faculty position that focuses on teaching courses within the psychosocial area of sport and physical activity as well as kinesiology-centred methods courses.

Craig A. Williams, PhD, is Professor of Paediatric Physiology and Health at the University of Exeter in the Department of Public Health and Sport Sciences. He is also Director of the Children's Health and Exercise Research Centre (CHERC), a world-leading centre for the investigation of children and young people's responses to exercise, sport, and health. His applied work on talent development and physiological bases of youth sports performance has involved organisations such as England Athletics, British Cycling, British Gymnastics, and the English Cricket Board. Current projects involve Manchester United Football, FC Barcelona and Canon Medical Systems Ltd examining cardiac functioning in young football players, as well as more locally with Exeter City Football Academy and their youth development squads.

Mark R. Wilson, PhD, is Professor in Performance Psychology at the University of Exeter, UK, where he is also Head of the Department of Public Health and Sports Sciences. He has an applied and theoretical interest in understanding the cognitive and emotional processes that underpin skill acquisition and performance under pressure. As a HCPC registered practitioner psychologist, he works with performers, leaders, and coaches in sport and business to help them perform at their best when it matters most.

Andrew Wood, PhD, is Senior Lecturer in Psychology at Manchester Metropolitan University. He is from the United Kingdom and earned a PhD at Staffordshire University examining the effects of rational emotive behaviour therapy on performance. Dr Wood provided psychological support to several para-football teams within the Football Association, in particular the Blind Squad.

Greg Wood, PhD, is Senior Lecturer in Motor Learning and Control at Manchester Metropolitan University, UK. His research examines the attentional processes underlying the learning and skilled performance of visually guided movement tasks in sport and everyday life. Current research projects are focused on exploring the application of virtual reality for improving performance and well-being in professional soccer, understanding the effects of soccer heading on cognitive and neurological function, and understanding the mechanisms behind movement impairments like developmental coordination disorder (DCD), stroke, and in patients learning to use prosthetic hands.

Matthew Wright, PhD, is Senior Lecturer in Biomechanics and Strength and Conditioning at Teesside University, United Kingdom. He is an accredited sports and exercise scientist (BASES) and a strength and conditioning coach (UKSCA) who has supported the physical development of girls' football players for over a decade, which was the focus of his PhD thesis. His research interests include the assessment and development of movement skills, physical activity, and physical performance in children and young people. Matt's current research spans the spectrum from physical activity and health to high performance sport.

FOREWORD

It is our pleasure to write the Foreword for Dr Adam L. Kelly's exciting book editorial on *Talent Identification and Development in Youth Soccer*. In line with our recent global analysis of the talent development ecosystem, coupled with the creation of FIFA's Talent Development Scheme, this text could not be timelier to help synthesise current knowledge and guide practical applications.

The need for greater global competitiveness in soccer is clear. Born as a 12-team tournament in 1991, 32 nations will compete in the Women's World Cup for the first time in 2023. Coincidingly, the 2026 Men's World Cup expands from 32 teams to 48. It is, therefore, our responsibility to ensure these competitions are even more spectacular than ever and feature finalists from as many FIFA Confederations as possible. In order to achieve these future outcomes, both in the short-term and long-term timescales, it is vital to support member associations to create successful talent development pathways to cultivate their national teams.

Based on our 14-month-long project that analysed talent development practices and organisational structures across 205 FIFA member associations, it is apparent that there are numerous areas for development in order to offer more opportunities for young players. The report found that a large number of talented players go undiscovered due to various factors, including the lack of planning, quality of education, infrastructure, and financial resources to train youngsters. This data-driven project, headed by FIFA's Chief of Global Football Development, Arsène Wenger, has delivered the message that every talented player deserves a chance to be identified and developed.

Having worked in both academic and applied settings, Dr Adam L. Kelly and his colleagues' wide-ranging knowledge and experiences help capture the current research in this field as well as offer practical suggestions to create more appropriate youth soccer environments. The book presents a range of chapters from world leading and emerging experts that allows the reader to reflect upon the many mono-, multi-, inter-, and trans-disciplinary approaches and areas of focus that are of importance to talent identification and development in youth soccer. It will be essential reading for those who are researching and working in this area to advance their understanding and future practices.

Ulf Schott
Head of High-Performance Programmes at FIFA
Patricia González
Group Leader Talent Development Programme at FIFA

ACKNOWLEDGEMENTS

Firstly, I'd like to thank my fellow authors for the opportunity to collaborate and their contributions towards this book. I would also like to acknowledge all the players, practitioners, researchers, and other stakeholders who have participated in all our soccer research and continue to strive for excellence in this field. Finally, I dedicate my contributions to my partner, Arabella, my son, Casey, and my daughter, Angelica, for their enduring love and support.

Adam L. Kelly

TESTIMONIALS

"This book will be an essential tool for those who endeavour to identify and develop top young talent in football. Having worked with Dr Adam L. Kelly at Exeter City Football Club and seeing first-hand his meticulous preparation and attention to detail, he was essential in helping ECFC become a conveyor belt of talent that continues to produce players for their first team and beyond."

Kwame Ampadu, Assistant Coach for CF Montreal, Canada

"Dr Adam L. Kelly has created a comprehensive summary of the research on the identification and development of soccer talent. This text involves most of the leading researchers from around the globe, highlighting the key issues and challenges in this area. I predict it will become the 'go to' resource for practitioners and researchers."

Joseph Baker, Director of the Lifespan Performance Lab at York University Toronto, Canada

"We have been seeking to further explore the minefield that is talent development, and Dr Adam L. Kelly has been a great companion to assist us through this journey. His passion to better advance the experiences and opportunities for young people has been clear. Working with us, he has been professional, objective, and a real ally in navigating this critical topic."

Donald Barrell, Head of Performance Pathways and Programmes at England Rugby, United Kingdom

"When I was tasked by FIFA to find the most talented researchers pertaining to the relative age effect in football, Dr Adam L. Kelly's work clearly stood out due to its novelty, robustness, but most importantly, its impact in football. Consequently, Adam has recorded numerous sessions for FIFA, in which his expertise and knowledge was clearly and effectively communicated. Dr Kelly remains a 'mover and shaker' in this space and I'm sure his work will continue to push boundaries."

Paul Bradley, Football Science Consultant (Various), United Kingdom

"Consideration towards talent identification and development within football has increased over recent times. This book examines the processes which connect research to impact industry through exploring talent identification and development across different environments, contexts, and perceptions. The areas of talent identification and development requires continual review, and this book, influenced and inspired by Dr Adam L. Kelly and colleagues, provides a broad understanding towards the many challenges experienced within this exciting field."

Kevin Braybrook, Senior Lecturer and Course Leader for Football Studies at Solent University, United Kingdom

"I have been involved in a number of projects with Dr Adam L. Kelly relating to talent identification systems in sports. Adam has a tremendous passion for this topic area which is infectious. The research carried out for this book makes essential reading for anyone involved in coaching, developing, or administering the youth game."

James Brayne, Head of Coaching (U13–U23) at Birmingham City Football Club, United Kingdom

"In *Talent Identification and Development in Youth Soccer*, Dr Adam L. Kelly has enlisted an impressive group of international scholars to understand athlete identification and development in youth soccer. The experts provide the building blocks for youth soccer coaches and practitioners to develop better athletes and better people but also to stimulate and advance research on the topic. As a competitive youth soccer coach, this book will be an invaluable resource to shape my coaching knowledge and practice."

Mark W. Bruner, Researcher at Nipissing University and Canada Research Chair, Canada

"Dr Adam L. Kelly has committed himself to the game he loves but specifically to the area of youth development. His focus on this area comes from a deep desire to help young people grow in positive football environments. His work will help those adults responsible for these environments and will shape the future of youth development globally."

Michael Cooper, Technical Director for Football South Australia and Assistant Coach for the U17 Australia Men's National team, Australia

"Talent identification and development is an area of research and practice that has evolved immensely over the last 50 years. During that period, methods to select, recruit, analyze, and foster talent have changed from 'talent detection models' to a more holistic understanding of how talent develops from early childhood to adulthood. This book contains the latest evidence related to the factors that affect the emergence of talent in youth soccer. Each chapter of the book accounts for the dynamic nature of talent, providing some valuable tools for coaches and practitioners. Additionally, the authors of the chapters address the research community by presenting different schools of thought and raising important issues that need further research and clarity. Overall, this book elegantly covers the complexity of evidence-based factors affecting youth soccer talent."

Jean Côté, Researcher in the Performance Lab for the Advancement of Youth in Sport (PLAYS) at Queen's University, Canada

"I have greatly enjoyed working with Dr Adam L. Kelly, both in practical football academy coaching and in an academic university setting. Adam's wide range of experience in both football-based talent identification research and as youth academy coach practitioner make him perfectly placed to lead this text. This innovative sport-specific publication is a particularly exciting development for students such as mine studying for a degree in football coaching disciplines."

Jack Gill, Programme Manager FdA Football Coaching and Development and Lead Academy Coach at Exeter College, United Kingdom

"In an age of youth sport coaches and administrators exercising more 'professionalism' and with career opportunities widening, Dr Adam L. Kelly attempts to make sense of recent and relevant research to aid practitioners in shaping youth sport pathways and best practice. Whilst I have been working with him, he has demonstrated huge passion and expertise in this area, in an attempt to better the development experience for our stars of the future."

Paul Greetham, High Performance Manager at Warwickshire County Cricket Club, United Kingdom

"Dr Adam L. Kelly is passionate about the topics of talent identification and development and I congratulate him on creating this book. Effective talent identification is crucial to all sports that wish to streamline and maximise their resources by making informed, efficient sporting decisions. Effective talent identification benefits teams, coaches, and the performers themselves. Soccer is lucky to have someone like Adam leading this book."

Carl Grosvenor, Head Coach at the City of Birmingham Swimming Club, United Kingdom

"I have been involved in a number of projects with Dr Adam L. Kelly relating to talent identification systems across a variety of sports. Adam has a tremendous passion for this topic area which is infectious. The research carried out for this book makes essential reading for anyone involved in coaching, developing, or administering the youth game."

Mark Jeffreys, Head of Sport and Physical Activity at Birmingham City University, United Kingdom

"Working with Dr Adam L. Kelly in the last couple of years has been one of my professional highlights. Collaborating in landmark events such as ICCE's Global Coaches House Birmingham 2022 and contributing to a guest editorial review on the event have allowed me to experience first-hand Adam's knowledge and passion for all things coaching and youth sport. This new book is a fantastic contribution to the talent identification and development literature at a time when it is most needed. Supporting researchers, coaches, and young people in performance sport is a key priority today, and this new text will go a long way to inform and guide all stakeholders."

Sergio Lara-Bercial, Researcher in Sport Coaching at Leeds Beckett University and Director of iCoachKids, United Kingdom

"Within a very competitive sporting environment such as football academies, developing the young individual's physical attributes enabling them to reach their potential is a key priority. Practitioners working in the field must have a strong understanding of the scientific underpinnings whilst translating this into practice. Dr Adam L. Kelly and PhD researcher Matthew North clearly demonstrate this within their research and the collaborative work we have done within the club

around nutritional research. Subsequently, our provisions, practices, and delivery of information has greatly improved aiding the young players development."
Dave Morrison, Head of Academy Sports Science at Wolverhampton Wanderers Football Club, United Kingdom

"This publication is a welcome addition to the topic of talent identification and development. Dr Adam L. Kelly and colleagues explore a range of key themes facing practitioners in talent pathways, and the insightful discussions are equally valuable for a range of sporting domains."
Alun Powell, National Talent Manager at the England and Wales Cricket Board, United Kingdom

"Dr Adam L. Kelly's extensive knowledge and innovative approach built the foundations for our 6-strand sports science model, which includes the highly acclaimed small-sided games conditioning programme. This model continues to deliver excellent results, alongside praise and recognition from external auditors as part of the EPPP. His work and research on growth and maturation as well as the relative age effect was way ahead of its time and has significantly contributed to the success of the Exeter City FC Academy in identifying and developing players for the professional game. As a friend and former colleague, I'm very proud to see the positive impact that Dr Kelly continues to provide for athlete development across youth and elite sport."
Arran Pugh, Academy Manager at Exeter City Football Club, United Kingdom

"I have had the great pleasure of collaborating with Dr Adam L. Kelly on the first mixed-methods study to investigate relative age effects in the Gaelic Athletic Association (GAA). The findings of this study have been invaluable to shaping current player development and organisational structures within the GAA. This book has important implications for talent identification and development, and, importantly, will act as a guide for those involved in youth sport to better understand the context of their environment and provide a holistic experience for all."
Jamie Queeney, The Gaelic Athletic Association Coaching and Games Development Manager, Ireland

"Talent identification is an increasingly competitive field for professional football clubs, and whilst it isn't a primary objective in the work of the Aston Villa Foundation, it is important that we are connected with our talent pathway and elite programmes for boys and girls. We are active in the space of identifying and educating a new generation of coaches with Dr Adam L. Kelly and his colleagues at Birmingham City University. Part of this education has to be focused on the understanding of talent identification and development, and Dr Kelly's research into this subject provides valuable insights for our students of today and coaches of tomorrow."
Guy Rippon, Head of Foundation and Community at Aston Villa Foundation, United Kingdom

"In my time working with Dr Adam L. Kelly at Exeter City Football Club, he showed a clear passion and understanding for the development of young players into professional footballers. In an elite sport such as professional football, so few transition from youth set-ups into the professional game. Therefore, being able to identify talented players early and provide them with a pathway through to the first team and support their development with a programme that provides effective practice on and off the grass can only increase their chances of maximising their potential and taking the opportunity given to them."

Lee Skyrme, B-Team Individual Development Coach at Southampton Football Club, United Kingdom

"Identifying young people with potential is a vital component of athlete development, regardless of the sport. Dr Adam L. Kelly has been at the forefront of the advances made in this discipline, and has combined a deep understanding of the coaching process with a desire to understand and overcome the many challenges that talent identification presents."

Peter Sturgess, National Lead Coach (5–11) for the England Football Association, United Kingdom

"Dr Adam L. Kelly and I have worked together for a number of years, firstly in the elite talent sector, in soccer academies in England, followed by setting up the Football Gene Project and working with a scientific group looking to better understand how genetic information can be utilised to further enhance talent development, engaging in a number of publications. *Talent Identification and Development in Youth Soccer: A Guide for Researchers and Practitioners* is a vital addition to the literature in a growing but little-understood area that is essential to the future development in the youth soccer sector, whereby we are now beginning to understand the holistic requirements of elite talent and how these can be developed through training and intervention."

Bruce Suraci, Head of Academy Coaching at AFC Bournemouth, United Kingdom

"Dr Adam L. Kelly continues to push the boundaries to understanding and ensuring that sports apply research and understanding to better the opportunity for all. Making sure we use research with direct practical application is critical as we look to better the environment for young people in the sporting ecosystems that we define. In working with Dr Kelly in my previous role with England Squash as National Performance Coach, I see that his deep passion and wish to see application runs clear."

Josh Taylor, Director of Squash at The Club, United Kingdom

"Talent identification and development within youth sport is a growing field, with many youths involved in such programmes. *Talent Identification and Development in Youth Soccer: A Guide for Researchers and Practitioners* provides an outstanding overview of the existing research within the field and provides a range of stake-holders' practical implications for improving practice. The text is comprehensive, with 22 chapters from world leading international authors, and covers a multitude of topics, including the technical, tactical, physical, psychological, and social aspects of talent identification and development to other recent hot topics, including genetics, player transitions to the COVID-19 pandemic. For anyone studying, researching, and practicing in talent identification and development—this is a must read!"

Kevin Till, Co-director of the Carnegie Applied Rugby Research (CARR) Centre and the Programme Lead for Doctor of Professional Practice in Sport (DProf) at Leeds Beckett University, United Kingdom

"Dr Adam L. Kelly obtained his PhD from the University of Exeter in 2018 under the supervision of myself and Professor Mark R. Wilson in the department of Sport and Health Sciences. His thesis, titled 'A multidisciplinary investigation into the talent identification and development process in an English football academy', comprised investigations into physiological, psychological, social, environmental, technical, and tactical factors. This research work was certainly a labour of love, as Adam was also concurrently employed as a head of Academy Sport Science at Exeter City Football Club, as well as being an accomplished player in his spare time. What has transpired since his graduation at Exeter is testament to his productivity and enthusiasm for research, which has not just been confined to football but includes a wider expansion into other sports such as squash, cricket, and rugby. Notable partnerships with leading regional and national organisations have ensued and it is encouraging to read of his approach to embedding research into his teaching. Opportunities like the writing of book chapters and editorials of books and special journal editions have all been accomplished enthusiastically and well received by practitioner and researchers alike. Given the renewed importance of the health and well-being of our youngest athletes, how we identify and develop talent in a pro-active but non-discriminatory and non-abusive approach is paramount. Continued research in this area by researchers like Adam can play a significant role in this approach, and I look forward to Adam contributing further to this field."

Craig A. Williams, Director of the Children's Health and Exercise Research Centre (CHERC) at the University of Exeter, United Kingdom

"This is an important book for a number of reasons. First, there is a recognition that it is very difficult to spot future expertise when looking at current potential. This is especially true in soccer, where some of the more easily measured physical attributes may be less relevant to future success than those which are more difficult to measure. Second, there has been a proliferation of research on talent identification and development in the last few years using various methodologies and access to more longitudinal data. As such, Dr Adam L. Kelly and his colleagues take stock of the current state of knowledge and make sure that this is of use to those for whom talent identification and development are key elements of their job.

Mark R. Wilson, Head of Department for Sport and Health Sciences at the University of Exeter, United Kingdom

"We had the pleasure to work together with Dr Adam L. Kelly on a research project regarding relative age effects in Dutch youth football. His expertise on this topic and his huge network with scientific experts in this domain were of great importance for conducting our modified Delphi study. The research project provided important insights for both science and practice, and supports the Royal Netherlands Football Association (KNVB) in our attempt to decrease relative age effects."

Frederike Zwenk, Head of Research at Royal Netherlands Football Association, Netherlands

1
DISCIPLINARY APPROACHES AND CHAPTER SUMMARIES

Introducing Talent Identification and Development in Youth Soccer

Adam L. Kelly

Introduction

Talent identification and development are rapidly increasing areas of research, particularly in the context of youth soccer. This is coincided with the ever-growing interest from practitioners regarding how to better identify and develop potential talent in real-life settings. However, there are a number of significant pitfalls with our current understandings and practices, such as early selection procedures, relative age effects, maturity-related biases, language games, and underrepresented populations (e.g., female players, para-soccer players, goalkeepers). Moreover, there is often a disconnect between researchers and practitioners regarding how objective data and guiding frameworks can help inform key stakeholder perspectives and facilitate evidence-informed practice.

Despite these possible drawbacks, it is also important to acknowledge that we do not have all the answers, and that a large proportion of stakeholders working in this field have a desire to learn and further develop their existing skillsets. The objective of this book is not to determine what researchers and practitioners *should* be doing or undermine present studies and practices; it is to act as a guide and offer possible considerations from a range of disciplinary approaches that *may* suit each individual in their respective environment. By doing so, it is hoped *Talent Identification and Development in Youth Soccer* will provide academics with a range of suggestions on how to advance this field of literature, as well as provide coaches and other stakeholders (e.g., coach educators, policy makers, support staff) with ideas and information of how they can translate contemporary knowledge into their applied settings.

The purpose of this chapter is to introduce *Talent Identification and Development in Youth Soccer*, through offering the reader an overview of the key processes and disciplinary approaches as well as providing a summary of each of the proceeding 21 chapters.

Talent Identification and Development Processes

Although often used interchangeably (such as the title of this book), it is important to recognise that talent identification and development are separate constructs. *Talent identification* can be considered as the process of recognising individuals with the potential to excel in soccer, whereas

DOI: 10.4324/9781032232799-1

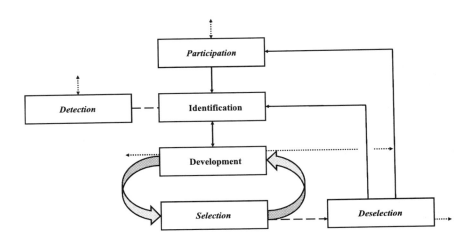

FIGURE 1.1 Key elements of the identification, selection, and development process in soccer (adapted from Williams et al., 2020).

Note: The arrows indicate possible player pathways, whereby heavy dashed lines indicate interlinked concepts and light dashed lines indicate exit or entry routes.

talent development is defined as the process of providing the most appropriate learning environment to realise this potential (Williams & Reilly, 2000). In practical terms, the two diverse concepts are related, since the effectiveness of one could directly impact the outcomes of the other. This interconnection can be explained by the fact that the progression of a player to top-level soccer is multi-contextual and multi-factorial (Dimundo et al., 2021). Thus, researchers and practitioners continue to search for the unique and dynamic factors responsible for optimum identification and development outcomes.

These processes have been dissected by Williams and colleagues (Williams & Reilly, 2000; Williams et al., 2020), who outline the key elements of identification, selection, and development in soccer (Figure 1.1). In addition to the identification and development processes outlined above, *detection* involves identifying those who have the potential to progress into development programmes from outside soccer, whereas *participation* refers to those who play soccer at a grassroots/recreational level for the purpose of fun and enjoyment. Additionally, *selection* involves the on-going process of choosing players who are already in a development programme (e.g., progression to the next age group in an academy, receiving a first team contract), whilst *deselection* refers to the process of removing players from a development programme (i.e., being released from an academy, not receiving a first team contract). These are typical processes that occur in talent pathways, such as professional youth academies (Ford et al., 2020). Since various factors can influence talent identification and development processes in youth soccer (see Sarmento et al., 2018 for a review), it is important to consider the different disciplinary approaches for research and practice.

Disciplinary Approaches

Traditionally, research methodologies in youth soccer would adopt a *mono-disciplinary* (i.e., working within a single discipline) approach, whereby a single area is explored. Hence, this book has focused on exploring such disciplinary approaches in youth soccer during the opening part of the book (e.g., technical, tactical, physical, psychological, social) to gain a deeper insight into specific topics. However, an obvious pitfall of using a mono-disciplinary approach is that it does not consider other factors (Barraclough et al., 2022); therefore, considering a broader range of aspects is warranted to better understand some of the more complex and interconnected processes during talent identification and development (e.g., activities and trajectories, career transitions, relative age effects, genetics).

Although various factors have been identified that influence talent identification and development processes in youth soccer, few *multi-disciplinary* (i.e., viewing one discipline from another) studies exist (Kelly et al., 2022b). Indeed, only recently have researchers and practitioners focused their attention on multi-disciplinary approaches to capture a variety of factors that could influence talent identification and development processes. One practically focused model that is particularly relevant to talent identification and development processes in youth soccer is the Four Corner Model (FCM) (The Football Association, 2020). The FCM is often adopted in professional soccer clubs and organisations, which advocates the assessment and development of players according to: (a) technical/tactical, (b) physical, (c) psychological, and (d) social attributes. Towlson et al. (2019) applied the FCM to their qualitative methodology when examining the perceived importance practitioners placed on the four sub-components during player selection in English academy soccer. Whilst the authors showed that the psychological sub-component was rated significantly higher than the other three sub-components, they also demonstrated the usefulness of considering the FCM from both a theoretical and practical perspective. This approach has been adopted in this book to explain some of the multi-disciplinary processes during talent identification and development (e.g., playing-up and playing-down, para-soccer). Although such multi-disciplinary approaches are useful to outline various factors in a practitioner-friendly manner, they often fail to appreciate how each of the element's influence, interact, or constrain each other. This is particularly relevant when contextual factors, such as ability, age, birthplace, gender, nationality, and playing position impact the external validity of research and practice across different populations (McAuley et al., 2021a).

Academics in this field of research have called for more *inter-disciplinary* (i.e., integrating knowledge and methods from different disciplines; see Piggott et al., 2019 for a review) and *trans-disciplinary* (i.e., unifying frameworks beyond disciplines; see Toohey et al., 2018 for a review) approaches. The involvement of practitioners, or non-academics, is seen as one of the most important features that distinguishes a trans-disciplinary approach from an inter-disciplinary approach (Stember, 1991). The inter-disciplinary and trans-disciplinary nature of talent identification and development processes are reflected in several theoretical models (e.g., biopsychosocial perspective, Collins & MacNamara, 2017; constraints-led approach, Davids et al., 2007; Personal Assets Framework, Côté et al., 2014). Using theoretical approaches can help encapsulate various 'mono-disciplinaries' and explain how they can influence, interact, and/or constrain one another based on the specific context. It also considers how they can integrate and involve different stakeholders from both within and beyond disciplinary perspectives to create new areas of knowledge and applied tools (Graham et al., 2006). Throughout this book, various chapters apply theoretical frameworks to capture the inter-disciplinary and trans-disciplinary nature of talent identification and development processes (e.g., creativity, gender, the COVID-19 pandemic). Overall, it is hoped that the proceeding chapters provide the reader with ideas or information from different disciplines in youth soccer to consider in their future research and practice (Figure 1.2).

4 Adam L. Kelly

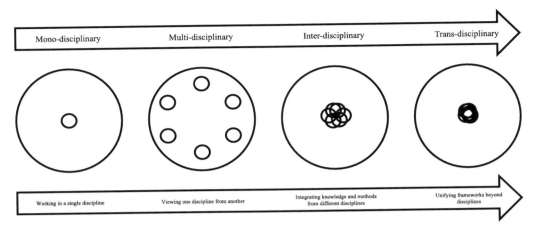

FIGURE 1.2 Disciplinary approaches that can be applied to talent identification and development in youth soccer (adapted from Stember, 1991).

Chapter Summaries

Only by involving end-users (e.g., practitioners, policymakers, stakeholders) in the process of knowledge creation can the proposed solutions be socially relevant, supported, and implemented (see Chapter 22). Therefore, a logical approach for this book was to develop a guide for both researchers and practitioners to help encourage collaboration and knowledge mobilisation. Each chapter is comprised of a consistent structure, which includes an introduction to its topic, a discussion of the key elements, considerations for researchers and practitioners, and concluding comments. In doing so, it was hoped the consistency ensured every chapter captured the most important aspects of their respective discipline, as well as clearly outlined future directions for both researchers and practitioners. The following is a summary of each chapter to offer the reader with an overview of the proceeding contents.

Chapter 2—Technical

Soccer is a sport that is comprised of many complex technical actions. In the context of youth soccer, these features have historically been measured and evaluated subjectively through the 'coach's eye' (Lath et al., 2021). However, objective tools are becoming increasingly more common to help compliment coaches' opinions (see McCalman et al., 2021 for a review), particularly since resources and technologies continue to evolve. Moreover, current research has illustrated how the technical demands of contemporary soccer have enhanced significantly in recent years (e.g., Zhou et al., 2020), which may have important implications on talent identification and development at youth levels. Thus, the purpose of this chapter is to underscore the subjective and objective performance parameters that contribute towards developmental outcomes and career progression in youth soccer. Specifically, the current literature is synthesised and focused on four key areas: (a) technical testing, (b) performance analysis, (c) indicators of potential and recruiter perspectives, and (d) laterality. Following the overview of these technical fields, possible directions for future research and considerations for applied practice are proposed.

Chapter 3—Tactical

The world's greatest professional soccer players are able to make effective decisions in unpredictable and pressurised situations. Determining more effective ways of assessing complex tactical skills is a difficult but important goal in helping to develop these attributes in youth soccer players (see Rechenchosky et al., 2021 for a review). There is also an increased interest in the application of contemporary virtual technologies in both the study and real-world practice of tactical skills (Wood et al., 2021). As such, the purpose of this chapter is to explore the current methodologies used to measure and develop tactical skills in youth soccer players. These are grouped as those focusing on: (a) tactical knowledge (derived from self-reports and perceptual-cognitive tests), (b) tactical performance (generally measured through game-based scenarios), and (c) virtual reality (computer-generated technology). Lastly, considerations for researchers and practitioners are offered in an attempt to advance this field of literature as well as the practical application of developing tactical skills, respectively.

Chapter 4—Physical

It is widely acknowledged that the attributes associated with maturity status play a significant role in the identification of potentially talented athletes, their retention within development pathways, and ultimately, their ability to achieve senior professional status (see Kelly & Williams, 2020 for a review). However, it is only more recently that strategies to determine and moderate disparities of maturity status between individuals of the same chronological age have become more popular (e.g., Cumming et al., 2017; Lloyd & Oliver, 2012). In light of the growing popularity of these strategies within both research and practice, this chapter provides an overview of the existing literature and practical considerations in the context of youth soccer. First, growth and maturation are defined, whilst the benefits and drawbacks of current methods for monitoring these processes are provided. Secondly, the discussion focuses on the impact of growth and maturation on physical performance and its subsequent influence on talent identification and development outcomes in both boys and girls. Third, the influence of maturation on injury risk is outlined, as well as conditions to protect players against potential maturity-related injury risks. Fourth, the strategies that have been proposed to accommodate for individual differences in growth and maturation are outlined, with a particular focus on the effectiveness of 'bio-banding' as an alternative grouping approach. Finally, potential areas for future research and key implications for practice are proposed.

Chapter 5—Psychological

Childhood and adolescence provide an opportunity for coaches and practitioners to positively impact the development and lives of youth athletes, as well as establish habits and behaviours to help youth cope with the inevitable highs and lows of being a competitive sportsperson (see Gledhill et al., 2017 for a review). Accordingly, this chapter provides an overview of psychological considerations for those working with young players towards the overarching aim of improving talent identification and development within the context of youth soccer. First, this chapter discusses psychosocial considerations pertinent to youth soccer populations. The general challenges and processes associated with childhood and adolescence are considered, along with those introduced (or magnified) via sport and athletic development. Second, the influence that external stakeholders (i.e., parents, coaches, and peers) may have on the psychosocial development of youth soccer players and how this may change throughout adolescence are discussed. Third, as youth soccer players approach transition to senior and professional sport, challenges associated with selection, deselection, and dropout in sport, including the potential psychological distress experienced during deselection and dropout, are outlined. Finally, recommendations for future research, along with limitations of existing literature, are identified, as well as practical applications and suggestions to help mitigate some of these issues in practice.

Chapter 6—Social

Talent and development in soccer are more typically considered from a technical, tactical, physical, and/or psychological perspective, with the social influences at play within a team often being overlooked. Despite its limited attention in the soccer literature, the importance of considering the social environment of a group is certainly not a novel suggestion, as it has been written about for nearly a century. In his field theory, Lewin (1939) posited that to understand individual behaviour, we must factor all 'fields' at play within the environment (e.g., physiological, psychological, and social). In this chapter, the importance and prevalence of groups and group membership are outlined before introducing and describing specific social constructs. These constructs provide a broad view of social influences as a function of internalising team membership (social identity), perceiving group unity (group cohesion), and considering performance-related interactions with important social agents (motivational climate). The chapter concludes with recommendations for future research and key takeaways for practitioners working in youth soccer.

Chapter 7—Sociocultural

Soccer occupies a unique position in society. Its global growth is, arguably, why and how it is able to assert influence and is chosen by nation states to exert soft power. The impact of globalisation has, undoubtedly, affected the costs associated with player transfers. Clubs have, therefore, sought to identify and develop players who can play in their first team. The social and cultural influences that affect the identification and development of talent in soccer are many and broad (see Reeves et al., 2018 for a review). Following a contextual overview, this chapter is comprised of three key sociocultural areas relevant to youth soccer: (a) sociodemographic influences, (b) cultural backgrounds, and (c) birthplace effects. Following these sections, considerations for researchers and practitioners are offered to advance this field of research and underscore key take-home messages. Most notably, although the impact of these areas is becoming better understood, it is important to recognise that social and cultural issues do not occur in isolation and future studies should attempt to better understand their interconnectedness.

Chapter 8—Activities and Trajectories

Pathways towards expertise in soccer can differ due to the diverse activities and trajectories that players engage in throughout childhood and adolescence (Côté et al., 2020). As in many other sports, researchers and youth soccer stakeholders are currently faced with a myriad of issues surrounding the competing developmental pathways of *early specialisation* (see Mosher et al., 2020 for a review) and *early sampling* (see Murata et al., 2021 for a review). For these individuals, early specialisation can be summarised as the intensified participation in soccer and soccer-specific training to the exclusion of other activities, whereas early sampling could be described as participation in soccer as well as a variety of other sports at varying levels of competition and intensity. A large and continually growing body of research exists describing both the benefits and drawbacks of each contrasting developmental pathway. The purpose of the present chapter is to assess prominent works within this literature in an attempt to help those involved with youth soccer programming (e.g., athletes, parents, coaches, administrators) to make informed decisions around what optimal participation might look like. Evidence outlining how each trajectory relates to player's overall personal development as well as their soccer specific development is discussed. Based on the evidence presented, considerations for researchers and practitioners are offered.

Chapter 9—Career Transitions

In England alone, there is an estimated 12,500 young players aged between nine and 16 years contracted to professional soccer academies. These players will encounter several critical career transitions throughout their lifespan that can potentially threaten their well-being and performance (Sothern & O'Gorman, 2021). With this in mind, this chapter will present three key career transitions, including: (a) deselection, (b) youth-to-senior, and (c) loans. In doing so, a definition, description, and comprehensive overview of each transition will be offered. Following this, the chapter presents considerations for future research, particularly regarding the utilisation of stress-based models and theories to design, deliver, and evaluate various interventions. From an applied perspective, this chapter will also offer key implications for practitioners to better support the transition experiences of academy soccer players that may influence both well-being and performance.

Chapter 10—Relative Age Effects

A common practice in youth soccer is to organise players into annual age groups using fixed cut-off dates. Such practices often result in 'relative age effects' (RAEs), which create an overrepresentation of players born at the beginning of the cut-off date and an underrepresentation of players born towards the end of the cut-off date (see Dixon et al., 2020 and Kelly et al., 2021 for editorials). Due to the increasing studies exploring RAEs in soccer, the purpose of this chapter is to synthesise the current literature to outline the contextual factors that impact RAEs, as well as offer possible solutions. As such, this chapter explores: (a) male youth soccer, (b) female youth soccer, (c) senior soccer, and (d) potential relative age solutions. Looking back at the existing literature, RAEs appear prevalent throughout both male and female youth soccer across the globe. Specifically, contextual factors (e.g., age, competition level, country, gender, playing position) as well as organisational structures (e.g., soccer clubs, governing bodies) and key stakeholders (e.g., coaches, scouts) can influence the extent to which RAEs occur. Further, it appears inconsistencies arise when exploring RAEs in senior levels, including the 'underdog hypothesis' and 'knock-on effects' on career success. Moving forward, researchers and practitioners are encouraged to work collaboratively to consider: (a) incorporating theoretical frameworks as part of their research methodologies to help better understand the explanatory factors of RAEs, (b) conducting qualitative and prospective studies to explore stakeholder perspectives and the long-term implications of RAEs, and (c) developing, implementing, and evaluating possible relative age solutions.

Chapter 11—Playing-Up and Playing-Down

There is often pressure from key stakeholders (e.g., players, coaches, parents, and policy makers) to search for more equitable competition and appropriate developmental settings in youth soccer. One common solution to these issues is for players to participate at higher or lower age levels (Goldman et al., 2022; Kelly et al., 2021). These practices are generally known as 'playing-up' or 'playing-down', respectively. Despite being widely used as strategies to create more developmentally appropriate settings, little research has focused on the potential outcomes of adopting such concepts in organised soccer (Goldman et al., 2021). Thus, the purpose of this chapter is to explore the phenomena of playing-up and playing-down, as well as to conceptualise a 'flexible chronological approach' to capture the dynamic nature of sport settings that allow players to participate outside their habitual age groups. Moreover, two brief, contrasting stories are offered based on two senior international players' experiences of playing-up and playing-down. By embedding these stories within the chapter, it is hoped that they will enable the reader to better understand some of the practical factors associated with playing-up and playing-down, as well as to recognise the diverse trajectories towards expertise that are dependent on individual circumstances. Finally, considerations for researchers and practitioners are proposed to extend the existing knowledge around the development and experiences of those who play-up and play-down in youth soccer.

Chapter 12—Creativity

The demand for creativity in team sports, and specifically in a highly unpredictable activity such as soccer, has generated great interest from academics and practitioners. Creative players can bring the unforeseeable into the game that can allow teams to keep an edge over their opponents and is considered a key element of performance. Current theoretical approaches highlight that nurturing creativity in soccer should be encouraged throughout youth developmental stages; thus, practitioners must create an enriching and supportive environment for creativity to thrive. The development of creativity comprises long-term work on the part of the young player, coupled with the corresponding planning, implementation, and patience from practitioners. As such, the first part of this chapter frames the concept and presents comprehensive frameworks (e.g., the Tactical Creativity Approach, Memmert, 2013; Creativity Developmental Framework, Santos et al., 2016) to aid creative play to flourish. The second part of this chapter provides a detailed description of small-sided games and movement variability features to encourage exploratory behaviour and complement soccer training tasks. Moreover, in this section, an overview of current evidence-based interventions is centrally discussed. The third part of this chapter offers a review across creativity training programmes, such as Skills4Genius (Santos et al., 2017) and The Creative Soccer Platform (Rasmussen & Østergaard, 2016), to provide further guidance and strategies for soccer practitioners to design for creativity developmental outcomes. Lastly, in order to advance this field of practice, considerations for researchers and practitioners are outlined.

Chapter 13—Transformational Coaching

The past two decades has seen an emergence of literature to support that coaches' implementation of transformational coaching behaviours is associated with a number of athlete developmental outcomes in youth sport. More recently, scholars have advocated coaches can learn to improve their use of transformational coaching in order to foster these developmental outcomes (see Turnnidge & Côté, 2018 for a review). To this end, the purpose of this chapter is to outline how coaches can monitor and improve their implementation of transformational coaching behaviours. First, this chapter discusses the theoretical and conceptual foundation of transformational coaching within the Full-Range Leadership Model Bass, 1985). Second, the chapter provides an overview of the Coach Leadership Assessment System (CLAS) (Turnnidge & Côté, 2019), along with the research that uses this assessment tool to observe transformational coaching behaviours. Given that the CLAS is a comprehensive observational tool primarily designed for research, the third section of this chapter proposes and describes a simplified Global Rating scale adapted from the CLAS (CLAS-GR), which can be used by coaches, practitioners, and sport organisations to observe and monitor coaches' leadership behaviours. In addition, this section suggests various complementary mechanisms wherein coaches can learn to improve their implementation of transformational behaviours, such as the use of mentoring relationships as an educational tool. Lastly, this chapter provides considerations for researchers and practitioners in the context of youth soccer.

Chapter 14—Genetics

Although inherited genetic variants are now generally accepted as influential on athlete development and attaining senior professional status in sport, they are often overlooked and less critically reviewed in the talent identification and development literature (see McAuley et al., 2021b for a review). In light of the general paucity of literature reviewing genetic studies in soccer, this chapter provides an overview of existing research in this field. The chapter begins with a brief explanation of some of the key terms and concepts that are important for understanding this topic. Subsequently, the concept of 'heritability' is introduced and the estimated genetic influence on traits associated with current performance and future success in soccer are discussed. Molecular genetic association studies are then explored, with a critical analysis provided on the most researched and evidenced genetic variant in soccer (i.e., ACTN3 R577X). This is followed by a discussion of the practical application of genetics in the context of soccer, with perspectives from key stakeholders (i.e., coaches, practitioners, and players) on genetic research and testing. Finally, limitations of current literature, proposed directions for future research, and implications for practice are outlined.

Chapter 15—Nutrition

A growing body of literature has drawn attention to the importance of appropriate nutrition to facilitate development and performance within youth soccer (see North et al., 2022 for a review). During youth development, whilst players are aiming to develop their soccer-specific skill set, they are also going through large growth and maturational changes, which can result in anatomical, physiological, and biological variations (Hannon et al., 2020). These growth and maturational changes, coupled with diverse training and competition loads, can result in large and diverse nutritional requirements based on individual needs (Hannon et al., 2021). Thus, it is critical practitioners are able support players to optimise their nutritional knowledge and intake to ensure peak development and performance outcomes are met. The aim of this chapter is to synthesise the current nutritional research within youth soccer by exploring: (a) energy balance (i.e., energy intake vs. energy expenditure), (b) hydration needs, (c) barriers, influences, and enablers, and (d) the female player. Moreover, recommendations for future research and considerations for practitioners are provided.

Chapter 16—International Perspectives

National youth sport culture plays an important role during talent identification and development. Despite its global popularity, nations often adopt diverse talent pathways in youth soccer depending on their country's philosophical approach and individual constraints (Bennett et al., 2019). Therefore, it is important to understand *what*, *how*, and *why* talent pathways operate across different nations and recognise it is not necessarily a 'one-size-fits-all' approach (Sullivan et al., 2022). Drawing from the international expertise of the authors, the purpose of this chapter is to provide an exploration of various national talent pathways in male soccer, including: (a) Canada, (b) England, (c) Germany, (d) Gibraltar, (e) India, (f) Republic of Ireland, (g) Scotland, (h) the Netherlands, and (i) the United States. Each exemplar will offer a critical analysis of the organisational structures that are embedded into their respective talent pathways by exploring considerations such as: (a) population, (b) popularity, (c) sociocultural influences, (c) formal selection age, (d) activities, (e) trajectories, (f) professional opportunities, and (g) specialist support. Finally, contextual and methodological considerations for researchers and practitioners are provided to help better understand the role of national youth sport culture as part of talent identification and development in youth soccer.

Chapter 17—Gender

Despite the increased growth and professionalism of women's and girls' soccer in recent years, there is still a paucity of research exploring talent identification and development (see Curran et al., 2019 for a review). It is widely acknowledged that growth and maturation influence the biopsychosocial development of girls and boys differently, which has important implications for talent identification and development in soccer (Emmonds et al., 2017, 2018, 2020). Therefore, this chapter disentangles gender by providing an overview of existing research in women's and girls' soccer as well as offering recommendations for talent identification and development practices. Firstly, the chapter explains how growth and maturation may impact physical development of young female soccer players. Secondly, the chapter considers the psychosocial development of female players. Lastly, the chapter proposes directions for future research and outlines implications for practice.

Chapter 18—Para-Soccer

Players who participate within para-soccer have highly individualised biomechanical, medical, physiological, and psychosocial characteristics (see Dehghansai et al., 2017 for a review). When compared with players without disabilities, the process of identifying and developing those with disabilities often requires a diverse perspective (Dehghansai et al., 2021). In this chapter, key research findings and implications for practice focused on identifying and developing players within para-soccer are presented using The Football Association (2020) FCM (i.e., technical/tactical, physical, psychological, and social). Specifically, the potential predictors of talent in para-soccer from sports science disciplines are discussed alongside some of the challenges in developing talented players within the para-soccer pathway. To support a better understanding, this chapter adopts a specific focus on blind soccer to help consider differences in developmental patterns between players with acquired and congenital disabilities. Moreover, the need for an interdisciplinary approach when working with players with disabilities is highlighted. Finally, considerations for researchers and practitioners are offered to help improve the knowledge and practice of talent identification and development in para-soccer.

Chapter 19—The Goalkeeper

Although goalkeepers (GKs) are an integral part of a soccer team, they require a diverse skill set when compared to their outfield peers (e.g., Gil et al., 2014). In light of their specialist demands, GKs are often discarded during talent identification and development research in youth soccer due to the different methodological approaches that are needed. As such, there is a limited evidence-base exploring the identification, development, and performance of soccer GKs. To help better understand their demands and requirements, this chapter analyses GKs through three main sub-topics: (a) talent identification, with a specific focus on anthropometric measures and relative age, fitness profiling, match demands, and skills testing, (b) talent development, with a specific focus on training load and training methods, and (c) performance tracking, with a specific focus on contextual factors (i.e., home vs. away, competition level, match outcome, offensive and defensive action, and minute of the match) during senior competitive match-play to help better understand the match demands on GKs and potentially inform youth development strategies. Following these three areas, the chapter offers methodological and practical considerations for researchers and practitioners, respectively.

Chapter 20—Language Games

The past two decades have seen a rapid rise in research exploring talent identification and development in youth soccer. Unfortunately, there are important limitations to the evidentiary foundations of the literature and practice in this area (e.g., Baker et al., 2018; Johnston et al., 2023; McAuley et al., 2021a; Till & Baker, 2020). In this chapter, there is a central focus on the need for clear and consistent language in how stakeholders (e.g., researchers and practitioners) talk about current issues in youth development in sport, particularly within youth soccer. Although the focus of this chapter is on three key areas (i.e., how we define talent, how we consider competition levels, and how we measure early specialisation), the larger rationale for clarity and standardisation is the same for issues outside the scope of this chapter. The chapter concludes with some recommendations for future work in this area and considerations for practitioners.

Chapter 21—The COVID-19 Pandemic

The COVID-19 pandemic significantly changed how youth soccer operated. Key stakeholders (i.e., parents, coaches, and administrators) were required to adapt their pre-existing approaches and create alternative provisions to ensure youth's participation continued (see Kelly et al., 2020, 2022a for a commentaries). Given these unprecedented circumstances, inquiries into how the pandemic affected stakeholders and their implications for youth soccer development is warranted. The Personal Assets Framework (PAF) (Côté et al., 2014, 2016) offers a useful tool to explore the practices of key stakeholders during COVID-19 and related processes of youth development through soccer, as well as the implications it may have in the future. The PAF proposes that development occurs through immediate sport experiences via three dynamic elements (i.e., personal engagement in activities, quality social dynamics, and appropriate settings and organisational structures), which can influence short-term (i.e., competence, confidence, connection, and character) and long-term (i.e., performance, participation, and personal development) athlete outcomes. The purpose of this chapter is to utilise the PAF as a conceptual framework to provide a critical synthesis of the implications of the COVID-19 pandemic on youth soccer development through the lens of: (a) parents, (b) coaches, and (c) administrators. Varying perspectives are synthesised and tensions among stakeholders are presented. Moreover, through analysing stakeholders' reflections, this chapter offers suggestions for future research directions and practical applications to advance the system of development in youth soccer.

Chapter 22—From Knowledge to Action

One of the principle aims of each chapter in this book is to offer a range of considerations for researchers and practitioners working in youth soccer. The purpose of this closing chapter is to reflect on these considerations and encourage researchers and practitioners to work collaboratively by designing, implementing, and evaluating evidence-informed practice to create more appropriate settings in youth soccer. The 'Knowledge to Action' framework (Graham et al., 2006) is introduced to guide the application of sustainable interventions in youth soccer via two processes: (a) knowledge creation (i.e., the refinement of primary studies into knowledge tools or products through the process of synthesising existing knowledge), and (b) the action cycle (i.e., the application of knowledge and skills previously created through informing future policy and systemic change). By embracing innovative approaches to knowledge design, implementation, and evaluation, we can enhance the quality of young players' experiences and, ultimately, the outcomes associated with talent identification and development in youth soccer.

Conclusion

How do talented youth soccer players achieve expertise at adulthood? The identification of young soccer players with the potential to develop and subsequently excel at senior level remains one of the major contemporary challenges for both researchers and practitioners. Indeed, the complex and multitudinous nature of these processes makes it extremely difficult to predict what youth are going to successfully transition to professional soccer at senior level (Kelly et al., 2018). By understanding the processes of talent identification and development as well as the different disciplinary approaches (i.e., mono-, multi-, inter-, and trans-disciplinary), researchers and practitioners can work together and benefit from more accurate informed decisions. As such, the overarching aim of this book is to synthesise the existing literature within this field and broaden our understanding of the methodological and practical considerations in youth soccer to help create more appropriate settings.

References

Baker, J., Schorer, J., & Wattie, N. (2018). Compromising talent: Issues in identifying and selecting talent in sport. *Quest*, 70(1), 48–63. https://doi.org/10.1080/00336297.2017.1333438

Barraclough, A. S., Till, K., Kerr, A., & Emmonds, S. (2022). Methodological approaches to talent identification in team sports: A narrative review. *Sports*, 10(6), 81. https://doi.org/10.3390/sports10060081

Bass, B. M. (1985). *Leadership and performance beyond expectations*. Free Press.
Bennett, K. J. M., Vaeyens, R., & Fransen, J. (2019). Creating a framework for talent identification and development in emerging football nations. *Science and Medicine in Football, 3*(1), 36–42. https://doi.org/10.1080/24733938.2018.1489141
Collins, D., & MacNamara, A. (2017). *Talent development: A practitioner guide*. Routledge.
Côté, J., Allan, V., Turnnidge, J., & Erickson, K. (2020). Early sport specialization and sampling. In G. Tenenbaum & R. C. Eklund (Eds.), *Handbook of sport psychology* (pp. 578–594). Wiley. https://doi.org/10.1002/9781119568124.ch27
Côté, J., Turnnidge, J., & Evans, M. B. (2014). The dynamic process of development through sport. *Kinesiologica Slovenica: Scientific Journal on Sport, 20*, 14–26.
Côté, J., Turnnidge, J., & Vierimaa, M. (2016). A personal assets approach to youth sport. In A. Smith & K. Green (Eds.), *Handbook of youth sport* (pp. 243–256). Routledge.
Cumming, S. P., Lloyd, R. S., Oliver, J. L., Eisenmann, J. C., & Malina, R. M. (2017). Bio-banding in sport: Applications to competition, talent identification, and strength and conditioning of youth athletes. *Strength & Conditioning Journal, 39*(2), 34–47. https://doi.org/10.1519/SSC.0000000000000281
Curran, O., MacNamara, A., & Passmore, D. (2019). What about the girls? Exploring the gender data gap in talent development. *Frontiers in Sports and Active Living, 1*, 3. https://doi.org/10.3389/fspor.2019.00003
Davids, K., Button, C., & Bennett, S. (2007). *Dynamics of skill acquisition: A constraints-led approach*. Human Kinetics.
Dehghansai, N., Pinder, R. A., & Baker, J. (2021). "Looking for a golden needle in the haystack": Perspectives on talent identification and development in paralympic sport. *Frontiers in Sports and Active Living, 3*, 635977. https://doi.org/10.3389/FSPOR.2021.635977
Dehghansai, N., Wattie, N., & Baker, J. (2017). A systematic review of influences on development of athletes with disabilities. *Adapted Physical Activity Quarterly, 34*, 72–90. https://doi.org/10.1123/APAQ.2016-0030
Dimundo, F., Cole, M., Blagrove, R. C., Till, K., McAuley, A. B. T., Hall, M., Gale, C., & Kelly, A. L. (2021). Talent identification and development in male rugby union: A systematic review. *Journal of Expertise, 4*(1), 33–55.
Dixon, J. C., Horton, S., Chittle, L., & Baker, J. (2020) *Relative age effects in sport: International perspective*. Routledge.
Emmonds, S., Morris, R., Murray, E., Robinson, C., Turner, L., & Jones, B. (2017). The influence of age and maturity status on the maximum and explosive strength characteristics of elite youth female soccer players. *Science and Medicine in Football, 1*(3), 209–215. https://doi.org/10.1080/24733938.2017.1363908
Emmonds, S., Scantlebury, S., Murray, E., Turner, L., Robsinon, C., & Jones, B. (2020). Physical characteristics of elite youth female soccer players characterized by maturity status. *The Journal of Strength & Conditioning Research, 34*(8), 2321–2328. https://doi.org/10.1519/jsc.0000000000002795
Emmonds, S., Till, K., Redgrave, J., Murray, E., Turner, L., Robinson, C., & Jones, B. (2018). Influence of age on the anthropometric and performance characteristics of high-level youth female soccer players. *International Journal of Sports Science & Coaching, 13*(5), 779–786. https://doi.org/10.1177/1747954118757437
Ford, P. R., Delgado Bordonau, J. L., Bonanno, D., Tavares, J., Groenendijk, C., Fink, C., Gualtieri, D., Gregson, W., Varley, M. C., Weston, M., Lolli, L., Platt, D., & Di Salvo, V. (2020). A survey of talent identification and development processes in the youth academies of professional soccer clubs from around the world. *Journal of Sports Sciences, 38*(11–12), 1269–1278. https://doi.org/10.1080/02640414.2020.1752440
Gil, S. M., Zabala-Lili, J., Bidaurrazaga-Letona, I., Aduna, B., Lekue, J. A., Santos-Concejero, J., & Granados, C. (2014). Talent identification and selection process of outfield players and goalkeepers in a professional soccer club. *Journal of Sports Sciences, 32*(20), 1931–1939. https://doi.org/10.1080/02640414.2014.964290
Gledhill, A., Harwood, C., & Forsdyke, D. (2017). Psychosocial factors associated with talent development in football: A systematic review. *Psychology of Sport and Exercise, 31*, 93–112. https://doi.org/10.1016/j.psychsport.2017.04.002

Goldman, D. E., Turnnidge, J., Côté, J., & Kelly, A. L. (2021). "Playing-up" in youth soccer. In A. L. Kelly, J. Côté, M. Jeffreys, & J. Turnnidge (Eds.), *Birth advantages and relative age effects in sport: Exploring organizational structures and creating appropriate settings* (pp. 77–94). Routledge.

Goldman, D. E., Turnnidge, J., Kelly, A. L., de Vos, J., & Côté, J. (2022). Athlete perceptions of "playing-up" in youth soccer. *Journal of Applied Sport Psychology, 34*(4), 862–885. https://doi.org/10.1080/10413200.2021.1875518

Graham, I. D., Logan, J., Harrison, M. B., Straus, S. E., Tetroe, J., Caswell, W., & Robinson, N. (2006). Lost in knowledge translation: Time for a map? *The Journal of Continuing Education in the Health Professions, 26*(1), 13–24. https://doi.org/10.1002/chp.47

Hannon, M. P., Carney, D. J., Floyd, S., Parker, L. J. F., McKeown, J., Drust, B., Unnithan, V. B., Close, G. L., & Morton, J. P. (2020). Cross-sectional comparison of body composition and resting metabolic rate in Premier League academy soccer players: Implications for growth and maturation. *Journal of Sports Sciences, 38*(11–12), 1326–1334. http://doi.org/10.1080/02640414.2020.1717286

Hannon, M. P., Parker, L. J. F., Carney, D. J., McKeown, J., Speakman, J. R., Hambly, C., Drust, B., Unnithan, V. B., Close, G. L., & Morton, J. P. (2021). Energy requirements of male academy soccer players from the English Premier League. *Medicine & Science in Sports & Exercise, 53*(1), 200–210. http://doi.org/10.1249/MSS.0000000000002443

Johnston, K., McAuley, A. B. T., Kelly, A. L., & Baker, J. (2023). Language games and blurry terminology: Can clarity enhance athlete development? *Frontiers in Sports and Active Living* [Advance online publication].

Kelly, A. L., Côté, J., Jeffreys, M., & Turnnidge, J. (2021). *Birth advantages and relative age effects in sport: Exploring organizational structures and creating appropriate settings*. Routledge.

Kelly, A. L., Erickson, K., & Turnnidge, J. (2022a). Youth sport in the time of COVID-19: Considerations for researchers and practitioners. *Managing Sport & Leisure, 27*(1–2), 62–72. https://doi.org/10.1080/23750472.2020.1788975

Kelly, A. L., Erickson, K., Pierce, S., & Turnnidge, J. (2020). Youth sport and COVID-19: Contextual, methodological, and practical considerations. *Frontiers in Sports and Active Living, 2*(584252), 1–4. https://doi.org/10.3389/fspor.2020.584252

Kelly, A. L., & Williams, C. A. (2020). Physical characteristics and the talent identification and development processes in male youth soccer: A narrative review. *Strength and Conditioning Journal, 42*(6), 15–34. https://doi.org/10.1519/SSC.0000000000000576

Kelly, A. L., Williams, C. A., Cook, R., Jiménez, S. L., & Wilson, M. R. (2022b). A multidisciplinary investigation into the talent development processes at an English football academy: A machine learning approach. *Sports, 10*(10), 159. https://doi.org/10.3390/sports10100159

Kelly, A. L., Wilson, M. R., Jackson, D. T., Goldman, D. E., Turnnidge, J., Côté, J., & Williams, C. A. (2021). A multidisciplinary investigation into "playing-up" a chronological age group in an English football academy. *Journal of Sports Sciences, 39*(8), 854–864. https://doi.org/10.1080/02640414.2020.1848117

Kelly, A. L., Wilson, M. R., & Williams, C. A. (2018). Developing a football-specific talent identification and development profiling concept—The Locking Wheel Nut Model. *Applied Coaching Research Journal, 2*(1), 32–41.

Lath, F., Koopman, T., Faber, I., Baker, J., & Scorer, J. (2021). Focusing on the coach's eye; Towards a working model of coach decision-making in talent selection. *Psychology of Sport and Exercise, 56*(102011), 1–13. https://doi.org/10.1016/j.psychsport.2021.102011

Lewin, K. (1939). Field theory and experiment in social psychology: Concepts and methods. *American Journal of Sociology, 44*(6), 868–896. https://doi.org/10.1086/218177

Lloyd, R. S., & Oliver, J. L. (2012). The youth physical development model: A new approach to long-term athletic development. *Strength & Conditioning Journal, 34*(3), 61–72. https://doi.org/10.1519/SSC.0b013e31825760ea

McAuley, A. B. T., Baker, J., & Kelly, A. L. (2021a). Defining "elite" status in sport: From chaos to clarity. *German Journal of Exercise and Sport Research, 52*, 193–197. https://doi.org/10.1007/s12662-021-00737-3

McAuley, A. B. T., Hughes, D. C., Tsaprouni, L. G., Varley, I., Suraci, B., Roos, T. R., Herbert, A. J., & Kelly, A. L. (2021b). Genetic association research in football: A systematic review. *European Journal of Sport Science, 21*(5), 714–752. https://doi.org/10.1080/17461391.2020.1776401

McCalman, W., Crowley-McHattan, Z. J., Fransen, J., & Bennett, K. J. M. (2022). Skill assessments in youth soccer: A scoping review. *Journal of Sports Sciences, 40*(6), 667–695. https://doi.org/10.1080/02640414.2021.2013617

Memmert, D. (2013). Tactical creativity. In T. McGarry, P. O'Donoghue, & J. Sampaio (Eds.), *Routledge handbook of sports performance analysis* (pp. 297–308). Routledge.

Mosher, A., Fraser-Thomas, J., & Baker, J. (2020). What defines early specialization: A systematic review of literature. *Frontiers in Sports and Active Living, 2*, 596229. https://doi.org/10.3389/fspor.2020.596229

Murata, A., Goldman, D. E., Martin, L. J., Turnnidge, J., Bruner, M. W., & Côté, J. (2021). Sampling between sports and athlete development: A scoping review. *International Journal of Sport and Exercise Psychology*, 1–25. https://doi.org/10.1080/1612197X.2021.1995021

North, M., Kelly, A. L., Ranchordas, M. K., & Cole, M. (2022). Nutritional consideration in high performance youth soccer: A systematic review. *Journal of Science in Sport and Exercise, 4*, 195–212. https://doi.org/10.1007/s42978-022-00171-3

Piggott, B., Müller, S., Chivers, P., Papaluca, C., & Hoyne, G. (2019). Is sports science answering the call for interdisciplinary research? A systematic review. *European Journal of Sport Science, 19*(3), 267–286. https://doi.org/10.1080/17461391.2018.1508506

Rasmussen, L., & Østergaard, L. (2016). The creative soccer platform: New strategies for stimulating creativity in organized youth soccer practice. *Journal of Physical Education, Recreation & Dance, 87*(7), 9–19. https://doi.org/10.1080/07303084.2016.1202799

Rechenchosky, L., Menezes Menegassi, V., de Oliveira Jaime, M., Borges, P. H., Sarmento, H., Mancha-Triguero, D., Serra-Olivares, J., & Rinaldi, W. (2021). Scoping review of tests to assess tactical knowledge and tactical performance of young soccer players. *Journal of Sports Sciences, 39*(18), 2051–2067. https://doi.org/10.1080/02640414.2021.1916262

Reeves, M. J., McRobert, A. P., Littlewood, M. A., & Roberts, S. J. (2018). A scoping review of the potential sociological predictors of talent in junior-elite football: 2000–2016. *Soccer & Society, 19*(8), 1–21. https://doi.org/10.1080/14660970.2018.1432386

Santos, S., Jiménez, S., Sampaio, J., & Leite, N. (2017). Effects of the Skills4Genius sports-based training program in creative behavior. *PLoS One, 12*(2). https://doi.org/10.1371/journal.pone.0172520

Santos, S., Memmert, D., Sampaio, J., & Leite, N. (2016). The spawns of creative behavior in team sports: A creativity developmental framework. *Frontiers in Psychology, 7*, 1282. https://doi.org/10.3389/fpsyg.2016.01282

Sarmento, H., Anguera, M., Pereira, A., & Araújo, D. (2018). Talent identification and development in male football: A systematic review. *Sports Medicine, 48*(4), 907–931. https://doi.org/10.1007/s40279-017-0851-7

Sothern, N. A., & O'Gorman, J. (2021). Exploring the mental health and wellbeing of professional academy footballers in England. *Soccer & Society, 22*(6), 641–654. https://doi.org/10.1080/14660970.2021.1952693

Stember, M. (1991). Advancing the social sciences through the interdisciplinary enterprise. *The Social Science Journal, 28*(1), 1–14. https://doi.org/10.1016/0362-3319(91)90040-B

Sullivan, M. O., Vaughan, J., Rumbold, J. L., & Davids, K. (2022). The learning in development research framework for sports organisations. *Sport, Education and Society, 27*(9), 1100–1114. https://doi.org/10.1080/13573322.2021.1966618

The Football Association. (2020). *The FA's 4 corner model [online]*. Retrieved from: https://thebootroom.thefa.com/resources/coaching/the-fas-4-corner-model

Till, K., & Baker, J. (2020). Challenges and [possible] solutions to optimizing talent identification and development in sport. *Frontiers in Psychology, 11*, 664. https://doi.org/10.3389/fpsyg.2020.00664

Toohey, K., MacMahon, C., Weissensteiner, J., Thomson, A., Auld, C., Beaton, A., Burke, M., & Woolcock, G. (2018) Using transdisciplinary research to examine talent identification and development in sport. *Sport in Society, 21*(2), 356–375, https://doi.org/10.1080/17430437.2017.1310199

Towlson, C., Cope, E., Perry, J. L., Court, D., & Levett, N. (2019). Practitioners' multi-disciplinary perspectives of soccer talent according to phase of development and playing position. *International Journal of Sports Science & Coaching*, *14*(4), 528–540. https://doi.org/10.1177/1747954119845061

Turnnidge, J., & Côté, J. (2018). Applying transformational leadership theory to coaching research in youth sport: A systematic literature review. *International Journal of Sport and Exercise Psychology*, *16*(3), 327–342. http://dx.doi.org/10.1080/1612197X.2016.1189948

Turnnidge, J., & Côté, J. (2019). Observing coaches' leadership behaviours in sport: The development of the Coach Leadership Assessment System (CLAS). *Measurement in Physical Education and Exercise Science*, *23*(3), 214–26. https://doi.org/10.1080/1091367X.2019.1602835

Williams, A. M., Ford, P. R., & Drust, B. (2020). Talent identification and development in soccer since the millennium. *Journal of Sports Sciences*, *38*(11–12), 1199–1210. https://doi.org/10.1080/02640414.2020.1766647

Williams, A. M., & Reilly, T. (2000). Talent identification and development in soccer. *Journal of Sports Sciences*, *18*(9), 657–667. https://doi.org/10.1080/02640410050120041

Wood, G., Wright, D. J., Harris, D., Pal, A., Franklin, Z. C., & Vine, S. J. (2021). Testing the construct validity of a soccer-specific virtual reality simulator using novice, academy, and professional soccer players. *Virtual Reality*, *25*(1), 43–51. https://doi.org/10.1007/s10055-020-00441-x

Zhou, C., Gómez, M., & Lorenzo, A. (2020). The evolution of physical and technical performance parameters in the Chinese soccer super league. *Biology of Sport*, *37*(2), 139–145. https://doi.org/10.5114/biolsport.2020.93039

2

TECHNICAL

Examining Subjective and Objective Performance Parameters That Contribute Towards Developmental Outcomes and Career Progression

Adam L. Kelly, Jan Verbeek, James H. Dugdale, and Matthew J. Reeves

Introduction

Soccer is an invasive sport comprised of many complex technical actions, such as passing, shooting, dribbling, and tackling (Ali, 2011). Research has shown how the technical demands of professional soccer have enhanced significantly over the years. As an example, Barnes et al. (2014) revealed an increase in the expertise required to perform in the English Premier League, with ~40% more successful passes completed in the 2012/13 season when compared to 2006/07 season. More recently, Zhou et al. (2020) demonstrated how there were ~23% more crosses, ~12% more shots on target, and ~11% more opponent penalty area entries during the 2017 season compared to the 2012 season in the Chinese Super League. As such, researchers and practitioners should be mindful of the increased demands and subsequent importance of technical actions during talent identification and development in order to prepare young players for the technical requirements at senior levels.

In the context of talent identification and development, technical ability is often evaluated through the 'coach's eye' (Jokuschies et al., 2017). This judgement and decision-making process is defined as *intuitive, experience-based, subjective,* and *holistic* (Lath et al., 2021), whilst often used parallel to terms such as 'gut instinct' (Roberts et al., 2021). However, since resources and technologies continue to be fast evolving, objective tools (e.g., technical testing and performance analysis) are becoming increasingly common throughout youth soccer settings to compliment the coach's eye (e.g., indicators of potential and recruiter perspectives). Other contextual factors, such as position-specific factors and laterality (i.e., the preferential use of one side of the body over the other) are also important characteristics when considering technical abilities of young players. Accordingly, the combination of subjective and objective data during youth soccer selection has been shown to be more accurate at predicting senior professional status when compared to their use in isolation (Sieghartsleitner et al., 2019).

The purpose of this chapter is to identify the objective and subjective technical performance parameters that contribute towards developmental outcomes and career progression in youth soccer. Specifically, four key sections have been synthesised based on the current literature to focus on: (a) technical testing, (b) performance analysis, (c) indicators of potential and recruiter

DOI: 10.4324/9781032232799-2

perspectives, and (d) laterality. As a result of this evidence-base, possible directions for future research and considerations for applied practice are proposed.

Technical Testing

Advanced technical skills are vital factors for succeeding in soccer and can be tested in isolation. The advantages of measuring technical attributes in soccer at youth levels include: (a) facilitating initial talent identification, (b) providing a strategy for skill acquisition, and (c) offering an alternative predictor for measuring technical ability compared to a skilled execution during competitive match-play (Ali, 2011). These benefits have been supported in many youth soccer studies, whereby an association between technical performance and playing level has been demonstrated (e.g., Coelho-e-Silva et al., 2010; Figueiredo et al., 2009; Höner et al., 2017; Huijgen et al., 2014; Kelly et al., 2021; Rebelo et al., 2013; Rubajczyk & Rokita, 2015). This section focuses on both the contextual factors and methodological considerations of technical testing studies in youth soccer.

Contextual Factors

Seminal work in this area was presented by Vaeyens et al. (2006), who applied a sequence of technical tests (i.e., ball juggle, slalom dribble, shooting accuracy, and lob pass) to explore the relationship between technical performance characteristics and playing level in male Belgian youth soccer players. They revealed that the tests distinguished three ability groups (i.e., elite: first and second division clubs; sub-elite: third and fourth division clubs; non-elite: regional teams) across U13–U16 age groups. Moreover, Keller et al. (2016) used the Loughborough Short Passing Test, long passing test, shooting test, and speed dribbling test with male U18 national-elite, state-elite, and sub-elite Australian youth soccer players. They reported that the national-elite group possessed higher scores compared to the other two cohorts across all tests. Indeed, such technical tests have shown to be a discriminative function across various countries, including Brazil, England, Germany, Portugal, Italy, and Spain (McCalman et al., 2021). Thus, technical tests can be considered as valuable measures for assessing young soccer players across a range of playing levels and national contexts.

Technical proficiency has also been illustrated to improve with age among youth soccer players (Kelly & Williams, 2020), with the greatest developments shown to occur in pre-pubertal years (Huijgen et al., 2010). For instance, Huijgen et al. (2010) longitudinal study measured male youth Dutch players (U12–U19) dribbling performance from two talent development programmes in Eredivisie clubs (the highest level of professional soccer in the Netherlands) on an annual basis for 7 years. They found that dribbling performance improved with age (especially from ages 12–14 years), as well as differentiating between players who achieved senior professional levels and those who reached amateur levels. Some studies have also reported that growth and maturation status may be associated with technical development, whereby biological maturity can impact upon the technical progression of young soccer players (e.g., Malina et al., 2005, 2007; Valente-dos-Santos et al., 2012, 2014). Furthermore, previous reviews have highlighted the relationship between advanced physical fitness and technical characteristics in both male and female youth soccer players (Farley et al., 2020; Meylan et al., 2010). Time spent within practice activities (e.g., deliberate practice, deliberate play, and multi-sports) is also reported to have a significant influence on the development of technical skills within a soccer player (e.g., Huijgen et al., 2010,

2013; Valente-dos-Santos et al., 2014). Taken together, this research highlights the importance of considering technical ability based on an age-specific perspective to support appropriate developmental strategies in youth soccer.

Given the importance of age when considering the technical abilities of youth soccer players, Kelly et al. (2020) examined how technical abilities contributed to coaches' ratings of potential in a male English category three soccer academy (U9–U16). The authors used a battery of four soccer-specific technical tests (Vaeyens et al., 2006) to compare 'higher-potentials' (i.e., top third of players) and 'lower-potentials' (i.e., bottom third of players) across the Foundation Development Phase (FDP) (U9–U11) and Youth Development Phase (YDP) (U12–U16). Data showed that higher-potentials performed significantly better on the lob pass test within the FDP, whereas higher-potentials performed significantly better on all four technical tests within the YDP (Table 2.1). These results indicate that soccer-specific technical tests may provide a discriminative tool to support the talent development process from an age-specific perspective, whilst also offering useful benchmarks for YDP players and an objective context for practitioners to consider for developmental purposes.

Methodological Considerations

A recent scoping review from McCalman et al. (2021) provides a particularly useful overview of skill assessment research in youth soccer. Although the inclusion of studies was not limited explicitly to technical testing (see Chapter 3 for tactical knowledge, tactical performance, and virtual reality; see Chapter 12 for creativity comprehensive frameworks and small-sided games), they showed the sample characteristics of skill assessments included: (a) a large proportion of the research was published between 2015 to 2020 (59%), (b) contained players from 25 countries across five continents, with Germany and Portugal possessing the equal largest proportion (11% each), (c) the collective sample was 129,232 (from U7–U23), with females (1.3%) considerably

TABLE 2.1 Technical test results, including z-scores and t-tests based on age phase (i.e., FDP and YDP) and non-standardised means based on age group (i.e., U9–U16) (adapted from Kelly et al., 2020)

Technical Tests	FDP				YDP					
	U9	U10	U11	z-score	U12	U13	U14	U15	U16	z-score
Ball juggle										
Higher-potentials	11	47.3	25.4	0.13 ± 1.08	93.5	80.8	164.8	160	200	0.43 ± 1.12*
Lower-potentials	13.2	12.7	19.2	-0.26 ± 0.79	28.8	96.3	54.8	126.3	112	-0.44 ± 0.89
Slalom dribble										
Higher-potentials	18.4	16.6	17.2	-0.18 ± 0.96	14.5	15.3	14.2	14.9	15.7	-0.4 ± 073**
Lower-potentials	19.4	18.1	16.7	0.01 ± 0.94	17.9	16	15.2	15.5	15.3	0.49 ± 0.97
Shooting accuracy										
Higher-potentials	21.8	24	23.4	0.22 ± 0.69	23.8	24.3	25.8	24.3	27	0.47 ±0.66**
Lower-potentials	23	23.7	20.2	-0.31 ± 1.10	21.8	22	23.8	24	24.5	-0.36 ± 0.98
Lob pass										
Higher-potentials	4.8	7.3	8	0.87 ± 0.77***	8	13.3	13.6	13.3	20	0.49 ± 1.08**
Lower-potentials	1	3.7	2.6	-0.63 ± 0.54	7.8	8.3	10.2	11.8	11.5	-0.54 ± 0.78

Significant difference in t-test denoted by $*=P < 0.05$, $**=P < 0.01$, $***=P < 0.001$.

underrepresented when compared to males (89.3%) (see Chapter 17 for gender considerations), whilst others studies did not report gender (9.4%), and (d) inconsistent terminology was used to define playing levels (see Chapter 20 for a discussion on the need for clear and consistent definitions). Furthermore, the methodological characteristics of studies showed: (a) 226 skill assessments were used across 93 studies, (b) isolated technical tests were commonly used (68%), whereas lab-based assessments and small-sided games were less common, and (c) dribbling, passing, and shooting measures appeared more regularly (49%) compared to other skills as part of testing batteries. Additionally, the authors also identified that the skill categories and measurement types comprised of: (a) offensive skills (99%) in all but one study, (b) only one documented study including goalkeeping skills (1%) (see Chapter 19 for goalkeeper considerations), and (c) notational systems incorporating criterion measures were used more by researchers (13%) compared to other methods such as observation sheets, checklists, and scoring charts.

While this section has presented various benefits of technical testing, it is important to acknowledge how they do not truly capture an ecological representation of soccer competition. For instance, such measures disregard the tactical (e.g., perceptual-cognitive skill), physical (e.g., fatigue), psychological (e.g., performing under pressure), and social (e.g., group dynamics) implications of a competitive game (Russell et al., 2010; Unnithan et al., 2012). As such, they generally apply to an environment that differs to the one that is illustrative to actual match-play (Kelly et al., 2020).

Performance Analysis

Analysis of performance in soccer, via the recording of competitive games and objectively analysing them, can provide both researchers and practitioners important data (Carling et al., 2007; Kempe et al., 2014). In the context of senior professional soccer, performance analysis has demonstrated how greater ball possession is associated with higher success in the Spanish La Liga (Liu et al., 2016) and Chinese Super League (Yang et al., 2018). Furthermore, players from more successful teams have been shown to complete a greater number of dribbles, passes, shots, and tackles in the Italian Serie A (Rampinini et al., 2009). In addition, superior ball possession, more ending actions, and lower individual challenges reflected a higher league ranking in the Greek Superleague (Gomez et al., 2018). Since match analysis provides useful indicators of successful performance, it is important to consider how this approach can be adapted within talent identification and development systems in youth soccer to prepare young players for the technical demands at senior levels.

Performance Analysis and Small-Sided Games

The notational style of performance analysis (i.e., a procedure that can be used in any discipline that requires assessment and analysis of performance; Hughes et al., 2007) that is generally applied within youth soccer settings is intended to provide objective data for player identification and development (Hughes, 1988; Waldron & Worsfold, 2010; Wright et al., 2014). The use of 4 vs. 4 small-sided games (SSGs) have been used to examine the skill behaviours of Australian male youth soccer players (aged 11–15 years) based on current performance levels (Bennett et al., 2018). They identified that professional academy players attempted and completed a significantly greater number of passes, touches, and total skill involvements compared with regional academy players. Moreover, Fenner et al. (2016) evaluated the technical attributes of U10 English male academy soccer players during 4 vs. 4 SSGs. They revealed that total points (based on match results and goals scored) had a very large significant relationship with the technical scoring chart (based on coach ratings). These studies suggest practitioners may apply performance analysis statistics during SSGs to help identify and differentiate talented young players.

Previous studies have explored the role of various simulated SSG formats (e.g., player number, pitch size, and work-rest ratio) on technical, tactical, and physical responses in youth soccer players (e.g., Clemente et al., 2018; Da Silva et al., 2011; Práxedes et al., 2018; Rowat et al., 2017; van Maarseveen et al., 2017). However, research has often overlooked the potential significance of performance analysis during *competitive* (i.e., organised competition) match-play, as well as the subsequent implications for identifying and developing talent in youth soccer (Atan et al., 2014; James, 2006; Kelly & Wilson, 2018). This is particularly surprising, since it is the most ecological approach and regularly used within applied settings across youth soccer organisations. Indeed, a large amount of data is captured through performance analysis departments (also commonly referred to as match analysis or video analysis) and, therefore, often readily available (see Robertson, 2020 for an overview). However, issues arise when considering there are no standardised tools or a consensus available regarding how to best measure overall technical performance when using performance analysis in youth soccer (Williams et al., 2020).

Performance Analysis and Competition

Only recently have age-related differences in technical match performance been examined in U13–U18 Japanese male soccer players (Goto & Saward, 2020). Using retrospective video analysis from 152 match files, these authors showed how pass accuracy significantly improved with age, from 73% at U13 to 85% at U18. Considering the importance of age-specific differences, Kelly et al. (2020) explored how match analysis statistics contributed to coach ratings of potential in a male English soccer academy (U9–U16) across an entire season. Their results revealed 'higher-potentials' possessed greater reliability in possession, pass completion, and accumulated more total touches compared to 'lower-potentials' within the FDP. In comparison, higher-potentials within the YDP possessed greater reliability in possession, dribble completion, and accumulated more total touches compared to lower-potentials (Table 2.2). Interestingly, whilst both cohorts showed some similar offensive findings (i.e., comparable differences for reliability in possession and total touches), there were no significant differences for defensive measures across age phases (e.g., tackles, blocks, and loose balls retrieved). These studies demonstrated how match analysis can support practitioners to identify talent, develop players, and support age-specific training and competition programmes.

An understanding of how researchers and practitioners can effectively and efficiently interact with match analysis technology to improve talent identification and development is constantly being developed (Robertson, 2020). Beyond the existing match analysis procedures that were presented in this section, it also important to note how it may offer additional avenues for player development (Williams et al., 2020). Many practitioners and soccer organisations can use videos of their players performing to relay information and reflect on performance parameters through re-watching clips, support with their planning and delivery of training sessions, and help inform preparation for match-play (Raya-Castellano et al., 2021). However, the benefits and drawbacks of these methods from a talent identification and development perspectives are scarce and requires further study. It is also important to emphasise the sensitive nature of recording young players and strict ethical procedures should always be followed by soccer clubs and organisations.

TABLE 2.2 Match analysis statistics, including z-scores and t-tests based on age phase (i.e., FDP and YDP) and non-standardised means based on age group (i.e., U9–U16) (adapted from Kelly et al., 2020)

Skill Behaviours	FDP				YDP					
	U9	U10	U11	z-score	U12	U13	U14	U15	U16	z-score
Reliability in possession (%)										
Higher-potentials	74.2	76.3	72	0.62 ± 0.83**	67.6	78.8	80.7	87.3	83.9	0.41 ± 0.98*
Lower-potentials	69.2	72	68.8	-0.33 ± 0.86	67.8	62.3	74	78.8	89.9	-0.33 ± 0.99
Pass completion (%)										
Higher-potentials	80.1	80.3	76.6	0.77 ± 0.81***	73	82.8	82.5	85.3	82.9	0.26 ± 0.97
Lower-potentials	72	72	73.8	-0.61 ± 0.89	75.3	69	78.6	75.2	90.8	-0.23 ± 1
Tackles										
Higher-potentials	13.2	6.8	5.2	0.21 ± 1.42	4.8	6.1	5.2	3.2	5.5	0.17 ± 1.11
Lower-potentials	7.1	9.9	5.5	-0.01 ± 0.65	2.6	3.1	5.4	2.5	4.9	-0.36 ± 0.77
Blocks										
Higher-potentials	2.2	1.3	0.8	-0.1 ± 0.95	1	1.2	1	0.4	0.6	-0.1 ± 0.7
Lower-potentials	1.2	2.7	0.9	-0.11 ± 1.16	0.8	1	1.2	0.5	1.8	0.01 ± 1.13
Loose balls retrieved										
Higher-potentials	4.9	2.7	2.2	-0.11 ± 1.21	2.2	3.9	2	0.5	3.1	-0.03 ± 1.28
Lower-potentials	2.9	3.2	3.3	-0.16 ± 0.78	1.2	2	2.7	1.2	1.4	-0.22 ± 0.63
Dribble completion (%)										
Higher-potentials	65.9	66	62.3	0.04 ± 0.79	58.4	79.5	82.5	94	83.6	0.62 ± 0.62**
Lower-potentials	64.6	66.7	60	-0.06 ± 1.32	33.8	48	67.6	91	78.9	-0.42 ± 1.07
Touches										
Higher-potentials	56.9	41.2	42.6	0.26 ± 1.26*	42	37.2	47.4	43	50	0.73 ± 0.95***
Lower-potentials	33.7	49.7	36.1	-0.62 ± 0.42	34.7	25.2	30.9	33.7	37.5	-0.65 ± 0.72
Goals										
Higher-potentials	1.9	0.9	0.5	0.28 ± 1.3	0.5	0.3	0.5	0.1	0.2	0.21 ± 1.08
Lower-potentials	0.9	1.1	0.2	-0.36 ± 0.7	0.3	0	0.1	0.1	0.2	-0.27 ± 0.54

Note: Significant difference in t-test denoted by *=$P < 0.05$, **=$P < 0.01$, ***=$P < 0.001$.

Indicators of Potential and Recruiter Perspectives

There has been increased interest in the indicators of potential talent in soccer over recent years. As formerly outlined, previous talent identification research sought to explore technical qualities that might discriminate between 'skilled' and 'less-skilled' players (e.g., Kelly et al., 2020; Vaeyens et al., 2006). In an attempt to gain insight in the attributes that scouts, recruitment staff, and coaches are looking for during talent identification, researchers have adopted subjective methods to better facilitate this understanding. This has included use of verbal reporting (Reeves et al., 2019) and expert consensus methods (Bergkamp et al., 2022; Larkin & O'Connor, 2017; Roberts et al., 2019). Indeed, such methods have aimed to move beyond the blurry concept of 'the coaches' eye' (Lath et al., 2021) and develop a more comprehensive and critical appreciation of talent identification in soccer.

In their study exploring attributes of young Australian players being identified for regional representative teams, Larkin and O'Connor (2017) asked 20 regional directors and coaches to participate in a three-stage, modified Delphi process comprising an interview and two questionnaires.

From these data, they generated a hierarchy of attributes that their participants believed to be important when identifying U13 players, which suggested a multidisciplinary approach to talent identification in Australian youth soccer. Their hierarchy of attributes, however, identified technical attributes (i.e., first touch, 1 vs. 1, and striking the ball) to be the top three most desired characteristics of recruiters, highlighting the fundamental importance of technical ability when identifying potential talent.

Building on the work of Larkin and O'Connor (2017), Roberts et al. (2019) sought to develop a consensus of the attributes that scouts use to inform their decisions by considering the position-specific nature of desired attributes. Here, expert consensus was sought using a modified, three-stage Delphi poll to determine the broad range of attributes considered most appropriate for identifying talent in youth soccer (see Table 2.3), and then what position-specific indicators exist (see Table 2.4). This approach brought together participants from both academia and applied practice in an effort to bridge the research-practice gap (Brocherie & Beard, 2021). This study found that perceptual-cognitive skills were considered the most important attribute for most positions, with the only exception being fullback where tackling was most important. All the second most important position-specific attributes were technical in nature (e.g., heading, tackling, technique under pressure, and shooting).

More recently, in their effort to understand the attributes that scouts identify when predicting potential future performance of players, Bergkamp et al. (2022) utilised an online questionnaire that was distributed to ten Dutch Eredivisie clubs' academy scouts. Due to the open nature of some questions within the questionnaire, participants were able to detail and then rank as many or as few attributes as they desired, as opposed to ranking against a pre-determined set of attributes as used in the previously presented studies. Data showed that the top three attributes identified for predicting future performance were technical skills or technique with the ball, games sense and awareness, and physiological or motor skills. Moreover, adopting a case study approach, Dugdale et al. (2021) explored differences in multidimensional attributes of players following closure of a

TABLE 2.3 Final list of agreed player attributes resulting from an e-Delphi poll (adapted from Roberts et al., 2019)

Physical	Psychological	Technical	Hidden
Acceleration	Aggression	First touch	Adaptability
Agility	Anticipation	Crossing	Consistency
Balance	Bravery	Corners (delivering)	Versatility
Fitness	Composure	Dribbling/running with the ball	Important matches
Speed	Concentration	Finishing	Coachability
Stamina	Decision-making	Free-kicks (delivering)	Communication
Strength	Determination	Heading	Flair
Jumping reach	Leadership	Long-range shooting	Creativity
	Off-the-ball thinking	Long throw-ins	
	Positioning	Passing accuracy	
	Teamwork	Marking	
	Attitude	Penalty taking	
	Vision	Tackling	
		1 vs. 1	
		Technique under pressure	

TABLE 2.4 Final list of agreed position-specific attributes resulting from an e-Delphi poll (adapted from Roberts et al., 2019)

Player Position	Attribute
Central Defender	Decision making
	Heading
	Marking
	Positioning
	First touch
	Strength
Full-back (Left/Right)	Tackling
	Crossing
	Passing accuracy
	Agility
	First touch
	Acceleration
Central Midfield	Decision-making
	Technique under pressure
	Passing accuracy
	Positioning
	First touch
	Stamina
Midfield (Left/Right)	Decision-making
	Technique under pressure
	Crossing
	Dribbling
	Agility
	Stamina
Central/Wide Attacking	Anticipation
	Shooting
	Finishing
	First touch
	1 vs. 1
	Speed

youth soccer academy. The authors found that players who were reselected into talent development programmes received higher coach subjective ratings for overall technical 'skill' ability, as well as receiving higher coach subjective ratings for all skill attributes selected within the study (see Table 2.5). These studies demonstrate the most obvious mixture of attributes (i.e., across different domains of performance) than had previously been reported.

It is important to note that the majority of the studies examining indicators of potential talent (Bergkamp et al., 2022; Larkin & O'Connor, 2017; Roberts et al., 2019) have collected data that were removed from the actual practice of identifying talent. Based on this ecological limitation, one study stands out for its experimental approach, utilising a verbal report protocol, and trying to understand the thought processes of two scouts during a live game (Reeves et al., 2019). The study yielded confirmatory data, supporting Roberts et al. (2019) in identifying perceptual-cognitive skills—specifically, decision-making—as the most important attribute scouts identify during the talent identification process. The most significant technical attributes, however, were passing accuracy, first touch, and dribbling/running with the ball, which finds some agreement

TABLE 2.5 Comparison between 'reselected' and 'deselected' players for coach subjective ratings of 'skill' attributes (adapted from Dugdale et al., 2021)

Skill	Reselected (n = 60)	Deselected (n = 19)	Effect Size (d)	
First Touch	3.4 ± 0.7	3.1 ± 0.8	0.4	*Small*
Striking the Ball	3.4 ± 0.7	3.3 ± 0.7	0.14	*Trivial*
1 vs. 1	3.2 ± 0.8	2.6 ± 0.7	0.8	*Moderate*
Decision Making	3.3 ± 0.8	2.6 ± 0.7	0.93	*Moderate*
Technique Under Pressure	3.2 ± 0.9	2.8 ± 0.4	0.57	*Small*
Running with the Ball	3.3 ± 0.9	2.8 ± 0.8	0.59	*Small*
X-Factor	2.9 ± 1.1	2.2 ± 0.7	0.76	*Moderate*
General Game Understanding	3.5 ± 0.9	2.7 ± 0.6	1.05	*Moderate*
Game Sense/Awareness	3.4 ± 0.8	2.6 ± 0.7	1.06	*Moderate*
Anticipation	3.3 ± 0.7	2.5 ± 0.7	1.14	*Moderate*
Consistent Execution	3.3 ± 0.8	2.8 ± 0.4	0.79	*Moderate*
Vision	3.2 ± 0.6	2.5 ± 0.7	1.07	*Moderate*
Team Understanding	3.5 ± 0.8	2.8 ± 0.5	1.05	*Moderate*
Defensive Ability	3.1 ± 0.9	2.8 ± 0.8	0.35	*Small*

Note: Data represent coach ratings of players relative to their age and stage of development on a 5-point Likert scale: 1—*poor*; 2—*below average*; 3—*average*; 4—*very good*; 5—*excellent*.

Data are presented as mean ± SD.

with previous studies (Larkin & O'Connor, 2017; Bergkamp et al., 2022). This reinforces the importance of considering technical attributes as part of a multidisciplinary approach when identifying potential talent in youth soccer.

Laterality

'Laterality' refers to the preferential use of one side of the body over the other for the execution of certain movements. This is evident in the case of limb-use such as hands and feet, which is rereferred to as 'handedness' and 'footedness' (Loffing et al., 2014). In the case of footedness, preferential use is often determined during a task, such as kicking a stationary ball in soccer (Musálek, 2014). The mobilising foot manipulates the object and is defined the preferred foot, while the other foot provides stabilising support and is referred to as the non-preferred foot (Hart & Gabbard, 1998). Typically, laterality is defined as a characteristic to group humans either in a dichotomous (e.g., right- or left-footedness) or trichotomous fashion (i.e., right-, left-, or mixed-footedness) (Utesch et al., 2016). In general, such laterality estimates are skewed, with approximately 80–90% of the global population reporting to be right-footed according to a recent meta-analysis (Packheiser et al., 2020). As such, studies have investigated the distribution of laterality in sporting contexts (Loffing et al., 2014). Generally, results show that, in interactive sports, where athletes can influence each other's actions, higher estimates of left-handedness are found (Schorer et al., 2016).

Footedness in soccer is also an interesting phenomenon, as players are free to use either foot (i.e., preferred or non-preferred foot). This might affect the relationship between laterality and soccer performance in several ways (Gabbard & Hart, 1996). First, performance differences have been found between preferred and non-preferred kicking, which stresses the need to have players execute on-the-ball actions with their preferred foot as much as possible. Hence, several playing positions are more suitable for left- or right-footed players. Second, due to the interaction with opponents, space, and time, certain situations require players to execute actions with their non-preferred foot. As such, if players could successfully complete actions with both feet, they could perform more efficiently and faster (Stöckel & Carey, 2016). These considerations might provide a laterality-related advantage in soccer for certain players. For instance, a GK–4–3–3 playing formation would preferably require a minimum of four left-footed field players (e.g., left-sided centre back, left fullback, left-sided central midfielder, and left-sided winger), which corresponds to 40% of outfield players. This, however, exceeds the prevalence of left-footedness in the general population (i.e., ~10–20%; Packheiser et al., 2020), and thus could increase likelihood of identification and selection for left- and mixed-footed soccer players (Schorer et al., 2016).

To test this hypothesis, research on player footedness within soccer is necessary. Preliminary research from Carey and colleagues (Carey et al., 2001, 2009; Stöckel & Carey, 2016) show that player footedness is skewed to the right side, as apparent in the general population. As an example, a study on foot use of players during matches from the 1998 World Cup showed that players are biased to using their preferred foot (Carey et al., 2001). This was most apparent for set pieces, as well as during dribbles, passes, and touches. Interestingly, on average, these players didn't show any difference in the successful execution of actions with their non-preferred or preferred foot. Moreover, while the study of Grouios et al. (2002) found almost half of Greek professional male soccer players being mixed-footed, this was done using a foot preference inventory instead of determining foot use on the field. In similar fashion, Bryson et al. (2012) found a prevalence of 20% mixed-footedness based on expert judgements in a sample of European soccer players. From a talent identification perspective, research from Verbeek et al. (2017) showed how left-foot preference increased the probability of selection in Dutch national youth soccer teams (i.e., U16 to U19), whereby 31% of selected players were left-footed when compared to an expected laterality distribution of left-foot preference of ~20% (Table 2.6).

TABLE 2.6 Players per Dutch national youth soccer team from the 2010–2011 to 2014–2015 competitive seasons based on footedness (adapted from Verbeek et al., 2017)

Season and Footedness	U16	U17	U18	U19	Total
Season 2010–2011 (n)	20	23	27	24	94
Left (%)	35	39.1	44.4	33.3	38.3
Right (%)	65	60.9	55.6	66.7	61.7
Season 2011–2012 (n)	21	34	19	30	104
Left (%)	28.6	29.4	26.3	36.7	30.8
Right (%)	71.4	70.6	73.7	63.3	69.2
Season 2012–2013 (n)	25	31	33	32	121
Left (%)	20	19.4	27.3	34.4	25.6
Right (%)	80	80.6	72.7	65.6	74.4
Season 2013–2014 (n)	28	28	25	29	110
Left (%)	50	32.1	12	27.6	30.9
Right (%)	50	67.9	88	72.4	69.1
Season 2014–2015 (n)	14	18	17	19	68
Left (%)	21.4	44.4	29.4	26.3	30.9
Right (%)	78.4	55.6	70.6	73.7	69.1
Total (n)	108	134	121	134	497
Left (%)	32.4	31.3	28.1	31.2	31
Right (%)	67.6	68.7	71.9	67.9	69

In sum, the effects of left- and mixed-footedness on soccer performance remains unclear. Although results show that prevalence of (self-) reported left- and mixed-footedness is higher amongst representative levels of soccer (i.e., professional, elite youth), studies on foot use during matches show similar estimates of footedness to population estimates. Nevertheless, left-footed players remain highly sought after. For instance, a study amongst professional soccer players' footedness on their salary showed that mixed-footed players were paid higher salaries when compared to right- or left-footed equivalents (Bryson et al., 2012). In addition, research into the technical skills (e.g., dribbling, shooting) of youth soccer players according to foot preference showed no differences on technical skills tests for left- and right-footed players (Bozkurt & Kucuk, 2018). Moving forward, further research is required to better understand the impact of footedness across various timelines (e.g., selection at youth level, transitions from youth levels to senior levels, and senior career duration), which will help inform practitioners working in youth soccer of best practice guidelines.

Laterality: A Case Study

In light of these findings, there have been examples of youth soccer academies organising trials solely for left-footed players (Port Vale, 2019). For instance, in the UK, Port Vale FC Academy published that, out of the 105 players from their U9s to U16s, 16% of those players were left-footed. Thus, in an attempt to search for "natural left-footed players between the ages of 7 to 14 years", they held a "left-footer talent identification day". Their Head of Recruitment suggested it was successful in identifying potential talent and it has made them think about how they should approach trials in the future. Moreover, they anecdotally suggested that "whatever the reason, there is something special about left-footed players", which highlights the lack of existing knowledge regarding what specifically differentiates players based on footedness, as well as the possible perception that left-footed players may be more talented. This might indicate that left-footed players are explicitly warranted in soccer and may be treated differently during selection procedures. Indeed, selecting left-footed players at youth level may also help smaller clubs financially in the long-term due to the transfer sales of 'home-grown' left-footed players to larger clubs. However, further research is required to substantiate some of these suggestions through both qualitative and quantitative research methods.

Considerations for Researchers

Evidence provided throughout this chapter demonstrates the importance of technical ability within talent identification and development. In order to build on this literature, future research should consider the technical attributes of youth soccer players through applying characteristics from other talent development variables (e.g., tactical, physical, psychological, and social). Furthermore, collecting these variables from a longitudinal perspective will also offer suggestions regarding what performance parameters are associated with individuals who achieve professional status and those who do not. This could be achieved through a combination of both subjective and objective performance parameters, which would help researchers to better understand how the combination of these methods can support greater accuracy during talent identification and development (e.g., Dugdale et al., 2020; Sieghartsleitner et al., 2019; Wilson et al., 2020).

The differences between markers of potential and position-specific indicators reflect the variances in the soccer philosophy of each country and where such studies were conducted (i.e.,

Australia, England, and the Netherlands). Thus, future research should consider how the role of organisational or national playing philosophy can influence practitioner's decision-making processes during the talent identification process. With regards to laterality, in accordance with Wattie et al.'s (2015) proposal, further empirical research is required to better understand left-footed (and both-footed) advantages in soccer and substantiate some of the anecdotal claims (e.g., Port Vale, 2019). By doing so, it may help inform micro-level approaches and organisational policies when identifying and developing talented players. It is also important to acknowledge how female samples are significantly underrepresented across all these technical fields. Therefore, researchers must prioritise female cohorts in order to level the playing field, particularly when it is readily understood that both genders develop at different rates (see Chapter 4). Likewise, goalkeepers remain underrepresented across the technical literature and require greater focus from researchers (see Chapter 19).

Considerations for Practitioners

In order to prepare young players for the demands at senior levels, it is important to consider technical attributes as part of a holistic approach to talent identification and development in youth soccer. The following considerations for practitioners are based on the extant literature presented throughout this chapter:

- The combination of subjective (e.g., the coach's eye and recruiter perspectives) and objective (e.g., technical testing, match analysis, and laterality) performance parameters may be more accurate for talent identification and development procedures, as well as negate the possible weaknesses of these different approaches when used in isolation.
- Technical tests can offer valuable objective measures for assessing young soccer players across various playing levels, nationalities, and age groups. These should be considered as part of a multidimensional battery of tests to offer a more holistic approach to talent identification and development procedures in youth soccer settings.
- Match analysis data provides useful information on individual skill behaviours in youth soccer. However, since the current talent identification and development literature has rarely incorporated match analysis procedures, organisations are encouraged to collaborate with researchers to help better understand how these tools and the subsequent data they provide can inform applied practice.
- Continual consideration should be given to the characteristics that practitioners (i.e., coaches, scouts, selectors) use to identify potential talent based on playing position. This process should be seen as one of constant iteration and refinement, not something that is set and stagnant.
- The tactical and positional considerations show that mixed- and left-footed players are scarce, but desirable, attributes. This, in turn, might have implications for selection procedures and squad management strategies in youth soccer.

Conclusion

Technical characteristics are vital aspects of talent identification and development in youth soccer. Practitioners are encouraged to adopt a unified application of both subjective (e.g., the coach's eye and recruiter perspectives) and objective (e.g., technical testing, match analysis, and laterality) performance parameters when identifying and developing talent to help inform more accurate decisions and refute the mutual weaknesses of these different approaches. Future studies should explore the possible outcomes of combining such technical measures, through adopting longitudinal, multidimensional research approaches, which will subsequently build on the existing evidence base that has been presented throughout this chapter.

References

Ali, A. (2011). Measuring soccer skill performance: A review. *Scandinavian Journal of Medicine & Science in Sports*, *21*(2), 170–183. https://doi.org/10.1111/j.1600-0838.2010.01256.x.

Atan, S. A., Foskett, A., & Ali, A. (2014). Special populations: Issues and considerations in youth soccer match analysis. *International Journal of Sports Science*, *4*(3), 103–114. https://doi.org/10.5923/j.sports.20140403.05

Barnes, C., Archer, D. T., Hogg, B., Bush, M., & Bradley, P. S. (2014). The evolution of physical and technical performance parameters in the English Premier League. *International Journal of Sports Medicine*, *35*(13), 1095–1100. https://doi.org/10.1055/s-0034-1375695

Bennett, K. J. M. novak, A. R., Pluss, M. A., Stevens, C. J., Coutts, A. J., & Fransen, J. (2018). The use of small-sided games to assess skill proficiency in youth soccer players: A talent identification tool. *Science and Medicine in Football*, *2*(3), 231–236. https://doi.org/10.1080/24733938.2017.1413246

Bergkamp, T. L. G., Frencken, W. G. P., Niessen, A. S. M., Meijer, R. R., & den Hartigh, R. J. R. (2022). How soccer scouts identify talented players. *European Journal of Sport Science*, *22*(7), 994–1004. https://doi.org/10.1080/17461391.2021.1916081

Bozkurt, S., & Kucuk, V. (2018). Comparing of technical skills of young football players according to preferred foot. *International Journal of Human Movement and Sports Sciences*, *6*(1), 19–22. https://doi.org/10.13189/saj.2018.060103

Brocherie, F., & Beard, A. (2021). All alone we go faster, together we go further: The necessary evolution of professional and elite sporting environment to bridge the gap between research and practice. *Frontiers in Sports and Active Living*, *2*(631147). https://10.3389/fspor.2020.631147

Bryson, A., Frick, B., & Simmons, R. (2012). The returns to scarce talent: Footedness and player remuneration in European soccer. *Journal of Sports Economics*, *14*(6), 606–628. https://doi.org/10.1177/1527002511435118

Carey, D. P., Smith, D. T., Martin, D., Smith, G., Skriver, J., Rutland, A., & Shepherd, J. W. (2009). The bi-pedal ape: Plasticity and asymmetry in footedness. *Cortex*, *45*(5), 650–661. https://doi.org/10.1016/j.cortex.2008.05.011

Carey, D. P., Smith, G., Smith, D. T., Shepherd, J. W., Skriver, J., Ord, L., & Rutland, A. (2001). Footedness in world soccer: An analysis of France' 98. *Journal of Sports Sciences*, *19*(11), 855–864. https://doi.org/10.1080/026404101753113804

Carling, C., Williams, M. A., & Reilly, T. (2007). *Handbook of soccer match analysis*. Routledge.

Clemente, F., Chen, Y., Bezerra, J., Guiomar, J., & Lima, R. (2018). Between-format differences and variability of technical actions during small-sided soccer games played by young players. *European Journal of Sport Science*, *19*(5), 114–120. https://doi.org/10.5114/hm.2018.83103

Coelho-e-Silva, M. J., Figueiredo, A. J., Simões, F., Seabra, A., Natal, A., Vaeyens, R., Philippaerts, R., Cumming, S. P., & Malina, R. M. (2010). Discrimination of U-14 soccer players by level and position. *International Journal of Sports Medicine*, *31*(11), 790–796. https://doi.org/10.1055/s-0030-1263139

Da Silva, C., Impellizzeri, F., Natali, A., de Lima, J., Bara-Filho, M., Silami- Garçia, E., & Marins, J. (2011). Exercise intensity and technical demands of small-sided games in young Brazilian soccer players: Effect of number of players, maturation, and reliability. *Journal of Strength and Conditioning Research*, *25*(10), 2746–2751. https://doi.org/10.1519/JSC.0b013e31820da061

Dugdale, J. H., McRobert, A. P., & Unnithan, V. B. (2021). Selected, deselected, and reselected: A case study analysis of attributes associated with player reselection following closure of a youth soccer academy. *Frontiers in Sports and Active Living*, *3*. https://doi.org/10.3389/fspor.2021.633124

Dugdale, J. H., Sanders, D., Myers, T., Williams, M. A., & Hunter, A. M. (2020). A case study comparison of objective and subjective evaluation methods of physical qualities in youth soccer players. *Journal of Sports Sciences*, *38*(11–12), 1304–1312. https://doi.org/10.1080/02640414.2020.1766177

Farley, J., Stein, J., Keogh, J., Woods, C., & Milne, N. (2020). The relationship between physical fitness qualities and sport-specific technical skills in female, team-based ball players: A systematic review. *Sports Medicine*, *6*(1), 1–20. https://doi.org/10.1186/s40798-020-00245-y

Fenner, J. S. J., Iga, J., & Unnithan, V (2016). The evaluation of small-sided games as a talent identification tool in highly trained prepubertal soccer players. *Journal of Sports Sciences*, *34*(20), 1983–1990. https://doi.org/10.1080/02640414.2016.1149602

Figueiredo, A. J., Goncalves, C. E., Coelho-e-Silva, M. J., & Malina, R. M. (2009). Characteristics of youth soccer players who drop out, persist or move up. *Journal of Sports Sciences*, *27*(9), 883–891. https://doi.org/10.1080/02640410902946469

Gabbard, C., & Hart, S. (1996). A question of foot dominance. *The Journal of General Psychology*, *123*(4), 289–296. https://doi.org/10.1080/00221309.1996.9921281

Gomez, M., Mitrotasios, M., Armatas, V., & Lago-Penas, C. (2018). Analysis of playing styles according to team quality and match location in Greek professional soccer. *International Journal of Performance Analysis in Sport*, *18*(6), 986–997. https://doi.org/10.1080/24748668.2018.1539382

Goto, H., & Saward, C. (2020). The running and technical performance of U13 to U18 elite Japanese soccer players during match play. *The Journal of Strength and Conditioning Research*, *34*(6), 1564–1573. https://doi.org/10.1519/JSC.0000000000003300

Grouios, G., Kollias, N., Koidou, I., & Poderi, A. (2002). Excess of mixed-footedness among professional soccer players. *Perceptual and Motor Skills*, *94*(2), 695–699. https://doi.org/10.2466/pms.2002.94.2.695

Hart, S., & Gabbard, C. (1998). Examining the mobilizing feature of footedness. *Perceptual and Motor Skills*, *86*(3), 1339–1342. https://doi.org/10.2466/pms.1998.86.3c.1339

Höner, O., Leyhr, D., & Kelava, A. (2017). The influence of speed abilities and technical skills in early adolescence on adult success in soccer: A long- term prospective analysis using ANOVA and SEM approaches. *PlOS One*, *12*(8), 1–15. https://doi.org/10.1371/journal.pone.0182211

Hughes, M. (1988). Computerised notation analysis in field games. *Ergonomics*, *31*(11), 1585–1592. https://doi.org/10.1080/00140138808966808

Hughes, M., Hughes, M. T., & Behan, H. (2007). The evolution of computerised notational analysis through the example of racket sports. *International Journal of Sports Science and Engineering*, *1*(1), 3–28. https://doi.org/10.21797/KSME.2008.10.3.001

Huijgen, B. C. H., Elferink-Gemser, M. T., Ali, A., & Visscher, C. (2013). Soccer skill development in talented players. *International Journal of Sports Medicine*, *34*(8), 720–726. https://doi.org/10.1055/s-0032-1323781

Huijgen, B. C. H., Elferink-Gemser, M. T., Lemmink, K. A. P. M., & Visscher, C. (2014). Multidimensional performance characteristics in selected and deselected talented soccer players. *European Journal of Sport Science*, *14*(1), 2–10. https://doi.org/10.1080/17461391.2012.725102

Huijgen, B. C. H., Elferink-Gemser, M. T., Post, W., & Visscher, C. (2010). Development of dribbling in talented youth soccer players aged 12–19 years: A longitudinal study. *Journal of Sports Sciences*, *28*(7), 689–698. https://doi.org/10.1080/02640411003645679

James, N. (2006). Notational analysis in soccer: Past, present and future. *International Journal of Performance Analysis in Sport*, *6*(2), 67–81. https://doi.org/10.1080/24748668.2006.11868373

Jokuschies, N., Gut, V., & Conzelmann, A. (2017). Systematizing coaches' 'eye for talent': Player assessments based on expert coaches' subjective talent criteria in top-level youth soccer. *International Journal of Sports Science & Coaching*, *12*(5), 565–576. https://doi.org/10.1177/1747954117727646

Keller, B. S., Raynor, A. J., Bruce, L., & Iredale, F. (2016). Technical attributes of Australian youth soccer players: Implications for talent identification. *International Journal of Sports Science & Coaching*, *11*(6), 819–824. https://doi.org/10.1177/1747954116676108

Kelly, A. L., & Williams, C. A. (2020). Physical characteristics and the talent identification and development processes in youth soccer: A narrative review. *Strength and Conditioning Journal*, *42*(6), 15–34. https://doi.org/10.1519/SSC.0000000000000576

Kelly, A. L., Williams, C. A., Jackson, D. T., & Wilson, M. R. (2020). Technical testing and match analysis statistics as part of the talent development process in an English football academy. *International Journal of Performance Analysis in Sport*, *20*(6), 1035–1051. https://doi.org/10.1080/24748668.2020.1824865

Kelly, A. L., & Wilson, M. R. (2018). Thinking inside the box: The effect of player numbers on locomotor activity and skill behaviour during competitive match-play in under-9 English academy football. *Journal of Sports Sciences*, *36*(S1), 51.

Kelly, A. L., Wilson, M. R., Jackson, D. T., Goldman, D. E., Turnnidge, J., Côté, J., & Williams, C. A. (2021). A multidisciplinary investigation into "playing-up" a chronological age group in an English football academy. *Journal of Sports Sciences*, *39*(8), 854–864. https://doi.org/10.1080/02640414.2020.1848117

Kempe, M., Vogelbein, M., Memmert, D., & Nopp, S. (2014). Possession vs. Direct play: Evaluating tactical behaviour in elite soccer. *International Journal of Sports Science*, *4*(6), 35–41. https://doi.org/10.5923/s.sports.201401.05

Larkin, P., & O'Connor, D. (2017). Talent identification and recruitment in youth soccer: Recruiter's perceptions of the key attributes for player recruitment. *PLOS One*, *12*(4), e0175716. https://doi.org/10.1371/journal.pone.0175716

Lath, F., Koopman, T., Faber, I., Baker, J., & Scorer, J. (2021). Focusing on the coach's eye; Towards a working model of coach decision-making in talent selection. *Psychology of Sport and Exercise*, *56*(102011), 1–13. https://doi.org/10.1016/j.psychsport.2021.102011

Liu, H., Hopkins, W. G., & Gomez, M. A. (2016). Modelling relationships between match events and match outcome in elite football. *European Journal of Sport Science*, *16*(5), 516–525. https://doi.org/10.1080/17461391.2015.1042527

Loffing, F., Sölter, F., & Hagemann, N. (2014). Left preference for sport tasks does not necessarily indicate left-handedness: Sport-specific lateral preferences, relationship with handedness and implications for laterality research in behavioural sciences. *PLoS One*, *9*(8), e105800. https://doi.org/10.1371/journal.pone.0105800

Malina, R. M., Cumming, S. P., Kontos, A. P., Eisenmann, J. C., Ribeiro, B., & Aroso, J. (2005). Maturity-associated variation in sport-specific skills of youth soccer players aged 13–15 years. *Journal of Sports Sciences*, *23*(5), 515–522. https://doi.org/10.1080/02640410410001729928

Malina, R. M., Ribeiro, B., Aroso, J., Cumming, S. P., Unnithan, V., & Kirkendall, D. (2007). Characteristics of youth soccer players aged 13–15 years classified by skill level. *British Journal of Sports Medicine*, *41*(5), 290–295. https://doi.org/10.1136/bjsm.2006.031294

McCalman, W., Crowley-McHattan, Z. J., Fransen, J., & Bennett, K. J. M. (2022). Skill assessments in youth soccer: A scoping review. *Journal of Sports Sciences*, *40*(6), 667–695. https://doi.org/10.1080/02640414.2021.2013617

Meylan, C., Cronin, J., Oliver, J., & Hughes, M. (2010). Talent identification in soccer: The role of maturity status on physical, physiological and technical characteristics. *International Journal of Sports Science & Coaching*, *5*(4), 571–592. https://doi.org/10.1260/1747-9541.5.4.571

Musálek, M. (2014). *Development of test batteries for diagnostics of motor laterality manifestation: Link between cerebellar dominance and hand performance*. Karolinum Press.

Packheiser, J., Schmitz, J., Berretz, G., Carey, D. P., Paracchini, S., Papadatou-Pastou, M., & Ocklenburg, S. (2020). Four meta-analyses across 164 studies on atypical footedness prevalence and its relation to handedness. *Scientific Reports*, *10*(1). https://doi.org/10.1038/s41598-020-71478-w

Port Vale. (2019). *Academy left-footed trials a huge success* [online]. Retrieved from: www.port-vale.co.uk/news/2019/may/left-footer-trial-succes/

Práxedes, A., Moreno, A., Gil-Arias, A., Claver, F., Del Villar, F., & Zagatto, A. (2018). The effect of small-sided games with different levels of opposition on the tactical behaviour of young footballers with different levels of sport expertise. *PloS One*, *13*(1), 1–14. https://doi.org/10.1371/journal.pone.0190157

Rampinini, E., Impellizzeri, F. M., Castagna, C., Couus, A. J., & Wisloff, U. (2009). Technical performance during soccer matches of the Italian Serie A league: Effect of fatigue and competitive level. *Journal of Science and Medicine in Sport*, *12*(1), 227–233. https://doi.org/10.1016/j.jsams.2007.10.002

Raya-Castellano, P. E., Reeves, M. J., Fradua-Uriondo, L., & McRobert, A. P. (2021). Post-match video-based feedback: A longitudinal work-based coach development program stimulating changes in coaches' knowledge and understanding. *International Journal of Sports Science & Coaching*, 16(6). https://doi.org/10.1177/17479541211017276

Rebelo, A., Brito, J., Maia, J., Coelho-e-Silva, M. J., Figueiredo, A. J., Bangsbo, J., Malina, R. M., & Seabra, A. (2013). Anthropometric characteristics, physical fitness and technical performance of under-19 soccer players by competitive level and field position. *International Journal of Sports Medicine*, 34(4), 312–317.

Reeves, M., McRobert, A. P., Lewis, C. J., & Roberts, S. J. (2019). A case study of the use of verbal reports for talent identification purposes in soccer: A Messi affair! *PLOS One*, 14(11), e0225033. http://doi.org/10.1371/journal.pone.0225033

Roberts, A. H., Greenwood, D., Stanley, M., Humberstone, C., Iredale, F., & Raynor, A. (2021). Understanding the "gut instinct" of expert coaches during talent identification. *Journal of Sports Science*, 39(4), 359–367. https://doi.org/10.1055/s-0032-1323729

Roberts, S. J., McRobert, A. P., Lewis, C. J., & Reeves, M. J. (2019). Establishing consensus of position-specific predictors for elite youth soccer in England. *Science and Medicine in Football*, 3(3), 205–213. https://doi.org/10.1080/24733938.2019.1581369

Robertson, S. (2020). Man & machine: Adaptive tools for the contemporary performance analyst. *Journal of Sports Sciences*, 38(18), 2118–2126. https://doi.org/10.1080/02640414.2020.1774143

Rowat, O., Fenner, J., & Unnithan, V. (2017). Technical and physical determinants of soccer match-play performance in elite youth soccer players. *The Journal of Sports Medicine and Physical Fitness*, 57(4), 369–379. https://doi.org/10.23736/S0022-4707.16.06093-X

Rubajczyk, K., & Rokita, A. (2015). Relationships between results of soccer-specific skill tests and game-related soccer skill assessment in young players aged 12 and 15 years. *Trends in Sport Sciences*, 22(4), 197–206.

Russell, M., Benton, D., & Kingsley, M. (2010). Reliability and construct validity of soccer skills tests that measure passing, shooting, and dribbling. *Journal of Sports Sciences*, 28(13), 1399–1408. https://doi.org/10.1080/02640414.2010.511247

Sieghartsleitner, R., Zuber, C., Zibung, M., & Conzelmann, A. (2019). Science or coaches' eye?—Both! Beneficial collaboration of multidimensional measurements and coach assessments for efficient talent selection in elite youth football. *Journal of Sports Science and Medicine*, 18(1), 32–43.

Schorer, J., Tirp, J., Steingröver, C., & Baker, J. (2016). Laterality and its role in talent identification and athlete development. In F. Loffing, N. Hagemann, B. Strauss, & C. MacMahon (Eds.), *Laterality in sports: Theories and applications* (pp. 87–105). Elsevier Academic Press.

Stöckel, T., & Carey, D. P. (2016). Laterality effects on performance in team sports: Insights from soccer and basketball. In F. Loffing, N. Hagemann, B. Strauss, & C. MacMahon (Reds.), *Laterality in sports: Theories and applications* (pp. 309–328). Academic Press.

Unnithan, V., White, J., Georgiou, A., Iga, J., & Drust, B. (2012). Talent identification in youth soccer. *Journal of Sports Sciences*, 30(15), 1719–1726. https://doi.org/10.1080/02640414.2012.731515

Utesch, T., Mentzel, S. V., Strauss, B., & Büsch, D. (2016). Measurement of laterality and its relevance for sports. In F. Loffing, N. Hagemann, B. Strauss, & C. MacMahon (Eds.), *Laterality in sports: Theories and applications* (pp. 65–86). Elsevier Academic Press.

Vaeyens, R., Malina, R. M., Janssens, M., van Renterghem, B., Bourgois, J., Vrijens, J., & Philippaerts, R. M. (2006). A multidisciplinary selection model for youth soccer: The ghent youth soccer project. *British Journal of Sports Medicine*, 40(11), 928–934. https://doi.org/10.1136%2Fbjsm.2006.029652

Valente-dos-Santos, J., Coelho-e-Silva, M. J., Simoes, F., Figueiredo, A. J., Leite, N., Elferink-Gemser, M. T., Malina, R. M., & Sherar, L. (2012). Modelling developmental changes in functional capacities and soccer-specific skills in male players aged 11–17 years. *Pediatric Exercise Science*, 24(4), 603–621. http://doi.org/10.1123/pes.24.4.603

Valente-dos-Santos, J., Coelho-e-Silva, M. J., Vaz, V., Figueiredo, A. J., Capranica, L., Sherar, L. B., Elferink-Gemser, M. T., & Malina, R. M. (2014). Maturity-associated variation in change of direction and dribbling speed in early pubertal years and 5-year developmental changes in young soccer players. *Journal of Sports Medicine and Physical Fitness*, 54(3), 307316.

van Maarseveen, M. J., Oudejans, R. R., & Savelsbergh, G. J. (2017). System for notational analysis in small-sided soccer games. *International Journal of Sports Science & Coaching*, *12*(2), 194–206. https://doi.org/10.1177/1747954117694922

Verbeek, J., Elferink-Gemser, M. T., Jonker, L., Huijgen, B. C. H., & Visscher, C. (2017). Laterality related to the successive selection of Dutch national youth soccer players. *Journal of Sports Sciences*, *35*(22), 2220–2224. https://doi.org/10.1080/02640414.2016.1262544

Waldron, M., & Worsfold, P. (2010). Differences in the game specific skills of elite and sub-elite youth football players: Implications for talent identification. *International Journal of Performance Analysis in Sport*, *10*(1), 9–24. https://doi.org/10.1080/24748668.2010.11868497

Wattie, N., Schorer, J., & Baker, J. (2015). The relative age effect in sport: A developmental systems model. *Sports Medicine*, *45*(1), 83–94. https://doi.org/10.1007/s40279-014-0248-9

Williams, M. A., Ford, P. R., & Drust, B. (2020). Talent identification and development in soccer since the millennium. *Journal of Sports Sciences*, *38*(11–12), 1199–1210. https://doi.org/10.1080/02640414.2020.1766647

Wilson, R., Souza, A., Santiago, P., Ignacio, D., & Smith, N. (2020). Individual performance in passing tests predicts age-independent success in small-sided soccer possession games. *Translational Sports Medicine*, *3*(4), 353–363. https://doi.org/10.1002/tsm2.142

Wright, C., Carling, C., & Collins, D. (2014). The wider context of performance analysis and it application in the football coaching process. *International Journal of Performance Analysis in Sport*, *14*(3), 709–733. https://doi.org/10.1080/24748668.2014.11868753

Yang, G., Leicht, A. S., Lago, C., & Gómez, M. (2018). Key team physical and technical performance indicators indicative of team quality in the soccer Chinese super league. *Research in Sports Medicine*, *26*(2), 158–167. https://doi.org/10.1080/15438627.2018.1431539

Zhou, C., Gómez, M., & Lorenzo, A. (2020). The evolution of physical and technical performance parameters in the Chinese Soccer Super League. *Biology of Sport*, *37*(2), 139–145. https://doi.org/10.5114/biolsport.2020.93039

3
TACTICAL

Measuring and Developing Tactical Knowledge and Performance in Youth Soccer Players

Adam L. Kelly, Mark R. Wilson, and Greg Wood

Introduction

Experts in ball games are characterised by extraordinary tactical knowledge and performance (Memmert & Perl, 2009). The application of these skills in sport can be referred to as the ability to recognise and execute the correct action at the optimal moment during competition (Grehaigne & Godbout, 1995). Tactical solutions, such as anticipation, decision-making, creativity, and game understanding, are crucially important in soccer (McPherson, 1994). These characteristics are generally acknowledged as tactical skills and are important features of contemporary talent identification and development strategies in youth soccer settings (e.g., Broadbent et al., 2014; Gonzalez-Villora et al., 2013; Huijgen et al., 2015; Savelsbergh et al., 2010).

There are ongoing discussions between researchers and practitioners focused on how to effectively measure and develop tactical skills in youth soccer (Barquero-Ruiz et al., 2020; González-Víllora et al., 2015). Despite attempts to advance research and practice, there is no consensus regarding the use of the terms related to the various tactical components of skill (Araújo et al., 2010). During their recent scoping review of tests to measure tactical knowledge and performance in young soccer players, Rechenchosky et al. (2021) suggested the term 'tactical knowledge' for methods based on interviews, questionnaires, images, and video-based simulation tests (e.g., declarative knowledge, cognitive skills) and the term 'tactical performance' for methods involving game-based situations (e.g., procedural knowledge, motor skills). As such, this chapter will use these definitions when describing the different research methods used in the literature.

Tactical knowledge research in youth soccer players (e.g., Williams & Ericsson, 2005Mann et al., 2007; Ward & Williams, 2003) generally uses lab-based settings to examine *perceptual-cognitive expertise* (PCE) (e.g., anticipation and decision-making). In comparison, tactical performance research is often conducted through *game-based situations* (e.g., modified small-sided games and representative designs) to observe characteristics such as awareness, creativity, and positioning (e.g., Memmert, 2015; Serra-Olivares et al., 2016). The increasing role of 'virtual reality' technologies (i.e., an artificial and fully immersive experience that can be similar to or completely different from the natural world) has also allowed researchers and practitioners to embed contemporary methods into their respective agendas to measure and develop tactical skills (Neumann

DOI: 10.4324/9781032232799-3

et al., 2018). The purpose of this chapter is to explore these approaches to measure and develop tactical knowledge and performance in youth soccer players, grouped by: (a) tactical knowledge, (b) tactical performance, and (c) virtual reality. Additionally, considerations for researchers and practitioners working in youth soccer are offered in an attempt to advance this field of literature and outline the principles for identifying and developing tactical skills in young players.

Tactical Knowledge

Through lab-based tests (using relevant images and video-based simulations) and asking athletes about their decision-making processes (via interviews and questionnaires), researchers can better understand athletes' use of situational probabilities, critical cues, and relevant patterns (e.g., Roca et al., 2013; Vaeyens et al., 2007; Williams & Davids, 1998; Williams & Ford, 2008). In the context of soccer, players must process information from the ball, teammates, and opponents before deciding on an appropriate response based upon the current objectives (e.g., playing position and opposition) and action potential (e.g., technical skill and physical capacity). These decisions are repeatedly made under pressure and under fatigue (especially later in a game; Kubayi & Toriola, 2019), with opponents trying to limit time and space accessible to execute the desired action (Williams, 2000).

Despite early equivocal findings (e.g., Helson & Starkes, 1999; Williams, 2000), research over the last two decades has supported a consensus that higher-performers, ranging from children (Wilson et al., 2012), athletes (Abernethy et al., 2005), and professional soccer players (Savelsbergh et al., 2002), possess superior tactical knowledge compared to their lower-performing counterparts. Within youth soccer, for example, Ward and Williams (2003) found superior PCE (assessed via the use of situational probabilities as well as tests of anticipation and memory recall) in male English Premier League academy players from as young as aged nine through to 17 years in comparison to sub-elite players (i.e., local elementary and secondary schools). Similarly, Keller et al. (2018) revealed how their video-based simulation test differentiated between three levels of male Australian youth soccer groups. Specifically, national elite players selected more correct responses than the state elite, while the state elite were more accurate than the sub-elite.

Competition level is not the only contextual factor that is important to consider when measuring tactical knowledge. García-López et al. (2010) showed that, despite national and international players revealing significantly more tactical knowledge than regional, provincial, and inexperienced young male Portuguese and Spanish soccer players, there were no differences between playing positions in any category. Bennett et al. (2019) also showed how response times were significantly faster in early- and mid-adolescent Australian male players when compared to those in the late childhood group. However, their video-based decision-making assessment lacked discriminant validity, as minimal differences between academies (i.e., A-League academy, National Premier League academy, and local academy) were evident for response accuracy and response time, while only response accuracy was able to differentiate the academy soccer players from the control group (i.e., no competitive soccer experience in the last 5 years). In sum, researchers and practitioners should consider contextual factors, such as age, competition level, playing position, and nationality, when evaluating tactical knowledge in youth soccer players.

Such video-based simulation tests are often used to measure anticipation and decision-making skill in soccer players by stopping (occluding) footage at a key moment and asking participants to select a response (Mann et al., 2007). Belling et al. (2014) Online Assessment of Strategic Skill in Soccer (OASSIS) is noteworthy in that it applied three occlusion phases to test decision-making

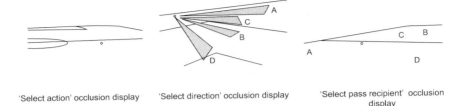

FIGURE 3.1 Occlusion displays for PCE tests (adapted from Kelly et al., 2021).

TABLE 3.1 Age group mean values and z-scores across PCE 'during' and 'post' tests (adapted from Kelly et al., 2021)

PCE Tests	FDP					YDP						
	U9	U10	U11	z-score	p	U12	U13	U14	U15	U16	z-score	p
PCE 'during'												
Higher-potentials	24.2	28.3	29.2	−0.05 ± 1.03	0.679	29	28.5	31.8	28.5	34	−0.2 ± 0.91	0.030
Lower-potentials	26.6	24.3	28.2	−0.2 ± 0.91		24.3	25.5	28.4	31	29.5	−0.29 ± 1.09	
PCE 'post'												
Higher-potentials	26.4	31	33	0.43 ± 0.93	0.042	32.8	35.3	33	32	35.5	−0.58 ± 0.89	0.052

ability (before, during, or after the player on the ball has executed the relevant action). These levels of difficulty (there is less definitive contextual information 'before' as opposed to 'after' an action) mean that testing environments are more sensitive to expertise-level differences. For example, Kelly et al. (2021) (Figure 3.1) showed that higher potential players in the foundation development phase (U9–U11) of a male soccer academy made significantly more accurate decisions in the 'post' activity phase compared to lower-potential players, whereas this expertise difference was achieved in the 'during' phase for older players in the youth development phase (U12–U16; see Table 3.1). Such nuances when planning tests are therefore critical and could have important implications for future research investigating tactical skills underpinning talent identification and development.

There are two important questions to consider when discussing tactical knowledge in the context of talent identification. First, can it be accurately measured, and second, can it be developed? While widely used, there is recent evidence that video-based simulations may not truly reflect the variety of tactical skills that are necessary on the field. For instance, Van Maarseveen et al. (2018) found that on-field performance could not be predicted based on PCE test performance in female Dutch youth soccer players. Further research is required to substantiate this preliminary research as well as help better understand how both of these tactical observations interact (i.e., knowledge *and* performance).

In terms of developing tactical knowledge, practice history might be an important element to explore and manipulate. Roca et al. (2012) found the average number of hours accumulated per year during childhood in soccer-specific play-like activity was the strongest predictor for greater PCE performance in semi-professional soccer players (see also Williams et al., 2012). Alongside practice history, psychological characteristics might play a role in the development of tactical knowledge. Larkin et al. (2016) showed that adolescent national players who scored higher on 'grit' (i.e., trait-level perseverance and passion toward long-term goals) accumulated significantly more time in soccer-specific activities, including competition, practice, and play, as well as performed better on assessments of decision making and situational probabilities, than less gritty players.

Tactical Performance

Although less developed than the tactical knowledge literature, there is a growing body of research, predominantly (but not exclusively) from Professor Daniel Memmert and colleagues (e.g., Memmert, 2007; 2010a; 2010b; 2011; 2013; 2015; Memmert & Furley, 2007; Memmert & Perl, 2009; Memmert & Roth, 2007; Perl et al., 2013), which looks specifically at using game-based situations to assess tactical performance in team sports. Rather than examining perceptual-cognitive skills, the focus of this research has been on the measurement and development of intelligent and creative behaviours in youth sport (Pain, 2013).

According to Memmert and Furley (2007), creative individuals set themselves apart during competitive situations. In soccer, for example, although Player A may intend to pass the ball to Player B, they are able to identify that Player C is suddenly unmarked and better positioned at the last moment and thus decide to pass the ball to them instead. Failure to spot Player C in this situation is called 'inattentional blindness', with practical tests demonstrating children with greater tactical performance being less prone to this lack of attention compared to children with lower tactical ability (Memmert & Furley, 2007). A wide focus of attention is therefore important to allow athletes to recognise a range of options in the sport environment (Aquino et al., 2016). Experiments in handball demonstrate that more tactical instructions from the coach can lead to a narrower breadth of attention and increased inattentional blindness, whereas fewer tactical instructions widen the breadth of attention and decrease inattentional blindness (Memmert, 2007). In the context of soccer, it may be suggested that vocal commands from practitioners could have a detrimental effect to the development of youth soccer players, through narrowing the breadth of attention and increasing inattentional blindness, and consequently, decreasing creativity and game intelligence. However, further research is required in youth soccer to validate these suggestions.

In order to test tactical performance, relevant and validated tests of in-game activities must be developed. Memmert (2010a) created two soccer-specific game test situations to examine creativity (ability to take advantage of openings) and game intelligence (positioning themselves optimally) in young players. Kannekens and colleagues (e.g., Kannekens et al., 2009; Kannekens et al., 2009; Kannekens et al., 2011) also developed the Tactical Skills Inventory for Sport (TACSIS) to assess differences across elements of tactical performance, such as 'knowing about the ball actions', 'knowing about others', and 'positioning and deciding'. As an example, Kannekens et al. (2011) analysed 105 male Dutch soccer players from Eredivisie clubs using the TACSIS to measure their eventual adult performance level (i.e., whether they became professionals or amateurs). Results showed 'positioning and deciding' was the greatest predictor for adult performance level, with an odds ratio indicating a 6.6 times greater likelihood that an individual became a professional player compared to those who reached amateur levels. This suggests that tactical performance measures can be a useful indicator of future potential, whereas a linked study (Kannekens et al., 2009) revealed differences in the development of tactical performance across positions. Specifically, defenders and midfielders did not improve their tactical scores, whereas attackers increased their overall score throughout the assessment years. This highlights the possible position-specific requirements for effective tactical performance. Taken together, age, nationality, competition level, and playing position are important considerations when measuring tactical performance in youth soccer players using game-based situations.

Research has shown that a greater varied sport-specific involvement can facilitate the development of advanced tactical performance (Memmert & Roth, 2007). For instance, Memmert et al. (2010) explored the practice history profiles of 72 professional athletes from various team sports, including soccer. During this study, coaches selected the most creative and the least creative players from their teams, with creative behaviour defined in terms of: (a) unusualness, innovativeness, statistical rareness, or even uniqueness of tactical solutions to a game related task, and (b) varying and flexible tactical solutions over different complex game situations. Results showed more creative athletes accumulated more hours in play-like *and* practice activities for their main sport than their less-creative counterparts. Memmert (2006) has also shown that tactical skills can be developed through different types of training. In the first intervention programme, they showed that players trained to participate in playful, self-determined, and diverse activities displayed a significant increase in tactical skills compared to a control group. In the second intervention, they revealed that creativity in game situations could be improved by an attention-broadening training programme. Overall, as with the research on tactical knowledge, it appears as though both unstructured play-like involvement *and* deliberate practice in soccer have crucial roles for the development of tactical performance.

Virtual Reality

With the increase in the development and availability of virtual reality (VR) platforms, it's unsurprising that such technologies are being applied in soccer contexts (Le Noury et al., 2022). For example, VR can provide practitioners with the ability to precisely replicate complex scenarios from the players viewpoint, thereby maintaining perception-action coupling (i.e., coinciding tactical knowledge and performance domains; Neumann et al., 2018). It can also provide practitioners with the opportunity for 'data-driven' coaching through the immediate availability of process-orientated performance metrics (e.g., decision time, visual scanning behaviour, and action preferences), which can be used to tailor coaching interventions in real time. These advantages can be combined to allow the formulation of standardised tests of tactical knowledge and performance that are more representative of the competitive game contexts, allowing the identification of areas for improvement and better predictions of skilled performers (see Figure 3.2 for examples of the virtual environment).

Despite these proposed benefits, there is still limited research evidence in relation to using VR for the identification and development of tactical knowledge and performance in sport. Most of this research has shown the benefits of this technology for training purposes compared to traditional training methods like 2D video. For example, the use of 360-degree video VR has been shown to be more beneficial for improving decision making skills of basketball players in novel situations (Pagé et al., 2019; Panchuk et al., 2018). Similar effects have been replicated in national level soccer players, whereby 360-degree VR video training led to greater improvement in passing decision making, compared to 2D video (Fortes et al., 2021). In a study using immersive VR, Tsai et al. (2022) successfully trained basketball players to learn tactics and then examined how players applied these tactics in real game scenarios. After training, the VR group showed

Tactical **39**

FIGURE 3.2 Representative examples of the virtual environments used in the study by Wood et al. (2021).

significant improvements in their tactical movement patterns in real game scenarios compared to more conventional coaching methods (e.g., whiteboard and 2D video). To summarise, the published studies to date support the use of VR over traditional video-based simulation methods for the training of tactical knowledge in sport.

There is less evidence supporting the use of VR for identifying tactical performance and sporting potential. The only study that has explored the ability of standardised VR tests to identify a performers skill level was carried out by Wood et al. (2021). They used a commercially available soccer-specific VR simulator and tested professional, academy, and novice players on standardised tests measuring passing accuracy, composure, reaction time, and adaptability (see Figure 3.3 for examples of the virtual environment). Results showed that the VR system differentiated between novice and academy players with a probability of 76%, between academy and professional players

40 Adam L. Kelly et al.

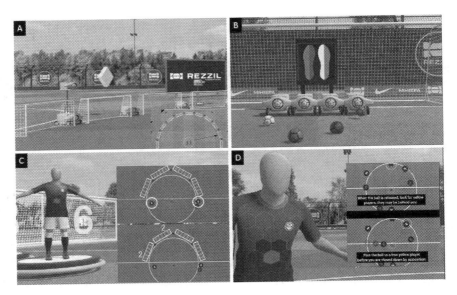

FIGURE 3.3 A visual representation of VR drills taken from the VR environment: (a) rondo scan, (b) colour combo, (c) shoulder sums, and (d) pressure pass (adapted from Wood et al., 2021).

with a probability of 85%, and between novice and professional players with a probability of 97%. However, this research had a small sample size (*n* = 17) in each of three 'extreme' groups of players where differences are probably easier to detect compared, for example, to a cohort of youth academy players. More research is therefore needed to examine the efficacy of VR for talent identification purposes. However, given previous evidence showing the effectiveness of video-based simulation methods for identifying soccer potential (Kelly et al., 2021), it is suggested that VR may offer added benefits in terms of identifying player potential over video-based simulation methods in a similar manner as in the training contexts previously described.

The paucity of research on the application of VR for identifying and developing expertise in soccer has not prevented professional clubs from adopting this technology in their practice. Recent research has suggested that coaches and players understand the potential value of VR, particularly in the rehabilitation and match analysis contexts (Greenhough et al., 2021; Thatcher et al., 2021). Anecdotally, this supports the experience of the current authors working with clubs who are currently using VR with their players. For example, several professional clubs are now applying VR during the rehabilitation of their players from injury (e.g., BBC News, 2017). In this context, VR is used to help to maintain the 'mental-sharpness' that coaches perceived to be lost when players solely focus on physical recovery. Providing exposure to virtual game-specific scenarios while preventing impact to an injury is thought to help maintain tactical skills (e.g., advance visual cue utilization, pattern recall and recognition, and visual scanning behaviour) and expedite a return to match fitness. While the benefits of VR for rehabilitation in terms of enjoyment, motivation, and adherence are well documented (Rose et al., 2018), the use of VR to maintain tactical knowledge and performance during injury needs to be evidenced.

Based on the experiences of the current authors, clubs are also using VR to develop the talent of young players by allowing players to watch previous game scenarios through the eyes of more experienced players. This practice, supported by feedback from coaches, is hoped to improve the situational awareness, positional sense, and game intelligence of the players. As an extension of this, VR is being used in the post-match analysis to enable players and coaches to revisit and reflect on critical match-related incidents from the perspective of players involved. Finally, teams are using VR platforms to elevate the strengths and weaknesses of their players before devising training goals based on their performance in the virtual world (e.g., iNews, 2022). In this context, information like action biases (e.g., foot/dive preferences for outfield players and goalkeepers) or situational weaknesses (e.g., curved free-kicks and corners) can be, and are being, recreated to expose players to situations to develop their perceptual-cognitive skill. It will be important for researchers to capture the application of these approaches in youth soccer to test their effectiveness and feasibility for talent identification and development.

Considerations for Researchers

Based on the literature presented throughout this chapter, there are a range of future research possibilities to assess the tactical knowledge and performance of young soccer players. Due to the variety of methods that can be used to measure tactical skills, it is important to offer a comparison between video-based simulation tests and game-based situations. According to Memmert (2013), video-based simulation tests are less complex with a distinct advantage of providing a clear test situation and response, with fewer confounding variables. However, it remains unclear what the most effective procedure is to measure PCE to accurately reflect the demands of on-field competitive performance. In comparison, the tactical solutions generated in the measurement of performance in game-based situations are influenced by the technical skills of each player and may be subject to coach bias when being rated. Although, it should be highlighted that coach rating of skill has been previously illustrated as a strong predictor for performance outcome in talent identification and development research (e.g., Sieghartsleitner et al., 2019; Tangalos et al., 2015). Thus, a combination of both observational and practical tests within tactical research may facilitate the application of a more holistic and accurate approach for talent identification and development in youth soccer.

Virtual reality environments are starting to be used by soccer clubs, despite the limited research evidence to support their efficacy in some contexts. It is clear, then, that a deeper examination of the validity of these systems is needed (e.g., Wood et al., 2021) using a systematic approach for testing their effectiveness (Harris et al., 2020). To achieve this, greater collaboration is needed between scientists, designers of VR environments, practitioners, and players to maximise the effectiveness of this developing technology. Lastly, according to Rechenchosky et al. (2021), current studies published on tactical domains in youth soccer are largely comprised of male (79.2%) and European cohorts (75%). Thus, the construction or adaptation of new tactical assessments should be prioritised with samples from females and other continents to ensure current findings are not generalised.

Considerations for Practitioners

This chapter has presented an overview of the literature to capture our current understanding of how tactical knowledge and performance can be identified and developed in young soccer players. As a result of this evidence base, the following considerations have been designed for practitioners to help inform their applied practice:

- Video-based simulation tests offer a useful tool to measure tactical knowledge in young soccer players. Practitioners should consider how they can objectively assess tactical knowledge in young players, which could help inform their talent identification strategies as markers of potential, as well as part of their talent development strategies to help inform individual development plans. Although, practitioners should also be cautious about the ecological validity of these tests and consider coinciding these with tactical performance markers for a more holistic approach.
- Game-based simulation tests provide an objective method to help assess tactical performance in youth soccer. Practitioners can use these tools to identify potential talent and help develop young players. It's also important to consider contextual factors, such as age, competition level, nationality, and playing position, when measuring tactical performance.
- Practitioners should consider the amount of verbal information that they are providing players with during competitive scenarios, since this could impact on their breadth of attention and inattentional blindness.
- Tactical skills can be developed through a varied soccer-specific involvement. Practitioners are encouraged to create a diverse learning environment for young soccer players in order to facilitate the development of advanced tactical skills. Specifically, play-like activity *and* soccer-specific practice should be considered in organised youth soccer settings, to offer a rich variety of experiences for young players to develop advanced tactical knowledge and performance.
- Although it's very much in its infancy, VR appears to offer practitioners a useful tool to help develop tactical skills in youth soccer players. This could be used to allow young players to watch game scenarios through the lens of professional soccer players as well as help players continue tactical development if they are side-lined due to injury or if their training is adapted due to ongoing injury (e.g., Osgood Schlatters) or possible injury risk (e.g., growth spurt).

Conclusion

The world's greatest professional soccer players can make effective decisions in unpredictable situations. In the context of talent identification and development, measuring and developing tactical knowledge and performance in youth soccer players can perhaps expedite this journey. Creating diverse learning environments for tactical skills to flourish should be at the fore of key stakeholders' (e.g., coaches, policy makers, support staff) agendas, alongside integrating subjective and objective methods into their programmes to help inform individual developmental plans. Further research is required to better understand the relationship between tactical knowledge and performance as well as a consensus of how to optimally measure and develop tactical skills in youth soccer players. The emerging role of VR also needs to be considered as a key part of this understanding to advance applied practice.

References

Abernethy, B., Baker, J., & Côté, J. (2005). Transfer of pattern recall skills may contribute to the development of sport expertise. *Applied Cognitive Psychology, 19*(6), 705–718. https://doi.org/10.1002/acp.1102

Araújo, D., Travassos, B., & Vilar, L. (2010). Tactical skills are not verbal skills: A comment on Kannekens and colleagues. *Perceptual and Motor Skills, 110*(3), 1086–1088. https://doi.org/10.2466/pms.110.C.1086-1088

Aquino, R., Marques, R., Petiot, G., Goncalves, L., Moraes, C., Santiago, P., & Puggina, E. (2016). Relationship between procedural tactical knowledge and specific motor skills in young soccer players. *Sports*, *4*(4), 52. https://doi.org/10.3390/sports4040052

Barquero-Ruiz, C., Arias-Estero, J. L., & Kirk, D. (2020). Assessment for tactical learning in games: A systematic review. *European Physical Education Review*, *26*(4), 827–847. https://doi.org/10.1177/1356336X19889649

BBC News. (2017). *Could VR help rehabilitate injured footballers?* [online]. Retrieved from: www.bbc.co.uk/news/av/technology-40814817

Belling, P. K., Suss, J., & Ward, P. (2014). Advancing theory and application of cognitive research in sport: Using representative tasks to explain and predict skilled anticipation, decision making, and option-generated behaviour. *Psychology of Sport and Exercise*, *16*, 45–59. http://doi.org/10.1016/j.psychsport.2014.08.001

Bennett, K., Novak, A. R., Pluss, M. A., Coutts, A. J., & Fransen, J. (2019). Assessing the validity of a video-based decision-making assessment for talent identification in youth soccer. *Journal of Science and Medicine in Sport*, *22*(6), 729–734. https://doi.org/10.1016/j.jsams.2018.12.011

Broadbent, D. P., Causer, J., Williams, A. M., & Ford, P. R. (2014). Perceptual-cognitive skill training and its transfer to expert performance in the field: Future research directions. *European Journal of Sport Science*, *15*(4), 322–331. https://doi.org/10.1080/17461391.2014.957727

Fortes, L. S., Almeida, S. S., Praça, G. M., Nascimento-Júnior, J. R., Lima-Junior, D., Barbosa, B. T., & Ferreira, M. E. (2021). Virtual reality promotes greater improvements than video-stimulation screen on perceptual-cognitive skills in young soccer athletes. *Human Movement Science*, *79*, 102856. https://doi.org/10.1016/j.humov.2021.102856

García López, L., Gutiérrez Díaz del Campo, D., Abellán Hernández, J., González, S., & Webb, L. (2010). Expert-novice differences in procedural knowledge in young soccer players from local to international level. *Journal of Human Sport and Exercise*, *5*(3), 444–452. https://doi.org/10.4100/jhse.2010.53.14

Gonzalez-Villora, S., Garcia-Lopez, L. M., Gutierrez-Diaz, D., & Pastor-Vicedo, J. C. (2013). Tactical awareness, decision making and skill in youth soccer players (under-14 years). *Journal of Human Sport and Exercise*, *8*(2), 412–426. https://doi.org/10.4100/jhse.2012.82.09

González-Víllora, S., Serra-Olivares, J., Pastor-Vicedo, J. C., & Teoldo, I. (2015). Review of the tactical evaluation tools for youth players, assessing the tactics in team sports: Football. *SpringerPlus*, *4*, 663. https://doi.org/10.1186/s40064-015-1462-0

Greenhough, B., Barrett, S., Towlson, C., & Abt, G. (2021). Perceptions of professional soccer coaches, support staff and players toward virtual reality and the factors that modify their intention to use it. *PloS One*, *16*(12), e0261378. https://doi.org/10.1371/journal.pone.0261378

Grehaigne, J. F., & Godbout, P. (1995). Tactical knowledge in team sports from a constructivist and cognitivist perspective. *Quest*, *47*(4), 490–505.

Harris, D. J., Bird, J. M., Smart, P. A., Wilson, M. R., & Vine, S. J. (2020). A framework for the testing and validation of simulated environments in experimentation and training. *Frontiers in Psychology*, *11*, 605. https://doi.org/10.1080/00336297.1995.10484171

Helson, W. F., & Starkes, J. L. (1999). A multidimensional approach to skilled perception and performance in sport. *Applied Cognitive Psychology*, *13*(1), 1–27. https://doi.org/10.1002/(SICI)1099-0720(199902)13:1%3C1::AID-ACP540%3E3.0.CO;2-T

Huijgen, B. C. H., Leemhuis, S., Kok, N. M., Verburgh, L., Oosterlaan, J., Elferink-Gemser, M. T., & Visscher, C. (2015). Cognitive functions in elite and sub-elite youth soccer players aged 13 to 17 years. *PLoS One*, *10*(12), e0144580. https://doi.org/10.1371/journal.pone.0144580

iNews. (2022). *Half of premier league clubs use virtual reality to heal injuries and recreate matchday pressure in training* [online]. Retrieved from: https://inews.co.uk/sport/football/premier-league-clubs-virtual-reality-heal-injuries-recreate-pressure-training-1635232

Kannekens, R., Elferink-Gemser., Post, W. J., & Visscher, C. (2009). Self-assessed tactical skills in elite youth soccer players: A longitudinal study. *Perceptual and Motor Skills*, *109*(2), 459–472. https://doi.org/10.2466/pms.109.2.459-472

Kannekens, R., Elferink-Gemser., & Visscher, C. (2009). Tactical skills of world-class youth soccer teams. *Journal of Sports Sciences*, *27*(8), 807–812. https://doi.org/10.1080/02640410902894339

Kannekens, R., Elferink-Gemser., & Visscher, C. (2011). Positioning and deciding: Key factors for talent development in soccer. *Scandinavian Journal for Medicine & Science in Sports, 21*(6), 846–852. https://doi.org/10.1111/j.1600-0838.2010.01104.x

Keller, B. S., Raynor, A. J., Iredale, F., & Bruce, L. (2018). Tactical skill in Australian youth soccer: Does it discriminate age-match skill levels? *International Journal of Sports Science & Coaching, 13*(6), 1057–1063. https://doi.org/10.1177%2F1747954118760778

Kelly, A. L., Wilson, M. R., Jackson, D. T., Turnnidge, J., & Williams, C. A. (2021). Speed of thought and speed of feet: Examining perceptual-cognitive expertise and physical performance in and English football academy. *Journal of Science in Sport and Exercise, 3*, 88–97. https://doi.org/10.1007/s42978-020-00081-2

Kubayi, A., & Toriola, A. (2019). Trends of goal scoring patterns in soccer: A retrospective analysis of five successive FIFA World Cup tournaments. *Journal of human kinetics, 69*, 231–238. https://doi.org/10.2478/hukin-2019-0015

Larkin, P., O'Connor, D., & Williams, A. M. (2016). Does grit influence sport-specific engagement and perceptual-cognitive expertise in elite youth soccer? *Journal of Applied Sport Psychology, 28*(2), 129–138. http://doi.org/10.1080/10413200.2015.1085922

Le Noury, P., Polman, R., Maloney, M., & Gorman, A. (2022). A narrative review of the current state of extended reality technology and how it can be utilised in sport. *Sports Medicine, 52*, 1473-1489. https://doi.org/10.1007/s40279-022-01669-0

Mann, D. T. Y., Williams, M. A., Ward, P., & Janelle, C. (2007). Perceptual-cognitive expertise in sport: A meta-analysis. *Journal of Sport & Exercise Psychology, 29*(4), 457–478. https://doi.org/10.1123/jsep.29.4.457

McPherson, S. L. (1994). The development of sport expertise: Mapping the tactical domain. *Quest, 46*(2), 223–240. https://doi.org/10.1080/00336297.1994.10484123

Memmert, D. (2006). Developing creative thinking in a gifted sport enrichment program and the crucial role of attention processes. *High Ability Studies, 17*(1), 101–115. http://dx.doi.org/10.1080/13598130600947176

Memmert, D. (2007). Can creativity be improved by an attention-broadening training program?—An exploratory study focusing on team sports. *Creativity Research Journal, 19*(2–3), 281–292. https://doi.org/10.1080/10400410701397420

Memmert, D. (2010a). Testing of tactical performance in youth elite football. *Journal of Sports Science and Medicine, 9*(2), 199–205.

Memmert, D. (2010b). Game test situations: Assessment of game creativity in ecological valid situations. *International Journal of Sport & Exercise Psychology, 41*, 94–95.

Memmert, D. (2011). Creativity, expertise, and attention: Exploring their development and their relationships. *Journal of Sports Sciences, 29*(1), 93–102. https://doi.org/10.1080/02640414.2010.528014

Memmert, D. (2013). Tactical creativity. In T. McGarry, P. O'Donoghue, & J. Sampaio (Eds.), *Routledge handbook of sports performance analysis* (pp. 297–308). Routledge.

Memmert, D. (2015). *Teaching tactical creativity in sport: Research and practice*. Routledge.

Memmert, D., Baker, J., & Bertsch, C. (2010). Play and practice in the development of sport-specific creativity in team ball sports. *High Ability Studies, 21*(1), 3–18. https://doi.org/10.1080/13598139.2010.488083

Memmert, D., & Furley, P. (2007). "I spy with my little eye!"—Breadth of attention, inattentional blindness, and tactical decision making in team sports. *Journal of Sport & Exercise Psychology, 29*(3), 365–347. https://doi.org/10.1123/jsep.29.3.365

Memmert, D., & Perl, J. (2009). Game creativity analysis using neural networks. *Journal of Sports Sciences, 27*(2), 139–149. https://doi.org/10.1080/02640410802442007

Memmert, D., & Roth, K. (2007). The effects of non-specific and specific concepts on tactical creativity in team ball sports. *Journal of Sports Sciences, 25*(12), 1423–1432. https://doi.org/10.1080/02640410601129755

Neumann, D. L., Moffitt, R. L., Thomas, P. R. loveday, K., Watling, D. P., Lombard, C. L., Antonova, S., & Tremeer, M. A. (2018). A systematic review of the application of interactive virtual reality to sport. *Virtual Reality, 22*, 183–198. https://doi.org/10.1007/s10055-017-0320-5

Pagé, C., Bernier, P. M., & Trempe, M. (2019). Using video simulations and virtual reality to improve decision-making skills in basketball. *Journal of sports sciences, 37*(21), 2403–2410. https://doi.org/10.1080/02640414.2019.1638193

Pain, M. A. (2013). Creativity in team sports. *The Boot Room*, *8*, 40–41.

Panchuk, D., Klusemann, M. J., & Hadlow, S. M. (2018). Exploring the effectiveness of immersive video for training decision-making capability in elite, youth basketball players. *Frontiers in Psychology*, *9*, 2315. https://doi.org/10.3389/fpsyg.2018.02315

Perl, J., Grunz, A., & Memmert, D. (2013). Tactics analysis in soccer: An advanced approach. *International Journal of Computer Science in Sport*, *12*(1), 33–44.

Rechenchosky, L., Menezes Menegassi, V., de Oliveira Jaime, M., Borges, P. H., Sarmento, H., Mancha-Triguero, D., Serra-Olivares, J., & Rinaldi, W. (2021). Scoping review of tests to assess tactical knowledge and tactical performance of young soccer players. *Journal of Sports Sciences*, *39*(18), 2051–2067. https://doi.org/10.1080/02640414.2021.1916262

Roca, A., Ford, P. R., McRobert, A. P., & Williams, A. M. (2013). Perceptual-cognitive skills and their interaction as a function of task constrains in soccer. *Journal of Sport & Exercise Psychology*, *35*(2), 144–155. https://doi.org/10.1123/jsep.35.2.144

Roca, A., Williams, A. M., & Ford, P. R. (2012). Developmental activities and the acquisition of superior anticipation and decision making in soccer players. *Journal of Sports Sciences*, *30*(15), 1643–1652. https://doi.org/10.1080/02640414.2012.701761

Rose, T., Nam, C. S., & Chen, K. B. (2018). Immersion of virtual reality for rehabilitation-review. *Applied Ergonomics*, *69*, 153–161. https://doi.org/10.1016/j.apergo.2018.01.009

Savelsbergh, G. J. P., Haans, S. H. A., Kooijman, M. K., & Van Kampen, P. M. (2010). A method to identify talent: Visual search and locomotion behaviour in young football players. *Human Movement Science*, *29*(5), 764–776. https://doi.org/10.1016/j.humov.2010.05.003

Savelsbergh, G. J. P., Williams, A. M., Van Der Kamp, J., & Ward, P. (2002). Visual search, anticipation and expertise in soccer goalkeepers. *Journal of Sports Sciences*, *20*(3), 279–287. https://doi.org/10.1080/026404102317284826

Serra-Olivares, J., Clemente, F. M., & González-Víllora, S. (2016). Tactical expertise assessment in youth football using representative tasks. *SpringerPlus*, *5*, 1301. https://doi.org/10.1186/s40064-016-2955-1

Sieghartsleitner, R., Zuber, C., Zibung, M., & Conzelmann, A. (2019). Science or coaches' eye?—Both! Beneficial collaboration of multidimensional measurements and coach assessments for efficient talent selection in elite youth football. *Journal of Sports Science and Medicine*, *18*(1), 32–43.

Tangalos, C., Robertson, S. J., Spittle, M., & Gastin, P. B. (2015). Predictors of individual player match performance in junior Australian football. *International Journal of Sports Physiology and Performance*, *10*(7), 853–859. https://doi.org/10.1123/ijspp.2014-0428

Thatcher, B., Ivanov, G., Szerovay, M., & Mills, G. (2021). Virtual reality technology in football coaching: Barriers and opportunities. *International Sport Coaching Journal*, *8*(2), 234–243. https://doi.org/10.1123/iscj.2020-0011

Tsai, W. L., Pan T. Y., & Hu, M. C. (2022). Feasibility study on virtual reality based basketball tactic training. *IEEE Transactions on Visualization and Computer Graphics*, *28*(8), 2970–2982. https://doi.org/10.1109/TVCG.2020.3046326

Vaeyens, R., Lenoir, M., Williams, A. M., Mazyn, L., & Philippaerts, R. M. (2007). The effects of task constraints on visual search behaviour and decision-making skill in youth soccer players. *Journal of Sport & Exercise Psychology*, *29*(2), 147–169. https://doi.org/10.1123/jsep.29.2.147

van Maarseveen, M. J. J., Oudejans, R. R. D., Mann, D. L., & Savelsbergh, G. J. P. (2018). Perceptual-cognitive skill and the in situ performance of soccer players. *The Quarterly Journal of Experimental Psychology*, *71*(2), 455–470. https://doi.org/10.1080/17470218.2016.1255236

Ward, P., & Williams, M. A. (2003). Perceptual and cognitive skill development in soccer: The multidimensional nature of expert performance. *Journal of Sport & Exercise Psychology*, *25*(1), 93–111. https://doi.org/10.1123/jsep.25.1.93

Williams, A. M. (2000). Perceptual skill in soccer: Implications for talent identification and development. *Journal of Sports Science*, *18*(9), 737–750. https://doi.org/10.1080/02640410050120113

Williams, A. M., & Davids, K. (1998). Visual search strategy, selective attention, and expertise in soccer. *Research Quarterly for Exercise and Sport*, *69*(2), 111–128. https://doi.org/10.1080/02701367.1998.10607677

Williams, A. M., & Ericsson, K. A. (2005). Perceptual-cognitive expertise in sport: Some considerations when applying the expert performance approach. *Human Movement Science*, *24*(3), 283–307. https://doi.org/10.1016/j.humov.2005.06.002

Williams, A. M., & Ford, P. R. (2008). Expertise and expert performance in sport. *International Review of Sport and Exercise Psychology*, *1*(1), 4–18. https://doi.org/10.1080/17509840701836867

Williams, A. M., Ward, P., Bell-Walker, J., & Ford, P. R. (2012). Perceptual-cognitive expertise, practice history profiles and recall performance in soccer. *British Journal of Psychology*, *103*(3), 393–411. https://doi.org/10.1111/j.2044-8295.2011.02081.x

Wilson, M. R., Miles, C. A. L., Vine, S. J., & Vickers, J. N. (2012). Quiet eye distinguishes children of high and low coordination abilities. *Medicine & Science in Sports & Exercise*, *45*(6), 1144–1151. https://doi.org/10.1249/mss.0b013e31828288f1

Wood, G., Wright, D. J., Harris, D., Pal, A., Franklin, Z. C., & Vine, S. J. (2021). Testing the construct validity of a soccer-specific virtual reality simulator using novice, academy, and professional soccer players. *Virtual Reality*, *25*(1), 43–51. https://doi.org/10.1007/s10055-020-00441-x

4

PHYSICAL

Considering the Influence of Maturity Status on Physical Performance

John M. Radnor, Adam L. Kelly, Craig A. Williams, and Jon L. Oliver

Introduction

Soccer academies are a central pathway in the long-term development of young players, with the primary objective of identifying and developing talented individuals to compete at senior levels (Carling et al., 2008; Reilly et al., 2000). One factor that influences player selection and progression through these academies is biological maturation (Clemente et al., 2021; Meylan et al., 2010). Research has demonstrated a number of inherent performance benefits associated with advanced maturation, which are summarised throughout this chapter. Due to the influence of maturation on physical performance, it is not surprising that early maturing males are more likely to be selected into talent pathways at youth levels (Clemente et al., 2021; Hill et al., 2020; Massa et al., 2022). However, there is some literature that suggests a greater proportion of late-maturing players actually make it to senior professional levels (Ostojic et al., 2014). Therefore, it is vital for practitioners to understand how to support the identification, development, and progression of early-, average-, and late-maturing players in youth soccer.

Due to the growing interest supporting the implementation and evaluation of physical development strategies in youth soccer (Thomas et al., 2021), this chapter provides an overview of the existing literature and practical considerations. First, growth and maturation are defined, whilst the benefits and drawbacks of current methods for monitoring these processes are provided. Second, the impact of growth and maturation on physical performance and its subsequent influence on talent identification and development outcomes in males and females is discussed. Third, the influence of maturation on injury risk is outlined alongside conditions to protect players against such maturity-related injury risks. Fourth, the strategies that have been proposed to accommodate for individual differences in growth and maturation are outlined, with a particular focus on the effectiveness of 'bio-banding' as an alternative grouping approach. Lastly, potential areas for future research and key implications for practice are proposed.

Growth and Maturation

Although the terms 'growth' and 'maturation' are often used interchangeably when describing the pathway from birth to adulthood, they are different concepts. *Growth* refers to quantifiable changes in body composition, either the size of the body as a whole or the size of specific regions of the body (Beunen & Malina, 2005), whereas *maturation* refers to qualitative system changes, both structural and functional, in the body's progress towards adulthood (Beunen & Malina, 2005; Malina et al., 2004a). All tissues, organs, and systems of the body mature with growth, but they do so at different rates (also known as tempo) and times (Malina et al., 2004a). Specifically, the timing and tempo of maturation can differ significantly, whereby *timing* defines when a particular maturation process occurs, whereas *tempo* is the rate at which maturation progresses.

Assessing Maturation

Despite 'chronological age' being predictable and easily calculated, and generally measured in years, months, or days at a single time point away from the date of birth, 'biological age' is significantly more problematic as it is less predictable and more difficult to assess. Furthermore, relative maturity differs between sexes, with females (on average) reaching their mature state 2 years before males, which indicates girls are generally more biologically mature than males at the same chronological age (Faigenbaum et al., 2020). There are a number of methods of assessing maturity status (i.e., biological age), none of which is the gold standard (Lloyd et al., 2014). Common measures of biological maturation that are reasonably well related include 'skeletal', 'sexual', and 'somatic' (Olivares et al., 2020).

Skeletal age assessment may be considered the preferable method of assessing maturity status (Malina et al., 2004a; Stratton & Oliver, 2020). This method is based upon the transition of the skeleton from cartilage at the prenatal stage to a fully developed skeleton in early adulthood (Malina et al., 2004a). A left hand-wrist radiograph is usually compared against standardised images to assess the degree of ossification of the anatomical area, and subsequently, a composite score of skeletal age is produced (Simoes et al., 2010). However, considering the expense and requirement for specialised radiographers, this method is difficult to implement and therefore other methods are often utilised.

Sexual age is defined as the progression towards a state of fully functional reproductive function. Tanner staging has been used to estimate sexual maturation and utilises a five-step ranking process that requires observations of secondary sexual characteristics and references against a criteria table (Tanner, 1990). However, the Tanner staging only provides categorical data and could be considered an unnecessarily invasive method of assessment.

Somatic age refers to the use of growth in stature or specific dimensions of the body for the estimation of maturity (Lloyd et al., 2014). Longitudinal assessment of growth can be used to create growth curves, and these can be used to identify the peak growth rate in children. The highest growth rate in stature is referred to as peak-height velocity (PHV), and the age at which this occurs is termed 'age at PHV'. Peak-height velocity can also be estimated from data collected at a single point in time, and predictive equations have been developed to estimate age at PHV (Mirwald et al., 2002; Moore et al., 2014). Predicted adult height can also be estimated, and the percentage of adult stature can be used to determine the maturational status of a young athlete (Khamis & Roche, 1994).

Growth Rates

The most simple level of assessment involves longitudinal anthropometric assessments (Lloyd et al., 2014). The repeated collection of height (e.g., every 3 months) over a period of time would enable the analysis of growth curves that allow information related to the initiation of the growth spurt and PHV to be obtained. On average, PHV will occur at age approximately 12 years in girls and 14 years in boys, with girls increasing stature at a rate of 8 cm/year and boys at 10 cm/year. However, it should be noted there is considerable variability in the timing and tempo of PHV. The age at which PHV occurs can vary from age approximately 10 to 15 years in girls and from 11 to 16 years in boys, with peak growth rates of 5–11 cm/year and 6–13 cm/year, respectively (Stratton & Oliver, 2020). While this is a relatively simple way of assessing PHV, one issue for practitioners is that the identification of age at PHV requires regular tracking of growth from middle childhood until late adolescence. Additionally, PHV can only be identified retrospectively, after a peak has been observed.

Predicting Age at Peak Height Velocity

Considering the limitations associated with collecting longitudinal data to identify PHV, predictive equations can be used to predict the age at PHV from single measurements of anthropometric variables (Mirwald et al., 2002; Moore et al., 2014). For instance, Mirwald et al. (2002) proposed a predictive equation based on the theory of differential growth rates between the lower limbs and torso. The calculation of PHV requires the collection of chronological age, body mass, standing height, and sitting height, with the equations providing a maturity offset, defined as the time before or after PHV in years (Kozieł & Malina, 2018). The maturity offset value derived from the equation can be converted into age at PHV by summing the maturity offset and chronological age. This approach to obtaining age at PHV has also been reported to possess an acceptable standard error of estimate ($\pm$ 0.6 years) (Mirwald et al., 2002). Thereafter, Moore et al. (2014) further developed the prediction equation, which no longer requires the inclusion of sitting height. However, this approach does not substantially improve the measurement accuracy of the maturity offset (standard error of estimates = 0.542 years), although it may allow practitioners to identify PHV when sitting height has not been calculated. Moreover, the equation has been shown to be biased to chronological age at the time of estimation, meaning that predictions may be more accurate around the time of PHV and less accurate further away from this event (Malina & Kozieł, 2014).

Predicting Adult Stature

The percentage of adult stature can be calculated at a given time point during childhood and adolescence, which can be used to determine the maturational status of a young player. This approach may be useful to differentiate between those who are early-maturing and those who are naturally predisposed to being tall, especially as it is possible that two individuals in this situation could present with the same absolute stature at a given chronological age (Lloyd et al., 2014). Khamis and Roche (1994) have proposed a prediction equation for somatic maturity using midparental height but also included the child's stature and body mass, in addition to specific coefficients for each of these variables at 0.5-year intervals, which serve to improve the accuracy of the prediction model (Khamis & Roche, 1994).

Research that has collated longitudinal data has highlighted that PHV occurs around 92%–93% of predicted adult height (PAH), with the linear growth-spurt lasting approximately 12 months pre-PHV and 12 months post-PHV (Cumming et al., 2017). It is possible to group athletes into maturity groups using PAH data: (a) pre-pubertal spurt is defined as < 85% (PH1), (b) early-pubertal ≥ 85–90% (PH2), (c) mid-pubertal ≥ 90–95% (PH3), and (d) late-pubertal ≥ 95% (PH4) (Cumming et al., 2017). It is important to note that caution is often required in the interpretation of the adult height predictions due to the accuracy of the adult stature that are often self-measured or self-reported, or in the case of one parent being absent, estimated by the other parent, but this can be mitigated by adjusting for over-estimation by using sex-specific equations (Epstein et al., 1995).

Influence of Maturation on Physical Performance

Youth can be classified as biologically 'ahead of' (referred to as an early maturer), 'on time' (referred to as an average maturer), or 'behind' (referred to as a late maturer) relative to their chronological age (Malina et al., 2004a). This inter-individual difference in biological maturation is evident when comparing a squad of young players of the same chronological age who may differ markedly in terms of their estimated maturation (Malina et al., 2000, 2015). During childhood, girls and boys experience similar rates of biological development and therefore display relatively similar levels of physical fitness and motor skill development (Faigenbaum et al., 2020). Following puberty, males experience superior gains in physical performance capabilities, owing to natural reductions in fat-mass, increases in muscle mass and stature, as well as increases in certain hormonal concentrations (e.g. testosterone and growth hormone) (Handelsman et al., 2018). Boys who mature in advance of their peers experience the adolescent growth-spurt at an earlier age and, thus, are invariably taller and heavier from late childhood and possess greater absolute and relative lean mass (Clemente et al., 2021; Malina et al., 2004; Meylan et al., 2010).

As a consequence of their advanced maturity, early-maturing boys also tend to outperform their less mature counterparts on tests of strength, power, speed, agility, and endurance (Guimarães et al., 2019; Meylan et al., 2010). However, research shows a similar pattern in girls is not as clear, with maturation enhancing some aspects of physical performance but not others, which may be explained by the natural increases in sex-specific fat-mass that girls experience that can negatively impact certain motor skills that involve the movement of body mass (Malina et al., 2004a).

Strength and Power

Muscular strength underpins a number of physical abilities and performance attributes in soccer (Murtagh et al., 2018; Wing et al., 2020). Consequently, weaker players may be less likely to reach their full athletic potential. Researchers have identified that measures of strength and power may determine the likelihood of players being selected at youth levels, proceeding to higher playing standards, and being awarded professional contracts in soccer (Deprez et al., 2015; Gil et al., 2014; le Gall et al., 2010). For example, Deprez et al. (2015) retrospective study on 388 Belgian youth soccer players found that participants who attained a professional contract jumped further compared to non-contracted players. They highlighted the importance of including the evaluation of physical performance characteristics between the ages of 8 and 16 years, since a combination of assessments can help distinguish high-level soccer players who progressed and succeeded within an academy environment (Deprez et al., 2015).

Strength and power increase naturally in youth soccer players as they transition towards adulthood (Emmonds et al., 2018; Morris et al., 2020; Parr et al., 2020). Research into male youth soccer players has demonstrated large to very large effect sizes between pre- to circa-, circa- to post-, and pre- to post-PHV groups for peak force during the isometric mid-thigh pull (IMTP). However, only small effect sizes were reported when force was made relative to body mass (Morris et al., 2020). Similar findings have been reported in girls, where peak force was greater in more mature female soccer players. However, when made relative to body mass, relative peak force did not increase linearly between consecutive maturity groups, with girls 0.5 years prior to PHV having greater relative force than girls 0.5 years post-PHV (Emmonds et al., 2018). This may be due to increases in body fat as girls mature (Malina et al., 2004a), and relative measures that divide performance by body mass may not account for this.

Research has demonstrated that muscle size is 104% greater in men than boys and only 57% greater in women than girls (O'Brien et al., 2010). Considering that muscle size is a primary factor in the improved capacity to produce force (O'Brien et al., 2010), these findings may suggest the sex differences in force production following puberty (Ramos et al., 1998). However, in boys, when force production is calculated relative to body mass, the more mature athletes still produce greater force, albeit to a lesser degree. This greater force may be due to changes in the specific architecture of muscles during maturation, as increases in fascicle length from childhood through to adolescence can improve force production at higher shortening speeds and over larger length ranges (Radnor et al., 2022). Additionally, as boys transition into adolescence, they will naturally improve their ability to recruit their high-threshold, type II motor units, thereby enhancing their ability to produce both the magnitude of force output and rate at which the force is developed (Dotan et al., 2012). These findings highlight the importance of considering relative versus absolute measures of peak force in youth soccer players, as maturation may not influence these qualities in the same way between the sexes.

Sprint and Change of Direction Speed

Speed is a desirable characteristic that has been associated with successful performance outcomes in young soccer players (Reilly et al., 2000). Sprinting and change of direction actions ($\geq 50°$) have been shown to be associated with goal scoring opportunities in soccer (Faude et al., 2012), highlighting the importance of developing sprint speed and change of direction speed (CODS) in young soccer players. Sprint speed has also been shown to differentiate youth soccer players who received a professional contract and those who did not (Deprez et al., 2015; Emmonds et al., 2016), those who were selected and non-selected (Gil et al., 2014), between high- and low-potentials (Kelly et al., 2021b), and those who play-up a chronological age group and those who do not (Kelly et al., 2021a). As an example, in a longitudinal study of 7 years, Emmonds et al. (2016) assessed 443 academy soccer players revealing that 10 m and 20 m sprint speed influenced obtaining a professional contract at aged 18 years. Furthermore, change of direction speed has been identified as the only physical performance quality that distinguished talented Spanish soccer players in U15 to U17 age groups (Gil et al., 2007), whilst it has also been identified as one of the major factors of predicting success in 11-year-old soccer players (Mirkov et al., 2010). A failure to fully develop speed during childhood may also restrict opportunities as an adult because speed is often reported to distinguish between adults of differing competitive standards (Pyne et al., 2005).

Improvements in both sprint and CODS during childhood follow a non-linear process for both boys and girls (Emmonds et al., 2018; Meyers et al., 2015; Vänttinen et al., 2011). Recently, research has shown that CODS may be similar in U15, U17, and U20 age groups, although senior players were significantly faster than all other groups (Loturco et al., 2020). In terms of sprint speed, research with young boys has shown the existence of a preadolescent spurt in speed, followed by a second adolescent spurt around the onset of maturation (Meyers et al., 2015; Nagahara et al., 2018). Furthermore, longitudinal data from boys have suggested that peak improvements in sprint speed occur around the period of peak height velocity (Meyers et al., 2016; Philippaerts et al., 2006). The pre-pubertal spurt has been attributed to rapid central nervous system development during the first decade of life, with the adolescent spurt primarily attributed to a rise in hormone levels and structural changes with maturity (Handelsman et al., 2018). Importantly, maximal sprint speed is the product of step length and step frequency (Hunter et al., 2004), and the latter is largely stable in youth, while increases in sprint speed are proportional to increases in step length (Meyers et al., 2016). Maximal sprint performance in pre-pubertal boys may be more step-frequency reliant, whilst post-pubertal boys may be marginally step-length reliant (Meyers et al., 2017), further highlighting the influence of maturation upon sprint performance in youth.

While CODS performance may distinguish between playing level in males, there is limited research available on the CODS ability of female soccer players as well as how this develops throughout maturation. However, the greatest difference in 30 m sprint speed between girls of consecutive maturity groups has been shown to be between 2.5 years pre-PHV and 1.5 years pre-PHV, with the smallest difference being between 0.5 to 1.5 years post-PHV (Emmonds et al., 2018). In contrast, girls 0.5 years prior to PHV had faster 10 m sprint times than girls 0.5 post-PHV, and this was in accordance with a likely moderate difference in relative peak force between these maturity groups, which may have had a negative influence on force production capabilities (Emmonds et al., 2018). These findings indicate that females will not experience a natural increase in speed throughout maturation, and exposure to strength and conditioning training to develop force production is vital for these athletes to improve sprint speed.

Endurance

Endurance is synonymous with the aerobic system and the ability to maintain lower-intensity exercise over a long duration. However, potentially more importantly for soccer performance, the aerobic system enables recovery to take place following bouts of high-intensity exercise. There is limited research on the improvement in endurance capacity with maturation in boys, but the Yo-Yo intermittent recovery test (YYIR) level-2 performance was greater in consecutive age groups from U14 up to U18 (Emmonds et al., 2016). In girls, the distance covered on the YYIR level-1 was greater for girls between 0.5 pre-PHV and 0.5 post-PHV, with all other groups reporting unclear differences in performance. Most importantly, endurance performance can be a distinguishing factor in players receiving a professional contract at U18 (Emmonds et al., 2016), and is therefore a key physical quality in soccer performance.

Endurance performance is determined by three physiological factors, including peak oxygen uptake (VO_2 peak), the anaerobic threshold, and economy. Absolute values of VO_2 peak increase by 150% in boys between the ages of 8 and 16 years and are underpinned by growth in body size, heart size and blood volume, and increasing cardiac output (Armstrong & Welsman, 2000). Pre-pubertal children have lower levels of glycolytic activity and are more reliant on aerobic energy, compared to more mature children and adults. Consequently, children experience less fatigue during exercise, recover more quickly, and can maintain exercise at a higher relative intensity. Running economy improves steadily with age in children and adolescents, with the oxygen cost of running at a set speed reducing approximately almost 20% from aged 5 to 18 years in boys and girls (Mahon, 2008). Changes in body size, improvements in technique, and reduced co-contraction may all help explain improvements in economy (Bar-Or & Rowland, 2004). The accumulation of the previously described physiological changes means that endurance performance improves markedly with maturation, with one mile run times decreasing by approximately 20% in boys between the ages of 9 and 17 years (Catley & Tomkinson, 2013).

Overall, this section highlights the general consensus that maturation positively influences physical performance, and the physical ability of players assists in their progression through soccer academies and into professional careers. Therefore, the development of physical abilities throughout childhood and adolescence should be at the forefront of all youth development programmes.

Trainability of Physical Qualities

In 2012, Lloyd and Oliver published the Youth Physical Development (YPD) model (Lloyd & Oliver, 2012), which is a framework for developing physical abilities throughout childhood. The YPD model (Figure 4.1a: males; Figure 4.1b: females) highlights the importance of considering training with respect to the maturational status of children, identified via the timing of PHV. The driving factor of the YPD model is that it is based on the fact that research highlights that most components of fitness are trainable, irrespective of the stage of maturation, while there is limited evidence to support the previous theory of 'windows of opportunity' (Ford et al., 2011). The

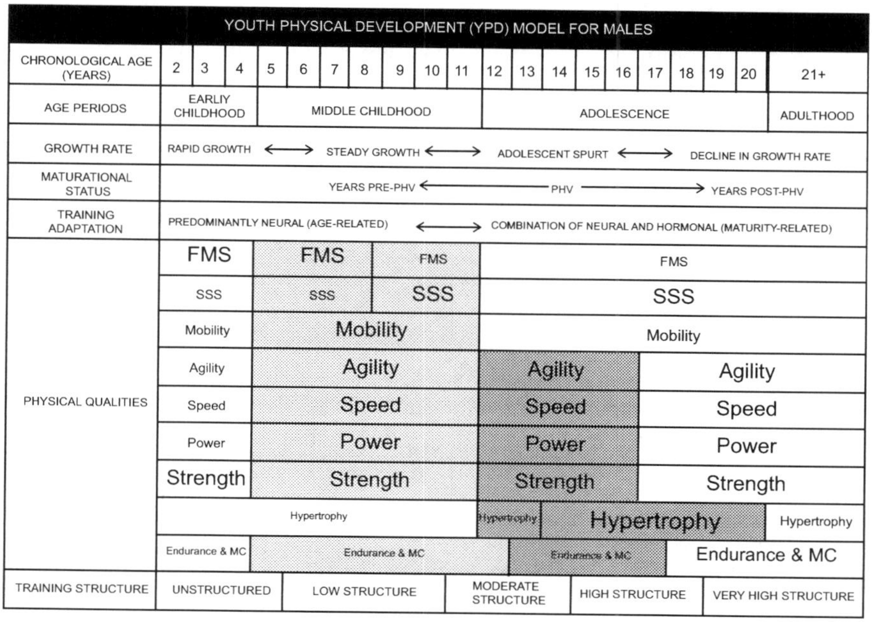

FIGURE 4.1A The Youth Physical Development model for males (Lloyd & Oliver, 2012).

Note: Font size refers to importance, whilst light shaded boxes refer to pre-adolescence periods of adaptation and dark shaded boxes refer to adolescent periods of adaptation.

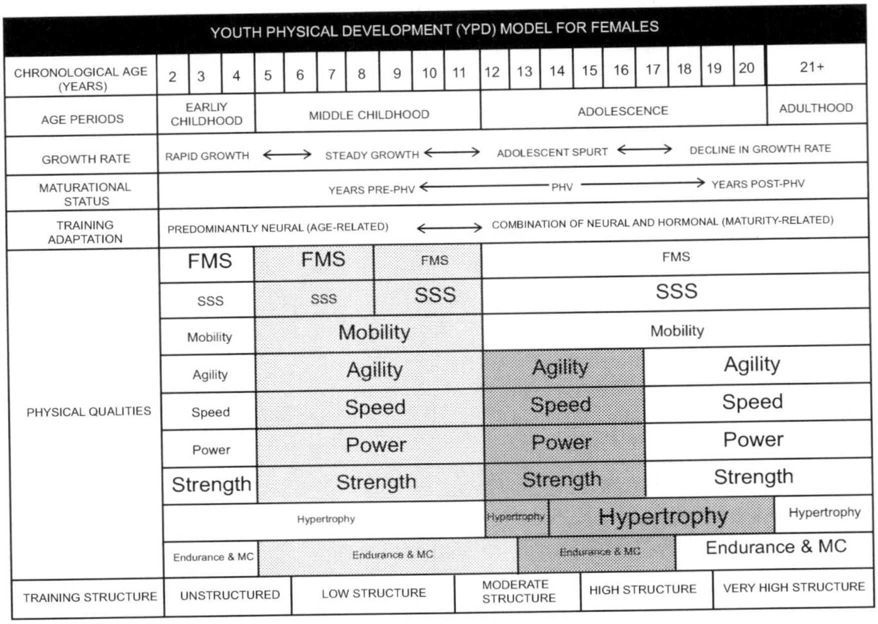

YOUTH PHYSICAL DEVELOPMENT (YPD) MODEL FOR FEMALES

CHRONOLOGICAL AGE (YEARS)	2	3	4	5	6	7	8	9	10	11	12	13	14	15	16	17	18	19	20	21+
AGE PERIODS	EARLY CHILDHOOD			MIDDLE CHILDHOOD							ADOLESCENCE									ADULTHOOD
GROWTH RATE	RAPID GROWTH ↔ STEADY GROWTH ↔ ADOLESCENT SPURT ↔ DECLINE IN GROWTH RATE																			
MATURATIONAL STATUS	YEARS PRE-PHV ← → PHV → YEARS POST-PHV																			
TRAINING ADAPTATION	PREDOMINANTLY NEURAL (AGE-RELATED) ← → COMBINATION OF NEURAL AND HORMONAL (MATURITY-RELATED)																			

Physical Qualities (in order): FMS, SSS, Mobility, Agility, Speed, Power, Strength, Hypertrophy, Endurance & MC

| TRAINING STRUCTURE | UNSTRUCTURED | LOW STRUCTURE | MODERATE STRUCTURE | HIGH STRUCTURE | VERY HIGH STRUCTURE |

FIGURE 4.1B The Youth Physical Development model for females (Lloyd & Oliver, 2012).

Note: Font size refers to importance, whilst light shaded boxes refer to pre-adolescence periods of adaptation and dark shaded boxes refer to adolescent periods of adaptation.

YPD model also highlights the process of 'synergistic adaptation', where the mechanisms that underpin training adaptations are likely to differ between the childhood and adolescent years (Lloyd et al., 2015). Research has indicated that, prior to adolescence, training adaptations will have a predominantly neural basis, whereas, once puberty has been reached, adaptations may also be attributed to morphological changes stimulated by the increase in circulating androgens interacting with training stimuli (Lloyd et al., 2015).

Recent meta-analyses have demonstrated improvements in strength and power measures following resistance training in youth (Behm et al., 2017; Granacher et al., 2016). Power (plyometric) training studies provide changes of a higher magnitude in jump performance than strength training studies in youth (Behm et al., 2017). Additionally, untrained individuals experienced greater jump height gains than trained participants, whilst children (boys: aged ≤ 13 years; girls: aged ≤ 11 years) experienced larger jump height gains than adolescents (boys: aged 14 to 18 years; girls: aged 12 to 18 years) (Behm et al., 2017). Strength training studies were shown to provide better sprint time results than power training, and untrained and child populations had greater improvements than trained and adolescents respectively for sprint performance (Behm et al., 2017). Furthermore, during a 6-month training intervention, athletes who trained twice per week achieved significantly larger improvements in movement competency, isometric strength, and concentric jump variables, compared with athletes who trained once per week. Furthermore, the training response was greater in those youth with lower baseline fitness and more advanced maturity status (Lloyd et al., 2021).

Influence of Maturation on Injury Risk

Another important factor in the talent-development pathway in soccer is the influence of maturation on injury risk. The period around PHV has been associated with a significantly higher risk of injury in youth soccer players compared with pre- and post-PHV players (Johnson et al., 2020; van der Sluis et al., 2014), although muscle injuries may be greatest in post-PHV players (Monasterio et al., 2021). More specifically, recent research has identified that growth-related injuries follow a distal to proximal pattern, with Sever's disease more prevalent in the less mature players, Osgood-Schlatter disease common in the pre- and circa-PHV group, and injuries to the hip and spine (e.g., Spondylolysis) more frequently at the post-PHV stage (Monasterio et al., 2021). Growth rates of ≥ 7.2 cm/year in stature or ≥ 0.3 kg/m^2 per month in body mass index are associated with increased injury risk (Kemper et al., 2015). Tracking growth rates (as mentioned in the foregoing section) can identify players 'at risk' of growth-related injuries and can assist practitioners in prescribing appropriate training during this stage. Sex-dependent injury risks may also start to become more evident during maturation, with adolescent female soccer players experiencing a three-fold higher rate of ACL injuries than their male counterparts (Gupta et al., 2020). The increased risk of injury surrounding the period of the growth spurt may also be elevated due to rapid growth of the limbs, causing a temporary disruption to motor coordination, termed 'adolescent awkwardness' (Quatman-Yates et al., 2012).

During the growth spurt, training may need to reinforce the re-learning of movement skills, conditioning players to protect them against specific injury risks (e.g., ACL), as well as reducing high-volume, repetitious training and potentially allowing for more recovery time between training sessions to prevent overuse injuries (Cumming et al., 2017). However, it is important to note that a youth development programme should not be solely designed based on maturity, since technical competency will always be the primary focus to help identify the most appropriate form of training (Lloyd & Oliver, 2012). Finally, it is key that practitioners understand that the growth spurt will influence young players technical and tactical abilities, and it is important that coaches do not deselect players during this stage or make decisions based solely on performance outcomes.

Bio-Banding

Given the inherent performance benefits associated with advanced maturation, it is not surprising that early-maturing males are more likely to be represented and selected for sports where greater size, strength, and power are desirable attributes, such as in soccer (Parr et al., 2020; Radnor et al., 2022). The selection bias towards advanced maturity in males emerges from late childhood/early adolescence and increase in size and magnitude with age and level of competition (Malina et al., 2004b). Those involved in the identification and development of academy players need to be aware of, and accommodate for, individual differences in maturation.

Bio-banding has been used as a method to ensure holistic development of soccer players in academies, which is the process of periodically grouping players on the basis of attributes associated with growth or maturation, rather than chronological age (Cumming et al., 2017). This method can theoretically benefit both early and late maturers by levelling out physical requirements, ensuring that players develop technical and tactical abilities as well as using their physical qualities. Bio-banding also present early and late maturing youth with new learning opportunities

TABLE 4.1 Maturation classifications for bio-banding pre-, circa-, and post-PHV youth players

Maturation Classification	Pre-PHV/Pre-Pubertal	Circa-PHV/Mid-Pubertal	Post-PHV/Post-Pubertal
Maturation offset	>-1 years from PHV	-1 to +1 years around PHV	<+1 years from PHV
Percentage of predicted adult height attained	≥85–90%	≥90–95%	≥95%

and challenges and provides coaches with the opportunity to evaluate and consider players within a different developmental context (Malina et al., 2019).

The two main bio-banding methods used to group athletes based on maturity are: (a) percentage of predicted adult height attained (%PAHA), and (b) maturity offset. The guidelines that are presented in Table 4.1 demonstrate how these methods can be used to band players into groups who are pre-, circa-, and post-PHV (Cumming et al., 2017). When using %PAHA, an additional band has been introduced, with 80–85% PAHA being used for early-prepubertal. However, a similar cut-off hasn't been used for pre-PHV, and if estimating maturity offset, this would be best being avoided as maturity offset prediction becomes less reliable the further it is from PHV (Mirwald et al., 2002).

Bio-banding literature has primarily been tested in the format of experimental tournaments in male youth soccer. Initial research from Cumming et al. (2018) revealed early-maturing players perceived bio-banded matches as more physically challenging in comparison to their normal chronological age group format, whereas later-maturing players perceived the bio-banded games to be less physically challenging. During their maturity-matched soccer tournament, Bradley et al. (2019) revealed later-maturing players perceived the bio-banded format afforded more opportunities to express themselves, adopt positions of leadership, and have a greater influence on gameplay when compared to their usual chronological age group format. In comparison, their early maturing but same-aged peers perceived the bio-banded games as more physically and technically challenging (Figure 4.2).

Since bio-banding exists as an adjunct to, and not a replacement for, age group competition, late maturing youth also continue to experience the challenges of competing against their more mature peers in the traditional formats. This observation may be key from an 'underdog hypothesis' perspective (Gibbs et al., 2012), whereby late-maturing youth must possess and/or develop superior technical, tactical, psychological, and/or social abilities if they are to remain competitive within their age groups, and hence developing these qualities generally results in them being more successful at the adult level (Cumming et al., 2018). It may be important for these later-maturing players to compete against more mature peers in order to develop these traits that result in their success transitioning towards adulthood. Equally, early-maturing players also need to benefit from such challenges, by either playing up an age group or competing in bio-banded competitions to develop technical skills, rather than relying on their physical dominance.

Preliminary and exploratory studies have revealed bio-banding may positively adapt the outcome of skill behaviours compared to chronological age grouping (Abbott et al., 2019; Romann et al., 2020; Thomas et al., 2017). For instance, initial research from Thomas et al. (2017) showed that, although a bio-banded format elicited a similar physiological (i.e., heart rate and distance covered across intensity zones) and perceptual (i.e., rate of perceived exertion) load to that of the chronological age group format, the technical demands were higher during bio-banding (e.g., an increase in the of number of passes, passes made from within the team's own half, and

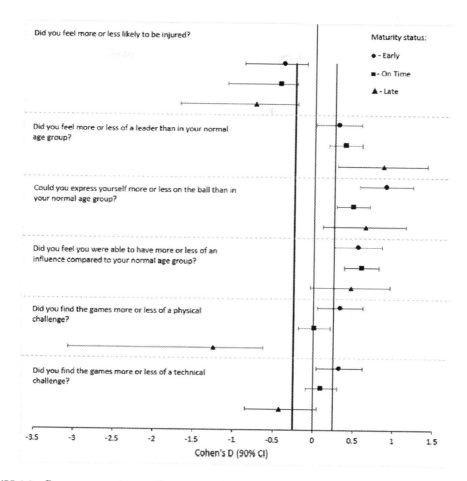

FIGURE 4.2 Responses to six specific questions by players of contrasting maturity status to participation in the bio-banded tournament (Bradley et al., 2019[1]).

Note: Data points represent Cohen's *d* effect size and confidence intervals. The vertical lines represent the threshold for the smallest worthwhile effect size (Cohens *d* effect size of 0.2 to -0.2 small).

total number of touches, as well as fewer headers) (see Table 4.2 for an overview). In addition, other studies have showed that bio-banded players completed more tackles and fewer long passes (Abbott et al., 2019), while covering less distance jogging, running, and high-speed running compared to those who were grouped by chronological age (Romann et al., 2020).

During bio-banding competitions, both early- and late-maturing players have identified that the format provided them with unique challenges (Cumming et al., 2018). Early-maturing players identified that games were more physically challenging and required them to rely more on technique, teamwork, and tactics over physicality (Cumming et al., 2018). Whereas, late-maturing players described their experience as less physically demanding than a normal format, but identified that they had more opportunity to use and demonstrate their complete skills set (i.e., technical, tactical, and physical) (Cumming et al., 2018). Collectively, these studies demonstrate that

TABLE 4.2 Technical performance measures of an U14 chronological age group competition compared to 85–90% bio-banded competition (Thomas et al., 2017[2])

Variable Groups	Performance Variable	Chronological Age Group	Bio-Banded Group (85–90%)	Increase/Decrease (%)
Variables related to goal scoring	Shot (no.)	19	23	21
	Shot on target (%)	54	70	16
Variables related to passing	Pass (no.)	259*	542*	109
	Pass accuracy (%)	75	78	3
	Pass in own half (no.)	150*	351*	134
	Pass in own half accuracy (%)	80	80	0
	Pass in opposition half (no.)	110	191	73
	Pass in opposition half accuracy (%)	68	74	6
	Touch (no.)	318*	623*	95
	Reliability in possession (%)	75	79	4
Variables related to dribbling	Dribbles (no.)	38	83	118
	Dribble accuracy (%)	61	58	-3
Variables related to defending	Tackles (no.)	46	41	-11
	Blocks (no.)	32	44	37
	Headers (no.)	35*	18*	-48

Note: *denotes statistically significant difference at $p < 0.05$.

when the method of grouping is manipulated to moderate maturity related biases, there may be important opportunities for players' technical, tactical, physical, psychological, and social development. That said, it may be important for later-maturing players to compete against more mature peers in order to develop key traits that result in their success transitioning towards adulthood, known as the 'underdog hypothesis' (Kelly et al., 2020). Equally, early-maturing players may also need to benefit from such challenges either by playing up an age group or competing in bio-banded competitions. Thus, a combination training and competing in biologically matched teams alongside regular chronological age groupings may result in the best-case scenario for player development.

Fitness testing has become integral within talent identification and development programmes in youth soccer to assess a player's current physical performance (Cobley et al., 2012). However, comparing two players within the same chronological age group without considering the individuals' biological maturity can be problematic, as maturity status has a significant influence on physical performance (Parr et al., 2020). Therefore, it is suggested that to better understand the fitness levels of a player relative to their peers, they are measured by comparing players of a similar maturity. Table 4.3 highlights benchmarking data from a male English Football League academy for a range of physical tests in youth soccer players of different maturity status. There data set included 88 players from U9 to U18. Mean and standard deviations of each test were created for all maturity groups, and z-scores of 0.5 and -0.5 were used to determine above-average and below-average performers. Practitioners can use this data to compare players against players in similar maturity groups if they do not have access to team data.

Considerations for Researchers

There has been a considerable amount of research into the influence of maturation on physical performance in male youth soccer players (Kelly & Williams, 2020). However, there are areas of research related to this that warrant further study. For example, a better understanding of how maturity and physical performance influence coaches' decisions when selecting or deselecting

TABLE 4.3 Benchmarking data from a male English Football League academy for a range of physical tests in youth soccer players of different maturity status

Age Group	Level	5 m (s)	10 m (s)	20 m (s)	30 m (s)	CMJ Height (cm)	IMTP Peak Force (N)	IMTP Relative PF (bw)	L-Run (Left)	L-Run (Right)	YoYo IE2 (Distance m)
PH4 (> 95% PAH)	Above Average	< 0.97	< 1.69	< 2.96	< 4.15	> 0.37	> 2553	> 35.9	< 5.7	< 5.68	> 2304
	Average	0.97–1.03	1.69–1.77	2.96–3.08	4.15–4.33	0.33–0.37	2003–2553	30.1–35.9	5.7–6.01	5.68–5.93	1606–2304
	Below Average	> 1.03	> 1.77	> 3.08	> 4.33	< 0.33	< 2003	< 30.1	> 6.01	> 5.93	< 1606
PH3 (90–95% PAH)	Above Average	< 1.01	< 1.78	< 3.13	< 4.43	> 0.32	> 1739	> 29.1	< 5.97	< 5.87	—
	Average	1.01–1.07	1.78–1.86	3.13–3.3	4.43–4.69	0.28–0.32	1489–1739	26.6–29.1	5.97–6.42	5.87–6.22	—
	Below Average	> 1.07	> 1.86	> 3.3	> 4.69	< 0.28	< 1489	< 26.6	> 6.42	> 6.22	—
PH2 (85–90% PAH)	Above Average	< 1.13	< 1.96	< 3.43	< 4.84	> 0.28	> 1459	> 31.3	< 6.17	< 6.12	—
	Average	1.13–1.2	1.96–2.06	3.43–3.59	4.84–5.08	0.24–0.28	1129–1459	25.3–31.3	6.17–6.47	6.12–6.39	—
	Below Average	> 1.20	> 2.06	> 3.59	> 5.08	< 0.24	< 1129	< 25.3	> 6.47	> 6.39	—
PH1 (< 85% PAH)	Above Average	< 1.19	< 2.11	< 3.71	< 5.3	> 0.23	> 996	> 26.7	< 6.04	< 6.06	—
	Average	1.19–1.26	2.11–2.19	3.71–3.84	5.3–5.55	0.2–0.23	803–996	23.2–26.7	6.04–6.38	6.06–6.4	—
	Below Average	> 1.26	> 2.19	> 3.84	> 5.55	< 0.2	< 803	< 23.2	> 6.38	> 6.4	—

players into talent pathways (e.g., academies) is warranted, which will also help inform coach education. Similarly, further research is required to recognise whether talent pathways in soccer develop the physical ability of players at a greater rate than those not selected, or whether academies simply identify and recruit players who possess superior physical characteristics at a young age, and then those players develop at the same rate as those who are not selected. Furthermore, the influence of training versus natural growth and maturation on physical performance is still unclear. As children transition towards adulthood, natural improvement in physical qualities is apparent, and therefore, training adaptations may be masked by these natural improvements. Understanding how training can develop physical qualities above and beyond natural growth and maturation is an important area for practitioners.

To date, the scientific inquiry into bio-banding in soccer has solely used male participants (Abbott et al., 2019; Bradley et al., 2019; Cumming et al., 2018; (Cumming et al., 2018; Romann et al., 2020), and as such, the influence of bio-banding upon female participants is unknown. Moreover, since bio-banding has only been trialled during short-term initiatives, there is a requirement for further knowledge on long-term outcomes during bio-banded interventions from a technical, tactical, physical, psychological, and social standpoint. Further, the majority of bio-banding research has been conducted in talent pathways within professional soccer academies, thus, further research is required beyond high-performance soccer (e.g., recreational soccer, schools), as it may have potential to benefit the wider population.

Considerations for Practitioners

It is key for practitioners to understand how maturity status can influence physical performance, and that there will be a large variation in the timing and tempo of maturation in children of similar chronological age. There are a number of maturity-related considerations that practitioners should be aware of to ensure a holistic development of a young soccer, including:

- At the time of maturation for boys and girls, increases in performance begin to diverge, with boys realising increases in physical performance, which is not the case in females. This has significant influence on the training and injury risk profile in sexes following puberty.
- Monitoring size is simple and accessible. Practitioners are encouraged to use this data to track growth rates and estimate maturity, which could serve as useful to consider the fitness of players relative to their maturity status rather than chronological age.
- Youth of all ages can experience positive improvements from many forms of training, but the response to training may differ between pre- and post-PHV youth. Therefore, it is important to initiate an age-appropriate athletic development programme during early childhood to stimulate the largest possible long-term gains.
- The increased injury risk around the time of the growth spurt, and associated adolescent awkwardness, may require coaches to reduce physical training volumes to reduce injury risk. Teaching fundamental movement skills during this stage is key to ensure balance and coordination is developed. Specifically, growth rates of ≥ 7.2 cm/year in stature or ≥ 0.3 kg/m^2 per month in body mass index are associated with increased injury risk.
- Consider the use of bio-banding to offer young players the opportunity to compete against players of the same maturity status, which may allow players to experience technical, tactical, physical, psychological, and social skills that they may not achieve within chronological age groups. Bio-banding could also provide coaches with a different perspective during talent identification procedures.

Conclusion

Most physical qualities will develop naturally with growth and maturation in both boys and girls as they experience maturation, but following the adolescent growth spurt, boys will see larger improvements in comparison to girls. Therefore, early-maturing boys tend to outperform their less mature counterparts in a range of physical performance tests and are more likely to be selected during talent identification and gain access to talent development pathways. While maturation will produce increases in physical performance, youth of all ages can experience positive improvements from many forms of training. Most importantly, practitioners must ensure that youth of all ages are prescribed varied, periodised, and developmentally appropriate training programmes (Brogden et al., 2020; Evans et al., 2021; Vahia et al., 2019). Bio-banding is a strategy that can be used to more even out different physical capabilities of players, by ensuring players compete against opponents of similar maturity status as well as encouraging the holistic development of young soccer players. Additionally, bio-banding fitness testing data can help practitioners to better understand the physical performance of players of a similar maturity.

Notes

1. The authors would like to thank Ben Bradley and colleagues for granting permissions to reproduce this figure.
2. The authors would like to thank Chris Thomas and colleagues for granting permissions to reproduce this table.

References

Abbott, W., Williams, S., Brickley, G., & Smeeton, N. (2019). Effects of bio-banding upon physical and technical performance during soccer competition: A preliminary analysis. *Sports*, 7(8), 193. https://doi.org/10.3390/sports7080193

Armstrong, N., & Welsman, J. R. (2000). Development of aerobic fitness during childhood and adolescence. *Pediatric Exercise Science*, 12, 128–149. https://doi.org/10.1123/pes.12.2.128

Bar-Or, O., & Rowland, T. W. (2004). *Pediatric exercise medicine: From physiological principles to health care application*. Human Kinetics.

Behm, D. G., Young, J. D., Whitten, J. H. D., Reid, J. C., Quigley, P. J., Low, J., Li, Y., Lima, C. D., Hodgson, D. D., Chaouachi, A., Prieske, O., & Granacher, U. (2017). Effectiveness of traditional strength vs. power training on muscle strength, power and speed with youth: A systematic review and meta-analysis. *Frontiers in Physiology*, 8, 423. https://doi.org/10.3389/fphys.2017.00423

Beunen, G. P., & Malina, R. M. (2005). Growth and biologic maturation: Relevance to athletic performance. In O. Bar-Or & H. Hebestreit (Eds.), *The child and adolescent athlete* (pp. 3–17). Blackwell Publishing.

Bradley, B., Johnson, D., Hill, M., McGee, D., Kana-ah, A., Sharpin, C., Sharp, P., Kelly, A., Cumming, S. P., & Malina, R. M. (2019). Bio-banding in academy football: Player's perceptions of a maturity matched tournament. *Annals of Human Biology*, 46(5), 400–408. https://doi.org/10.1080/03014460.2019.1640284

Brogden, C., Gough, L. A., & Kelly, A. L. (2020). The effects of a soccer-specific fitness test on eccentric knee-flexor strength. *Journal of Sport Rehabilitation*, 30(4), 568–572. https://doi.org/10.1123/jsr.2019-0532

Carling, C., Le Gall, F., Reilly, T., & Williams, A. M. (2008). Do anthropometric and fitness characteristics vary according to birth date distribution in elite youth academy soccer players?: Relative age effect in elite youth soccer. *Scandinavian Journal of Medicine & Science in Sports*, 19(1), 3–9. https://doi.org/10.1111/j.1600-0838.2008.00867.x

Catley, M. J., & Tomkinson, G. R. (2013). Normative health-related fitness values for children: Analysis of 85347 test results on 9–17-year-old Australians since 1985. *British Journal of Sports Medicine*, 47, 98–108. https://doi.org/10.1136/bjsports-2011-090218

Clemente, F. M., Clark, C. C. T., Leão, C., Silva, A. F., Lima, R., Sarmento, H., Figueiredo, A. J., Rosemann, T., & Knechtle, B. (2021). Exploring relationships between anthropometry, body composition, maturation, and selection for competition: A study in youth soccer players. *Frontiers in Physiology*, *12*, 651735. https://doi.org/10.3389/fphys.2021.651735

Cobley, S., Schorer, J., & Baker, J. (2012). *Talent identification and development in sport: International perspectives*. Routledge.

Cumming, S. P., Brown, D. J., Mitchell, S., Bunce, J., Hunt, D., Hedges, C., Crane, G., Gross, A., Scott, S., Franklin, E., Breakspear, D., Dennison, L., White, P., Cain, A., Eisenmann, J. C., & Malina, R. M. (2018). Premier League academy soccer players' experiences of competing in a tournament bio-banded for biological maturation. *Journal of Sports Sciences*, *36*(7), 757–765. https://doi.org/10.1080/02640414.2017.1340656

Cumming, S. P., Lloyd, R. S., Oliver, J. L., Eisenmann, J. C., & Malina, R. M. (2017). Bio-banding in sport: Applications to competition, talent identification, and strength and conditioning of youth athletes. *Strength & Conditioning Journal*, *39*(2), 34–47. https://doi.org/10.1519/SSC.0000000000000281

Cumming, S. P., Searle, C., Hemsley, J. K., Haswell, F., Edwards, H., Scott, S., Gross, A., Ryan, D., Lewis, J., White, P., Cain, A., Mitchell, S. B., & Malina, R. M. (2018). Biological maturation, relative age and self-regulation in male professional academy soccer players: A test of the underdog hypothesis. *Psychology of Sport and Exercise*, *39*, 147–153. https://doi.org/10.1016/j.psychsport.2018.08.007

Deprez, D., Valente-Dos-Santos, J., Coelho-e-Silva, M., Lenoir, M., Philippaerts, R., & Vaeyens, R. (2015). Longitudinal development of explosive leg power from childhood to adulthood in soccer players. *International Journal of Sports Medicine*, *36*(08), 672–679. https://doi.org/10.1055/s-0034-1398577

Dotan, R., Mitchell, C., Cohen, R., Klentrou, P., Gabriel, D., & Falk, B. (2012). Child—adult differences in muscle activation — A review. *Pediatric Exercise Science*, *24*(1), 2–21. https://doi.org/10.1123/pes.24.1.2

Emmonds, S., Scantlebury, S., Murray, E., Turner, L., Robsinon, C., & Jones, B. (2018). Physical characteristics of elite youth female soccer players characterized by maturity status. *Journal of Strength and Conditioning Research*, *34*(8), 2321–2328. https://doi.org/10.1519/JSC.0000000000002795

Emmonds, S., Till, K., Jones, B., Mellis, M., & Pears, M. (2016). Anthropometric, speed and endurance characteristics of English academy soccer players: Do they influence obtaining a professional contract at 18 years of age? *International Journal of Sports Science & Coaching*, *11*(2), 212–218. https://doi.org/10.1177/1747954116637154

Epstein, L., Valoski, S., Kalarchian, M., & McCurley, J. (1995). Do children lose and maintain weight easier than adults?: A comparison of child and parent weight changes from six months to ten years. *Obesity Research*, *3*(5), 411–417.

Evans, D., Jackson, D., Kelly, L. A., Williams, C. A., McAuley, A. B. T., Knapman, H., & Morgan, P. (2021). Monitoring post-match fatigue during a competitive season in elite youth soccer players. *Journal of Athletic Training*, *57*(2), 184–190. https://doi.org/10.4085/1062-6050-0245.21

Faigenbaum, A. D., Lloyd, R. S., & Oliver, J. L. (2020). *Essentials of youth fitness: American college of sports medicine human kinetics*. Human Kinetics.

Faude, O., Koch, T., & Meyer, T. (2012). Straight sprinting is the most frequent action in goal situations in professional football. *Journal of Sports Sciences*, *30*(7), 625–631. https://doi.org/10.1080/02640414.2012.665940

Ford, P., De Ste Croix, M., Lloyd, R., Meyers, R., Moosavi, M., Oliver, J., Till, K., & Williams, C. (2011). The Long-Term Athlete Development model: Physiological evidence and application. *Journal of Sports Sciences*, *29*(4), 389–402. https://doi.org/10.1080/02640414.2010.536849

Gibbs, B. G., Jarvis, J. A., & Dufur, M. J. (2012). The rise of the underdog? The relative age effect reversal among Canadian-born NHL hockey players: A reply to Nolan and Howell. *International Review for the Sociology of Sport*, *47*(5), 644–649. https://doi.org/10.1177/1012690211414343

Gil, S. M., Badiola, A., Bidaurrazaga-Letona, I., Zabala-Lili, J., Gravina, L., Santos-Concejero, J., Lekue, J. A., & Granados, C. (2014). Relationship between the relative age effect and anthropometry, maturity and performance in young soccer players. *Journal of Sports Sciences*, *32*(5), 479–486. https://doi.org/10.1080/02640414.2013.832355

Gil, S. M., Ruiz, F., Irazusta, A., Gil, J., & Irazusta, J. (2007). Selection of young soccer players in terms of anthropometric and physiological factors. *The Journal of Sports Medicine and Physical Fitness*, 47(1), 25–32.

Granacher, U., Lesinski, M., Busch, D., Muehlbauer, T., Prieske, O., Puta, C., Gollhofer, A., & Behm, D. G. (2016). Effects of resistance training in youth athletes on muscular fitness and athletic performance: A conceptual model for long-term athlete development. *Frontiers in Physiology*, 7. https://doi.org/10.3389/fphys.2016.00164

Guimarães, E., Ramos, A., Janeira, M. A., Baxter-Jones, A. D. G., & Maia, J. (2019). How does biological maturation and training experience impact the physical and technical performance of 11–14-year-old male basketball players? *Sports*, 7(12), 243. https://doi.org/10.3390/sports7120243

Gupta, A. S., Pierpoint, L. A., Comstock, R. D., & Saper, M. G. (2020). Sex-based differences in anterior cruciate ligament injuries among United States high school soccer players: An epidemiological study. *Orthopaedic Journal of Sports Medicine*, 8(5), 232596712091917. https://doi.org/10.1177/2325967120919178

Handelsman, D. J., Hirschberg, A. L., & Bermon, S. (2018). Circulating testosterone as the hormonal basis of sex differences in athletic performance. *Endocrine Reviews*, 39(5), 803–829. https://doi.org/10.1210/er.2018-00020

Hill, M., Scott, S., Malina, R. M., McGee, D., & Cumming, S. P. (2020). Relative age and maturation selection biases in academy football. *Journal of Sports Sciences*, 38(11–12), 1359–1367. https://doi.org/10.1080/02640414.2019.1649524

Hunter, J. P., Marshall, R. N., & Mcnair, P. J. (2004). Interaction of step length and step rate during sprint running. *Medicine & Science in Sports & Exercise*, 36(2), 261–271. https://doi.org/10.1249/01.MSS.0000113664.15777.53

Johnson, D. M., Williams, S., Bradley, B., Sayer, S., Murray Fisher, J., & Cumming, S. (2020). Growing pains: Maturity associated variation in injury risk in academy football. *European Journal of Sport Science*, 20(4), 544–552. https://doi.org/10.1080/17461391.2019.1633416

Kelly, A. L., & Williams, C. A. (2020). Physical characteristics and the talent identification and development processes in male youth soccer: A narrative review. *Strength and Conditioning Journal*, 42(6), 15–34. https://doi.org/10.1519/SSC.0000000000000576

Kelly, A. L., Wilson, M. R., Gough, L. A., Knapman, H., Morgan, P., Cole, M., Jackson, D. T., & Williams, C. A. (2020). A longitudinal investigation into the relative age effect in an English professional football club: Exploring the 'underdog hypothesis'. *Science and Medicine in Football*, 4(2), 111–118. https://doi.org/10.1080/24733938.2019.1694169

Kelly, A. L., Wilson, M. R., Jackson, D. T., Goldman, D. E., Turnnidge, J., Côté, J., & Williams, C. A. (2021a). A multidisciplinary investigation into "playing-up" in academy football according to age phase. *Journal of Sports Sciences*, 39(8), 854–864. https://doi.org/10.1080/02640414.2020.1848117

Kelly, A. L., Wilson, M. R., Jackson, D. T., Turnnidge, J., & Williams, C. A. (2021b). Speed of thought and speed of feet: Examining perceptual-cognitive expertise and physical performance in an English Football academy. *Journal of Science in Sport and Exercise*, 3(1), 88–97. https://doi.org/10.1007/s42978-020-00081-2

Kemper, G., van der Sluis, A., Brink, M., Visscher, C., Frencken, W., & Elferink-Gemser, M. (2015). Anthropometric injury risk Factors in elite-standard youth soccer. *International Journal of Sports Medicine*, 36(13), 1112–1117. https://doi.org/10.1055/s-0035-1555778

Khamis, H., & Roche, A. (1994). Predicting adult stature without using skeletal age: The Khamis-Roche method. *Pediatrics*, 94(4), 504–507.

Kozieł, S. M., & Malina, R. M. (2018). Modified maturity offset prediction equations: Validation in independent longitudinal samples of boys and girls. *Sports Medicine*, 48(1), 221–236. https://doi.org/10.1007/s40279-017-0750-y

le Gall, F., Carling, C., Williams, M., & Reilly, T. (2010). Anthropometric and fitness characteristics of international, professional and amateur male graduate soccer players from an elite youth academy. *Journal of Science and Medicine in Sport*, 13(1), 90–95. https://doi.org/10.1016/j.jsams.2008.07.004

Lloyd, R. S., Dobbs, I. J., Wong, M. A., Moore, I. S., & Oliver, J. L. (2021). Effects of training frequency during a 6-month neuromuscular training intervention on movement competency, strength and power in male youth. *Sports Health*, 12.

Lloyd, R. S., & Oliver, J. L. (2012). The Youth Physical Development Model: A new approach to long-term athletic development. *Strength & Conditioning Journal*, 34(3), 61–72. https://doi.org/10.1519/SSC.0b013e31825760ea

Lloyd, R. S., Oliver, J. L., Faigenbaum, A. D., Myer, G. D., & De Ste Croix, M. B. A. a. (2014). Chronological age vs. Biological maturation: Implications for exercise programming in youth. *Journal of Strength and Conditioning Research*, 28(5), 1454–1464. https://doi.org/10.1519/JSC.0000000000000391

Lloyd, R. S., Radnor, J. M., De Ste Croix, M., Cronin, J. B., & Oliver, J. L. (2015). Changes in sprint and jump performances after traditional, plyometric, and combined resistance training in male youth pre- and post-peak height velocity. *Journal of Strength & Conditioning Research*, 30(5), 1239–1247. https://doi.org/10.1519/jsc.0000000000001216

Loturco, I., Jeffreys, I., Abad, C. C. C., Kobal, R., Zanetti, V., Pereira, L. A., & Nimphius, S. (2020). Change-of-direction, speed and jump performance in soccer players: A comparison across different age-categories. *Journal of Sports Sciences*, 38(11–12), 1279–1285. https://doi.org/10.1080/02640414.2019.1574276

Mahon, A. D. (2008). Aerobic training. In N. Armstrong & W. van Mechelen (Eds.), *Paediatric exercise science and medicine* (pp. 513–530). Oxford University Press.

Malina, R. M., Bouchard, C., & Bar-Or, O. (2004a). *Growth, maturation and physical activity* (2nd ed.). Human Kinetics.

Malina, R. M., Cumming, S. P., Rogol, A. D., Coelho-E-Silva, M. J., Figueiredo, A. J., Konarski, J. M., & Kozieł, S. M. (2019). Bio-banding in youth sports: Background, concept, and application. *Sports Medicine (Auckland, N.Z.)*, 49(11), 1671–1685. https://doi.org/10.1007/s40279-019-01166-x

Malina, R. M., Eisenmann, J. C., Cumming, S. P., Ribeiro, B., & Aroso, J. (2004b). Maturity-associated variation in the growth and functional capacities of youth football (soccer) players 13–15 years. *European Journal of Applied Physiology*, 91(5–6), 555–562. https://doi.org/10.1007/s00421-003-0995-z

Malina, R. M., Peña Reyes, M. E., Eisenmann, J. C., Horta, L., Rodrigues, J., & Miller, R. (2000). Height, mass and skeletal maturity of elite Portuguese soccer players aged 11-16 years. *Journal of Sports Sciences*, 18(9), 685–693. https://doi.org/10.1080/02640410050120069

Malina, R. M., Rogol, A. D., Cumming, S. P., Coelho e Silva, M. J., & Figueiredo, A. J. (2015). Biological maturation of youth athletes: Assessment and implications. *British Journal of Sports Medicine*, 49(13), 852–859. https://doi.org/10.1136/bjsports-2015-094623

Malina, R. M., & Kozieł, S. M. (2014). Validation of maturity offset in a longitudinal sample of Polish boys. *Journal of Sports Sciences*, 32(5), 424–437. https://doi.org/10.1080/02640414.2013.828850

Massa, M., Moreira, A., A. Costa, R., R. Lima, M., R. Thiengo, C., Q. Marquez, W., J. Coutts, A., & S. Aoki, M. (2022). Biological maturation influences selection process in youth elite soccer players. *Biology of Sport*, 39(2), 435–441. https://doi.org/10.5114/biolsport.2022.106152

Meyers, R. W., Oliver, J. L., Hughes, M. G., Cronin, J. B., & Lloyd, R. S. (2015). Maximal sprint speed in boys of increasing maturity. *Pediatric Exercise Science*, 27(1), 85–94. https://doi.org/10.1123/pes.2013-0096

Meyers, R. W., Oliver, J. L., Hughes, M. G., Lloyd, R. S., & Cronin, J. B. (2016). The influence of maturation on sprint performance in boys over a 21-month period. *Medicine & Science in Sports & Exercise*, 48(12), 2555–2562. https://doi.org/10.1249/MSS.0000000000001049

Meyers, R. W., Oliver, J. L., Hughes, M. G., Lloyd, R. S., & Cronin, J. B. (2017). Influence of age, maturity, and body size on the spatiotemporal determinants of maximal sprint speed in boys. *Journal of Strength and Conditioning Research*, 31(4), 1009–1016. https://doi.org/10.1519/JSC.0000000000001310

Meylan, C., Cronin, J., Oliver, J., & Hughes, M. (2010). Talent identification in soccer: The role of maturity status on physical, physiological and technical characteristics. *International Journal of Sports Science & Coaching*, 5(4), 571–592. https://doi.org/10.1260/1747-9541.5.4.571

Mirkov, D. M., Kukolj, M., Ugarkovic, D., J. Koprivica, V., & Jaric, S. (2010). Development of anthropometric and physical performance profiles of young elite male soccer players: A longitudinal study. *Journal of Strength and Conditioning Research*, 24(10), 2677–2682. https://doi.org/10.1519/JSC.0b013e3181e27245

Mirwald, R. L., G. Baxter-Jones, A. D., Bailey, D. A., & Beunen, G. P. (2002). An assessment of maturity from anthropometric measurements. *Medicine and Science in Sports and Exercise*, *34*(4), 689–694. https://doi.org/10.1097/00005768-200204000-00020

Monasterio, X., Gil, S. M., Bidaurrazaga-Letona, I., Lekue, J. A., Santisteban, J., Diaz-Beitia, G., Martin-Garetxana, I., Bikandi, E., & Larruskain, J. (2021). Injuries according to the percentage of adult height in an elite soccer academy. *Journal of Science and Medicine in Sport*, *24*(3), 218–223. https://doi.org/10.1016/j.jsams.2020.08.004

Moore, S. A., McKay, H. A., Macdonald, H., Nettlefold, L., Baxter-Jones, A. D. G., Cameron, N., & Brasher, P. M. A. (2014). Enhancing a somatic maturity prediction model. *Medicine & Science in Sports & Exercise*, *47*(8), 1755–1764. https://doi.org/10.1249/MSS.0000000000000588

Morris, R. O., Jones, B., Myers, T., Lake, J., Emmonds, S., Clarke, N. D., Singleton, D., Ellis, M., & Till, K. (2020). Isometric midthigh pull characteristics in elite youth male soccer players: Comparisons by age and maturity offset. *Journal of Strength and Conditioning Research*, *34*(10), 2947–2955. https://doi.org/10.1519/JSC.0000000000002673

Murtagh, C. F., Brownlee, T. E., O'Boyle, A., Morgans, R., Drust, B., & Erskine, R. M. (2018). The importance of speed and power in elite youth soccer depends on maturation status. *Journal of Strength & Conditioning Research*, *32*(2), 297–303. http://doi.org/10.1519/JSC.0000000000002367

Nagahara, R., Takai, Y., Haramura, M., Mizutani, M., Matsuo, A., Kanehisa, H., & Fukunaga, T. (2018). Age-related differences in spatiotemporal variables and ground reaction forces during sprinting in boys. *Pediatric Exercise Science*, *30*(3), 335–344. https://doi.org/10.1123/pes.2017-0058

O'Brien, T. D., Reeves, N. D., Baltzopoulos, V., Jones, D. A., & Maganaris, C. N. (2010). Muscle-tendon structure and dimensions in adults and children. *Journal of Anatomy*, *216*(5), 631–642. https://doi.org/10.1111/j.1469-7580.2010.01218.x

Olivares, L. A. F., De León, L. G., & Fragoso, M. I. (2020). Skeletal age prediction model from percentage of adult height in children and adolescents. *Scientific Reports*, *10*(1), 15768. https://doi.org/10.1038/s41598-020-72835-5

Ostojic, S. M., Castagna, C., Calleja-González, J., Jukic, I., Idrizovic, K., & Stojanovic, M. (2014). The biological age of 14-year-old boys and success in adult soccer: Do early maturers predominate in the top-level game? *Research in Sports Medicine*, *22*(4), 398–407. https://doi.org/10.1080/15438627.2014.944303

Parr, J., Winwood, K., Hodson-Tole, E., Deconinck, F. J. A., Hill, J. P., Teunissen, J. W., & Cumming, S. P. (2020). The main and interactive effects of biological maturity and relative age on physical performance in elite youth soccer players. *Journal of Sports Medicine*, *2020*, 1–11. https://doi.org/10.1155/2020/1957636

Philippaerts, R. M., Vaeyens, R., Janssens, M., Van Renterghem, B., Matthys, D., Craen, R., Bourgois, J., Vrijens, J., Beunen, G., & Malina, R. M. (2006). The relationship between peak height velocity and physical performance in youth soccer players. *Journal of Sports Sciences*, *24*(3), 221–230. https://doi.org/10.1080/02640410500189371

Pyne, D., Gardner, A., Sheehan, K., & Hopkins, W. (2005). Fitness testing and career progression in AFL football. *Journal of Science and Medicine in Sport*, *8*(3), 321–332. https://doi.org/10.1016/S1440-2440(05)80043-X

Quatman-Yates, C. C., Quatman, C. E., Meszaros, A. J., Paterno, M. V., & Hewett, T. E. (2012). A systematic review of sensorimotor function during adolescence: A developmental stage of increased motor awkwardness? *British Journal of Sports Medicine*, *46*(9), 649–655. https://doi.org/10.1136/bjsm.2010.079616

Radnor, J. M., Oliver, J. L., Waugh, C. M., Myer, G. D., & Lloyd, R. S. (2022). Muscle architecture and maturation influences sprint and jump ability in young boys: A multi-study approach. *Journal of Strength and Conditioning Research*, *36*(10), 2741–2751. https://doi.org/10.1519/jsc.0000000000003941

Radnor, J. M., Staines, J., Bevan, J., Cumming, S. P., Kelly, A. L., Lloyd, R. S., & Oliver, J. L. (2021). Maturity has a greater association than relative age with physical performance in English male academy soccer players. *Sports*, *9*(12), 171. https://doi.org/10.3390/sports9120171

Ramos, E., Frontera, W., Llopart, A., & Feliciano, D. (1998). Muscle strength and hormonal levels in adolescents: Gender related differences. *International Journal of Sports Medicine*, *19*(08), 526–531. https://doi.org/10.1055/s-2007-971955

Reilly, T., Williams, A. M., Nevill, A., & Franks, A. (2000). A multidisciplinary approach to talent identification in soccer. *Journal of Sports Sciences*, *18*(9), 695–702. https://doi.org/10.1080/02640410050120078

Romann, M., Lüdin, D., & Born, D.-P. (2020). Bio-banding in junior soccer players: A pilot study. *BMC Research Notes*, *13*(1), 240. https://doi.org/10.1186/s13104-020-05083-5

Simoes, F., Santos, J., dos Vaz, V., Figueiredo, A. J., Reyes, M., Malina, R. M., & Coelho E Silva, M. (2010). Assessment of biological maturation in adolescent athletes: Application of different methods with soccer and hockey players. In Youth sports: Growth, Maturation and Talent (pp. 33–50). Coimbra University Press.

Stratton, G., & Oliver, J. L. (2020). The impact of growth and maturation on physical performance. In R. Lloyd & J. L. Oliver (Eds.), *Strength and conditioning for young athletes: Science and application* (2nd ed., pp. 1–5). Routledge.

Tanner, J. (1990). *Foetus into man: Physical growth from conception to maturity*. Harvard University Press.

Thomas, C., Oliver, J., & Kelly, A. L. (2021). Bio-banding in youth soccer: Considerations for researchers and practitioners. In A. L. Kelly, J. Côté, M. Jeffreys, & J. Turnnidge (Eds.), *Birth advantages and relative age effects in sport: Exploring organizational structures and creating appropriate settings* (pp. 125–156). Routledge.

Thomas, C., Oliver, J. L., Kelly, A. L., & Knapman, H. (2017). A pilot study of the demands of chronological age group and bio-banded match play in elite youth soccer. *Graduate Journal of Sport, Exercise & Physical Education Research*, *5*(1), 211.

Vahia, D., Kelly, A. L., Knapman, H., & Williams, C. (2019). Variation in the correlation between heart rate and session rating of perceived exertion based estimations of internal training load in youth soccer players. *Pediatric Exercise Science*, *31*(1), 91–98. https://doi.org/10.1123/pes.2018-0033

van der Sluis, A., Elferink-Gemser, M., Coelho-e-Silva, M., Nijboer, J., Brink, M., & Visscher, C. (2014). Sport injuries aligned to peak height velocity in talented pubertal soccer players. *International Journal of Sports Medicine*, *35*(04), 351–355. https://doi.org/10.1055/s-0033-1349874

Vänttinen, T., Blomqvist, M., Nyman, K., & Häkkinen, K. (2011). Changes in body composition, hormonal status, and physical fitness in 11-, 13-, and 15-year-old Finnish regional youth soccer players during a two-year follow-up. *Journal of Strength and Conditioning Research*, *25*(12), 3342–3351. https://doi.org/10.1519/JSC.0b013e318236d0c2

Wing, C. E., Turner, A. N., & Bishop, C. J. (2020). Importance of strength and power on key performance indicators in elite youth soccer. *Journal of Strength and Conditioning Research*, *34*(7), 2006–2014. https://doi.org/10.1519/JSC.0000000000002446

5
PSYCHOLOGICAL

Supporting Psychosocial Growth, Development, and Potential Challenges Experienced in Youth Soccer

James H. Dugdale, Alban C. S. Dickson, Alex Murata, Adam L. Kelly, and Kacey C. Neely

Introduction

Childhood and adolescence are phases of life defined by change. In addition to physical growth, psychological changes emerge as interests adapt, priorities shift, and distractions are introduced. The environment surrounding a young person also evolves, which is characterised by a transition in social support requirements, resultant of the continuous psychosocial development of independence and maturity during this time. In soccer, specifically, young players may experience being identified, (de)selected, and immersed in intensive development systems from the age of just 4 years old (Mitchell et al., 2020). Therefore, it is essential to ensure there is appropriate support for this population during childhood and throughout adolescence. From dealing with challenges experienced at this formative time in life to the pressures and potential setbacks of being an aspiring athlete, understanding ways for coaches and practitioners to positively impact youth have never been more necessary.

Talent development is considered as a process of providing specialist support to those with the potential to become elite performers in their field (Williams & Reilly, 2000). Positive talent development environments are those which intentionally facilitate psychosocial growth (Larsen et al., 2012). The emergent term *psychosocial* captures the internal psychological characteristics of the individual with the related external social or environmental influence that shapes their behaviour (Gledhill et al., 2017). Examples include self-regulation and the player's relationship with their coach, parents, and peers (Gledhill et al., 2017; Zibung & Conzelman, 2013). Literature has highlighted the benefits of psychosocial development in youth soccer, such as determining which players may progress into elite performers (e.g., Höner et al., 2021; Ivarsson et al., 2020; Murr et al., 2021; van Yperen, 2009). Recently, further implications have suggested the importance of integrating psychosocial skills as part of a multidisciplinary approach. Here, psychosocial skills are not viewed independently, but rather advocating the utilisation of psychology to enhance other areas of importance for progression in soccer (Musculus & Lobinger, 2018). Yet, even with the best intentions, the competitive, social, and financial pressures of soccer across all levels may distract focus away from optimal strategies for talent development. From an applied perspective, whilst sport psychology is now positioned as a cornerstone of best practice in talent development environments, its endorsement remains dependent on coach and club attitudes as well as player resistance (Cooper, 2021).

Accordingly, this chapter aims to discuss psychosocial considerations pertinent to aspiring and developing soccer players and provides practical suggestions to help researchers and practitioners working in this domain. Next, the chapter acknowledges the influence of external stakeholders on the experiences and development of young soccer players by discussing the impact of parents, coaches, and peers. The process of (de)selection in soccer and the potential psychosocial implications this may have on developing soccer players is then considered. Lastly, recommendations for future research, along with limitations of existing literature, are identified, as well as practical applications and suggestions to help mitigate some of these issues in practice.

Psychosocial Development of Youth Soccer Players

For effective talent development, coaches and practitioners must adopt a multidimensional approach to foster development across technical, tactical, physical, social, and psychological elements (Williams & Reilly, 2000; Williams et al., 2020). The players' personal environment is also critical, with research advocating for a long-term, supportive, individualised, and developmental focus to talent development (Martindale et al., 2005). Holt and Dunn (2004) identified four key concepts that reflect the individual qualities and environmental conditions required for progression in elite adolescent soccer: (a) discipline, (b) social support, (c) resilience, and (d) commitment. Related to these concepts, the authors provide an overview of sub-categories and categories, along with identifying key stakeholders pertaining to psychosocial competencies associated with success in soccer (Figure 5.1). However, what may appear as solely psychological factors are influenced by social aspects of the environment (Gledhill et al., 2017). Young players are required to navigate a successful transition to senior soccer by managing perceptions, impressions, and the features of the environment (Røynesdal et al., 2018). Psychosocial skills have been found to show a difference across selected and deselected players, indicating application from the

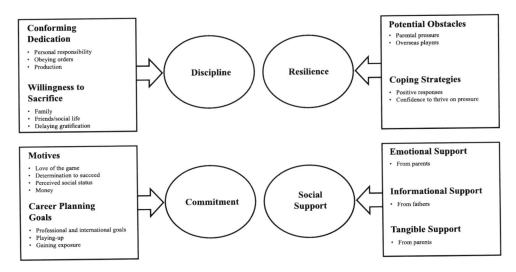

FIGURE 5.1 An overview of concepts, sub-categories, and categories pertaining to psychosocial competencies associated with soccer success during adolescence (adapted from Holt & Dunn, 2004).

point of talent identification (Platvoet et al., 2020). Acknowledging the importance and potential value of psychosocial development in youth soccer, it is necessary to identify and understand the methods of instilling, promoting, and facilitating the emergence of these skills and characteristics (Elbe & Wikman, 2017; Sarmento et al., 2018).

During early childhood, individuals may experience entry into a sport. Initial exposure to soccer may be through a local participation team (e.g., grassroots level) or via physical education in school. Whilst research demonstrates consequential risks associated with early specialisation (e.g., burnout or withdrawal from the sport), this trend remains common throughout childhood in soccer (Platvoet et al., 2020; see Chapter 8). Knowledge of developmental stages and both the challenges and opportunities that each stage brings is paramount to ensuring effective progression of these qualities. Developmental stages of youth athletes and corresponding chronological ages include: (a) early childhood (aged 3–6 years), (b) middle childhood (aged 7–9 years), (c) late childhood (aged 10–12 years), (d) early adolescence (aged 12–14 years), (e) middle adolescence (aged 15–17 years), and (f) late adolescence (aged 18–21 years) (Harter, 1999; Kipp, 2018). Psychosocial considerations and challenges may evolve or transform during and between these stages. Consideration of these phases is evident in applied talent development models for soccer, such as the Premier League's Elite Player Performance Plan (2011), which demonstrates altering psychological priorities across the foundation, development, and performance phases. However, these ages should not be viewed as fixed, given inter-individual differences in tempo and timing of physical, emotional, and social development.

During early-to-middle childhood, however, cognitive thinking is considered fixed. For example, a team of 5-year-old soccer players may chase a ball around the pitch because kicking the ball is a concrete task (Kipp, 2018). This is opposed to the abstract idea of holding their positions or defending a goal. Perception of ability for young children again revolves around concrete sources, such as simple task performance (e.g., successfully kicking a ball) and personal effort (e.g., I worked hard so I must be good) (Kipp, 2018). Socially, during early childhood, peer relationships are simply viewed as shared activities (i.e., they are in my class/on my team; therefore, they are my friend). This 'black and white' approach to sport during this stage lends itself to play-based activities and may not be conducive to overly structured or complex practice environments; further questioning the suitability of highly structured talent development pathways at this stage. Upon reaching late childhood and adolescence, young soccer players considered as talented may enter talent development environments (e.g., academies), which often follow a multidimensional selection process that considers physical, coordination, technical, and psychosocial attributes (Fortin-Guichard et al., 2022). Comparisons of age-matched school and academy soccer players suggest that there remain similar psychosocial outcomes (e.g., needs satisfaction, well-being, social support), with athletic identity one of few distinguishing features (Rongen et al., 2020). As an athletic identity emerges, particularly during the adolescent years, there is a requirement of support from a variety of sources to ensure a healthy and sustainable tenure in sport (Edison et al., 2021). This underlines the importance of getting the young soccer player's environment right, and social support remains a key feature that promotes their development (Erikstad et al., 2018; Flatgård et al., 2020; Steptoe et al., 2018).

Interventions promoting psychosocial development in youth soccer span a broad range of adopted models, populations, and methodologies. One popular model is the '5Cs' of Harwood (2008), where applicable studies have promoted the development of communication, commitment, concentration, control, and confidence. The 5Cs offers a practitioner-friendly and evidence-informed framework to help better understand how to incorporate psychosocial development strategies into real-life soccer practice (see Figure 5.2 for examples; Harwood et al.,

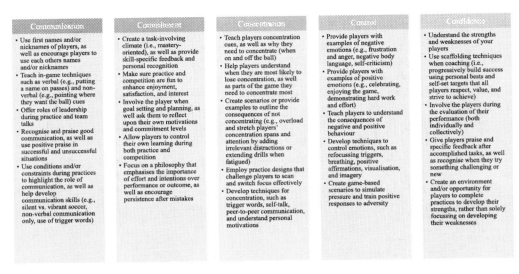

FIGURE 5.2 Examples of how to promote the development of psychosocial skills in youth soccer using the '5Cs' (Harwood, 2008; Harwood et al., 2015).

2015). Acknowledging the foundations identified in Holt and Dunn (2004), the 5Cs are often delivered through parents or coaches within professional soccer academies (Harwood et al., 2015; Kramers et al., 2022; Mitchell et al., 2022; Steptoe et al., 2018). Associated literature goes far beyond one shared approach, with some case studies including Mindful Sport Performance Enhancement (Kaufman et al., 2009; Spencer et al., 2019) as well as other interventions addressing team cohesion (Wickman et al., 2017). Nonetheless, it is evident that interpretation of the term psychosocial is subjective, with studies promoting such characteristics across a very broad range of topics (Thelwell et al., 2006). What is apparent is that promoting psychosocial development requires attending to both internal (psychological) and external (interpersonal or social) skills (Holt et al., 2017; Larsen et al., 2012). This is best achieved in an appropriately constructed, holistic environment that encourages the early adoption of these characteristics, is permeated by support from multiple sources, and bears a long-term developmental focus (Harwood, 2008; Henriksen et al., 2010; Larsen et al., 2012; Martindale et al., 2005).

Influence of External Stakeholders on Psychosocial Development

The transition from childhood through adolescence requires young athletes to rely on a variety of support structures and systems to aid their development and success both inside and outside of sport. Quality social interactions with peers and teammates appear to play a significant role in shaping development across an athlete's entire youth sport career (Smith et al., 2006). Whereas child athletes typically rely on most support from their parents at an early age, the importance of appropriate support from their coaches is also necessary as they crossover into adolescence (Murray et al., 2020). Acknowledging the plethora of ways in which external, proximal individuals can aid (and/or inhibit) young athletes in their development, the following section will provide a more detailed account of how those closest to young soccer players (i.e., their parents, coaches, and peers) may behave to best help them excel in sport.

Parent Influences

The effects of parental actions and behaviours have been shown to greatly influence the experiences and outcomes of youth athletes in sport (Erdal, 2018; Harwood & Knight, 2015). When considering the social agents most critical in dictating a developing athlete's sport-related experiences, Côté et al. (2020) suggest that, in many cases, parents (and legal guardians) should be considered among the most influential stakeholders responsible for shaping a child's sporting trajectory. In addition to being responsible for creating a climate conducive to sport participation (Côté, 1999; Wiersma & Fifer, 2008), both a sport parent's social proximity to and influence on their child-athlete creates a multitude of opportunities for behaviour- and role-modelling (Bricheno & Thornton, 2007; Rodrigues et al., 2018). These associations are explored further by Strandbu et al. (2020), who observed the importance of family culture in dictating the degree of a child's sport involvement. Here, the researchers reported that, while overall sport participation seems to decline as children enter their teenage years, those children with active parents and/or parents who perceive sport to be highly important appear more likely to remain involved.

In addition to influencing the degree to which their children may remain engaged in sport, parents also appear to play a direct role in shaping how their children experience sporting activities. As outlined by Sánchez-Miguel et al. (2013), young athletes who perceived their parents to be supportive and actively involved in their sport programming reported increased sport-related motivation and higher levels of enjoyment when participating in sport. Conversely, athletes who felt negative parental pressure to perform as well as athletes who experienced a lack of support from their parents (i.e., disinterest, lack of sport comprehension) were more likely to report sport-related amotivation and lower levels of interest (Sánchez-Miguel et al., 2013; Witt & Dangi, 2018). Adopting the 5Cs model (Harwood, 2008), researchers have identified how parents can embrace a series of congruent strategies to support young soccer players. This includes providing tailored feedback, setting expectations, creating an autonomy-supportive environment, and promoting participation in activities beyond those typically inherent within a soccer academy (Kramers et al., 2022). Each of these strategies embraces different components of the 5Cs and, therefore, offers consistency for young soccer players both on and off the pitch.

Looking deeper into the specific choices parents can make to aid their children to develop as successful young athletes, previous research has identified several actionable behaviours that may be beneficial. After a setback or defeat, athletes have reported feeling the need for parents to provide them with empathy and encouragement rather than correction or critique (Omli et al., 2011). Additionally, athletes also preferred parents to be somewhat reserved as spectators of their sport instead of drawing attention to them or anything else (e.g., poor officiating, bad luck) in any overt way (Omli et al., 2011). Research also indicates that athletes value emotionally intelligent communication (i.e., clear, calm, timely conversation) with their parents when discussing sport, and that parents who emphasise talent development and winning over fun and learning may be perceived as both less positive and less supportive (Lauer et al., 2010).

Similar outcomes have been reported within soccer, with players preferring that parents refrain from being disruptive spectators and providing negative 'coaching' to their children (Knight et al., 2011). In their study exploring factors influencing soccer academy players' confidence at U11 and U12 levels, Greenlees et al. (2021) showed that social support from parents in the form of positive feedback was critical in building confidence. Conversely, it was found that sustained negativity and criticism from parents greatly reduced players' confidence in this environment. Considering these congruent findings and reports from youth athletes and soccer players, parents are considered to play a vital role in fostering constructive environments for young soccer players (e.g., through positive psychological methods), particularly within the context of the stressful high-performance academy system.

Coach Influences

The role of the coach upon young soccer players is evidently critical in their progression, which extends beyond the establishment of skills and characteristics to forming the environment that surrounds a player inclusive of promoting all attributes required for progression (Flatgård et al., 2020; Larsen et al., 2012; Musculus & Lobinger, 2018). However, coaches have been found to largely focus on delivering technical aspects and may be unclear how to establish psychological practices and their role in this regard (Feddersen et al., 2021; Mitchell et al., 2022). In addition to a responsibility for explicitly developing skills, coaches may implicitly shape their players' development through displays of transformational leadership (see Chapter 13). Introduced by Bass and Riggio (2006), this approach requires coaches to stimulate, develop, and inspire young athletes (Arthur et al., 2017). Such behaviours mapped to this model are associated with improved perceived relationships and positive developmental experiences (Vella et al., 2013). In practice, it is proposed that coaches regularly display transformational leadership to foster positive outcomes in youth soccer (Erikstad et al., 2021). Example behaviours might reflect role-modelling respect, expressing confidence in players' potential, and stimulating new ways of thinking. Coaches displaying such illustrations of transformational leadership may inspire, challenge, and motivate young soccer players in their pursuit of development (Erikstad et al., 2021; Vella et al., 2013).

During middle-to-late childhood, youth athletes integrate more sources of information, whereby peers and coaches become more important while parents become less significant sources of feedback (Kipp, 2018; Murray et al., 2020). A coach may influence the psychosocial development of a young soccer player in explicit (e.g., through teaching of skills) and implicit (e.g., through their involvement in the player's environment) ways (Holt et al., 2017). In addition to discussing the importance of parents in instilling confidence within developing academy soccer players, Greenlees et al. (2021) highlighted the power that coaches have in influencing young athletes. These authors reported that players identified coach recognition and praise as critical behaviours that both instilled confidence and acted as an indicator of their performance. Conversely, unsupportive coach behaviours or incongruent coach-athlete relationships have been identified as some of the most common reasons for young athletes to disengage from sport (Fraser-Thomas et al., 2008; Gardner et al., 2017; Wekesser et al., 2021). The prevalence of toxic coaching behaviours (i.e., the use of fear, intimidation, or other unethical leadership behaviours) appears to be positively correlated with athlete burnout as well as negatively correlated with sport commitment and academic performance in elite university-level athletes (Rusbasan et al., 2021).

Motivational climate has been a steady area of interest in youth sport, with examples arising across the spectrum of performance environments (Ames, 1992; Kipp & Bolter, 2020). Established by athletes and coaches, this captures the influence of the social environment and can be defined based on the goal orientation (or priority) of that context. Differences are observed between those being either performance- or mastery-focused on their orientation. A performance environment compels the pursuit of achievement with an ego-related emphasis upon external measures of success or social comparison, whereas a mastery environment promotes effort and progression with respect to the required tasks (Ommundsen et al., 2013). An intervention promoting the display of task-related behaviours of youth soccer coaches was found to increase task and social cohesion in young male and female recreational players (McLaren et al., 2015). As key social agents, coaches can initiate motivational climates for their players (see Chapter 6).

Peer Influences

Peer interactions can provide youth with opportunities to acquire a range of skills, attitudes, and behaviours that influence their development (Rubin et al., 1998, 2006). Peer group experiences may also represent some of the most meaningful aspects of participation in youth sport. For instance, youth sport provides individuals with opportunities to expand their social networks, develop friendships, and learn a range of social skills, such as how to work with other people (e.g., Holt et al., 2009). For the young soccer player, peers may include fellow athletes or friends outside of the sport. The role of these social relations is integral, forming part of the young soccer player's micro-environment (Flatgård et al., 2020). Compared to coach and parental influences, peer group experiences in youth soccer remain relatively unexplored. As Smith (2003) suggested, "it is puzzling the degree to which research on peers has paled in comparison [to research on coaches and parents] given the relevance of these social agents" (p. 26). From a social perspective, most youth go through a process of becoming less reliant on their parents as they gain an increasing level of independence. Simultaneously, peers (i.e., individuals of equal standing; Smith, 2007) begin to fulfil a more important role in their lives (see Lerner et al., 2005). Despite this transition, it is not to say parents are no longer important.

Although parents are still required to maintain many caregiving roles and responsibilities, acceptance and affirmation is sought more so from peers (Neely & Holt, 2016). By the end of late childhood, children can compare feedback from significant adults to other sources of information, including peer comparison. This process of peer referencing allows for a more accurate perception of sporting ability. Peer referencing refers to individuals making comparisons to others regarding ability, social acceptance, or potential. The importance that young athletes give to the weighting of peer acceptance develops through late childhood and into adolescence. In soccer, young players may develop an interest in how they compare with others, which may have a motivating or deterring effect, depending on their conclusions. Contextual factors such as playing position, leadership roles, and ability may introduce variations in standing and power among peers (Smith & Delli Paoli, 2018). Coaches and practitioners may be mindful to consider this and the potential implications on interactions and dynamics while striving to optimise talent development environments in young soccer players.

Qualitative research of child and adolescent athletes shows that peers can influence motivation not only through feedback and collaboration but also during competition (Keegan et al., 2010). In youth soccer, for instance, Ommundsen and Vaglum (1991) suggested that a performance-oriented motivational climate can lead to negative peer relationships. Thus, to best facilitate young players' development and experiences, talent development programmes in soccer should consider how to promote long-term engagement and foster positive interactions amongst peers (Martindale et al., 2005).

Selection, Deselection, and Dropout in Youth Soccer

This chapter has highlighted the occurrence of early selection and identification in soccer. Accordingly, a pertinent issue to consider during childhood and adolescence is the psychosocial impact of (de)selection and dropout. Youth soccer is selective across all levels of competition, whether that be school teams, club teams, regional squads, or academy programmes. Typically, soccer players vie for a place in the squad through a trial match or training period, at which time they are either selected or deselected (Neely et al., 2016). Deselection can also occur during transitions across age groups or competitive stages (Williams et al., 2020; see Figure 1.1 in Chapter 1 for an illustration of the identification, selection, and development processes in soccer).

Butt and Molnar (2009) highlighted that, given the pyramidal structure of competitive sport, there are fewer places available the further athletes work their way 'up' the competitive system. Therefore, selection and deselection often become more pronounced and significant for those playing at a higher competitive level. Although youth soccer infrastructures often comprise of many competitive levels allowing players to continue to play in the sport after being deselected, players must cope with a range of potentially negative psychosocial and emotional consequences. Those who are selected and move 'up' in competition standard must also swiftly adapt to the demands elicited by their new environment while continuing to perform at a high level. Understandably, (de)selection may be disruptive, difficult, and demanding, particularly for youth soccer players already navigating their way through childhood and adolescence and the varied challenges these formative years pose.

In order to better understand the deselection process during athlete trials in girls' competitive youth sport, Neely et al. (2016) interviewed head coaches from Canadian provincial teams, including soccer. Based on the coaches' perspectives, the authors revealed that the deselection process involved four phases: (a) pre-try-out meeting, (b) evaluation and decision-making, (c) communication of deselection, and (d) post-deselection reflections (see Table 5.1). Notably, coaches made programmed and nonprogrammed decisions under conditions of certainty and uncertainty during the evaluation and decision-making phase, whilst they relied on intuition when faced with uncertainty. These findings suggest how coaches could consider using more objective and evidence-informed rationales during their evaluation and decision-making, as well as ensure appropriate strategies are in place to support players during and following their deselection.

Within and outside of soccer, research has shown the negative psychological and emotional impact deselection can have on adolescent athletes. For example, deselected athletes have reported a loss of identity, friendships, connectedness to school, and decreased academic performance (Blakelock et al., 2019). Moreover, athletes have reported a range of negative emotions, such as feelings of anxiety and depression, embarrassment, humiliation, and anger (Barnett, 2007; Brown & Potrac, 2009; Grove et al., 2004; Neely et al., 2017). Deselected athletes have also been shown to be 'at risk' of developing clinical levels of psychological distress following deselection (Blakelock et al., 2016), posing a significant threat to athletes' mental health. There have been severe instances of this in popular culture, whereby soccer players as young as 18-years-old have completed suicide following being released from their professional academies. Thus, there is clearly an urgent need to improve support for players during and following the deselection phase, as well as consider how early selection practice can impact youth's mental health and wellbeing in the long-term.

One disruption caused by deselection during adolescence is related to identity. Several researchers have documented the negative influence of deselection on athletic identity (i.e., the degree to which an individual identifies with an athletic role; Brewer et al., 1993). Athletic identity begins to develop during late childhood and becomes stronger as individuals commit to an athletic role through late adolescence (Houle & Kluck, 2015). Hence, the process of identity formation that is a central task during adolescence may be disrupted because of deselection (Erikson, 1968), leaving athletes to deal with a loss of identity and the task of 'rebuilding' a sense of 'who they are'. Within a soccer population, Brown and Potrac (2009) explored players' experiences

TABLE 5.1 High- and low-order themes describing coach perceptions of the deselection process in girls' competitive youth sport (adapted from Neely et al., 2016)

High-Order Themes	Low-Order Themes	Example Quotations
Pre-try-out meeting	Explaining expectation	"It needs to be clear what you're looking for. Okay, so whatever criteria you're using to evaluate the players, that needs to be clear."
Evaluation and decision-making	Evaluating athletes	"Make yourself visible, make yourself active in the selection process so that all athletes that are involved know that you're there observing them and spending time working with them. Don't let any athlete feel like they're being left out."
	Documentation	"Take time taking notes and if you feel it's difficult to do when you're walking around doing the drills and that kind of stuff, make sure that you're taking time after the session is done because there is time to pull out the list and write down one or two key words about that athlete because the paper trail will save you in the end)."
	Dealing with certainty	"When the athlete hasn't met the criteria you're looking for, she doesn't shoot the ball well enough, or she's not a good ball handler [it was an obvious decision that they could make with certainty]."
	Dealing with uncertainty	"We try to make the decisions that are best on that day. Do we always hit a home run [make the correct decision] and get it right? Not always, but we're trying to. . . . So we're trying under restrictions of the amount of evaluation periods to make a very difficult decision."
Communication of deselection	Informing players	"The tough part of communication, I think the toughest part for me . . . is communicating that they're not going make the team and seeing the tears and emotion."
	Providing feedback	"You can't just leave someone hanging, for me that's wrong. Tell me what I did wrong. Explain your rationale."
	Dealing with parents	"The parent interaction is one that definitely stresses me out. I don't often know the parents as well as I know the kid, and so I don't know what interaction they might want to have, and they're usually way less reasonable than the athlete is. The athlete often knows where they sit, they might be upset about the decision, but they often know where they sit in the scenario, and the parent has jaded views."
Post deselection reflections	Reflecting on athlete development	". . . we encourage [athletes] to retry in future events and making them understand that it's not the be all end all, and we [coaches] really do that at the U16 level as well, helping them recognize that OK, just because you don't move from the U16 camp to the U18 your very first time you get released, doesn't mean it can't happen the year after. So really trying to make sure that they don't stop participating, don't stop trying in subsequent years."
	Reflecting on the process	"I would also say having girls continually come back and try out even when they have been cut in the past by you . . . I think it's definitely a good sign if the kids are still able to come back and do that."

of deselection and loss of athletic identity. Specifically, the authors examined how a strong athletic identity influenced athletes' responses to deselection from professional soccer clubs. In-depth interviews with four former male youth soccer players (mean age 16 years) revealed they began to identify with an athletic role when they started playing competitive soccer at age 10 years. Early success in soccer was a key contributor to their developing identities. The players emphasised how the responses of significant others and peers towards their soccer prowess, as well as the recognition they received from coaches, reinforced their self-esteem and the importance of soccer in their lives. Following deselection, the players described a loss in their sense of self and feelings of anxiety, humiliation, and anger. Given the players' strong athletic identity and the influence of others in its development and maintenance, feelings of failure and embarrassment following deselection were perhaps not surprising, since it has negative implications for personal and social identity.

Due to the limited capacity of team sport and talent development programmes, many perceive deselection as 'necessary' but with the potential to exhibit 'unhealthy' outcomes given their design and implementation (Rongen et al., 2018). Therefore, from a coaching perspective, the way selection and deselection processes in soccer are carried out can be adapted/modified to better support player development. Given deselection can be such a sensitive and challenging aspect of soccer, coaches can approach deselection with more care and must consider a variety of psychological, social, and emotional factors during the deselection process. Specifically, communicating deselection face-to-face, providing players with specific reasons they were not selected, and supporting them in their transition should be prioritised (Neely & Dugdale, 2022).

Considerations for Researchers

Research into youth soccer is embracing an exciting range of approaches. Consideration of the holistic and ecological approach lends itself well to conducting detailed case studies into successful club environments (e.g., Erikstad et al., 2018; Flatgård et al., 2020; Larsen et al., 2012; Mitchell et al., 2022; Vaughan et al., 2022). In addition, substantial understanding has been gained from adopting grounded theory and through engaging with experts in their field (Holt & Dunn, 2004; Martindale et al., 2005). Moving beyond a cross-sectional approach and conducting longitudinal studies to better track and predict development based on psychosocial factors is of current interest (Fortin-Guichard et al., 2022; Murr et al., 2018; Rongen et al., 2020). Researchers should continue to adopt diverse and novel approaches to research as well as present their findings with an applied lens to help accelerate research and shape practical changes for young soccer players, their parents, and coaches. It is also worthwhile to consider relevant psychological and social theories to help advance our understanding of psychosocial growth and development in youth soccer.

While literature surrounding sport parent behaviour and its impact on the developing athlete is both comprehensive and extensive (Dorsch et al., 2021), opportunities to conduct novel research projects remains ongoing. First, continued research should be completed within the specific context of girls' soccer. As many previous studies in youth soccer have been exclusively completed with boys and, since results often differ within the studies that include both girls and boys in sport (e.g., Strandbu et al., 2020), it is necessary to explore the impact that various adjustments within the youth soccer system may have specifically on girls. Future research projects may also benefit from more meaningful collaborations with stakeholders within the youth soccer context. As discussed by Harwood et al. (2019), more purposeful discussion with those individuals currently working to address contemporary issues in youth soccer (e.g., overinvolved parents) may yield more easily actionable results and strategies to aid in improving youth soccer for all those involved.

Finally, given the potential psychological, social, and emotional consequences of deselection for athletes (Neely et al., 2018), future research on player deselection in the specific context of soccer is warranted. Considerations for best practices for deselection processes need to be developed. Importantly, research examining athletes' perspectives on deselection processes, along with establishing methods of how deselection is communicated within talent development pathways, is needed (Neely & Dugdale, 2022).

Considerations for Practitioners

It is important for all adult stakeholders (e.g., coaches, support staff, policy makers, parents) involved in youth soccer to adopt a collaborative approach, and act and behave in ways best suited to support optimal development of young soccer players. Creation of organisational norms and programme policy informed from the perspective of developing players themselves is an excellent place to start. The following considerations are offered to help practitioners incorporate relevant psychological strategies into their respective environments:

- While it may be difficult for many practitioners within the youth soccer system to collaborate with external figures (i.e., parents and peers), it is critical that these relationships be functional for young players to develop and thrive (Knight et al., 2011).
- Those involved in the delivery of youth soccer programming may benefit from learning how young players prefer their parents to behave before formulating policy, practice, and programme norms to encourage and enforce these behaviours.
- Should a youth soccer organisation choose to formulate evidence-informed policy regarding sport parent codes of conduct, practitioners could caution parents against criticising their children following setbacks and, instead, advise them to be empathetic and encouraging (e.g., Knight et al., 2011; Omli et al., 2011).
- Practitioners working with players within a club or academy setting should acknowledge the requirement for psychological support for players during and following their release. A highly structured deselection process communicating deselection face-to-face, providing players with specific reasons they were not selected, and supporting them in their transition should be prioritised (Neely & Dugdale, 2022).
- Practitioners may reflect on the following questions to stimulate the development of psychosocial skills in young soccer players:
  - In addition to the development of mental skills, how can you integrate sport psychology components to practice and competition (e.g., the 5Cs; refer to Figure 5.2)?
  - What coach behaviours are required, or incompatible, with the environment or motivational climate you want to establish?
  - How can you create a synergy of player support across parents, coaches, and peers?

Conclusion

This chapter has discussed psychosocial growth and development, acknowledged the influence of external stakeholders, and considered the process of (de)selection in soccer and its potential psychosocial implications for young soccer players. The authors have acknowledged that psychosocial considerations and challenges may evolve or transform during and between developmental stages, established that the players' environment is also critical, and provided practical examples of programmes and models that may help embed these within practice. The importance of external stakeholders to the long-term development of players' psychosocial skills was also highlighted, which acknowledges the range of different ways in which individuals can aid (and/or inhibit) young players in their development, as well as demonstrates how these figures may change in importance throughout childhood and adolescence. Lastly, the prevalence of early selection and identification in soccer was illustrated, which presents many challenges and potential implications of (de)selection decision-making. Coaches and practitioners working with youth soccer players are encouraged to recognise the important yet often overlooked area of psychosocial development as a principal element within talentdevelopment.

References

Ames, C. (1992). Achievement goals and the classroom motivational climate. In D. H. Schunk & J. L. Meece (Eds.), *Student perceptions in the classroom* (pp. 327–348). Lawrence Erlbaum Associates Inc.

Arthur, C. A., Bastardoz, N., & Eklund, R. (2017). Transformational leadership in sport: Current status and future directions. *Current Opinion in Psychology*, *16*, 78–83. https://doi.org/10.1016/j.copsyc.2017.04.001

Barnett, L. (2007). "Winners" and "losers": The effects of being allowed or denied entry into competitive extracurricular activities. *Journal of Leisure Research*, *39*(2), 316–344. https://doi.org/10.1080/00222216.2007.11950110

Bass, B. M., & Riggio, R. E. (2006). *Transformation leadership* (2nd ed.). Lawrence Erlbaum Associates Publishers.

Blakelock, D. J., Chen, M. A., & Prescott, T. (2016). Psychological distress in elite adolescent soccer players following deselection. *Journal of Clinical Sport Psychology*, *1*(10), 59–77. https://doi.org/10.1123/jcsp.2015-0010

Blakelock, D. J., Chen, M. A., & Prescott, T. (2019). Coping and psychological distress in elite adolescent soccer players following professional academy deselection. *Journal of Sport Behavior*, *41*(1), 1–26.

Brewer, B. W., Van Raalte, J. L., & Linder, D. E. (1993). Athletic identity: Hercules' muscle or Achilles' heel? *International Journal of Sport Psychology*, *24*(2), 237–254.

Bricheno, P., & Thornton, M. (2007). Role model, hero or champion? Children's views concerning role models. *Educational Research*, *49*(4), 383–396. https://doi.org/10.1080/00131880701717230

Brown, G., & Potrac, P. (2009). You've not made the grade son: De-selection and identity disruption in elite level youth football. *Soccer & Society*, *10*, 143–159. https://doi.org/10.1080/14660970802601613

Butt, J., & Molnar, G. (2009). Involuntary career termination in sport: A case study of the process of structurally induced failure. *Sport in Society*, *12*(2), 240–257. https://doi.org/10.1080/17430430802591027

Cooper, A. (2021). An investigation into the factors affecting player development within each phase of the academy pathway in English football academies. *Soccer and Society*, *22*(5), 429–441. https://doi.org/10.1080/14660970.2020.1822342

Côté, J. (1999). The influence of the family in the development of talent in sport. *The Sport Psychologist*, *13*(4), 395–417. https://doi.org/10.1123/tsp.13.4.395

Côté, J., Turnnidge, J., Murata, A., S. Mcguire, C., J. Martin, L. (2020). Youth sport research: Describing the integrated dynamic elements of the personal assets framework. *International Journal of Sport Psychology*, *51*(6), 562–578. https://doi.org/10.7352/IJSP.2020.51.562

Dorsch, T. E., Wright, E., Eckardt, V. C., Elliott, S., Thrower, S. N., & Knight, C. J. (2021). A history of parent involvement in organized youth sport: A scoping review. *Sport, Exercise, and Performance Psychology*, *10*(4), 536–557. https://doi.org/10.1037/spy0000266

Edison, B. R., Christino, M. A., & Rizzone, K. H. (2021). Athletic identity in youth athletes: A systematic review of the literature. *International Journal of Environmental Research and Public Health*, *18*, 1–18. https://doi.org/10.3390/ijerph18147331

Elbe, A. M., & Wikman, J. M. (2017). Psychological factors in developing high performance athletes. In J. Baker, S. Cobley, J. Schorer, & Wattie, N. (Eds.), *Routledge handbook of talent identification and development in sport* (pp. 169–180). Routledge.

Erdal, K. (2018). *The adulteration of children's sports: Waning health and well-being in the age of organized play*. Ronan & Littlefield.

Erikson, E. (1968). *Identity, youth, and crisis*. W. W. Norton.

Erikstad, M. K., Høigaard, R., Côté, J., Turnnidge, J., & Haugen, T. (2021). An examination of the relationship between coaches' transformational leadership and athletes' personal and group characteristics in elite youth soccer. *Frontiers in Psychology, 12*, https://doi.org/10.3389/fpsycg.2021.707669

Erikstad, M. K., Høigaard, R., Johansen, B. T., Kandala, N. B., & Haugen, T. (2018). Childhood football play and practice in relation to self-regulation and national team selection; a study of Norwegian elite youth players. *Journal of Sports Sciences, 36*(20), 2304–2310. https://doi.org/10.1080/02640414.2018.1449563

Feddersen, N. B., Keis, M. A. B., & Elbe, A. M. (2021). Coaches' perceived pitfalls in delivering psychological skills training to high-level youth athletes in fencing and football. *International Journal of Sports Science and Coaching, 16*(2), 249–261. https://doi.org/10.1177/1747954120959524

Flatgård, G., Larsen, C. H., & Sæther, S. A. (2020). Talent development environment in a professional football club in Norway. *Scandinavian Journal of Sport and Exercise Psychology, 2*, 8–15. https://doi.org/10.7146/sjsep.v2i0.114470

Fortin-Guichard, D., Huberts, I., Sanders, J., van Elk, R., Mann, D. L., & Savelsbergh, G. J. P. (2022). Predictors of selection into an elite level youth football academy: A longitudinal study. *Journal of Sports Sciences, 40*(9), 984–999. https://doi.org/10.1080/02640414.2022.2044128

Fraser-Thomas, J., Côté, J., & Deakin, J. (2008). Understanding dropout and prolonged engagement in adolescent competitive sport. *Psychology of Sport and Exercise, 9*(5), 645–662. https://doi.org/10.1016/j.psychsport.2007.08.003

Gardner, L. A., Magee, C. A., & Vella, S. A. (2017). Enjoyment and behavioral intention predict organized youth sport participation and dropout. *Journal of Physical Activity and Health, 14*(11), 861–865. https://doi.org/10.1123/jpah.2016-0572

Gledhill, A., Harwood, C., & Forsdyke, D. (2017). Psychosocial factors associated with talent development in football: A systematic review. *Psychology of Sport and Exercise, 31*, 93–112. https://doi.org/10.1016/j.psychsport.2017.04.002

Greenlees, I., Parr, A., Murray, S., & Burkitt, E. (2021). Elite youth soccer players' sources and types of soccer confidence. *Sports, 9*(11), 146. https://doi.org/10.3390/sports9110146

Grove, J., Fish, M., & Eklund, R. (2004). Changes in athletic identity following team selection: Self-protection versus self-enhancement. *Journal of Applied Sport Psychology, 16*, 75–81. https://doi.org/10.1080/10413200490260062

Harter, S. (1999). *The construction of the self: A developmental perspective*. Guilford Press.

Harwood, C. G. (2008). Developmental consulting in a professional football academy: The 5Cs coaching efficacy program. *The Sport Psychologist, 22*(1), 109–133.

Harwood, C. G., Barker, J. B., & Anderson, R. (2015). Psychosocial development in youth soccer players: Assessing the effectiveness of the 5Cs intervention program. *Sport Psychologist, 29*(4), 319–334. https://doi.org/10.1123/tsp.2014-0161

Harwood, C. G., & Knight, C. J. (2015). Parenting in youth sport: A position paper on parenting expertise. *Psychology of Sport and Exercise, 16*, 24–35. https://doi.org/10.1016/j.psychsport.2014.03.001

Harwood, C. G., Knight, C. J., Thrower, S. N., & Berrow, S. R. (2019). Advancing the study of parental involvement to optimise the psychosocial development and experiences of young athletes. *Psychology of Sport and Exercise, 42*, 66–73. https://doi.org/10.1016/j.psychsport.2019.01.007

Henriksen, K., Stambulova, N., & Roessler, K. K. (2010). Holistic approach to athletic talent development environments: A successful sailing milieu. *Psychology of Sport and Exercise, 11*, 212–222. https://doi.org/10.1016/j.psychsport.2009.10.005

Holt, N. L., & Dunn, J. G. H. (2004). Toward a grounded theory of the psychosocial competencies and environmental conditions associated with soccer success. *Journal of Applied Sport Psychology, 16*(3), 199–219. https://doi.org/10.1080/10413200490437949

Holt, N. L., Neely, K. C., Slater, L. G., Camiré, M., Côté, J., Fraser-Thomas, J., MacDonald, D., Strachan, L., & Tamminen, K. A. (2017). A grounded theory of positive youth development through sport based on results from a qualitative meta-study. *International Review of Sport and Exercise Psychology*, *10*(1), 1–49. https://doi.org/10.1080/1750984X.2016.1180704

Holt, N. L., Tamminen, K. A., Tink, L. N., & Black, D. E. (2009). An interpretive analysis of life skills associated with sport participation. *Qualitative Research in Sport and Exercise*, *1*(2), 160–175. https://doi.org/10.1080/19398440902909017

Höner, O., Murr, D., Larkin, P., Schreiner, R., & Leyhr, D. (2021). Nationwide subjective and objective assessments of potential talent predictors in elite youth soccer: An investigation of prognostic validity in a prospective study. *Frontiers in Sports and Active Living*, *3*. https://doi.org/10.3389/fspor.2021.638227

Houle, J. L. W., & Kluck, A. S. (2015). An examination of the relationship between athletic identity and career maturity in student-athletes. *Journal of Clinical Sport Psychology*, *9*(1), 24–40. https://doi.org/10.1123/jcsp.2014-0027

Ivarsson, A., Kilhage-Persson, A., Martindale, R., Priestley, D., Huijgen, B., Ardern, C., & McCall, A. (2020). Psychological factors and future performance of football players: A systematic review with meta-analysis. *Journal of Science and Medicine in Sport*, *23*(4), 415–420. https://doi.org/10.1016/j.jsams.2019.10.021

Kaufman, K. A., Glass, C. R., & Arnkoff, D. B. (2009). Evaluation of mindful sport performance enhancement (MSPE): A new approach to promote flow in athletes. *Journal of Clinical Sport Psychology*, *3*(4), 334–356.

Keegan, R., Spray, C., Harwood, C., & Lavallee, D. (2010). The motivational atmosphere in youth sport: Coach, parent, and peer influences on motivation in specializing sport participants. *Journal of Applied Sport Psychology*, *1*, 87–105. https://doi.org/10.1080/10413200903421267

Kipp, L. E. (2018). Developmental considerations for working with young athletes. In C. J. Knight, C. G. Harwood, & D. Gould (Eds.), *Sport psychology for young athletes* (pp. 33–42). Routledge.

Kipp, L. E., & Bolter, N. D. (2020). Motivational climate, psychological needs, and personal and social responsibility in youth soccer: Comparisons by age group and competitive level. *Psychology of Sport and Exercise*, *51*. https://doi.org/10.1016/j.psychsport.2020.101756

Knight, C. J., Neely, K. C., & Holt, N. L. (2011). Parental behavior in team sports: How do female athletes want parents to behave? *Journal of Applied Sport Psychology*, *23*, 76–92. https://doi.org/10.1080/10413200.2010.525589

Kramers, S., Thrower, S. N., Steptoe, K., & Harwood, C. G. (2022). Parental strategies for supporting children's psychosocial development within and beyond elite sport. *Journal of Applied Sport Psychology*, 1–23. https://doi.org/10.1080/10413200.2022.2043486

Larsen, C., Alfermann, D., & Christensen, M. (2012). Psychosocial skills in a youth soccer academy: A holistic ecological perspective. *Sport Science Review*, *21*(3–4), 51–74. https://doi.org/10.2478/v10237-012-0010-x

Lauer, L., Gould, D., Roman, N., & Pierce, M. (2010). Parental behaviors that affect junior tennis player development. *Psychology of Sport and Exercise*, *11*(6), 487–496. https://doi.org/10.16/j.psychsport.2010.06.008

Lerner, R. M., Brown, J. D., & Kier, C. (2005). *Adolescence: Development, diversity, context, and application*. Pearson.

Martindale, R. J., Collins, D., & Daubney, J. (2005). Talent development: A guide for practice and research within sport. *Quest*, *57*(4), 353–375. https://doi.org/10.1080/00336297.2005.10491862

McLaren, C. D., Eys, M. A., & Murray, R. A. (2015). A coach-initiated motivational climate intervention and athletes' perceptions of group cohesion in youth sport. *Sport, Exercise, and Performance Psychology*, *4*(2), 113–126. https://doi.org/10.1037/spy0000026

Mitchell, T. O., Cowburn, I. H. J., Piggott, D., Littlewood, M. A., Cook, T., & Till, K. (2022). Fostering psychosocial characteristics within an English soccer academy. *The Sport Psychologist*, 1–11. https://doi.org/10.1123/tsp.2021-0105

Mitchell, T.O., Gledhill, A., Nesti, M., Richardson, D., & Littlewood, M. (2020). Practitioner perspectives on the barriers associated with youth-to-senior transition in elite soccer academy players. *International Sport Coaching Journal*, *19*(7), 273–282. https://doi.org/10.1123/iscj.2019-0015

Murr, D., Feichtinger, P., Larkin, P., O'Connor, D., & Höner, O. (2018). Psychological talent predictors in youth soccer: A systematic review of the prognostic relevance of psychomotor, perceptual-cognitive and personality-related factors. *PLoS One, 13*(10). https://doi.org/10.1371/journal.pone.0205337

Murr, D., Larkin, P., & Höner, O. (2021). Decision-making skills of high-performance youth soccer players: Validating a video-based diagnostic instrument with a soccer-specific motor response. *German Journal of Exercise and Sport Research, 51*(1), 102–111. https://doi.org/10.1007/s12662-020-00687-2

Murray, R.M., Dugdale, J.H., Habeeb, C.M., & Arthur, C.A. (2020). Transformational parenting and coaching on mental toughness and physical performance in adolescent soccer players: The moderating effect of athlete age. *European Journal of Sport Science, 21*(4), 580–589. https://doi.org/10.1080/17461391.2020.1765027

Musculus, L., & Lobinger, B. H. (2018). Psychological characteristics in talented soccer players—Recommendations on how to improve coaches' assessment. *Frontiers in Psychology, 9*. https://doi.org/10.3389/fpsyg.2018.00041

Neely, K. C., & Dugdale, J. H. (2022). Making the cut: Coaches and the deselection of young athletes. In M. Toms & R. Jeane (Eds.), *Routledge handbook of coaching children in sport.* Routledge.

Neely, K. C., Dunn, J. G. H., McHugh, T. L. F., & Holt, N. L. (2016). The deselection process in competitive female youth sport. *The Sport Psychologist, 30*, 141–153. https://doi.org/10.1123/tsp.2015-0044

Neely, K. C., Dunn, J. G. H., McHugh, T. L. F., & Holt, N. L. (2018). Female athletes' experiences of positive growth following deselection. *Journal of Sport & Exercise Psychology, 40*, 173–185. https://doi.org/10.1123/jsep.2017-0136

Neely, K. C., & Holt, N. L. (2016). Peer group experiences in youth sport. In K. Green & A. Smith (Eds.), *Handbook of youth sport* (pp. 218–226). Routledge.

Neely, K. C., McHugh, T. L. F, Dunn, J. G. H., & Holt, N. L. (2017). Athletes and parents coping with deselection in competitive youth sport: A communal coping perspective. *Psychology of Sport and Exercise, 30*, 1–9. https://doi.org/10.1016/j.psychsport.2017.01.004

Omli, J., & Wiese-Bjornstal, D. M. (2011). Kids speak: Preferred parental behavior at youth sport events. *Research Quarterly for Exercise and Sport, 82*(4), 702–711. https://doi.org/10.1080/02701367.2011.10599807

Ommundsen, Y., Lemyre, P., Abrahamsen, F., & Roberts, G.C. (2013). The role of motivational climate for sense of vitality in organized youth grassroots football players: Do harmonious and obsessive types of passion play a mediating role? *International Journal of Applied Sports Sciences, 25*(2), 102–117. https://doi.org/10.24985/ijass.2013.25.2.102

Ommundsen, Y., & Vaglum, P. (1991). The influence of low perceived soccer and social competence on later dropout from soccer: A prospective study of young boys. *Scandinavian Journal of Medicine & Science in Sports, 1*(3), 180–188. https://doi.org/10.1111/j.1600-0838.1991.tb00293.x

Platvoet, S. W. J., Opstoel, K., Pion, J., Elferink-Gemser, M. T., & Visscher, C. (2020). Performance characteristics of selected/deselected under 11 players from a professional youth football academy. *International Journal of Sports Science and Coaching, 15*(5–6), 762–771. https://doi.org/10.1177/1747954120923980

Rodrigues, D., Padez, C., & Machado-Rodrigues, A. M. (2018). Active parents, active children: The importance of parental organized physical activity in children's extracurricular sport participation. *Journal of Child Health Care, 22*(1), 159–170. https://doi.org/10.1177/1367493517741686

Rongen, F., McKenna, J., Cobley, S., Tee, J. C., & Till, K. (2020). Psychosocial outcomes associated with soccer academy involvement: Longitudinal comparisons against aged matched school pupils. *Journal of Sports Sciences, 38*(11–12), 1387–1398. https://doi.org/10.1080/02640414.2020.1778354

Rongen, F., McKenna, J., Cobley, S., & Till, K. (2018). Are youth sport talent identification and development systems necessary and healthy? *Sports Medicine—Open, 18*, 1–4. https://doi.org/10.1186/s40798-018-0135-2

Røynesdal, Ø., Toering, T., & Gustafsson, H. (2018). Understanding players' transition from youth to senior professional football environments: A coach perspective. *International Journal of Sports Science and Coaching, 13*(1), 26–37. https://doi.org/10.1177/1747954117746497

Rubin, K. H., Bukowski, W. M., & Parker, J. G. (1998). Peer interactions, relationships, and groups. In W. Damon, & N. Eisenberg (Ed.), *Handbook of child psychology: Social, emotional, and personality development* (pp. 619–700). John Wiley & Sons, Inc.

Rubin, K. H., Bukowski, W. M., & Parker, J. G. (2006). Peer Interactions, Relationships, and Groups. In N. Eisenberg, W. Damon, & R. M. Lerner (Eds.), *Handbook of child psychology: Social, emotional, and personality development* (pp. 571–645). John Wiley & Sons, Inc.

Rusbasan, D., Collisson, B., & Ham, E. (2021). Toxic coaching of collegiate student-athletes: Burnout mediates the relation between school/sport conflict and commitment. *Journal of Issues in Intercollegiate Athletics, 14*, 365–386. https://csri-jiia.org/wp-content/uploads/2021/08/RA_2021_19.pdf

Sánchez-Miguel, P. A., Leo, F. M., Sánchez-Oliva, D., Amado, D., & García-Calvo, T. (2013). The importance of parents' behavior in their children's enjoyment and amotivation in sports. *Journal of Human Kinetics, 36*(1), 169–177. https://doi.org/10.2478/hukin-2013-0017

Sarmento, H., Anguera, M. T., Pereira, A., & Araújo, D. (2018). Talent identification and development in male football: A systematic review. *Sports Medicine, 48*(4), 907–931. https://doi.org/10.1007/s40279-017-0851-7

Smith, A. L. (2003). Peer relationships in physical activity contexts: a road less traveled in youth sport and exercise psychology research. *Psychology of Sport and Exercise, 4*(1), 25–39.

Smith, A. L. (2007). Youth peer relationships in sport. In D. Lavallee & S. Jowett (Eds.), *Social psychology in sport*. Human Kinetics.

Smith, A. L., & Delli Paoli, A. G. (2018). Fostering adaptive peer relationships in youth sport. In C. J. Knight, C. G. Harwood, & D. Gould (Eds.), *Sport psychology for young athletes* (pp. 196–205). Routledge.

Smith, A. L., Ullrich-French, S., Walker, E., & Hurley, K. S. (2006). Peer relationship profiles and motivation in youth sport. *Journal of Sport and Exercise Psychology, 28*(3), 362–382. https://doi.org/10.1123/jsep.28.3.362

Spencer, A. L., Kaufman, K. A., & Glass, C. R. (2019). Mindful sport performance enhancement in action: A case study with an elite football academy. In K. Henriksen, J. Hansen, & C. V. Larsen (Eds.), *Mindfulness and acceptance in sport*. Routledge.

Steptoe, K., King, T., & Harwood, C.G. (2018). The consistent psycho-social development of young footballers: Implementing the 5C's as a vehicle for interdisciplinary cohesion. In E. Konter, J. Beckmann, & T. Loughead (Eds.), *Football psychology: From theory to practice*. Routledge.

Strandbu, Å., Bakken, A., & Stefansen, K. (2020). The continued importance of family sport culture for sport participation during the teenage years. *Sport, Education and Society, 25*(8), 931–945. https://doi.org/10.1080/13573322.2019.1676221

The Premier League. (2011). *Elite player performance plan*. Retrieved from: www.premierleague.com/youth/EPPP [accessed 14th January 2022].

Thelwell, R. C., Greenlees, I. A., & Weston, N. J. V. (2006) Using psychological skills training to develop soccer performance. *Journal of Applied Sport Psychology, 18*(3), 254–270. https://doi.org/10.1080/10413200600830323

van Yperen, N. W. (2009). Why some make it and others do not: Identifying psychological factors that predict career success in professional adult soccer. *Sport Psychologist, 23*(3), 317–329. https://doi.org/10.1123/tsp.23.3.317

Vaughan, J., Mallett, C. J., Potrac, P., Woods, C., O'Sullivan, M., & Davids, K. (2022). Social and cultural constraints on football player development in Stockholm: Influencing skill, learning, and wellbeing. *Frontiers in Sports and Active Living, 4*(832111), 1–18. https://doi.org/10.3389/fspor.2022.832111

Vella, S.A., Oades, L. G., & Crowe, T. P. (2013). The relationship between coach leadership, the coach–athlete relationship, team success, and the positive developmental experiences of adolescent soccer players. *Physical Education and Sport Pedagogy, 18*(5), 549–561, https://doi.org/10.1080/17408989.2012.726976

Wekesser, M. M., Harris, B. S., Langdon, J., & Wilson Jr, C. H. (2021). Coaches' impact on youth athletes' intentions to continue sport participation: The mediational influence of the coach-athlete relationship. *International Journal of Sports Science & Coaching, 16*(3), 490–499. https://doi.org/10.1177/1747954121991817

Wickman, J. M., Stelter, R., Petersen, N. K., & Elbe, A. (2017). Effects of a team building intervention on social cohesion in adolescent elite football players. *Swedish Journal of Sport Research*.

Wiersma, L. D., & Fifer, A. M. (2008). "The schedule has been tough but we think it's worth it": The joys, challenges, and recommendations of youth sport parents. *Journal of Leisure Research, 40*(4), 505–530. https://doi.org/10.1080/00222216.2008.11950150

Williams, A. M., Ford, P. R., & Drust, B. (2020). Talent identification and development in soccer since the millennium. *Journal of Sports Sciences*, *38*(11–12), 1199–1210. https://doi.org/10.1080/02640414.2020.1766647

Williams, A. M., & Reilly, T. (2000). Talent identification and development in soccer. *Journal of Sports Sciences*, *18*(9), 657–667. https://doi.org/10.1080/02640410050120041

Witt, P. A., & Dangi, T. B. (2018). Why children/youth drop out of sports. *Journal of Park and Recreation Administration*, *36*(3). https://doi.org/10.18666/JPRA-2018-V36-I3-8618

Zibung, M., & Conzelmann, A. (2013). The role of specialisation in the promotion of young football talents: A person-oriented study. *European Journal of Sport Science*, *13*(5), 452–460. https://doi.org/10.1080/17461391.2012.749947

6
SOCIAL

Investigating Social Influences on Talent and Development in Soccer

Colin D. McLaren, Mark W. Bruner, Luc J. Martin, Adam L. Kelly, Achuthan Shanmugaratnam, and Mathieu Simard

Introduction

Talent identification and development in soccer are often considered from a technical, tactical, physical, and/or psychological perspective, whereas social influences at play within a team are often overlooked. The importance of considering the social environment of a group is certainly not a novel suggestion, as it has been written about for nearly a century. In his field theory, Lewin (1939) posited that, to understand individual behaviour, all 'fields' at play within the environment must be factored (e.g., physiological, psychological, and social). Groups (i.e., two or more individuals who are connected by social relationships) represent a pervasive aspect of modern society, with conservative estimates suggesting the current existence of around 30 billion groups (Forsyth, 2014). Membership and involvement in groups span the boundaries of family, education, work, physical activity, and social endeavours. Given its ubiquity throughout society, it is likely not surprising that belonging to a group has been identified as a fundamental human need (e.g., Baumeister & Leary, 1995). Thus, attempts to understand individual behaviour, developmental pathways, and talent would also benefit from knowledge of the group to which individuals belong.

In this chapter, three important and highly researched constructs that have received a great deal of attention in soccer (and other comparable sports) are the primary focus, which include: (a) social identity, (b) group cohesion, and (c) motivational climate. In doing so, the social forces that exist in a group setting are examined from unique angles. First, social identity relates to how an individual internalises their membership within a soccer team. Conversely, group cohesion relates to an individual's perceptions that their soccer team is on the same page in terms of performance tasks and social relationships. Finally, motivational climate relates to the behaviours of important social agents regarding what it means to be successful in that soccer team environment (performance or growth). After detailing these constructs, the chapter summarises key implications regarding the utility of each construct in a soccer context. This chapter then concludes by offering a range of considerations for researchers and practitioners to advance the field of social research and practice in youth soccer.

Social Identity

As part of a sport team, one social consideration is the degree to which an individual comes to internalise that membership as a meaningful part of their social makeup. Social identity is defined as "that part of an individual's self-concept which derives from his/her knowledge of his/her membership of a social group (or groups) together with the value and emotional significance attached to that membership" (Tajfel, 1981, p. 255). More specifically, when a soccer player places significance on their team membership and that membership becomes integrated into their sense of self (i.e., 'us members of this team'), it can fundamentally shape their thoughts, attitudes, and behaviours (e.g., Beauchamp, 2019). Social Identity Theory (SIT) (Tajfel, 1981) explains the mechanisms through which people identify with membership to particular social groups (e.g., school soccer teams) as well as the personal and collective outcomes that result from that identification (Bruner et al., 2014). The central premise of SIT is that people define and evaluate themselves based on the groups to which they belong (Hogg & Abrams, 2001). Questions of social identity are critical because, when people internalise a sense of shared group membership (i.e., strong social identity), it results in a change to oneself that can serve as a foundation for a variety of positive individual outcomes (Haslam, 2004). Through elevated social identity, people experience greater psychological connection to fellow group members, receive social support, and feel a sense of meaning, purpose, and control (Haslam et al., 2005).

One widely adopted model of social identity was initially advanced by Cameron (2004) and later adapted to sport by Bruner and Benson (2018). According to this model, social identity strength can be understood and measured using three dimensions, referred to as ingroup ties (perceptions of connections and belongingness experienced with other group members), cognitive centrality (the frequency with which the group comes to mind and the importance that individuals place on group membership), and ingroup affect (the positive feelings or emotions associated with group membership). A growing body of literature specific to sport has adopted this model to demonstrate important consequences for their thoughts, feelings, and behaviours (Bruner et al., 2020). As an illustration, outcomes that have been explored in relation to social identity include interpersonal factors (e.g., moral behaviour; Bruner et al., 2018), team factors (e.g., group norms; Täuber & Sassenberg, 2012), leadership factors (e.g., formal and informal leaders; Martin et al., 2017), and performance (e.g., Zuccian teams, social identity contributes to the frequency with which youth engage in prosocial and antisocial behaviour. Bruner et al. (2014) examined the effects of the three dimensions of social identity (i.e., ingroup ties, cognitive centrality, ingroup affect) on prosocial and antisocial behaviour towards teammates and opponents in a sample of adolescent male and female sport team athletes, including high school soccer players. Findings revealed that positive feelings associated with group membership (i.e., ingroup affect) had a positive effect on prosocial behaviour toward teammates (Bruner et al., 2014). Further, by additionally examining whether any effects of social identity on prosocial and antisocial behaviour were mediated by cohesion, Bruner et al. (2014) found that task cohesion mediated a positive effect of ingroup ties on prosocial teammate behaviour, and a negative effect of ingroup ties and ingroup effect on antisocial behaviour toward teammates and opponents. In relation to team factors, Täuber and Sassenberg (2012) assessed competitive German adult women soccer players' identification with their team, adherence to group norms, and disengagement from the team over the course of a competitive season. Results of the study revealed that those who identified strongly with the team were more likely to deviate from potentially harmful group goals (and thus protecting the best interests of the group) and remained more committed to the team across the season.

For leadership factors that have been explored as an outcome of social identity, Martin et al. (2017) investigated leadership status and perceptions of social identity among a sample of multi-sport school athletes. Their results revealed that being a formal or informal leader positively related to increased feelings of social identity (Martin et al., 2017). Moreover, Zucchermaglio (2005) undertook a qualitative, ethnographic approach to investigate social identities arising in the interactions between members of a professional soccer team in Italy. Interactions between the players were audio recorded after a victory, after a defeat, and in a pre-game situation. Zucchermaglio (2005) coded the conversations, paying particular attention to the pronouns used within the conversations (e.g., 'I', 'we'). Results revealed that match outcome influenced how soccer players referenced team membership and specific sub-groups. For example, after a loss, players were more likely to distance themselves from the team and identify specific sub-groups to account for the loss (e.g., forwards were responsible for the loss for not scoring goals), whereas, post-victory, the group was considered as a whole, and fewer differentiations were made regarding team membership. Additionally, in relation to personal outcomes, stronger social identity perceptions were related to positive mental health in adolescent male athletes in Australia, which included competitive soccer players (Vella et al., 2021; see Table 6.1). Specifically, a global measure of social identity (which combined ingroup ties, cognitive centrality, and ingroup affect scores) was positively related to athlete wellbeing and negatively related to psychological distress.

Despite the significance of athletes' social identities, gaps in our understanding remain pertaining to how social identities form and can be influenced to promote positive outcomes for athletes. In essence, the question of how one comes to identify more strongly with a particular social group is not as clear, especially in the context of soccer. Social identity leadership is one option that applies well to the sport context.

Identity Leadership

Within social psychology, there is theoretical and empirical evidence supporting peer leaders as active agents in establishing a shared sense of social identity within a group (Steffens & Haslam, 2017). A key tenet of the Social Identity Approach to Leadership asserts that leaders are effective in their mission to motivate and mobilise followers towards common goals insofar that those followers see their capability to represent, advance, create, and embed a shared sense of social identity for group members (Haslam et al., 2011; Slater et al., 2014). These behaviours are captured

TABLE 6.1 Relationships between motivation, social identity, and mental health among adolescent male athletes (adapted from Vella et al., 2021)

Variable	M	SD	Range	1	2	3	4
1. Self-determined motivation	13.39	5.91	−8 to 18	—			
2. Social identity	17.22	3.43	0–21	.41**	—		
3. Psychological distress	10.68	3.83	6–30	−0.28**	−0.15**	—	
4. Wellbeing	67.58	11.87	14–84	0.28**	0.36**	−0.51**	—

Note: ** $p < .001$.

under what is called identity leadership, a multidimensional construct centred on four key principles: (a) identity prototypicality—embodying the distinct qualities that define the group and what it means to be a group member (e.g., 'being one of us'), (b) identity advancement—being an ingroup champion by promoting the shared interests of the group (e.g., 'doing it for us'), (c) identity entrepreneurship—creating and maintaining a sense of 'we' and 'us' by defining what us means (and does not mean) for followers (e.g., 'crafting a sense of us'), and (d) identity impresarioship—developing and promoting events and activities that give weight to the group's existence (e.g., 'making us matter'; Steffens et al., 2014). Identity leadership has been shown to positively predict social identity, which, in turn, was related through this research to outcomes such as adherence (Stevens et al., 2018), social support (Miller et al., 2020), moral behaviour among teammates (McLaren et al., 2021), and measures of teamwork, resilience, and satisfaction with team performance (Fransen et al., 2020).

Group Cohesion

In sport group dynamics research, one specific variable that has received a great deal of attention is the degree to which members perceive the cohesiveness of their team (Carron et al., 1985). In fact, group cohesion has been identified as the most important small group variable by some researchers (Lott & Lott, 1965). In sport, group cohesion is defined as an emergent state that "is reflected in the tendency for a group to stick together and remain united in pursuit of its instrumental objectives and/or for the satisfaction of member affective needs" (Carron et al., 1998, p. 213). The process of forming cohesion perceptions has been described in general at the conceptual level. According to Carron and colleagues (e.g., Carron & Brawley, 2000; Carron et al., 2002a), athletes will consider information from two sources in formulating cohesion perceptions. First, they will consider their own personal experiences within the social situation of the team. In addition, they also will expand on their own experiences and consider the nature of the team as a collective unit. Together, these individual and team aspects are selectively filtered and interpreted in a way that informs the athlete's perception as to the unity of the team in its pursuit of different team objectives.

Sport team cohesion has been conceptualised as being multidimensional in nature with one key distinction drawn between task and social cohesion (Carron et al., 1985). A task orientation captures the degree to which members are united towards achieving the team's objectives (e.g., winning matches), whereas a social orientation represents members developing and maintaining social relationships within the team. Given this distinction, it is possible that different aspects of the group will serve as cues for each orientation. Further, Carron and Brawley (2000) noted that multidimensional does not imply that both task and social cohesion are equally present in all teams, at all times. As described in the subsequent sections, cohesion has been related to personal factors (e.g., acceptance, commitment, enjoyment; Donkers et al., 2015), social factors (e.g., positive youth development; Taylor & Bruner, 2012), team factors (e.g., performance; Dobersek et al., 2014), and potential maladaptive factors (e.g., groupthink; Rovio et al., 2009).

As it relates to talent and development in sport, task cohesion has been found to mediate the relationship between social acceptance, commitment, and enjoyment, whereas social cohesion did not in a sample of adolescent recreational soccer players (Donkers et al., 2015). Relating to social factors of cohesion in sport teams, Taylor and Bruner (2012) conducted a cross-sectional study in order to examine social-contextual correlates of players' developmental experiences in a youth soccer context. Youth soccer players from four academies associated with professional

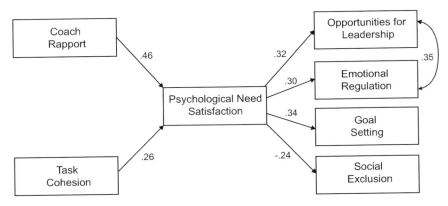

FIGURE 6.1 Relationships between task cohesion, psychological need satisfaction, and positive youth development outcomes in youth soccer (adapted from Taylor & Bruner, 2012).

soccer clubs in the United Kingdom completed a multi-section questionnaire to assess coach rapport, task cohesion, psychological needs satisfaction, and developmental experiences. Results found a positive relationship between players' psychological need fulfilment and three positive developmental experiences (Taylor & Bruner, 2012). Additionally, Taylor and Bruner (2012) found a negative relationship between psychological need satisfaction and social exclusion, which ultimately highlights an important area of coaching practice that should foster autonomy, competence, and relatedness within youth soccer players (see Figure 6.1). Although many questions remain regarding the relative impact of group cohesion towards team factors and outcomes (Eys & Brawley, 2018), multiple studies help reinforce the relationship of group cohesion and team performance (e.g., Carron et al., 2002b; Dobersek et al., 2014).

Through meta-analysis, Carron et al. (2002b) and Dobersek et al. (2014) have examined the direction and magnitude of the cohesion and team performance relationship in sport-based research. Overall, both studies reported a significant moderate relationship between cohesion and performance (Carron et al., 2002b; Dobersek et al., 2014). Further, these reviews support the bidirectional nature of the cohesion-performance link. This means that greater group cohesion leads to greater team performance but also that greater performance leads to greater cohesion. In fact, it appears that the inverse relationship (performance to cohesion) is slightly stronger (i.e., teams who win will see themselves as more united towards team objectives).

Up until this point, the discussion has painted a rather advantageous picture of group cohesion. However, there are similar findings in the sports literature and other domains that also describe some debilitating aspects and a maladaptive side of too much cohesion (e.g., groupthink; Hardy et al., 2005; Rovio et al., 2009). For instance, Rovio et al. (2009) conducted a case study of a junior ice-hockey team to investigate the relationships between performance in a team sport and social psychological group phenomena, such as cohesion, conformity, groupthink, and group polarisation. Their results displayed that pressure to conform, groupthink, and group polarisation increased due to a high level of social cohesion, which, in turn, was also associated with the deterioration of the group's performance. Ultimately, Rovio et al. (2009) concluded that high cohesion may not always be beneficial to the team and does not necessarily lead to better performance in all situations, thus providing a perspective of the maladaptive side to cohesion.

Motivational Climate

One final social construct to highlight involves the salience of different types of interactions athletes have and the behaviours they witness within the team environment related to successful performance. A growing body of literature has examined motivational climate as an indicator of positive and negative experiences in sport (e.g., Harwood & Thrower, 2020; Smith et al., 2009). Motivational climate has its theoretical roots in Achievement Goal Theory (AGT) (Nicholls, 1984). Achievement Goal Theory describes the pursuit of different individual goals across two different perspectives. Specifically, performance (ego) goals emphasise success as outperforming others, whereas mastery (task) goals emphasise success as learning and improvement, independent of performance outcome (Nicholls, 1984).

As an illustration, consider a youth soccer player who aims to increase their individual performance for a segment of the season. In the case of a performance/ego-related goal pursuit, this individual would be more likely to feel as though the goal is achieved when they are one of the best performing players, compared to the other players on their team (e.g., score the most goals, have the highest passing accuracy). Alternatively, in the case of a mastery/task-related goal pursuit, the individual would feel as though the goal is achieved when they have improved their own skill level over a previous segment of the season. Generally speaking, there is an understanding from existing theory and research that ego-related behaviours are seen as deleterious within a youth sport context (e.g., Smith et al., 2008) and refer to those behaviours as promoting social comparison and outcome-first attitudes. Conversely, task-related behaviours are seen as more acceptable in youth sport and refer to the promotion of effort, cooperation, teamwork, and self-referenced comparisons.

To situate the AGT research that led to the emergence of the motivational climate, we can look to the foundational research of Ames and Ames (1984). In their qualitative research investigating motivation and its influences on forming the environment in a classroom setting, they offered preliminary evidence that the classroom environments could be characterised as task- or ego-related. They described the construct motivational climate as an indicator of the degree to which the salient group environment (e.g., the classroom) is perceived to promote the achievement of either task- or ego-related goals (Ames & Ames, 1984). Selfriz et al. (1992) later extended that research into the context of sport and found evidence that the behaviours of key social agents (i.e., coaches, parents, and peers) were responsible for crafting a task- and/or ego-climate. More studies are now beginning to explore the specific behaviours of these social agents and the unique influence they have on the motivational climate (e.g., Keegan et al., 2010). In fact, the simultaneous influences from each respective climate has been labelled the motivational 'atmosphere' (Keegan et al., 2010).

As highlighted by Keegan and colleagues (Keegan et al., 2009, 2010), the broader motivational atmosphere surrounding youth sport participants encases the relative influence of three different climates initiated by the coach, parents, and peers (i.e., teammates). Through a series of qualitative investigations, Keegan and colleagues suggested that coaches play a specific role, predicated on instruction and pedagogic considerations, while parents play a role more suited to supporting participation and learning. Peers, in contrast, uniquely influence motivation through competitive and collaborative behaviours, evaluative communication, and social relationships. As a result, Keegan and colleagues contend that the specific contributions of coaches, parents, and peers offer important insight into the youth sport environment.

When looking at existing research in sport, various outcomes have been explored in relation to motivational climate (e.g., Isoard-Gautheur et al., 2021; Jõesaar et al., 2012; Kolayiş et al.,

2017; Reinboth & Duda, 2004; Rottensteiner et al., 2015). Importantly, these outcomes have been explored through the perspective of the coach- (e.g., McLaren et al., 2015), parent- (e.g., O'Rourke et al., 2013), and peer-initiated motivational climate (e.g., McLaren et al., 2017). For instance, multiple studies have examined team factors—namely, group cohesiveness—as an outcome of motivational climate in sport (e.g., García-Calvo et al., 2014; McLaren et al., 2015, 2017). Using semi-professional Spanish soccer players, García-Calvo et al. (2014) found that a task-related motivational climate as initiated by the coach was positively related to perceived group cohesion and players' satisfaction with their participation within their team (García-Calvo et al., 2014). Additionally, a task-related peer climate was also related positively to perceived cohesion (García-Calvo et al., 2014). A comparable pattern of relationships was found by McLaren et al. (2015) using an experimental study design. They showed recreational youth soccer coaches from Canada who participated in a workshop designed to develop a task-related motivational climate had players who perceived higher task and social cohesion by the end of season compared with attention-control and control condition athletes. As illustrated in Figure 6.2, both task and social cohesion perceptions were significantly higher by the end of season measure for players of a coach trained to promote a task-related motivational climate.

In a sample of young Spanish soccer players, Alvarez et al. (2012) examined the relationship of a coach-initiated motivational climate, player's well-being, and intentions to continue participation. The findings of this study revealed that a perceived task-related climate was a positive predictor of psychological well-being (subjective vitality), satisfaction of basic psychological needs of autonomy, competence, and relatedness, and future intentions to play. Conversely, a perceived ego climate was a negative predictor of relatedness satisfaction (Alvarez et al., 2012). Through the perspective of a parent-created motivational climate, one sample study by O'Rourke et al. (2013) found that young swimming athletes whose parents created a task-related climate, focused on enjoyment, self-improvement, and effort, reported higher intrinsic motivation than did those whose parent exhibited ego-related behaviours that emphasised winning, avoiding mistakes, and social comparisons. On the other hand, ego climate scores were related to greater extrinsic motivation. Taken together, these examples illustrate the different ways that important social agents in any sport environment can impact outcomes for the athlete, in this case specific to how successful performance is defined.

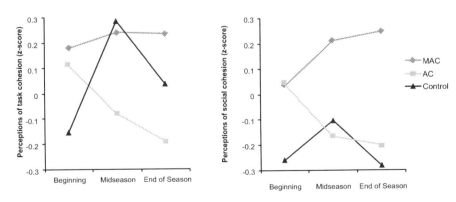

FIGURE 6.2 Comparing task and social cohesion among recreational soccer athletes of coaches trained to promote a task-related motivational climate (MAC) and controls (AC and Control) (adapted from McLaren et al., 2015).

Implications for Talent Development

Each of the three social constructs identified in this chapter—social identity, group cohesion, and motivational climate—hold important value in helping to unlock the soccer team as a powerful vehicle for talent and positive youth development. Whereas much of this research is not conducted through the lens of talent identification or development per se, it stands that soccer players who train and compete in a healthy social environment will be better suited to reach their potential, both physically and mentally. In addition, constructs such as cohesion have been tied to greater performance, which may increase the possibility that players are identified to continue along a particular competitive trajectory. In the following paragraph, some potential strategies are highlighted to foster social identity, cohesion, and a task motivational climate.

Coaches and practitioners working with soccer teams should consider the team and player developmental benefits of building strong team identities (e.g., performance, teammate behaviour, mental health) by fostering the importance of the team (cognitive centrality), the sense of belonging (ingroup ties), and the positive feelings associated with group membership (ingroup affect). Coaches and practitioners play a vital role in shaping a strong sense of unity on the pitch (task cohesion) and among the teammate relationships off the field (social cohesion). When players are on the same page, they can work together more effectively towards team goals. Team-building activities led by the coach or a sport psychology practitioner are a viable option to strengthen cohesiveness (see Eys et al., 2022; Martin et al., 2009 for examples). As detailed earlier, too much cohesion must be carefully considered by practitioners employed in youth soccer settings to promote talent and healthy development. Indeed, a blanket assumption that improved cohesion is good might not be appropriate. Finally, coaches should reflect on how they define what it means to be successful (i.e., is success about improvement and skill mastery, or winning at any cost). When soccer players feel that their coach promotes improvement and effort (i.e., task motivational climate), positive outcomes are more likely to follow.

Considerations for Researchers

As players move along developmental trajectories in soccer, both physical and mental wellbeing are of utmost importance. Along this line, studies focused on social influences in youth soccer will continue to benefit from collaboration with researchers who focus on physical, talent-related outcomes and greater consideration of player mental health as a fundamental outcome of the research. This inclusion of mental health is particularly true for group cohesion research, which lags behind social identity and motivational climate research in terms of the quantity of literature to illustrate how the constructs relate to athlete mental health.

In terms of the motivational climate specifically, research would benefit from greater consideration of the additive effects of task and ego climates together (see Chicau Borrego et al., 2021 as an example). Although ego climates are typically considered to be detrimental to athlete development, is it possible that a high task climate acts as a buffer when an ego climate also is perceived as higher? At the current time, task and ego climates are typically treated as independent constructs to predict outcomes. For instance, if a soccer coach places emphasis on winning and performance as markers of success, do the negative outcomes consistent with this climate erode if that same coach also preaches improvement and teamwork?

In terms of study design, social influence research would benefit from greater use of second- (moderation) and third-generation research (mediation; Zanna & Fazio, 1982) to understand the boundary conditions of the relationships described in this chapter as well as the mechanisms through which the relationships exist (see Eys & Spink, 2016). Further, given the dynamic nature of these constructs (i.e., social identity, group cohesion, and motivational climate), longitudinal research is needed to unpack relationships across time within soccer teams as well as to help understand the potential bidirectional nature of these same relationships (e.g., group cohesion predicts performance and performance predicts cohesion; Carron et al., 2002b).

Considerations for Practitioners

Related to the social constructs discussed in this chapter, the following considerations are made for coaches and/or practitioners to help create a positive environment in youth soccer:

- Following matches, whether the result ends in a win, draw, or loss, emphasise the team and not individual performances. Promote 'we' over 'I'.
- Establish a sense of belonging within the team by identifying the values of each member. This will help in promoting prosocial behaviours and interaction within teammates.
- Clarify goals and objectives for the group, such that members can be on the same page. Team-building activities can be used to target specific team process weaknesses (e.g., interaction and communication, leadership, role clarity).
- Reward effort over performance. Focus on player progression and effort relative to themselves rather than in comparison with their peers and based on performance.
- Educate parents on positive interactions with their child, which should entail rewarding effort and self-improvement rather than focusing on comparing performances and winning.

Conclusions

In early group dynamics research, Lewin (1939) expressed the importance of the social environment through field theory, stating that, if we are to understand individual behaviour, we must factor the influence of all fields (e.g., psychological, physiological, biological, and social). As players are inherently social beings, soccer offers the opportunity for youth players to engage in interpersonal interaction and therefore develop connections with fellow members, the provision of social support, and a sense of meaning and purpose. This chapter has detailed three social constructs as examples that could be of interest for scholars and practitioners. Specifically, it has been highlighted that the way a youth soccer player internalises their team membership (social identity), the level of perceived cohesiveness within the team (task and social cohesion), and the behaviours that important social agents (coaches, parents, and peers) exhibit related to defining success in soccer all play an important role in physical and psychological outcomes and the subsequent developmental trajectories of young players. Although psychological, physiological, and biological markers may help identify a talented player, it is critical that the social environment in which an individual competes and learns is conducive to positive development over time.

References

Alvarez, M. S., Balaguer, I., Castillo, I., & Duda, J. L. (2012). The coach-created motivational climate, young athletes' well-being, and intentions to continue participation. *Journal of Clinical Sport Psychology*, 6(2), 166–179. http://doi.org/10.1123/jcsp.6.2.166

Ames, C., & Ames, R. (1984). Systems of student and teacher motivation: Toward a qualitative definition. *Journal of Educational Psychology*, 76(4), 535–556. https://doi.org/10.1037/0022-0663.76.4.535

Baumeister, R. F., & Leary, M. R. (1995). The need to belong: Desire for interpersonal attachments as a fundamental human motivation. *Psychological Bulletin*, 11(3), 497–529. http://doi.org/10.1037/0033-2909.117.3.497

Beauchamp, M. R. (2019). Promoting exercise adherence through groups: A self-categorization theory perspective. *Exercise and Sport Sciences Reviews*, 47(1), 54–61. http://doi.org/10.1249/JES.0000000000000177

Bruner, M. W., & Benson, A. J. (2018). Evaluating the psychometric properties of the Social Identity Questionnaire for Sport (SIQS). *Psychology of Sport and Exercise*, 35(2), 181–188. https://doi.org/10.1016/j.psychsport.2017.12.006

Bruner, M. W., Boardley, I. D., Benson, A. J., Wilson, K. S., Root, Z., Turnnidge, J., Sutcliffe, J., & Côté, J. (2018). Disentangling the relations between social identity and prosocial and antisocial behavior in competitive youth sport. *Journal of Youth and Adolescence*, 47(5), 1113–1127. https://doi.org/10.1007/s10964-017-0769-2

Bruner, M. W., Boardley, I. D., & Côté, J. (2014). Social identity and prosocial and antisocial behavior in youth sport. *Psychology of Sport and Exercise*, 15(1), 56–64. https://doi.org/10.1016/j.psychsport.2013.09.003

Bruner, M. W., Dunlop, W. L., & Beauchamp, M. R. (2014). A social identity perspective on group processes in sport and exercise. In M. Beauchamp & M. Eys (Eds.), *Group dynamics in exercise and sport psychology* (pp. 38–52). Routledge.

Bruner, M. W., Eys, M., Carreau, J. M., McLaren, C., & Van Woezik, R. (2020). Using the Team Environment AssessMent (TEAM) to enhance team building in sport. *The Sport Psychologist*, 34(1), 62–70. https://doi.org/10.1123/tsp.2018-0174

Cameron, J. E. (2004). A three-factor model of social identity. *Self and Identity*, 3(3), 239–262. https://doi.org/10.1080/13576500444000047

Carron, A. V., & Brawley, L. R. (2000). Cohesion: Conceptual and measurement issues. *Small Group Research*, 31(1), 89–106. http://doi.org/10.1177/104649640003100105

Carron, A. V., Brawley, L. R., & Widmeyer, W. N. (1998). The measurement of cohesiveness in sport groups. In J. L. Duda (Ed.), *Advances in sport and exercise psychology measurement* (pp. 213–226). Fitness Information Technology.

Carron, A. V., Bray, S. R., & Eys, M. A. (2002a). Team cohesion and team success in sport. *Journal of Sports Sciences*, 20(2), 119–126. https://doi.org/10.1080/026404102317200828

Carron, A. V., Colman, M. M., Wheeler, J., & Stevens, D. (2002b). Cohesion and performance in sport: A meta analysis. *Journal of Sport and Exercise Psychology*, 24(2), 168–188. https://doi.org/10.1123/jsep.24.2.168

Carron, A. V., Widmeyer, W. N., & Brawley, L. R. (1985). The development of an instrument to assess cohesion in sport teams: The group environment questionnaire. *Journal of Sport and Exercise Psychology*, 7(3), 244–266. https://doi.org/10.1123/jsp.7.3.244

Chicau Borrego, C., Monteiro, D., Benson, A. J., Miguel, M., Teixeira, E., & Silva, C. (2021). Disentangling the effects of ego and task-involving climate perceptions on cohesion in youth sport. *Sport, Exercise, and Performance Psychology*, 10(4), 558–570. https://doi.org/10.1037/spy0000270

Dobersek, U., Gershgoren, L., Becker, B., & Tenenbaum, G. (2014). The cohesion–performance relationship in sport: A 10-year retrospective meta-analysis. *Sport Sciences for Health*, 10(3), 165–177. https://doi.org/10.1007/s11332-014-0188-7

Donkers, J. L., Martin, L. J., Paradis, K. F., & Anderson, S. H. (2015). The social environment in children's sport: Cohesion, social acceptance, commitment, and enjoyment. *International Journal of Sport Psychology*, 46(4), 275–294. http://doi.org/10.7352/IJSP.2015.46.275

Eys, M. A., & Brawley, L. R. (2018). Reflections on cohesion research with sport and exercise groups. *Social and Personality Psychology Compass*, 12(4), e12379. https://doi.org/10.1111/spc3.12379

Eys, M. A., Coleman, T., & Crickard, T. (2022) Group cohesion: The glue that helps teams stick together. *Frontiers Young Minds*, 10, 685318. https://doi.org/10.3389/frym.2022.685318

Eys, M. A., & Spink, K. S. (2016). Forecasts to the future: Group dynamics. In R. J. Schinke, K. R. McGannon, & B. Smith (Eds.), *Routledge international handbook of sport psychology* (pp. 572–580). Routledge

Forsyth, D. L. (2014). *Group dynamics* (6th ed.). Wadsworth Cengage Learning.

Fransen, K., McEwan, D., & Sarkar, M. (2020). The impact of identity leadership on team functioning and well-being in team sport: Is psychological safety the missing link? *Psychology of Sport and Exercise, 51*, 101763. https://doi.org/10.1016/j.psychsport.2020.101763

García-Calvo, T., Leo, F. M., Gonzalez-Ponce, I., Sánchez-Miguel, P. A., Mouratidis, A., & Ntoumanis, N. (2014). Perceived coach-created and peer-created motivational climates and their associations with team cohesion and athlete satisfaction: Evidence from a longitudinal study. *Journal of Sports Sciences, 32*(18), 1738–1750. https://doi.org/10.1080/02640414.2014.918641

Hardy, J., Eys, M. A., & Carron, A. V. (2005). Exploring the potential disadvantages of high cohesion in sports teams. *Small Group Research, 36*(2), 166–187. https://doi.org/10.1177/1046496404266715

Harwood, C. G., & Thrower, S. N. (2020). Motivational climate in youth sport groups. In M. Bruner, L. Martin, & M. Eys (Eds.), *The power of groups in youth sport* (pp. 145–163). Academic Press.

Haslam, C., Jetten, J., Haslam, S. A., Pugliese, C., & Tonks, J. (2011). 'I remember therefore I am, and I am therefore I remember': Exploring the contributions of episodic and semantic self-knowledge to strength of identity. *British Journal of Psychology, 102*(2), 184–203. https://doi.org/10.1348/000712610X508091

Haslam, S. A. (2004). *Psychology in organizations*. Sage.

Haslam, S. A., O'Brien, A., Jetten, J., Vormedal, K., & Penna, S. (2005). Taking the strain: Social identity, social support, and the experience of stress. *British Journal of Social Psychology, 44*(3), 355–370. https://doi.org/10.1348/014466605X37468

Hogg, M. A., & Abrams, D. (2001). *Intergroup relations: Essential readings* (Vol. 1). Psychology Press.

Isoard-Gautheur, S., Ginoux, C., & Trouilloud, D. (2021). Associations between peer motivational climate and athletes' sport-related well-being: Examining the mediating role of motivation using a multi-level approach. *Journal of Sports Sciences, 40*(5), 550–560. https://doi.org/10.1080/02640414.2021.2004680

Jõesaar, H., Hein, V., & Hagger, M. S. (2012). Youth athletes' perception of autonomy support from the coach, peer motivational climate and intrinsic motivation in sport setting: One-year effects. *Psychology of Sport and Exercise, 13*(3), 257–262. https://doi.org/10.1016/j.psychsport.2011.12.001

Keegan, R. J., Harwood, C. G., Spray, C. M., & Lavallee, D. E. (2009). A qualitative investigation exploring the motivational climate in early career sports participants: Coach, parent and peer influences on sport motivation. *Psychology of Sport and Exercise, 10*(3), 361–372. https://doi.org/10.1016/j.psychsport.2008.12.003

Keegan, R. J., Spray, C., Harwood, C., & Lavallee, D. (2010). The motivational atmosphere in youth sport: Coach, parent, and peer influences on motivation in specializing sport participants. *Journal of Applied Sport Psychology, 22*(1), 87–105. https://doi.org/10.1080/10413200903421267

Kolayiş, H., Sarı, İ., & Çelik, N. (2017). Parent-initiated motivational climate and self-determined motivation in youth sport: How should parents behave to keep their child in sport? *Kinesiology, 49*(2), 217–224. https://doi.org/10.26582/k.49.2.4

Lewin, K. (1939). Field theory and experiment in social psychology: Concepts and methods. *American Journal of Sociology, 44*(6), 868–896. https://doi.org/10.1086/218177

Lott, A. J., & Lott, B. E. (1965). Group cohesiveness as interpersonal attraction: A review of relationships with antecedent and consequent variables. *Psychological Bulletin, 64*(4), 259–309. https://doi.org/10.1037/h0022386

Martin, L. J., Balderson, D., Hawkins, M., Wilson, K., & Bruner, M. W. (2017). Groupness and leadership perceptions in relation to social identity in youth sport. *Journal of Applied Sport Psychology, 29*(3), 367–374. https://doi.org/10.1080/10413200.2016.1238414

Martin, L. J., Carron, A. V., & Burke, S. M. (2009). Team building interventions in sport: A meta-analysis. *Sport and Exercise Psychology Review, 5*(2), 3–18.

McLaren, C. D., Boardley, I. D., Benson, A. J., Martin, L. J., Fransen, K., Herbison, J. D., Slatcher, R. B., Carré, J. M., Côté, J., & Bruner, M. W. (2021). Follow the leader: Identity leadership and moral behaviour in social situations among youth sport teammates. *Psychology of Sport and Exercise, 55*, 101940. https://doi.org/10.1016/j.psychsport.2021.101940

McLaren, C. D., Eys, M. A., & Murray, R. A. (2015). A coach-initiated motivational climate intervention and athletes' perceptions of group cohesion in youth sport. *Sport, Exercise, and Performance Psychology, 4*(2), 113. https://doi.org/10.1037/spy0000026

McLaren, C. D., Newland, A., Eys, M., & Newton, M. (2017). Peer-initiated motivational climate and group cohesion in youth sport. *Journal of Applied Sport Psychology, 29*(1), 88–100. https://doi.org/10.1080/10413200.2016.1190423

Miller, A. J., Slater, M. J., & Turner, M. J. (2020). Coach identity leadership behaviours are positively associated with athlete resource appraisals: The mediating roles of relational and group identification. *Psychology of Sport and Exercise, 51*, 101755. https://doi.org/10.1016/j.psychsport.2020.101755

Nicholls, J. G. (1984). Achievement motivation: Conceptions of ability, subjective experience, task choice, and performance. *Psychological Review, 91*(3), 328–346. https://doi.org/10.1037/0033-295X.91.3.328

O'Rourke, D. J., Smith, R. E., Smoll, F. L., & Cumming, S. P. (2013). Parent-initiated motivational climate and young athletes' intrinsic- extrinsic Motivation: Cross-sectional and longitudinal relations. *Journal of Child and Adolescent Behaviour, 1*(109). https://doi.org/10.4172/2375-4494.1000109

Reinboth, M., & Duda, J. L. (2004). The motivational climate, perceived ability, and athletes' psychological and physical well-being. *Sport Psychologist, 18*(3), 237–251.

Rottensteiner, C., Konttinen, N., & Laakso, L. (2015). Sustained participation in youth sports related to coach-athlete relationship and coach-created motivational climate. *International Sport Coaching Journal, 2*(1), 29–38. https://doi.org/10.1123/iscj.2014-0060

Rovio, E., Eskola, J., Kozub, S. A., Duda, J. L., & Lintunen, T. (2009). Can high group cohesion be harmful? A case study of a junior ice-hockey team. *Small Group Research, 40*(4), 421–435. https://doi.org/10.1177/1046496409334359

Selfriz, J. J., Duda, J. L., & Chi, L. (1992). The relationship of perceived motivational climate to intrinsic motivation and beliefs about success in basketball. *Journal of Sport and Exercise Psychology, 14*(4), 375–391. https://doi.org/10.1123/jsep.14.4.375

Slater, M. J., Coffee, P., Barker, J. B., & Evans, A. L. (2014). Promoting shared meanings in group memberships: A social identity approach to leadership in sport. *Reflective Practice, 15*(5), 672–685. https://doi.org/10.1080/14623943.2014.944126

Smith, R. E., Cumming, S. P., & Smoll, F. L. (2008). Development and validation of the motivational climate scale for youth sports. *Journal of Applied Sport Psychology, 20*(1), 116–136. https://doi.org/10.1080/10413200701790558

Smith, R. E., Smoll, F. L., & Cumming, S. P. (2009). Motivational climate and changes in young athletes' achievement goal orientations. *Motivation and Emotion, 33*(2), 173–183. https://doi.org/10.1007/s11031-009-9126-4

Steffens, N. K., & Haslam, S. A. (2017). Building team and organisational identification to promote leadership, citizenship and resilience. In M. Crane (Ed.), *Managing for resilience: A practical guide for employee wellbeing and organizational performance* (pp. 150–167). Routledge.

Steffens, N. K., Haslam, S. A., Reicher, S. D., Platow, M. J., Fransen, K., Yang, J., Ryan, M. K., Jetten, J., Peters, K., & Boen, F. (2014). Leadership as social identity management: Introducing the Identity Leadership Inventory (ILI) to assess and validate a four-dimensional model. *The Leadership Quarterly, 25*(5), 1001–1024. https://doi.org/10.1016/j.leaqua.2014.05.002

Stevens, M., Rees, T., Coffee, P., Haslam, S. A., Steffens, N. K., & Polman, R. (2018). Leaders promote attendance in sport and exercise sessions by fostering social identity. *Scandinavian Journal of Medicine & Science in Sports, 28*(9), 2100–2108. https://doi.org/10.1111/sms.13217

Tajfel, H. (1981). *Human groups and social categories*. Cambridge University Press.

Täuber, S., & Sassenberg, K. (2012). The impact of identification on adherence to group norms in team sports: Who is going the extra mile? *Group Dynamics: Theory, Research, and Practice, 16*(4), 231–240. https://doi.org/10.1037/a0028377

Taylor, I. M., & Bruner, M. W. (2012). The social environment and developmental experiences in elite youth soccer. *Psychology of Sport and Exercise, 13*(4), 390–396. https://doi.org/10.1016/j.psychsport.2012.01.008

Vella, S. A., Benson, A., Sutcliffe, J., McLaren, C., Swann, C., Schweickle, M. J., Miller, A., & Bruner, M. (2021). Self-determined motivation, social identification and the mental health of adolescent male team sport participants. *Journal of Applied Sport Psychology, 33*(4), 452–466. https://doi.org/10.1080/10413200.2019.1705432

Zanna, M., & Fazio, R. (1982). The attitude-behavior relation: Moving toward a third generation of research. In M. Zanna, E. Higgins, & C. Harman (Eds.), *Consistency in social behavior: The ontario symposium* (Vol. 2, pp. 283–301). Erlbaum.

Zucchermaglio C., (2005). Who wins and who loses: The rhetorical manipulation of social identities in a soccer team. *Group Dynamics: Theory, Research, and Practice*, 9(4), 219–238. https://doi.org/10.1037/1089-2699.9.4.219

7

SOCIOCULTURAL

Reflecting on the Social and Cultural Influences on Talent in Soccer

Matthew J. Reeves, Simon J. Roberts, and Adam L. Kelly

Introduction

Due to its worldwide popularity, soccer has emerged as a sport capable of exporting social and cultural influences across the far-flung corners of the globe. Whether this be high levels of performance or health-prescribing interventions designed to deliver social reform, the growth of soccer clubs and leagues as multinational brands has enabled soccer to assert its influence on a worldwide scale. From a purely economic perspective, the marketisation of soccer requires all concerned to ensure that the quality of the 'product' doesn't decline (Lath et al., 2021). This means that there is a continual drive for clubs to field teams and players that can perform at the highest standard based on their level of competition.

The consequences of soccer's ongoing march toward multi-modal commodification have seen net outlay on player transfer fees increase significantly (McHale & Holmes, 2022). As such, clubs and federations are paying increased attention to how players are identified and developed within academy environments (Reeves & Roberts, 2020), with a view to limiting spending in the transfer market. This has meant some clubs and federations have reconfigured their talent identification and development processes and practices to look beyond just the technical, tactical, physical, and psychological aspects of performance (Reeves et al., 2018). The purpose of this chapter is, therefore, to examine more closely the sociocultural influences of talent identification and development in soccer.

Contextual Overview

Despite the worldwide popularity of soccer, when compared to mainstream businesses such as those listed on the London 250 stock market, soccer clubs (even those in the English Premier League) are relatively small, with very few returning a profit. With soaring transfer fees and increases in player salaries, efforts have been made to stem the increasing costs associated with purchasing players. For example, some clubs have implemented transfer policies and their own wage caps to help mitigate spiralling budget costs. One example is Tottenham Hotspur FC in the English Premier League. Their chairperson, Daniel Levy, has made it clear to players, other clubs, and the media what they are and are not prepared to do to retain or purchase a player. Arguably, this might have contributed to the club's lack of success (i.e., trophies won), but it has helped them to build a new training ground and stadium as well as prove themselves to be one of the most financially stable teams in the English Premier League, despite posting a net loss of £80 million in 2021 that was attributable to the new stadium development. A similar picture is emerging across national and international federations. For example, UEFA have been trying for over a decade to increase the quality and quantity of 'homegrown players' (HGP) in an effort to protect young players and restrict migration at early ages. However, there has been an indirect effect, with some players who qualify as being homegrown for European competitions attracting a transfer fee premium. A recent example of this would be Jack Grealish, whose reported £100 million transfer from Aston Villa FC to Manchester City FC made him the most expensive British soccer player in history. The move not only recognised Grealish's performances at Aston Villa FC, but also ensured Manchester City FC would remain compliant of the HGP rule in domestic and European competitions. Other examples from national federations include: (a) the Deutscher Fußball-Bund (DFB) mandating that all German clubs in the top three tiers must operate an academy, (b) the Fédération Française de Football (FFF) and Ligue de Football Professionnel (LPF) implementing the 'Charte du Football Professionnel' in France, and (c) the English Premier League 'Elite Player Performance Plan' (EPPP).

Evidently, there have been multiple influences upon clubs and how they operate their talent identification and development practices. One perennial question that remains unanswered, however, is the overall effectiveness of academies for producing players who transition to the first team (Morris et al., 2015). From a United Kingdom context, recent data from the English Premier League suggest that 97% of players who progress through the academy system never play a single minute of top-flight soccer, while 70% of those never receive a professional contract (Cunningham, 2022). Consequently, researchers and practitioners have tried to understand the influence that different factors have upon the identification and development of young players to help improve the youth-to-senior transition process (see Chapter 9). Each academy has its own way of operating, but usually within parameters set by the national federation or league. They do, however, all utilise a range of specialist practitioners within these structures, including coaches, sports medics, performance analysts, psychologists, and educationalists, amongst others, with the intention of supporting player development. As specialist practitioners' influence upon individuals advances, so does our need to fully understand that influence. One area where this remains limited is within the sociocultural domain (Reeves et al., 2018).

A useful starting point for first considering the potential social predictors of future performance was initially proposed by Williams and Reilly (2000), which was recently reinvigorated by Williams et al. (2020). In the discussion that follows, several of these proposed sociocultural factors are considered, with a view to understanding more about how researchers and practitioners can utilise this knowledge to inform processes and practices that might lead to better talent-related outcomes. More specifically, three sub-topics focused on sociocultural influences on talent in soccer are presented, including: (a) sociodemographic influences, (b) cultural backgrounds, and (c) birthplace effects. Following these sections, considerations for researchers and practitioners are offered to advance this field of research and underscore key take-home messages.

Sociodemographic Influences

The influence of sociodemographic features has, until recently, been largely overlooked within soccer talent identification and development research. Whilst there is strong evidence relating to engagement in and drop out from grassroots sport based on social class (e.g., Lammle et al., 2012;

Pabayo et al., 2014; Pabayo et al., 2014; Vandendriessche et al., 2012), there is little examination of this issue from a talent development or elite performance perspective. In other sports, scientists have reported that athletes' sociodemographic markers, such as ethnicity and relative access to wealth, favour white, privately educated athletes (e.g., Brown & Kelly, 2021; Brown et al., 2022; Lawrence, 2017; Winn et al., 2017). However, this change within soccer has been slow to occur; since its inception, soccer has been the quintessential working-class sport. For instance, less than two decades ago, it was suggested that, in Ireland, young soccer players tended to be targeted from working-class families (Bourke, 2003), perhaps, due to soccer's historical roots as one of the few sporting opportunities available to those from lower socioeconomic backgrounds (Hodkinson & Sparkes, 1997), though current evidence from other regions challenges that notion.

In the United States, there have been material, geographic, and cultural changes in soccer since the 1970s that has included the expansion of private leagues, pushing competitive structures into the suburbs and away from larger cities, with obvious implications for the demographic of players participating (e.g., Andrews, 1999; Andrews et al., 1997; Reck & Dick, 2015). A recent study of the socioeconomic, racial, and geographic composition of professional female soccer players in the United States found support for these claims (Allison & Barranco, 2021). The study examined longitudinal data from the National Women's Super League (NWSL) rosters and combined these with United States Census data, concluding that those at the highest levels of women's soccer in the United States derived from "places ('hometowns') that are whiter, less black or Latino, more suburban, and less socioeconomically disadvantaged than the national average, with higher per capita, median household, and median family incomes" (pp. 464–465). Interestingly, despite earlier claims that soccer in the United Kingdom and Ireland has its roots in the working-class traditions, recent research conducted in academies in England suggest that this might be changing, as youngsters entering talent development programmes were perceived by some recruitment staff as being increasingly from middle-class backgrounds (Reeves et al., 2018).

There is only one study, of which the authors are aware, that has specifically focused on issues of socioeconomic status of academy soccer players from Europe (Kelly et al., 2023). This study explored socioeconomic status and psychological characteristics in academy players in England. Players' home postcodes were used to determine socioeconomic status (i.e., social classification via the General Registrar Classification system and financial risk via credit rating) and the Psychological Characteristics for Developing Excellence Questionnaire (PCDEQ) to explore psychological constructs of coach-rated 'high' and 'low' potential players. Players rated as having a higher potential were from families with a significantly lower socioeconomic status (social classification) and scored higher on factor three of the PCDEQ (coping with performance and developmental pressures), compared to players considered to have lower potential (Table 7.1). These results suggest a possible causal link between socioeconomic status, psychological characteristics, and perceived potential to become a professional player.

Similar suggestions have recently been reported in Brazil, where it was proposed that the poverty of young Brazilian soccer players might help shape their level of skill and expertise (Uehara et al., 2021). The authors suggested that poverty created an exosystem, whereby young players increased the likelihood of participation in soccer-specific activities and, thus, their engagement in deliberate practice and play, both of which have been shown to facilitate the development of expertise (e.g., Ford et al., 2012; Hornig et al., 2016). It has also been suggested such situational factors might facilitate some psychological characteristics, such as overcoming adversity, motivation, mental toughness, and resilience (Collins & MacNamara, 2012). However, it is difficult to assess such claims, as there is a lack of sufficient relevant high-quality studies and data.

TABLE 7.1 Age group mean scores for socioeconomic markers (adapted from Kelly et al., 2023)

Socioeconomic Markers	Age Group U12	U13	U14	U15	U16	Overall	P
Social classification							
Higher-potentials	2.5 ± 0.58	3.25 ± 0.96	2.6 ± 0.89	3.25 ± 0.96	2.5 ± 2.12	2.84 ± 0.96	0.014
Lower-potentials	2.5 ± 1.29	2.25 ± 0.96	1.8 ± 1.3	1.25 ± 0.5	2.5 ± 0.71	2 ± 1.05	
Financial risk							
Higher-potentials	796 ± 131.41	765.50 ± 77.83	858.6 ± 65.53	890 ± 23.64	864.5 ± 77.08	833.05 ± 89.73	0.076
Lower-potentials	883.25 ± 19.19	877.25 ± 17.41	839.8 ± 42.37	898.25 ± 36.95	887 ± 16.97	874.11 ± 35.36	

Note: For this study, the UK General Registrar Classification system was adopted that uses the average credit rating applying the Cameo™ geodemographic database. This provided a social classification (A, B, C1, C2, D, and E) determined by the UK's Office for National Statistics and an average credit score (out of 999) for where each participant lives (i.e., based on their home postcode). The social classification was scored numerically, with a higher score relating to a lower social classification (i.e., A = 1, B = 2, C1 = 3, C2 = 3, D = 4, and E = 5). The credit score denotes those with a higher score to have lower financial risk from '0' (low) to '999' (high).

There are obvious differences between the socioeconomic statuses of players and their families around the world, but it is imperative that those involved in academies and development programmes recognise the influence that socioeconomic status might have when designing, implementing, and evaluating talent development pathways (Rees et al., 2016). By exploring such issues, it will help practitioners to create wider opportunities and more equitable talent systems for all young players to flourish.

Cultural Backgrounds

The cultural makeup of soccer teams around the world has been changing over the last few decades (Poli, 2010b). Until recently, there had been little effort to try and understand the impact this might have upon team performance and success. Modern teams include players from different countries, with unique cultural and religious backgrounds, different languages, and social and behavioural norms, and they are thrust together and expected to perform as a team with little understanding of each other that might instead lead to misunderstanding and conflict (Lazear, 1999).

When considering the 'big five' leagues in Europe, it has been suggested that culturally homogenous teams achieve higher average performances. Furthermore, managers of more culturally diverse teams, it is recommended, should consider the potential implications associated with striving to achieve cultural integration (Maderer et al., 2014). Indeed, the effect of cultural heterogeneity amongst teams in the Bundesliga has been shown to negatively (Haas & Nüesch, 2012) and positively (Andresen & Altmann, 2006) affect team performance. However, it is proposed that there is a more complex interaction of cultural influences upon team performance when we look deeper into the macro-level of a team's cultural diversity (Brandes et al., 2009). For example, when taking playing positions into consideration, more homogenous defensive formations were shown to perform better, whereas the opposite was true for attacking formations. Whilst these findings were shown across league- and club-level competitions, examination of teams in the UEFA Champions League showed that more diverse and more valuable teams tended to outperform their less diverse and less valuable counterparts (Ingersoll et al., 2017). Thus, it is suggested that the cost of players also acts as a mediator to performance outcome alongside cultural diversity. Whilst cultural diversity and team performance has been examined across twelve European leagues (Gerhards & Mutz, 2017), it has been further claimed that a team's market value could be a better predictor of success, especially in leagues where financial inequalities between clubs is greater. However, whilst their study showed that market value and relative team salary have a positive effect on team performance, whereas squad size had a negative effect, cultural diversity was shown to have no significant correlation to performance.

It is fair to say that the limited results and findings surrounding cultural and ethnic diversity are inconclusive and the evidence is, at best, mixed. Consequently, further examination of this area is required. Whilst a non-linear relationship appears to exist between cultural/ethnic diversity and team performance, it is unclear where the tipping-point between benefits and disadvantages lie, as well as what or how much other factors might be influential (e.g., player/team value). Moreover, most studies in this area have been confined to elite teams rather than development environments, despite the growth of player migration, including youth players, over the last 20 years. Whilst development environments have been examined in relation to the influence of geographic location upon talent identification and development, there have been no efforts to understand the effects of cultural background during critical development periods of younger players. Such studies would be a welcomed addition to improve our understanding of the role of cultural diversity during players' development. This would undoubtedly have value as soccer's globalised state continues to grow and interest, participation, and investment increases from countries that have, previously, had little influence in soccer, such as China and the Arab States of the Persian Gulf.

A final point to make is related to player migration. There is evidence of wealthy European clubs recruiting young talent from regions such as Africa, Asia, and South America (Acheampong et al., 2019; Elliott & Maguire, 2008; Ungruhe, 2016). In the English Premier Academy League, for instance, Elliot and Weedon (2011) suggested the concept of 'feet exchange', whereby skills and knowledge are shared to improve the overall performance of indigenous and foreign players, which favours both the host and donor nations by enhancing the development potential of all talent. Conversely, however, Milanovic (2005) proposed how developing countries often capture 'leg-drain' when their natives pursue a professional career elsewhere, leaving them unable to grow and develop their own talent development pathways and domestic leagues. Indeed, the transit of African soccer players to Europe and the role of soccer academies in this process has been suggested as a form of neo-colonial exploitation and impoverishment of the developing world by the developed world (Darby, 2000). This largely Western view has been challenged for disregarding local perceptions from African settings. It is not only the top clubs that are importing players, either. For instance, lower level and less wealthy clubs are recruiting a broad range of African players with varying ability, mainly as they are cheaper to purchase, demand lower wages, are willing to negotiate shorter-term contracts, and have also been found to be left vulnerable and exploited following their release (Poli, 2010a). This is particularly concerning, as the possible benefits of ethnic diversity to talent development and performance should not be at the expense of exploiting developing nations or vulnerable individuals. As such, clubs and stakeholders should always prioritise player well-being and positively support their migratory experience (Lally et al., 2022; van der Meij & Darby, 2017).

Birthplace Effects

Another important environmental factor that has been associated with the development of expertise in soccer is the place of birth. To be specific, 'where' a player is born can impact their opportunities to engage in youth soccer and developmental activities, which can either enhance or constrain potential talent (Côté et al., 2006). These *birthplace effects* (see Baker & Horton, 2004 for a review) are generally influenced by the athlete's 'community size' (i.e., the total number of people living within the area) and 'community density' (i.e., the number of people living within a specific unit of area). To examine the impact of community size and community density, research has traditionally observed the birthplace of professional and/or national-level athletes against the expected values from their location of birth as a proxy for talent development (Baker et al., 2014). Although work on the influence of community density is relatively novel, the impact of community size is not a new phenomenon. For instance, Curtis and Birch (1987) showed how Canadian-born professional and Olympic ice hockey players from larger cities (> 500,000) and rural communities (< 1,000) were underrepresented when compared to small and medium-sized cities (1,000–499,999) that were overrepresented. Similarly, other studies in sports have shown comparable community size effects (e.g., Côté et al., 2006; Lidor et al., 2014; MacDonald et al., 2009; MacDonald et al., 2009).

In the context of soccer, Rossing et al. (2016) suggested how male professional players were more likely to derive from a community size of > 30,000 inhabitants. When considering the role of community density, Finnegan et al. (2017) revealed an increased likelihood of selection into talent development pathways with a lower population density in Irish national youth male soccer players, which reflected the inequitable distribution of opportunities to access talent pathways across the country. Rossing et al. (2018) showed it was important to consider birthplace effects from a sport-specific perspective, as optimal community size and community density for talent development differed between soccer and handball. More specifically, in soccer, the authors observed a trend towards larger and more densely populated cities for professional (> 30,000 members; > 250 people/km^2) and national (> 50,000 inhabitants; ≥ 1,000 people/km^2) players. Smith and Weir (2020) demonstrated how community size and community density are unique and separate constructs. Their findings revealed medium-sized communities (i.e., 10,000–249,999 inhabitants) offered the best odds of participation and continued engagement in Canadian female youth soccer, whereas less densely populated communities (i.e., 50–<400 population/km^2) were the greatest for facilitating participation at age 10 years but not for engagement at age 16 years.

Potential explanations for birthplace effects suggest that community size impacts the availability of youth soccer experiences. For instance, small, rural communities may lack facilities and resources (e.g., soccer pitches, changing rooms, equipment, coaches, volunteers) to sustain organised competition, whereas larger cities may possess an inadequate number of facilities and resources to meet the demands of young players, which potentially leads to competition to access these among inhabitants. In comparison, small- to medium-sized cities likely facilitate greater availability of soccer facilities and resources to their inhabitants during development, as well as offer provision of a social structure that promotes athletic expertise (Smith & Weir, 2020). Moreover, advantages for less densely populated communities have been reported to offer greater opportunities for free play and organised participation during the earlier stages of development (Hancock et al., 2018), although the benefits of this environment may be reduced if these communities are not dense enough to provide the necessary resources for talent development programmes (Smith & Weir, 2020). Qualitative studies have shed light on the potential mechanisms of birthplace effects and the benefits of deriving from small- to medium-sized cities (e.g., Balish & Côté, 2014; Maayan et al., 2022; McCalpin et al., 2017). For example, based on the perception of stakeholders from a small and successful sport community in Canada, Balish and Côté (2014) showed how residents contributed to the development of local athletes through: (a) developmental experiences (i.e., youth engaging in organised and unorganised sport activities where teammates remained stable throughout development), (b) community influences (i.e., the interdependence between the local schools and the community), and (c) sociocultural influences (i.e., youth possessing a collective identity coupled with an intense inter-community rivalry).

Since individual regions possess broad and diverse social and cultural norms, it is important to consider the sociocultural mechanisms of countries independent of one another when exploring birthplace effects (Baker & Logan, 2007). As an example, Morganti et al. (in press) explored the 'southern question' (i.e., the expression used to label southern Italy's underdevelopment compared to the north and the centre of the country; Pescosolido, 2019) and whether it had an impact on selection in Italian national soccer. The authors examined the birthplace distribution of 2,012 Italian soccer players who have played in any of their male youth (U15–U21) or senior national teams. Findings revealed an overrepresentation of players born in the north and centre across all youth and senior cohorts, whereby players were up to 3.2 times more likely of being selected when compared to those from the south (see Figure 7.1). Likely explanations are the sociocultural divide between the north, the centre, and the south of Italy, which leaves inhabitants from the south with a reduced number of facilities and resources that leads to fewer developmental opportunities in soccer. Generally, however, there appears to be a lack of research focused on sociocultural influences within specific organisations and contexts in soccer and thus warrants further study.

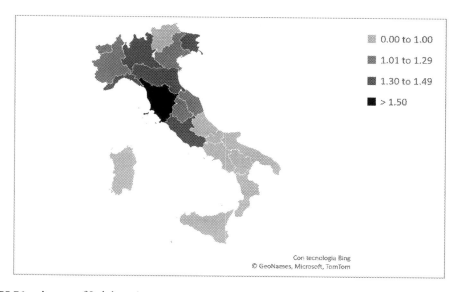

FIGURE 7.1 A map of Italy's regions.

Note: Regions are coloured with different gradations according to odd ratios (a darker gradient indicates a higher odds ratio). These were calculated on the likelihood of players being selected for Italy's male youth (U15–U21) or senior national teams (adapted from Morganti et al., in press).

Since contextual factors, such as country (Finnegan et al., 2017), gender (Hancock et al., 2018), sport popularity (Maayan et al., 2022), and sport type (Rossing et al., 2018), can have a varying influence on birthplace effects, it is important that the impact of community size and community density is not considered as homogenous. Moving forward, practitioners should be cautious of the influence of birthplace effects during talent identification and development in soccer, whilst researchers should focus on advancing our understanding of the potential barriers across and within different countries (see Chapter 16).

Considerations for Researchers

There is a limited understanding of the role socioeconomic status plays in talent identification and development. The limited yet growing data paints a picture of an increased number of middle-class participants from less diverse backgrounds entering academies and development programmes in developed countries. However, it is noted that poverty in developing nations, like Brazil, is suggested to be, at least in part, responsible for the development of more skilful players, through promotion of an ecosystem that promotes deliberate play and practice. That said, the causal relationship between poverty and skill development in soccer has not been established, despite calls for such examinations in the literature, and it thus offers a worthy direction for future research.

It is important to recognise that not all academies and development programmes are created equal and that the sociocultural determinants (e.g., ethnicity, relative access to wealth, birthplace effects) have a significant role to play in the identification and development of soccer players. In order that researchers and practitioners do not miss or prevent any individual from succeeding in soccer, it's imperative to continue to enhance our understanding of the complexity and interconnectedness of sociocultural factors with technical, tactical, physical, and psychological determinants of talent in soccer. Here, it is suggested that there needs to be more comprehensive, inclusive, and inter-/trans-disciplinary thought given to the sociocultural factors that affect the identification and development of players; and that thought extends into the elite professional game, too. The notion of a sociologist working within an academy or development environment might seem alien, particularly as sports science disciplines and sub-disciplines continue to fight for recognition and to be embraced. Yet, such a role would be truly trans-disciplinary, cutting across all departments with the potential to positively impact and influence possibilities for players to achieve their full potential.

Considerations for Practitioners

In comparison to other elements of talent identification and development in youth soccer (e.g., technical, tactical, physical, and psychological), sociocultural influences are less understood and/or measured. The following considerations are provided to help practitioners employed in youth soccer settings to better understand how social and cultural factors can impact player identification and development, as well as ensure strategies are adopted to facilitate equitable opportunities and appropriate settings for all individuals:

- Sociodemographic influences have the potential to bias scouts and coaches when identifying potentially talented players. Players with greater financial means are more likely to be recruited into development programmes in some countries (e.g., United States), whereas other regions (e.g., Brazil) show lower socioeconomic status may be key to progression as a professional

player. Clubs are encouraged to look in different environments and across the breadth of soccer provision when looking to identify players.
- Integrating players from different cultures and backgrounds is not restricted to first team environments, particularly as opportunities arise for potentially talented youngsters to move across national borders increases. Practitioners need to consider the potential impact of multiple cultures and backgrounds and how they understand and manage their own and their teams' relationships.
- Caution should be taken when migrating foreign talent. Player welfare must remain paramount, and formal policies should always be followed to support young players before, during, and after any trial or contract period.
- Where a player comes from matters. It could assist or limit their opportunities to engage in soccer-specific and other developmental activities. At club level, practitioners should consider how this could impact each individual and recognise how they could potentially be supported. At governing body level, policy makers are encouraged to ensure young players from all areas have access to soccer facilities and resources or invest where necessary.
- Inter- and trans-disciplinary approaches to talent identification and development are crucial for understanding the whole player. Practitioners must ensure their working practices encompass input from multiple professional domains, including sociology, and don't operate in isolation.

Conclusion

In this chapter, social and cultural influences upon talent identification and development in soccer were explored and demonstrated they can have widespread implications, which can be individual and context specific. The range, breadth, and interconnectedness of these factors can be a confounding factor and researchers have only recently begun to explore some of these issues. Sociocultural influences do not occur in isolation, and so neither can our efforts to examine these matters. It is emphasised that the impact upon the development and performance of individuals and teams can be greatly influenced by these issues, and thus, should be considered a central aspect during talent identification and development in youth soccer.

References

Acheampong, E. Y., Bouhaouala, M., & Raspaud, M. (2019). Socioeconomic analysis of African footballers' migration to Europe. In C. Onwumechili (Ed.), *Africa's elite football* (pp. 58–73). Routledge.

Allison, R., & Barranco, R. (2021). 'A rich white kid sport?' Hometown socioeconomic, racial, and geographic composition among U.S. women's professional soccer players. *Soccer & Society, 22*(5), 457–469. https://doi.org/10.1080/14660970.2020.1827231

Andresen, M., & Altmann, T. (2006). Diversity and success in professional football. *Leadership and Organization Magazine: ZfO, 75*(6), 325–332.

Andrews, D. L. (1999). Contextualizing suburban soccer: Consumer culture, lifestyle differentiation and suburban America. *Culture, Sport, Society, 2*(3), 31–53. https://doi.org/10.1080/14610989908721846

Andrews, D. L., Pitter, R., Zwick, D., & Ambrose, D. (1997). Soccer's racial frontier: Sport and the suburbanization of contemporary America. In G. Armstrong & R. Giulianotti (Eds.), *Entering the field: New perspectives on world football* (pp. 261–282). Berg.

Baker, J., & Horton, S. (2004). A review of primary and secondary influences on sport expertise. *High Ability Studies, 15*(2), 211–228. https://doi.org/10.1080/1359813042000314781

Baker, J., & Logan, A. J. (2007). Developmental contexts and sporting success: Birth date and birthplace effects in national hockey league draftees 2000–2005. *British Journal of Sports Medicine, 41*(8), 515–517. https://doi.org/10.1136/bjsm.2006.033977

Baker, J., Shuiskiy, K., & Schorer, J. (2014). Does size of one's community affect likelihood of being drafted into the NHL? Analysis of 25 years of data. *Journal of Sports Sciences, 32*(16), 1570–1575. https://doi.org/10.1080/02640414.2014.908319

Balish, S., & Côté, J. (2014) The influence of community on athletic development: An integrated case study. *Qualitative Research in Sport, Exercise and Health, 6*(1), 98–120. https://doi.org/10.1080/2159676X.2013.766815

Bourke, A. (2003). The dream of being a professional soccer player. *Journal of Sport and Social Issues, 27*(4), 399–419. https://doi.org/10.1177/0193732503255478

Brandes, L., Franck, E. P., & Theiler, P. (2009). The effect from national diversity on team production—empirical evidence from the sports industry. *Schmalenbach Business Review, 61*, 225–246.

Brown, T. W., Greetham, P., Powell, A., Gough, L., Khawaja, I., & Kelly, A. L. (2022). The sociodemographic profile of the England and Wales Cricket Board (ECB) talent pathways and first-class counties. *Managing Sport and Leisure*. https://doi.org/10.1080/23750472.2021.1949382

Brown, T. W., & Kelly, A. L. (2021). Relative access to wealth and ethnicity in professional cricket. In A. L. Kelly, J. Côté, M. Jeffreys, & J. Turnnidge (Eds.), *Birth advantages and relative age effects in sport: Exploring organizational structures and creating appropriate settings* (pp. 184–206). Routledge.

Collins, D., & MacNamara, Á. (2012). The rocky road to the top: Why talent needs trauma. *Sports Medicine, 42*(11), 907–914. https://doi.org/10.1007/bf03262302

Côté, J., Macdonald, D. J., Baker, J., & Abernethy, B. (2006). When "where" is more important than "when": Birthplace and birthdate effects on the achievement of sporting expertise. *Journal of Sports Sciences, 24*(10), 1065–1073. https://doi.org/10.1080/02640410500432490

Cunningham, S. (2022). *Premier League reveal 97% of players who come through top academies never play a minute of top-flight football [online]*. Retrieved from: https://inews.co.uk/sport/football/premier-league-academy-players-figures-appearances-numbers-1387302 [accessed 17th October 2022].

Curtis, J. E., & Birch, J. S. (1987). Size of community of origin and recruitment to professional and Olympic hockey in North America. *Sociology of Sport Journal, 4*(3), 229–244. https://doi.org/10.1123/ssj.4.3.229

Darby, P. (2000). The new scramble for Africa: African football labour to Europe. *European Sports History Review, 3*(2), 217–244.

Elliott, R., & Maguire, J. (2008). Thinking outside the box: Exploring a conceptual synthesis for research in the area of athletic labour migration. *Sociology of Sport Journal, 25*(4), 482–497. https://doi.org/10.1123/ssj.25.4.482

Elliott, R., & Weedon, G. (2011). Foreign players in the English premier academy league: "Feet-drain" or "feet-exchange?" *International Review for the Sociology of Sport, 46*(1), 61–75. https://doi.org/10.1177/1012690210378268

Finnegan, L., Richardson, D., Littlewood, M., & McArdle, J. (2017). The influence of date and place of birth on youth player selection to a national football association elite development programme. *Science and Medicine in Football, 1*(1), 30–39. https://doi.org/10.1080/02640414.2016.1254807

Ford, P. R., Carling, C., Garces, M., Marques, M., Miguel, C., Farrant, A., Stenling, A., Moreno, J., Le Gall, F., Holmstrom, S., Salmela, J. H., & Williams, A. M. (2012). The developmental activities of elite soccer players aged under-16 years from Brazil, England, France, Ghana, Mexico, Portugal and Sweden. *Journal of Sports Sciences, 30*(15), 1653–1663. https://doi.org/10.1080/02640414.2012.701762

Gerhards, J., & Mutz, M. (2017). Who wins the championship? Market value and team composition as predictors of success in the top European football leagues. *European Societies, 19*(3), 223–242. https://doi.org/10.1080/14616696.2016.1268704

Haas, H., & Nüesch, S. (2012). Are multinational teams more successful? *The International Journal of Human Resource Management, 23*(15), 3105–3113. https://doi.org/10.1080/09585192.2011.610948

Hancock, D. J., Coutinho, P., Côté, J., & Mesquita, I. (2018). Influences of population size and density on birthplace effects. *Journal of Sports Sciences, 36*(1), 33–38. https://doi.org/10.1080/02640414.2016.1276614

Hodkinson, P., & Sparkes, A. C. (1997). Careership: A sociological theory of career decision making. *British Journal of Sociology of Education, 18*(1), 29–44. https://doi.org/10.1080/0142569970180102

Hornig, M., Aust, F., & Güllich, A. (2016). Practice and play in the development of German top-level professional football players. *European Journal of Sport Science, 16*(1), 96–105. https://doi.org/10.1080/17461391.2014.982204

Ingersoll, K., Malesky, E., & Saiegh, S. M. (2017). Heterogeneity and team performance: Evaluating the effect of cultural diversity in the world's top soccer league. *Journal of Sports Analytics*, *3*(2), 67–92. https://doi.org/10.3233/JSA-170052

Kelly, A. L., Williams, C. A., Jackson, D. T., Turnnidge, J., Reeves, M. J., Dugdale, J. H., & Wilson, M. R. (2023). Exploring the role of socioeconomic status and psychological characteristics on talent development in an English soccer academy. *Science and Medicine in Football*.

Lally, A., Smith, M., & Parry, K. D. (2022). Exploring migration experiences of foreign footballers to England through the use of autobiographies. *Soccer & Society*, *23*(6), 529–544. https://doi.org/10.1080/14660970.2021.1930535

Lammle, L., Worth, A., & Bos, K. (2012). Socio-demographic correlates of physical activity and physical fitness in German children and adolescents. *The European Journal of Public Health*, *22*(6), 880–884. https://doi.org/10.1093/eurpub/ckr191

Lath, F., Koopman, T., Faber, I., Baker, J., & Scorer, J. (2021). Focusing on the coach's eye; Towards a working model of coach decision-making in talent selection. *Psychology of Sport and Exercise*, *56*(102011), 1–13. https://doi.org/10.1016/j.psychsport.2021.102011

Lawrence, D. W. (2017). Sociodemographic profile of an Olympic team. *Public Health*, *148*, 149–158. https://doi.org/10.1016/j.puhe.2017.03.011

Lazear, E. P. (1999). Globalisation and the market for team-mates. *The Economic Journal*, *109*(454), 15–40. https://doi.org/10.1111/1468-0297.00414

Lidor, R., Arnon, M., Maayan, Z., Gershon, T., & Côté, J. (2014). Relative age effect and birthplace effect in division 1 female ballgame players—The relevance of sport-specific factors. *International Journal of Sport and Exercise Psychology*, *12*(1), 19–33. https://doi.org/10.1080/1612197X.2012.756232

Maayan, Z., Lidor, R., & Arnon, M. (2022). The birthplace effect in 14–18-year-old athletes participating in competitive individual and team sports. *Sports*, *10*(59), 1–14. https://doi.org/10.3390/sports10040059

MacDonald, D. J., Cheung, M., Côté, J., & Abernethy, B. (2009). Place but not date of birth influences the development and emergence of athletic talent in American football. *Journal of Applied Sport Psychology*, *21*(1), 80–90. https://doi.org/10.1080/10413200802541868

MacDonald, D. J., King, J., Côté, J., & Abernethy, B. (2009). Birthplace effects on the development of female athletic talent. *Journal of Science and Medicine in Sport*, *12*(1), 234–237. https://doi.org/10.1016/j.jsams.2007.05.015

Maderer, D., Holtbrügge, D., & Schuster, T. (2014). Professional football squads as multicultural teams. *International Journal of Cross Cultural Management*, *14*(2), 215–238. https://doi.org/10.1177/1470595813510710

McCalpin, M., Evans, B., & Côté, J. (2017). Young female soccer players' perceptions of their modified sport environment. *The Sport Psychologist*, *31*(1), 65–77. https://doi.org/10.1123/tsp.2015-0073

McHale, I. G., & Holmes, B. (2022). Estimating transfer fees of professional footballers using advanced performance metrics and machine learning. *European Journal of Operational Research* [advance online publication]. https://doi.org/10.1016/j.ejor.2022.06.033

Milanovic, B. (2005). Globalisation and goals: Does soccer show the way? *Review of International Political Economy*, *12*(5), 829–850. https://doi.org/10.1080/09692290500339818

Morganti, G., Kelly, A. L., Apollaro, G., Pantanella, L., Esposito, M., Grossi, A., & Ruscello, B. (in press). Exploring birthplace effects in a national context: Is there a 'southern question' in Italian soccer?

Morris, R., Tod, D., & Oliver, E. (2015). An analysis of organizational structure and transition outcomes in the youth-to-senior professional soccer transition. *Journal of Applied Sport Psychology*, *27*(2), 216–234. https://doi.org/10.1080/10413200.2014.980015

Pabayo, R., Janosz, M., Bisset, S., & Kawachi, I. (2014). School social fragmentation, economic deprivation and social cohesion and adolescent physical inactivity: A longitudinal study. *PLoS ONE*, *9*(6), e99154. https://doi.org/10.1371/journal.pone.0099154

Pabayo, R., Molnar, B. E., Cradock, A., & Kawachi, I. (2014). The relationship between neighborhood socioeconomic characteristics and physical inactivity among adolescents living in Boston, Massachusetts. *American Journal of Public Health*, *104*(11), e142–e149. https://doi.org/10.2105/AJPH.2014.302109

Pescosolido, G. (2019). Italy's southern question: Long-standing thorny issues and current problems. *Journal of Modern Italian Studies*, *24*(3), 441–455. https://doi.org/10.1080/1354571X.2019.1605726

Poli, R. (2010a). African migrants in Asian and European football: Hopes and realities. *Sport in Society*, *13*(6), 1001–1011. https://doi.org/10.1080/17430437.2010.491269

Poli, R. (2010b). Understanding globalization through football: The new international division of labour, migratory channels and transnational trade circuits. *International Review for the Sociology of Sport*, *45*(4), 491–506. https://doi.org/10.1177/1012690210370640

Reck, G. G., & Dick, B. A. (2015). *American soccer: History, culture, class*. McFarland & Company, Inc.

Rees, T., Hardy, L., Güllich, A., Abernethy, B., Côté, J., Woodman, T., Montgomery, H., Laing, S., &Warr, C. (2016). The great British medalists project: A review of current knowledge on the development of the world's best sporting talent. *Sports Medicine*, *46*(8), 1041–1058. https://doi.org/10.1007/s40279-016-0476-2

Reeves, M. J., McRobert, A. P., Littlewood, M. A., & Roberts, S. J. (2018). A scoping review of the potential sociological predictors of talent in junior-elite football: 2000–2016. *Soccer & Society*, *19*(8), 1–21. https://doi.org/10.1080/14660970.2018.1432386

Reeves, M. J., & Roberts, S. J. (2020). A bioecological perspective on talent identification in junior-elite soccer: A Pan-European perspective. *Journal of Sports Sciences*, *38*(11–12), 1259–1268. https://doi.org/10.1080/02640414.2019.1702282

Reeves, M. J., Roberts, S. J., McRobert, A. P., & Littlewood, M. A. (2018). Factors affecting the identification of talented junior-elite footballers: a case study. *Soccer & Society*, *19*(8), 1106–1121. https://doi.org/10.1080/14660970.2018.1432383

Rossing, N. N., Nielsen, A. B., Elbe, A.-M., & Karbing, D. S. (2016). The role of community in the development of elite handball football players in Denmark. *European Journal of Sport Science*, *16*(2), 237–245. https://doi.org/10.1080/17461391.2015.1009492

Rossing, N. N., Stentoft, D., Flattum, A., Côté, J., & Karbing, D. S. (2018). Influence of population size, density, and proximity to talent clubs on the likelihood of becoming an elite youth athlete. *Scandinavian Journal of Medicine and Science in Sports*, *28*(2), 1304–1313. https://doi.org/10.1111/sms.13009

Smith, K. L., & Weir, P. L. (2020). Female youth soccer participation and continued engagement: Association with community size, community density, and relative age. *Frontiers in Sports and Active Living*, *2*(552597), 1–10. https://doi.org/10.3389/fspor.2020.552597

Uehara, L., Falcous, M., Button, C., Davids, K., Araújo, D., de Paula, A. R., & Saunders, J. (2021). The poor "wealth" of Brazilian football: How poverty may shape skill and expertise of players. *Frontiers in Sports and Active Living*, *3*. https://doi.org/10.3389/fspor.2021.635241

Ungruhe, C. (2016) Mobilities at play: The local embedding of transnational connections in West African football migration. *The International Journal of the History of Sport*, *33*(15), 1767–1785. https://doi.org/10.1080/09523367.2017.1330262

Vandendriessche, J. B., Vandorpe, B. F. R., Vaeyens, R., Malina, R. M., Lefevre, J., Lenoir, M., & Philippaerts, R. M. (2012). Variation in sport participation, fitness and motor coordination with socioeconomic status among Flemish children. *Pediatric Exercise Science*, *24*(1), 113–128. https://doi.org/10.1123/pes.24.1.113

van der Meij, N., & Darby, P. (2017). Getting in the game and getting on the move: Family, the intergenerational contract and internal migration into football academies in Ghana. *Sport in Society*, *20*(11), 1580–1595. https://doi.org/10.1080/17430437.2017.1284807

Williams, A. M., Ford, P. R., & Drust, B. (2020). Talent identification and development in soccer since the millennium. *Journal of Sports Sciences*, *38*(11–12), 1199–1210. https://doi.org/10.1080/02640414.2020.1766647

Williams, A. M., & Reilly, T. (2000). Talent identification and development in soccer. *Journal of Sports Sciences*, *18*(9), 657–667. https://doi.org/10.1080/02640410050120041

Winn, C. O. N., Ford, P. R., McNarry, M. A., Lewis, J., & Stratton, G. (2017). The effect of deprivation on the developmental activities of adolescent rugby union players in Wales. *Journal of Sports Sciences*, *35*(24), 2390–2396. https://doi.org/10.1080/02640414.2016.1271136

8
ACTIVITIES AND TRAJECTORIES

Exploring Pathways of Athlete Development in Youth Soccer

Alex Murata, Alexander B. T. McAuley, Matthew P. Ferguson, Martin R. Toms, and Adam L. Kelly

Introduction

Research into *early specialisation* (i.e., participation in a single sporting activity during childhood) has been critical of narrowing children's sporting engagement before their adolescent years (Côté et al., 2020; Kliethermes et al., 2021; LaPrade et al., 2016). Previous studies have indicated that youth sport specialisation may increase an athlete's chances of experiencing overuse injuries, lower levels of motivation, higher levels of emotional stress, and burnout (Bell et al., 2018; Gould, 2010). Despite this, it is also argued that athletes may benefit from early specialisation in: (a) sports where peak performance occurs at an early age (e.g., figure skating, gymnastics, skateboarding, swimming) and/or (b) sporting contexts wherein high-performance is valued over long-term participation (Law et al., 2007; Morrice & Andronikos, 2021; Starkes et al., 1996).

Although the outcomes associated with early specialisation remain somewhat controversial, many contemporary youth sport programmes continue to discourage the practice of its alternative, *early sampling* (i.e., participation in more than one organised sport during childhood), in hopes of giving young athletes a performance edge, regardless of age or level of competition (DiSanti & Erickson, 2019; Murata et al., 2021). While it may seem intuitive that increased involvement in sport should equate to higher performance, in many team sports—including soccer—research indicates that few differences in performance can be seen between groups of early samplers and early specialisers over time (Ginsburg et al., 2014; Güllich et al., 2022; Haugaasen et al., 2014).

Given both the inconsistent messages and many contrasting opinions surrounding the subject of early specialisation and early sampling in youth soccer, the purpose of this chapter is to present previous research exploring this contentious topic. In doing so, it is hoped that players, parents, coaches, administrators, and other important stakeholders within the youth soccer space might formulate their own, evidence-informed opinions on how early specialisation and early sampling may affect players' long-term participation and development of sport-specific expertise. Research outlining how each trajectory relates to both youth soccer as well as personal developmental opportunities for young people more broadly will also be discussed. Finally, considerations for researchers and practitioners will be offered based on the evidence presented.

DOI: 10.4324/9781032232799-8

The Early Specialisation Advantage

Previous definitions describe early specialisation in sport as the activity of athletes focusing on one sport during childhood (i.e., ages 6 to 12 years), which is practised, trained, and competed in all year-round (Hill, 1993) to the exclusion of other sport and non-sport related activities (Wiersma, 2000). This pathway can also be characterised by its emphasis on *deliberate practice*, which refers to domain-specific, highly structured activities targeted towards improving performance (Ericsson et al., 1993). More recently, the idea of measuring the degree to which young athletes could be considered specialised was put forth by Jayanthi et al. (2015) as well as Myer et al. (2015). Here, athletes who had not yet reached physical maturity were considered highly (i.e., dangerously) specialised should they: (a) participate in sport more than 8 months per year, (b) participate and practice in a single sport only, and (c) have recently quit all other sports to pursue their main sport. Athletes meeting two of the three criteria mentioned previously were considered moderately specialised and moderately at risk of sustaining a sport-related injury, while athletes meeting one or zero were considered low specialisers with a low risk for injury (see Table 8.1 for soccer-specific examples).

Along with its evolving definitions, early specialisation has become a key topic of interest within the youth sport and athlete development literature in recent years. In a review conducted by Kliethermes et al. (2021), the authors found that 196 articles were published on the topic of early specialisation between the years of 2017 and 2019, whereas only 179 articles were published between 2010 and 2016. Researchers have speculated that the changing norms of youth sport participation and increasing expectation for athletes to professionalise at increasingly younger ages may have resulted in an increase of both early specialisers as well as early specialisation research (Brenner et al., 2016; Erdal, 2018).

As alluded to previously, some academic works exploring early specialisation in youth sport have suggested that engagement in sport-specific, deliberate practice from an early age may provide athletes with a viable pathway to develop high levels of sport expertise (i.e., elite performance) (Côté et al., 2009b; Haugaasen & Jordet, 2012; Huard Pelletier & Lemoyne, 2022). As such, the primary rationale applied to support the practice of early specialisation is the perceived relationship between the total duration in time individuals have spent practising a task and the resulting attainment of improved competence (Baker et al., 2003; Baker et al., 2003). For example, research from Schmidt and Lee (2011) suggested that individuals who spent more time in purposeful physical

TABLE 8.1 Degree of soccer specialisation and risk of injury (adapted from Myer et al., 2015)

Degree of Soccer Specialisation	*Risk of Injury*
Low specialisation (0 or 1 of the following): • Year-round training (> 8 months per year in soccer) • Chooses soccer as their single main sport • Quits all sports to focus on soccer	Low
Moderately specialised (2 of the following): • Year-round training (> 8 months per year in soccer) • Chooses soccer as their single main sport • Quits all sports to focus on soccer	Moderate
Highly specialised (each of the following): • Year-round training (> 8 months per year in soccer) • Chooses soccer as their single main sport • Quits all sports to focus on soccer	High

practice and training gained larger improvements in skill, competency, and physical fitness, compared to inactive controls. In the context of sport specifically, as discussed by Ford and Williams (2017), athletes who engaged in early sport specialisation in childhood were found to display a higher level of ability, while also obtaining a greater number of sport-related achievements in their adolescent years, compared to both early samplers and athletes who started in sport later.

With regard to youth sport selection at the high-performance level, findings reported by Archer et al. (2016) revealed that technical proficiency and physical abilities were the most prominent influences in determining athlete evaluations in children as young as 3- to 5-years-old. In line with this, Sieghartsleitner et al. (2017) summarised these criteria as the 'early specialised bird catches the worm' in their assessment of how young soccer players may gain advantages over their age-matched peers. These ideas also appear to persist upwards into the professional senior level of soccer. As shown by Forsman et al. (2016), players with more sport-specific practice (as well as play) during childhood were found to possess superior technical, tactical, and psychological skills, whilst also being more likely to be selected for national teams.

Early Sampling and Athlete Development

As discussed in a review describing what is known about early sampling in the youth sport literature, neither a singular definition of the concept nor established parameters for athletes hoping to follow a 'sampling pathway' appear to exist (Murata et al., 2021). As such, many researchers have, instead, encompassed and/or classified all activities and practices that do not fall under the umbrella of early specialisation, broadly, as early sampling or early sport diversification. In hopes of rectifying this issue, McLaren et al. (2022) have begun to advocate for the formulation of a more concrete definition of early sampling for young athletes to follow as a developmental pathway. At minimum, the research team proposed that athletes may be considered early samplers should they be: (a) engaged in more than one sport, (b) have sampled a variety of positions *within* (e.g., striker *and* goalkeeper) or versions *of* (e.g., 11 vs. 11 soccer *and* futsal) a single sport, and (c) that the choice to sample has been child-led rather than adult-led. It was also suggested that these patterns of behaviour should occur consistently (i.e., not only in one off situations) when an athlete is between the ages of 6 and 12 years (see Table 8.2).

TABLE 8.2 Ingredients of the early sampling pathway (adapted from McLaren et al., 2022)

Component	*Early Sampler*	*Non-Early Sampler*
Sport engagement	Engaged in more than one organised sport Engaged in more than one unorganised sport Engaged in various versions of the same sport (i.e., soccer *and* futsal) Engaged in multiple sporting positions (i.e., striker *and* goalkeeper)	Engaged in a single sport Not engaged in unorganised sport—Plays a single position exclusively
Time	Engaged in sport sampling at least 1-hour per week Engaged in sport sampling at least 3-months out of twelve Engaged in sport sampling for at least 2-years consecutively	—
Decision-making	Child-led decisions around sport participation	Adult-led decisions around sport participation

Although a formalised definition has yet to be established, many studies have previously explored how participation in multiple sports rather than a single sport might affect athlete development. Some of the primary works to establish the benefits of this developmental pathway were those centred around the conceptualisation of the Developmental Model of Sport Participation (DMSP) by Côté and colleagues (Côté, 1999; Côté & Vierimaa, 2014; Côté et al., 2009a, 2009b). Here, researchers looking into the developmental histories of athletes competing at the highest levels of sport found that many appeared to sample a variety of sports in childhood before choosing a single sport to focus on late in adolescence. Additionally, it was also speculated that early sampling, combined with participation in unstructured sporting activities (i.e., play), might be useful in preventing injury, maintaining sport-related motivation, and therefore, be conducive to long-term sport participation and personal development across an athletes' lifetime. For athletes hoping to follow along the most optimal developmental trajectory laid out within the DMSP, it is suggested that they: (a) begin by participating in multiple sports recreationally until their pre-pubescent years, (b) continue participating recreationally or start the process of specialising in early adolescence, (c) only specialise completely in late adolescence, and (d) only introduce deliberate practice when sport becomes less recreational (see Figure 8.1).

Looking closer into findings reported within the previously mentioned review from Murata et al. (2021), evidence appears to exist that supports the idea that early sampling may be conducive to the development of sport-specific skill (i.e., sport performance), as well as both short- and long-term participation. These ideas are further unpacked by Fransen et al. (2012), who speculated that the varied range of activities and movement patterns performed by early samplers could be beneficial in developing higher levels of fitness and improved gross motor coordination compared to early specialisers. As discussed by DiStefano et al. (2018), this broader inventory of movement abilities and subsequent improved neuromuscular control could also play a critical role in reducing injury risk.

Within the sport of soccer specifically, previous research further indicates that a healthy balance of play (i.e., child-led, informal, unstructured soccer activities) *and* deliberate practice may

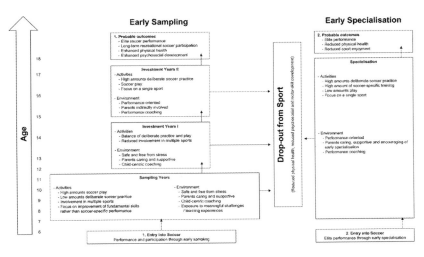

FIGURE 8.1 Soccer trajectories within the Developmental Model of Sport Participation (adapted from Côté & Fraser-Thomas, 2016).

be most effective in developing expertise and skill (Hendry & Hodges, 2019; Hendry et al., 2019). This is supported by Ford and colleagues (Ford & Williams, 2012; Ford et al., 2009, 2010, 2012), who proposed the *early engagement* hypothesis. Early engagement involves athletes participating in a high amount of singular sporting involvement during childhood through deliberate play-like activities (with little deliberate practice and competition), whilst also partaking in a low to medium amount of time in other sports alongside their favoured activity (Ford et al., 2009). Following a re-examination of data from Ward et al. (2007) on participation histories from youth soccer players, Ford et al. (2009) distinguished 11 players from the original number of 33 participants that had gone on to achieve full-time professional status. The purpose of this study was to identify what developmental activities differentiated the players who progressed and the ones who didn't. They revealed the players who attained professional status accumulated more hours per year in deliberate play-like activities, specifically in soccer, but not in deliberate soccer practice, competition, or other sports between the ages of 6 to 12 years, compared to those who did not progress. Further research from Ford et al. (2012) explored the backgrounds of elite and non-elite soccer players from seven different nations (i.e., Brazil, England, France, Ghana, Mexico, Portugal, and Sweden). For these players, elements of early specialisation did appear to occur in some of their backgrounds, as did both high amounts of play and participation in multiple sports. As such, the research team concluded that early sampling should not be thought of as an obstacle barring players from recruitment into world-class soccer academies.

These sentiments have been supported in studies on the participation histories of German professional and national soccer players in both female (Güllich, 2019) and male (Hornig et al., 2016) cohorts. For instance, Güllich (2019) found female national team players differed from their professional (Bundesliga) peers through completing less physical conditioning and greater proportions of playing forms within soccer practice. Moreover, national team players accumulated less total soccer practice until aged 18 years but more peer-led soccer and coach-led practice in other sports, compared to their professional counterparts. Similarly, in males, Hornig et al. (2016) revealed that professional players performed moderate amounts of organised soccer practice throughout their career, whereby they accumulated an average of 4,264 hours over ~16 years before debuting in the Bundesliga, whereas German national team debut was preceded by an average of 4,532 hours over ~17 years. In addition, the national team differed from amateurs through engaging in more non-organised soccer activities during childhood, more engagement in other sports during adolescence, later specialisation, and in more organised soccer only at age 22+ years.

On a different note, through a detailed research paradigm constructed by Güllich et al. (2020), it was found that the acquisition of soccer-specific skills appeared most easily learned for athletes that had previously participated in formalised, coach-led programming within other sporting contexts. Here, researchers collected data that assessed 100 youth soccer players' (aged 10 to 13 years) ability to learn a variety of skills (e.g., ball control, tackling, decision-making) and compared this information to each players' previous sporting history. Interestingly, while coach-led participation in other sports appeared beneficial, it was found that neither the number of other sports each player sampled, the amount of coach-led soccer they had previously played, nor the amount of youth-led or play-like soccer activities they engaged in seemed to contribute to their ability to learn soccer-related skills. From a psychosocial perspective, Erikstad et al. (2018) sought to examine whether soccer-specific activities during childhood (aged 6 to 12 years) was related to self-regulatory skills and national U14 and U15 team selection in Norwegian youth soccer players. Their results showed that high self-regulated players were more likely to be selected for national initiatives as well as an increased involvement in peer-led soccer play and adult-led soccer practice during childhood when compared to players with lower levels of self-regulation. Collectively, these findings shed some light on how participation in a variety of sports and soccer-specific activities during childhood may contribute to the short- and long-term development of technical, tactical, and psychosocial skills in soccer.

Contemporary Issues and Concerns

Although there is evidence to suggest that both early specialisation and early sampling can positively influence sport performance, it is important to acknowledge the negative effects associated with selecting one pathway over the other. Unfortunately, when exploring the literature related to each topic, it is evident that early specialisation may be associated with several negative athlete outcomes, including: (a) overuse injuries (Carder et al., 2020; Jayanthi, et al., 2015; Pasulka et al., 2017; Post et al., 2017), (b) burnout and overtraining syndrome (Myer et al., 2015, 2016), (c) negative psychological states (i.e., decreased motivation and achievement-oriented behaviours; Hendry et al., 2014; Horn, 2015; LaPrade et al., 2016), and (d) poor social development (Carlson, 1988; Sheridan et al., 2014). Indeed, as reported by Read et al. (2016) in their paper exploring the health risks associated with early specialisation in youth soccer, it was suggested that factors such as prolonged, repetitive movements and overtraining could be detrimental to the physical development of young athletes—particularly should high intensity, deliberate soccer practice commence before a player has reached physical maturity. Further, in a study exploring the injury histories of non-specialised and specialised soccer players between the ages of 12 and 18 years, Bell et al. (2018) found that specialised athletes were approximately 5 times more likely to report a soccer-related injury than their non-specialised peers.

Outside of the negative physical effects associated with early specialisation, research also indicates that certain components of an athlete's mental health may also suffer. As reported within the findings of a meta-analysis completed by Giusti et al. (2020), it was found that specialised athletes experienced greater burnout profiles (i.e., a reduced sense of accomplishment, exhaustion, and sport devaluation) than athletes who sampled. Further, in qualitative interviews involving both professional soccer players and soccer players of a similar calibre who had left the sport (i.e., dropped out), researchers found that early specialisation, highly pressurised environments, and an over-emphasis on winning were commonly reported as factors leading to their attrition (Morrice & Andronikos, 2021).

For youth soccer players, coaches, parents, and others close to the sport, findings from the early specialisation and sampling literature indicate that careful and thoughtful consideration is required when selecting the types of soccer programming that should be engaged in by young players. As such, a summative chart listing the broad pros and cons of each pathway can be found in Table 8.3. Additionally, as outlined within the aforementioned work by McLaren et al. (2022), the choice to specialise, sample, or engage in any other form of sport participation should be child-led, rather than adult-led, or should, at the very least, be decided upon collaboratively between parents and children with children having the final say.

Considerations for Researchers

As concerns related to the growing intensity associated with youth sport participation have increased, a number of academic position papers and consensus statements have been released that emphasise the dangers associated with early specialisation for the developing athlete

TABLE 8.3 Pros and cons of early specialisation and early sampling

Soccer Pathway	Positive Outcomes from the Literature	Negative Outcomes from the Literature
Early Specialisation	Chance at achieving high-performance levels in soccer Meaningful soccer-related experiences—	Increased risk of injury Increased risk of negative psychological state(s) Increased chance of dropout
Early Sampling	Chance at achieving high-performance levels in soccer Meaningful soccer-related experiences Increased chance of long-term soccer participation	Less soccer success at a younger age——

(e.g., Bergeron et al., 2015; Brenner et al., 2016; DiFiori et al., 2017; Jayanthi et al., 2019; LaPrade et al., 2016). However, to further complicate these issues, a number of recent articles have also highlighted several research gaps, prevalent limitations, and trends of note associated with previous works within the early specialisation literature (Baker et al., 2021; Kliethermes et al., 2021; Mosher et al., 2021). For example, a recent systematic review from Mosher et al. (2020) reported that prevalent limitations within early sport specialisation research include: (a) inconsistencies in the definitions and components used for *specialisation*, (b) discrepancies in the arbitrary parameters used to categorise *early*-specialising athletes, (c) a lack of data-driven, primary research as well as a overrepresentation of non-systematic reviews (i.e., editorials, summaries), and (d) a lack of knowledge regarding the mechanisms underpinning the relationships between early specialisation and its associated negative outcomes (also see Chapter 20). In a similarly timed review from Murata et al. (2021), the authors found parallel issues associated with the current literature focused on early sampling, such as: (a) the usage of inconsistent definitions and terminology, (b) an overrepresentation of certain research paradigms (i.e., retrospective studies, quantitative studies), and (c) an overrepresentation of homogenous samples. As such, while a substantial body of work has identified many notable drawbacks associated with early specialisation and several advantages associated with early sampling, more targeted and detailed research is needed to gain a better understanding of each pathway.

In regard to soccer specifically, future studies should evaluate both early specialisation and early sampling through more diverse and precise social and cultural contexts (i.e., age, gender, ability level, success rate of players). Additionally, more longitudinal rather than cross-sectional studies should be designed and produced. Similarly, more work on the concept of 'talent transfer' (i.e., a formalised process used to identify and develop talented athletes by selecting individuals who have already succeeded in one sport and transferring them to another; see Collins et al., 2014) must be completed, as exploring diversification retrospectively may not allow for an accurate assessment of the specific mechanisms behind the youth soccer skill and talent-transfer processes. Whilst this will aid the development of improved soccer appropriate skills in developing athletes, it will also allow players to better understand what might be more or less beneficial in terms of their training programmes. Finally, future studies also need to acknowledge the broader context and sporting histories of the athletes they will work with in the future. Only after considering the full socio-political and socio-cultural context from which their athletes come will researchers possess better data describing more of the mechanisms involved within a soccer players' talent journey (Bridge & Toms, 2013).

Considerations for Practitioners

For practitioners, there is an additional level of consideration required when it comes to endorsing early specialisation or early sampling. As each pathway has its own selection of pros and cons, communication with players and their families is paramount before prescribing adherence to one or the other. Overall, coaches should carefully consider and be able to justify any recommendation they make regarding early specialisation and/or early sampling. Further, any decision around the selection of either pathway should be made in conjunction with an athlete's personal goals. With these ideas in mind, all youth soccer practitioners should reflect on the following considerations within their respective settings:

- Be observant: Do you see any concerning differences in your specialised and non-specialised athletes?
- Be aware of your athletes' personal goals: Do you think they will be better served to early specialise or to early sample?
- Be safe: Do you know your individual athletes' injury histories? Could specialisation be an issue?
- Be mental-health aware: Do you see signs of mental distress or burnout in your athletes?
- Be self-reflexive: Is long-term participation more or less important than short-term success?

Conclusion

The primary purpose of the present chapter was to provide readers with a broad picture of what is known about both the early specialisation and early sampling developmental pathways, which are particularly pertinent to talent identification and development in youth soccer. It was also hoped that the presentation of this information would provide youth soccer stakeholders (e.g., players, parents, coaches, administrators) with the tools to formulate their own, evidence-informed opinions regarding each topic. A large body of research appears to indicate that a myriad of negative outcomes may be associated with early specialisation (e.g., greater risk of acute, sport-related injury, overuse injury, burnout, and premature sport attrition). Several studies have also reported that athletes who engage in early sampling may: (a) have longer sport careers than early specialisers, (b) be more satisfied with sport compared to early specialisers, and (c) be no less likely to achieve high levels of sport performance than early specialisers. Despite this, it also seems apparent that earlier, higher-volume, structured (i.e., deliberate practice), and adult-led sport programming may be helpful in allowing athletes to build the skills necessary to compete at sports' highest levels. While many rigorous, creative, and informative studies have been produced exploring both of these developmental pathways, recent research has also highlighted areas which could be improved upon in the future. Examples of these include the development of more specific definitions and parameters for each pathway, the inclusion of more diverse athlete participants and sporting contexts, and, finally, a greater selection and usage of research methodologies.

The debate about early sampling and early specialisation is one that continues to polarise academics and youth soccer stakeholders alike. Hopefully, with a continued exploration into the effects that each developmental pathway can have on talent development, both inside as well as outside of the sporting context, future soccer players and their families may be better equipped to make informed choices regarding which path is more conducive to their lifestyles and goals. In the meantime, it is important for all those associated with the youth soccer context to remain informed of the risks involved in selecting one pathway over the other and to carefully consider how they choose to engage in soccer, as well as all other sports, in the safest and most enjoyable ways that they can.

References

Archer, D. T., Drysdale, K., & Bradley, E. J. (2016). Differentiating technical skill and motor abilities in selected and non-selected 3–5 year old team-sports players. *Human Movement Science*, 47, 81–87. https://doi.org/10.1016/j.humov.2016.02.001

Baker, J., Côté, J., & Abernethy, B. (2003). Sport-specific practice and the development of expert decision-making in team ball sports. *Journal of Applied Sport Psychology*, 15(1), 12–25. http://hdl.handle.net/1974/14437

Baker, J., Horton, S., Robertson-Wilson, J., & Wall, M. (2003). Nurturing sport expertise: Factors influencing the development of elite athlete. *Journal of Sports Science and Medicine*, 2(1), 1–9.

Baker, J., Mosher, A., & Fraser-Thomas, J. (2021). Is it too early to condemn early sport specialisation? *British Journal of Sports Medicine*, 55(3), 179–180. http://doi.org/10.1136/bjsports-2020-102053

Bell, D. R., Lang, P. J., Valovich McLeod, T. C., McCaffrey, K. A., Zaslow, T. L., McKay, S. D., & PRiSM Sport Specialization Interest Group. (2018). Sport specialization is associated with injury history in youth soccer athletes. *Athletic Training & Sports Health Care*, 10(6), 241–246. https://doi.org/10.3928/19425864-20180813-01

Bergeron, M. F., Mountjoy, M., Armstrong, N., Chia, M., Côté, J., Emery, C. A., Faigenbaum, A., Hall, G., Kriemler, S., Léglise, M., Malina, R. M., Pensgaard, A. M., Sanchez, A., Soligard, T., Sundgot-Borgen, J., van Mechelen, W., Weissensteiner, J. R., & Engebretsen, L. (2015). International Olympic committee consensus statement on youth athletic development. *British Journal of Sports Medicine*, 49(13), 843–851. https://doi.org/10.1136/bjsports-2015-094962

Brenner, J. S., & Council on Sports Medicine and Fitness. (2016). Sports specialization and intensive training in young athletes. *Pediatrics*, 138(3), e20162148. https://doi.org/10.1542/peds.2016-2148

Bridge, M., & Toms, M. (2013). The specialising or sampling debate: A retrospective analysis of adolescent sports participation in the UK. *Journal of Sports Sciences*, 31(1), 15–28. https://doi.org/10.1080/02640414.2012.721560

Carder, S. L., Giusti, N. E., Vopat, L. M., Tarakemeh, A., Baker, J., Vopat, B. G., & Mulcahey, M. K. (2020). The concept of sport sampling versus sport specialization: Preventing youth athlete injury: A systematic review and meta-analysis. *The American Journal of Sports Medicine*, 48(11), 2850–2857. https://doi.org/10.1177/0363546519899380

Carlson, R. (1988). The socialisation of elite tennis players in Sweden: An analysis of the players' backgrounds and development. *Sociology of Sport Journal*, 5(3), 241–256. https://doi.org/10.1123/ssj.5.3.241

Collins, R., Collins, D., MacNamara, A., & Jones, M. I. (2014). Change of plans: An evaluation of the effectiveness and underlying mechanisms of successful talent transfer. *Journal of Sports Sciences*, 32(17), 1621–1630. https://doi.org/10.1080/02640414.2014.908324

Côté, J. (1999). The influence of the family in the development of talent in sport. *The Sport Psychologist*, 13(4), 395–417. https://doi.org/10.1123/tsp.13.4.395

Côté, J., Allan, V., Turnnidge, J., & Erickson, K. (2020). Early sport specialization and sampling. In G. Tenenbaum & R. C. Eklund (Eds.), *Handbook of sport psychology* (pp. 578–594). Wiley. https://doi.org/10.1002/9781119568124.ch27

Côté, J., & Fraser-Thomas, J. (2016). Youth involvement and positive development in sport. In P. R. E. Crocker (Ed.), *Sport and exercise psychology: A Canadian perspective* (3rd ed.). Pearson.

Côté, J., Horton, S., MacDonald, D., & Wilkes, S. (2009a). The benefits of sampling sports during childhood. *Physical & Health Education Journal*, 74(4), 6.

Côté, J., Lidor, R., & Hackfort, D. (2009b). ISSP position stand: To sample or to specialize? Seven postulates about youth sport activities that lead to continued participation and elite performance. *International Journal of Sport and Exercise Psychology*, 7(1), 7–17. https://doi.org/10.1080/1612197X.2009.9671889

Côté, J., & Vierimaa, M. (2014). The developmental model of sport participation: 15 years after its first conceptualization. *Science & Sports, 29*, S63–S69. https://doi.org/10.1016/j.scispo.2014.08.133

DiFiori, J. P., Brenner, J. S., Comstock, D., Côté, J., Gullich, A., Hainline, B., & Malina, R. (2017). Debunking early single sport specialisation and reshaping the youth sport experience: An NBA perspective. *British Journal of Sports Medicine, 51*(3), 142. http://doi.org/10.1136/bjsports-2016-097170

DiSanti, J. S., & Erickson, K. (2019). Youth sport specialization: A multidisciplinary scoping systematic review. *Journal of Sports Sciences, 37*(18), 2094–2105. https://doi.org/10.1080/02640414.2019.1621476

DiStefano, L. J., Beltz, E. M., Root, H. J., Martinez, J. C., Houghton, A., Taranto, N., Pearce, K., McConnell, E., Muscat, C., Boyle, S., & Trojian, T. H. (2018). Sport sampling is associated with improved landing technique in youth athletes. *Sports Health: A Multidisciplinary Approach, 10*(2), 160–168. https://doi.org/10.1177/1941738117736056

Erdal, K. (2018). *The adulteration of children's sports: Waning health and well-being in the age of organized play*. Ronan & Littlefield.

Ericsson, K. A., Krampe, R. T., & Tesch-Romer, C. (1993). The role of deliberate practice in the acquisition of expert performance. *Psychological Review, 100*(3), 363–406. https://doi.org/10.1037/0033-295X.100.3.363

Erikstad, M. K., Høigaard, R., Johansen, B. T., Kandala, N. B., & Haugen, T. (2018). Childhood football play and practice in relation to self-regulation and national team selection; A study of Norwegian elite youth players. *Journal of Sports Sciences, 36*(20), 2304–2310. https://doi.org/10.1080/02640414.2018.1449563

Ford, P. R., Carling, C., Garces, M., Marques, M., Miguel, C., Farrant, A., Stenling, A., Moreno, J., Le Gall, F., Holmstrom, S., Salmela, J. H., & Williams, A. M. (2012). The developmental activities of elite soccer players aged under-16 years from Brazil, England, France, Ghana, Mexico, Portugal and Sweden. *Journal of Sports Sciences, 30*(15), 1653–1663. https://doi.org/10.1080/02640414.2012.701762

Ford, P. R., Ward, P., Hodges, N. J., & Williams, A. M. (2009). The role of deliberate practice and play in career progression in sport: The early engagement hypothesis. *High Ability Studies, 20*(1), 65–75. https://doi.org/10.1080/13598130902860721

Ford, P. R., & Williams, M. A. (2017). Sport activity in childhood: Early specialization and diversification. In J. Baker, S. Cobley, J. Schorer, & N. Wattie (Eds.), *Routledge handbook of talent identification and development in sport* (pp. 117–132). Routledge.

Ford, P. R., & Williams, M. A. (2012). The developmental activities engaged in by elite youth soccer players who progressed to professional status compared to those who did not. *Psychology of Sports & Exercise, 13*(3), 349–352. https://doi.org/10.1016/j.psychsport.2011.09.004

Ford, P. R., Yates, I., & Williams, A. M. (2010). An analysis of practice activities and instructional behaviours used by youth soccer coaches during practice: Exploring the link between science and application. *Journal of Sports Sciences, 28*(5), 483–495. https://doi.org/10.1080/02640410903582750

Forsman, H., Blomqvist, M., Davids, K., Konttinen, N., & Liukkonen, J. (2016). The role of sport-specific play and practice during childhood in the development of adolescent Finnish team sport athletes. *International Journal of Sports Science & Coaching, 11*(1), 69–77. https://doi.org/10.1177/1747954115624816

Fransen, J., Pion, J., Vandendriessche, J., Vandorpe, B., Vaeyens, R., Lenoir, M., & Philippaerts, R. M. (2012). Differences in physical fitness and gross motor coordination in boys aged 6–12 years specializing in one versus sampling more than one sport. *Journal of Sports Sciences, 30*(4), 379–386. https://doi.org/10.1080/02640414.2011.642808

Ginsburg, R. D., Smith, S. R., Danforth, N., Ceranoglu, T. A., Durant, S. A., Kamin, H., Babcock, R., Robin, L., & Masek, B. (2014). Patterns of specialization in professional baseball players. *Journal of Clinical Sport Psychology, 8*(3), 261–275. https://doi.org/10.1123/jcsp.2014-0032

Giusti, N. E., Carder, S. L., Vopat, L., Baker, J., Tarakemeh, A., Vopat, B., & Mulcahey, M. K. (2020). Comparing burnout in sport-specializing versus sport-sampling adolescent athletes: A systematic review and meta-analysis. *Orthopaedic Journal of Sports Medicine, 8*(3). https://doi.org/10.1177/2325967120907579

Gould, D. (2010). Early sport specialization: A psychological perspective. *Journal of Physical Education, Recreation & Dance, 81*(8), 33–37. https://doi.org/10.1080/07303084.2010.10598525

Güllich, A. (2019). "Macro-structure" of developmental participation histories and "micro-structure" of practice of German female world-class and national-class football players. *Journal of Sports Sciences, 37*(12), 1347–1355. https://doi.org/10.1080/02640414.2018.1558744

Güllich, A., Cronauer, R., Diehl, J., Gard, L., & Miller, C. (2020). Coach-assessed skill learning progress of youth soccer players correlates with earlier childhood practice in other sports. *International Journal of Sports Science & Coaching, 15*(3), 285–296. https://doi.org/10.1177/1747954120912351

Güllich, A., Macnamara, B. N., & Hambrick, D. Z. (2022). What makes a champion? Early multidisciplinary practice, not early specialization, predicts world-class performance. *Perspectives on Psychological Science, 17*(1), 6–29. https://doi.org/10.1177/1745691620974772

Haugaasen, M., & Jordet, G. (2012). Developing football expertise: A football-specific research review. *International Review of Sport Exercise Psychology, 5*(2), 177–201. https://doi.org/10.1080/1750984X.2012.677951

Haugaasen, M., Toering, T., & Jordet, G. (2014). From childhood to senior professional football: A multi-level approach to elite youth football players' engagement in football-specific activities. *Psychology of Sport and Exercise, 15*(4), 336–344. https://doi.org/10.1016/j.psychsport.2014.02.007

Hendry, D. T., Crocker, P. R. E., & Hodges, N. J. (2014). Practice and play as determinants of self-determined motivation in youth soccer players. *Journal of Sports Sciences, 32*(11), 1091–1099. https://doi.org/10.1080/02640414.2014.880792

Hendry, D. T., & Hodges, N. J. (2019). Pathways to expert performance in soccer. *Journal of Expertise, 2*(1), 14.

Hendry, D. T., Williams, A. M., Ford, P. R., & Hodges, N. J. (2019). Developmental activities and perceptions of challenge for National and varsity women soccer players in Canada. *Psychology of Sport and Exercise, 43*, 210–218. https://doi.org/10.1016/j.psychsport.2019.02.008

Hill, G. M. (1993). Youth sport participation of professional baseball players. *Sociology of Sport Journal, 10*(1), 107–114. https://doi.org/10.1123/ssj.10.1.107

Horn, T. S. (2015). Social psychological and developmental perspectives on early sport specialization. *Kinesiology Review, 4*(3), 248–266. https://doi.org/10.1123/kr.2015-0025

Hornig, M., Aust, F., & Güllich, A. (2016). Practice and play in the development of German top-level professional football players. *European Journal of Sport Science, 16*(1), 96–105. https://doi.org/10.1080/17461391.2014.982204

Huard Pelletier, V., & Lemoyne, J. (2022). Early sport specialization and relative age effect: Prevalence and influence on perceived competence in ice hockey players. *Sports, 10*(4), 62. https://doi.org/10.3390/sports10040062

Jayanthi, N. A., Labella, C. R., Fischer, D., Pasulka, J., & Dugas, L. R. (2015). Sports-specialized intensive training and the risk of injury in young athletes: A clinical case-control study. *American Journal of Sports Medicine, 43*(4), 794–801. https://doi.org/10.1177/0363546514567298

Jayanthi, N. A., Post, E. G., Laury, T. C., & Fabricant, P. D. (2019). Health consequences of youth sport specialization. *Journal of Athletic Training, 54*(10), 1040–1049. https://doi.org/10.4085/1062-6050-380-18

Kliethermes, S. A., Marshall, S. W., LaBella, C. R., Watson, A. M., Brenner, J. S., Nagle, K. B., Jayanthi, N., Brooks, M. A., Tenforde, A. S., Herman, D. C., DiFiori, J. P., & Beutler, A. I. (2021). Defining a research agenda for youth sport specialisation in the USA: the AMSSM youth early sport specialization summit. *British Journal of Sports Medicine, 55*(3), 135–143. https://bjsm.bmj.com/content/bjsports/55/3/135.full.pdf

LaPrade, R. F., Agel, J., Baker, J., Brenner, J. S., Cordasco, F. A., Côté, J., Engebretsen, L., Feely, B. T., Gould, D., Hainline, B., Hewett, T., Jayanthi, N., Kocher, M. S., Myer, G. D., Nissen, C. W., Philippon, M. J., & Provencher, M. T. (2016). AOSSM early sport specialization consensus statement. *Orthopaedic Journal of Sports Medicine, 4*(4), 1–8. https://doi.org/10.1177/2325967116644241

Law, M., Côté, J., & Ericsson, K. A. (2007). Characteristics of expert development in rhythmic gymnastics: A retrospective study. *International Journal of Sport and Exercise Psychology, 5*(1), 82–103. https://doi.org/10.1080/1612197X.2008.9671814

McLaren, C. D., Bruner, M. W., Murata, A., Martin, L. J., & Côté, J. (2022). Sampling and specialising in children's sport: Implications for research and coaching practice. In M. Toms & R. Jeanes (Eds.), *Routledge handbook of coaching children in sport*. Routledge.

Morrice, E., & Andronikos, G. (2021). Investigating the impact of early specialization on career progression in football. *The International Journal of Sport and Society*, *12*(2), 167–184. https://doi.org/10.18848/2152-7857/CGP/v12i02/167-184

Mosher, A., Fraser-Thomas, J., & Baker, J. (2020). What defines early specialization: A systematic review of literature. *Frontiers in Sports and Active Living*, *2*, 596229. https://doi.org/10.3389/fspor.2020.596229

Mosher, A., Till, K., Fraser-Thomas, J., & Baker, J. (2021). Revisiting early sport specialization: What's the problem? *Sports Health*, *14*(1), 13–19. https://doi.org/10.1177/19417381211049773

Murata, A., Goldman, D. E., Martin, L. J., Turnnidge, J., Bruner, M. W., & Côté, J. (2021). Sampling between sports and athlete development: A scoping review. *International Journal of Sport and Exercise Psychology*, 1–25. https://doi.org/10.1080/1612197X.2021.1995021

Myer, G. D., Jayanthi, N., DiFiori, J. P., Faigenbaum, A. D., Kiefer, A. W., Logerstedt, D., & Micheli, L. J. (2015). Sport specialization, part I: Does early sports specialization increase negative outcomes and reduce the opportunity for success in young athletes? *Sports Health*, *7*(5), 437–442. https://doi.org/10.1177/1941738115598747

Myer, G. D., Jayanthi, N., DiFiori, J. P., Faigenbaum, A. D., Kiefer, A. W., Logerstedt, D., & Micheli, L. J. (2016). Sports specialization, part II: Alternative solutions to early sport specialization in youth athletes. *Sports Health*, *8*(1), 65–73. https://doi.org/10.1177/1941738115614811

Pasulka, J., Jayanthi, N., McCann, A., Dugas, L. R., & LaBella, C. (2017). Specialization patterns across various youth sports and relationship to injury risk. *Physician and Sportsmedicine*, *45*(3), 344–352. https://doi.org/10.1080/00913847.2017.1313077

Post, E. G., Trigsted, S. M., Riekena, J. W., Hetzel, S., McGuine, T. A., Brooks, M. A., & Bell, D. R. (2017). The association of sport specialization and training volume with injury history in youth athletes. *American Journal of Sports Medicine*, *45*(6), 1405–1412. https://doi.org/10.1177/0363546517690848

Read, P. J., Oliver, J. L., De Ste Croix, M. B. A., Myer, G. D., & Lloyd, R. S. (2016). The scientific foundations and associated injury risks of early soccer specialization. *Journal of Sports Sciences*, *34*(24), 2295–2302. https://doi.org/10.1080/02640414.2016.1173221

Schmidt, R. A., & Lee, T. D. (2011). *Motor control and learning: A behavioural emphasis* (5th ed.). Human Kinetics.

Sheridan, D., Coffee, P., & Lavallee, D. (2014). A systematic review of social support in youth sport. *International Review of Sport and Exercise Psychology*, *7*(1), 198–228. https://doi.org/10.1080/1750984X.2014.931999

Sieghartsleitner, R., Zuber, C., Zibung, M., Conzelmann, A. (2017). Talent development in football: The early specialized bird catches the worm! [Online]. Retrieved from: https://boris.unibe.ch/96404/1/Talent%20development%20in%20football.pdf

Starkes, J. L., Deakin, J. M., Allard, F., Hodges, N. J., & Hayes, A. (1996). Deliberate practice in sports: What is it anyway? In K. A. Ericsson (Ed.), *The road to excellence: The acquisition of expert performance in the arts and sciences, sports, and games* (pp. 81–106). Psychology Press.

Ward, P., Hodges, N. J., Starkes, J. L., & Williams, M. A. (2007). The road to excellence: Deliberate practice and the development of expertise. *High Ability Studies*, *18*(2), 119–153. https://doi.org/10.1080/13598130701709715

Wiersma, L. D. (2000). Risks and benefits of youth sport specialization: Perspectives and recommendations. *Pediatric Exercise Science*, *12*(1), 13–22. https://doi.org/10.1123/pes.12.1.13

9
CAREER TRANSITIONS
Navigating Players from Youth Team to First Team

Sofie Kent, Robert Morris, and Adam L. Kelly

Introduction

Within the UK, male soccer players may join an academy programme from the age of 8 years old. However, only 15% of those players obtain an U18 scholarship, whilst just 1% of those players typically transition into the senior first team (Green, 2009). Such statistics highlight the complexity and arduous nature of the talent development pathway within soccer that is reflective across the globe. Therefore, understanding the various career transitions that occur throughout the soccer talent pathway (e.g., academy) experience is of significance to better support those individuals who enter, exit, or progress.

In sport psychology literature, a career transition is defined as a turning phase in an athletes' development that brings a set of demands beyond those experienced in everyday life, which requires adequate coping processes in order to continue the pursuit of the career (Stambulova & Wylleman, 2014). Career transitions are typically classified based by two forms: (a) *normative transitions*, referring to the changes that an athlete would be normally expected to undertake during their career (e.g., academy to first team), and (b) *non-normative*, referring to the unpredictable transitions that an athlete may experience (e.g., deselection) (Stambulova & Wylleman, 2014). Adding to this notion more recently, Stambulova and Ryba (2020) recognised that this taxonomy inadequately reflects the various transitions athletes may have, and thus introduced a new category of *quasi-normative transitions*. Quasi-normative transitions are predictable transitions but only for particular groups of athletes (e.g., temporary loan to another club).

Based on these definitions, while appreciating that a youth soccer player may experience many different transitions throughout their lifespan, this chapter will present three key career transitions, including: (a) deselection, (b) youth-to-senior, and (c) loans. Before discussing these processes, however, it is important to firstly understand the characteristics of selected and deselected youth soccer players to help inform the potential career transitions.

Characteristics of Selected and Deselected Players

The youth-to-senior transition is arguably the most defining moment in a promising young player's career (Morris et al., 2017). By receiving a professional contact, a youth team player moves one step closer to fulfilling their aspirations of representing their respective first team. To better understand this career transition, it is important to consider the characteristics that differentiate those who achieve professional status (i.e., selected, successful) and those who do not (i.e., deselected, unsuccessful). By doing so, it will enable stakeholders employed in talent development programmes to allocate resources more efficiently as well as facilitate a science-based support system (Kelly & Williams, 2020).

There are a number of qualitative studies that have attempted to underscore the characteristics that positively support the youth-to-senior transition. For instance, Mills et al. (2012) interviewed ten expert coaches who revealed six factors that were perceived to either positively or negatively influence player development, including: (a) awareness (e.g., self-awareness, awareness of others), (b) resilience (e.g., coping with setbacks, optimistic attitude), (c) goal-directed attributes (e.g., passion, professional attitude), (d) intelligence (e.g., sport intelligence, emotional competence), (e) sport-specific attributes (e.g., coachability, competitiveness), and (f) environmental factors (e.g. significant others, culture of game). Moreover, Cook et al. (2014) reported four general dimensions of mental toughness that were deemed crucial in securing a professional contract in the English Premier League, including: (a) competitiveness with self and others, (b) mind-set, (c) resilience, and (d) personal responsibility. Additionally, early research from Holt and Dunn (2004) showed that Canadian and English soccer coaches and players outlined four major psychosocial competencies that were central to success, including: (a) discipline (e.g., conforming dedication to the sport and a willingness to sacrifice), (b) commitment (e.g., strong motives and career-planning goals), (c) resilience (e.g., the ability to use coping strategies to overcome obstacles), and (d) social support (e.g., the ability to use emotional, informational, and tangible support). Overall, research through interviews exploring the opinions of people with lived experiences (e.g., coaches and players) appears to consistently show that psychological skills, amongst other multidimensional factors, are of vital importance.

Quantitative studies in youth soccer have also aimed to shed some light on the factors that differentiate selected and deselected players, which may aid our understanding of the youth-to-senior transition. As an example, Huijgen et al. (2014) applied a battery of objective field tests and questionnaires within the four domains of technical, tactical, physical, and psychological characteristics to players aged 16 to 18 years. It was revealed that selected players outperformed their deselected counterparts, whereby performance in the technical skill of dribbling, the tactical characteristics of positioning and decision-making, and the physical attribute of sprinting correctly classified 69% of talented players. Moreover, Forsman et al. (2016) examined multiple factors of youth soccer players at aged 15 years that eventually contributed to successful soccer performance at aged 19 years. They showed performance at aged 19 years was associated with technical (i.e., passing), tactical (i.e., centring), physical (i.e., agility), and psychological (i.e., motivation) characteristics that were displayed at aged 15 years. In addition, Zuber et al. (2016) observed holistic patterns as an instrument for predicting the performance in promising young soccer players over a 3-year period. They revealed that highly skilled players scored above average on all technical, physical, and psychological characteristics. Collectively, this research reinforces the usefulness of applying objective data and the importance of conducting a multidimensional assessment when considering first team contract decisions.

With talent development being inherently multifactorial, explorative studies must employ analysis techniques that can handle multiple competing and possible correlated features. To analyse the factors that contributed to U18 players achieving a professional contract at the end of their academy scholarship (i.e., selected n = 8; deselected: n = 10), Kelly et al. (2022) used a novel

TABLE 9.1 Summary of non-zero coefficients for the likelihood of signing a professional contract (adapted from Kelly et al., 2022)

Feature	Coefficient/SD of Feature	Odds Ratio/SD of Feature
43 progression steps rating	0.64	1.89
Slalom dribble	0.01	1.01
PCDEQ Factor 3	0.44	1.55
Home postcode social grade 2	-0.12	0.89

machine learning approach (i.e., a cross-validated Lasso regression using the glmnet package in R) to examine 53 factors cumulated from eight data collection methods across two seasons. Key findings revealed that the Psychological Characteristics for Developing Excellence Questionnaire (PCDEQ) Factor 3 (i.e., coping with performance and developmental pressures) and PCDEQ Factor 4 (i.e., an ability to organise and engage in quality practice) were important contributing factors towards achieving a professional contract. Moreover, player review ratings (i.e., higher coach scores), slalom dribble (i.e., quicker dribble times), and a lower home social classification (i.e., derived from more deprived areas) also provided a small contribution to successfully obtaining a professional contract (see Table 9.1). Overall, it appears the key factors associated with positive developmental outcomes are not always technical and tactical in nature, which is generally where coaches have their expertise (Lefebvre et al., 2016). The machine learning approach used here also serves as an alternative method when analysing large, multidimensional databases.

Deselection and Exit from the Academy System

A high percentage of youth soccer players are released before obtaining a scholarship (99%) or after their scholarship (85%) (Wilkinson, 2021). Deselection and exiting an academy system are common yet non-normative (e.g., unpredicted, unanticipated, and involuntary) transitions. Based on a number of empirical studies and literature reviews, it is evident that deselection can evoke a number of unpleasant emotions (e.g., anger, fear, humiliation; Brown & Potrac, 2009) and adverse outcomes to health and well-being (e.g., anxiety, depression; Brown & Potrac, 2009). As such, it is of utmost importance for stakeholders employed in youth soccer settings (e.g., coaches, support staff, education staff, welfare officers) to better understand what factors (e.g., coping resources) may influence transition quality and outcomes following deselection. Further to this, it is also important to understand how such factors may impact upon the transition quality and outcomes following deselection (see Chapter 5 for an overview of the deselection process).

Due to the significant time that a player invests within the soccer environment, a characteristic that has been associated with a problematic transition is athletic identity (Calvin, 2017). An athletic identity is when a salient part of an individual's identity becomes grounded in their participation, in this instance during soccer, throughout childhood and adolescence (Mitchell et al., 2020). The athletic identity can be shaped through the extensive engagement in the sport and/or by family members, peers, teammates, and coaches (Morris et al., 2015). An athletic identity has been associated with some performance benefits (e.g., commitment) and could contribute to a successful transition into a senior first team (Mitchell et al., 2020). However, a number of studies have identified that players who have an exclusive athletic identity to soccer are vulnerable to experience significant emotional disturbances and increased difficulty in coping with deselection (Wilkinson, 2021).

Deselection may also be a challenging transition for youth soccer players due to the perceived lack of control and choice (Wilkinson, 2021). Players who perceived their deselection to be unexpected or chose not to acknowledge deselection cues (e.g., lack of game time) are likely to appraise this transition as harmful and threatening (Blakelock et al., 2016). Subsequently, to understand how players attempted to cope with deselection, Blakelock et al. (2019) looked to explore the range of coping strategies utilised by academy soccer players within their first month of deselection. The authors identified that, although players engaged in range of coping strategies, it was avoidance coping during the first month of deselection that was positively associated with higher levels of psychological distress and unpleasant emotions such as anger, anxiety, depression, fear, and humiliation Blakelock et al. (2019). However, problem-focused coping (e.g., seeking out trials with other clubs or increased involvement in vocational or educational programmes) allowed some players to enhance their perceived control over their deselection as well as serve as an opportunity to increase psychological well-being (e.g., greater relaxation and enjoyment of life) and life-skill development (Blakelock et al., 2019).

Academy soccer players may experience deselection in contrasting ways at different points in time. Appraisal (e.g., challenge and threat) is argued to underpin the variability upon transition quality and adjustment post-deselection due to the implications this has upon perceived coping options available (Blakelock et al., 2016). Research that explored experiences of academy soccer players post-deselection has identified several characteristics that can impact upon the appraisal of deselection (Brown & Potrac, 2009). Specifically, athletic identity is one characteristic that can heighten harm/loss and threat associated with goals, values, and beliefs (Brown & Potrac, 2009). Given the high probability of experiencing deselection, it is proposed that academies and practitioners should emphasise the development of a broad identity (e.g., being a friend, other interests) and psychological characteristics (e.g., problem-focused coping, confidence) to reduce the threat, harm/loss associated with deselection (Williams & MacNamara, 2020).

The Youth-to-Senior Transition

The nature of the youth-to-senior transition is multifaceted, complex, and dynamic. Swainston et al. (2021) suggested this transition consists of four phases: (a) preparation, (b) orientation, (c) adaptation, and (d) stabilisation. The 'preparation phase' occurs before the full-time move to the senior environment, beginning with the first experience in the senior team (Stambulova et al., 2017). During the 'orientation phase', players look to find their role in the team and understand the requirements of senior competition. The 'adaptation phase' is where players seek to establish themselves in the team and gain experience of senior competition (Pehrson et al., 2017). Finally, through the 'stabilisation phase', players seek to perform consistently, take more responsibility in the group such as evolving leadership roles, and potentially look to further their career at a new level. Players will go through a period of adaption within each of these transition phases. However, in one specific study by Mitchell et al. (2020), who looked to explore the challenges associated with the progression through such phases, adaption can be influenced by the cultural climate (e.g., limited playing opportunities), working practices (e.g., increased training intensity), occupational hazards (e.g., injury), and social issues (e.g., parents). Furthermore, to navigate this transition, a young player requires a corresponding set of personal characteristics and psychological resources to manage the fluctuating levels of anxiety and confidence (Morris et al., 2015).

Finn and McKenna (2010) identified that the coping strategies utilised by players could positively influence the youth-to-senior transition. More specifically, adaptive coping strategies in the form of problem solving, self-control, acceptance of responsibly, and positive re-appraisal help to successfully influence the transition process. Such strategies promote the use of actions to try and reduce the appraisal of threat and harm of the transition demands, increase self-confidence, and help to interpret anxiety symptoms as facilitative. Conversely, distancing and escape-avoidance coping strategies have been typically associated with players that may distance themselves from inevitable transition challenges as well as avoid responsibility for their own development and performances (Finn & McKenna, 2010). Moreover, the motivation for transition has also been identified as a valuable psychological resource (Morris et al., 2015). Typically, players who have an intrinsic or self-determined motivation to succeed report being dedicated to their sport and working hard in training and matches. For instance, Morris et al. (2015) identified that players' motives may change pre- and post-transition; however, successful players post-transition maintain self-determined motivation to not just to get into the first team, but to be a successful senior squad member and move to better teams.

Resources in the form of organisational and coach support also appear to be highly influential for transition success (Swainston et al., 2020). Most notably, many players have discussed challenges in utilising coaching staff as emotional support during this transition. This is due to the players perceived impact that seeking help could have upon their playing time or this being used against them in deciding contracts (Swainston et al., 2020). Therefore, transition support could be improved by developing a positive coach-athlete relationship in order to help ease the power dynamics at play during this transition. Furthermore, organisational support, in the form of playing time and opportunity, has been identified as an important transition mechanism (Swainston et al., 2021). Within soccer, players have discussed how opportunity can create challenges to motivation and confidence due to the lack of perceived success or being able to demonstrate progression (Swainston et al., 2020). Within the youth-to-senior transition in professional soccer, prolonged periods without playing opportunities are commonplace (Swainston et al., 2020). Subsequently, soccer clubs should improve on utilising different strategies to create playing opportunities (e.g., the loan system; Kent et al., 2022), improve communication and access to support systems, as well as continue to provide players with psychological support for the development of adaptive psychological coping skills to improve transition success.

Overall, practitioners should be mindful of the many factors that could influence the youth-to-senior transition. Due to the growing amount of literature, Drew et al. (2019) conducted a systematic review on the qualitative research on the youth-to-senior transition in sport. The authors identified 59 factors that were perceived to impact the youth-to-senior transition, which were subsequently allocated into one of 13 sub-themes and then categorised into four overarching themes: (a) individual factors (e.g., perceptions of transition, psychological factors), (b) external factors (e.g., sources of stress, social support), (c) cultural factors (e.g., organisational, youth development), and (d) intervention strategies (e.g., coping strategies, educational programmes). Based on their synthesis of the current knowledge, Drew et al. (2019) created the 'individual, external, culture model of the youth-to-senior transition', which is offers a useful tool to explain this process and help understand the aforementioned facilitative and debilitative factors in soccer (see Figure 9.1).

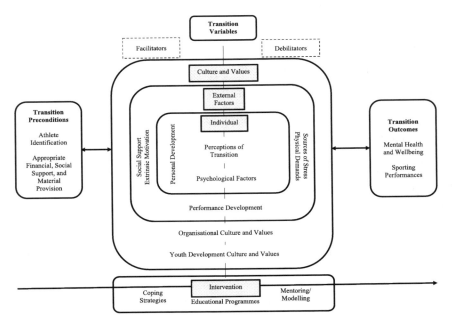

FIGURE 9.1 The individual, external, culture model of the youth-to-senior transition (adapted from Drew et al., 2019).

Loan Transition

A successful transition to first team remains a challenge for players in professional soccer environments. One possible reason for this challenge is the limited opportunities to train and compete with the first team. This is likely due to the pressure for first team managers to achieve immediate results that can mean a reliance on proven senior first team players (Prendergast & Gibson, 2022). In order to foster a young player's development and prepare them for senior soccer within their respective club, a growing number of players are experiencing a loan transition (Kent et al., 2022). The loan transition is a quasi-normative temporal transition, whereby soccer clubs temporarily transfer playing talent to another club to experience a new training and competition environment (Bond et al., 2020). Although, the loan transition can potentially provide opportunities for much-needed competitive game time and socialisation with senior players, this transition can also bring a unique set of demands and requires adequate coping processes in order to transition successfully (Stambulova & Wylleman, 2014). Interestingly, coping skills and protective factors were recognised by Prendergast and Gibson (2022) as essential competencies that a player needs to successfully progress into a first team environment; however, they were not typically being developed within an U23 environment. Subsequently, a loan transition may serve as a holistic developmental tool for players' technical, tactical, physical, psychological, and social development (Swainston et al., 2021).

Due to the increasing number of players undertaking a loan transition, Kent et al. (2022) developed the Demands, Resources, and Individual Effects (DRIVE) model during a qualitative

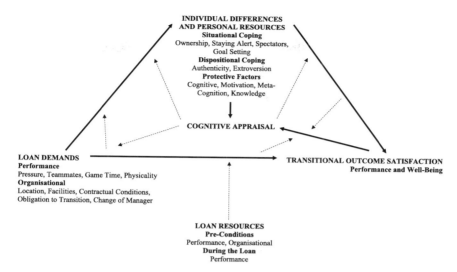

FIGURE 9.2 The DRIVE model illustrating loan demands, loan resources, individual differences, personal resources and demands, and transition outcomes (adapted from Kent et al., 2022).

examination of loan players stress process (e.g., demands, appraisals, and coping), with consideration of both performance and well-being responses during the loan transition (Figure 9.2). The DRIVE model identifies the performance (e.g., pressure, teammates, game time, and physicality) and organisational (e.g., location, facilities, contract conditions, and obligation to transition) demands of the loan transition. The exposure to such loan demands may facilitate the development of psychosocial and physical attributes of the players due to the development of coping strategies, coping flexibility, developing knowledge of when to utilise different strategies, and enhancing confidence in their application (Kent et al., 2022). However, the degree to which players may develop strategies that are helpful to managing performance and well-being is influenced by their primary appraisal. For instance, harm/loss appraisals can negatively impact upon well-being due to the projection of unpleasant emotions (e.g., anxiety). Alternatively, the appraisal of loan demands perceived as beneficial or a challenge can maintain well-being and performance through adaptive cognitions and behaviours (e.g., increased effort). Subsequently, this presents how players' evaluation, relational meaning, and interpretation of the loan environment can influence the appraisals of loan demands (e.g., harm, benefit, challenge, or threat) (Kent et al., 2022).

The DRIVE model also captures how transition pre-conditions and during-the-loan resources could mediate the appraisal of loan transition demands. Pre-transition conditions include social support (i.e., manager, professional advice), recommendation to the club, and contractual conditions. Loan transition resources could also influence both performance and well-being outcomes during the loan and include teammates and parent club staff (e.g., loan manager, sport scientist, physiotherapist). Specifically, Kent et al. (2022) showed that players who received adequate pre-transition informational support discussed perceptions of personal control, awareness of the perceived benefits of the loan, and anticipated demands. Moreover, players alluded to different types of situational coping, dispositional coping, and protective factors, which influenced their loan transition experiences. Situational coping, referred to as players' ability to take ownership (e.g., self-discipline, responsibility), was a significant resource in managing their loan transition. Dispositional coping also referred to the players' extraversion and ability to be authentic, whilst protective factors included self-efficacy, meta-cognition, and understanding of the loan.

Based on the limited loan literature, soccer clubs are encouraged to recognise the unique demands and wider social and cultural landscape that surrounds the loan player (e.g., identity, accommodation, social awareness). It is also important to acknowledge that professional soccer clubs have recently implemented loan-agreement strategies as well as employ a loan manager to manage such transitions (Bond et al., 2020). Moving forward, it will be important to capture the effectiveness of these processes and how they facilitate long-term player development.

Considerations for Researchers

A high proportion of academy soccer players will be deselected from their club, which may increase their vulnerability to mental health issues (Blakelock et al., 2019). To date, research has sought to explore the experiences of young players during various normative, non-normative, and quasi-transitions across the lifespan. While such research has allowed clubs and organisations to take note of the severity of unsuccessful transitions, there is a lack of soccer-specific transition intervention literature. Currently, Morris et al. (2015) has identified that soccer clubs who utilise and implement transition support have better transition outcomes (e.g., player financial value, retention rates) and spend less on player assistance, compared to when a club does not have a transition programme in place. This provides support to the idea that intervening to facilitate transitions could be valuable to soccer organisations. In this respect, future research should begin to design, deliver, and evaluate the effectiveness of such interventions.

Research has discussed how stress-based models and theories may help researchers to develop a stronger understanding of transitions and interventions (e.g., Kent et al., 2022). Thus, the use of a stress-based perspective (or other relevant theories) to develop interventions would be a fruitful avenue in exploring the effectiveness of transition interventions that focus on the development of coping flexibility. Additionally, the majority of the current literature on transitions in soccer has focused on male populations from developed soccer nations, most notably from England. Therefore, it is important that future research captures the career transitions of young soccer players across a variety of sociocultural contexts as well as prioritise women's and girls' provision.

In addition to understanding individuals' transition experiences, it becomes important to also acknowledge the role of key stakeholders in supporting transition processes, including coaches and support staff (e.g., physiotherapists and loan managers). Future research may, therefore, be directed towards the development of psychological-educational interventions that may assist such individuals in understanding how they could better prepare players for normative, non-normative, and quasi-transitions. Moreover, there are an increasing number of stakeholder roles within the soccer academy that have been developed to support various within-career transitions of academy players (e.g., loan manager; Kent et al., 2022). Thus, future research should also seek to explore the perceived roles and responsibilities of such staff and any barriers and facilitators they may experience when trying to carry out their role.

Considerations for Practitioners

Based on the literature presented throughout this chapter, the following suggestions for practitioners may support the transition processes for their players and colleagues:

- The development of a rigid athletic identity within the youth soccer context can be deleterious for adjustment following non-normative transitions, such as deselection. Practitioners are advised to ensure players continue to experiment with other interests and roles outside of soccer.
- It is important to complete a multidimensional assessment (i.e., technical, tactical, physical, psychological, social) to help inform transition decisions (e.g., deselection, first team contract, loan). This should be communicated between and agreed amongst all staff (e.g., coach, performance analyst, psychologist, sport scientist, strength and conditioning coach) to support holistic decision-making.
- Opportunity and playing time are critical factors to help athletes cope with soccer transitions. Practitioners should continue to evaluate and manage the clubs' overall scope to ensure there are routes into the first team for players. One method in which this could be achieved is through the loan system.
- Throughout the lifespan, key individuals have significant influence upon the transition experience of players. Practitioners are encouraged to provide players with suitable support when adapting to their new environment and potential changes to their identity.
- Proactive (e.g., planning) and problem-focused (e.g., mobilise available resources) coping appear to be the most effective coping strategies for successful transitions. Practitioners are encouraged to help players (e.g., understanding, confidence) in how they can maximize the support that is available in their network (e.g., sport psychologist, loan manager) to engage in such coping strategies.

Conclusion

This chapter aimed to provide an insight into the transition experiences of young players within youth soccer. By presenting three key transitions—namely deselection, youth-to-senior, and loans—this chapter has underscored key literature to demonstrate how and why various experiences occur. Key areas of future research include the need for transition-intervention research and the evaluation of success as well as examining the effectiveness of psychological-education interventions with key stakeholders. With regards to applied practice, practitioners are encouraged to ensure players engage in psychological provision that develops coping skills, which will, in turn, limit the impact that some transitions may have on mental health and well-being.

References

Blakelock, D., Chen, M., & Prescott, T. (2016). Psychological distress in elite adolescent soccer players following deselection. *Journal of Clinical Sport Psychology, 10*(1), 59–67. https://doi.org/10.1123/jcsp.2015-0010

Blakelock, D., Chen, M., & Prescott, T. (2019). Coping and psychological distress in elite adolescent soccer players following professional academy deselection. *Journal of Sport Behavior, 41*(1), 1–26.

Bond, A. J., Widdop, P., & Parnell, D. (2020). Topological network properties of the European football loan system. *European Sport Management Quarterly, 20*(5), 655–678. https://doi.org/10.1080/16184742.2019.1673460

Brown, G., & Potrac, P. (2009). 'You've not made the grade, son': De-selection and identity disruption in elite level youth football. *Soccer & Society, 10*(2), 143–159. https://doi.org/10.1080/14660970802601613

Calvin, M. (2017). *No hunger in paradise. The players. The journey. The dream.* Arrow Books.

Cook, C., Crust, L., Littlewood, M., Nesti, M., & Allen-Collinson, J. (2014). 'What it takes': Perceptions of mental toughness and its development in an English premier league soccer academy. *Qualitative Research in Sport, Exercise & Health, 6*(3), 329–347. https://doi.org/10.1080/2159676X.2013.857708

Drew, K., Morris, R., Tod, D. A., & Eubank, M. R. (2019). A meta-study of qualitative research on the junior-to-senior transition in sport. *Psychology of Sport and Exercise, 45*, 101556. https://doi.org/10.1016/j.psychsport.2019.101556

Finn, J., & McKenna, J. (2010). Coping with academy-to-first-team transitions in elite English male team sports: The coaches' perspective. *International Journal of Sports Science & Coaching, 5*(2), 257–279. https://doi.org/10.1260/1747-9541.5.2.257

Forsman, H., Grasten, A., Blomqvist, M., Davids, K., Liukkonen, J., & Konttinen, N. (2016). Development of perceived competence, tactical skills, motivation, technical skills, and speed and agility in young soccer players. *Journal of Sports Sciences, 34*(14), 1311–1318. https://doi.org/10.1080/02640414.2015.1127401

Green, C. (2009). *Every boy's dream.* Bloomsbury Publishing Plc.

Holt, N. L., & Dunn, J. G. H. (2004). Towards a grounded theory of the psychosocial competencies and environmental conditions associated with soccer success. *Journal of Applied Sport Psychology, 16*(3), 199–219. https://doi.org/10.1080/10413200490437949

Huijgen, B. C. H., Elferink-Gemser, M. T., Lemmink, K. A. P. M., & Visscher, C. (2014). Multidimensional performance characteristics in selected and deselected talented soccer players. *European Journal of Sport Science, 14*(1), 2–10. https://doi.org/10.1080/17461391.2012.725102

Kelly, A. L., & Williams, C. A. (2020). Physical characteristics and the talent identification and development processes in male youth soccer: A narrative review. *Strength and Conditioning Journal, 42*(6), 15–34. https://doi.org/10.1519/SSC.0000000000000576

Kelly, A. L., Williams, C. A., Cook, R., Jiménez, S. L., & Wilson, M. R. (2022). A multidisciplinary investigation into the talent development processes at an English football academy: A machine learning approach. *Sports, 10*(10), 159. https://doi.org/10.3390/sports10100159

Kent, S., Neil, R., & Morris, R. (2022). Coping with the loan transition in professional association football. *Psychology of Sport and Exercise, 60*, 102–158. https://doi.org/10.1016/j.psychsport.2022.102158

Lefebvre, J. S., Evans, M. B., Turnnidge, J., Gainforth, H. L., & Côté, J. (2016). Describing and classifying coach development programmes: A synthesis of empirical research and applied practice. *International Journal of Sports Science & Coaching, 11*(6), 887–899. https://doi.org/10.1177/1747954116676116

Mills, A., Butt, J., Maynard, I., & Harwood, C. (2012). Identifying factors perceived to influence the development of elite youth football academy players. *Journal of Sports Sciences, 30*(15), 1593–1604. https://doi.org/10.1080/02640414.2012.710753

Mitchell, T., Gledhill, A., Nesti, M., Richardson, D., & Littlewood, M. (2020). Practitioner perspectives on the barriers associated with youth-to-senior transition in elite youth soccer academy players. *International Sport Coaching Journal, 7*(3), 273–282. https://doi.org/10.1123/iscj.2019-0015.

Morris, R., Tod, D., & Oliver, E. (2015). An analysis of organizational structure and transition outcomes in the youth-to-senior professional soccer transition. *Journal of Applied Sport Psychology, 27*(2), 216–234. https://doi.org/10.1080/10413200.2014.980015

Morris, R., Tod, D., & Eubank, M. (2017). From youth team to first team: An investigation into the transition experiences of young professional athletes in soccer. *International Journal of Sport and Exercise Psychology, 15*(5), 523–539. https://doi.org/10.1080/1612197X.2016.1152992

Pehrson, S., Stambulova, N. B., & Olsson, K. (2017). Revisiting the empirical model 'Phases in the junior-to-senior transition of Swedish ice hockey players': External validation through focus groups and interviews. *International Journal of Sports Science & Coaching, 12*(6), 747–761. https://doi.org/10.1177/1747954117738897

Prendergast, G., & Gibson, L. (2022). A qualitative exploration of the use of player loans to supplement the talent development process of professional footballers in the under 23 age group of English football academies. *Journal of Sports Sciences*, *40*(4), 422–430. https://doi.org/10.1080/02640414.2021.1996985

Stambulova, N. B., Pehrson, S., & Olsson, K. (2017). Phases in the junior-to-senior transition of Swedish ice hockey players: From a conceptual framework to an empirical model. *International Journal of Sports Science & Coaching*, *12*(2), 231–244. https://doi.org/10.1177/1747954117694928

Stambulova, N. B., & Ryba, T. V. (2020). Identity and cultural transition: Lessons to learn from a negative case analysis. *Journal of Sport Psychology in Action*, *11*(4), 266–278. https://doi.org/10.1080/21520704.2020.1825025

Stambulova, N. B., & Wylleman, P. (2014). Athletes' career development and transitions. In *Routledge companion to sport and exercise psychology* (pp. 629–644). Routledge.

Swainston, S. C., Wilson, M. R., & Jones, M. I. (2020). Player experience during the junior to senior transition in professional football: a longitudinal case study. *Frontiers in Psychology*, *11*, 1672. https://doi.org/10.3389/fpsyg.2020.01672

Swainston, S. C., Wilson, M. R., & Jones, M. I. (2021). "It's all about opportunity": From professional contract to first-team regular. *Journal of Applied Sport Psychology*, 1–21. https://doi.org/10.1080/10413200.2021.1934914

Williams, G. G., & MacNamara, Á. (2020). Coaching on the talent pathway: Understanding the influence of developmental experiences on coaching philosophy. *International Sport Coaching Journal*, *8*(2), 141–152. https://doi.org/10.1123/iscj.2019-0099

Wilkinson, R. J. (2021). A literature review exploring the mental health issues in academy football players following career termination due to deselection or injury and how mcounselling could support future players. *Counselling and Psychotherapy Research*, *21*(4), 859–868. https://doi.org/10.1002/capr.12417

Zuber, C., Zibung, M., & Conzelmann, A. (2016). Holistic patterns as an instrument for predicting the performance of promising young soccer players—A 3-years longitudinal study. *Frontiers in Psychology*, *7*(1088), 1–10. https://doi.org/10.3389%2Ffpsyg.2016.01088

10
RELATIVE AGE EFFECTS
Looking Back and Moving Forward

Adam L. Kelly, Laura Finnegan, Kevin Till, and Kristy L. Smith

Introduction

Relative age effects (RAEs) are a well-established phenomenon in organised youth sport (Musch & Grondin, 2001). To be specific, when individuals are allocated into annual age groups, relatively older athletes (i.e., those born at the beginning of the cut-off date) are often overrepresented throughout recreational and talent pathways when compared to their relatively younger peers (i.e., those born at the end of the cut-off date) (Barnsley et al., 1985). As a result, relatively older athletes become exposed to a wealth of opportunities (e.g., greater access to coaching, competition, facilities, specialist support), which can have a positive impact upon subsequent developmental outcomes (Furley & Memmert, 2016; Wattie et al., 2008). Conversely, studies have shown detrimental effects for relatively younger athletes, such as limited selection opportunities, lower participation, and higher dropout rates (e.g., Delorme et al., 2010a; Hancock et al., 2013b).

The relationship between birthdate and success was first identified by Grondin et al. (1984) during their study of competitive youth and professional ice hockey league in North America. They showed how those born in the first months of the selection year were overrepresented, whereas there was an underrepresentation of athletes born in the last months of the selection year. In the almost 40 years since then, several authors have studied the presence of RAEs across a range of sports, including (but not limited to) baseball (BoLun et al., 2018), basketball (Delorme & Raspaud, 2009), handball (de la Rubia et al., 2021), rugby league (Cobley & Till, 2017), rugby union (Kelly et al., 2021c), tennis (Gerdin et al., 2018), and water polo (Barrenetxea-Garcia et al., 2018).

Early relative age research in youth sport generally assumed that an advanced maturity status was the major underlying cause (e.g., the *maturation-selection hypothesis*; Cobley et al., 2009). Thereafter, Hancock et al. (2013a) proposed the *Social Agents model* to suggest how social agents, including athletes (i.e., Galatea effect; Merton, 1957), coaches (i.e., Pygmalion effect; Rosenthal & Jacobson, 1968), and parents (i.e., Matthew effect; Merton, 1968), are responsible for perpetuating RAEs. A more holistic suggestion was put forward by Wattie et al. (2015), who theorised a *constraints-based developmental systems model* to describe various factors that influence the emergence of RAEs within a particular context, based on environmental (e.g., popularity of sport), individual (e.g., gender), and task (e.g., playing position) constraints. More recently, Kelly et al. (2022) used the *Personal Assets Framework* to explain the immediate (i.e., personal engagement in activities, appropriate settings and organisational structures, and quality social dynamics), short-term (i.e., competence, confidence, connection, and character), and long-term (i.e., performance, participation, and personal development) developmental outcomes due to RAEs. Despite these explanatory efforts, limited empirical studies are available to show the exact causes of RAEs in youth sport.

The purpose of this chapter is to look back at the existing literature to outline the contextual factors that can impact RAEs in soccer as well as examine possible relative age solutions. As such, this chapter is comprised of four sections, including: (a) male youth soccer, (b) female youth soccer, (c) senior soccer, and (d) potential relative age solutions. Based on this extant literature, considerations for researchers and practitioners are presented to help this area of research and practice move forward.

Male Youth Soccer

Perhaps due to its broad international popularity, soccer has received the largest academic attention on RAEs. The first study was published in 1992, where Barnsley et al. (1992) analysed the rosters of soccer teams at the male 1990 World Cup and the 1989 U17 and U20 youth equivalents. They revealed almost 45% of U17 players were born in the first 3 months of the annual selection year, whereas only 7.7% were born in the last 3 months of the annual selection year, with similar results shown across the U20 team rosters. Senior squads also showed inequities of representation across the four birth quarters, although to a lesser extent than the youth cohorts. The authors concluded by suggesting that parents could take a 'family planning approach' to ensure that their children were born favourably earlier in the soccer selection year. Since this preliminary work, the percentages of male youth soccer players born in the first half of the selection year have been reported as between 55–60% (Hirose, 2009), 60–70% (Gil et al., 2014), and 70–80% (Skorski et al., 2016).

Relative age research in male youth soccer has generally applied a cross-sectional approach using birth quarters (BQs) to compare the observed and expected distributions (i.e., BQ1, representing those born in the first 3 months of an annual age group and BQ4, representing those born in the last 3 months). As an example, Finnegan et al. (2017) showed how the Irish U14 national development programme was comprised of 38.2% of players born in BQ1 and only 12.6% born in BQ4 (Figure 10.1a and 10.1b). Moreover, Patel et al. (2019) found that BQ1 players were approximately 6 times more likely to be represented than BQ4 players within a male category one English professional soccer club (overall sample of 11 age groups ranging from U9 to senior level). Most notably, in the U9 group, there was a 19-times-greater likelihood of being selected as a BQ1, compared to BQ4. Similarly, Lovell et al. (2015) showed that almost 50% of all U9 to U18 male players in English professional soccer academies were born in BQ1. As such, it is plausible to suggest that there is a systematic selection bias towards relatively older players throughout talent pathways in male youth soccer. Thus, it is important to explore the contextual factors that underpin these RAEs to better understand how they operate throughout these settings.

Relative age effects in male youth soccer occur on an international scale and have been identified across several countries, including America (Vincent & Glamser, 2006), Brazil (Massa et al., 2014), Germany (Augste & Lames, 2011), France (Delorme et al., 2010a), Holland (Verbeek

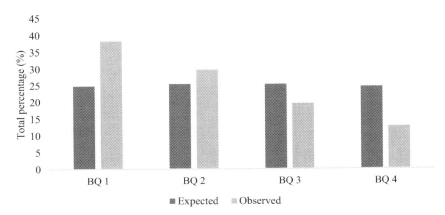

FIGURE 10.1A The percentage of players selected onto a male youth soccer development programme within each BQ, compared to the expected national BQ distribution (adapted from Finnegan et al., 2017).

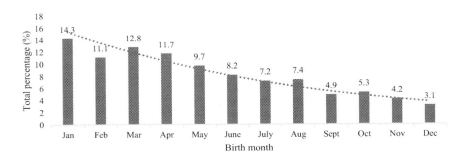

FIGURE 10.1B The birth month distribution of U14 players selected into a male youth soccer development programme in Ireland (adapted from Finnegan et al., 2017).

et al., 2021), Scotland (Dugdale et al., 2021), Slovakia (Mikulič et al., 2015), Spain (Jimenez & Pain, 2008), and Switzerland (Romann & Fuchslocher, 2013a). This effect is shown consistently, despite a variety of cut-off dates in youth soccer being utilised worldwide (i.e., September 1 in England, April 1 in Japan, and, most commonly, January 1 across Australia, Europe, and North America) (Kelly et al., 2021b; Musch & Hay, 1999). Furthermore, RAEs have also been revealed throughout a range of competition levels, such as recreational, academy, professional, and international (e.g., Figueiredo et al., 2019; Fumarco & Rossi, 2018; Helsen et al., 2012; Ostapczuk & Musch, 2013; Yagüe et al., 2018).

Player selection procedures can play an important role in exacerbating RAEs. In England, for instance, 30% of U8 recreational players were born in BQ1, compared to 57% of academy players born in BQ1 (Jackson & Comber, 2020). Similarly, Doncaster et al. (2020) observed that 53% of male soccer players from the FC Barcelona academy were born in BQ1, compared to the Spanish BQ1 general population values of 24%. In a study of Scottish soccer players, significant

RAEs were found at youth academy, development, and performance levels but not recreational or professional levels (Dugdale et al., 2021). Additionally, Romann et al. (2020) found that clubs who used coach selections and trials to form their youth soccer squads showed small RAEs with an overrepresentation of BQ1 players in the first team and inverse RAEs with an underrepresentation of BQ1 players in the lower teams. This research indicates the role of coach selections and the upward pressure for places on a representative squad can have on perpetuating RAEs. Moreover, RAEs in male youth soccer have shown to be stronger for traditionally 'successful' teams (i.e., those with a reputation for their youth teams) and those within bigger cities (Bennett et al., 2019; Finnegan et al., 2017; Jimenez & Pain, 2008). It has also been suggested that RAEs are more prevalent when a desire for a competitive advantage is presented (Sæther, 2016; Verbeek et al., 2021). For example, Augste and Lames (2011) discovered a positive correlation between RAEs and league position, reinforcing the interpretation that success in the first German male U17 league may be due, to some extent, to a higher relative age of the players. Similarly, Söderström et al. (2019) showed how the birthdate distribution of the Swedish male national U15 soccer team was also impacted by competitive success.

Female Youth Soccer

Female youth soccer research has documented RAEs for the past two decades (e.g., Helsen et al., 2005; Romann & Fuchslocher, 2013a). A systematic review and meta-analysis of female RAEs in sport identified soccer as one of the most studied contexts (i.e., 33 samples from the total of 308 available in published literature) (Smith et al., 2018), with updated data confirming soccer to be the activity with the greatest number of studies examining female athletes (Wattie & Baker, 2020). Samples are available from around the world, such as China (Liu & Liu, 2008), Japan (Nakata & Sakamoto, 2012), Israel (Lidor et al., 2014), North America (Vincent & Glamser, 2006), and throughout Europe (Delorme et al., 2010b; Helsen et al., 2005; Sedano et al., 2015). For example, Helsen et al. (2005) reported BQ1 comprised 31% of female players participating in the female UEFA U18 tournament, while only 17% were born in BQ4. Moreover, Romann and Fuchslocher (2013a) provided data from the female U17 World Cup, which offers comparisons of RAEs for players across various geographical regions. Specifically, BQ distributions were relatively equal in the collapsed sample, yet trends varied considerably by region. For instance, North/Central America and Europe showed the classic overrepresentation in BQ1 (34% and 33%, respectively), while Africa was observed to have a reversed pattern with an overrepresentation in BQ4 (45%).

Most female youth soccer studies have reported RAEs, which favour the relatively older players within the respective selection year (Smith et al., 2018). Generally, researchers have focused on high-performance players in post-adolescent and senior age groups, while investigations of pre-adolescent/adolescent and recreational-level players are less common. The findings from the Smith et al. (2018) review in sport imply that players in soccer have a notably high risk of experiencing relative age related (dis)advantages, with estimates suggesting female players are 31% more likely to be born in BQ1 of the selection year when compared to BQ4 in this sport context.[1] This level of risk may be related to the subjective nature of talent selections that occur on the field of play in team sports (discussed further in Baker et al., 2014), as well as also due in part to the undeniable popularity of soccer around the world, which increases competition for opportunities to participate. A notable exception to the consistent reporting of RAEs among females that also illustrates the role of sport popularity is found in a study of Israeli players, where no RAEs were observed among the highest senior levels. The authors noted that opportunities for females to play soccer were relatively recent, and thus, competition for positions on high-performance Israeli soccer teams may have been low at that time (i.e., in comparison to other nations), therefore reducing the likelihood of RAEs (Lidor et al., 2014).

The role of moderating variables on the magnitude of observed RAEs has been noted in the existing literature (e.g., Cobley et al., 2009). Age and competition level are amongst the more commonly discussed moderating variables for female soccer players. Smith et al. (2018) conducted subgroup analyses for both age and competition level. They found that, while soccer-specific analyses were not performed, subgroup analyses for all compiled female sport samples suggested the greatest magnitude of risk is present in pre-adolescent categories for females (i.e., age 11 years and younger), and decreases thereafter[2]. The authors attributed these trends to the normal physical- and psychosocial-development differences found prior to maturation between age-grouped peers, along with parental decisions regarding early sport involvement. Further, the greatest likelihood of encountering relative age inequities was identified at the most high-performance levels. Smith and Weir (2022) showed that these moderating trends might extend to soccer-specific contexts in a longitudinal examination of all female soccer players belonging to a 1-year, same-age cohort from the province of Ontario, Canada. An overrepresentation of registrants with relatively earlier birthdates[3] was observed in the overall sample at age 10 years, suggesting higher participation among the relatively oldest members of this group. These trends persisted throughout the years examined (i.e., up to and including age 16 years) in both the competitive and recreational trajectories. However, RAEs were descriptively stronger among the competitive players, suggesting a greater magnitude of risk at higher levels of competition in this sample (Figure 10.2a and 10.2b).

Studies offering direct comparisons of female and male youth soccer samples are lacking in the literature, and thus, represent a consideration for future work. The available evidence

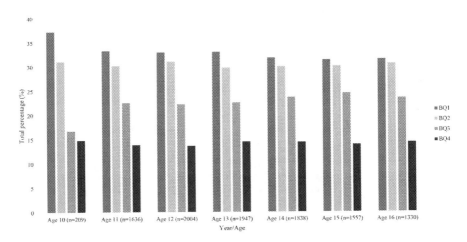

FIGURE 10.2A Birth quartile distribution for competitive female soccer players in Ontario, Canada, aged 10–16 years[4] (longitudinal, 1-year cohort) (adapted from Smith & Weir, 2022).

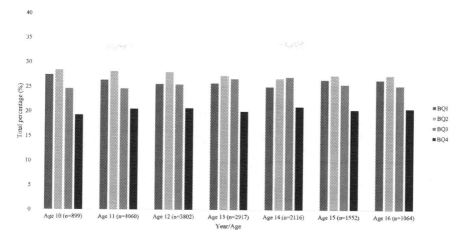

FIGURE 10.2B Birth quartile distribution for recreational female soccer players in Ontario, Canada, aged 10–16 years[4] (longitudinal, 1-year cohort) (adapted from Smith & Weir, 2022).

from analogous samples supports that male RAEs are greater in magnitude. For instance, Li et al. (2020) reported a strong overrepresentation of BQ1 among elite Chinese U18 and U20 male soccer players (39% and 43% born in BQ1, respectively), while lesser RAEs were noted for females in U19 and adult categories (35% and 32%, respectively). The work of Andrew et al. (2022) also supports male RAEs being greater in magnitude compared to females, as evidenced in analyses of players qualifying for the 2019 U17 European Championships, U19 European Championships, and the 2021 (male) and 2022 (female) European Championships (Table 10.1). Strong RAEs were noted for U17 and U19 males (i.e., ranging from 42–46% for BQ1) in comparison to the female sample (i.e., 26–32% in BQ1). These trends in the context of soccer may be intricately entwined with maturational processes and associated (dis)advantages following the completion of maturation for each sex (see Vincent & Glamser, 2006 for further discussion), along with cultural and social norms (e.g., greater popularity of male soccer versus female).

Senior Soccer

There appears to be a complicated relationship between selection at youth levels and the successful transition to senior levels across sports (Kelly & Williams, 2020). Compared to the traditional RAEs often observed at youth levels, occurrences in senior soccer appear mixed. On the one hand, a larger pool of evidence suggests how there are *knock-on effects* of relative age at senior levels due to its prevalence at youth levels (e.g., Brustio et al., 2018, 2019; de la Rubia et al., 2021). On the other hand, however, a growing body of literature has suggested possible *reversal effects* of relative age at senior levels in sport, including a higher proportion of relatively younger athletes who achieved professional contracts (Kelly et al., 2021b, 2021d, 2021e; McCarthy & Collins, 2014; McCarthy et al., 2016; Wrang et al., 2018), earlier selection during drafts (Baker & Logan,

TABLE 10.1 Birth quartile distribution based on gender, age group, and qualification status in European U17, U19, and senior tournaments (adapted from Andrew et al., 2022)

Gender	Age	Status	n	Birth Quartile Distribution (%)				Odds Ratios				Chi-square	P
				BQ1	BQ2	BQ3	BQ4	BQ1 vs. BQ4	BQ2 vs. BQ4	BQ3 vs. BQ4	S1 vs. S2		
Female	U17	Qual	165	42 (25.5)	52 (31.5)	37 (22.4)	34 (20.6)	1.2 (0.6–2.8)	1.5 (0.7–3.4)	1.1 (0.5–2.5)	1.3 (0.8–2.3)	2.6	0.467
		Non	159	45 (28.3)	42 (23.3)	37 (23.3)	35 (22)	1.3 (0.6–2.8)	1.2 (0.5–2.7)	1.1 (0.5–2.4)	1.2 (0.7–2.1)	1.3	0.735
		All	324	87 (26.9)	94 (29)	74 (22.8)	69 (21.3)	1.3 (0.6–2.8)	1.4 (0.6–3)	1.1 (0.5–2.4)	1.3 (0.7–2.2)	1.5	0.68
	U19	Qual	160	51 (31.9)	37 (23.1)	37 (23.1)	35 (21.9)	1.5 (0.7–3.2)	1.1 (0.5–2.4)	1.1 (0.5–2.4)	1.2 (0.7–2.1)	3.0	0.383
		Non	133	46 (34.6)	39 (29.3)	26 (19.5)	22 (16.5)	2.1 (0.9–4.7)	1.8 (0.8–4)	1.2 (0.5–2.8)	1.8 (1–3.1)	8.9*	0.03
		All	293	97 (33.1)	76 (25.9)	63 (21.5)	57 (19.5)	1.7 (0.8–3.7)	1.3 (0.6–3.0)	1.1 (0.5–2.5)	1.4 (0.8–2.5)	4.8	0.187
	Sen	Qual	669	165 (24.7)	201 (30)	144 (21.5)	159 (23.8)	1.1 (0.5–2.3)	1.3 (0.6–2.7)	0.9 (0.4–2)	1.2 (0.7–2.1)	1.6	0.654
		Non	1,101	275 (25)	317 (28.8)	259 (23.5)	250 (22.7)	1.1 (0.5–2.4)	1.3 (0.6–2.8)	1.0 (0.5–2.3)	1.2 (0.7–2)	0.8	0.849
		All	1,770	440 (24.9)	518 (29.3)	403 (22.8)	409 (23.1)	1.1 (0.5–2.4)	1.3 (0.6–2.8)	1.0 (0.4–2.2)	1.2 (0.7–2.1)	1.1	0.788
Male	U17	Qual	323	147 (45.5)	94 (29.1)	58 (18)	24 (7.4)	6.1 (2.4–15.9)	3.9 (1.5–10.4)	2.4 (0.9–6.7)	2.9 (1.6–5.3)	32.9*	<0.001
		Non	864	366 (42.4)	230 (26.6)	173 (20)	95 (11)	3.9 (1.6–9.2)	2.4 (1.0–5.9)	1.8 (0.7–4.6)	2.2 (1.3–4)	21.9*	<0.001
		All	1,187	513 (43.2)	324 (27.3)	231 (19.5)	119 (10)	4.3 (1.8–10.4)	2.7 (1.1–6.8)	1.9 (0.8–5)	2.4 (1.3–4.3)	24.6*	<0.001
	U19	Qual	159	66 (41.5)	41 (25.8)	33 (20.8)	19 (11.9)	3.5 (1.5–8.1)	2.2 (0.9–5.2)	1.7 (0.7–4.3)	2.1 (1.2–3.7)	19.3*	<0.001
		Non	1,070	421 (39.3)	297 (27.8)	186 (17.4)	166 (15.5)	2.5 (1.1–5.7)	1.8 (0.8–4.1)	1.1 (0.5–2.7)	2.0 (1.2–3.6)	15.3*	0.002
		All	1,229	487 (39.6)	338 (27.5)	219 (17.8)	185 (15.1)	2.6 (1.2–5.9)	1.8 (0.8–4.2)	1.2 (0.5–2.9)	2.0 (1.2–3.6)	15.7*	0.001
	Sen	Qual	923	295 (32)	239 (25.9)	219 (23.7)	170 (18.4)	1.7 (0.8–3.9)	1.4 (0.6–3.2)	1.3 (0.6–2.9)	1.4 (0.8–2.4)	4.0	0.265
		Non	820	229 (27.9)	208 (25.4)	215 (26.2)	168 (20.5)	1.4 (0.6–3)	1.2 (0.6–2.8)	1.3 (0.6–2.9)	1.1 (0.7–2)	1.1	0.784
		All	1,743	524 (30.1)	447 (25.6)	434 (24.9)	338 (19.4)	1.6 (0.7–3.4)	1.3 (0.6–3)	1.3 (0.6–2.9)	1.3 (0.7–2.2)	2.3	0.506

2007; Coutts et al., 2014; Deaner et al., 2013), a longer career duration (Steingröver et al., 2016), earned higher salaries (Fumarco et al., 2017), and performed better (e.g., Bjerke et al., 2017; Jones et al., 2018). Gibbs et al. (2012) put forward the *underdog hypothesis* to explain how relatively younger athletes who are initially selected into talent pathways may benefit in the long-term by engaging in more competitive play against relatively older peers throughout their development.

In the context of youth soccer, recent research showed traditional RAEs within an English category-three academy, whereby BQ1s were almost 3 times more likely to be recruited compared to BQ4s across the U9 to U18 age groups (Kelly et al., 2020). Interestingly, when observing the conversion rates, BQ4s were 4 times more likely to achieve a professional contract once they were selected at youth level compared to BQ1s (Figure 10.3). Kelly et al. (2020) used the *underdog hypothesis* to theorise how relatively younger players may be required to develop technical and tactical skills in order to counteract relative age biases when playing against relatively older peers. Moreover, relatively younger players may maintain a desire to compete with those of a greater physical stature at youth level, which could facilitate the development of psychological and social skills that are more complimentary to the challenges individuals may encounter in adulthood (Kelly et al., 2021e). These benefits may equip relatively younger players, or 'underdogs', to overcome subsequent obstacles and succeed in senior soccer (Schorer et al., 2009).

Similar findings have been revealed by Gil et al. (2019), who demonstrated that, although their Spanish professional soccer academy had a significant overrepresentation of BQ1s from U12 to U19, compared to any other for the last 20 years (e.g., U16 BQ1 = 51% vs. BQ4 = 6%), the odds for BQ4s achieving professional status were 3 times more compared to any other BQ. Likewise, Grossman and Lames (2013) demonstrated almost twice as many relatively younger players

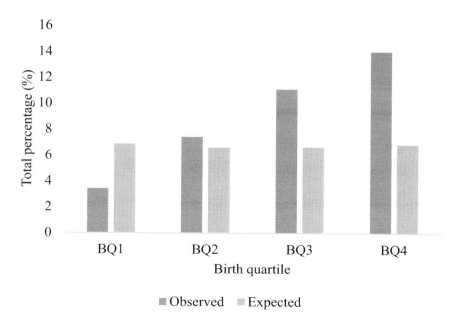

FIGURE 10.3 The percentage of professional contracts awarded based on the total number of academy players within each BQ, compared with the expected BQ distribution based on national norms (adapted from Kelly et al., 2020).

transitioned from academy to senior professional teams in the Bundesliga (Germany) when compared to relatively older players. This reinforces that, despite RAEs continuing to be prevalent across male youth soccer academies, once a relatively younger player enters a talent pathway, they may be more likely to graduate with a professional contract. It is important, however, to highlight that research in female settings remains absent.

Better performance in male professional soccer (i.e., measured by the total number of games in their career) has also been positively associated with relatively younger players in Brazil, although this was not apparent in relation to their market value (Ramos-Filho & Ferreira, 2021). With regards to career earnings, Ashworth and Heyndels (2007) revealed relatively younger male German professional soccer players earned systematically higher wages than their relatively older counterparts, which was strongest for goalkeepers and defenders. This suggests that although relatively younger players may have to overcome a system that discriminates against them, it could have subsequent long-term benefits. Moreover, it may be suggested that relatively younger players are likely to be positively selected, whereby they are chosen from 'the right tail of the ability distribution' (Fumarco et al., 2017).

A recent overview of these possible late-birthday benefits was offered by Smith and Weir (2020), who suggested potential explanations for the *underdog hypothesis* as three-fold: (a) relatively younger athletes may possess superior performance skills, (b) relatively younger athletes may develop superior psychological skills, and (c) perceived advantages of being relatively older may be detrimental to the athlete's overall well-being. However, it's important to note that the authors emphasised that being required to overcome pitfalls as a relatively younger athlete only benefits a small proportion, and that the inequities occurring through RAEs are largely tied to the negative outcomes that have been previously outlined throughout this chapter.

Despite the exploratory suggestions of possible late-birthday benefits in soccer, *knock-on effects* of relative age at senior levels are well evidenced (Wiium et al., 2010). For instance, López de Subijana and Lorenzo (2018) demonstrated BQ1s were overrepresented (31%) across the entire population of Spain's highest male division (La Liga) in comparison to BQ4s (18%); albeit to a lesser extent when compared to Spain's national youth team players (BQ1 = 46 vs. BQ4 = 10%). Similarly, in Italy, Lupo et al. (2019) revealed the beginning of a senior career in male soccer was affected by relative age, whereby players born close to the start of the selection year were 2.7 times more likely to reach first and second Italian division, when compared to those born towards the end of the selection year. In fact, Yagüe et al. (2018) showed RAEs in nine of the top ten male senior professional leagues in Europe (Figure 10.4). Their results confirmed a greater representation of players born in BQ1 (ranging from 29–34%), compared to BQ4 (ranging from 14–27%) for all the leagues studied (with the exception of the Eerste Klasse A, Belgium). Interestingly, however, team ranking did not impact upon any RAEs across the leagues, which is converse to data at youth levels (e.g., Augste & Lames, 2011; Söderström et al., 2019; Verbeek et al., 2021).

Further knock-on effects of relative age were presented by Rađa et al. (2018), who analysed the birthdates of 1,332 first-tier and 1,992 second-tier players across England, France, Germany, Italy, and Spain. They found the number of players born in the first month of the calendar year to be twice the number of those born in the last month. Since RAEs in the second tiers were the same as the first tiers, the authors suggest that there is no 'second chance' for later born players. Similarly, Pérez-González et al. (2021) showed RAEs across the majority of U19–U21 international competitions, suggesting that the next generation of senior professional soccer talent is born under a relative age bias. With regards to market value, Gyimesi and Kehl (2021) showed an earlier birth date within the calendar year resulted in a higher value across several countries.

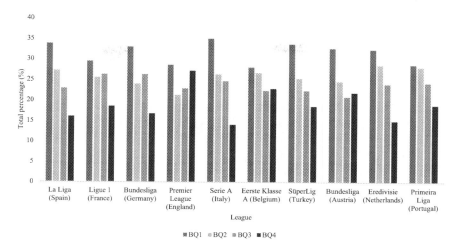

FIGURE 10.4 Birth quartile distribution of the ten best male European professional soccer leagues (adapted from Yagüe et al., 2018[5]).

Likewise, Romann et al. (2021) showed how the market value of young BQ1 players was initially overvalued in terms of performance and monetary, although this levelled out as players became older and more established.

Relative age effects can also vary according to playing position. For example, in male soccer, higher RAEs have been reported among defenders, whereas the impact varies across other playing positions (i.e., goalkeepers, midfielders, forwards) based on country and playing styles (Padrón-Cabo et al., 2016; Salinero et al., 2013; Yagüe et al., 2018). Several studies have also evaluated the role of playing position in moderating RAEs in female soccer and increased risk has been noted in some instances, particularly among female goalkeepers and defenders (e.g., Baker et al., 2009; Sedano et al., 2015), although results vary (Romann & Fuchslocher, 2013b). The exact mechanisms contributing to these trends has yet to be determined, but generally, a higher risk of RAEs is attributed to increased physical demands for a particular position (see Schorer et al., 2009 and Till et al., 2010 for discussion of playing position in other sport contexts).

Potential Relative Age Solutions

Since there appears to be pronounced RAEs across male and female soccer contexts, it is important to consider possible relative age solutions at youth levels. Grossmann and Lames (2013) advised governing bodies to include the relative age phenomena in *coach education*, with the purpose of enhancing grassroots practitioners' knowledge and understanding of RAEs as part of formal coaching courses. Mann and van Ginneken (2017) designed an *age-ordered shirt numbering system* as an explicit cue, which provides practitioners with knowledge that the numbers on individuals' playing shirts corresponded with their relative age. Tribolet et al. (2019) proposed *avoiding early deselection*, through encouraging practitioners to refrain releasing players at young ages to ensure they have continued exposure to practice, competition, and resources without the option or pressures of being deselected. Bennett et al. (2019) recommended a *selection quota*, whereby practitioners endorse policies that ensure clubs select a minimum number of players from each

BQ. Romann et al. (2020) suggested clubs and governing bodies should *delay the selection process* preferentially until post-maturation, in order to make more fair and accurate decisions based on potential and negate the possible drawbacks of early specialisation. Despite many suggestions in the literature, however, little research has evaluated such proposals in applied settings.

Literature on alternative grouping strategies to moderate RAEs is also limited when compared to the body of research demonstrating its prevalence. Where grouping strategies have been proposed, little evidence has documented their effectiveness or directly implemented such approaches (Webdale et al., 2020). Boucher and Halliwell (1991) presented the *novem system* as an age band modification tool through applying 9-month age groups, which would create a shift in relative age for each BQ every consecutive year. Hurley et al. (2001) suggested the *relative age fair cycle system* to rotate cut-off dates, with the purpose of each player spending time as both the oldest and youngest player across a given cohort. Kelly et al. (2020) conceptualised a *flexible chronological approach*, whereby early birth quartiles (i.e., BQ1 and BQ2) and late birth quartiles (i.e., BQ3 and BQ4) should be offered the opportunity to 'play-up' (e.g., Goldman et al., 2021; Kelly et al., 2021f) and 'play-down' annual age groups, respectively (see Chapter 11). Kelly et al. (2020) introduced birthday-banding, where young athletes move up to their next birthdate group on their birthday, with the aim to remove particular selection time-points and specific chronological age groups. Helsen et al. (2000) proposed setting the average age of a team to a predetermined maximum, which was thereafter designed more precisely as the *average team age* (ATA) (Figure 10.5) method by Lawrence et al. (2019)[6], which has since offered some positive outcomes during preliminary organised in-house youth soccer competitions[7],[8] (Verbeek et al., 2021).

Another useful strategy that may be utilised in soccer could be from the organisational policies incorporated in youth American football. More specifically, contrary to many other youth team sports, previous research has identified no RAEs in American football, which may lend credibility

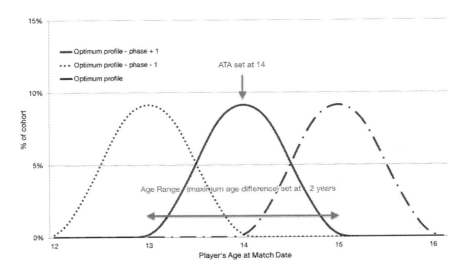

FIGURE 10.5 Optimum age profile (mean + range) during ATA competitions.

Note: The solid curve represents the age profile of the teams in any ATA competition, whereas the dotted curve represents the age profile of the ATA minus one competition, and the long-dash curve represents the age profile of the ATA plus one competition[9] (adapted from Verbeek et al., 2021[10]).

to the *age and anthropometric* bandings that are often employed to group their players (e.g., Jones et al., 2019; MacDonald et al., 2009). A similar grouping approach that has produced promising results in youth soccer is *bio-banding* (Bradley et al., 2019; Malina et al., 2019; Thomas et al., 2021), which groups young players based on anthropometric and maturational status (see Chapter 4). Both age and anthropometric banding and bio-banding appear to systematically address one of the key mechanisms of RAEs, whereby relatively older athletes may have an advanced growth status (Cobley et al., 2009). Although these approaches remain unproven in their impact on RAEs, an introduction to grouping players by height, weight, and/or some maturational variables may prove beneficial in moderating RAEs in youth soccer and thus warrants further study. Interestingly, preliminary research from Helsen et al. (2021) used both chronological age and maturity status to determine players' *estimated developmental birth dates*, revealing that BQs were more equally distributed once they were reallocated into these groups.

Considerations for Researchers

Despite the large amount of literature that has explored the presence of RAEs, few researchers have put forward theories to hypothesise how RAEs occur (e.g., Cobley et al., 2009; Hancock et al., 2013a; Kelly et al., 2022; Wattie et al., 2015). Moreover, only preliminary and exploratory studies have tested such hypotheses in applied settings as part of their empirical research. Thus, researchers are encouraged to incorporate theoretical frameworks as part of their methodologies to help better understand the explanatory factors of RAEs (Kelly et al., 2021a). By doing so, it will assist researchers and practitioners when designing, implementing, and evaluating strategies so they can directly moderate these effects.

The need to better understand the explanatory factors of RAEs is also underscored by the lack of qualitative and prospective studies. Researchers could utilise a qualitative approach to examine stakeholder perspectives to learn more about *how* and *why* RAEs operate in their respective settings (Turnnidge & Kelly, 2021). Moreover, prospective studies would enable the exploration of *how* and *why* RAEs evolve throughout talent development (e.g., reversal effects, stages of selection/deselection and dropout, career progression and longevity, performance outcomes at adulthood) (Schorer et al., 2020). Indeed, these approaches may shed light on the potential mechanisms (e.g., sport activities, social dynamics, growth and maturation) that may contribute to or detract from RAEs (Turnnidge et al., 2021).

What we do currently know, however, is that RAEs exist and that they are producing an inequitable youth soccer system. Therefore, researchers and practitioners are encouraged to work collaboratively to design, implement, and evaluate a range of alternative grouping strategies and relative age solutions in the immediate timescale. Although some proposed solutions demonstrate their potential to mitigate RAEs in youth soccer, it is important for future studies to consider how these approaches may also look in the long-term. In addition, since female cohorts remain underrepresented across relative age research, priority should be placed on these populations in order to capture an even-handed understanding about RAEs in soccer.

Considerations for Practitioners

The extent of RAEs have been shown to be contingent on several contextual factors, including age, competition level, country, gender, and playing position. Organisational structures and key stakeholders also influence RAEs through encouraging early selection procedures and emphasising performance-related outcomes. As such, the following considerations are offered to help mitigate such effects:

- Look beyond the misconception that physical characteristics are solely responsible for RAEs. Instead, consider holistic profiling (e.g., technical, tactical, physical, psychological, and social) to better understand how they occur.
- Some of the most prevalent RAEs occur during the youngest age groups at the highest competition levels (e.g., initial enrolment into an U9 academy). Since these players will (most likely) form the core of each successive age group for the proceeding years, relatively younger players will continue to be overlooked in the long-term. As a result, practitioners should reconsider the efficacy of formal selection practices at these ages.
- Although preliminary research has underscored the possible late-birthday benefits of RAEs (e.g., the underdog hypothesis), it appears the knock-on effects at senior levels are far more substantiated and, thus, should be acknowledged when designing age group structures and relative age strategies in youth soccer.
- Consider how to offer relatively younger players opportunities within talent development pathways, as well as how to leverage relative age differences to challenge all players to promote positive developmental outcomes.
- Work collaboratively with researchers to design, implement, and evaluate a range of potential relative age solutions. Indeed, research collaborations need to be prioritised by soccer organisations to develop and test interventions that could be adopted on a larger scale.

Conclusion

Looking back at the existing literature and observing the marked overrepresentation of early-born players across male and female talent development pathways, the findings challenge the efficacy of an unconscious bias towards relatively older players that permeates youth soccer. It also appears the implications of RAEs at youth levels have long-lasting effects at senior levels. This is particularly concerning, since the fate of a child's date of birth should not have enduring consequences on their subsequent opportunities in adulthood. Moving forward, it is vital that researchers and practitioners work collaboratively to challenge the existing annual age group structures that are commonly used by governing bodies and organisations in youth soccer.

Notes

1 See Table 5 in Smith et al. (2018).
2 This finding differs from comparable estimates for male athletes, where the greatest magnitude of risk has been identified in adolescent age groups (see Cobley et al., 2009 for a review).
3 A Chi-square analysis and visual inspection of the birth distribution were conducted to determine whether RAEs might be present in the initial cohort for this study. The analysis suggested an overrepresentation of relatively older participants was present in this sample with a small effect size.
4 Between ages ten–12 years, many players are not yet classified as competitive or recreational under Ontario Soccer's organisational structure and the birth distribution for these ages should be interpreted with caution.
5 The authors would like to thank José Yagüe, Alfonso de la Rubia, and colleagues for granting permissions to use their data to produce this figure.
6 In the ATA grouping method, the bandings apply to the team and not the individual, which comprises two components: (a) the average (mean) age of the starting team in a competition match shall

be no more than 'Y' years. In addition to setting the ATA, this grouping method also addresses the maximum range of players' ages competing in a team: (b) no player in the squad shall be more than 'Z' years older than the youngest player in the squad (see Verbeek et al., 2021 for an overview of the ATA method).
7 Stoke City Football Club Academy: www.stokecityfc.com/news/academy-trial-birth-bias-concept
8 Football Club Weesp and the Royal Dutch Football Association (KNVB): https://decorrespondent.nl/10913/waarom-deze-voetbalclub-experimenteert-met-een-gemiddelde-leeftijd-voor-jeugdteams/963707004645-0dbc4ba4
9 A player aged 13–15 years has the opportunity of playing in each of the ATA bands; as the oldest in the first team, as the average age in the second team, and as the youngest in the third team.
10 The authors would like to thank Jan Verbeek, Steve Lawrence, and colleagues for granting permissions to use their figure.

References

Andrew, M., Finnegan, L., Datson, N., & Dugdale, J. H. (2022). Men are from quartile one, women are from? Relative age effect in European soccer and the influence of age, success, and playing status. *Children*, *9*, 1747. https://doi.org/10.3390/children9111747

Ashworth, J., & Heyndels, B. (2007). Selection bias and peer effects in team sports: The effect of age grouping on earnings of German soccer players. *Journal of Sports Economics*, *8*(4), 355–377. https://doi.org/10.1177/1527002506287695

Augste, C., & Lames, M. (2011). The relative age effect and success in German elite U-17 soccer teams. *Journal of Sports Sciences*, *29*(9), 983–987. https://doi.org/10.1080/02640414.2011.574719

Baker, J., Janning, C., Wong, H., Cobley, S., & Schorer, J. (2014). Variations in relative age effects in individual sports: Skiing, figure skating and gymnastics. *European Journal of Sport Science*, *14*(1), 183–190. https://doi.org/10.1080/17461391.2012.671369

Baker, J., & Logan, A. (2007). Developmental contexts and sporting success: Birth date and birth-place effects in national hockey league draftees 2000–2005. *British Journal of Sports Medicine*, *41*(8), 515–517. https://doi.org/10.1136/bjsm.2006.033977

Baker, J., Schorer, J., Cobley, S., Bräutigam, H., & Büsch, D. (2009). Gender, depth of competition and relative age effects in team sports. *Asian Journal of Exercise & Sports Science*, *6*(1), 1–7.

Barnsley, R. H., Thompson, A. H., & Barnsley, P. E. (1985). Hockey success and birthdate: The relative age effect. *Canadian Association Health Physical Education & Recreation Journal*, *51*(8), 23–28.

Barnsley, R. H., Thompson, A. H., & Legault, P. (1992). Family planning: Football style. The relative age effect in football. *International Review for the Sociology of Sport*, *27*(1), 77–87. https://doi.org/10.1177/101269029202700105

Barrenetxea-Garcia, J., Torres-Unda, J., Esain, I., & Gil, S. M. (2018). Relative age effect and left-handedness in world class water polo male and female players. *Laterality*, *24*, 259–273. https://doi.org/10.1080/1357650X.2018.1482906

Bennett, K. J. M., Vaeyens, R., & Fransen, J. (2019). Creating a framework for talent identification and development in emerging football nations. *Science and Medicine in Football*, *3*(1), 36–42. https://doi.org/10.1080/24733938.2018.1489141

Bjerke, Ø., Pedersen, A. V., Aune, T. K., & Lorås, H. (2017). An inverse relative age effect in male alpine skiers at the absolute top level. *Frontiers in Psychology*, *8*, 1210. https://doi.org/10.3389/fpsyg.2017.01210

BoLun, Z., Lemez, S., Wattie, N., & Baker, J. (2018). A historical examination of relative age effects in major league baseball. *International Journal of Sport Psychology*, *49*(5), 448–463. https://doi.org/10.7352/IJSP2018.49.448

Boucher, J., & Halliwell, W. (1991). The Novem system: A practical solution to age grouping. *Canadian Association Health Physical Education & Recreation Journal*, *57*(1), 16–20.

Bradley, B., Johnson, D., Hill, M., McGee, D., Kana-ah, A., Sharpin, C., Sharp, P., Kelly, A., Cumming, S., & Malina, R. (2019). Bio-banding in academy football: Player's perceptions of a maturity matched tournament. *Annals of Human Biology*, *46*(5), 400–408. https://doi.org/10.1080/03014460.2019.1640284

Brustio, P. R., Kearney, P. E., Lupo, C., Ungureanu, A. N., Mulasso, A., Rainoldi, A., & Boccia, G. (2019). Relative age influences performance of world-class track and field athletes even in the adulthood. *Frontiers in Psychology, 10,* 1395. https://doi.org/10.3389/fpsyg.2019.01395

Brustio, P. R., Lupo, C., Ungureanu, A. N., Frati, R., Rainoldi, A., & Boccia, G. (2018). The relative age effect is larger in Italian soccer top-level youth categories and smaller in Serie a. *PLoS One, 13,* e0196253. https://doi.org/10.1371/journal.pone.0196253

Cobley, S. P., Baker, J., Wattie, N., & McKenna, J. (2009). Annual age-grouping and athlete development: A meta-analytical review of relative age effects in sport. *Sports Medicine, 39*(3), 235–256. https://doi.org/10.2165/00007256-200939030-00005

Cobley, S. P., & Till, K. (2017). Participation trends according to relative age across youth UK Rugby League. *International Journal of Sports Science & Coaching, 12*(3), 339–343. https://doi.org/10.1177%2F1747954117710506

Coutts, A., Kempton, T., & Vaeyens, R. (2014). Relative age effects in Australian football league national draftees. *Journal of Sports Sciences, 32*(7), 623–628. https://doi.org/10.1080/02640414.2013.847277

de la Rubia, A., Calvo, A. L., Bjørndal, C. T., Kelly, A. L., García-Aliaga, A., & Lorenzo-Calvo, J. (2021). The impact and evolutionary trend of relative age effects on the competition performance of Spanish international handball players: A longitudinal study from 2005 to 2020. *Frontiers in Psychology, 12,* 673434. https://doi.org/10.3389/fpsyg.2021.673434

Deaner, R., Lowen, A., & Cobley, S. (2013). Born at the wrong time: Selection bias in the NHL draft. *PLoS One, 8*(2), e57753. https://doi.org/10.1371/journal.pone.0057753

Delorme, N., Boiché, J., & Raspaud, M. (2010a) Relative age and dropout in French male soccer. *Journal of Sports Sciences, 28*(7), 717–722. https://doi.org/10.1080/02640411003663276

Delorme, N., Boiché, J., & Raspaud, M. (2010b). Relative age effects in female sport: A diachronic examination of soccer players. *Scandinavian Journal of Medicine & Science in Sports, 20*(3), 509–515. https://doi.org/10.1111/j.1600-0838.2009.00979.x.

Delorme, N., & Raspaud, M. (2009). The relative age effect in young French basketball players: a study on the whole population. *Scandinavian Journal of Medicine & Science in Sports, 19*(2), 235–242. https://doi.org/10.1111/j.1600-0838.2008.00781.x

Doncaster, G., Medina, D., Drobnic, F., Gómez-Díaz, A. J., & Unnithan, V. (2020). Appreciating factors beyond the physical in talent identification and development: Insights from the FC Barcelona sporting model. *Frontiers in Sports and Active Living, 2,* 91. https://doi.org/10.3389/fspor.2020.00091

Dugdale, J. H., McRobert, A. P., & Unnithan, V. B. (2021). "He's just a wee laddie": The relative age effect in male Scottish soccer. *Frontiers in Psychology, 12,* 633469. https://doi.org/10.3389/fpsyg.2021.633469

Figueiredo, A. J., Coelho-e-Silva, M. J., Cumming, S. P., & Malina, R. M. (2019). Relative age effect: Characteristics of youth soccer players by birth quarter and subsequent playing status. *Journal of Sports Sciences, 37*(6), 677–684. https://doi.org/10.1080/02640414.2018.1522703

Finnegan, L., Richardson, D., Littlewood, M., & McArdle, J. (2017). The influence of date and place of birth on youth player selection to a National Football Association elite development programme. *Science and Medicine in Football, 1,* 30–39. https://doi.org/10.1080/02640414.2016.1254807

Fumarco, L., Gibbs, B. G., Jarvis, J. A., & Rossi, G. (2017) The relative age effect reversal among the National Hockey League elite. *PLoS One, 12*(8), e0182827. https://doi.org/10.1371/journal.pone.0182827

Fumarco, L., & Rossi, G. (2018) The relative age effect on labour market outcomes—evidence from Italian football. *European Sport Management Quarterly, 18*(4), 501–516. https://doi.org/10.1080/16184742.2018.1424225

Furley, P., & Memmert, D. (2016). Coaches' implicit associations between size and giftedness: Implications for the relative age effect. *Journal of Sports Sciences, 34*(5), 459–466. https://doi.org/10.1080/02640414.2015.1061198

Gerdin, G., Hedberg, M., & Hageskog, C.A. (2018). Relative age effect in Swedish male and female tennis players born in 1998–2001. *Sports, 6,* 38. https://doi.org/10.3390/sports6020038

Gibbs, B. G., Jarvis, J. A., & Dufur, M. J. (2012). The rise of the underdog? The relative age effect reversal among Canadian-born NHL hockey players: A reply to Nolan and Howell. *International Review for the Sociology of Sport, 47*(5), 644–649. https://doi.org/10.1177/1012690211414343

Gil, S. M., Badiola, A., Bidaurrazaga-Letona, I., Zabala-Lili, J., Gravina, L., Santos-Concejero, J., & Granados, C. (2014). Relationship between the relative age effect and anthropometry, maturity and performance in young soccer players. *Journal of Sports Sciences, 32*(5), 479–485. https://doi.org/10.1080/02640414.2013.832355

Gil, S. M., Bidaurrazaga-Letona, I., Martin-Garetxana, I., Lekue, J. A., & Larruskain, J. (2019). Does birth date influence career attainment in professional soccer? *Science and Medicine in Football, 4*, 119–126. https://doi.org/10.1080/24733938.2019.1696471

Goldman, D. E., Turnnidge, J., Kelly, A. L., de Vos, J., & Côté, J. (2021). Athlete perceptions of "playing-up" in youth soccer. *Journal of Applied Sport Psychology, 34*(4), 862–885. https://doi.org/10.1080/10413200.2021.1875518

Grondin, S., Deshaies, P., & Nault, L. (1984). Trimestres de naissance et participation au hockey et au volleyball. *La Revue Quebecoise de l'Activite Physique, 2*, 97–103.

Grossmann, B., & Lames, M. (2013). Relative age effect (RAE) in football talents: The role of youth academies in transition to professional status in Germany. *International Journal of Performance Analysis in Sport, 13*(1), 120–134. https://doi.org/10.1080/24748668.2013.11868636

Gyimesi, A., & Kehl, D. (2021). Relative age effect on the market value of elite European football players: A balanced sample approach. *European Sport Management Quarterly* [ePub ahead of print]. https://doi.org/10.1080/16184742.2021.1894206

Hancock, D. J., Adler, A. L., & Côté, J. (2013a). A proposed theoretical model to explain relative age effects in sport. *European Journal of Sport Science, 13*(6), 630–637. https://doi.org/10.1080/17461391.2013.775352

Hancock, D. J., Ste-Marie, D. M., & Young, B. W. (2013b). Coach selections and the relative age effect in male youth ice hockey. *Research Quarterly for Exercise and Sport, 84*(1), 126–130. https://doi.org/10.1080/02701367.2013.762325

Helsen, W. F., Baker, J., Michiels, S., Scorer, J., Van Winckel, & Williams, M. A. (2012). The relative age effect in European professional soccer: Did ten years of research make any difference? *Journal of Sports Sciences, 30*(15), 1665–1671. https://doi.org/10.1080/02640414.2012.721929

Helsen, W. F., Starkes, J. L., & Van Winckel, J. (2000). Effect of a change in selection year on success in male soccer players. *American Journal of Human Biology, 12*(6), 729–735. https://doi.org/10.1002/1520-6300(200011/12)12:6<729::aid-ajhb2>3.0.co;2-7

Helsen, W. F., Thomis, M., Starkes, J. L., Vrijens, S., Ooms, G., MacMaster, C., & Towlson, C. (2021). Leveling the playing field: A new proposed method to address relative age- and maturity-related biases in soccer. *Frontiers in Sports and Active Living, 3*, 635379. https://doi.org/10.3389/fspor.2021.635379

Helsen, W. F., van Winckel, J., & Williams, A.M. (2005). The relative age effect in youth soccer across Europe. *Journal of Sports Sciences, 23*(6), 629–636. https://doi.org/10.1080/02640410400021310

Hirose, N. (2009). Relationships among birth-month distribution, skeletal age and anthropometric characteristics in adolescent elite soccer players. *Journal of Sports Sciences, 27*(11), 1159–1166. https://doi.org/10.1080/02640410903225145

Hurley, W., Lior, D., & Tracze, S. (2001). A proposal to reduce the age discrimination in Canadian minor hockey. *Canadian Public Policy—Analyse de Politiques, 27*(1), 65–75. https://doi.org/10.2307/3552374

Jackson, R. C., & Comber, G. (2020). Hill on a mountaintop: A longitudinal and cross-sectional analysis of the relative age effect in competitive youth football. *Journal of Sports Sciences, 38*, 1352–1358. https://doi.org/10.1080/02640414.2019.1706830

Jimenez, I. P., & Pain, M. T. (2008). Relative age effect in Spanish association football: Its extent and implications for wasted potential. *Journal of Sports Sciences, 26*(10), 995–1003. https://doi.org/10.1080/02640410801910285

Jones, B. D., Lawrence, G. P., & Hardy, L. (2018). New evidence of relative age effects in "super-elite" sportsmen: A case for the survival and evolution of the fittest. *Journal of Sports Sciences, 36*(6), 697–703. https://doi.org/10.1080/02640414.2017.1332420

Jones, C., Visek, A. J., Barron, M. J., Hyman, M., & Chandran, A. (2019). Association between relative age effect and organisational practices of American youth football. *Journal of Sports Sciences, 37*(10), 1146–1153. https://doi.org/10.1080/02640414.2018.1546545

Kelly, A. L., Brown, T., Reed, R., Côté, J., & Turnnidge, J. (2022). Relative age effects in male cricket: A personal assets approach to explain immediate, short-term, and long-term developmental outcomes. *Sports*, *10*(3), 39. https://doi.org/10.3390/sports10030039

Kelly, A. L., Côté, J., Turnnidge, J., & Hancock, D. (2021a). Editorial: Birth advantages and relative age effects. *Frontiers in Sports and Active Living*, *3*, 721704. https://doi.org/10.3389/fspor.2021.721704

Kelly, A. L., Jackson, D. T., Barrell, D., Burke, K., & Baker, J. (2021b). The relative age effect in international rugby union: Consequences of changing the cut-off date and exploring youth to senior transitions. *High Ability Studies* [ePub ahead of print]. http://doi.org/10.1080/13598139.2021.1997722

Kelly, A. L., Jackson, D. T., Barrell, D., Burke, K., & Till, K. (2021c). The relative age effect in male and female English age-grade rugby union: Exploring the gender-specific mechanisms that underpin participation. *Science and Medicine in Football*, *6*(3), 277–284. https://doi.org/10.1080/24733938.2021.1955145

Kelly, A. L., Jiménez Sáiz, S. L., Calvo, A. L., de la Rubia, A., Jackson, D. T., Jeffreys, M. A., Ford, C., Owen, D., & dos Santos, S. D. L. (2021d). Relative age effects in basketball: Exploring the selection into and successful transition out of a national talent pathway. *Sports*, *9*(7), 101. https://doi.org/10.3390/sports9070101

Kelly, A. L., Till, K., Jackson, D., Barrell, D., Burke, K., & Turnnidge, J. (2021e). Talent identification and relative age effects in English male rugby union pathways: From entry to expertise. *Frontiers in Sports and Active Living*, *3*, 640607. https://doi.org/10.3389/fspor.2021.640607

Kelly, A. L., & Williams, C. A. (2020). Physical characteristics and the talent identification and development processes in youth soccer: A narrative review. *Strength and Conditioning Journal*, *42*(6), 15–34. https://doi.org/10.1519/SSC.0000000000000576

Kelly, A. L., Wilson, M. R., Gough, L. A., Knapman, H., Morgan, P., Cole, M., Jackson, D. T., & Williams, C. A. (2020). A longitudinal investigation into the relative age effect in an English professional football club: Exploring the 'underdog hypothesis'. *Science and Medicine in Football*, *4*(2), 111–118. https://doi.org/10.1080/24733938.2019.1694169

Kelly, A. L., Wilson, M. R., Jackson, D. T., Goldman, D. E., Turnnidge, J., Côté, J., & Williams, C. A. (2021f). A multidisciplinary investigation into "playing-up" a chronological age group in an English football academy. *Journal of Sports Sciences*, *39*(8), 854–864. https://doi.org/10.1080/02640414.2020.1848117

Lawrence, S., Jonker, L., & Verbeek, J. (2019). The age advantage in youth football. In D. Karlis, I. Ntzoufras, & S. Drikos (Eds.), *Proceedings of the mathsport international congress* (pp. 228–233). Propobos Publications.

Li, Z., Mao, L., Steingröver, C., Wattie, N., Baker, J., Schorer, J., & Helsen, W. (2020). Relative age effects in Elite Chinese soccer players: Implications of the 'one-child' policy. *PLoS ONE*, *15*(2), e0228611. https://doi.org/10.1371/journal.pone.0228611

Lidor, R., Arnon, M., Maayan, Z., Gershon, T., & Côté, J. (2014). Relative age effect and birthplace effect in division 1 female ballgame players—The relevance of sport-specific factors. *International Journal of Sports and Exercise Psychology*, *12*(1), 19–33. https://doi.org/10.1080/1612197X.2012.756232

Liu, W., & Liu D. (2008). A research on the relative age effect among excellent youth female football players in China. *Journal of Beijing Sport University*, *31*(1), 135–7.

López de Subijana, C., & Lorenzo, J. (2018). Relative age effect and long-term success in the Spanish soccer and basketball national teams. *Journal of Human Kinetics*, *65*(1), 197–204. https://doi.org/10.2478/hukin-2018-0027

Lovell, R., Towlson, C., Parkin, G., Portas, M., Vaeyens, R., & Cobley, S. (2015). Soccer player characteristics in English lower-league development programmes: The relationships between relative age, maturation, anthropometry and physical fitness. *PLoS One*, *10*(9), e0137238. https://doi.org/10.1371/journal.pone.0137238

Lupo, C., Boccia, G., Ungureanu, A. N., Frati, R., Marocco, R., & Brustio, P. R. (2019). The beginning of senior career in team sport is affected by relative age effect. *Frontiers in Psychology*, *10*, 1465. https://doi.org/10.3389/fpsyg.2019.01465

MacDonald, D. J., Cheung, M., Côté, J., & Abernethy, B. (2009). Place but not date of birth influences the development and emergence of athletic talent in American football. *Journal of Applied Sport Psychology*, *21*(1), 80–90. https://doi.org/10.1080/10413200802541868

Malina, R. M., Cumming, S. P., Rogol, A. D., Coelho-e-Silva, M. J., Figueiredo, A. J., Konarski, J. M., & Kozieł, S. M. (2019). Bio-banding in youth sports: Background, concept, and application. *Sports Medicine*, *49*(11), 1671–1685. https://doi.org/10.1007/s40279-019-01166-x

Mann, D. L., & van Ginneken, P. J. M. A. (2017). Age-ordered shirt numbering reduces the selection bias associated with the relative age effect. *Journal of Sports Sciences*, *35*(8), 784–790. http://doi.org/10.1080/02640414.2016.1189588

Massa, M., Costa, E. C., Moreira, A., Thiengo, C. R., Lima, M. R., Marquez, W. Q., & Aoki M. S. (2014). The relative age effect in soccer: A case study of the Sao Paulo Football Club. *Revista Brasileira Cineantropometria e Desempenho Humano*, *16*(4), 399–405. http://doi.org/10.5007/1980-0037.2014v16n4p399

McCarthy, N., & Collins, D. (2014). Initial identification & selection bias versus the eventual confirmation of talent: Evidence for the benefits of a rocky road? *Journal of Sports Sciences*, *32*(17), 1604–1610. https://doi.org/10.1080/02640414.2014.908322

McCarthy, N., Collins, D., & Court, D. (2016). Start hard, finish better: Further evidence for the reversal of the RAE advantage. *Journal of Sports Sciences*, *34*(15), 1461–1465. https://doi.org/10.1080/02640414.2015.1119297

Merton, R. K. (1957). Priorities in scientific discovery: A chapter in the sociology of science. *American Sociological Review*, *22*(6), 635–659. https://doi.org/10.2307/2089193

Merton, R. K. (1968). The Matthew effect in science: The reward and communication systems of science are considered. *Science*, *159*(3810), 56–63. https://doi.org/10.1126/science.159.3810.56

Mikulič, M., Gregora, P., Benkovský, Ľ., & Peráček, P. (2015). The relative age effect on the selection in the slovakia national football teams. *Acta Facultatis Educationis Physicae Universitatis Comenianae*, *55*, 122–131. https://doi.org/10.1515/afepuc-2015-0013

Musch, J., & Grondin, S. (2001). Unequal competition as an impediment to personal development: A review of the relative age effect in sport. *Developmental Review*, *21*, 147–167. https://doi.org/10.1006/drev.2000.0516

Musch, J., & Hay, R. (1999). The relative age effect in soccer: Cross-cultural evidence for a systematic discrimination against children born late in the competition year. *Sociology of Sport Journal*, *16*(1), 54–64. https://doi.org/10.1123/ssj.16.1.54

Nakata, H., & Sakamoto, K. (2012). Sex differences in relative age effects among Japanese athletes. *Perceptual & Motor Skills*, *115*(1), 179–86. https://doi.org/10.2466/10.05.17.PMS.115.4.179-186

Ostapczuk, M., & Musch, J. (2013). The influence of relative age on the composition of professional soccer squads. *European Journal of Sport Science*, *13*(3), 249–255. https://doi.org/10.1080/17461391.2011.606841

Padrón-Cabo, A., Rey E., García-Soidán, J. L., & Penedo-Jamardo, E. (2016). Large scale analysis of relative age effect on professional soccer players in FIFA designated zones. *International Journal of Performance Analysis in Sport*, *16*(1), 332–346. https://doi.org/10.1080/24748668.2016.11868890

Patel, R., Nevill, A., Cloak, R., Smith, T., & Wyon, M. (2019). Relative age, maturation, anthropometry and physical performance characteristics of players within an elite youth football academy. *International Journal of Sports Science & Coaching*, *14*(6), 714–725. https://doi.org/10.1177/1747954119879348

Pérez-González, B., León-Quismondo, J., Bonal, J., Burillo, P., & Fernández-Luna, Á. (2021). The new generation of professional soccer talent is born under the bias of the RAE: Relative age effect in international male youth soccer championships. *Children*, *8*(12), 1117.

Rađa, A., Padulo, J., Jelaska, I., Ardigò, L. P., & Fumarco, L. (2018). Relative age effect and second-tiers: No second chance for later-born players. *PLoS One*, *13*(8), e0201795. https://doi.org/10.1371/journal.pone.0201795

Ramos-Filho, L., & Ferreira, M. P. (2021). The reverse relative age effect in professional soccer: An analysis of the Brazilian national league of 2015. *European Sport Management Quarterly*, *21*(1), 78–93. https://doi.org/10.1080/16184742.2020.1725089

Romann, M., & Fuchslocher, J. (2013a). Influences of player nationality, playing position, and height on relative age effects at women's under-17 FIFA World Cup. *Journal of Sports Sciences*, *31*(1), 32–40. https://doi.org/10.1080/02640414.2012.718442

Romann, M., & Fuchslocher, J. (2013b). Relative age effects in Swiss junior soccer and their relationship with playing position. *European Journal of Sport Science*, *13*(4), 356–363. https://doi.org/10.1080/17461391.2011.635699

Romann, M., Javet, M., Cobley, S., & Born, D. (2021). How relative age effects associate with football players' market values: Indicators of losing talent and wasting money. *Sports, 9*(7), 99. https://doi.org/10.3390/sports9070099

Romann, M., Rüeger, E., Hintermann, M., Kern, R., & Faude, O. (2020). Origins of relative age effects in youth football—A nationwide analysis. *Frontiers in Sports and Active Living, 2*, 591072. https://doi.org/10.3389/fspor.2020.591072

Rosenthal, R., & Jacobson, L. (1968). Pygmalion in the classroom. *The Urban Review, 3*(1), 16–20. https://doi.org/10.1007/BF02322211

Sæther, S. A. (2016). Relative age effect and its effect on playing time. *Montenegrin Journal of Sports Science and Medicine, 5*(1), 11–15.

Salinero, J. J., Pérez, B., Burillo, P., & Lesma, M. L. (2013). Relative age effect in European professional football. Analysis by position. *Journal of Human Sport & Exercise, 8*(4), 966–973. https://doi.org/10.4100/jhse.2013.84.07

Schorer, J., Cobley, S., Büsch, D., Bräutigam, H., & Baker, J. (2009). Influences of competition level, gender, player nationality, career stage, and player position on relative age effects. *Scandinavian Journal of Medicine & Science in Sports, 19*(5), 720–730. https://doi.org/10.1111/j.1600-0838.2008.00838.x

Schorer, J., Roden, I., Büsch, D., & Faber, I. (2020). Relative age effects are developmental! The necessity of looking at more than one time point. In J. C. Dixon, S. Horton, L. Chittle, & J. Baker (Eds.), *Relative age effects in sport: International perspective* (pp. 33–45). Routledge.

Sedano, S., Vaeyens, R., & Redondo, J. C. (2015). The relative age effect in Spanish female soccer players. Influence of the competitive level and a playing position. *Journal of Human Kinetics, 46*(1), 129–37. https://doi.org/10.1515/hukin-2015-0041

Skorski, S., Skorski, S., Faude, O., Hammes, D., & Meyer, T. (2016). The relative age effect in elite German youth soccer: Implications for a successful career. *International Journal of Sports Physiology and Performance, 11*, 370–376. https://doi.org/10.1123/ijspp.2015-0071

Smith, K. L., & Weir, P. L. (2020). Late birthday benefits: The "underdog hypothesis". In J. C. Dixon, S. Horton, L. Chittle, & J. Baker (Eds.), *Relative age effects in sport: International perspective* (pp. 71–82). Routledge.

Smith, K. L., & Weir, P. L. (2022). An examination of relative age and athlete dropout in female development soccer. *Sports, 10*(5), 79. https://doi.org/10.3390/sports10050079

Smith, K. L., Weir, P. L., Till, K., Romann, M., & Cobley, S. (2018). Relative age effects across and within female sport contexts: A systematic review and meta-analysis. *Sports Medicine, 48*(6), 1451–1478. https://doi.org/10.1007/s40279-018-0890-8

Söderström, T., Brusvik, P., & Lund, S. (2019). Factors underlying competitive success in youth football. A study of the Swedish national U15 football talent system. *Scandinavian Sport Studies Forum, 10*, 139–162.

Steingröver, C., Wattie, N., Baker, J., & Schorer, J. (2016). Does relative age affect career length in North American professional sports? *Sports Medicine—Open, 2*(1), 1–7. https://doi.org/10.1186/s40798-016-0042-3

Thomas, C., Oliver, J., & Kelly, A. L. (2021). Bio-banding in youth soccer: Considerations for researchers and practitioners. In A. L. Kelly, J. Côté, M. Jeffreys, & J. Turnnidge (Eds.), *Birth advantages and relative age effects in sport: Exploring organizational structures and creating appropriate settings* (pp. 125–156). Routledge.

Till, K., Cobley, S., Wattie, N., O'Hara, J., Cooke, C. B., & Chapman, C. (2010). The prevalence, influential factors and mechanisms of relative age effects in UK Rugby League. *Scandinavian Journal of Medicine & Science in Sports, 20*(2), 320–329. https://doi.org/10.1111/j.1600-0838.2009.00884.x

Tribolet, R., Watsford, M. L., Coutts, A. J., Smith, C., & Fransen, J. (2019). From entry to elite: The relative age effect in the Australian football talent pathway. *Journal of Science and Medicine in Sport, 22*(6), 741–745. https://doi.org/10.1016/j.jsams.2018.12.014

Turnnidge, J., & Kelly, A. L. (2021). Organizational structures: Looking back and looking ahead. In A. L. Kelly, J. Côté, M. Jeffreys, & J. Turnnidge (Eds.), *Birth advantages and relative age effects in sport: Exploring organizational structures and creating appropriate settings* (pp. 239–246). Routledge.

Turnnidge, J., Wright, E., & Matthews, E. (2021). Organizational structures in sport: Methodological considerations. In A. L. Kelly, J. Côté, M. Jeffreys, & J. Turnnidge (Eds.), *Birth advantages and relative age effects in sport: Exploring organizational structures and creating appropriate settings* (pp. 30–56). Routledge.

Verbeek, J., Lawrence, S., van der Breggen, J., Kelly, A. L., & Jonker, L. (2021). The average team age method and its potential to reduce relative age effects. In A. L. Kelly, J. Côté, M. Jeffreys, & J. Turnnidge (Eds.), *Birth advantages and relative age effects in sport: Exploring organizational structures and creating appropriate settings* (pp. 107–124). Routledge.

Vincent, J., & Glamser, F. D. (2006). Gender differences in the relative age effect among U.S. Olympic development program youth soccer players. *Journal of Sports Sciences, 24*(4), 405–413. https://doi.org/10.1080/02640410500244655

Wattie, N., & Baker, J. (2020). Relative age effects in female athletes. Similarities and differences highlight the nuances of this effect . . . If you know where to look. In J. C. Dixon, S. Horton, L. Chittle, & J. Baker (Eds.), *Relative age effects in sport: International perspectives* (pp. 46–56). Routledge.

Wattie, N., Cobley, S., & Baker, J. (2008). Towards a unified understanding of relative age effects. *Journal of Sports Sciences, 26*(13), 1403–1409. https://doi.org/10.1080/02640410802233034

Wattie, N., Schorer, J., & Baker, J. (2015). The relative age effect in sport: A developmental systems model. *Sports Medicine, 45*(1), 83–94. https://doi.org/10.1007/s40279-014-0248-9

Webdale, K., Baker, J., Schorer, J., & Wattie, N. (2020). Solving sport's "relative age" problem: A systematic review of proposed solutions. *International Review of Sport and Exercise Psychology, 13*(1), 187–204. https://doi.org/10.1080/1750984X.2019.1675083

Wiium, N., Atle-Lie, S., Ommundsen, Y., & Enksen, H. R. (2010). Does relative age effect exist among Norwegian professional soccer players? *International Journal of Applied Sports Sciences, 22*(2), 66–76. https://doi.org/10.24985/ijass.2010.22.2.66

Wrang, C., Rossing, N., Diernæs, R., Hansen, C., Dalgaard-Hansen, C., & Karbing, D. (2018). Relative age effect and the re-selection of Danish male handball players for national teams. *Journal of Human Kinetics, 63*(1), 33–41. https://doi.org/10.2478/hukin-2018-0004

Yagüe, J. M., de la Rubia, A., Sánchez-Molina, J., Maroto-Izquierdo, S., & Molinero, O. (2018). The relative age effect in the 10 best leagues of male professional football of the Union of European Football Associations (UEFA). *Journal of Sports Science & Medicine, 17*(3), 409–416.

11

PLAYING-UP AND PLAYING-DOWN

Conceptualising a 'Flexible Chronological Approach'

Adam L. Kelly, Daniel E. Goldman, Jean Côté, and Jennifer Turnnidge

Introduction

Young athletes are often clustered into fixed chronological age groups during organised youth sport in an attempt to foster equitable competition. Despite these efforts, biases in selection and participation remain prevalent throughout youth soccer (Baxter-Jones, 1995). Specifically, relative age effects (RAEs) have been widely reported, whereby players born earlier in the selection year are overrepresented in talent pathways, compared to those born later (see Cobley et al., 2009 for a review; see Chapter 10 for an overview). Moreover, early-maturing players are often identified as 'talented' due to their advanced physiological and psychosocial skill-sets, and are thus often selected ahead of their late-maturing, age-matched peers (see Cumming et al., 2017 for a review; see Chapter 4 for an overview). As such, it is important to consider practical solutions to these relative age and maturity-related biases by looking beyond fixed chronological age grouping in youth soccer.

In addition to these existing biases, it is also essential to consider the possible developmental drawbacks that are exacerbated by fixed chronological age groups. For example, there is often pressure from key stakeholders (e.g., players, coaches, parents, and policy makers) to search for more appropriate levels of challenge and developmental opportunities for high-achieving players (Taylor & Collins, 2019). One regular solution to this issue is for players to participate at higher age levels, which is commonly known as *playing-up* (Kelly et al., 2021b). In contrast, *playing-down* occurs when players participate at lower age levels. Playing-down may create more suitable developmental settings by promoting greater selection opportunities and increased participation amongst low-achieving players (Goldman et al., 2021).

The purpose of this chapter is to explore the concepts of playing-up and playing-down as well as to introduce a *flexible chronological approach* to capture the dynamic nature of sport settings that allow athletes to play-up and play-down, as necessary. Moreover, current research is supplemented with a discussion of the experiences of two male international soccer players who have played-up and played-down, respectively. Overall, this chapter is organised into three sections. First, an education context is used to introduce the topic of playing-up, propose considerations based on the Four Corner Model (i.e., technical/tactical, physical, psychological, and social sub-components;

The Football Association, 2020), and present a lived example of how playing-up has been experienced by an international soccer player. Second, the concept of playing-down is discussed, and another practical example is offered to showcase the possible outcomes of this method. Third, the phenomena of playing-up and playing-down are used to conceptualise a flexible chronological approach that can be applied to youth soccer organisations. Based on these key areas, considerations for both researchers and practitioners are provided to advance knowledge in this field.

Playing-Up

Playing-up involves adjusting athlete groupings so that dominant athletes in a given age group are offered the opportunity to play with older peers and experience more challenging learning environments. Although studies on playing-up are sparse, current literature in education suggests that, when students are grouped by ability rather than chronological age, there may be numerous benefits as well as drawbacks for youth. Methods of student grouping in education that compare to playing-up in sport include *ability grouping* (i.e., whereby students are placed into classes based on academic achievement; Neihart, 2007) and *acceleration* (i.e., whereby students enter into school early or skip a grade; Steenbergen-Hu et al., 2016). Although the research in schools is complex, findings generally indicate that ability grouping may benefit students' academic achievement (Tieso, 2005) and attitudes toward their schoolwork (Kulik & Kulik, 1982). More recently, however, Becker et al. (2014) noted that students who transferred to an academically selective school reported higher anxiety and lower self-concept than those who did not. This evidence suggests that, while ability grouping may improve students' academic performance, their self-concept may decrease when they compare themselves to similarly high-achieving peers and realise that they do not stand out.

With regards to acceleration, past studies in education have shown promising results in terms of its effects on students' academic achievement and psychosocial development. Meta-analyses conducted by Kulik and Kulik (1982) and Steenbergen-Hu and Moon (2011) suggested that high-achieving, accelerated students recorded higher academic achievement than their non-accelerated peers. From a psychosocial perspective, researchers have suggested that a youth's mental age (i.e., how old an average person with their intellect would be) may be a greater determinant of their emotional maturity compared to their chronological age (e.g., Janos & Robinson, 1985). This suggestion is supported by the findings of Sayler and Brookshire (1993), who found that high-achieving students who skipped a grade had greater socio-emotional development and engaged in fewer problem behaviours than those who did not.

Collectively, the bodies of literature on ability grouping and acceleration in schools suggest that accelerated learning has the potential to facilitate youth's holistic development, but it can also lead to diminished psychosocial assets. In an attempt to further understand the mechanisms of playing-up in sport, two studies were conducted to investigate *what* factors differentiated players who played-up from those who did not, as well as *how* and *why* playing-up may have affected players' sport-specific skill and psychosocial outcomes.

Playing-Up in Youth Soccer

In the context of soccer, Kelly et al. (2021b) and Goldman et al. (2022) explored playing-up from a quantitative and qualitative perspective, respectively. First, Kelly et al. (2021b) collected data from 98 male players ($n = 28$ playing-up; $n = 70$ non-playing-up) from an English professional soccer academy. The participants represented two age phases, including the foundation development phase (FDP) (from U9 to U11) and the youth development phase (YDP) (from U12 to U16). The authors measured 27 developmental factors over the course of one season, and they used univariate regression and t-tests to assess significant differences between players who did and did not play-up. They then used multivariate regression to test the percentage variance predicted by playing-up amongst the factors that were significant or near-significant. Their results revealed a wide range of factors that differentiated English academy soccer players who played-up from those who did not. Broadly, their study highlighted the multidimensional nature of the player development process that was implicated through playing-up and dependent on age phase.

Second, Goldman et al. (2022) conducted semi-structured interviews with 17 players who played-up ($n = 5$ females; $n = 12$ males) from four soccer clubs in Ontario, Canada. During the interviews, players discussed the activities, social dynamics, and settings involved in playing-up. The researchers sought to investigate the players' perceptions of playing-up and the processes by which it may have affected their development. Overall, the players perceived playing-up to involve a combination of *challenge* and *progress*. However, the authors noted that participants' perceptions of playing-up varied greatly from player to player. As such, Goldman et al. (2022) emphasised their understanding of playing-up as a heterogeneous experience that would be inappropriate to examine using a 'one-size-fits-all' approach. Therefore, it is important to adopt a multidisciplinary approach to playing-up by contextualising its different processes and outcomes. A multidisciplinary approach to athlete development has been emphasised in many developmental models over the years (Bruner et al., 2010). Specific to soccer, the Four Corner Model (The Football Association, 2020) can be used to understand global player development and acts as a salient framework that is useful for practitioners to interpret academic findings in soccer, which is particularly important for integrating theory into practice (Turnnidge & Kelly, 2021).

From a technical/tactical perspective, players who play-up may exhibit greater ball maintenance and execution of accurate actions, compared to those who do not (Kelly et al., 2020b). Technical and tactical outcomes may differentiate players who play-up from those who do not because coaches may place greater value on these outcomes, compared to others. Indeed, previous research has noted that coach education tends to focus more on teaching technical and tactical skills over psychosocial development, which may contribute to this finding (Côté et al., 2010; Lefebvre et al., 2016). In addition, playing-up may benefit players' sport-specific skill development by exposing them to diverse experiences and environments. Previous research shows that athletes' sampling of diverse activities within a sport may benefit their continued engagement in that sport (Côté & Vierimaa, 2014; Murata et al., 2021). In addition, when youth soccer players are surrounded by highly skilled peers, current evidence suggests that they may adjust their self-expectations and develop positive habits related to self-regulation (Cumming et al., 2018). However, when the time demands of playing-up become overwhelming, players may no longer have fun when they play-up, which could lead to dropout (Goldman et al., 2022). Overall, preliminary findings suggest that playing-up may facilitate diverse sport experiences and contribute to higher expectations for performance, both of which may be conducive to player development. In contrast, the increased responsibilities of playing-up may negatively affect players' enjoyment and motivation.

Playing-up in soccer may benefit players' physical development in similar ways to how it may benefit their technical/tactical development. For example, players' engagement with faster and stronger peers may affect their expectations for fitness as well as skill (Kelly et al., 2021b). Additionally, players who play-up may outperform those who do not because they have attained a higher percentage of their predicted adult height (i.e., an indicator of early-maturity status), resulting in greater physical capabilities (Malina et al., 2019). Kelly et al. (2021b) noted that enhanced maturity and fitness may contribute to playing-up in soccer amongst players aged 12–16 years. Coaches may select players to play-up to encourage them to rely on their skills, rather than their physical strength, to succeed; however, they may also mistake players' maturity for ability (Baxter-Jones et al., 1995; Cobley et al., 2009). Conversely, soccer players may perceive playing-up to involve a greater risk of injury—which represents an impairment to physical development—due to more aggressive play or overtraining (Goldman et al., 2022). Thus, players who play-up may have advanced maturity status and greater fitness measures, but they may also face a higher risk of injury compared to players who compete in their chronological age group.

In terms of the psychological benefits of playing-up, soccer players may perceive improvements in their ability to cope with pressure, and they may also gain access to an effective support system that allows them to compete to their potential. These trends are more likely to be observed amongst players who have accumulated more years of playing-up, and thus, had more time to develop their sport-specific skill and psychosocial outcomes (Kelly et al., 2021b). Furthermore, players who perform well and interact socially with older peers may perceive large increases in competence and confidence, as they recognise they are overcoming adversity by being relatively younger (Collins et al., 2016). This effect is supported by previous research on ability grouping in education, whereby high-achieving students may experience increased self-confidence because they feel proud to be grouped with other high-achievers (Cialdini et al., 1976). Contrastingly, when players fall short of the standards set by older peers, they may experience discouragement or burnout. This result is consistent with previous findings in motivation research that showed that athletes who assess their sport success based on peer comparisons or performance, rather than goal orientation or athlete identity, may be more likely to burn out or drop out (Duda, 1987; Gustafsson et al., 2018). As such, when players who play-up compare themselves to older peers, these comparisons may increase players' competence and confidence when they are successful, but they may decrease these outcomes when players make mistakes or fail to connect with older peers.

Finally, playing-up in soccer may offer social benefits to players because it represents a source of social capital and provides a context for players to learn about the social standards of older peer groups. For one, players may gain confidence if they are recognised for playing-up by their coaches or same-aged peers. From a different perspective, playing-up in youth soccer is associated with greater involvement in diverse soccer activities (e.g., coach-led practice and peer-led play), compared to playing at one's chronological age level (Kelly et al., 2021b). When players engage in a wide range of activities within the same sport, they are exposed to rich social experiences that may help them interact more confidently with different peer groups (Goldman et al., 2022). However, when players first start to play-up, they may find it hard to connect with older peers due to a lack of common ground. Therefore, while playing-up may enhance players' social capital and expose them to diverse social comparisons (e.g., Gibbs et al., 2012; Jarvis, 2007), they may become isolated if they are not provided with opportunities to engage socially with others.

Preliminary Guidelines for Playing-Up

Based on our emerging knowledge of the benefits and drawbacks of playing-up, it is recommended that coaches and practitioners consider a variety of factors when assessing youth soccer players' suitability to play-up. Figure 11.1 contextualises research from Kelly et al. (2021b) quantitative findings and Goldman et al. (2022) qualitative analysis within the context of the Four

156 Adam L. Kelly et al.

Technical/Tactical
- Advanced skill behaviors (i.e., dribble completion; pass completion; reliability in possession; total touches)
- Higher performance on technical tests (i.e., ball juggling; lob pass; shooting accuracy; slalom dribble)
- Superior perceptual-cognitive expertise

Psychological
- Greater motivation to develop expertise
- Higher perceived ability to cope with performance and developmental pressures
- Higher perceived support from others (e.g., coaches, teammates, and parents) to compete to their potential
- More experiences of sport-specific and psychosocial success

Physical
- Ability to cope with intensity
- Faster sprint speed (i.e., 0-10 m; 0-30 m)
- Greater percentage of estimated adult height attained (i.e., advanced maturity status)
- Higher countermovement jump height

Social
- Ability to fit in with older peers
- Higher level of recognition from others
- More engagement in sport-related activities (i.e., coach-led practice; peer-led play; total soccer and multisport hours)
- Relatively older (i.e., first or second birth quarter)

FIGURE 11.1 Considerations for coaches and practitioners to reflect upon when selecting players to play-up within the context of the Four Corner Model.

Corner Model. This figure provides a visual representation of some of the technical/tactical, physical, psychological, and social factors that soccer coaches and practitioners may consider when making decisions about whether players should play-up. Given the limited body of evidence on which these factors are based, it is advised that coaches and practitioners do not consider this list to be exhaustive. Rather, Figure 11.1 shows a list of considerations that could be used as a guide for policies about playing-up in organised youth soccer. In the following section, a case study is presented to illustrate how the factors shown in Figure 11.1 are considered in the real-life experiences of a professional soccer player who has participated in playing-up.

Playing-Up: A Case Study

In order to better understand the long-term development outcomes of playing-up, it is important to draw from the experiences of those who have participated at higher age levels and subsequently achieved expertise. One such example is England international and Manchester United FC defender Harry Maguire. When a television interviewer questioned Maguire about his "first memory" in soccer, he reflected on playing-up for his local youth club:

> I always played a year above because my brother was a year older than me, so I played in his team, which made it easier for travel for my parents. It probably helped me in the long run to get used to playing with better players and better ability.
>
> *(Sky Sports, 2020, 0:57–1:11)*

Maguire's experiences of playing-up resonate with Goldman et al. (2022) higher order themes of challenge and progress. For instance, Maguire states how playing-up may have supported his development through "playing with better players" who have "better ability", which may contribute to perceptions of challenge. Moreover, Maguire suggests that he "always played a year above", which he believed may have "helped" his development in the "long run" towards expertise. This example highlights the possible benefits of playing-up as a strategy to facilitate perceptions of progress.

Overall, Maguire's story provides a practical example of how the playing-up experience may shape athletes' developmental trajectories. Nonetheless, it is important to be cognizant of potential 'survivorship bias' (e.g., Smith, 2014), in that we are more likely to hear the stories of those for whom playing-up was a positive experience. Furthermore, Maguire's account of his experiences also does not fully capture the mechanisms by which playing-up may have affected his long-term development. How, if at all, did competing with and against older players facilitate his development? In what ways was he supported by his social network (e.g., teammates, coaches, parents, and siblings)? If he perceived playing-up as an opportunity to progress in soccer, how did this perception affect his psychosocial development? While it is beyond the scope of this chapter to answer these questions, the phenomenon of playing-up certainly offers a host of possible directions for future research.

Playing-Down

Drawing from an education context, playing-down in youth soccer may be compared to *grade retention* (i.e., being held back a grade in school) or *academic redshirting* (i.e., delaying entry into school). Interestingly, previous research shows that grade retention may have negative effects on student outcomes. As an example, Jimerson et al. (2002) conducted a systematic review on the relationship between grade retention and dropout amongst high school students. Across 17 studies, students who were held back were 2–11 times more likely to drop out than those who were not. More recently, researchers showed that grade retention had neither positive nor negative effects on students' attendance and discipline, although it was associated with a decrease in students' motivation (Kretschmann et al., 2019; Martorell & Mariano, 2018). In contrast, academic redshirting may increase children's likelihood of success in school by affording them an extra year of development (Datar, 2006). Youth's delayed entry into school may also prevent them from facing negative emotions as a result of being held back later in their academic career.

In the context of sport, parents may 'redshirt' their children if they are relatively younger within their chronological age group or if they lack the athletic or social skills needed to flourish amongst their same-aged peers (Hancock et al., 2021; McNamara et al., 2004). While the potential influence of academic redshirting on youth's development in sport is unclear and warrants further investigation, there appears to be a common perception amongst parents that academic redshirting helps youth develop physically as well as cognitively (NICHD Early Child Care Research Network, 2007). Overall, current literature in education and sport outlines the potential benefits and drawbacks of moving relatively younger individuals into lower age groups, such as in the case of playing-down. As the implications of playing-down have yet to be empirically evaluated in youth soccer, some foundational knowledge is offered to inform future directions.

Playing-Down in Youth Soccer

Playing-down is primarily used to moderate growth and maturation as well as relative age biases in youth soccer (e.g., Malina et al., 2019). From a growth and maturation perspective, playing-down could be a useful strategy for late-maturing players. Indeed, matching players based on maturity status has revealed positive developmental outcomes for late-maturing individuals. For example, following their experiences of competing in 'bio-banded' tournaments, late-maturing soccer players reported greater opportunities to engage in leadership behaviours, influence gameplay, and express themselves on the ball. Moreover, the players perceived bio-banded games to be less physically challenging than chronological age-banded games (Bradley et al., 2019; Cumming et al., 2018). In addition, two recent studies showed that bio-banded players in youth soccer completed significantly more tackles and fewer long passes (Abbott et al., 2019), while covering significantly less distance jogging, running, and high-speed running, compared to players who were grouped by chronological age (Romann et al., 2020). Collectively, these examples demonstrate that, when the method of grouping is manipulated to moderate maturity biases, there may be significant implications for athletes' technical/tactical, physical, psychological, and social development.

With regards to moderating RAEs, youth soccer players who are born later in the selection year may warrant the opportunity to play-down due to being considerably younger than their age-matched peers. As such, playing-down may create a more suitable developmental setting by moderating RAEs (i.e., promoting greater selection opportunities and increased participation) and preventing dropout amongst relatively younger players (Delorme et al., 2011; Hancock et al., 2013). More specifically, if a player is born in the last month of the selection year, they are only 1 month away from being in the annual age-group below, whereas they could be up to 12 months younger than their age-matched peers in their chronological age group (Kelly et al., 2020a). Logically, if those players who are selected to play-up are more physically developed, earlier-maturing, and relatively older than others in their age group (e.g., Kelly et al., 2021b), the opposite of these variables might be considered when deciding to play-down youth soccer players. Further research is required to explore whether playing-down may be a useful option for those who are less physically developed, later-maturing, and relatively younger than their same-aged peers.

Besides physical characteristics, as highlighted previously, technical/tactical, psychological, and social factors must also be considered for players who may play-down. For example, skill development opportunities, emotional maturity, and existing peer relationships are additional factors that could be measured and should be considered (Sarmento et al., 2018). Indeed, young players should be viewed in a holistic manner through understanding the potential variation and interaction of these characteristics. It is also important to recognise that selecting a player to compete against relatively younger peers may create a perception that they are less able or do not have the potential to succeed at senior professional levels. Malina et al. (2019) suggest that such concerns can be educated through highlighting how several 'late-developing' professional soccer players have played-down during various stages of their development, such as Alex Oxlade-Chamberlain (Southampton FC Academy), Jesse Lingard, and Danny Welbeck (both Manchester United FC Academy).

Playing-Down: A Case Study

Another successful example of a player who played-down is England international and Manchester City FC defender John Stones. When a television interviewer questioned Stones about his "first tears" in soccer, he reflected on his youth experience at Barnsley FC Academy when his coach told him he was going to play-down:

> When I got dropped actually . . . I was about, from, say 12 to 13 years old, and I got told I was going to be playing-down for a few years because I was too small. And my coach actually told me that session, and I had to still train with my mates and all my teammates, and I was so upset. . . . People don't realise that you have those setbacks and how much it means to you, but it definitely made me stronger.

(Sky Sports, 2019, 0:59–1:31)

Based on this short quotation, there are three interesting observations to take away from Stones' playing-down experience. First, he was asked to play-down because he was "too small" during key pubertal years for boys (e.g., aged 12–16 years), which suggests that he may have relatively younger (i.e., he was born in the third birth quartile [March to May in England] for his chronological age group) as well as potentially late-maturing. During these adolescent years, there can be up to 5 years' difference in biological age between athletes in the same chronological age groups, which may exacerbate physiological biases (Kelly & Williams, 2020). As such, playing-down at these age levels may be advantageous because it allows late-developers to compete against maturity-matched peers.

Second, it is evident that Stones remembers playing-down as a challenging experience during his development, thus highlighting the possible stigma associated with playing-down. In fact, Stones labelled playing-down as being "dropped", and since being dropped can be associated with negative emotions (e.g., disheartenment, embarrassment, and rejection), this term may not accurately capture the intended outcomes of playing-down. Therefore, it is necessary to educate stakeholders (e.g., athletes, teammates, coaches, and parents) to better understand and positively support the playing-down process. Lastly, it is interesting to hear Stones' story of how the playing-down experience was an important part of his athletic journey. His experiences highlight the dynamic nature of the athlete development process, in which athletes can be exposed to a 'rocky road' effect (i.e., an opportunity to develop psychosocial skills in response to adversity), which could be considered an important process for preparing athletes to overcome future challenges (Collins et al., 2016). In considering these experiences, it is important for researchers and practitioners to create support systems for athletes throughout their developmental trajectory.

Just as not all soccer players who play-up achieve expertise, so, too, does playing-down not guarantee successful development. Thus, Stones' experiences must not be interpreted as a recipe for achieving professional status. More information is needed to understand *how* and *why* playing-down may have affected Stones' development. How, if at all, did the physical environment suit his developmental needs? In what ways did his social network support his confidence? If he perceived playing-down as a setback, how did this perception affect his psychosocial development? The existing literature is not comprehensive enough to answer these questions in this chapter; however, they provide several avenues for further research.

Conceptualising a Flexible Chronological Approach

Together, playing-up and playing-down offer useful strategies to promote equity in youth soccer and may provide players with a more appropriate learning environment. In the context of education, *multi-age classes* have been shown to benefit students' development, especially at the primary school level (Song et al., 2009). For instance, Ong et al. (2000) revealed that students had greater achievement in mathematics when they engaged in multi-age classes, compared to single-age classes. In addition, Aina (2001) suggested that students in multi-age classes created realistic self-expectations because they recognised that their peers were all at different levels. In the context of playing-up and playing-down, this evidence suggests that youth soccer players may benefit in terms of their sport-specific skill and psychosocial outcomes if coaches and practitioners apply flexible age groups (see also Balish & Côté, 2014).

Within a youth soccer setting, Kelly et al. (2020b) termed the adoption of playing-up and playing-down as a *flexible chronological approach* (FCA), as opposed to a traditional fixed chronological approach. During their investigation into RAEs at a professional soccer academy, the authors suggested that playing-up may facilitate greater development for players born early in the selection year by creating a 'birth quarter four effect' (i.e., players who are relatively older within their age group become relatively younger by playing-up against older peers). If the relatively oldest players in a given age group play-up, this may provide more openings for relatively younger players to be selected into youth soccer academies at their chronological age levels. In this way, playing-up may mediate the lower participation levels and higher dropout rates that have been documented amongst relatively younger players (e.g., Figueiredo et al., 2009; Helsen et al., 1998).

Likewise, playing-down may offer a more suitable developmental setting for later-born players whilst they 'catch-up' with their relatively older peers, while possibly offering a more challenging environment for earlier-born players in a younger age group. Moreover, rather than competing in a 'fixed' chronological age group (i.e., being relatively older or relatively younger throughout development), playing-up and playing-down facilitate more diverse experiences throughout players' developmental pathways (i.e., opportunities to be both relatively older *and* relatively younger; Jarvis, 2007; Kelly et al., 2020b, 2021b). Whilst these examples focus on how RAEs could be moderated, other performance-related outcomes could also be mediated through a FCA, such as maturation status, technical and tactical skills, and psychosocial behaviours. Therefore, further empirical research is required to explore how a FCA can be used to foster rich sport experiences that facilitate long-term athlete development. Collaboration between researchers and practitioners is encouraged to explore the lived sport experiences of those who play-up and play-down, to gain a better understanding of the technical/tactical, physical, psychological, and social processes that affect their development.

This chapter has offered two contrasting experiences of international players (i.e., Harry Maguire and John Stones) who have played-up and played-down during their respective trajectories towards expertise. When considering the diverse nature of Maguire (i.e., played-up) and Stones' (i.e., played-down) experiences, they have both led to the same outcome of achieving senior professional status at two high-profile English clubs. Moreover, to illustrate the similar nature of their performance outcomes at adulthood, both players competed together as England's first-choice central defenders at the 2018 World Cup in Russia. Although it is important to highlight that playing-up and playing-down do not necessarily lead to expertise and may not benefit certain individuals, the examples of Maguire and Stones illustrate that the talent pathway towards expertise is not a one-size-fits-all approach (Goldman et al., 2022; Kelly et al., 2021b). Thus, stakeholders employed in youth soccer settings should consider how a FCA *may* create more appropriate settings based on individual and contextual circumstances (Kelly et al., 2021a). Coaches and practitioners should strive to use a FCA to ensure that athletes' sport experiences are developmentally appropriate, meaningful for the individual, and aligned with their specific sport context.

When designing, implementing, and evaluating a FCA, it is important to consider the activities, social dynamics, and settings (Côté et al., 2014, 2020; Vierimaa et al., 2017), along with the youth sport policies and organisational structures that currently exist. Within the context of youth soccer, practice and competition are generally constructed around fixed chronological age groups, which directly impacts the potential for young soccer players to play-up and play-down. However, professional youth soccer academies in England offer a more flexible approach to allow players to move freely between age groups based on the decisions of stakeholders (The Premier League, 2011), which are mainly constructed through their subjective opinions and objective data (Sieghartsleitner et al., 2019). This is possibly due to the non-competitive nature of English academy soccer formats from U9 to U15 (e.g., no league tables) as well as the ownership placed on an individual club's philosophy, rather than competition-driven policies (e.g., league regulations; The Premier League, 2011).

A FCA could be utilised to create a more developmentally friendly environment, as opposed to adopting a performance-focused approach. However, particularly in the case of playing-down, some stakeholders have the potential to exploit a FCA system by selecting players to play outside their chronological age groups to gain a competitive advantage (e.g., to try and win at all costs). Accordingly, stakeholders are encouraged to work collaboratively when implementing a FCA to ensure the most appropriate learning environment is available for every player to achieve their full potential (Verbeek et al., 2021). Moreover, the removal of performance-related outcomes (e.g., no scores kept) and a greater emphasis placed on developmental outcomes (e.g., psychosocial skills) may help to achieve these intended aims (McCalpin et al., 2017). Education programmes could also be required in order to help stakeholders better understand the mechanisms of a FCA (Kelly et al., 2021a).

Considerations for Researchers

Further study is needed to advance what is currently known about the relationship between playing-up, playing-down, and youth soccer players' holistic development. For example, research is warranted to explore differences in player, coach, parent, and teammate perceptions of playing-up based on context (e.g., sport, race, gender, socioeconomic status, and sociocultural status) (Côté & Gilbert, 2009). Future studies are also needed to examine the influence of playing-up on players' immediate (e.g., enjoyment, interest), short-term (e.g., competence, confidence, connection, and character; the 4Cs) and long-term (e.g., performance, participation, and personal development; the 3Ps) developmental outcomes (Côté et al., 2014, 2020; Vierimaa et al., 2017). The data from these studies could then be used to reform playing-up policies so that players can benefit from their own recommendations (Goldman et al., 2021).

With regards to playing-down, research is needed to examine the characteristics of players who have played-down, compared to those who have not, to inform an evidence-based support system and decision-making process. Moreover, by qualitatively exploring players' playing-down experiences, researchers and practitioners could better understand the mechanisms that underlie this strategy. In addition, since playing-down can be coupled with the stigma of being 'dropped', effective educational approaches require further investigation. Lastly, the conceptualisation of a FCA is proposed to capture the phenomena of playing-up and playing-down. In light of this new concept, it is important to design, implement, and evaluate its effectiveness before it is formally incorporated into youth sport policies. Researchers are encouraged to work collaboratively with practitioners, clubs, and governing bodies to better understand the immediate, short-term, and long-term developmental outcomes of a FCA.

Considerations for Practitioners

These practical considerations for playing-up, playing-down, and a FCA are based on the available, yet limited, pool of evidence. Therefore, youth soccer organisations and practitioners are encouraged to interpret these considerations as guidelines that should be adapted to different contexts:

- In the FDP, technical/tactical and social characteristics appear to differentiate players who play-up compared to those who do not. In the YDP, however, there are significant measures representing all four sub-components of the Four Corner Model. It is important that

practitioners consider these holistic factors when considering to play-up youth soccer players within both age phases.
- Players perceived playing-up to involve a combination of challenge and progress. Youth players are more likely to experience sport-specific skill and psychosocial development as a result of playing-up when practitioners and teammates provide them with welcoming introductions, constructive feedback, and opportunities to show their skills.
- Playing-up and playing-down may offer a more suitable developmental setting for players to engage with peers of a similar relative age (i.e., relatively older or younger) or maturity level (i.e., earlier- or later-maturing).
- It is important to recognise that selecting a player to play-down may create a perception that they are less able or do not have the same potential as their age-matched peers. Thus, it is necessary to treat the subject sensitively, as it could lead to unintended consequences. Education amongst stakeholders (e.g., players, teammates, parents, and practitioners) and a positive support network are required to constructively facilitate the playing-down process.
- Youth soccer practitioners should consider how a FCA *may* create more appropriate settings that support players in improving engagement and reaching their full potential. Practitioners are encouraged to collaborate with researchers to design, implement, and evaluate the impact of a FCA before it is formally incorporated into youth soccer policies.

Conclusion

While often adopted as strategies to create more appropriate learning environments, little is known about the mechanisms and experiences associated with playing-up and playing-down in youth soccer. Preliminary and exploratory studies that have examined playing-up in youth soccer illustrate its possible benefits and drawbacks. Playing-up may benefit youth development by engaging players in diverse sport and social activities with skilled peers. However, playing-up may also contribute to burnout or dropout due to negative peer comparisons, social isolation, or injury (e.g., Goldman et al., 2022; Kelly et al., 2021b; Sky Sports, 2020). In contrast, playing-down is yet to be empirically studied in sport. Evidence from grey literature suggests that, although it may offer useful long-term developmental outcomes, there may be potential negative consequences during players' immediate and short-term experiences (e.g., Malina et al., 2019; Sky Sports, 2019). The terminology of a FCA is used to represent the malleable nature and policy of allowing players to compete outside their fixed chronological age groups. Moving forward, future research is warranted to explore the lived experiences of players who have played-up and played-down, as well as design, implement, and evaluate the organisational structures that capture a FCA.

References

Abbott, W., Williams, S., Brickley, G., & Smeeton, N. (2019). Effects of bio-banding upon physical and technical performance during soccer competition: A preliminary analysis. *Sports*, 7(8), 8–10. https://doi.org/10.3390/sports7080193

Aina, O. E. (2001). Maximizing learning in early childhood multiage classrooms: Child, teacher, *and parent perceptions. Early Childhood Education Journal*, 28(4), 219–224. https://doi.org/10.1023/A:1009590724987

Balish, S., & Côté, J. (2014). The influence of community on athletic development: An integrated case study. *Qualitative Research in Sport, Exercise, and Health*, 6, 98–120. https://doi.org/10.1080/2159676X.2013.766815

Baxter-Jones, A. (1995). Growth and development of young athletes: Should competition be age related? *Sports Medicine, 20*(2), 59–64. https://doi.org/10.2165/00007256-199520020-00001

Becker, M., Neumann, M., Tetzner, J., Böse, S., Knoppick, H., Maaz, K., Baumert, J., & Lehmann, R. (2014). Is early ability grouping good for high-achieving students' psychosocial development? Effects of the transition into academically selective schools. *Journal of Educational Psychology, 106*(2), 555–568. https://doi.org/10.1037/a0035425

Bradley, B., Johnson, D., Hill, M., McGee, D., Kana-ah, A., Sharpin, C., Sharp, P., Kelly, A. L., Cumming, S. P., & Malina, R. M. (2019). Bio-banding in academy football: Player's perceptions of a maturity matched tournament. *Annals of Human Biology, 46*(5), 400–408. https://doi.org/10.1080/03014460.2019.1640284

Bruner, M., Wilson, B., Erickson, K., & Côté, J. (2010). An appraisal of athlete development models through citation network analysis. *Psychology of Sport and Exercise, 11*, 133–139. https://doi.org/10.1016/j.psychsport.2009.05.008

Cialdini, R. B., Borden, R. J., Thorne, A., Walker, M. R., Freeman, S., & Sloan, L. R. (1976). Basking in reflected glory: Three (football) field studies. *Journal of Personality and Social Psychology, 34*(3), 366–375. https://doi.org/10.1037/0022-3514.34.3.366

Cobley, S., Baker, J., Wattie, N., & McKenna, J. (2009). Annual age-grouping and athlete development: A meta-analytical review of relative age effects in sport. *Sports Medicine, 39*(3), 235–256.

Collins, D. J., MacNamara, Á., & McCarthy, N. (2016). Putting the bumps in the rocky road: *Optimizing the pathway to excellence*. *Frontiers in Psychology, 7*(1482), 1–6. https://doi.org/10.3389/fpsyg.2016.01482

Côté, J., Bruner, M., Erickson, K., Strachan, L., & Fraser-Thomas, J. (2010). Athlete development and coaching. In C. Cushion, & J. Lyle (Eds.), *Sports coaching: Professionalism and practice* (pp. 63–78). Elsevier.

Côté, J., & Gilbert, W. (2009). An integrative definition of coaching effectiveness and expertise. *International Journal of Sports Science & Coaching, 4*(3), 307–323. https://doi.org/10.1260/174795409789623892

Côté, J., Turnnidge, J., Murata, A., McGuire, C., & Martin, L. (2020). Youth sport research: Describing the integrated dynamics elements of the personal assets framework. *International Journal of Sport Psychology, 51*(6), 562–578. https://doi.org/10.1002/9781119568124.ch27

Côté, J., & Vierimaa, M. (2014). The developmental model of sport participation: 15 years after its first conceptualization. *Science & Sports, 29*(1), S63-S69. https://doi.org/10.1016/j.scispo.2014.08.133

Cumming, S. P., Brown, D. J., Mitchell, S., Bunce, J., Hunt, D., Hedges, C., Crane, G., Gross, A., Scott, S., Franklin, E., Breakspear, D., Dennison, L., White, P., Cain, A., Eisenmann, J. C., & Malina, R. M. (2018). Premier League academy soccer players' experiences of competing in a tournament bio-banded for biological maturation. *Journal of Sports Sciences, 36*(7), 757–765. https://doi.org/10.1080/02640414.2017.1340656

Cumming, S. P., Lloyd, R. S., Oliver, J. L., Eisenmann, J. C., & Malina, R. M. (2017). Bio-banding in sport: Applications to competition, talent identification, and strength and conditioning of youth athletes. *Strength & Conditioning Journal, 39*(2), 34–47. https://doi.org/10.1519/SSC.0000000000000281

Datar, A. (2006). Does delaying Kindergarten entrance give children a head start? *Economics of Education Review, 25*(1), 43–62. https://doi.org/10.1016/j.econedurev.2004.10.004

Delorme, N., Chalabaev, A., & Raspaud, M. (2011). Relative age is associated with sport dropout: Evidence from youth categories of French basketball. *Scandinavian Journal of Medicine & Science in Sports, 21*(1), 120–128. https://doi.org/10.1111/j.1600-0838.2009.01060.x

Duda, J. L. (1987). Toward a developmental theory of children's motivation in sport. *Journal of Sport and Exercise Psychology, 9*(2), 130–145. https://doi.org/10.1123/jsp.9.2.130

Figueiredo, A. J., Goncalves, C. E., Coelho-e-Silva, M. J., & Malina, R. M. (2009). Characteristics of youth soccer players who drop out, persist or move up. *Journal of Sports Sciences, 27*(9), 883–891. https://doi.org/10.1080/02640410902946469

Gibbs, B. G., Jarvis, J. A., & Dufur, M. J. (2012). The rise of the underdog? The relative age effect reversal among Canadian-born NHL hockey players: A reply to Nolan and Howell. *International Review for the Sociology of Sport, 47*(5), 644–649. https://doi.org/10.1177/1012690211414343

Goldman, D. E., Turnnidge, J., Côté, J., & Kelly, A. L. (2021). "Playing-up" in youth soccer. In A. L. Kelly, J. Côté, M. Jeffreys, & J. Turnnidge (Eds.), *Birth advantages and relative age effects in sport: Exploring organizational structures and creating appropriate settings* (pp. 77–94). Routledge.

Goldman, D. E., Turnnidge, J., Kelly, A. L., deVos, J., & Côté, J. (2022). Athlete perceptions of playing-up in youth soccer. *Journal of Applied Sport Psychology*, *34*(4), 862–885. https://doi.org/10.1080/10413200.2021.1875518

Gustafsson, H., Martinent, G., Isoard-Gautheur, S., Hassmén, P., & Guillet-Descas, E. (2018). Performance based self-esteem and athlete-identity in athlete burnout: A person-centered approach. *Psychology of Sport and Exercise*, *38*, 56–60. https://doi.org/10.1016/j.psychsport.2018.05.017

Hancock, D. J., Adler, A. L., & Côté, J. (2013). A proposed theoretical model to explain relative *age effects in sport*. *European Journal of Sport Science*, *13*(6), 630–637. https://doi.org/10.1080/17461391.2013.775352

Hancock, D. J., Murata, A., & Côté, J. (2021). Parents' roles in creating socio-environmental birth advantages for their children. In A. L. Kelly, J. Côté, M. Jeffreys, & J. Turnnidge (Eds.), *Birth advantages and relative age effects in sport: Exploring organizational structures and creating appropriate settings* (pp. 207–221). Routledge.

Helsen, W. F., Starkes, J. L., & Van Winckel, J. (1998). The influence of relative age on success and dropout in male soccer players. *American Journal of Human Biology*, *10*(6), 791–798. https://doi.org/10.1002/(SICI)1520-6300(1998)10:6<791::AID-AJHB10>3.0.CO;2-1

Janos, P. M., & Robinson, N. M. (1985). Psychosocial development in intellectually gifted children. In F. D. Horowitz & M. O'Brien (Eds.), *The gifted and talented: Developmental perspectives* (pp. 149–195). American Psychological Association.

Jarvis, P. (2007). Dangerous activities within and invisible playground: A study of emergent male football play and teachers' perspectives of outdoor free play in the early years of primary school. *International Journal of Early Years Education*, *15*, 245–259. https://doi.org/10.1080/09669760701516918

Jimerson, S. R., Anderson, G. E., & Whipple, A. D. (2002). Winning the battle and losing the war: Examining the relation between grade retention and dropping out of high school. *Psychology in the Schools*, *39*(4), 441–457. https://doi.org/10.1002/pits.10046

Kelly, A. L., Jackson, D. T., Taylor, J. J., Jeffreys, M. A., & Turnnidge, J. (2020a). "Birthday-banding" as a strategy to moderate the relative age effect: A case study into the England Squash Talent Pathway. *Frontiers in Sports and Active Living*, *2*(573890), 1–9. https://doi.org/10.3389/fspor.2020.573890

Kelly, A. L., Verbeek, J., & Goldman, D. (2021a, May 12). Looking beyond traditional chronological age grouping: International perspectives [Symposium]. *Expertise and Skill Acquisition Network (ESAN) Online 2021*.

Kelly, A. L., & Williams, C. A. (2020). Physical characteristics and the talent identification and *development processes in male youth soccer: A narrative review*. *Strength and Conditioning Journal*, *42*(6), 15–34. https://doi.org/10.1519/SSC.0000000000000576

Kelly, A. L., Wilson, M. R., Gough, L. A., Knapman, H., Morgan, P., Cole, M., Jackson, D. T., & Williams, C. A. (2020b). A longitudinal investigation into the relative age effect in an English professional football club: Exploring the 'underdog hypothesis'. *Science and Medicine in Football*, *4*(2), 111–118. https://doi.org/10.1080/24733938.2019.1694169

Kelly, A. L., Wilson, M. R., Jackson, D. T., Goldman, D. E., Turnnidge, J., Côté, J., & Williams, C. A. (2021b). A multidisciplinary investigation into "playing-up" in academy football according to age phase. *Journal of Sports Sciences*, *39*(8), 854–864. https://doi.org/10.1080/02640414.2020.1848117

Kretschmann, J., Vock, M., Lüdtke, O., Jansen, M., & Gronostaj, A. (2019). Effects of grade retention on students' motivation: A longitudinal study over 3 years of secondary school. *Journal of Educational Psychology*, *111*(8), 1432–1446. https://doi.org/10.1037/edu0000353

Kulik, C. L. C., & Kulik, J. A. (1982). Effects of ability grouping on secondary school students: A meta-analysis of evaluation findings. *American Educational Research Journal*, *19*(3), 415–428. https://doi.org/10.3102/00028312019003415

Lefebvre, J. S., Evans, M. B., Turnnidge, J., Gainforth, H. L., & Côté, J. (2016). Describing and classifying coach development programmes: A synthesis of empirical research and applied practice. *International Journal of Sports Science & Coaching*, *11*(6), 887–899. https://doi.org/10.1177/1747954116676116

Malina, R. M., Cumming, S. P., Rogol, A. D., Coelho-e-Silva, M. J., Figueiredo, A. J., Konarski, J. M., & Kozieł, S. M. (2019). Bio-banding in youth sports: Background, concept, and application. *Sports Medicine, 49*(11), 1671–1685. https://doi.org/10.1007/s40279-019-01166-x

Martorell, P., & Mariano, L. T. (2018). The causal effects of grade retention on behavioral outcomes. *Journal of Research on Educational Effectiveness, 11*(2), 192–216. https://doi.org/10.1080/19345747.2017.1390024

McCalpin, M., Evans, B., & Côté, J. (2017). Young female soccer players' perceptions of their modified sport environment. *The Sport Psychologist, 31*(1), 65–77. https://doi.org/10.1123/tsp.2015-0073

McNamara, J. K., Scissons, M., & Simonot, S. (2004). Should we "redshirt" in Kindergarten? A study of the effect of age on Kindergarteners' reading readiness. *The Alberta Journal of Educational Research, 50*(2), 128–140.

Murata, A., Goldman, D. E., Martin, L. J., Turnnidge, J., Bruner, M. W., & Côté, J. (2021). Sampling between sports and athlete development: A scoping review. *International Journal of Sport and Exercise Psychology, 11*(2), 133–139. https://doi.org/10.1080/1612197X.2021.1995021

Neihart, M. (2007). The socioaffective impact of acceleration and ability grouping: Recommendations for best practice. *Gifted Child Quarterly, 51*(4), 330–341. https://doi.org/10.1177/0016986207306319

NICHD Early Child Care Research Network. (2007). Age of entry to kindergarten and children's academic achievement and socioemotional development. *Early Education and Development, 18*(2), 337–368. https://doi.org/10.1080/10409280701283460

Ong, W., Allison, J., & Haladyna, T. M. (2000). Student achievement of 3rd-graders in comparable single-age and multiage classrooms. *Journal of Research in Childhood Education, 14*(2), 205–215. https://doi.org/10.1080/02568540009594764

Romann, M., Lüdin, D., & Born, D. P. (2020). Bio-banding in junior soccer players: A pilot study. *BMC Research Notes, 13*(1), 240. https://doi.org/10.1186/s13104-020-05083-5

Sarmento, H., Anguera, M. T., Pereira, A., & Araujo, D. (2018). Talent identification and development in male football: A systematic review. *Sports Medicine, 48*(4), 907–931. https://doi.org/10.1007/s40279-017-0851-7

Sayler, M. F., & Brookshire, W. K. (1993). Social, emotional, and behavioral adjustment of accelerated students, students in gifted classes, and regular students in eighth grade. *Gifted Child Quarterly, 37*(4), 150–154. https://doi.org/10.1177/001698629303700403

Sieghartsleitner, R., Zuber, C., Zibung, M., & Conzelmann, A. (2019). Science or coaches' eye?—Both! Beneficial collaboration of multidimensional measurements and coach assessments for efficient talent selection in elite youth football. *Journal of Sports Science & Medicine, 11*(1), 32–43.

Sky Sports. (2019, January 5). Stones first. *Soccer AM*. Retrieved from: www.youtube.com/watch?v=6ZF07DlUn1g [accessed 14th January 2021].

Sky Sports. (2020, December). Maguire first. *Soccer AM*. Retrieved from: www.youtube.com/watch?v=RVQruDjEKQQ [accessed 12th May 2021].

Smith, G. (2014). *Standard deviations*. Duckworth.

Song, R., Spradlin, T. E., & Plucker, J. A. (2009). The advantages and disadvantages of multiage classrooms in the era of NCLB accountability. *Center for Evaluation & Education Policy, 7*(1), 1–8.

Steenbergen-Hu, S., Makel, M. C., & Olszewski-Kubilius, P. (2016). What one hundred years of research says about the effects of ability grouping and acceleration on K–12 students' academic achievement: Findings of two second-order meta-analyses. *Review of Educational Research, 86*(4), 849–899. https://doi.org/10.3102/0034654316675417

Steenbergen-Hu, S., & Moon, S. M. (2011). The effects of acceleration on high-ability learners: A meta-analysis. *Gifted Child Quarterly, 55*(1), 39–53. https://doi.org/10.1177/0016986210383155

Taylor, J., & Collins, D. (2019). Shoulda, coulda, didnae—Why don't high-potential players make it? *The Sport Psychologist, 33*(2), 85–96. https://doi.org/10.1123/tsp.2017-0153

The Football Association. (2020). *The FA's 4 corner model*. Retrieved from: https://thebootroom.thefa.com/resources/coaching/the-fas-4-corner-model [accessed 14th January 2021].

The Premier League. (2011). *Elite player performance plan*. Retrieved from: www.premierleague.com/youth/EPPP [accessed 14th January 2021].

Tieso, C. (2005). The effects of grouping practices and curricular adjustments on achievement. *Journal for the Education of the Gifted, 29*(1), 60–89. https://doi.org/10.1177/016235320502900104

Turnnidge, J., & Kelly, A. L. (2021). Organizational structures: Looking back and looking ahead. In A. L. Kelly, J. Côté, M. Jeffreys, & J. Turnnidge (Eds.), *Birth advantages and relative age effects in sport: Exploring organizational structures and creating appropriate settings* (pp. 239–246). Routledge.

Verbeek, J., Lawrence, S., van der Breggen, J., Kelly, A. L., & Jonker, L. (2021). The average team age method and its potential to reduce relative age effects. In A. L. Kelly, J. Côté, M. Jeffreys, & J. Turnnidge (Eds.), *Birth advantages and relative age effects in sport: Exploring organizational structures and creating appropriate settings* (pp. 107–124). Routledge.

Vierimaa, M., Turnnidge, J., Bruner, M., & Côté, J. (2017). Just for the fun of it: Coaches' perceptions of an exemplary community youth sport program. *Physical Education and Sport Pedagogy, 22*(6), 603–617. https://doi.org/10.1080/17408989.2017.1341473

12
CREATIVITY

Creating Supportive and Enriching Environments

Sara Santos, Diogo Coutinho, Adam L. Kelly, Sergio L. Jiménez Sáiz, Alberto Lorenzo Calvo, and Jaime Sampaio

Introduction

Soccer is the world's most popular sport and has been driven by creativity since its infancy. As such, it should be understood as a developmental resource in practice and recognised as a crucial attribute during the selection process (Leso et al., 2017; Santos et al., 2016). During the male World Cup (2010 and 2014) and male European Championship (2016), creative behaviours were shown to be decisive in order to advance to the later rounds and proved to be the best predictor for game success (Kempe & Memmert, 2018). However, the concept of creativity is not consensual and may entail a broader scope of application in soccer (Fardilha & Allen, 2020). Grounded in cognitive science, a common way to define creativity is the ability to produce something that is both new/original and task/domain appropriate (Sternberg & Lubart, 1999). In team sports, creativity has been described as a search process of generating several solutions to solve a game or training problem in an appropriate, unpredictable, and authentic way under the environmental conditions (Santos et al., 2016). In this regard, creativity should be understood as the process of perceiving, exploring, and generating novel affordances (i.e., opportunities for action) within a given context, taking into consideration the importance of contemplating the experiential process (Glăveanu, 2012; Rasmussen et al., 2019).

The first part of this chapter frames this concept and presents the developmental trends of creativity in soccer, encompassing comprehensive frameworks (e.g., the *Tactical Creativity Approach* and the *Creativity Developmental Framework*) to encourage creativity to thrive. The second part of this chapter provides a detailed description of small-sided games and movement variability features to encourage exploratory behaviour and complement soccer training tasks. The third part of this chapter offers a review across creativity training programmes, specifically *Skills4Genius* and *The Creative Soccer Platform*, to provide further guidance and strategies for soccer practitioners to design for creativity. Lastly, in order to advance this field of practice, considerations for researchers and practitioners are outlined.

Creativity Comprehensive Frameworks

A key role for soccer practitioners is to design their session plans for creativity to flourish. For that, coaches and other practitioners should nurture the 'Personal-creativity' (P-type) into their practices. This creative expression leads to the self-exploration of novel solutions that allow players to overcome personal limitations. Thus, most of the players' actions and decisions are novel to them but not necessary to society (Boden, 1994). To support the P-type expression, soccer practitioners are encouraged to cultivate an environment with a positive development climate to explore new behaviours, favour the openness to fresh challenges, and inspire confidence to engage in unfamiliar training routines (Santos & Monteiro, 2020; Santos et al., 2020). To achieve this, comprehensive frameworks have been designed to offer specific approaches in which practitioners might grasp and nurture creativity into their practices.

The *Tactical Creativity Approach* (TCA) (Memmert, 2013, 2015) and the *Creativity Developmental Framework* (CDF) (Santos et al., 2016) are two comprehensive models that have emerged to ignite creative behaviours across the lifespan in sport. The TCA emerges from Professor Daniel Memmert's extensive empirical research on sports creativity and enclosed the 'Seven D's': (a) deliberate play, (b) one-dimension games, (c) diversification, (d) deliberate coaching, (e) deliberate memory, (f) deliberate motivation, and (g) deliberate practice (for an overview, see Memmert, 2015). More recently, the CDF, which is outlined in Figure 12.1, provides the general guidelines that can lead to a long-term creativity improvement process (Santos et al., 2016). This framework describes five creative developmental stages: (a) beginner (age 2–6 years), (b) explorer (age 7–9 years), (c) illuminati (age 10–12 years), (d) creator (age 13–15 years), and (e) rise (over age 16 years). The CDF is driven by the goal to promote a creativity-nurturing environment through the combination of different training approaches embodied on creative assumptions: (a) practice pathway (e.g., diversification and specialisation), (b) physical literacy, (c) nonlinear-pedagogy, including *Teaching Games for Understanding* (TGfU) and differential learning, and (d) creative thinking, considering divergent and convergent thinking roles (Santos et al., 2016).

The CDF has been partially put into practice (explorer stage) through the *Skills4Genius* pedagogical programme, which is extensively described later in the chapter. Both highlighted the benefits of early diversification, taking into consideration that players should 'sample' in a variety of movements and sports activities involving higher levels of deliberate play and unstructured activities, as a suitable route to unleash creativity (Memmert, 2015; Memmert et al., 2010). In support of this notion, Roca and Ford (2021) showed that highly-creative soccer players accumulated more time in free play and unstructured soccer-specific activities, whereas no differences were identified in soccer-specific formal practice and competition, in comparison to low-creative soccer players. Accordingly, practitioners should be aware that, during the early years, an exclusive focus on early specialisation and deliberate practice can be detrimental for creativity, since it is generally grounded in rigid skills-based approaches, with the main focus on short-term results (Côté & Erickson, 2015; Richard et al., 2018; see Chapter 8 for an overview). Further, both frameworks support the manipulation of constraints that form boundary conditions, which offers challenging environments for youth soccer players to fulfil their creative potential. In this regard, the following section provides an overview of the benefits related to constraints-based coaching.

Creativity **169**

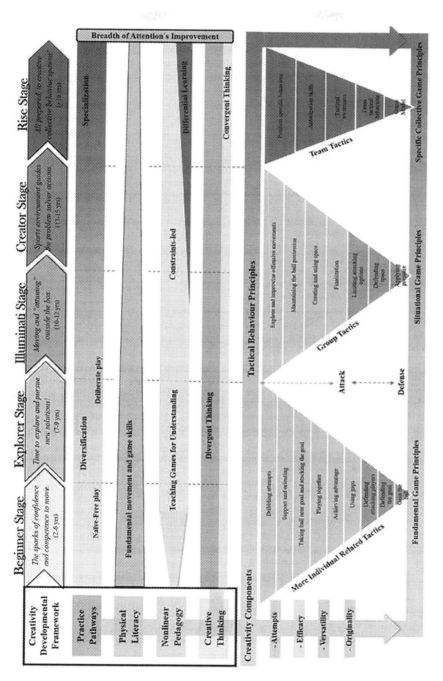

FIGURE 12.1 Representation of the Creativity Developmental Framework structure (Santos et al., 2016).

Note: (1) Developmental creativity stages: (a) beginner, (b) explorer, (c) illuminati, (d) creator, and (e) rise. (2) Tenets of the Creativity Developmental Framework: (a) practice pathways, (b) physical literacy, (c) nonlinear pedagogy, including Teaching Games for Understanding and differential learning, and (d) creative thinking, considering divergent and convergent thinking roles. (3) Creativity training components: (a) attempts, (b) efficacy, (c) versatility, and (d) originality. And, (4) tactical behaviour principles: (a) fundamental game principles, (b) situational game principles, and (c) specific collective game principles.

FIGURE 12.2 Lionel Messi, using the referee to create space and dribble past his opponent during a game between Barcelona and Celta from the 2016/17 season.

Using Small-Sided Games to Unleash Creativity

Small-sided games (SSGs) have been widely used during soccer sessions as a training approach to develop and refine players' skills and movements (Coutinho et al., 2019; Santos et al., 2020; Travassos et al., 2012). One of the main reasons for its popularity is that practitioners can model the game-based rules to create enriching environments that guide players towards specific learning goals (Travassos et al., 2012). The majority of studies into SSGs have focused on the effects of different manipulations (e.g., pitch size, player numbers, and game duration) on physical, technical, and tactical behaviours (Kelly & Wilson, 2018; Murata et al., 2021). More recently, however, researchers have shifted their attention towards better understanding what boundary conditions release or restrain creative behaviours (Santos et al., 2016; Torrents et al., 2020).

The environment appears to be a core feature to generate creative behaviour. One example of how the environment can guide players towards unique behaviours is presented by Lionel Messi's actions during a game between Barcelona and Celta from the 2016/17 season in Figure 12.2. Here, he had the referee close to him, so he decided to use them as an obstacle to create space and dribble past his opponent. It may be plausible to assume that Lionel Messi would also be able to beat his opponent without the referee; however, this is a useful example of how the environment contains information that players can use to guide their behaviours (Fajen, 2005; Fajen et al., 2009; Newell, 1986).

The rules applied by practitioners during their practices may amplify or limit the number of available possibilities for action and, consequently, the likelihood that a creative behaviour emerges (Torrents et al., 2020). Therefore, it would be worthwhile for soccer coaches and other practitioners to better understand the conditions that trigger or refrain creative behaviour according to players age or experience. At this point, it is important to consider that creativity has been tracked during game-based situations, according to four components: (a) *attempts*, recognised as any effort of a player attempting to perform a novel action, however, without success (e.g., a player trying to use his back to receive and dribble past an opponent without success), (b) *fluency*, known as standardised successful actions (e.g., regular pass that reach the intended target player), (c) *versatility*, encompasses the non-regular or the variety of actions performed with success (e.g., Mesut Özil bounce pass), and (d) *originality*, which not only consider an action as novel but relates it to its uniqueness in the team (Caso & van der Kamp, 2020; Santos et al., 2017, 2018). Under these components, some research has started to address how different game-based rules affects the players' creative predisposition. For example, playing with limited touches (i.e., one or two touches per ball possession) can foster the players' ability to perform fluent actions; however, it refrains them to explore and performing novel movement patterns (i.e., attempts or versatility) (Coutinho et al., 2021). These results do not mean that practitioners should not restrain touches, as it favours one of the creative components (i.e., fluency); although, it may limit the development of other relevant creative components when considering a long-term perspective.

During soccer training sessions, practitioners often vary the number of players on each team to elicit different outcomes. For instance, Caso and van der Kamp (2020) explored how varying the number of players during balanced scenarios (i.e., 5 vs. 5, 6 vs. 6, 7 vs. 7, and 11 vs. 11) affected the versatility and originality of the actions performed by players. They found that players do not only perform more versatile actions during smaller game-based situations, but it also enhanced the emergence of novel actions (i.e., original skills). Moreover, Torrents et al. (2016) explored how different number of players affects players versatile actions; however, the authors considered different unbalanced scenarios between the confronting teams (i.e., 3 vs. 4, 5 vs. 4, and 7 vs. 4). These results suggest that players adopt more predictable and fewer varied actions when they face less demanding scenarios (e.g., playing in superiority during a 7 vs. 4 SSG), whereas they appear to explore different technical and tactical actions when facing more challenging scenarios (e.g., 3 vs. 4 or 5 vs. 4) (Torrents et al., 2016).

More recently, Santos et al. (forthcoming) studied how the creative behaviour of a control team was affected with the progressive increase in the number of creative players in the opposing team during a 4 vs. 4 with goalkeepers (GKs) SSG based on the following conditions: (a) playing against one creative player plus three intermediate players (1 Creative), (b) playing against two creative players plus two intermediate players (2 Creatives), (c) playing against three creative players plus one intermediate player (3 Creatives), and (d) playing against four creative players (4 Creatives). An increase in the players' fluency, attempts, and versatile actions during low (i.e., against 1 Creative) to moderate scenarios (i.e., against 2 and 3 Creatives), while extremely high demanding scenarios (i.e., against 4 Creatives) suppressed all the creative components (Figure 12.3). The main findings from this study suggest that an appropriate level of difficulty is necessary to trigger players creative components. In this regard, it seems vital to expose players to varied and dynamic contexts that challenge them to think and behave beyond the typical.

Sparking Creativity with Variability

Over the last decade, a new theoretical perspective has been generating attention across the sports science domain, which highlights the role of *variability* to aid learning (e.g., Herzfeld & Shadmehr, 2014; Tumer & Brainard, 2007; Wu et al., 2014) and creativity (e.g., Coutinho et al., 2018; Orth et al., 2017; Santos et al., 2016, 2018, 2020). Movement variability can be depicted from the different variations in a movement or skill while performing a specific task (Newell & Corcos,

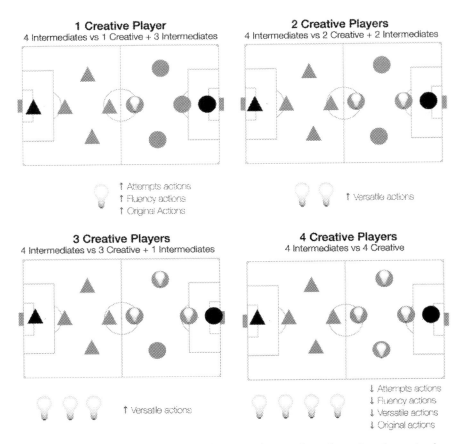

FIGURE 12.3 Main results from the effects of varying the number of creative players in the creative components performed by a control team during a 4 vs. 4 plus goalkeepers small-sided game (Santos et al., forthcoming).

1993; Stergiou et al., 2013). In soccer, players' predisposition to explore also seems to be awakened when they are exposed to a wide range and unpredictable scenarios (Santos et al., 2016). In this respect, variability may be added by asking players to perform novel movement variations in a specific movement pattern (e.g., receiving a pass in a different way) (Schöllhorn et al., 2012), by promoting variations that would lead to adaptive patterns (e.g., game-based situations focused on travelling with the ball but using a different type of ball that will force the player to continuously adjust their movement) (Santos et al., 2020), or even in the performance environment (e.g., varying dynamically the number of players involved or even the pitch size, such as performing on various pitches with different shapes and sizes) (Coutinho et al., 2019).

Figure 12.4 shows some possibilities related to adding variability during the training tasks. Adopting the tenets presented earlier in this chapter, a small group of researchers has started to explore how variability (more and less functional) affects players' creative behaviour from both short- to mid- and long-term perspectives. From the acute viewpoint, Santos et al. (2020) analysed the impact of using different types of balls (i.e., soccer ball, handball ball, and rugby ball) on youth players' creative components during two different SSGs situations (i.e., 4 vs. 4 with GKs and 6 vs. 6 with GKs). In addition, the authors also had a condition with dynamic variability, whereby the players

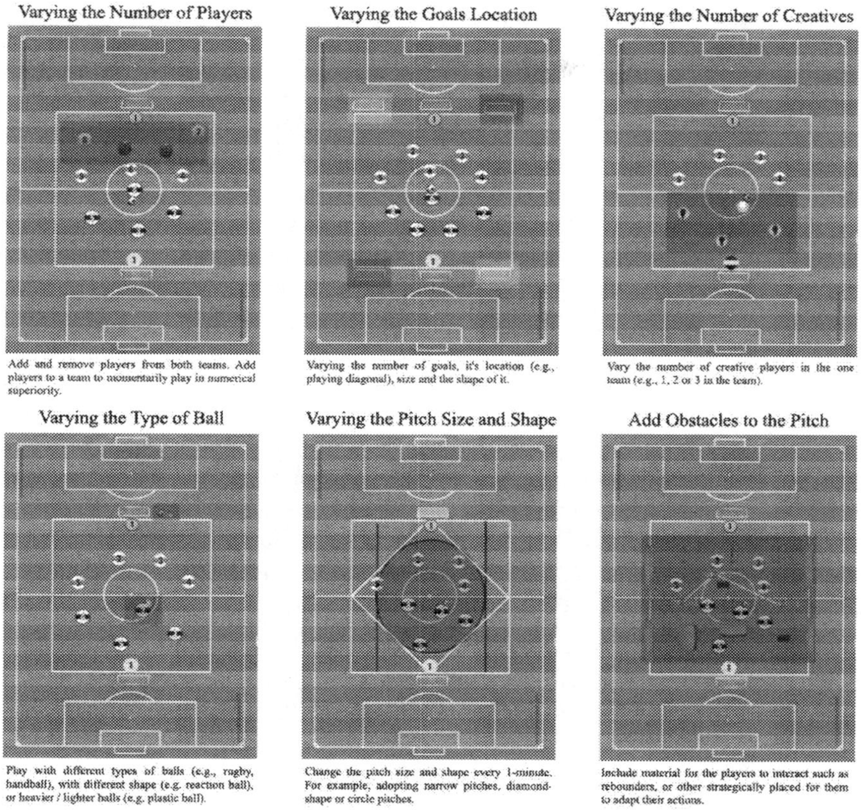

Creativity 173

FIGURE 12.4 Examples of boundary conditions that coaches can manipulate to emphasise different creative components (e.g., Canton et al., 2019; Caso & Van der Kamp, 2020; Coutinho et al., 2018; Santos et al., 2020; Torrents et al., 2016).

varied the type of ball every 2 minutes. In spite of playing with different balls, unaffected by the creative components, players explored different strategies to create goal opportunities. For instance, there was an increase in the number of shots on target when playing with the handball ball, possibly because its smaller size limited the opening for the defender to intercept the ball during the shot, amplifying the opportunities for scoring. Similarly, playing with the rugby ball or during the condition in which the balls vary every 2 minutes led players towards more compact behaviours, possibly as an adaptive behaviour resulting from the ball shape. These results highlight how players were able to adapt their actions as a result of the environmental information, suggesting that the variability may enhance their adaptability to changes in the performance environment.

Studies exploring chronic adaptations of variability have emerged during the recent years, which have attempted to understand how players may benefit from mid- to long-term interventions that complement regular training routines. For example, Santos et al. (2018) exposed U13 and U15 soccer players to a 5-month intervention embedded into SSGs with additional variability (differential learning), which consisted of three sessions per week with a duration of 30 minutes each. Some of the variations used during the intervention consisted in dynamically varying the number of players during a situation (i.e., starting with a 3 vs. 3 and after 1-minute performed a 6 vs. 2), performing on pitches with different shapes (e.g., circle, triangle, diamond, or hexagon), sizes and surfaces (e.g., grass or sand), varying the type of goals and playing with distinct body restrictions (e.g., with visual occlusion or both hands on the chest), or inclusively playing on pitches with obstacles. The control group performed the same number of sessions and duration adopting regular SSG situations (e.g., progressively increasing the number of players or limiting the number of touches). From the creative components perspective, the differential learning programme showed positive results as players enhanced the attempts, versatility, and originality of their actions, while also decreasing the number of fails (Santos et al., 2018). Using the same principles, Coutinho et al. (2018) applied a 3-month intervention grounded on differential learning to improve strikers' performance. In this study, U15 and U17 players were exposed to two sessions per week with a 25-minute duration each. The authors found improvements in fluency and versatility in the U15 age group, while the creative components remained unaffected in the U17 players (Coutinho et al., 2018).

Altogether, these studies provide important results regarding the impact of training programmes underpinned by additional variability to ignite creative behaviour, mainly in younger age groups. The weaker effects found in older age groups may be a result of the higher time spent in structured and less variable practices, which may stifle their ability to adapt and readjust the movement and behavioural patterns in more dynamic, complex, and unfamiliar scenarios. Exposing players to a broad range of configurations cannot only amplify their creative thinking and adaptive motor repertoire, but it could also contribute to their individual and personal development plans. This approach is widely used by recognised soccer head coaches, such as Thomas Tuchel and Jürgen Klopp, in order to develop creative and unpredictable teams (Boon, 2021; Meuren & Schächter, 2021). Whereas the previous boundary conditions disrupt what is usually appropriate and amplify players' affordances, the following section will provide coaches and other practitioners guidance on specific coaching models, principles, and active play strategies to design for creativity within youth soccer.

Creativity-Supportive Learning Environments

Creative behaviour is often developed in an environment that encourages well-adjusted, sufficiently new, movement-varied, and challenging boundary conditions. This is demonstrated in the following two sports creativity-based programmes: (a) the *Skills4Genius* programme (Santos et al., 2017) and (b) *The Creative Soccer Platform* (Rasmussen & Østergaard, 2016).

The Skills4Genius Programme

Skills4Genius is a training programme intended to develop social and emotional skills, such as creative thinking, as well as in-game creativity under the CDF assumptions in children from aged 5 to 10 years. Santos et al. (2017) applied this creativity-based programme for 5 months (for a total of 60 sessions) in primary school-aged children, with their overall findings demonstrating an increase in the participants motor performance and creative thinking. Specifically, children developed in-game creativity measured through the four previously mentioned components (i.e., attempts, fluency, versatility, and originality), which were complemented with other positional variables that aligned to several specific skills (i.e., pass, dribble, and shot) in SSGs (Santos et al., 2017). The findings support an interplay between thinking and sports creativity, revealing commonalities in the underlying processes responsible for driving creative thinking and children's novel behaviours in the field, which is further explored by Richard et al. (2018) and Santos and Monteiro (2020).

The Skills4Genius programme combines creative thinking strategies (i.e., cognitive assumptions), with a set of three constructivist models; namely, TGfU, Student-Designed Games, and Sport Education, aligned with CDF approaches (i.e., motor assumptions). In this regard, a typical Skills4Genius session begins with a 10-minute energiser presented in the creative thinking booklet. The activities booklet encompasses the use of drawing, oral, written, and motor tasks to boost imagination through exploration (Santos et al., 2017). Finally, several active-play strategies are incorporated in the session to ignite the emergence of creative behaviours, such as building material (e.g., create different balls, goals, captain band, or referee cards), storytelling (e.g., create an embodied history during the practice), LEGO Serious Play methodology (e.g., children can co-create by building the field, goals, or circuits with bricks), and social priming (e.g., playing with superpowers). Figure 12.5 displays several examples of the Skills4Genius practice design combining the previous approaches, which can be easily adapted to youth soccer practices[1].

A typical soccer-specific Skills4Genius session begins with rescuing the street soccer assumptions by creating a starter 'mysterious field' in the club setting, in which players from different age groups can play under daily challenges. For example, players and coaches can incorporate loose parts (e.g., boxes, water bottles, or rebounders), change the shape (e.g., circular, square, or diamond), and add missions (e.g., playing without soccer boots or with balloons to complete a mission) to their game design. Thereafter, the players perform a 10-minute energiser grounded in motor divergent tasks to boost creative thinking and motor creativity (e.g., use as many different variations as possible to put a ball into a box or show as many different feints as possible during a 1 vs. 1 competition). These tasks enhance a wide range of cognitive, social, and motor dimensions as well as nurture an atmosphere to ensure that players are feeling comfortable and competent in this type of environment since it is an important factor related to adaptability (Bournelli et al., 2009).

The main part of a soccer-specific Skills4Genius session is designed to develop movement creativity features through improvisation, discovery, and problem solving (Santos et al., 2016). It is manipulated specific-task constraints with extra variability to trigger a player's discovery of novel and functional movement patterns (Hristovski et al., 2011). In this regard, all the aforementioned boundary conditions presented in the variability section of this chapter could be applied. Playing SSG situations, through embodying the co-design and social priming, can promote different boundary conditions. For example, after scoring a goal, the team roll a dice, where each face holds a superhero picture empowering the team by playing under different constraints, such as: (a) *spider-man*, whereby the opposing team must play in pairs holding their hands, (b) *flash*, whereby opponents must play with the non-dominant limb, (c) *ant-man*, whereby the team reduce their own target or opponents scoring zone, and (d) *captain America*, whereby players create a new constraint to apply to the other team. The 'spider-man' constraint could emphasise the offensive principles of play related to width and mobility. The previous approach aids players to explore different strategies (i.e., technical actions, displacements on the pitch, and collective behaviours), which allows them to afford new goal opportunities to trigger a self-organising process. It seems that, when players are exposed to unfamiliar situations, it will prompt the emergence of new behaviours, and in turn, they perform more regular actions under more familiar scenarios (Coutinho et al., 2018).

During the extension part of a soccer-specific Skills4Genius session (following the main part), players receive street soccer balls from practitioners to play in unfamiliar places (e.g., beach, park, or school playground). As illustrated in Figure 12.6, several creative strategies could be incorporated during the soccer session, although assumptions are adjustable to other team sports.

176 Sara Santos et al.

FIGURE 12.5 Representation of the Skills4Genius practice design (adapted from Santos et al., 2017).

Note: Images include: (a) creative thinking booklets to fuel children's imagination, (b) activities supported on the Lego Serious Play foundations and student-designed games, in which children are creating their own games, circuits, and other activities, (c) building material approach; namely, a field hockey stick to play at tournament, (d) primming approach at the carnival session, whereas children play unconventional SSGs (with extra variability) incorporating super powers given by their own masks, and (e) Building material session; namely, a ball made of journal, captain band, referees cards, and defining roles such as coach, player, captain, referee, and cheerleaders, grounded in the Sports Education Model.

FIGURE 12.6 Representation of the Skills4Genius practice design applied in soccer.

Note: Images include: (a) playing SSGs with superhero powers adding extra variability, and (b) activities based on the Lego Serious Play foundations in which players create their changeable field or receive bricks when they score to be placed on the field.

The Creative Soccer Platform

The Creative Soccer Platform (TCSP) focuses on creating a playful, judgement-free, and autonomy-supportive training environment to blossom soccer players creative potential (Rasmussen & Østergaard, 2016). The TCSP was applied in an U15 recreational soccer team and the players' perceptions were gathered from a focus group (for an overview, see Rasmussen & Østergaard, 2016). Findings revealed that players and practitioners understand the importance of displaying creative and unexpected behaviours to keep an edge over their opponents. These behaviours were designed taking into consideration the four TCSP pedagogical assumptions that are presented in Table 12.1.

To provide soccer practitioners with further guidance when implementing creative-supportive activities, the research from Rasmussen et al. (2020) examined the conditions that enable or obstruct the design and application of creative strategies in U17 soccer players. Their findings resulted in the development of six generic design principles. The TCSP and six design principles, outlined in Table 12.2, are intended to create risk-friendly and challenging environments and can be used to design new or adjust existing soccer activities (Rasmussen et al., 2020). In general, they support players to engage in unfamiliar activities and try to perform new technical skills in competitive matches with no fear of making mistakes. However, creative behaviour can be prevented when coaches provide negative feedback towards their players when confronted with unsuccessful actions (mistakes), whilst exploratory behaviour inhibited when feedback from coaches focuses on the result due to promoting frustration and anxiety among soccer players.

TABLE 12.1 Description of the TCSP assumptions applied in youth soccer teams

TCSP Assumptions	Description
Task focus	Consists of focusing players attention towards to the task at hand and avoiding external disturbances. Task focus can generate more attention to a demanding task, increasing the likelihood for a player to dive into the creative process.
Parallel thinking	Splits all tasks into sub-tasks and whereby coaches perform examples step by step to ensure that all players understand the unfamiliar task. This creates a deep commitment to the ongoing activity.
Horizontal thinking	Aims to trigger ideas through several stimuli to break with typical cognitive or motor patterns (e.g., buzzwords, pictures, or materials), which rarely occur in organised soccer-specific practice settings. This can inspire players to explore outside the box.
No experienced judgment	Highlights mistakes as an opportunity to evolve and underlines their importance for the creative process. This can create a judgement-free environment, since the fear of receiving negative feedback can be detrimental to creativity.

TABLE 12.2 Description of the six design principles derived from applied in youth soccer teams (adapted from Rasmussen et al., 2020)

Design Principles	Description
Play with quantity	Solve a game problem by performing as many variants as possible of technical skill.
Improvised scenarios	Do not to use the same solution more than once in order to improvise diverse solutions.
Plan and break	Create an action plan to outplay and surprise opponents (e.g., during the build-up phase, players must plan how to create space against different opposing team playing formations).
Instant problems	Act instantaneously on particular prompts (e.g., stimulus related with words, colours, or numbers) provided by practitioners or peers while players are playing modified games (e.g., after a goal is scored, players state a number from one to five to decide the number of touches).
Unhabitualisation	Boundary conditions (individual or team level) that perturb player's behaviours (e.g., do a turn or a pre-feint before passing or play with a tennis ball in the hand).
Secret missions	Co-create situations recognised as rare and receive extra points for doing it (e.g., three consecutive first touch passes before shooting).

To design for creativity, recent evidence claimed the importance of regulating the feedback towards the process to highlight the importance to discover new actions and fuel players' self-challenge (e.g., recognise the mistakes as a form to evolve) (Lago, 2020). As such, the type of feedback should be considered as an essential factor to develop a culture of creativity. Further, based on Rasmussen et al. (2020) research, six factors emerged when applying creativity routines in U17 elite soccer players, namely: (a) support autonomy and ownership, (b) revitalise curiosity, (c) contribute to de-robotisation, (d) support the evolution of trademarks, (e) form a playful atmosphere, and (f) facilitate rare (inter)actions. Moreover, eight potential obstacles for creativity were highlighted, including: (a) soccer-specific curriculum, (b) tight tournament program, (c) result and performance pressure, (d) beliefs about quality coaching, (e) demands for a high transfer-value, (f) coach perceptions of player preferences, (g) requirements to integrate creativity in established practice, and (h) soccer-specific views about creativity and its development.

Considerations for Researchers

Grounded on sports creativity evidence, the first challenge for researchers is to uncover the role of boundary conditions in releasing creative behaviours according to the players' age or previous experiences. This will help practitioners to better understand the impact of different manipulations on players' environmental exploration, and ultimately, on their ability to explore and create. As such, further studies should explore the dynamic interaction between constraints (e.g., varying the pitch size and format on a temporal basis), to underscore what scenarios are more likely to promote individual and/or team creativity.

Variability has been considered as a key feature for the creative process to blossom. However, the optimal training dose of variability to be induced remains unknown. Therefore, future studies should expose players to different mid- to long-term interventions embedded in variability to underpin its periodisation on the players' developmental path. Lastly, in order to advance this field of practice, it is essential to address the gender bias towards male players, since there is, concerningly, yet to be a single study exploring the creative process among female players.

Considerations for Practitioners

Based on the evidence and intervention programmes presented throughout this chapter, the following considerations for practitioners are offered to help inform future practice:

- Act as a facilitator rather than an instructor. This will increase the players' autonomy and their capacity to actively co-design and analyse training activities or game situations.
- Embrace variability during training routines. This can help promote creativity and innovation as well as empower exploratory behaviour.
- Encourage creativity components and allow room for mistakes during training sessions or competiton. This is particularly important, since learning from mistakes should be seen as part of the long-term creative development process.
- The creative process begins with the practitioner's predisposition to be innovative during the session design and convey to soccer players an encouraging climate to engage in creative play.
- To cultivate enriching and supportive environments, practitioners do not necessarily need to completely change their game vision or training sessions, since the CDF approach, TCSP, and the six design principles can be used to modify existing soccer tasks aligned with an effective team climate and process-based feedback.

Conclusion

This chapter provides an overview of comprehensive frameworks, principles, boundary conditions, and strategies that will guide and support soccer organisations and practitioners to design for creativity. From a developmental view, there seems to be a vital need to increase creativity in youth soccer settings, which may not only contribute to enhancing overall performance through specific skills, but also a wide range of benefits related to long-term participation and personal development. In this regard, soccer players need innovative environments to discover novel techniques and adapt known behaviours during the training session. In terms of cultivating a creativity-supportive learning environment, adult stakeholders may need to rethink their role. For that, the Skills4Genius programme and the Creative Soccer Platform provide further guidance for practitioners to take players out of their comfort zone.

To develop creativity at all levels, players need to be exposed to more challenging scenarios. Indeed, soccer practices benefit greatly from using a wide variety of boundary conditions embedded in variability. Nurturing creativity should be seen as an integrated part of coaching philosophies and not treated as a separated element of training routine (e.g., warm-up, arrival, or restitution activities), as this vision could be detrimental to creativity. To avoid that, governing bodies, soccer clubs, and practitioners should remove barriers by creating normative guidelines that encourage and reward clubs that implement these enriching and supportive environments (e.g., valuing the most creative player in the formal competition and not the one with the highest performance). Finally, soccer organisations should apply evidence-informed approaches in a long-term perspective and decrease the pressure among practitioners and players to win games, especially in the early ages, while also involving the parents in this process. These creative efforts could be central to talent identification and development, in order to reach a world-class performance.

Note

1 The Skills4Genius promotional video (Portuguese language) can be accessed in the following link: https://gulbenkian.pt/academias/videos/utad-cidesd/

References

Boden, A. (1994). What is creativity? In *Dimensions of creativity* (pp. 75–117). The MIT Press.

Boon, J. (2021). Inside Chelsea boss Thomas Tuchel's unique coaching methods that have led Blues to FA Cup and Champions League finals. *The Sun.* www.thesun.co.uk/sport/14931911/chelsea-thomas-tuchel-coaching-methods-fa-cup-champions-league/

Bournelli, P., Makri, A., & Mylonas, K. (2009). Motor creativity and self-concept. *Creativity Research Journal*, 21(1), 104–110. https://doi.org/10.1080/10400410802633657

Canton, A., Torrents, C., Ric, A., Gonçalves, B., Sampaio, J., & Hristovski, R. (2019). Effects of temporary numerical imbalances on collective exploratory behavior of young and professional football players. *Frontiers in Psychology*, 10, 1968. https://doi.org/10.3389/fpsyg.2019.01968

Caso, S., & van der Kamp, J. (2020). Variability and creativity in small-sided conditioned games among elite soccer players. *Psychology of Sport and Exercise*, 48, 101645. https://doi.org/https://doi.org/10.1016/j.psychsport.2019.101645

Côté, J., & Erickson, K. (2015). Diversification and deliberate play during the sampling years. In J. Baker & D. Farrow (Eds.), *Routledge handbook of sport expertise*. Routledge. https://doi.org/10.4324/9781315776675.ch27

Coutinho, D., Gonçalves, B., Santos, S., Travassos, B., Folgado, H., & Sampaio, J. (2021). Exploring how limiting the number of ball touches during small-sided games affects youth football players' performance across different age groups. *International Journal of Sports Science & Coaching*, 17479541211037001. https://doi.org/10.1177/17479541211037001

Coutinho, D., Gonçalves, B., Santos, S., Travassos, B., Wong, D., & Sampaio, J. (2019). Effects of the pitch configuration design on players' physical performance and movement behaviour during soccer small-sided games. *Research in Sports Medicine*, 27(3), 298–313. https://doi.org/10.1080/15438627.2018.1544133

Coutinho, D., Santos, S., Gonçalves, B., Travassos, B., Wong, D., Schöllhorn, W., & Sampaio, J. (2018). The effects of an enrichment training program for youth football attackers. *PLoS One*, *13*(6), e0199008. https://doi.org/10.1371/journal.pone.0199008

Fajen, B. (2005). Perceiving possibilities for action: On the necessity of calibration and perceptual learning for the visual guidance of action. *Perception*, *34*(6), 717–740. https://doi.org/10.1068/p5405

Fajen, B., Riley, M., & Turvey, M. (2009). Information, affordances, and the control of action in sport. *International Journal of Sport Psychology*, *40*, 79–107. http://panda.cogsci.rpi.edu/resources/papers/Fajen-RileyTurvey2009.pdf

Fardilha, F., & Allen, J. (2020). Defining, assessing, and developing creativity in sport: A systematic narrative review. *International Review of Sport and Exercise Psychology*, *13*(1), 104–127. https://doi.org/10.1080/1750984X.2019.1616315

Glăveanu, V. P. (2012). What can be done with an egg? Creativity, material objects, and the theory of affordances. *The Journal of Creative Behavior*, *46*(3), 192–208. https://doi.org/10.1002/jocb.13

Herzfeld, D., & Shadmehr, R. (2014). Motor variability is not noise, but grist for the learning mill. *Nature Neuroscience*, *17*(2), 149–150. https://doi.org/10.1038/nn.3633

Hristovski, R., Davids, K., Araujo, D., & Passos, P. (2011). Constraints-induced emergence of functional novelty in complex neurobiological systems: A basis for creativity in sport. *Nonlinear Dynamics, Psychology and Life Science*, *15*(2), 175–206.

Kelly, A. L., & Wilson, M. R. (2018). Thinking inside the box: The effect of player numbers on locomotor activity and skill behaviour during competitive match-play in under-9 English academy football. *Journal of Sports Sciences*, *36*(S1), 51.

Kempe, M., & Memmert, D. (2018). "Good, better, creative": The influence of creativity on goal scoring in elite soccer. *Journal of Sports Sciences*, *36*(21), 2419–2423. https://doi.org/10.1080/02640414.2018.1459153

Lago, C. (2020). La influencia del entrenador en el aprendizaje de los futebolistas. Cómo dar los feedbacks em el entrenamiento. *Barca Innovation Hub*. https://barcainnovationhub.com/pt/a-influencia-do-treinador-durante-a-preparacao-dos-atletas-como-fornecer-feedbacks-nos-treinamentos/

Leso, G., Dias, G., Ferreira, J., Gama, J., & Couceiro, M. (2017). Perception of creativity and game intelligence in soccer. *Creativity Research Journal*, *29*(2), 182–187. https://doi.org/10.1080/10400419.2017.1302779

Memmert, D. (2013). Tactical creativity. In T. McGarry, P. O'Donoghue, & J. Sampaio (Eds.), *Routledge handbook of sports performance analysis* (pp. 297–308). Routledge.

Memmert, D. (2015). *Teaching tactical creativity in sport: Research and Practice*. Taylor & Francis.

Memmert, D., Baker, J., & Bertsch, C. (2010). Play and practice in the development of sport-specific creativity in team ball sports. *High Ability Studies*, *21*(1), 3–18. https://doi.org/10.1080/13598139.2010.488083

Meuren, D., & Schächter, T. (2021). Thomas Tuchel at Mainz: 'You need A-levels for some of these exercises!'. *The Guardian*. www.theguardian.com/football/2021/sep/24/thomas-tuchel-at-mainz-chelsea-manager-training-sessions

Murata, A., Herbison, J. D., Côté, J., Turnnidge, J., & Kelly, A. L. (2021). Competitive engineering in the youth sport context: Theory, practice, and future directions. In A. L. Kelly, J. Côté, M. Jeffreys, & J. Turnnidge (Eds.), *Birth advantages and relative age effects in sport: Exploring organizational structures and creating appropriate settings* (pp. 222–236). Routledge.

Newell, K. (1986). Constraints on the development of coordination. In M. Wade & A. Whiting (Eds.), *Motor development in children: Aspects of coordination and control* (pp. 341–360). Martinus Nijhoff. https://doi.org/10.1007/978-94-009-4460-2_19

Newell, K., & Corcos, D. (1993). Issues in variability and motor control. In K. Newell, & D. M. Corcos (Eds.), *Variability and motor control* (pp. 1–12). Human Kinetics.

Orth, D., van der Kamp, J., Memmert, D., & Savelsbergh, G. (2017). Creative motor actions as emerging from movement variability. *Frontiers in Psychology*, *8*(1903). https://doi.org/10.3389/fpsyg.2017.01903

Rasmussen, L., Glăveanu, V., & Østergaard, L. (2020). "The principles are good, but they need to be integrated in the right way": Experimenting with creativity in elite youth soccer. *Journal of Applied Sport Psychology*, 1–23. https://doi.org/10.1080/10413200.2020.1778135

Rasmussen, L., & Østergaard, L. (2016). The creative soccer platform: New strategies for stimulating creativity in organized youth soccer practice. *Journal of Physical Education, Recreation & Dance*, 87(7), 9–19. https://doi.org/10.1080/07303084.2016.1202799

Rasmussen, L., Østergaard, L., & Glăveanu, V. (2019). Creativity as a developmental resource in sport training activities. *Sport, Education and Society*, 24(5), 491–506. https://doi.org/10.1080/13573322.2017.1403895

Richard, V., Lebeau, J., Becker, F., Inglis, E., & Tenenbaum, G. (2018). Do more creative people adapt better? An investigation into the association between creativity and adaptation. *Psychology of Sport and Exercise*, 38, 80–89. https://doi.org/https://doi.org/10.1016/j.psychsport.2018.06.001

Roca, A., & Ford, P.R. (2021). Developmental activities in the acquisition of creativity in soccer players. *Thinking Skills and Creativity*, 41, 100850. https://doi.org/https://doi.org/10.1016/j.tsc.2021.100850

Santos, S., Coutinho, D., Gonçalves, B., Abade, E., Pasquarelli, B., & Sampaio, J. (2020). Effects of manipulating ball type on youth footballers' performance during small-sided games. *International Journal of Sports Science & Coaching*, 15(2), 170–183. https://doi.org/10.1177/1747954120908003

Santos, S., Coutinho, D., Gonçalves, B., & Sampaio, J. (forthcoming). How many creatives are enough? Exploring how manipulating the number of creative players in the opposing team impacts footballers' performance during small-sided games [Manuscript submitted for publication]. *Human Movement Science*.

Santos, S., Coutinho, D., Gonçalves, B., Schöllhorn, W., Sampaio, J., & Leite, N. (2018). Differential learning as a key training approach to improve creative and tactical behavior in soccer. *Research Quarterly for Exercise and Sport*, 89(1), 11–24. https://doi.org/10.1080/02701367.2017.1412063

Santos, S., Jiménez, S., Sampaio, J., & Leite, N. (2017). Effects of the Skills4Genius sports-based training program in creative behavior. *PLoS One*, 12(2). https://doi.org/10.1371/journal.pone.0172520

Santos, S., Memmert, D., Sampaio, J., & Leite, N. (2016). The spawns of creative behavior in team sports: A creativity developmental framework. *Frontiers in Psychology*, 7, 1282. https://doi.org/10.3389/fpsyg.2016.01282

Santos, S., & Monteiro, D. (2020). Uncovering the role of motor performance and creative thinking on sports creativity in primary school-aged children. *Creativity Research Journal*, 1–15. https://doi.org/10.1080/10400419.2020.1843125

Schöllhorn, W., Hegen, P., & Davids, K. (2012). The nonlinear nature of learning—A differential learning approach. *The Open Sports Sciences Journal*, 5, 100–112.

Stergiou, N., Yu, Y., & Kyvelidou, A. (2013). A perspective on human movement variability with applications in infancy motor development. *Kinesiology Review*, 2(1), 93. https://doi.org/10.1123/krj.2.1.93 10.1123/krj.2.1.93

Sternberg, R., & Lubart, T. (1999). The concept of creativity: Prospects and paradigms. In R. Sternberg (Ed.), *Handbook of creativity* (pp. 3–15). Cambridge University Press.

Torrents, C., Balagué, N., Ric, Á., & Hristovski, R. (2020). The motor creativity paradox: Constraining to release degrees of freedom. *Psychology of Aesthetics, Creativity, and the Arts*, 340–351. https://doi.org/10.1037/aca0000291

Torrents, C., Ric, A., Hristovski, R., Torres-Ronda, L., Vicente, E., & Sampaio, J. (2016). Emergence of exploratory, technical and tactical behavior in small-sided soccer games when manipulating the number of teammates and opponents. *PLoS One*, 11(12), e0168866. https://doi.org/10.1371/journal.pone.0168866

Travassos, B., Duarte, R., Vilar, L., Davids, K., & Araújo, D. (2012). Practice task design in team sports: Representativeness enhanced by increasing opportunities for action. *Journal of Sports Sciences*, 30(13), 1447–1454. https://doi.org/10.1080/02640414.2012.712716

Tumer, E., & Brainard, M. (2007). Performance variability enables adaptive plasticity of 'crystallized' adult birdsong. *Nature*, 450, 1240–1244. https://doi.org/10.1038/nature06390

Wu, H., Miyamoto, Y., Castro, L., Ölveczky, B., & Smith, M. (2014). Temporal structure of motor variability is dynamically regulated and predicts motor learning ability. *Nature Neuroscience*, 17, 312–321. https://doi.org/10.1038/nn.3616

13
TRANSFORMATIONAL COACHING

Developing a Global Rating Scale to Observe Coach Leadership Behaviours

Jordan S. Lefebvre, Adam L. Kelly, Jean Côté, and Jennifer Turnnidge

Introduction

The past two decades has seen an emergence of literature to support that coaches' implementation of transformational coaching behaviours is associated with a number of positive athlete developmental outcomes in youth sport (e.g., Arthur et al., 2011; Callow et al., 2009; Price & Weiss, 2013; Rowold, 2006; Stenling & Tafvelin, 2014; Vella et al., 2013). More recently, scholars have demonstrated that transformational coaching behaviours can be observed through systematic observation as well as learned and integrated into coaching practice (Lawrason et al., 2019; Turnnidge & Côté, 2018, 2019).

The purpose of this chapter is to outline how youth soccer coaches can use a global rating scale—derived from a systematic observation tool called the Coach Leadership Assessment System (CLAS)—to observe, monitor, and improve their implementation of transformational coaching behaviours. First, this chapter discusses the theoretical and conceptual foundation of transformational coaching within the full-range leadership model. Second, the chapter provides an overview of the CLAS, along with the research that uses this assessment tool to observe transformational coaching behaviours. Given that the CLAS is a comprehensive observational tool primarily designed for research, the third section of this chapter proposes and describes a simplified global rating scale adapted from the CLAS (CLAS-GR), which can be used by practitioners and sport organisations to observe and monitor coaches' leadership behaviours in practical settings. In addition, this section suggests various complementary mechanisms wherein coaches can learn to improve their implementation of transformational behaviours, such as the use of mentoring relationships as an educational tool. Lastly, this chapter provides considerations for researchers and practitioners in the context of youth soccer.

Transformational Coaching

Organised youth sport provides a valuable avenue through which youth can become competent athletes and social human beings (Holt & Neely, 2011; Larson, 2000). Accordingly, coaches' leadership behaviours play an important role in creating high-quality sport experiences that facilitate long-term performance, participation, and personal development outcomes (Côté & Gilbert, 2009; Horn, 2008). Effective coaches lead their teams in such a way that benefits athletes' personal assets, such as their competence, confidence, connection, and character (Côté et al., 2020). There are various conceptual frameworks that have examined leadership behaviours within sporting environments, such as the Multidimensional Model of Leadership (Chelladurai, 1993), the Cognitive-Mediational Model of Leadership (Smoll et al., 1978), and the Social Identity Approach to Leadership (Hogg, 2001). Although each of these models have greatly contributed to our understanding of leadership in sport, they are mainly transactional and focused on goals, feedback, and performance outcomes (e.g., Barling, 2014; Chelladurai, 2007). As such, researchers have advocated that it may be beneficial to explore alternative approaches to the study of leadership in sport that focused on contemporary issues, such as personal development and relationships (Rowold, 2006; Turnnidge & Côté, 2018).

One particular approach that may be useful for examining and comparing the large spectrum of leadership behaviours in sport is the Full-Range Leadership Model (Avolio, 1999; Bass, 1985). Informed by Burns' (1978) early work on political leadership, this model suggests that leadership behaviours can be understood along two axes, whereby one axis ranges from passive to active, whereas the other axis ranges from least effective to most effective. This model is comprised of three distinct forms of leadership: (a) laissez-faire, (b) transactional, and (c) transformational (Figure 13.1).

Laissez-faire leadership refers to a passive and ineffective form of leadership in which leaders are unresponsive to followers needs (e.g., avoiding one's responsibilities, withholding feedback). This form of leadership has been associated with negative outcomes, such as role stress, psychological fatigue, and reduced well-being (Barling & Frone, 2017; Fosse et al., 2019; Kaluza et al., 2020). Moving along the axes, transactional leadership relates to behaviours such as assigning

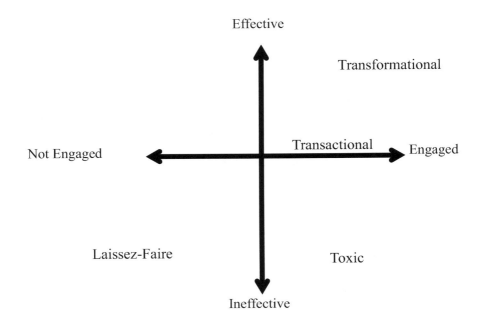

FIGURE 13.1 Full-Range Leadership Model (adapted from Bass, 1985).

consequences for certain types of behaviours (i.e., contingent reward) or monitoring followers to detect deviations from specific standards (i.e., management-by-exception). Transactional leadership focuses on providing rewards and/or punishments in relation to followers' abilities to meet leaders' expectations or standards. Although previous studies suggest that these behaviours can be an important component of leadership, they may be insufficient for optimal follower development (Judge & Piccolo, 2004). At the end of the two axes is transformational leadership, which represents an approach to leadership designed to empower, challenge, and inspire followers (Bass & Riggio, 2006). Although there are various interpretations of transformational leadership (e.g., Bass, 1985; Callow et al., 2009; Podsakoff et al., 1990), this chapter will focus on the conceptualisation of transformational leadership put forward by Bass (1985; Bass & Riggio, 2006).

A transformational leadership approach to coaching is one method of sports coaching that is associated with improvements in athletes' personal assets (Price & Weiss, 2013). Through the transformational leadership lens, the role of a coach is to help athletes acquire the interpersonal skills they need to become effective leaders. Transformational leadership is a unique style of leadership in that it may facilitate the interpersonal development of coaches and their athletes. Transformational leadership theory is grounded in four principles that are known as 'the 4I's': (a) idealised influence, (b) inspirational motivation, (c) intellectual stimulation, and (d) individualised consideration (Bass, 1999). First, *idealised influence* reflects a leader's ability to act as a positive role model and gain the trust and respect of their followers (Bass & Riggio, 2006; Becker, 2009). As an example, coaches can model respectful behaviours to athletes by speaking respectfully to officials. Second, *inspirational motivation* occurs when leaders encourage self-belief in followers and express a compelling vision. For instance, coaches who are inspirational motivators may discuss short-term goals with athletes as well as link these to the achievement of a long-term goal in the future. Third, *intellectual stimulation* involves leaders helping followers to look at challenges from many points of view to find the best solution (Bass, 1999). As an example, coaches can ask athletes open-ended questions during training activities to facilitate critical thinking. Finally, *individualised consideration* emphasises the importance for leaders to interact with followers on a personal level (Hoption et al., 2007). For instance, coaches can show interest in their athletes' lives outside of sport, such as having conversations about school, hobbies, or other extracurricular activities.

There is growing evidence to support the use of transformational behaviours to facilitate positive developmental outcomes in sport (e.g., Callow et al., 2009; Charbonneau et al., 2001; Erikstad et al., 2021; Haugen et al., 2020; Price & Weiss, 2013; Rowold, 2006; Stenling & Tafvelin, 2014). The majority of studies have used self-report questionnaires to assess transformational leadership in sport (Turnnidge & Côté, 2018). For example, Arthur et al. (2011) used questionnaire data to show that youth athletes, including soccer players from the Singapore Sports Academy, placed more effort into their performances when their coaches are perceived as transformational. Data from similar questionnaires also linked youth soccer coaches' inspirational motivation and individualised consideration behaviours to improvements in players' task and social cohesion (Álvarez et al., 2019). Regarding personal development, Vella et al. (2013) demonstrated that players' perception of transformational leadership advanced the social skills, goal setting, and initiative of Australian adolescent soccer players. They also recommended that coaches could use transformational leadership behaviours to create inclusive soccer environments that provide rich opportunities for players to grow. Transformational leadership has also been shown to have a positive impact on participation in soccer. As an example, You (2021) found perceived transformational leadership had a positive effect on organisational team culture in Korean University soccer teams, and suggested it is a likely factor in the successful development of organisational effectiveness. Moreover, Martínez-Moreno et al. (2021) showed how presidents from amateur Spanish sports clubs (which were largely comprised of soccer organisations) who were perceived to demonstrate transformational behaviours increased their subordinates' effort, effectiveness, and satisfaction.

Clearly, the capacity of transformational leadership to produce effective outcomes in sport, and in particular soccer, has been a key focus of previous research (Turnnidge & Côté, 2018). Unfortunately, self-report measures tend to assess perceived coach behaviours only in terms of their effectiveness; that is, *what* they can do for athletes, without tapping into the actual occurrence of transformational behaviours and their effectiveness (e.g., Leadership Scale for Sport: Chelladurai & Saleh, 1980; Multifactorial Leadership Questionnaire: Bass & Avolio, 1995; Transformational Teaching Questionnaire: Beauchamp et al., 2010). However, few studies have explored how observed transformational behaviours may affect athletes in real-world contexts and bypass the limitations of self-report questionnaires (Vierimaa et al., 2016). Fortunately, researchers in sport have begun to examine transformational leadership using observational methods to better understand *how* coaches' leadership behaviours may influence players' outcomes.

Coach Leadership Assessment System

The Coach Leadership Assessment System (Turnnidge & Côté, 2019) is a systematic observation system designed to assess the coaches' leadership behaviours in their interactions with their athletes. The CLAS was developed through an iterative process of literature reviews, interviews with sport coaches, and observations of coach behaviours (Turnnidge & Côté, 2019). The behavioural categories of the CLAS include eleven categories encompassing the 4Is of transformational leadership, two categories representing transactional (i.e., behaviours that are oriented toward reward and punishment, such as searching for and responding to deviations from rules or standards), and one category representing laissez-faire leadership behaviours (e.g., passive behaviours that deflect responsibility, such as showing disinterest). In addition, given that the CLAS is designed to be exhaustive and requires continuous coding—each behaviour needs to be assigned a category. In developing the tool, there were coach behaviours that did not align with the dimensions of the full-range leadership model, which included toxic and neutral leadership. Accordingly, the CLAS includes two categories representing toxic (i.e., behaviours that model anti-social values, such as expressing anger or hostility), and two categories representing neutral (i.e., behaviours that do not fall into any other category) leadership behaviours (Table 13.1). Overall, the CLAS provides useful information regarding the duration, frequency, and sequence of coaches' leadership behaviours (Turnnidge & Côté, 2019). It is also important to note that the CLAS includes a set of content modifiers to provide context for each behaviour code and identify the behaviour recipient.

When developing the CLAS, Turnnidge and Côté (2019) employed several strategies to establish initial measures of validity and reliability. Specifically, they examined the content and face validity of the instrument by: (a) undertaking pilot testing, (b) consulting with a panel of expert reviewers, and (c) consulting with youth sport coaches and organisation stakeholders to ensure that the final system reflected coaching behaviours. Next, examining reliability across four coders, Turnnidge and Côté (2019) reported inter-rater reliability ranging from 78–84% and intra-rater reliability ranging from 75–76%. Collectively, these estimates demonstrated preliminary evidence for good psychometric properties of the tool.

As a systematic observation tool, the CLAS observational data is typically coded continuously (i.e., every second of a person's behaviours are accounted for). Coders are required to

TABLE 13.1 Leadership dimensions of the Coach Leadership Assessment System (CLAS) (adapted from Lefebvre et al., 2021)

Higher-Order Dimension	Lower-Order Dimension	Example Behaviour Code
Idealized Influence	Discussing/modelling pro-social values or behaviours	"Alright folks, any guesses for our last drill? I'll give you a clue: What kind of tea do soccer players drink? . . . Penal-Tea! That's right, to finish today's training we will be practising penalty kicks!"
	Showing vulnerability/humility	"Sorry Blair, I'll take responsibility for that, that was my mistake."
Inspirational Motivation	Discussing goals/expectations	"For today's game, I want you to focus on two things: clean passes and possession."
	Expressing confidence in athlete(s) potential	"Jean, I think you should take the penalty kick. I know you can do this."
	Promoting team concept	"It's important that we work together. There is no 'I' in 'team'."
	Providing rationales/explanations	"We committed too many turnovers last weekend, so today we will focus on ball control."
Intellectual Stimulation	Eliciting athlete input	"That was a good try Michelle, but what do you think you could have done differently?"
	Sharing decision making/leadership responsibilities	"Alright everyone, we have 15 minutes left in practice. Would you rather finish with a scrimmage or do you want to practice penalty kicks?"
	Emphasising learning/process	"Don't worry about it Liz, we learn from our mistakes. Better now than in a game."
Individualized Consideration	Showing interest in athletes' feelings/needs/concerns	"Hey Matthew, how did your exam go today? I remember you said you were a bit worried about it."
	Recognising athlete achievements/contributions	"That was excellent, Chantal! That is exactly what I am looking for, great work!"
Transactional	Discussing rewards/penalties	"Every time you turn over the ball, I want to see 10 push-ups."
	Searching for/responding to deviations from rules or standards	"Ian, stop messing around. Focus please."
Neutral	Silent observation	*Coach observes his/her athletes as they attempt a new drill.*
	Interactive	"Veronica, today you will play on the left side." or "Luc, take a couple steps back."
Laissez-faire	Showing disinterest	*Coach looks at his phone during practice while players wait for instructions.*
Toxic	Expressing anger/hostility	"JORDAN! Get off the field! That was the worst play I've ever seen in my life!"
	Modelling anti-social behaviours	"Common ref, that was a terrible call, open your damn eyes for once."

be rigorously trained to ensure adequate skill and knowledge of the system, which consists of reading pre-determined materials about the full-range leadership model and observational coding, participating in group discussions about the coding process and engaging in group-based coding sessions, followed by independent coding of video segments. To be considered 'reliable', coders are required to attain 75% intra-rater reliability as well as 75% inter-rater reliability with another 'reliable' coder across multiple 10-minute video segments (e.g., Hollenstein et al., 2004). Agreement required the activation of the same complete three-sequence code (i.e., leadership behaviour + content modifier + recipient) within a 3-second window as well as the subsequent deactivation of this coding sequence within a 3-second window. Agreement represented concurrence on five coding decisions: (a) time of behaviour initiation, (b) leadership behaviour, (c) content, (d) recipient, and (e) time of behaviour discontinuation.

A number of studies have used the CLAS to examine the leaderships behaviours of sport coaches (e.g., Hummell et al., 2023; Lawrason et al., 2019; Lefebvre et al., 2021; McGuckin et al., 2022; Turnnidge & Côté, 2019). As an example, Lefebvre et al. (2021) used the CLAS to establish a descriptive behavioural baseline of leadership behaviours of youth soccer coaches. After observing 9,760 behaviours across seven male coaches, their findings identified that 75% of coaches' behaviours in training and competition were 'neutral', whereby they did not characterise any leadership style (e.g., organisation, technical feedback, silent observation). Nonetheless, when displaying leadership, coaches used a greater quantity of individualised consideration and inspirational motivation, followed by idealised influence and intellectual stimulation. Building from these findings, McGuckin et al. (2022) combined the CLAS with a video-stimulated recall methodology to identify youth coaches' intended outcomes when using leadership behaviours. Specifically, 11 competitive youth soccer and volleyball coaches' behaviours were systematically observed and coded using the CLAS and then clips were extracted from the video footage and used to stimulate the memory of coaches within semi-structured interviews. Their findings indicated that, when coaches display a particular leadership behaviour, it was intended to be associated with distinct objectives, such as engaging in transformational leadership to promoting confidence or engaging in transactional leadership to establishing respect. In another study, Lawrason et al. (2019) used the CLAS to evaluate the effectiveness of Turnnidge and Côté's (2017) transformational coaching workshop. They systematically observed the leadership behaviours of eight male head youth soccer coaches before and after participating in the transformational coaching workshop. The observational findings from the CLAS data revealed that coaches increased the frequency of use of transformational leadership behaviours after participating in the workshop.

Collectively, the aforementioned studies shed insight into the possible application of systematic observation and how a tool, such as how the CLAS "can be implemented to explore real-world changes in behaviours" (Lawrason et al., 2019, p. 304). Despite the many advantages of the CLAS, there are also many limitations inherent in the application of systematic observation that detract from the applied utility of the CLAS. Systematic observation is quite time-consuming and typically requires considerable resources, which makes it challenging to observe and analyse large samples (Frick et al., 2010). For instance, the process of training coders to learn coding software and become proficient and reliable in following the coding protocols for systematic observation is challenging. In addition, the detail required in the coding process for the CLAS is time-consuming. For these reasons, systematic observation requires a detailed and tightly controlled setup that is inherently more applicable for research-focused endeavours, where frequency and duration of behaviours are of most importance. Alternatively, global rating observation systems require more summary judgements of larger intervals of behaviours, with the purpose of providing a more general quality assessment of the behaviours that are being displayed. Global rating systems are a viable alternative to systematic observation for real-world applications and for practical use in applied settings, such as soccer competition and practice, which will be presented in the following section.

Global Rating Scale

Global rating scales have been developed and implemented across a number of disciplines, such as education (e.g., Allen et al., 2013; Hafen et al., 2015; Wright & Irwin, 2018), parenting (e.g., Dishion et al., 2017; Lotzin et al., 2015; Ryu & Lombardi, 2015; Tryphonopoulos et al., 2016), medical education (Gerard et al., 2013; Kim et al., 2009), and sport (Smith et al., 2015, 2017). For example, Kim et al. (2009) developed the Crisis Resource Management global rating scale. The tool is designed to assess the non-medical skills required for the management of medical emergencies and was used to compare the differences between medical residents in their first year with residents in their third year. Residents were evaluated by attending physicians trained in the use of the observational tool. The global rating scale included five categories of crisis management skills that were measured on a 7-point Likert scale: (a) problem-solving, (b) situational awareness, (c) leadership, (d) resource utilisation, and (e) communication. As another example, Morawska et al. (2010, 2014) developed a global rating scale alternative to the systematic observation tool called the 'family observation schedule', which is designed to measure maternal parenting behaviours. The scale is composed of four dimensions of behaviours that were coded on a 9-point Likert scale: (a) permissiveness, (b) use of positive parenting strategies, (c) appropriate use of strategies, and (d) parent-child interaction quality. Interestingly, Morawska et al. (2010, 2014) contrasted the global rating scale and the systematic observation scale and found that both scales exhibited similar findings and demonstrated adequate psychometric properties, indicating that global rating can be a suitable and complementary alternative to systematic observation coding. In essence, a global rating scale is most appropriate when the subjective quality and meaning of the behaviours are required in addition to the quantity or duration. Because of its ease of use, global rating scales can also be employed live during actual events instead of being coded from recordings.

In the sport domain, Smith et al. (2015) developed the multidimensional motivational climate observational system, a global rating scale designed for observing the behaviours of sport coaches grounded in self-determination theory and achievement goal theory. The scale consists of two higher-order factors, including empowering and disempowering behaviours. Empowering behaviours include autonomy-supportive, task-involving, and relatedness-supportive behaviours. Disempowering coaching includes controlling, ego-involving, and relatedness-thwarting behaviours. The scale has demonstrated adequate levels of reliability (inter- and intra-observer) and validity (factorial and predictive). In addition, Smith et al. (2017) implemented the multidimensional motivational climate observational system to examine the differences in 17 youth soccer coach behaviours in the training context, compared to the competitive context. Accordingly, the coaches were found to be less empowering (lower in autonomy support, task involvement, and relatedness support) and more disempowering (higher in control, ego-involvement, and relatedness thwarting) in competition compared to training. These studies provide the most robust to date for the use of global rating in the team sport context and, in particular, demonstrate utility for the sport of soccer. Accordingly, this paves the way for the development of other global rating scales for the sport context. Accordingly, in the remainder of this chapter, the initial development of a global rating version of the CLAS is proposed, hereby referred to as the CLAS-GRS.

Coach Leadership Assessment System—Global Rating Scale (CLAS-GRS)

Analogous to the CLAS, the CLAS-GRS examines the leadership behaviours of coaches across the full-range leadership model (i.e., transformational, transactional, laissez-faire, and toxic leadership) (see Table 13.1). With the CLAS-GRS, however, coach leadership behaviours are assessed

190 Jordan S. Lefebvre et al.

Name:		Evaluator:						
Date:		Venue/Competition:						

Leadership	Coaching Behavior	Segment 1						
		L		M				H
Idealized Influence (TFL)	Discussing and modelling prosocial values/behaviors	1	2	3	4	5	6	7
	Showing vulnerability and humility	1	2	3	4	5	6	7
	Discussing goals and expectations	1	2	3	4	5	6	7
Inspirational Motivation (TFL)	Expressing confidence in athlete capabilities	1	2	3	4	5	6	7
	Implementing a collective vision	1	2	3	4	5	6	7
	Providing meaningful and challenging tasks and roles	1	2	3	4	5	6	7
Intellectual Stimulation (TFL)	Eliciting athlete input	1	2	3	4	5	6	7
	Sharing decision making and leadership responsibilities	1	2	3	4	5	6	7
	Emphasizing the learning process	1	2	3	4	5	6	7
Individualized Consideration (TFL)	Showing interest in athletes needs	1	2	3	4	5	6	7
	Recognizing individual roles and contributions	1	2	3	4	5	6	7
Transactional	Discussing rewards and penalties	1	2	3	4	5	6	7
	Searching for and responding to deviations	1	2	3	4	5	6	7
Laissez-faire	Showing disinterest	1	2	3	4	5	6	7
Toxic	Expressing anger/hostility	1	2	3	4	5	6	7
	Discussing and modelling anti-social values/behaviors	1	2	3	4	5	6	7

Evaluator Observations and Reflections

Segment 1	
Goals and Suggestions for Next Attempt	

FIGURE 13.2 Coach Leadership Assessment System—Global Rating Scale (CLAS-GRS).

using a potency scale that combines frequency, duration, and meaning of behaviours across a 10-minute segment, using a 7-point Likert scale ranging from 1 (low potency) to 7 (high potency) (see Figure 13.2). That is, the potency takes into account how many times a coach engages in a behaviour, how long a coach engages in a behaviour, and how meaningful the execution a behaviour appears to be. As an example, a coach may frequently recognise the efforts of athletes in brief, encouraging statements (e.g., good try, keep going) in line with intellectual stimulation (emphasising the learning process), which would correspond to a high potency rating. Alternatively, there may be one instance of showing humility (e.g., apologising for a mistake or sharing a personal story), which is longer in duration and meaningful for those involved. This would also lead to a higher potency rating.

An assessor typically uses the CLAS-GRS to assess coaches for three 10-minute segments (e.g., beginning, middle, end) per event (e.g., practice, competition). For each 10-minute segment, assessors are provided with an opportunity to deliver thoughts and feedback. In addition, at the end of an event, assessors provide a final assessment based on the potency evaluations across all three segments. Similar to the CLAS, coders are trained using an in-depth coding manual designed specifically for the CLAS-GRS[1]. During the training, assessors are provided with: (a) a short tutorial about the full-range leadership model and relevant leadership theoretical principles, (b) the CLAS-GRS manual, (c) reading materials on transformational coaching and behavioural observation, (d) time to engage in self-directed practice with the tool, and (e) the opportunity to receive coding feedback with a gold standard coder. Assessors are also provided with companion material to facilitate the interpretation of scores.

The CLAS-GRS is designed to be used by a wide range of assessors looking to examine the leadership behaviours of a coach in any context. An assessor might include a technical director, a colleague, a coach mentor, or a coach who can examine their own behaviours. As an example, a technical director might use the CLAS-GRS as a means for cursory assessment of interpersonal competencies (e.g., using findings to inform coach development plans, training needs). Ultimately, the tool is designed as a means for stimulating discussion between an assessor and coach or as a means for self-reflection, suggesting there are various mechanisms wherein coaches can learn to improve their implementation of transformational behaviours.

Considerations for Researchers

Given the novelty of the CLAS-GRS, there are a number of considerations for future research endeavours. As a next step, it will be important for scholars to engage in research efforts that attempt to demonstrate estimates of validity (e.g., construct, discriminate validity) and reliability (e.g., inter- and intra-observer) for the CLAS-GRS. Researchers are also encouraged to engage, examine, and solidify the value proposition of the CLAS-GRS using qualitative methodology, such as its ability to stimulate feedback discussions that promote coaches' interpersonal development (also see considerations for practitioners). Another valuable avenue for future work would be to work with sport stakeholders (e.g., coaches, coach developers, and organisational administrators) to explore the value, usability, and feasibility of the tool. This aligns with a knowledge mobilisation approach in which knowledge tools, such as the CLAS-GRS, are adapted to diverse local contexts (Graham et al., 2006). It is also important for future work to examine how the tool can be disseminated, implemented, and adapted over time in real-world settings.

Interpersonal coach behaviours, such as leadership behaviours, are inherently a reciprocal process (e.g., Jones et al., 2010). Therefore, it would be interesting for future research to observe athlete's behavioural responses along with transformational coaching behaviours. This could pave the way for the implementation of state space grid methodology (see Hollenstein, 2007), which could uncover the structural features of leadership-based interactions (e.g., effective behaviour sequencing of leadership).

Considerations for Practitioners

Many benefits have been presented throughout this chapter with regards to *why* practitioners should consider implementing transformational coaching behaviours into their coaching. This has been reinforced with strategies of *how* they can be monitored and developed. In order to develop their transformational coaching behaviours, practitioners should consider the following suggestions:

- Incorporate a range of transformational behaviours (i.e., the 4Is) into applied practice. This can be achieved through acting as a positive role model (idealised influence), encouraging self-belief and a compelling vision (inspirational motivation), helping players look at challenges from many points of view (intellectual stimulation), and interacting with players on a personal level (individualised consideration).
- Consider the benefits of implementing the CLAS-GRS into applied practice. This will allow practitioners to document live or retrospective observation and analysis of transformational leadership behaviours.
- Practitioners could use the CLAS-GRS for the purpose of self-assessment and to stimulate self-reflection of one's own transformational coaching behaviours.
- A coach developer, mentor coach, or colleague could use the CLAS-GRS as a learning tool to facilitate feedback discussions and foster continued coach development. This would help soccer organisations or clubs embed transformational coaching behaviours into their coaching philosophy at a broader level. Indeed, this tool may be a suitable alternative to more time-consuming systematic observation coding.
- Organisations could use the CLAS-GRS as a component of an educational programme to facilitate coaches' development of leadership behaviours.

Conclusion

There are different observation methodologies available to researchers and practitioners seeking to assess and reflect on coach leadership behaviours. In research settings, the CLAS (Turnnige & Côté, 2019) employs a continuous coding strategy that requires the analysis of recorded interactions in games or practices. The CLAS was rigorously developed over several years and provides a wealth of objective and highly detailed information that can be analysed, in a laboratory setting, from recorded competition or practice. The purpose of this chapter was to build upon the CLAS to offer a user-friendly version, the CLAS-GRS instrument, which can be primarily used in applied settings to offer coaches real-time feedback on their interactions and leadership behaviours. The CLAS-GRS provides sport organisations with a convenient and accessible observational tool, which has been adapted from an evidence-based instrument that was rigorously developed and validated. The advantages of the CLAS-GRS are that it is quick to learn, simple to use, and can be widely implemented by practitioners and sport organisations. The CLAS-GRS aims to bridge the gap between research and applied settings to ensure that the observation data used by practitioners in the real world are measuring what they are intended to measure in the most effective way possible. The rigorous application of an evidence-based rating scale observation system such as the CLAS-GRS would provide useful, meaningful, and reliable data to soccer organisations across a range of leadership behaviours that can be used to build better interpersonal culture.

Note

1 The CLAS-GRS coding manual can be obtained via the Queen's University Sport Psychology PLAYS Research Group website: www.queensu.ca/sportpsych/resources.

References

Allen, J., Gregory, A., Mikami, A., Lun, J., Hamre, B., & Pianta, R. (2013). Observations of effective teacher–student interactions in secondary school classrooms: Predicting student achievement with the classroom assessment scoring system—Secondary. *School Psychology Review*, *42*(1), 76–98.

Álvarez, O., Castillo, I., Molina-García, V., & Tomás, I. (2019). Transformational leadership, task-involving climate, and their implications in male junior soccer players: A multilevel approach. *International Journal of Environmental Research and Public Health*, *16*(19), 3649. https://doi.org/10.3390/ijerph16193649

Arthur, C. A., Woodman, T., Ong, C. W., Hardy, L., & Ntoumanis, N. (2011). The role of athlete narcissism in moderating the relationship between coaches' transformational leader behaviors and athlete motivation. *Journal of Sport and Exercise Psychology*, *33*(1), 3–19. http://dx.doi.org/10.1123/jsep.33.1.3

Avolio, B. J. (1999). *Full leadership development: Building the vital forces in organizations*. Sage.

Barling, J. (2014). *The science of leadership: Lessons from research for organizational leaders*. Oxford University Press.

Barling, J., & Frone, M. R. (2017). If only my leader would just do something! Passive leadership undermines employee well-being through role stressors and psychological resource depletion. *Stress and Health*, *33*(3), 211–222. https://doi.org/10.1002/smi.2697

Bass, B. M. (1985). *Leadership and performance beyond expectations*. Free Press.

Bass, B. M. (1999). Two decades of research and development in transformational leadership. *European Journal of Work and Organizational Psychology*, *8*(1), 9–32. https://doi.org/10.1080/135943299398410

Bass, B. M., & Avolio, B. J. (1995). *Multifactor leadership questionnaires (MLQ)*. APA PsycTests.

Bass, B. M., & Riggio, R. E. (2006). *Transformational leadership*. Psychology Press.

Beauchamp, M. R., Barling, J., Li, Z., Morton, K. L., Keith, S. E., & Sumbo, B. D. (2010). Development and psychometric properties of the transformational teaching questionnaire. *Journal of Health Psychology*, *15*(8), 1123–1134. https://doi.org/10.1177%2F1359105310364175

Becker, A. J. (2009). It's not what they do, it's how they do it: Athlete experiences of great coaching. *International Journal of Sports Science & Coaching*, *4*(1), 93–119. https://doi.org/10.1260%2F1747-9541.4.1.93

Burns, J. M. (1978). *Leadership*. Harper and Row.

Callow, N., Smith, M. J., Hardy, L., Arthur, C. A., & Hardy, J. (2009). Measurement of transformational leadership and its relationship with team cohesion and performance level. *Journal of Applied Sport Psychology*, *21*(4), 395–412. https://doi.org/10.1080/10413200903204754

Charbonneau, D., Barling, J., & Kelloway, E. K. (2001). Transformational leadership and sports performance: The mediating role of intrinsic motivation. *Journal of Applied Sport Psychology*, *31*, 1521–1534. https://doi.org/10.1111/j.1559-1816.2001.tb02686.x

Chelladurai, P. (1993). Leadership. In R. N. Singer, M. Murphey, & L. K. Tennant (Eds.), *Handbook of research on sport psychology* (pp. 647–671). MacMillan.

Chelladurai, P. (2007). Leadership in sports. In G. Tenenbaum & R. C. Eklund (Eds.), *Handbook of sport psychology* (pp. 113–135). Wiley.

Chelladurai, P., & Saleh, S. D. (1980). Dimensions of leader behavior in sports: Development of a leadership scale. *Journal of Sport Psychology*, 2(1), 34–45. https://doi.org/10.1123/jsp.2.1.34

Côté, J., & Gilbert, W. (2009). An integrative definition of coaching effectiveness and expertise. *International Journal of Sports Science & Coaching*, 4(3), 307–323. https://doi.org/10.1260%2F174795409789623892

Côté, J., Turnnidge, J., Murata, A., McGuire, C., Martin, L. (2020). Youth sport research: Describing the integrated dynamics elements of the personal assets framework. *International Journal of Sport Psychology*, 51(2), 562–578. https://doi.org/10.7352/IJSP.2020.51.562

Dishion, T. J., Mun, C. J., Tein, J. Y., Kim, H., Shaw, D. S., Gardner, F., Wilson, M. H., & Peterson, J. (2017). The validation of macro and micro observations of parent–child dynamics using the relationship affect coding system in early childhood. *Prevention Science*, 18(3), 268–280. https://doi.org/10.1007/s11121-016-0697-5

Erikstad, M. K., Høigaard, R., Côté, J., Turnnidge, J., & Haugen, T. (2021). An examination of the relationship between coaches' transformational leadership and athletes' personal and group characteristics in elite youth soccer. *Frontiers in Psychology*, 3010. https://doi.org/10.3389/fpsyg.2021.707669

Fosse, T. H., Skogstad, A., Einarsen, S. V., & Martinussen, M. (2019). Active and passive forms of destructive leadership in a military context: A systematic review and meta-analysis. *European Journal of Work and Organizational Psychology*, 28(5), 708–722. https://doi.org/10.1080/1359432X.2019.1634550

Frick, P. J., Barry, C. T., & Kamphaus, R. W. (2010). *Clinical assessment of child and adolescent personality and behavior*. Springer.

Gerard, J., Kessler, D., Braun, C., Mehta, R., Scalzo, A., & Auerbach, M. (2013). Validation of global rating scale and checklist instruments for the infant lumbar puncture procedure. *The Journal of the Society for Simulation in Healthcare*, 8(3), 148–154. https://doi.org/10.1097/sih.0b013e3182802d34

Graham, I. D., Logan, J., Harrison, M. B., Straus, S. E., Tetroe, J., Caswell, W., & Robinson, N. (2006). Lost in knowledge translation: Time for a map? *Journal of Continuing Education in the Health Professions*, 26(1), 13–24. https://doi.org/10.1002/chp.47

Hafen, C. A., Hamre, B. K., Allen, J. P., Bell, C. A., Gitomer, D. H., & Pianta, R. C. (2015). Teaching through interactions in secondary school classrooms: Revisiting the factor structure and practical application of the classroom assessment scoring system–secondary. *The Journal of Early Adolescence*, 35(5–6), 651–680. https://doi.org/10.1177/0272431614537117

Haugen, T., Riesen, J. F., Østrem, K., Høigaard, R., & Erikstad, M. K. (2020). The relationship between motivational climate and personal treatment satisfaction among young soccer players in Norway: The moderating role of supportive coach-behaviour. *Sports*, 8(12), 162. https://doi.org/10.3390/sports8120162

Hogg, M. A. (2001). A social identity theory of leadership. *Personality and Social Psychology Review*, 5, 184–200. https://doi.org/10.1207%2FS15327957PSPR0503_1

Hollenstein, T. (2007). State space grids: Analyzing dynamics across development. *International Journal of Behavioral Development*, 31, 384–396. https://doi.org/10.1177%2F0165025407077765

Hollenstein, T., Granic, I., Stoolmiller, M., & Snyder, J. (2004). Rigidity in parent-child interactions and the development of externalizing and internalizing behavior in early childhood. *Journal of Abnormal Child Psychology*, 32(6), 595–607. https://doi.org/10.1023/b:jacp.0000047209.37650.41

Holt, N. L., & Neely, K. C. (2011). Positive youth development through sport: A review. *Revista Iberoamericana de Psicología del Ejercicio y el Deporte*, 6(2), 299–316.

Hoption, C., Phelan, J., & Barling, J. (2007). Transformational leadership in sport. In M. R. Beauchamp & M. A. Eys (Eds.), *Group dynamics in exercise and sport psychology: Contemporary themes* (pp. 45–60). Routledge.

Horn, T. S. (2008). *Advances in sport psychology*. Human Kinetics.

Hummell, C., Herbison, J. D., Turnnidge, J., & Côté, J. (2023). Assessing the effectiveness of the transformational coaching workshop using behavior change theory. *International Journal of Sports Science & Coaching*, *18*(1), 3–12. https://doi.org/10.1177/17479541221122435

Jones, R. L., Bowes, I., & Kingston, K. (2010). Complex practice in coaching: Studying the chaotic nature of coach-athlete interactions. In J. Lyle & C. Cushion (Eds.), *Sport coaching: Professionalization and practice* (pp. 15–25). Elsevier.

Judge, T. A., & Piccolo, R. F. (2004). Transformational and transactional leadership: A meta-analytic test of their relative validity. *Journal of Applied Psychology*, *89*, 755–768. https://psycnet.apa.org/doi/10.1037/0021-9010.89.5.755

Kaluza, A. J., Boer, D., Buengeler, C., & van Dick, R. (2020). Leadership behaviour and leader self-reported well-being: A review, integration and meta-analytic examination. *Work & Stress*, *34*(1), 34–56. https://doi.org/10.1080/02678373.2019.1617369

Kim, J., Neilipovitz, D., Cardinal, P., & Chiu, M. (2009). A comparison of global rating scale and checklist scores in the validation of an evaluation tool to assess performance in the resuscitation of critically ill patients during simulated emergencies. *Simulation in Healthcare*, *4*(1), 6–16. https://doi.org/10.1097/sih.0b013e3181880472

Larson, R. W. (2000). Toward a psychology of positive youth development. *American Psychologist*, *55*(1), 170–183. https://psycnet.apa.org/doi/10.1037/0003-066X.55.1.170

Lawrason, S., Turnnidge, J., Martin, L. J., & Côté, J. (2019). A transformational coaching workshop for changing youth sport coaches' behaviours: A pilot intervention study. *The Sport Psychologist*, *33*(4), 304–312. https://doi.org/10.1123/tsp.2018-0172

Lefebvre, J. S., Turnnidge, J., & Côté, J. (2021). A systematic observation of coach leadership behaviours in youth sport. *Journal of Applied Sport Psychology*, *33*(3), 377–386. https://doi.org/10.1080/10413200.2019.1609620

Lotzin, A., Lu, X., Kriston, L., Schiborr, J., Musal, T., Romer, G., & Ramsauer, B. (2015). Observational tools for measuring parent–infant interaction: A systematic review. *Clinical Child and Family Psychology Review*, *18*(2), 99–132. https://doi.org/10.1007/s10567-015-0180-z

Martínez-Moreno, A., Cavas-García, F., & Díaz-Suárez, A. (2021). Leadership style in amateur club sports: A key element in strategic management. *Sustainability*, *13*(2), 730. https://doi.org/10.3390/su13020730

McGuckin, M. E. C., Turnnidge, J., Bruner, M. W., Lefebvre, J. S., & Côté, J. (2022). Exploring youth sport coaches' perceptions of intended outcomes of leadership behaviours. *International Journal of Sport Science & Coaching*, *17*(3), 377–386. https://doi.org/10.1177%2F17479541221076247

Morawska, A., Adamson, M., & Winter, L. (2010). *Observation global rating scale*. Parenting and Family Support Centre, University of Queensland.

Morawska, A., Basha, A., Adamson, M., & Winter, L. (2014). Microanalytic coding versus global rating of maternal parenting behaviour. *Early Child Development and Care*, *185*(3), 448–463. https://doi.org/10.1080/03004430.2014.932279

Podsakoff, P. M., MacKenzie, S. B., Moorman, R. H., & Fetter, R. (1990). Transformational leader behaviors and their effects on followers' trust in leader, satisfaction, and organizational citizenship behaviors. *The Leadership Quarterly*, *1*, 107–142. https://doi.org/10.1016/1048-9843(90)90009-7

Price, M. S., & Weiss, M. R. (2013). Relationships among coach leadership, peer leadership, and adolescent athletes' psychosocial and team outcomes: A test of transformational leadership theory. *Journal of Applied Sport Psychology*, *25*(2), 265–279. https://doi.org/10.1080/10413200.2012.725703

Rowold, J. (2006). Transformational and transactional leadership in martial arts. *Journal of Applied Sport Psychology*, *18*(4), 312–325. https://doi.org/10.1080/10413200600944082

Ryu, S., & Lombardi, D. (2015). Coding classroom interactions for collective and individual engagement. *Educational Psychologist*, *50*(1), 70–83. http://dx.doi.org/10.1080/00461520.2014.1001891

Smith, N., Quested, E., Appleton, P. R., & Duda, J. L. (2017). Observing the coach-created motivational environment across training and competition in youth sport. *Journal of Sports Sciences*, *35*(2), 149–158. https://doi.org/10.1080/02640414.2016.1159714

Smith, N., Tessier, D., Tzioumakis, Y., Quested, E., Appleton, P., Sarrazin, P., Papaioannou, A., & Duda, J. L. (2015). Development and validation of the multidimensional motivational climate observation system. *Journal of Sport and Exercise Psychology*, *37*(1), 4–22. https://doi.org/10.1123/jsep.2014-0059

Smoll, F. L., Smith, R. E., Curtis, B., & Hunt, E. (1978). Toward a mediational model of coach-player relationships. *Research Quarterly. American Alliance for Health, Physical Education and Recreation*, *49*(4), 528–541. https://doi.org/10.1080/10671315.1978.10615567

Stenling, A., & Tafvelin, S. (2014). Transformational leadership and well-being in sports: The mediating role of need satisfaction. *Journal of Applied Sport Psychology*, *26*, 182–196. https://doi.org/10.1080/10413200.2013.819392

Tryphonopoulos, P. D., Letourneau, N., & DiTommaso, E. (2016). Caregiver-infant interaction quality: A review of observational assessment tools. *Comprehensive Child and Adolescent Nursing*, *39*(2), 107–138. https://doi.org/10.3109/01460862.2015.1134720

Turnnidge, J., & Côté, J. (2017). Transformational coaching workshop: Applying a person-centred approach to coach development programs. *International Sport Coaching Journal*, *4*(3), 314–325. https://doi.org/10.1123/iscj.2017-0046

Turnnidge, J., & Côté, J. (2018). Applying transformational leadership theory to coaching research in youth sport: A systematic literature review. *International Journal of Sport and Exercise Psychology*, *16*(3), 327–342. http://dx.doi.org/10.1080/1612197X.2016.1189948

Turnnidge, J., & Côté, J. (2019). Observing coaches' leadership behaviours in sport: The development of the Coach Leadership Assessment System (CLAS). *Measurement in Physical Education and Exercise Science*, *23*(3), 214–26. https://doi.org/10.1080/1091367X.2019.1602835

Vella, S. A., Oades, L. G., & Crowe, T. P. (2013). The relationship between coach leadership, the coach-athlete relationship, team success, and the positive developmental experiences of adolescent soccer players. *Physical Education and Sport Pedagogy*, *18*(5), 549–561. http://doi.org/10.1080/17408989.2012.726976

Vierimaa, M., Turnnidge, J., Evans, M. B., & Côté, J. (2016). Tools and techniques used in the observation of coach behavior. In P. Davis (Ed.), *The psychology of effective coaching and management* (pp. 111–132). Nova.

Wright, P. M., & Irwin, C. (2018). Using systematic observation to assess teacher effectiveness promoting personally and socially responsible behavior in physical education. *Measurement in Physical Education and Exercise Science*, *22*(3), 250–262. https://doi.org/10.1080/1091367X.2018.1429445

You, K. W. (2021). The effect of transactional and transformational leadership behaviours on factors establishing teams' cultural aspects to promote organizational effectiveness. *Sport Mont*, *19*(3), 35–40. https://doi.org/10.26773/smj.211008

14
GENETICS

Understanding the Influence and Application of Genetics in Soccer

Alexander B. T. McAuley, Joseph Baker, Bruce Suraci, and Adam L. Kelly

Introduction

The process of reaching senior professional status in sports such as soccer is both dynamic and multifactorial (Kelly & Williams, 2020; McAuley et al., 2022a; Williams et al., 2020). The complexity involved when identifying athlete potential has become even more convoluted with advances in research disciplines such as genetics. The influence of genetics on expertise is now generally accepted (Georgiades et al., 2017; Hambrick et al., 2018; Tucker & Collins, 2012); however, it is often overlooked and less critically reviewed throughout the talent identification and development literatures in soccer (McAuley et al., 2021b; Sarmento et al., 2018). This is despite early and more recent definitions and conceptualisations describing 'talent' as at least partly 'innate' (e.g., Baker & Wattie, 2018; Baker et al., 2019; Howe et al., 1998). In light of the general paucity of talent identification and development literature reviewing soccer specific genetic studies, the purpose of this chapter is to provide an overview of contemporary investigations in this field of research. The chapter begins with a discussion of key terms and concepts that are important for understanding this topic, before discussing the practical application of genetics in soccer contexts, the limitations of current understanding, and directions for future research and practice.

Principal Genetic Concepts

All genetic information a human possesses, represented by the entirety of DNA coded sequences, is contained in the 'genome'. The DNA molecules are predominantly found inside a cell's nucleus, where there are 23 different pairs of chromosomes and ~25,000 pairs of 'genes' (i.e., an interval of DNA ranging from hundreds to millions of base pairs, which produces a product that has a biological function; Gibson, 2016). Human genome sequencing has revealed that the DNA sequence between individuals is more than 99% identical (International Human Genome Sequencing Consortium, 2004). That said, due to the size of the human genome (~3,000,000,000 base pairs), there are millions of potential base pair variations between individuals (Attia et al., 2009). 'Base pairs' are one set of nucleotides (i.e., Adenine [A], Cytosine [C], Guanine [G], and Thymine [T]) connected to each other via the opposite DNA strand (Gibson, 2016). Nucleotides

DOI: 10.4324/9781032232799-14

are bound in sequence adjacent to one another (e.g., ACAGTTCGA), forming a human's double-stranded DNA code (Guilherme et al., 2014). Significantly, 'A' always pairs with 'T', and 'C' always pairs with 'G', so once the order of nucleotides is identified on one DNA strand, the other strand is automatically known (Attia et al., 2009).

Common inter-individual variations that appear in DNA are: (a) single base-pair alterations (i.e., ACAG*G*TCGA—ACAG*T*TCGA), (b) base-pair insertions (i.e., ACAGTTCGA—ACAG*C*TTCGA), and (c) base-pair deletions (i.e., ACAGTTCGA—ACAG_TCGA). Different sequences in DNA at a specific chromosomal location (i.e., locus) on each gene are known as 'alleles', which collectively denote an individual's 'genotype'. As such, the genotype of an individual will be either homozygous (i.e., same copy of both alleles, such as C/C or T/T) or heterozygous (i.e., different copies of both alleles, such as C/T), which will influence associated 'phenotypes' (i.e., observable traits, such as height, strength, speed, and endurance). The most common genetic variation in humans is an alteration in one base pair known as a single nucleotide polymorphism (SNP) (Salisbury et al., 2003). The term 'polymorphism' is used describe a variant with a frequency above 1% in the population (i.e., common variant), whereas a variant with a frequency under 1% in the population is called a 'mutation' (i.e., rare variant) (Gibson, 2016). A SNP is one of the easiest types of variation to determine, and therefore, are widely investigated in human genetic studies (Johnson, 2009). Due to the abundance of SNPs, each one is usually assigned an unambiguous 'rs' (i.e., referenceSNP) number (e.g., rs1815739) (Gibson, 2016).

The similarity and frequency of genetic variations are not universal across all population groups. Genetic variation is contingent on a number of factors, such as geographical ancestry (i.e., ethnicity) and sex. As such, depending on the characteristics that define particular cohorts, distinct genetic associations may emerge if the allele frequency of a specific genetic variant differs between population substructures (e.g., population stratification) (Attia et al., 2009). If a significant association is found in a specific population, replication is required in other populations to substantiate findings and identify the underpinning biological mechanisms (Guilherme et al., 2014). A failure to replicate associations may also indicate that methodological limitations were present in the original study (Ioannidis et al., 2001). For instance, polymorphisms generally have small effects (i.e., odds ratios [OR] of ~1.2 and R^2 of ~1%) on complex traits (i.e., athletic performance) (Bouchard, 2011; Tanisawa et al., 2020). Thus, it is essential that studies are sufficiently powered with an adequate sample size and athlete cohorts are homogenous in characteristics influencing associations with performance (e.g., sex, ethnicity, maturation, sport, and playing level) to reduce false positive and/or negative results.

Heritability of Soccer Characteristics

Early studies examining the role of genetics on human performance (i.e., classical genetics) investigated the differences between pairs of monozygotic (i.e., identical) and dizygotic (i.e., fraternal) twins or members of nuclear families (i.e., familial aggregation studies) (Bouchard & Malina, 2014). The overall purpose of these studies was to calculate a 'heritability' estimate for the particular trait(s) of interest within each investigation. The heritability statistic was introduced by Fisher (1918) to quantify the overall phenotypic variance that is attributable to genetics in specific environmental contexts. Several heritability studies have now been conducted on a wide range of traits that are relevant in youth soccer contexts. For instance, anthropometric heritability studies have estimated that ~80% of the variation in height is due to genetic factors (Silventoinen et al., 2008; Visscher et al., 2006). Other examples of relatively high anthropometric heritability estimates include mesomorphy (~80%), skeletal muscle mass (~80%), body mass (~60%), and body mass index (~60%) (Livshits et al., 2016; Peeters et al., 2007). In physiological research, heritability studies have often focused on investigating maximal endurance, strength, and power capacities. Recent meta-analyses have reported relatively high weighted heritability estimates. For instance, Schutte et al. (2016) meta-analysis of VO_2 max revealed a weighted heritability estimate of ~72%. Similarly, Zempo et al. (2017) meta-analysis produced an overall weighted heritability estimate of 52% for strength and power measurements.

Heritability estimates have also been reported for a wide range of relevant psychological, technical, and tactical traits for youth soccer development and performance. Specifically, studies have produced heritability estimates for intracortical facilitation (~90%), intracortical inhibition (80%), motor control (~70%), motor learning (~70%), motor cortex plasticity (~70%), personality traits (~50%), and cognitive abilities (~50%) (Missitzi et al., 2013; Pellicciari et al., 2009; Polderman et al., 2015). In addition, although data on the heritability of injuries is more limited, a recent study on a large number of twins (n = 88,414) reported a heritability estimate of 69% for lifetime risk of ACL rupture (Magnusson et al., 2021). Overall, heritability studies emphasise the contribution of genetics to a number of factors related to athletic status in soccer. This is exemplified by an overall heritability estimate of ~66% for athletic status, irrespective of the sport (De Moor et al., 2007). Furthermore, the most comprehensive heritability meta-analysis conducted to date, which comprised ~14 million twin pairs and 17,804 human traits, reported a weighted heritability estimate of 49% across all traits (Polderman et al., 2015). Moreover, no trait produced a weighted heritability estimate of 0%, indicating that all human traits are influenced by genetic factors to some extent (Polderman et al., 2015).

Molecular Genetic Associations

While heritability studies establish a foundation of the potential genetic influence on human traits, they do not reveal what specific biological variants directly contribute to the observed differences in investigated traits (Guilherme et al., 2014). However, the more sophisticated molecular biology techniques developed over the past two decades have removed this constraint. Genetic researchers now have access to advanced scientific tools that enable the analysis and evaluation of specific alterations in DNA sequences, both within and between distinct athletic groups as well as their consequent influence on selected traits (i.e., genotype-phenotype associations) (Pitsiladis & Wang, 2011). The most common experimental approach employed to identify genetic associations is the candidate gene association study (CGAS) (Guilherme et al., 2014). This design uses pre-selected (i.e., candidate) genetic variants according to their known or postulated biological function and previous results with a relevant trait in a particular cohort (Attia et al., 2009). In soccer, three main types of investigations have been performed: (a) *case-control*, which compare the genotype/allele frequency between categorical variables (e.g., soccer players and non-soccer players; Egorova et al., 2014; Gineviciene et al., 2014; Juffer et al., 2009; Santiago et al., 2008), (b) *cross-sectional*, which compare genotype/allele associations with quantitative variables (e.g., sprint time and jump height; Dionísio et al., 2017; Massidda et al., 2012; McAuley et al., 2022b, 2022c; Micheli et al., 2011; Pimenta et al., 2013), and (c) *longitudinal*, which compare genotype/allele associations with responses to specific interventions (e.g., resistance training and aerobic training modifications; Jones et al., 2016; Pickering et al., 2018; Pimenta et al., 2012; Suraci et al., 2021).

The positives of CGAS include its inexpensiveness and relative ease to conduct (Guilherme et al., 2014). However, the major limitation is the limited number of genetic variants that can be assessed in each study. This limitation has led to new experimental approaches, with the genome-wide association study (GWAS) becoming one of the most common (e.g., Al-Khelaifi et al., 2019, 2020; Pickering et al., 2019; Rodas et al., 2019). A GWAS does not involve the pre-selection of genetic variants based upon contemporary theoretical suggestions regarding their possible influence on particular traits (Attia et al., 2009). Instead, a GWAS is 'hypothesis-free', so it can analyse an extremely large number (i.e., > 1,000,000) of genetic polymorphisms and suggest genotype-phenotype associations based solely on observed data (Visscher et al., 2012). This makes the GWAS a more robust genetic association tool, as it increases the chance of finding novel genetic variants associated with investigated traits (Bouchard et al., 2011). However, a GWAS is more expensive and requires large homogenous samples in order to reach adequate statistical power (i.e., 5×10^{-8}), due to the number of multiple comparisons being performed (McCarthy et al., 2008). This can be problematic, since high-performance cohorts in sports such as soccer are very small and heterogenic by nature (Hughes et al., 2011).

Genetic association studies have grown extensively in sport since the first polymorphism associated with performance (i.e., *ACE* I/D) was discovered in 1998 (Gayagay et al., 1998; Montgomery et al., 1998). Indeed, a literature review reported that, from the period of 1998–2015, a total of 155 polymorphisms associated with athletic status in sport had been identified (Ahmetov et al., 2016). Interestingly, 77% were identified between 2010 and 2015, which showcased a remarkable rise of interest within this field of research. Most of the research conducted on genetic associations involves athletes from individual sports, such as sprinting, long-distance running, cycling, rowing, and swimming (Ahmetov et al., 2016). However, following a similar trend with overall sport genomic research, genetic association studies in soccer are on the rise (McAuley et al., 2021b). The first genetic association study involving soccer players was conducted over two decades ago (Fatini et al., 2000). In 2020, it was estimated there were at least 80 genetic association studies conducted involving soccer players. More significantly, over 50% of these studies have been conducted within the last 4 years (McAuley et al., 2021b). This increase has been accompanied by an increase in the number of genes and phenotypes investigated, alongside the utilisation of players defined by diverse population characteristics (i.e., sex, ethnicity, nationality, maturation, and playing level).

It is estimated that at least 103 different genes have been investigated in soccer contexts (McAuley et al., 2021b). The most frequently investigated genes (i.e., ≥ five studies) include: *ACTN3, ACE, COL5A1, PPARA, IL6, PPARAG1A, VDR, AMPD1, COL1A1, IGF2,* and *MCT1* (see Figure 14.1). The phenotypes examined include athletic status, career progression, strength, power, endurance, agility, body composition, trainability, cardiac morphology and function, personality, anxiety, impulse control, cognitive abilities, bone phenotypes, concussion, and musculoskeletal injuries. These studies have involved males and females from youth (both pre- and post-peak height velocity) and senior cohorts, competing at various playing levels (e.g., elite, sub-elite, and amateur) within and across a wide range of countries (e.g., UK, USA, Russia, China, and Brazil) and ethnicities (e.g., Caucasian, African, and Asian). Collectively, the most frequently conducted study has utilised a case-control CGAS to investigate the association of the *ACTN3* R577X polymorphism with athletic status in senior elite male players of Caucasian ethnicity. Given the amount of data that exists on the association of the *ACTN3* R577X polymorphism within a soccer context, the results of these studies are a useful indicator of the evidence base in this field.

The *ACTN3* R577X polymorphism is a SNP (rs1815738) identified within the *ACTN3* gene located on chromosome 11q13.2 (North et al., 1999). More specifically, this SNP occurs within the gene in codon 577 at the nucleotide position 1747 (Yang et al., 2003). The common

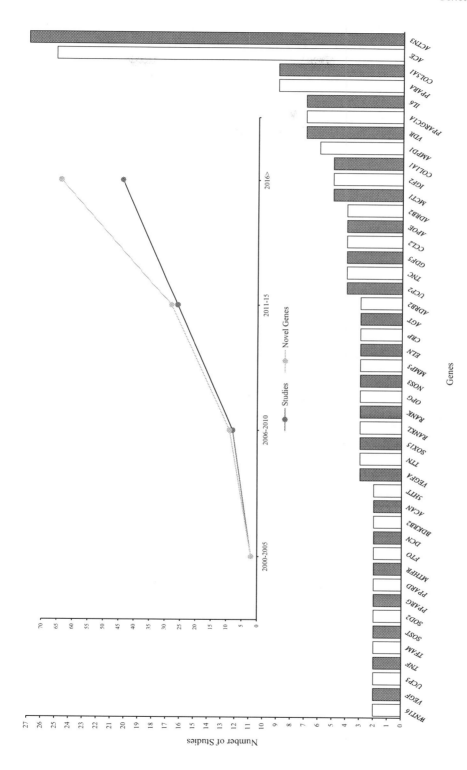

FIGURE 14.1 Progress of genetic research in soccer.

nucleotide at this position is the C allele and the variant is the T allele (Mills et al., 2001). The two alleles are commonly referred to as 'R' and 'X', as the presence of the C allele results in the encoding of the amino acid arginine (R) and the T allele introduces a 'stop codon' (X). A stop codon, produced in this instance by the T allele, prematurely ends the polypeptide chain, which can potentially produce a less functional or completely defective protein (North et al., 1999). Indeed, the rs1815738 SNP can result in an individual being deficient in a sarcomeric protein that is expressed in muscle tissue (Beggs et al., 1992). One of the functions of this protein is crosslinking fast-twitch (type II) actin filaments in skeletal muscle fibres (Mills et al., 2001). As such, it is hypothesised that *ACTN3* protein expression is a contributing factor in the generation of powerful and explosive muscle contractions, and as a consequence, performance in activities where extensive force production is required (e.g., sprinting and jumping) (Garton et al., 2014). Numerous studies of power-oriented sports have reported significant associations between the R allele and athletic status, supporting this hypothesis (e.g., Ahmetov et al., 2011; Chiu et al., 2011; Cięszczyk et al., 2011; Druzhevskaya et al., 2008; Eynon et al., 2009; Massidda et al., 2009; Mikami et al., 2014; Niemi & Majamaa, 2005; Papadimitriou et al., 2008; Roth et al., 2008).

Subsequent meta-analyses of power athletes further substantiate associations with the R allele (see Ma et al., 2013 and Tharabenjasin et al., 2019 for reviews). Studies in soccer, however, have been inconsistent, reporting contrasting allelic associations (McAuley et al., 2021c). This may be due to the intermittent nature of soccer, and consequently, the requirement of both power- and endurance-related capacities (Bangsbo et al., 2006; Buchheit et al., 2010; Dellal et al., 2011; Mallo et al., 2015), which could reduce the importance of a strictly power-orientated genotype. Despite some inconsistency, results of a recent meta-analysis indicate that the *ACTN3* R allele is associated with athletic status in soccer to some extent (McAuley et al., 2021c). To be specific, there was an overrepresentation of the R allele in professional soccer players of Caucasian ethnicity and Brazilian nationality.

It is notable, however, that the *ACTN3* R577X SNP has only a minor influence on athletic status in soccer, as reflected in the small ORs (i.e., 1.35) in the meta-analysis. It is estimated this SNP only accounts for 1–3% of the variance in speed and power performance (Moran et al., 2007; Papadimitriou et al., 2016). As such, even though it is the most evidenced SNP, it would be futile to use *ACTN3* in isolation for talent identification purposes within soccer (McAuley et al., 2021c). Indeed, even Olympic athletes in power-orientated events (i.e., 100 m sprint and long jump) do not all possess an R allele (Lucia et al., 2007; Papadimitriou et al., 2016); likely because several additional genetic variants compensate the produced biological alterations. As previously mentioned, athletic performance is a complex, 'polygenic' trait, which is influenced by the cumulative interactions of a number of genes and variants. Accordingly, a few studies have used polygenic profiling approaches (e.g., total genotype score [TGS]) (Williams & Folland, 2008) in soccer and have found some success (e.g., Egorova et al., 2014; Jones et al., 2016; Massidda et al., 2014; Murtagh et al., 2020; Pickering et al., 2018). However, due to the small number of these studies, a lack of certainty over which variants should be included within a profile, and the exact weight each variant should have in the algorithm, current profiles lack the required specificity and sensitivity (Pickering et al., 2019).

In the future, it is likely more genetic variants will be discovered and incorporated into polygenic profiles, with more accurate weightings applied, consequently enhancing prognostic capabilities (Pickering et al., 2019). However, it is important to remember that the 'degenerate' (i.e., structurally different elements performing similar functions) nature of biology is also present during athlete development (Davids & Baker, 2007); more specifically, *how* athletes with distinct genetics and/or environmental exposures achieve the same level of performance. Indeed, the so-called 'compensation phenomenon' (see Williams & Ericsson, 2005) can be observed within soccer, whereby a player who performs poorly in one performance test (e.g., speed) can compensate by being strong in another (e.g., technical skill) (Williams et al., 2020). Players have individual strengths and weaknesses, and as a consequence, there are different pathways towards achieving particular playing levels (Sarmento et al., 2018). As such, it is likely there will be distinct polygenic profiles associated with athletic status in soccer due to associations with one or several different performer constraints. Therefore, the utilisation of cross-sectional and longitudinal study designs to investigate more specific and quantifiable traits that characterise soccer performance may be more appropriate (McAuley et al., 2021a).

Practical Application and Stakeholder Perspectives

Coupled with the important contributions genetics have on multiple facets of performance and the identification of genetic variants that may be responsible for some of the observed inter-individual differences in specific traits, several companies provide direct-to-consumer (DTC) genetic testing services to athletes and sporting organisations (Pickering et al., 2019). Some of these companies claim they can identify a child's genetic predisposition for success in particular sports and determine optimal training programme design for enhanced adaptation and recovery (Webborn et al., 2015). However, as previously discussed, current understanding is confounded by numerous methodological flaws and inconsistent findings. Moreover, there are ethical, legal, and social concerns that accompany the genetic testing of children and adolescents (Botkin et al., 2015). This has resulted in several consensus statements deeming that the utilisation of genetic testing for athlete selection and development is inappropriate and without scientific credibility (Vlahovich et al., 2017; Webborn et al., 2015). Despite a limited evidence base, there is anecdotal support that suggests genetic testing may have been used in soccer contexts for talent identification (Scott & Kelso, 2008) as well as that FC Barcelona (Miller, 2016) and the Egyptian National team (Holmes, 2018) use genetic testing for training optimisation and injury prevention.

In the scientific literature, recent surveys have sought to elucidate the extent to which genetic testing is currently implemented within sport generally. Varley et al. (2018) reported that, of 72 high-performance athletes and 95 support staff from multiple sports based within the UK, 17% of athletes and 8% of support staff had utilised genetic testing. More recently, Pickering and Kiely (2021) reported that, of 110 athletes and 133 support staff from varying levels of performance, countries, and sports, 10% of athletes and 11% of support staff had utilised genetic testing. In a soccer-specific context, these studies have little applicability, as they only included 22 and 23 stakeholders employed in soccer, respectively. However, a recent study from the authors research group (McAuley et al., 2022d) surveyed 122 key stakeholders (i.e., coaches, practitioners, and players) in professional soccer, reporting that 10% of stakeholders and 14% of organisations have used genetic testing to aid performance and/or mitigate injury risk. Collectively, these studies suggest genetic testing is rarely utilised within soccer, although further studies are required using larger and/or more diverse cohorts to assess the broader prevalence of genetic testing in soccer.

In addition to assessing the prevalence of genetic testing in soccer, McAuley et al. (2022d) also examined the perspectives of key stakeholders in professional soccer on other aspects of genetic testing and research, with 75% of stakeholders believing it would have some value in the future. Moreover, 35% and 72% believed genetic testing should be used for talent identification and development, respectively. However, 89% of stakeholders perceived their knowledge on genetic research as insufficient. The anticipated rise in the utilisation of genetic testing, coupled by the lack of knowledge by stakeholders in soccer, emphasises the value of education programs as well as more accessible and/or digestible summaries of the genetic literature moving forward.

Considerations for Researchers

The field of soccer genetics is comprised of several methodological shortcomings and under-researched populations and playing levels (see Figure 14.2). For instance, there is a need to incorporate advanced genomic technology (e.g., GWAS) and polygenic profiling approaches (e.g., TGS) to facilitate the discovery of important novel genetic variants as well as assess their combined effect on specific performance traits. Moreover, a transition to cross-sectional and longitudinal study designs with more detailed phenotypes will allow more nuanced relationships to be established. It is also important that more diverse populations are investigated, as most research has examined Caucasian males at senior playing levels. In particular, further research is required with females, ethnicities other than Caucasian, and youth populations.

The heterogeneity within genetic research in soccer is also an issue, as several studies include soccer players amongst other individual and team sport athletes. As such, future studies should solely include soccer players in their samples; or, at the very least, provide a soccer-specific sub-analysis. Moreover, further research should incorporate inter-positional analysis, since there are inter- and intra-sport differences in performer constraints that may dilute any potential findings and/or produce spurious associations. The inclusion of multiple sports and failure to conduct position-specific analysis (or GWAS) reflects issues with sample size. Indeed, sample size is regularly cited as the most prominent limitation in all sport genetic research as well as elite athlete research

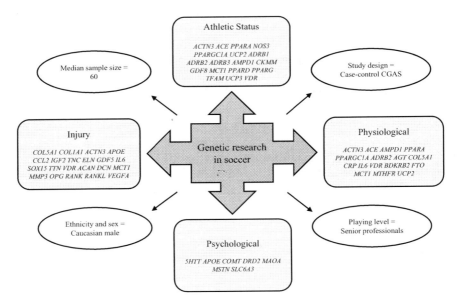

FIGURE 14.2 Prominent characteristics of genetic research in soccer.

generally. Therefore, it is imperative that organisations participate in national and international collaborations (e.g., Football Gene Project; McAuley et al., 2021b) to facilitate increased sample sizes, improved methodological approaches, and superior statistical power.

Considerations for Practitioners

In light of the current genetic evidence within the context of talent identification and development in soccer, the following considerations for practitioners employed in youth settings are proposed:

- Current research in soccer does not provide sufficient evidence to utilise genetic information within talent identification and development systems.
- In the future, it is unlikely an all-encompassing genetic profile will be discovered that warrants the implementation of genetic testing for talent identification purposes.
- Further research may provide evidence for the application of genetic testing to facilitate a more individualised talent development process, such as personalised training programs, managing athlete welfare, and reducing injury susceptibility.
- Genetic information should not be seen as an isolated determinant, but rather, as an additional objective tool when designing, implementing, and evaluating subjective development decisions.
- Participation in genomic educational programs and enhanced engagement with genetic literature will be valuable to remain informed of progress in this emerging field.

Conclusion

It is apparent that genetic variation has a significant influence on several performer constraints within soccer. There has been an increased interest in recent years to identify the specific genetic variants associated with playing status and various parameters of performance in soccer. At present, evidence is limited by numerous methodological flaws and under-researched populations. The participation of research centres and key stakeholders in a major collaborative initiative will be required to overcome these limitations. Genetic information should be seen as an additional objective tool to inform subjective assessment decisions to enhance the talent-development process, similar to that of other performance profiling methods that are currently adopted in youth soccer settings (i.e., fitness testing, nutrition status, psychological profiling, and performance analysis). A shift towards more robust study designs aimed at establishing genotypic associations with detailed phenotypes may facilitate individualised training programs to optimise exercise adaptations, monitor athlete welfare, and reduce injury susceptibility. Even with improved methodological approaches, it is unlikely genetic profiling alone will ever be able to predict future sporting prowess, due to the complex, multifactorial, and dynamic nature of talent development in soccer.

References

Ahmetov, I. I., Druzhevskaya, A. M., Lyubaeva, E. V., Popov, D. V., Vinogradova, O. L., & Williams, A. G. (2011). The dependence of preferred competitive racing distance on muscle fibre type composition and ACTN3 genotype in speed skaters. *Experimental Physiology*, *96*(12), 1302–1310. https://doi.org/10.1113/expphysiol.2011.060293

Ahmetov, I. I., Egorova, E. S., Gabdrakhmanova, L. J., & Fedotovskaya, O. N. (2016). Genes and athletic performance: An update. *Medicine and Sport Science*, *61*, 41–54. https://doi.org/10.1159/000445240

Al-Khelaifi, F., Diboun, I., Donati, F., Botrè, F., Abraham, D., Hingorani, A., Albagha, O., Georgakopoulos, C., Suhre, K., Yousri, N. A., & Elrayess, M. A. (2019). Metabolic GWAS of elite athletes reveals novel genetically-influenced metabolites associated with athletic performance. *Scientific Reports, 9*(1), 19889. https://doi.org/10.1038/s41598-019-56496-7

Al-Khelaifi, F., Yousri, N. A., Diboun, I., Semenova, E. A., Kostryukova, E. S., Kulemin, N. A., Borisov, O. V., Andryushchenko, L. B., Larin, A. K., Generozov, E. V., Miyamoto-Mikami, E., Murakami, H., Zempo, H., Miyachi, M., Takaragawa, M., Kumagai, H., Naito, H., Fuku, N., Abraham, D., Hingorani, A., Donati, F., Costas Georgakopoulos, F., Suhre, K., Ahmetov, I. I., Albagha, O., & Elrayess, M. A. (2020). Genome-wide association study reveals a novel association between MYBPC3 gene polymorphism, endurance athlete status, aerobic capacity and steroid metabolism. *Frontiers in Genetics, 11*, 595. https://doi.org/10.3389/fgene.2020.00595

Attia, J., Ioannidis, J. P. A., Thakkinstian, A., McEvoy, M., Scott, R. J., Minelli, C., Thompson, J., Infante-Rivard, C., & Guyatt, G. (2009). How to use an article about genetic association: B: Are the results of the study valid? *JAMA, 301*(2), 191–197. https://doi.org/10.1001/jama.2008.946

Baker, J., & Wattie, N. (2018). Innate talent in sport: Separating myth from reality. *Current Issues in Sport Science, 3*, 6.

Baker, J., Wattie, N., & Schorer, J. (2019). A proposed conceptualization of talent in sport: The first step in a long and winding road. *Psychology of Sport and Exercise, 43*, 27–33. https://doi.org/10.1016/j.psychsport.2018.12.016

Bangsbo, J., Mohr, M., & Krustrup, P. (2006). Physical and metabolic demands of training and match-play in the elite football player. *Journal of Sports Sciences, 24*(7), 665–674. https://doi.org/10.1080/02640410500482529

Beggs, A. H., Byers, T. J., Knoll, J. H., Boyce, F. M., Bruns, G. A., & Kunkel, L. M. (1992). Cloning and characterization of two human skeletal muscle alpha-actinin genes located on chromosomes 1 and 11. *The Journal of Biological Chemistry, 267*(13), 9281–9288.

Botkin, J. R., Belmont, J. W., Berg, J. S., Berkman, B. E., Bombard, Y., Holm, I. A., Levy, H. P., Ormond, K. E., Saal, H. M., Spinner, N. B., Wilfond, B. S., & McInerney, J. D. (2015). Points to consider: Ethical, legal, and psychosocial implications of genetic testing in children and adolescents. *American Journal of Human Genetics, 97*(1), 6–21. https://doi.org/10.1016/j.ajhg.2015.05.022

Bouchard, C. (2011). Overcoming barriers to progress in exercise genomics. *Exercise and Sport Sciences Reviews, 39*(4), 212–217. https://doi.org/10.1097/JES.0b013e31822643f6

Bouchard, C, & Malina, R. M. (2014). Genomics, genetics, and exercise biology. In C. M. Tipton (Ed.), *History of exercise physiology* (pp. 105–135). Human Kinetics.

Bouchard, C, Rankinen, T., & Timmons, J. A. (2011). Genomics and genetics in the biology of adaptation to exercise. *Comprehensive Physiology, 1*(3), 1603–1648. https://doi.org/10.1002/cphy.c100059

Buchheit, M., Mendez-villanueva, A., Simpson, B. M., & Bourdon, P. C. (2010). Repeated-sprint sequences during youth soccer matches. *International Journal of Sports Medicine, 31*(10), 709–716. https://doi.org/10.1055/s-0030-1261897

Chiu, L. L., Wu, Y. F., Tang, M. T., Yu, H. C., Hsieh, L. L., & Hsieh, S. S. Y. (2011). ACTN3 genotype and swimming performance in Taiwan. *International Journal of Sports Medicine, 32*(6), 476–480. https://doi.org/10.1055/s-0030-1263115

Cięszczyk, P., Eider, J., Ostanek, M., Arczewska, A., Leońska-Duniec, A., Sawczyn, S., Ficek, K., & Krupecki, K. (2011). Association of the ACTN3 R577X polymorphism in polish power-orientated athletes. *Journal of Human Kinetics, 28*, 55–61. https://doi.org/10.2478/v10078-011-0022-0

Davids, K., & Baker, J. (2007). Genes, environment and sport performance: Why the nature-nurture dualism is no longer relevant. *Sports Medicine, 37*(11), 961–980. https://doi.org/10.2165/00007256-200737110-00004

De Moor, M. H. M., Spector, T. D., Cherkas, L. F., Falchi, M., Hottenga, J. J., Boomsma, D. I., & Geus, E. J. C. D. (2007). Genome-wide linkage scan for athlete status in 700 British female DZ twin pairs. *Twin Research and Human Genetics, 10*(6), 812–820. https://doi.org/10.1375/twin.10.6.812

Dellal, A., Chamari, K., Wong, D. P., Ahmaidi, S., Keller, D., Barros, R., Bisciotti, G. N., & Carling, C. (2011). Comparison of physical and technical performance in European soccer match-play: FA Premier

League and La Liga. *European Journal of Sport Science, 11*(1), 51–59. https://doi.org/10.1080/17461391.2010.481334

Dionísio, T. J., Thiengo, C. R., Brozoski, D. T., Dionísio, E. J., Talamoni, G. A., Silva, R. B., Garlet, G. P., Santos, C. F., & Amaral, S. L. (2017). The influence of genetic polymorphisms on performance and cardiac and hemodynamic parameters among Brazilian soccer players. *Applied Physiology, Nutrition, and Metabolism, 42*(6), 596–604. https://doi.org/10.1139/apnm-2016-0608

Druzhevskaya, A. M., Ahmetov, I. I., Astratenkova, I. V., & Rogozkin, V. A. (2008). Association of the ACTN3 R577X polymorphism with power athlete status in Russians. *European Journal of Applied Physiology, 103*(6), 631–634. https://doi.org/10.1007/s00421-008-0763-1

Egorova, E. S., Borisova, A. V., Mustafina, L. J., Arkhipova, A. A., Gabbasov, R. T., Druzhevskaya, A. M., Astratenkova, I. V., & Ahmetov, I. I. (2014). The polygenic profile of Russian football players. *Journal of Sports Sciences, 32*(13), 1286–1293. https://doi.org/10.1080/02640414.2014.898853

Eynon, N., Duarte, J. A., Oliveira, J., Sagiv, M., Yamin, C., Meckel, Y., Sagiv, M., & Goldhammer, E. (2009). ACTN3 R577X polymorphism and Israeli top-level athletes. *International Journal of Sports Medicine, 30*(9), 695–698. https://doi.org/10.1055/s-0029-1220731

Fatini, C., Guazzelli, R., Manetti, P., Battaglini, B., Gensini, F., Vono, R., Toncelli, L., Zilli, P., Capalbo, A., Abbate, R., Gensini, G. F., & Galanti, G. (2000). RAS genes influence exercise-induced left ventricular hypertrophy: An elite athletes study. *Medicine and Science in Sports and Exercise, 32*(11), 1868–1872. https://doi.org/10.1097/00005768-200011000-00008

Fisher, R. A. (1918). The correlation between relatives on the supposition of mendelian inheritance. *Earth and Environmental Science Transactions of The Royal Society of Edinburgh, 52*(2), 399–433. https://doi.org/10.1017/S0080456800012163

Garton, F. C., Seto, J. T., Quinlan, K. G. R., Yang, N., Houweling, P. J., & North, K. N. (2014). α-Actinin-3 deficiency alters muscle adaptation in response to denervation and immobilization. *Human Molecular Genetics, 23*(7), 1879–1893. https://doi.org/10.1093/hmg/ddt580

Gayagay, G., Yu, B., Hambly, B., Boston, T., Hahn, A., Celermajer, D. S., & Trent, R. J. (1998). Elite endurance athletes and the ACE I allele—The role of genes in athletic performance. *Human Genetics, 103*(1), 48–50. https://doi.org/10.1007/s004390050781

Georgiades, E., Klissouras, V., Baulch, J., Wang, G., & Pitsiladis, Y. (2017). Why nature prevails over nurture in the making of the elite athlete. *BMC Genomics, 18*(S8), 835. https://doi.org/10.1186/s12864-017-4190-8

Gibson, W. T. (2016). Core concepts in human genetics: Understanding the complex phenotype of sport performance and susceptibility to sport injury. *Medicine and Sport Science, 61*, 1–14. https://doi.org/10.1159/000445237

Gineviciene, V., Jakaitiene, A., Tubelis, L., & Kucinskas, V. (2014). Variation in the ACE, PPARGC1A and PPARA genes in Lithuanian football players. *European Journal of Sport Science, 14*(1), S289–295. https://doi.org/10.1080/17461391.2012.691117

Guilherme, J. P. L. F., Tritto, A. C. C., North, K. N., Lancha Junior, A. H., & Artioli, G. G. (2014). Genetics and sport performance: Current challenges and directions to the future. *Revista Brasileira de Educação Física e Esporte, 28*(1), 177–193. https://doi.org/10.1590/S1807-55092014000100177

Hambrick, D. Z., Burgoyne, A. P., Macnamara, B. N., & Ullén, F. (2018). Toward a multifactorial model of expertise: Beyond born versus made. *Annals of the New York Academy of Sciences.* https://doi.org/10.1111/nyas.13586

Holmes, E. (2018). *In the blood: How DNAFit is using gene testing to prepare Egypt for their world cup return.* www.sportspromedia.com/interviews/dnafit-gene-testing-egypt-world-cup

Howe, M. J., Davidson, J. W., & Sloboda, J. A. (1998). Innate talents: Reality or myth? *The Behavioral and Brain Sciences, 21*(3), 399–407; 407–442. https://doi.org/10.1017/s0140525x9800123x

Hughes, D. C., Day, S. H., Ahmetov, I. I., & Williams, A. G. (2011). Genetics of muscle strength and power: Polygenic profile similarity limits skeletal muscle performance. *Journal of Sports Sciences, 29*(13), 1425–1434. https://doi.org/10.1080/02640414.2011.597773

International Human Genome Sequencing Consortium. (2004). Finishing the euchromatic sequence of the human genome. *Nature, 431*(7011), 931–945. https://doi.org/10.1038/nature03001

Ioannidis, J. P., Ntzani, E. E., Trikalinos, T. A., & Contopoulos-Ioannidis, D. G. (2001). Replication validity of genetic association studies. *Nature Genetics, 29*(3), 306–309. https://doi.org/10.1038/ng749

Johnson, A. D. (2009). Single-nucleotide polymorphism bioinformatics: A comprehensive review of resources. *Circulation. Cardiovascular Genetics, 2*(5), 530–536. https://doi.org/10.1161/CIRCGENETICS.109.872010

Jones, N., Kiely, J., Suraci, B., Collins, D. J., de Lorenzo, D., Pickering, C., & Grimaldi, K. A. (2016). A genetic-based algorithm for personalized resistance training. *Biology of Sport, 33*(2), 117–126. https://doi.org/10.5604/20831862.1198210

Juffer, P., Furrer, R., González-Freire, M., Santiago, C., Verde, Z., Serratosa, L., Morate, F. J., Rubio, J. C., Martin, M. A., Ruiz, J. R., Arenas, J., Gómez-Gallego, F., & Lucia, A. (2009). Genotype distributions in top-level soccer players: A role for ACE? *International Journal of Sports Medicine, 30*(5), 387–392. https://doi.org/10.1055/s-0028-1105931

Kelly, A. L., & Williams, C. A. (2020). Physical characteristics and the talent identification and development processes in male youth soccer: A narrative review. *Strength & Conditioning Journal, 42*(6), 15–34. https://doi.org/10.1519/SSC.0000000000000576

Livshits, G., Gao, F., Malkin, I., Needhamsen, M., Xia, Y., Yuan, W., Bell, C. G., Ward, K., Liu, Y., Wang, J., Bell, J. T., & Spector, T. D. (2016). Contribution of heritability and epigenetic factors to skeletal muscle mass variation in United Kingdom twins. *The Journal of Clinical Endocrinology & Metabolism, 101*(6), 2450–2459. https://doi.org/10.1210/jc.2016-1219

Lucia, A., Oliván, J., Gómez-Gallego, F., Santiago, C., Montil, M., & Foster, C. (2007). Citius and longius (faster and longer) with no alpha-actinin-3 in skeletal muscles? *British Journal of Sports Medicine, 41*(9), 616–617. https://doi.org/10.1136/bjsm.2006.034199

Ma, F., Yang, Y., Li, X., Zhou, F., Gao, C., Li, M., & Gao, L. (2013). The association of sport performance with ACE and ACTN3 genetic polymorphisms: A systematic review and meta-analysis. *PloS One, 8*(1), e54685. https://doi.org/10.1371/journal.pone.0054685

Magnusson, K., Turkiewicz, A., Hughes, V., Frobell, R., & Englund, M. (2021). High genetic contribution to anterior cruciate ligament rupture: Heritability ~69%. *British Journal of Sports Medicine, 55*(7), 385–389. https://doi.org/10.1136/bjsports-2020-102392

Mallo, J., Mena, E., Nevado, F., & Paredes, V. (2015). Physical demands of top-class soccer friendly matches in relation to a playing position using global positioning system technology. *Journal of Human Kinetics, 47*, 179–188. https://doi.org/10.1515/hukin-2015-0073

Massidda, M., Corrias, L., Ibba, G., Scorcu, M., Vona, G., & Calò, C. M. (2012). Genetic markers and explosive leg-muscle strength in elite Italian soccer players. *The Journal of Sports Medicine and Physical Fitness, 52*(3), 328–334.

Massidda, M., Scorcu, M., & Calò, C. M. (2014). New genetic model for predicting phenotype traits in sports. *International Journal of Sports Physiology and Performance, 9*(3), 554–560. https://doi.org/10.1123/ijspp.2012-0339

Massidda, M., Vona, G., & Calò, C. M. (2009). Association between the ACTN3 R577X polymorphism and artistic gymnastic performance in Italy. *Genetic Testing and Molecular Biomarkers, 13*(3), 377–380. https://doi.org/10.1089/gtmb.2008.0157

McAuley, A. B. T., Baker, J., & Kelly, A. L. (2021a). How nature and nurture conspire to influence athletic success. In A. L. Kelly, J. Côté, M. Jeffreys, & J. Turnnidge (Eds.), *Birth advantages and relative age effects in sport: Exploring organizational structures and creating appropriate settings* (pp. 159–183). Routledge.

McAuley, A. B. T., Baker, J., & Kelly, A. L. (2022a). Defining "elite" status in sport: From chaos to clarity. *German Journal of Exercise and Sport Research, 52*(1), 193–197. https://doi.org/10.1007/s12662-021-00737-3

McAuley, A. B. T., Hughes, D. C., Tsaprouni, L. G., Varley, I., Suraci, B., Baker, J., Herbert, A. J., & Kelly, A. L. (2022b). Genetic associations with technical capabilities in English academy football players: A preliminary study. *The Journal of Sports Medicine and Physical Fitness, 63*(2), 230–240. https://doi.org/10.23736/S0022-4707.22.13945-9

McAuley, A. B. T., Hughes, D. C., Tsaprouni, L. G., Varley, I., Suraci, B., Baker, J., Herbert, A. J., & Kelly, A. L. (2022c). Genetic associations with personality and mental toughness profiles of English academy football players: An exploratory study. *Psychology of Sport and Exercise, 61*, 102209. https://doi.org/10.1016/j.psychsport.2022.102209

McAuley, A. B. T., Hughes, D. C., Tsaprouni, L. G., Varley, I., Suraci, B., Roos, T. R., Herbert, A. J., & Kelly, A. L. (2021b). Genetic association research in football: A systematic review. *European Journal of Sport Science*, *21*(5), 714–752. https://doi.org/10.1080/17461391.2020.1776401

McAuley, A. B. T., Hughes, D. C., Tsaprouni, L. G., Varley, I., Suraci, B., Roos, T. R., Herbert, A. J., & Kelly, A. L. (2021c). The association of the ACTN3 R577X and ACE I/D polymorphisms with athlete status in football: A systematic review and meta-analysis. *Journal of Sports Sciences*, *39*(2), 200–211. https://doi.org/10.1080/02640414.2020.1812195

McAuley, A. B. T., Hughes, D. C., Tsaprouni, L. G., Varley, I., Suraci, B., Roos, T. R., Herbert, A. J., & Kelly, A. L. (2022d). Genetic testing in professional football: Perspectives of key stakeholders. *Journal of Science in Sport and Exercise*, *4*(1), 49–59. https://doi.org/10.1007/s42978-021-00131-3

McCarthy, M. I., Abecasis, G. R., Cardon, L. R., Goldstein, D. B., Little, J., Ioannidis, J. P. A., & Hirschhorn, J. N. (2008). Genome-wide association studies for complex traits: Consensus, uncertainty and challenges. *Nature Reviews Genetics*, *9*(5), 356–369. https://doi.org/10.1038/nrg2344

Micheli, M. L., Gulisano, M., Morucci, G., Punzi, T., Ruggiero, M., Ceroti, M., Marella, M., Castellini, E., & Pacini, S. (2011). Angiotensin-converting enzyme/vitamin D receptor gene polymorphisms and bioelectrical impedance analysis in predicting athletic performances of Italian young soccer players. *Journal of Strength & Conditioning Research*, *25*(8), 2084–2091. https://doi.org/10.1519/JSC.0b013e31820238aa

Mikami, E., Fuku, N., Murakami, H., Tsuchie, H., Takahashi, H., Ohiwa, N., Tanaka, H., Pitsiladis, Y. P., Higuchi, M., Miyachi, M., Kawahara, T., & Tanaka, M. (2014). ACTN3 R577X genotype is associated with sprinting in elite Japanese athletes. *International Journal of Sports Medicine*, *35*(2), 172–177. https://doi.org/10.1055/s-0033-1347171

Miller, A. (2016). *Barcelona breaking the mould with DNA testing as La Liga giants prepare for Champions league clash with Arsenal | Daily mail online*. www.dailymail.co.uk/sport/football/article-3456465/Barcelona-breaking-mould-DNA-testing-La-Liga-giants-prepare-Champions-League-clash-Arsenal.html

Mills, M., Yang, N., Weinberger, R., Vander Woude, D. L., Beggs, A. H., Easteal, S., & North, K. (2001). Differential expression of the actin-binding proteins, alpha-actinin-2 and -3, in different species: Implications for the evolution of functional redundancy. *Human Molecular Genetics*, *10*(13), 1335–1346. https://doi.org/10.1093/hmg/10.13.1335

Missitzi, J., Gentner, R., Misitzi, A., Geladas, N., Politis, P., Klissouras, V., & Classen, J. (2013). Heritability of motor control and motor learning. *Physiological Reports*, *1*(7), e00188. https://doi.org/10.1002/phy2.188

Montgomery, H. E., Marshall, R., Hemingway, H., Myerson, S., Clarkson, P., Dollery, C., Hayward, M., Holliman, D. E., Jubb, M., World, M., Thomas, E. L., Brynes, A. E., Saeed, N., Barnard, M., Bell, J. D., Prasad, K., Rayson, M., Talmud, P. J., & Humphries, S. E. (1998). Human gene for physical performance. *Nature*, *393*(6682), 221–222. https://doi.org/10.1038/30374

Moran, C. N., Yang, N., Bailey, M. E. S., Tsiokanos, A., Jamurtas, A., MacArthur, D. G., North, K., Pitsiladis, Y. P., & Wilson, R. H. (2007). Association analysis of the ACTN3 R577X polymorphism and complex quantitative body composition and performance phenotypes in adolescent Greeks. *European Journal of Human Genetics: EJHG*, *15*(1), 88–93. https://doi.org/10.1038/sj.ejhg.5201724

Murtagh, C. F., Brownlee, T. E., Rienzi, E., Roquero, S., Moreno, S., Huertas, G., Lugioratto, G., Baumert, P., Turner, D. C., Lee, D., Dickinson, P., Lyon, K. A., Sheikhsaraf, B., Biyik, B., O'Boyle, A., Morgans, R., Massey, A., Drust, B., & Erskine, R. M. (2020). The genetic profile of elite youth soccer players and its association with power and speed depends on maturity status. *PloS One*, *15*(6), e0234458. https://doi.org/10.1371/journal.pone.0234458

Niemi, A.-K., & Majamaa, K. (2005). Mitochondrial DNA and ACTN3 genotypes in Finnish elite endurance and sprint athletes. *European Journal of Human Genetics: EJHG*, *13*(8), 965–969. https://doi.org/10.1038/sj.ejhg.5201438

North, K. N., Yang, N., Wattanasirichaigoon, D., Mills, M., Easteal, S., & Beggs, A. H. (1999). A common nonsense mutation results in alpha-actinin-3 deficiency in the general population. *Nature Genetics*, *21*(4), 353–354. https://doi.org/10.1038/7675

Papadimitriou, I. D., Lucia, A., Pitsiladis, Y. P., Pushkarev, V. P., Dyatlov, D. A., Orekhov, E. F., Artioli, G. G., Guilherme, J. P. L. F., Lancha, A. H., Ginevičienė, V., Cieszczyk, P., Maciejewska-Karlowska, A., Sawczuk, M., Muniesa, C. A., Kouvatsi, A., Massidda, M., Calò, C. M., Garton, F., Houweling, P. J., . . . &

Eynon, N. (2016). ACTN3 R577X and ACE I/D gene variants influence performance in elite sprinters: A multi-cohort study. *BMC Genomics, 17*(1), 285. https://doi.org/10.1186/s12864-016-2462-3

Papadimitriou, I. D., Papadopoulos, C., Kouvatsi, A., & Triantaphyllidis, C. (2008). The ACTN3 gene in elite Greek track and field athletes. *International Journal of Sports Medicine, 29*(4), 352–355. https://doi.org/10.1055/s-2007-965339

Peeters, M. W., Thomis, M. A., Loos, R. J. F., Derom, C. A., Fagard, R., Claessens, A. L., Vlietinck, R. F., & Beunen, G. P. (2007). Heritability of somatotype components: A multivariate analysis. *International Journal of Obesity, 31*(8), 1295–1301. https://doi.org/10.1038/sj.ijo.0803575

Pellicciari, M. C., Veniero, D., Marzano, C., Moroni, F., Pirulli, C., Curcio, G., Ferrara, M., Miniussi, C., Rossini, P. M., & De Gennaro, L. (2009). Heritability of intracortical inhibition and facilitation. *The Journal of Neuroscience: The Official Journal of the Society for Neuroscience, 29*(28), 8897–8900. https://doi.org/10.1523/JNEUROSCI.2112-09.2009

Pickering, C., & Kiely, J. (2021). The frequency of, and attitudes towards, genetic testing amongst athletes and support staff. *Performance Enhancement & Health, 8*(4), 100184. https://doi.org/10.1016/j.peh.2020.100184

Pickering, C., Kiely, J., Grgic, J., Lucia, A., & Del Coso, J. (2019). Can genetic testing identify talent for sport? *Genes, 10*(12). https://doi.org/10.3390/genes10120972

Pickering, C., Kiely, J., Suraci, B., & Collins, D. (2018). The magnitude of Yo-Yo test improvements following an aerobic training intervention are associated with total genotype score. *PloS One, 13*(11), e0207597. https://doi.org/10.1371/journal.pone.0207597

Pickering, C., Suraci, B., Semenova, E. A., Boulygina, E. A., Kostryukova, E. S., Kulemin, N. A., Borisov, O. V., Khabibova, S. A., Larin, A. K., Pavlenko, A. V., Lyubaeva, E. V., Popov, D. V., Lysenko, E. A., Vepkhvadze, T. F., Lednev, E. M., Leońska-Duniec, A., Pająk, B., Chycki, J., Moska, W., . . . & Ahmetov, I. I. (2019). A genome-wide association study of sprint performance in elite youth football players. *Journal of Strength & Conditioning Research, 33*(9), 2344–2351. https://doi.org/10.1519/JSC.0000000000003259

Pimenta, E. M., Coelho, D. B., Cruz, I. R., Morandi, R. F., Veneroso, C. E., de Azambuja Pussieldi, G., Carvalho, M. R. S., Silami-Garcia, E., & De Paz Fernández, J. A. (2012). The ACTN3 genotype in soccer players in response to acute eccentric training. *European Journal of Applied Physiology, 112*(4), 1495–1503. https://doi.org/10.1007/s00421-011-2109-7

Pimenta, E. M., Coelho, D. B., Veneroso, C. E., Barros Coelho, E. J., Cruz, I. R., Morandi, R. F., De A Pussieldi, G., Carvalho, M. R. S., Garcia, E. S., & De Paz Fernández, J. A. (2013). Effect of ACTN3 gene on strength and endurance in soccer players. *Journal of Strength & Conditioning Research, 27*(12), 3286–3292. https://doi.org/10.1519/JSC.0b013e3182915e66

Pitsiladis, Y., & Wang, G. (2011). Necessary advances in exercise genomics and likely pitfalls. *Journal of Applied Physiology, 110*(5), 1150–1151. https://doi.org/10.1152/japplphysiol.00172.2011

Polderman, T. J. C., Benyamin, B., de Leeuw, C. A., Sullivan, P. F., van Bochoven, A., Visscher, P. M., & Posthuma, D. (2015). Meta-analysis of the heritability of human traits based on fifty years of twin studies. *Nature Genetics, 47*(7), 702–709. https://doi.org/10.1038/ng.3285

Rodas, G., Osaba, L., Arteta, D., Pruna, R., Fernández, D., & Lucia, A. (2019). Genomic prediction of tendinopathy Risk in elite team sports. *International Journal of Sports Physiology and Performance, 15*(4), 1–7. https://doi.org/10.1123/ijspp.2019-0431

Roth, S. M., Walsh, S., Liu, D., Metter, E. J., Ferrucci, L., & Hurley, B. F. (2008). The ACTN3 R577X nonsense allele is under-represented in elite-level strength athletes. *European Journal of Human Genetics, 16*(3), 391–394. https://doi.org/10.1038/sj.ejhg.5201964

Salisbury, B. A., Pungliya, M., Choi, J. Y., Jiang, R., Sun, X. J., & Stephens, J. C. (2003). SNP and haplotype variation in the human genome. *Mutation Research/Fundamental and Molecular Mechanisms of Mutagenesis, 526*(1), 53–61. https://doi.org/10.1016/S0027-5107(03)00014-9

Santiago, C., González-Freire, M., Serratosa, L., Morate, F. J., Meyer, T., Gómez-Gallego, F., & Lucia, A. (2008). ACTN3 genotype in professional soccer players. *British Journal of Sports Medicine, 42*(1), 71–73. https://doi.org/10.1136/bjsm.2007.039172

Sarmento, H., Anguera, M. T., Pereira, A., & Araújo, D. (2018). Talent identification and development in male football: A systematic review. *Sports Medicine, 48*(4), 907–931. https://doi.org/10.1007/s40279-017-0851-7

Schutte, N. M., Nederend, I., Hudziak, J. J., Bartels, M., & de Geus, E. J. C. (2016). Twin-sibling study and meta-analysis on the heritability of maximal oxygen consumption. *Physiological Genomics*, *48*(3), 210–219. https://doi.org/10.1152/physiolgenomics.00117.2015

Scott, M., & Kelso, P. (2008, April 25). One club wants to use a gene-test to spot the new Ronaldo. Is this football's future? *The Guardian*. www.theguardian.com/football/2008/apr/26/genetics

Silventoinen, K., Magnusson, P. K. E., Tynelius, P., Kaprio, J., & Rasmussen, F. (2008). Heritability of body size and muscle strength in young adulthood: A study of one million Swedish men. *Genetic Epidemiology*, *32*(4), 341–349. https://doi.org/10.1002/gepi.20308

Suraci, B. R., Quigley, C., Thelwell, R. C., & Milligan, G. S. (2021). A comparison of training modality and total genotype scores to enhance sport-specific biomotor abilities in under 19 male soccer players. *Journal of Strength & Conditioning Research*, *35*(1), 154–161. https://doi.org/10.1519/JSC.0000000000003299

Tanisawa, K., Wang, G., Seto, J., Verdouka, I., Twycross-Lewis, R., Karanikolou, A., Tanaka, M., Borjesson, M., Luigi, L. D., Dohi, M., Wolfarth, B., Swart, J., Bilzon, J. L. J., Badtieva, V., Papadopoulou, T., Casasco, M., Geistlinger, M., Bachl, N., Pigozzi, F., & Pitsiladis, Y. (2020). Sport and exercise genomics: The FIMS 2019 consensus statement update. *British Journal of Sports Medicine*, *54*(16), 969–975. https://doi.org/10.1136/bjsports-2019-101532

Tharabenjasin, P., Pabalan, N., & Jarjanazi, H. (2019). Association of the ACTN3 R577X (rs1815739) polymorphism with elite power sports: A meta-analysis. *PLoS One*, *14*(5), e0217390. https://doi.org/10.1371/journal.pone.0217390

Tucker, R., & Collins, M. (2012). What makes champions? A review of the relative contribution of genes and training to sporting success. *British Journal of Sports Medicine*, *46*(8), 555–561. https://doi.org/10.1136/bjsports-2011-090548

Varley, I., Patel, S., Williams, A. G., & Hennis, P. J. (2018). The current use, and opinions of elite athletes and support staff in relation to genetic testing in elite sport within the UK. *Biology of Sport*, *35*(1), 13–19. https://doi.org/10.5114/biolsport.2018.70747

Visscher, P. M., Brown, M. A., McCarthy, M. I., & Yang, J. (2012). Five years of GWAS discovery. *The American Journal of Human Genetics*, *90*(1), 7–24. https://doi.org/10.1016/j.ajhg.2011.11.029

Visscher, P. M., Medland, S. E., Ferreira, M. A. R., Morley, K. I., Zhu, G., Cornes, B. K., Montgomery, G. W., & Martin, N. G. (2006). Assumption-free estimation of heritability from genome-wide identity-by-descent sharing between full siblings. *PLoS Genetics*, *2*(3), e41. https://doi.org/10.1371/journal.pgen.0020041

Vlahovich, N., Fricker, P. A., Brown, M. A., & Hughes, D. (2017). Ethics of genetic testing and research in sport: A position statement from the Australian Institute of Sport. *British Journal of Sports Medicine*, *51*(1), 5–11. https://doi.org/10.1136/bjsports-2016-096661

Webborn, N., Williams, A., McNamee, M., Bouchard, C., Pitsiladis, Y., Ahmetov, I., Ashley, E., Byrne, N., Camporesi, S., Collins, M., Dijkstra, P., Eynon, N., Fuku, N., Garton, F. C., Hoppe, N., Holm, S., Kaye, J., Klissouras, V., Lucia, A., . . . & Wang, G. (2015). Direct-to-consumer genetic testing for predicting sports performance and talent identification: Consensus statement. *British Journal of Sports Medicine*, *49*(23), 1486–1491. https://doi.org/10.1136/bjsports-2015-095343

Williams, A. G., & Folland, J. P. (2008). Similarity of polygenic profiles limits the potential for elite human physical performance. *The Journal of Physiology*, *586*(1), 113–121. https://doi.org/10.1113/jphysiol.2007.141887

Williams, A. M., & Ericsson, K. A. (2005). Perceptual-cognitive expertise in sport: Some considerations when applying the expert performance approach. *Human Movement Science*, *24*(3), 283–307. https://doi.org/10.1016/j.humov.2005.06.002

Williams, A. M., Ford, P. R., & Drust, B. (2020). Talent identification and development in soccer since the millennium. *Journal of Sports Sciences*, *38*(11–12), 1199–1210. https://doi.org/10.1080/02640414.2020.1766647

Yang, N., MacArthur, D. G., Gulbin, J. P., Hahn, A. G., Beggs, A. H., Easteal, S., & North, K. (2003). ACTN3 genotype is associated with human elite athletic performance. *American Journal of Human Genetics*, *73*(3), 627–631. https://doi.org/10.1086/377590

Zempo, H., Miyamoto-Mikami, E., Kikuchi, N., Fuku, N., Miyachi, M., & Murakami, H. (2017). Heritability estimates of muscle strength-related phenotypes: A systematic review and meta-analysis. *Scandinavian Journal of Medicine & Science in Sports*, *27*(12), 1537–1546. https://doi.org/10.1111/sms.12804

15

NUTRITION

Optimising Development and Performance Through Nutrition

Matthew North, Adam L. Kelly, Jennie Carter, Lewis Gough, and Matthew Cole

Introduction

The prioritisation of developing players has led to a large emphasis being placed upon talent pathways to realise each individual's potential (Kelly et al., 2018). In the context of soccer, developmental pathways are mapped by governing bodies that begin at grassroot levels and progress towards high performance youth soccer (HPYS) environments, such as academies. Over the last decade within these HPYS environments, there has been a growing awareness regarding the impact of a multidisciplinary approach, which has resulted in further research aimed to seek out these marginal gains (e.g., Gledhill et al., 2017; Sarmento et al., 2018; The Premier League, 2011; Trakman et al., 2016; Wrigley et al., 2012). This has led to the implementation of nutritional practice in applied HPYS settings to support optimal development and performance outcomes (see North et al., 2022 for a review).

During the youth development phases, players not only need to support their training demands with appropriate nutritional intake, but they are also undergoing rapid growth and maturational changes that result in physiological, anatomical, and biological adaptations (Hannon et al., 2020). Subsequently, this leads to players exhibiting increased nutritional requirements to support the energy demands of growth and performance in their sport (Malina et al., 2004), thus reinforcing the importance to optimise and support development through nutritional practice. The purpose of this chapter is to synthesise the current nutritional research within youth soccer by exploring: (a) energy balance (i.e., energy intake vs. energy expenditure), (b) hydration needs, (c) barriers, influences, and enablers, and (d) the female player. Moreover, recommendations for future research and considerations for practitioners are provided.

Dietary Intake

In HPYS environments, players undergo rapid changes in growth and maturation, which, when coupled with increasing training and match loads, can result in extremely high energy requirements (Hannon et al., 2021). Insufficient energy intake (EI) has been shown to result in body and muscle mass loss, injury, illness, increased prevalence of overtraining, and severely impaired performance (Kreider et al., 2010). Therefore, ensuring young players consume adequate EI to support development, training, and competition is vital. Furthermore, inadequate EI coinciding with increasing energy requirements may be associated with low energy availability (LEA), resulting in impaired growth and maturation of tissues and organs, delayed sexual maturation, decreases in immune function, and reduced bone mineral density over a chronic period (Loucks, 2007). Low energy availability not only has the ability to limit physical development but also reduce training output and adaptation, thus limiting soccer-specific development.

Dietary practices of male youth soccer players are well documented within the literature. Multiple studies have assessed EI in single age groups of differing populations and ages (Bettonviel et al., 2016; Briggs et al., 2015; Caccialanza et al., 2007; Iglesias-Gutiérrez et al., 2005). More specifically, when comparing EI to estimated energy expenditure (EE), it has been shown that players did not meet their requirements, with results presenting mean energy deficits of up to -788 ± 174 kcal·day^{-1} in English HYPS players (Russell & Pennock, 2011) and -890 ± 734 kcal·day^{-1} in Italian HYPS players (Caccialanza et al., 2007). However, as developmental stages span across large age ranges, and given sociocultural differences apparent in differing populations, it is hard to understand a true representation of youth soccer players energy balance.

To understand a true picture of the nutritional intakes of youth soccer players, research has been performed in multiple age groups to negate possible age differences (e.g., Garrido et al., 2007; Hannon et al., 2021; Iglesias-Gutiérrez et al., 2012; Naughton et al., 2017; Ruiz et al., 2005). Within these studies, EI appears to vary based upon nationality, which may indicate cultural influences. However, within each population, EI appears to stay consistent irrespective of age between the U13 to U20 age groups (Hidalgo et al., 2015; Naughton et al., 2016; Ruiz et al., 2005). Therefore, when growth and maturational differences are considered and express EI in relative terms to body weight (BW), a reduction in overall EI is observed as players grow and progress through the age groups. For instance, Hannon et al. (2021) showed a stepwise reduction in EI when expressed relative to BW between U12/U13 (68 ± 8 kcal·kg^{-1}·day^{-1}), U15 (50 ± 7 kcal·kg^{-1}·day^{-1}), and U18 (44 ± 7 kcal·kg^{-1}·day^{-1}) English Premier League (EPL) academy players.

It is common within soccer for training weeks and sessions to be periodised through macro- and mesocycles, leading to differing EE dependant on training and match schedules and demands. This also occurs within youth soccer through a mixture of natural variations in training, rest, and match days as well as conscious periodisation (Nobari et al., 2021; Wrigley et al., 2012). Therefore, practitioners must ensure that players account for increases in EE with appropriate EI. Current findings would indicate training load has a direct impact upon energy balance, where heavier training and match days led to negative energy balance in U14 and U16 players (Briggs et al., 2015; Granja et al., 2017).

Briggs et al. (2015) showed heavy training days and match days to be at greatest risk of overall energy balance, inducing energy deficits of -505 ± 539 kcal·day^{-1} and -544 ± 551 kcal·day^{-1}, respectively, which resulted in a mean energy deficit of -311 ± 397 kcals·day^{-1} across a competitive week. In relation to body mass, this would equate to a mean weekly loss of -0.04 ± 0.05 kg per player, which may appear trivial, but is of concern during a phase where growth and development are key. Indeed, this may be counterproductive and could have severe health and performance consequences over a prolonged period. Granja et al. (2017) showed similar issues in U16 male Portuguese academy players; however, energy deficits were much larger at -1030 kcals·day^{-1} on heavy training days and -1009 kcal·day^{-1} on match days. Between the U14 and U16 male age groups, there can be significant differences in maturational status and training load (Hannon et al., 2020, 2021; Kelly & Williams, 2020). Therefore, although both studies investigated heavy training and match days, the exact training loads and subsequent energy requirements may differ.

Many of the aforementioned studies estimated EE through predictive resting metabolic rate (RMR) equations, population predicted EE, and through indirect measures, such as accelerometery and activity diaries (Briggs et al., 2015; Russell & Pennock, 2011), all of which have a degree of inaccuracy. RMR accounts for around 60% of total daily energy expenditure, whilst Hannon et al. (2020) has shown the use of current predicative equations in this population to underestimate requirements. Given RMR has been shown to increase by approximately 400 kcal·day^{-1} between ages 12 and 16 years (Hannon et al., 2020), it is important to assess total EE through more accurate measures.

Through indirect calorimetry and doubly labelled water, Hannon et al. (2021) reported average daily total EE values of 2859 ± 265 kcal·day^{-1} (range: 2275–3903 kcal·day^{-1}), 3029 ± 262 kcal·day^{-1} (range: 2738–3726 kcal·day^{-1}), and 3586 ± 487 kcal·day^{-1} (range: 2542·5172 kcal·day^{-1}), in U12/U13, U15, and U18 male EPL players, respectively. This, coupled with the previously stated EI findings in the same cohort (Hannon et al., 2021), may put the older age groups at risk of energy deficits and potential LEA. As with EI, large ranges are apparent within age groups, and there is considerable overlap between different age groups, which may be further influenced by contextual factors, such as playing position and training load as well as individual constraints, including growth and maturational differences. Based on these findings, practitioners need to be aware of individual changes and not make assumptions based on group mean responses.

Within youth soccer, players are generally still grouped by chronological age. Within these age groups, there are large differences in growth and maturation between players (see Chapter 4), which can have a significant impact on their size and development and subsequent energy requirements. Future studies should consider the growing concept of 'bio-banding' within academy soccer (Bradley et al., 2019) and assess nutritional requirements and intakes based upon biological age of players, in order to better consider the impact of growth and maturation on energy requirements. By identifying key biological ages at which nutritional requirements and eating habits are impacted, this would allow for more appropriate nutritional interventions to be implemented for the optimal growth, development, and performance of individual players. Currently, EE has been shown to increase as players progress throughout an academy (Hannon et al., 2021). However, further research is required to understand whether this is largely due to increases in training load, a product of growth and maturation, or a combination of both. Nonetheless, the main challenge is to ensure that EE is being met by EI on an individual basis, which is most likely to be compromised on match days and/or heavy training days. Table 15.1 provides an overview of studies examining EI and/or EE in HPYS players.

Protein Intake

Sufficient protein intake is required to support growth and development and aid recovery from training and competition (Aerenhouts et al., 2011). Currently, there are no youth-specific protein guidelines, although preliminary research has showed U14 male HPYS players require 1.4g·kg^{-1}·day-1 to obtain nitrogen balance (Boisseau et al., 2002, 2007). Therefore, it would appear that all studies investigating nutritional intakes (displayed in Table 15.1) demonstrated that players met or exceeded their requirements. In order to facilitate maximal muscle protein synthesis (MPS) and promote recovery, individuals must not only meet absolute protein requirements but also regularly distribute protein throughout the day (Areta et al., 2013)—around every

3–4 hours—and achieve intakes of 0.25–0.3 g·kg⁻¹ BM per meal with a high leucine content (Murphy et al., 2015).

Based on the current literature, HPYS eating habits do not meet these requirements, with an uneven spread of protein intake throughout the day deriving from sub-optimal leucine sources (Naughton et al., 2016). For instance, differences in protein intake were observed in U18s who displayed higher intakes at lunch and dinner than their younger counterparts, whilst the younger ages' protein intake was low at breakfast and increased at each meal throughout the day (Naughton et al., 2016). Differences in eating habits between ages could potentially be influenced by contact time within the respective club or organisation, as more staff are often available to older age groups and thus have a greater control over their food quality and options. However, there is currently no study investigating the impact of food provision supplied by clubs or organisation on youth soccer players protein intake.

Carbohydrate Intake

Less mature youth soccer players have lower glycogen storage capacities (Eriksson & Saltin, 1974) and a greater reliance on fat as fuel (Timmons et al., 2003), compared to more mature players. Surprisingly, there are currently no carbohydrate (CHO) guidelines specific to the youth population. Current recommendations for adult soccer players range between 5–10g·kg⁻¹·day⁻¹ (Oliveira et al., 2017); however, it appears that male youth players currently consume between 5–7g·kg⁻¹·day⁻¹ CHO daily with the majority currently around 5g·kg⁻¹·day⁻¹, irrespective of age or nationality. If practitioners assume adult guidelines can be applied to the youth population, players may exhibit reduced recovery capabilities on heavier training days, sub-optimal fuelling strategies, and limited growth. This may be further exacerbated in older age groups who have displayed a decreased CHO intake as players age when expressed relative to body mass (Hannon et al., 2021; Hidalgo et al., 2015; Naughton et al., 2016; Ruiz et al., 2005).

Overall, youth soccer players do not appear to be meeting their CHO and energy requirements (particularly in older age groups). Furthermore, with the day before a game and game day adult CHO recommendations ranging between 6–8g·kg⁻¹·day⁻¹ (Collins et al., 2021), players may be starting the game with sub-optimal glycogen stores, potentially limiting performance. Therefore, this is key area practitioners need to implement effective interventions to prevent this.

Hydration Needs

Younger individuals appear to be able to withstand similar thermal loads to their adult counterparts (Inbar et al., 2004; Rowland et al., 2008), although the mechanism by which they do so differs (Inbar et al., 2004). Whilst adults rely on evaporative cooling (i.e., sweating), younger individuals dissipate heat via radiative and conductive cooling (Falk & Dotan, 2008). Therefore, players in developmental stages may display lower sweat rates than adults, and, coupled with higher metabolic cost of locomotion, it can make thermoregulation harder in children (Falk & Dotan, 2008). Data suggests children can dehydrate to similar levels as adults if no fluid is ingested (Meyer & Bar-Or, 1994). Even mild dehydration (-2% of body mass) can have adverse effects on cognitive function and physical performance, which are important to soccer performance (Edwards et al., 2007). Thus, hydration is evidently a key area to assess in youth soccer, since the onset of dehydration can result in a greater increase in core temperature (Bar-Or, 1980).

TABLE 15.1 Overview of studies examining EI and/or EE in HPYS players

Reference	Aim	Sample Size	Population	Dietary Assessment Tool	Energy Intake (kcal·day⁻¹)	Energy Expenditure (kcal·day⁻¹)
(Leblanc et al., 2002)	Characterise nutritional intake in terms of energy, macronutrients, calcium, and iron of adolescent French soccer players.	N = 180	French 13–16 years	5-day food diary	Range: 2352–3395	Not measured
(Iglesias-Gutiérrez et al., 2005)	Accurately assess the food habits and nutritional status of high-level adolescent soccer players living in their home environment during the competitive season.	N = 33	Spanish 14–16 years	6-day food diary	3,003 Range: 2,261–4,007	2,983 Range: 2,705–3,545
(Ruiz et al., 2005)	Characterise the diet of the growing soccer player and to examine how it varies during the course of adolescent development.	N = 81	Spanish U15: 14.0 ± 0.3 years U16: 14.9 ± 0.2 years U17: 16.6 ± 0.6 years	3-day food diary	U15:3,456 ± 309 U15: 3,418 ± 182 U17:3,478 ± 223	Not measured
(Caccialanza et al., 2007)	Assess the dietary intake of a sample of young male Italian high-level soccer players on two time points to evaluate the degree of under-reporting, using the EEI/EEE ratio.	N = 43	Italian 16 ± 1 years	4-day food diary	2,560 ± 636	Not measured

(Russell & Pennock, 2011)	Investigate the dietary and activity regimes of professional soccer players who played for the youth department team (under-18s) of a professional club based within the United Kingdom during a 7-day period.	N = 10	English 17 ± 1 years	7-day food diary	2,831 ± 164	3,618 ± 61
(Iglesias-Gutiérrez et al., 2012)	Evaluate the nutritional intake and eating patterns of young high-level soccer players according to their playing position in the team.	N = 87	Spanish 18 ± 2 years	6-day food diary	2,794 ± 526	Not measured
(Briggs et al., 2015)	Assess energy balance in male adolescent, academy-level soccer players over a 7-day period that included four training days, one match day, and two rest days.	N = 10	English 15.4 ± 0.3 years	7-day food diary with 24-hour recall	2,245 ± 321	2,543 ± 244

(Continued)

Reference	Aim	Sample Size	Population	Dietary Assessment Tool	Energy Intake (kcal·day⁻¹)	Energy Expenditure (kcal·day⁻¹)
(Hidalgo et al., 2015)	Analyse anthropometric characteristics and evaluate nutritional intake and status, as well as dietary habits, and finally, to evaluate pre- and post-training and game meals.	N = 72	Mexican Team A (N = 24): 15.5 ± 0.06 years Team B (N = 24): 16.5 ± 0.04 years Team C (N = 18): 17.3 ± 0.04 years Team D (N = 6): 19.3 ± 0.17 years	4-day food diary	Team A: 3,067 ± 151 Team B: 2,930 ± 73 Team C: 2,715 ± 131 Team D: 3,042 ± 117	Team A: 3,118 ± 41 Team B: 3,246 ± 55 Team C: 3,286 ± 39 Team D: 3,103 ± 56
(Naughton et al., 2016)	Quantify the total daily energy and macronutrient intakes of elite youth English academy players of different ages (U13/14, U15/16, and U18 playing squads) and to quantify the daily distribution of energy and macronutrient intake.	N = 59	English U13/14: 12.7 ± 0.6 years U15/16: 14.4 ± 0.5 years U18: 16.4 ± 0.5 years	7-day food diary	U13/14: 1,903 ± 432 U15/16: 1,927 ± 317 U18: 1,958 ± 390	Not measured

(Granja et al., 2017)	Investigate the dietary intake of academy-level soccer players from a Portuguese first league soccer club on match day (MD) and on the highest training load day (HTLD) during three consecutive weeks of the final phase of a competitive season.	N = 10	Portuguese 15.8 ± 0.4 years	2-week food diary and photographic record	MD: 2,667 ± 170 Range: 2,256–2,810 HTLD: 2,646 ± 415 Range: 2,043–3,234	Not measured
(Hannon et al., 2020)	Quantify the energy expenditure, energy intake, and training loads of elite youth soccer players over a 14-day in-season period.	N = 24	English U12/13 (N = 8): 12.2 ± 0.4 years U15 (N = 8): 15.0 ± 0.2 years U18 (N = 8): 17.5 ± 0.4 years	Food photography	U12/13: 2,659 ± 187 U15: 2,821 ± 338 U18: 3,180 ± 279	U12/13: 2,859 ± 265 Range: 2,275–3,903 U15: 3,029 ± 262 Range: 2,738–3,726 U18: 3,586 ± 487 Range: 2,542–5,172

Note: EEI = Estimated Energy Intake; EEE = Estimated Energy Expenditure; HTLD = Heavy Training Load Day; MD = Match Day.

Due to the adverse impact of heat on hydration status, the majority of research in youth soccer has been performed in tropical conditions (~30°C and > 50% relative humidity). More specifically, multiple studies have investigated hydration in U18 Brazilian male youth soccer players (Da Silva et al., 2012; Guttierres et al., 2011; Silva et al., 2011). Across three studies, dehydration levels were reported as -1.77 ± 0.70%.BW following training (Silva et al., 2011), whereas it was -1.62 ± 0.78%.BW (Da Silva et al., 2012) and 1.35 ± 0.87%.BW (Iglesias-Gutiérrez et al., 2012) following a match. This indicates a slight risk of dehydration, though none reach the critical -2%.BW level. Although mean data would present hydration levels as adequate, individuals displayed up to -3.15%.BW across the course of a match (Da Silva et al., 2012), which has been shown to be detrimental to performance.

It would appear the hydration status players achieve prior to training and competition has a considerable influence on overall hydration level. Da Silva et al. (2012) showed all players attended the match dehydrated, with ~45% classed as moderately dehydrated (USG = 1.010–1.020 g·ml-1), ~50% significantly dehydrated (USG = 1.021–1.030 g·ml-1), and ~5% presented a condition of serious dehydration (USG > 1.030 g·ml-1) in the pre-match period. Even with an increased fluid intake that exceeded sweat losses, ~65% of the players reached significant dehydration levels, while ~17% presented a serious dehydration condition. However, in moderate conditions, it appears youth players currently match their fluid requirements (Ersoy et al., 2016; Phillips et al., 2014).

Given the differences in thermoregulation mechanisms between children, adolescents, and adults, further research is required in younger ages. Currently, there are no specific youth hydration guidelines; therefore, it is advised players start exercise in a well-hydrated state and continually develop individual hydration strategies to limit more than 2%.BW loss.

Barriers, Influences, and Enablers

From the extensive research into dietary intakes of HPYS male players discussed earlier in this chapter, it is clear current practices are inadequate and do not meet the energy demands of training and competition, which highlights the need for improved nutritional support. Therefore, in order to design and implement effective interventions, researchers and practitioners must understand the influences, barriers, and enablers to achieving adequate EI. In the context of sports nutrition, this is a relatively novel area, and specific to the youth soccer population, research is extremely limited (Carter et al., 2021).

One of the most commonly cited barriers to achieving appropriate nutritional intake is nutritional knowledge (Bentley et al., 2019). However, existing literature in the present male youth soccer population is exceptionally limited and conflicting. For instance, Noronha et al. (2020) found a correlation between better nutritional knowledge and the appropriate dietary intake of some key nutrients. Players cited 'lack of willpower' as a main barrier, although, as nutrition knowledge was low, some players may be unaware that they needed to improve their dietary intake. Specifically, CHO intake (3.9 g·kg^{-1}) was far below recommended values, and although protein consumption appeared adequate (1.4 g·kg^{-1}), on average only 3.7 eating occasions were documented, which potentially limits opportunities to maximise muscle protein synthesis. Contrastingly, Murphy and Jeanes (2006) found a poor correlation between nutritional knowledge and appropriate EI, especially with regards to CHO intake. Discrepancies in findings between the two studies may be influenced by a multitude of factors. However, each study assessed nutritional knowledge via different questionnaires, neither of which have been validated as an appropriate measure of nutrition knowledge. Findings in youth soccer players show a poor correlation between knowledge and healthier food choices (Heaney et al., 2011); therefore, it is pertinent to understand other factors limiting adequate nutritional behaviours across different age groups.

Across a broad athletic population, the COM-B model (Capability, Opportunity, Motivation-Behaviour) has been implemented to explore key influencers to dietary behaviours (Bentley et al., 2019, 2021). Preliminary findings from Carter et al. (2022) have built upon this research specifically in male English youth academy soccer players. During an investigation into sport nutritionists, players, and coaches' perspectives of barriers and enablers to nutritional adherence, three high-order and seven low-order themes were identified: (1) *capability*—(a) nutritional knowledge, and (b) cooking skills; (2) *opportunity*—(c) training venue food provision, (d) nutritionist accessibility and approachability, and (e) living status; and, (3) *motivation*—(f) performance implications, and (g) role modelling.

Interestingly, the importance of nutritional knowledge was once again reported with soccer players, coaches, and sports nutritionists, whereby they all stated it as a factor for capability (Carter et al., 2022). Physical food environments have a significant impact upon nutritional behaviours as well as inadequate food provision within the training and home environment cited as key barriers. Furthermore, the importance of the volume of nutrition support players received, alongside the amount of time spent with the sports nutritionist, were all recorded as key influencers, whilst limited time with the sports nutritionist was a key barrier (Carter et al., 2022). Overall, to improve nutritional adherence, environments looking to facilitate optimal development should look to seek the support of a sports nutritionist and allocate sufficient time with players. Moreover, sports nutritionists should aim to control the players environment to support optimal nutritional intake. See Figure 15.1 for key practical considerations for sports nutritionists and soccer clubs to consider.

The Female Player

Female representation within existing sport science literature is significantly under-reported (Costello et al., 2014; see Chapter 17) and is evident even more so in female youth soccer. Given their diverse and differing requirements in comparison to their male counterparts (Lewis et al., 1986), it is not appropriate to simply apply findings from male soccer players across both genders. Especially at the youth level as females, on average, reach maturity approximately 2 years earlier than their male counterparts (Malina et al., 2004). Of the limited research within female youth soccer, it would appear there are similar nutritional issues. As an example, Canadian HPYS female players were shown to not meet energy demands, with mean daily energy deficits of ~500kcal.day^{-1} being reported with certain individuals displaying EI of only ~1,292kcal·day^{-1} (Gibson et al., 2011). This would indicate a large energy deficit and potentially low energy availability. These findings were supported by Braun et al. (2018), who found insufficient EI and CHO intake in female youth soccer players, with over 50% displaying low EA (< 30 kcal·kg^{-1} lean body mass). This would pose a threat to the issues highlighted previously in relation to low EA. Furthermore, inadequate levels of Vitamin D and Calcium were recorded, which highlights the need for future research in the female population.

Of the extremely limited research (one study) investigating hydration status of youth female soccer players, Gibson et al. (2012) showed U15, U16, and U18 players experienced mild dehydration and low sodium losses, even in cool conditions (9.8 ± 3.3 °C). Players displayed mean sweat and sodium losses of −0.69 ± 0.54 L and 48 ± 12 mmol.L^{-1}, respectively. However, only

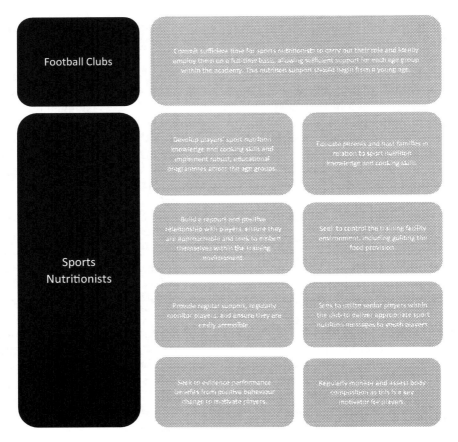

FIGURE 15.1 The key practical considerations for sports nutritionists and soccer clubs to consider when developing nutrition support for soccer players (adapted from Carter et al., 2022).

12.1% of participants lost more than −2% of the body mass, which has been associated with negative physiological and mental performance in soccer athletes (Edwards et al., 2007). These results are most likely due to mild conditions and players attending the session in a hypo-hydrated state, and thus, indicates the need for an individualised based approach.

Considerations for Researchers

Future investigations into nutritional intakes of youth soccer players should look to build upon the existing evidence-base to understand the impact of maturation upon energy requirements and subsequent EI of players. Following a 'bio-banding' approach (Malina et al., 2019) whilst assessing EI and EE may allow for identification of key age groups and individuals who require further support. Moreover, further research is required to understand the key reasons why current youth player are not meeting their nutritional requirements and build upon the novel findings of Carter et al. (2022), which will allow for improved development of interventions and support. Finally, with the increase in female participation within the sport, coinciding with the under-reported research, a greater understanding of current nutritional practices and requirements in women's and girls' soccer is needed to allow for appropriate support and guidelines.

Considerations for Practitioners

Coaches should work collaboratively with nutritionists as part of a multi-/inter-disciplinary team to achieve optimal nutrition outcomes for their young players. In light of the current nutritional research in soccer, the following considerations are proposed for practitioners employed in youth soccer settings:

- Strategies should be implemented to promote more optimal dietary behaviours to help ensure that HPYS players consume sufficient EI to meet their energy requirements. Moreover, practitioners should aim to identify scenarios that pose a significant threat to the energy demands of HPYS players (e.g., heavier training days, match days, tournaments, fixture congestion) and encourage increased energy and carbohydrate intakes around these periods.
- Consider the differences that are required in EI and EE based on growth and maturation status rather than chronological age, since there can be up to 5 years' difference in biological age within a single annual age group.
- Ensure players attend training and matches well-hydrated and look to develop individual hydration targets, especially through puberty and in environments that pose a greater risk to < 2% body mass loss during exercise.
- Aim to understand the key barriers and influencers of players achieving adequate EI and aim to develop educational programmes and interventions to combat these. Indeed, educational programmes and interventions should be implemented based on maturation status rather than chronological age groups to support growth and development based on each individual's needs.
- Practitioners working with female players should follow individual- and population-specific guidelines. Since the research within this area is limited, they should implement practical and informed practices where possible.

Conclusion

During phases of growth and development, it is paramount youth soccer players meet energy requirements, particularly due to increased energy expenditure from training and matches. At present, research indicates soccer players do not match their energy requirements, which may limit growth, development, and performance in their sport. As maturation onset and growth rates are extremely variable, it is hard to provide nutritional advice on a mass level based upon chronological age groups and, therefore, should seek to be implemented on an individual basis via biological age. Furthermore, the underpinnings of why players currently do not meet their requirements are not fully understood but it would appear the support of a qualified nutrition practitioner plays a vital role. Lastly, the female population is extremely underrepresented in current sports nutrition; thus, further exploration of the differing requirements of female youth soccer players will improve guidelines and the support provided.

References

Aerenhouts, D., Deriemaeker, P., Hebbelinck, M., & Clarys, P. (2011). Energy and macronutrient intake in adolescent sprint athletes: A follow-up study. *Journal of Sports Sciences, 29*(1), 73–82. http://doi.org/10.1080/02640414.2010.521946

Areta, J. L., Burke, L. M., Ross, M. L., Camera, D. M., West, D. W. D., Broad, E. M., Jeacocke, N. A., Moore, D. R., Stellingwerff, T., Phillips, S. M., Hawley, J. A., & Coffey, V. G. (2013). Timing and distribution of protein ingestion during prolonged recovery from resistance exercise alters myofibrillar protein synthesis. *The Journal of Physiology, 591*(9), 2319–2331. http://doi.org/10.1113/jphysiol.2012.244897

Bar-Or, O. (1980). Climate and the exercising child-a review. *International Journal of Sports Medicine, 1*(02), 53–65. http://doi.org/10.1055/s-2008-1034631

Bentley, M. R. N., Mitchell, N., Sutton, L., & Backhouse, S. H. (2019). Sports nutritionists' perspectives on enablers and barriers to nutritional adherence in high performance sport: A qualitative analysis informed by the COM-B model and theoretical domains framework. *Journal of Sports Sciences, 37*(18), 2075–2085. http://doi.org/10.1080/02640414.2019.1620989

Bentley, M. R. N., Patterson, L. B., Mitchell, N., & Backhouse, S. H. (2021). Athlete perspectives on the enablers and barriers to nutritional adherence in high-performance sport. *Psychology of Sport and Exercise, 52*, 101831. http://doi.org/10.1016/j.psychsport.2020.101831

Bettonviel, A. E. O., Brinkmans, N. Y. J., Russcher, K., Wardenaar, F. C., & Witard, O. C. (2016). Nutritional status and daytime pattern of protein intake on match, post-match, rest and training days in senior professional and youth elite soccer players. *International Journal of Sport Nutrition & Exercise Metabolism, 26*(3), 285–293. http://doi.org/10.1123/ijsnem.2015-0218

Boisseau, N., Le Creff, C., Loyens, M., & Poortmans, J. R. (2002). Protein intake and nitrogen balance in male non-active adolescents and soccer players. *European Journal of Applied Physiology, 88*(3), 288–293. https://doi.org/10.1007/s00421-002-0726-x

Boisseau, N., Vermorel, M., Rance, M., Duché, P., & Patureau-Mirand, P. (2007). Protein requirements in male adolescent soccer players. *European Journal of Applied Physiology, 100*(1), 27–33. https://doi.org/10.1007/s00421-007-0400-4

Bradley, B., Johnson, D., Hill, M., McGee, D., Kana-ah, A., Sharpin, C., Sharp, P., Kelly, A. L., Cumming, S. P., & Malina, R. M. (2019). Bio-banding in academy football: Player's perceptions of a maturity matched tournament. *Annals of Human Biology, 46*(5), 400–408. https://doi.org/10.1080/03014460.2019.1640284

Braun, H., von Andrian-Werburg, J., Schänzer, W., & Thevis, M. (2018). Nutrition status of young elite female german football players. *Pediatric Exercise Science, 30*(1), 157–167. http://doi.org/10.1123/pes.2017-0072

Briggs, M. A., Cockburn, E., Rumbold, P. L. S., Rae, G., Stevenson, E. J., & Russell, M. (2015). Assessment of energy intake and energy expenditure of male adolescent academy-level soccer players during a competitive week. *Nutrients, 7*(10), 8392–8401. https://doi.org/10.3390/nu7105400

Caccialanza, R., Cameletti, B., & Cavallaro, G. (2007). Nutritional intake of young Italian high-level soccer players: Under-reporting is the essential outcome. *Journal of Sports Science & Medicine, 6*(4), 538–542.

Carter, J. L., Kelly, A. L., Williams, R. A., Ford, T. J., & Cole, M. (2021). Exploring sports nutritionists' and players' perspectives of nutrition practice within English professional football during the COVID-19 pandemic. *Science and Medicine in Football, 5*(S1), 32–37. https://doi.org/10.1080/24733938.2021.1984559

Carter, J. L., Lee, D. J., Ranchordas, M. K., & Cole, M. (2022). Perspectives of the barriers and enablers to nutritional adherence in professional male academy football players. *Science & Medicine in Football*, 1–12. https://doi.org/10.1080/24733938.2022.2123554

Collins, J., Maughan, R. J., Gleeson, M., Bilsborough, J., Jeukendrup, A., Morton, J. P., Phillips, S. M., Armstrong, L., Burke, L. M., Close, G. L., Duffield, R., Larson-Meyer, E., Louis, J., Medina, D., Meyer, F., Rollo, I., Sundgot-Borgen, J., Wall, B. T., Boullosa, B., Dupont, G., Lizarraga, A., Res, P., Bizzini, M., Castagna, C., Cowie, C. M., D'Hooghe, M., Geyer, H., Meyer, T., Papadimitriou, N., Vouillamoz, M., & McCall, A. (2021). UEFA expert group statement on nutrition in elite football. Current evidence to inform practical recommendations and guide future research. *British Journal of Sports Medicine, 55*(8), 416–416. http://doi.org/10.1136/bjsports-2019-101961

Costello, J. T., Bieuzen, F., & Bleakley, C. M. (2014). Where are all the female participants in Sports and Exercise Medicine research? *European Journal of Sport Science, 14*(8), 847–851. http://doi.org/10.1080/17461391.2014.911354

Da Silva, R. P., Mündel, T., Natali, A. J., Bara Filho, M. G., Alfenas, R. C. G., Lima, J. R. P., Belfort, F. G., Lopes, P. R. N. R., & Marins, J. C. B. (2012). Pre-game hydration status, sweat loss, and fluid intake in elite Brazilian young male soccer players during competition. *Journal of Sports Sciences, 30*(1), 37–42. http://doi.org/10.1080/02640414.2011.623711

Edwards, A. M., Mann, M. E., Marfell-Jones, M. J., Rankin, D. M., Noakes, T. D., & Shillington, D. P. (2007). Influence of moderate dehydration on soccer performance: physiological responses to 45 min of outdoor match-play and the immediate subsequent performance of sport-specific and mental concentration tests. *British Journal of Sports Medicine, 41*(6), 385–391. http://doi.org/10.1136/bjsm.2006.033860

Eriksson, O., & Saltin, B. (1974). Muscle metabolism during exercise in boys aged 11 to 16 years compared to adults. *Acta Paediatrica Belgica, 28*, 257.

Ersoy, N., Ersoy, G., & Kutlu, M. (2016). Assessment of hydration status of elite young male soccer players with different methods and new approach method of substitute urine strip. *Journal of the International Society of Sports Nutrition, 13*, 1–6. http://doi.org/10.1186/s12970-016-0145-8

Falk, B., & Dotan, R. (2008). Children's thermoregulation during exercise in the heat—a revisit. *Applied Physiology, Nutrition, and Metabolism, 33*(2), 420–427. http://doi.org/10.1139/H07-185

Garrido, G., Webster, A. L., & Chamorro, M. (2007). Nutritional adequacy of different menu settings in elite Spanish adolescent soccer players. *International Journal of Sport Nutrition & Exercise Metabolism, 17*(5), 421–432. http://doi.org/10.1123/ijsnem.17.5.421

Gibson, J. C., Stuart-Hill, L., Martin, S., & Gaul, C. (2011). Nutrition status of junior elite Canadian female soccer athletes. *International Journal of Sport Nutrition & Exercise Metabolism, 21*(6), 507–514. http://doi.org/10.1123/ijsnem.21.6.507

Gibson, J. C., Stuart-Hill, L. A., Pethick, W., & Gaul, C. A. (2012). Hydration status and fluid and sodium balance in elite Canadian junior women's soccer players in a cool environment. *Applied Physiology, Nutrition, and Metabolism, 37*(5), 931–937. https://doi.org/10.1139/h2012-073

Gledhill, A., Harwood, C., & Forsdyke, D. (2017). Psychosocial factors associated with talent development in football: A systematic review. *Psychology of Sport and Exercise, 31*, 93–112. http://doi.org/10.1016/j.psychsport.2017.04.002

Granja, D. S., Cotovio, R., Pinto, R., Borrego, R., Mendes, L., Carolino, E., Macedo, P., Ferreira, D., Caetano, C., & Mendes, B. (2017). Evaluation of young elite soccer players food intake on match day and highest training load days. *Journal of Human Sport & Exercise, 12*(4), 1238–1247. http://doi.org/10.14198/jhse.2017.124.10

Guttierres, A. P. M., Natali, A. J., Vianna, J. M., Reis, V. M., & Marins, J. C. B. (2011). Dehydration in soccer players after a match in the heat. *Biology of Sport, 28*(4), 249–254. http://doi.org/10.5604/965483

Hannon, M. P., Carney, D. J., Floyd, S., Parker, L. J. F., McKeown, J., Drust, B., Unnithan, V. B., Close, G. L., & Morton, J. P. (2020). Cross-sectional comparison of body composition and resting metabolic rate in Premier League academy soccer players: Implications for growth and maturation. *Journal of Sports Sciences, 38*(11–12), 1326–1334. http://doi.org/10.1080/02640414.2020.1717286

Hannon, M. P., Parker, L. J. F., Carney, D. J., McKeown, J., Speakman, J. R., Hambly, C., Drust, B., Unnithan, V. B., Close, G. L., & Morton, J. P. (2021). Energy requirements of male academy soccer players from the English Premier League. *Medicine & Science in Sports & Exercise, 53*(1), 200–210. http://doi.org/10.1249/MSS.0000000000002443

Heaney, S., O'Connor, H., Michael, S., Gifford, J., & Naughton, G. (2011). Nutrition knowledge in athletes: A systematic review. *International Journal of Sport Nutrition and Exercise Metabolism, 21*(3), 248–261. http://doi.org/10.1123/ijsnem.21.3.248

Hidalgo y Teran Elizondo, R., Martín Bermudo, F. M., Peñaloza Mendez, R., Berná Amorós, G., Lara Padilla, E., & Berral de la Rosa, F. J. (2015). Nutritional intake and nutritional status in elite

Mexican teenagers soccer players of different ages. *Nutricion Hospitalaria*, *32*(4), 1735–1743. https://doi.org/10.3305/nh.2015.32.4.8788

Iglesias-Gutiérrez, E., García, A., García-Zapico, P., Pérez-Landaluce, J., Patterson, A. M., & García-Rovés, P. M. (2012). Is there a relationship between the playing position of soccer players and their food and macronutrient intake? *Applied Physiology, Nutrition, and Metabolism*, *37*(2), 225–232. https://doi.org/10.1139/h11-152

Iglesias-Gutiérrez, E., García-Rovés, P. M., Rodríguez, C., Braga, S., García-Zapico, P., & Patterson, Á. M. (2005). Food habits and nutritional status assessment of adolescent soccer players. A necessary and accurate approach. *Canadian Journal of Applied Physiology*, *30*(1), 18–32. http://doi.org/10.1139/h05-102

Inbar, O., Morris, N., Epstein, Y., & Gass, G. (2004). Comparison of thermoregulatory responses to exercise in dry heat among prepubertal boys, young adults and older males. *Experimental Physiology*, *89*(6), 691–700. http://doi.org/10.1113/expphysiol.2004.027979

Kelly, A. L., & Williams, C. A. (2020). Physical characteristics and the talent identification and development processes in male youth soccer: A narrative review. *Strength & Conditioning Journal*, *42*(6), 15–34. http://doi.org/10.1519/SSC.0000000000000576

Kelly, A. L., Williams, C. A., & Wilson, M. (2018). Developing a football-specific talent identification and development profiling concept–the locking wheel nut model. *Applied Coaching Research Journal*, *2*, 32–41.

Kreider, R. B., Wilborn, C. D., Taylor, L., Campbell, B., Almada, A. L., Collins, R., Cooke, M., Earnest, C. P., Greenwood, M., Kalman, D. S., Kersick, C. M., Kleiner, S. M., leutholtz, B., Lopez, H., Lowery, L. M., mendel, R., Smith, A., Spano, M., Wildman, R., Willoughby, D. S., Ziegenfuss, T. N., & Kalman, D. S. (2010). ISSN exercise & sport nutrition review: research & recommendations. *Journal of the International Society of Sports Nutrition*, *7*(1), 7. http://doi.org/10.1186/s12970-017-0173-z

Leblanc, J. Ch, Le Gall, F., Grandjean, V., & Verger, P. (2002). Nutritional intake of French soccer players at the clairefontaine training center. *International Journal of Sport Exercise Metabolism*, *12*(3), 268–280. https://doi.org/10.1123/ijsnem.12.3.268

Lewis, D. A., Kamon, E., & Hodgson, J. L. (1986). Physiological differences between genders implications for sports conditioning. *Sports Medicine*, *3*(5), 357–369.

Loucks, A. B. (2007). Low energy availability in the marathon and other endurance sports. *Sports Medicine*, *37*(4–5), 348–352. http://doi.org/10.2165/00007256-200737040-00019

Malina, R. M., Bouchard, C., & Bar-Or, O. (2004). *Growth, maturation, and physical activity*. Human Kinetics.

Malina, R. M., Cumming, S. P., Rogol, A. D., Coelho-E-Silva, M. J., Figueiredo, A. J., Konarski, J. M., & Kozieł, S. M. (2019). Bio-banding in youth sports: Background, concept, and application. *Sports Medicine (Auckland, N.Z.)*, *49*(11), 1671–1685. https://doi.org/10.1007/s40279-019-01166-x

Meyer, F., & Bar-Or, O. (1994). Fluid and electrolyte loss during exercise. *Sports Medicine*, *18*(1), 4–9. http://doi.org/10.2165/00007256-199418010-00002

Murphy, C. H., Hector, A. J., & Phillips, S. M. (2015). Considerations for protein intake in managing weight loss in athletes. *European Journal of Sport Science*, *15*(1), 21–28. https://doi.org/10.1080/17461391.2014.936325

Murphy, S., & Jeanes, Y. (2006). Nutritional knowledge and dietary intakes of young professional football players. *Nutrition & Food Science*, *36*(5), 343–348. http://doi.org/10.1108/00346650610703199

Naughton, R. J., Drust, B., O'Boyle, A., Abayomi, J., Mahon, E., Morton, J. P., & Davies, I. G. (2017). Free-sugar, total-sugar, fibre, and micronutrient intake within elite youth British soccer players: A nutritional transition from schoolboy to fulltime soccer player. *Applied Physiology, Nutrition & Metabolism*, *42*(5), 517–522. http://doi.org/10.1139/apnm-2016-0459

Naughton, R. J., Drust, B., O'Boyle, A., Morgans, R., Abayomi, J., Davies, I. G., Morton, J. P., & Mahon, E. (2016). Daily distribution of carbohydrate, protein and fat intake in elite youth academy soccer players over a 7-day training period. *International Journal of Sport Nutrition & Exercise Metabolism*, *26*(5), 473–480. http://doi.org/10.1123/ijsnem.2015-0340

Nobari, H., Barjaste, A., Haghighi, H., Clemente, F. M., Carlos-Vivas, J., & Perez-Gomez, J. (2021). Quantification of training and match load in elite youth soccer players: A full-season study. *The Journal of Sports Medicine and Physical Fitness*, *62*(4), 448–456. https://doi.org/10.1186/s12970-021-004415

Noronha, D. C., Santos, M. I. A. F., Santos, A. A., Corrente, L. G. A., Fernandes, R. K. N., Barreto, A. C. A., Santos, R. G. J., Santos, R. S., Gomes, L. P. S., & Nascimento, M. V. S. (2020). Nutrition knowledge is correlated with a better dietary intake in adolescent soccer players: A cross-sectional study. *Journal of Nutrition and Metabolism, 3519781.* http://doi.org/10.1155/2020/3519781

North, M., Kelly, A. L., Ranchordas, M. K., & Cole, M. (2022). Nutritional consideration in high performance youth soccer: A systematic review. *Journal of Science in Sport and Exercise, 4,* 195–212.

Oliveira, C. C., Ferreira, D., Caetano, C., Granja, D., Pinto, R., Mendes, B., & Sousa, M. (2017). Nutrition and supplementation in soccer. *Sports, 5*(2), 28. http://doi.org/10.3390/sports5020028

Phillips, S. M., Sykes, D., & Gibson, N. (2014). Hydration status and fluid balance of elite European youth soccer players during consecutive training sessions. *Journal of Sports Science & Medicine, 13*(4), 817–882.

Rowland, T., Hagenbuch, S., Pober, D., & Garrison, A. (2008). Exercise tolerance and thermoregulatory responses during cycling in boys and men. *Medicine and Science in Sports and Exercise, 40*(2), 282–287. http://doi.org/10.1249/mss.0b013e31815a95a7

Ruiz, F., Irazusta, A., Gil, S., Irazusta, J., Casis, L., & Gil, J. (2005). Nutritional intake in soccer players of different ages. *Journal of Sports Sciences, 23*(3), 235–242. http://doi.org/10.1080/02640410410001730160

Russell, M., & Pennock, A. (2011). Dietary analysis of young professional soccer players for 1 week during the competitive season. *The Journal of Strength & Conditioning Research, 25*(7), 1816–1823. http://doi.org/10.1519/JSC.0b013e3181e7fbdd

Sarmento, H., Clemente, F. M., Araújo, D., Davids, K., McRobert, A., & Figueiredo, A. (2018). What performance analysts need to know about research trends in association football (2012–2016): A systematic review. *Sports Medicine, 48*(4), 799–836. http://doi.org/10.1007/s40279-017-0836-6

Silva, R., Mündel, T., Natali, A., Bara Filho, M., Lima, J. P., Alfenas, R. G., Lopes, P. R. N. R., Belfort, F. G., & Marins, J. B. (2011). Fluid balance of elite Brazilian youth soccer players during consecutive days of training. *Journal of Sports Sciences, 29*(7), 725–732. http://doi.org/10.1080/02640414.2011.552189

The Premier League. (2011). *Elite player performance plan* [online]. Retrieved from: www.premierleague.com/youth/EPPP [accessed 22nd June 2019].

Timmons, B. W., Bar-Or, O., & Riddell, M. C. (2003). Oxidation rate of exogenous carbohydrate during exercise is higher in boys than in men. *Journal of Applied Physiology, 94*(1), 278–284. http://doi.org/10.1152/japplphysiol.00140.2002

Trakman, G. L., Forsyth, A., Devlin, B. L., & Belski, R. (2016). A systematic review of athletes' and coaches' nutrition knowledge and reflections on the quality of current nutrition knowledge measures. *Nutrients, 8*(9), 570. http://doi.org/10.3390/nu8090570

Wrigley, R., Drust, B., Stratton, G., Scott, M., & Gregson, W. (2012). Quantification of the typical weekly in-season training load in elite junior soccer players. *Journal of Sports Sciences, 30*(15), 1573–1580. http://doi.org/10.1080/02640414.2012.709265

16
INTERNATIONAL PERSPECTIVES
Evaluating Male Talent Pathways from Across the Globe

Adam L. Kelly, Chris Eveleigh, Fynn Bergmann, Oliver Höner, Kevin Braybrook, Durva Vahia, Laura Finnegan, Stephen Finn, Jan Verbeek, Laura Jonker, Matthew P. Ferguson, and James H. Dugdale

Introduction

Various sociocultural perspectives have been presented throughout this book (see Chapter 7). One particularly important consideration during talent identification and development is national youth sport culture. Countries often adopt diverse talent pathways, depending on their history, national philosophy, and individual constraints. For instance, there are emerging nations where the popularity of soccer is very much in its infancy, whereas there are other established soccer nations who have had the sport entrenched into their society for many years. It is also essential to recognise the constraints of respective nations—most notably, the socioeconomic limitations and populations of countries. As a result of the different international perspectives, it is important that stakeholders understand the impact of sociocultural factors on talent pathways whilst appreciating it is not necessarily a 'one-size-fits-all' approach (Sullivan et al., 2022).

Drawing from the international expertise of the authors, the purpose of this chapter is to provide an exploration of various national talent pathways in male soccer, including: (a) Canada, (b) England, (c) Germany, (d) Gibraltar, (e) India, (f) Republic of Ireland, (g) Scotland, (h) the Netherlands, and (i) the United States. Each example will offer an overview of the organisational structures that are embedded into their respective talent pathways by exploring considerations such as: (a) population, (b) popularity, (c) sociocultural influences, (c) formal selection age, (d) activities, (e) trajectories, (f) professional opportunities, and (g) specialist support. Finally, contextual and methodological considerations for researchers and practitioners are provided to help better understand the role of national youth sport culture as part of talent identification and development in youth soccer.

Canada

Canada is known as one of the most diverse countries in the world. It boasts the inclusion of many cultures and different sports, with the second largest land mass globally. Although the general belief is that ice hockey is the most popular sport in Canada, soccer actually has the highest participation (Hanley, 2022). Specifically, it was reported in January 2022 that there are approximately

DOI: 10.4324/9781032232799-16

1,000,000 registered soccer players in Canada, which is far greater than the ~650,000 players registered in ice hockey. These participation numbers may be a testament to the fact that soccer has a wide range of offerings for youth in Canada, such as various game formats (e.g., interactive games with family members, club festivals, futsal, beach soccer, indoor leagues) (Ontario Soccer, 2018) and developmental stages (i.e., U4–U6—active start, U6–U10—fundamentals, U9–U12—learning to train, U12–U15—training to train, U16–U20—training to compete, U19+—training to win, adulthood—active for life) (Canada Soccer, 2022a) for different ages. Also, the cost to participate, although rising, is still much lower than that of ice hockey. The country is comprised of many clubs with thousands of members, although most of those members are only playing recreationally. The recent professionalisation of soccer in Canada, via provincial player development leagues and the formation of the Canadian Premier League (founded in 2017), has certainly contributed towards the growth of the sport, with many clubs now investing in paid coaches for sessions with children as young as aged 3 years. Although not entirely soccer focused, sessions with young children are leading many parents who may have had their child play ice hockey (or other sports) remain within soccer.

The country's diversity can provide contrasting opinions on how the sport should be played and developed. However, strong leadership from Canada Soccer has produced the first World Cup qualification in 36 years for the men's team in 2022. Many people have worked hard to change the culture that is embedded across sport and soccer in Canada to achieve this recent success. Soccer in Canada changed its approach in 2013 by moving to keep no scores and league standings for those aged under 12 years, which was initially met with outrage from parents (Toronto Star, 2013). Indeed, this led to a small decline in registrations, but those who stayed have recognised the new focus on long-term player development, where coaches and players can compete in games with little pressure.

Slowly but surely, players from Canada are being recognised and making the leap across the Atlantic to play in Europe. Alphonso Davies, Jonathan David, and Tajon Buchanan are just three on the male side who have had success in Europe. With only three Major League Soccer Clubs in Canada (CF Montréal, Toronto FC, and Vancouver Whitecaps FC), the youth development for those organisations differs, whereby their academy teams play in various leagues inside and outside of Canada but rarely against each other. This is mainly due to the distance between all three clubs and the associated travel costs, which, understandably, has important implications on the talent pathways for professional clubs. Canada Soccer have invested in coaching staff to visit these three clubs regularly, who work directly with the Canadian players within those youth teams to support the national pathway as part of the new 'NEX-PRO' programme (Canada Soccer, 2022b). Canada also continues to develop domestically, with the formation of the Canadian Premier League steadily growing the number of teams across the country and attendances rising for every game.

England

Soccer academies in England are specialist-training programmes established and funded by professional soccer clubs and the Premier League, with the primary objective of developing home-grown players for their respective senior team. Between the ages of 8 and 16 years, young players join an academy on schoolboy terms (i.e., part-time attendance), then, at aged 16 years, those players who show continued progress are selected to undertake a 2-year, full-time youth training scheme known as an academy scholarship. Upon completion of their scholarship, players either sign a professional contract or are released. These developmental stages have been divided into three phases: (a) foundation development phase (FDP) (U9 to U11), (b) youth development phase (YDP) (U12 to U16), and (c) professional development phase (PDP) (U17 to U21). Because of the difficulties in achieving a professional contract, over 90% of players who join an academy fail to make it into their respective senior team (Mills et al., 2012). Therefore, it is each academy's responsibility to provide their youth soccer players the maximum opportunity to develop and reach their full potential.

The complex process of identifying and developing soccer players from youth levels to senior professional status has advanced over the last decade, with the implementation of contemporary multidisciplinary paradigms being a mandatory requirement in England (Kelly & Williams, 2020). One such example is the design and implementation of the Elite Player Performance Plan (EPPP) amongst professional soccer academies (The Premier League, 2011). The EPPP policy provides recommendations for the multifaceted components of player development, with adherence to these standards assessed to categorise each academy in return for financial investment from the Premier League. Although the EPPP mandates contextual and environmental approaches, these prescriptions are non-specific in their design and open to interpretation, thus allowing academies to adapt their own philosophy and 'best-practice' strategies. Academies are audited every 3 years and subsequently categorised from one to four based on: (a) productivity rates, (b) training facilities, (c) coaching, (d) education, and (e) welfare provisions. As part of the EPPP, all clubs are required to track information that is relevant to their academy (e.g., player reviews, fitness testing, growth and maturation, performance analysis statistics) via the Performance Management Application (PMA). Although the PMA has been used for almost 10 years and holds a wealth of data, it remains a relatively untapped resource with regards to collating information for research purposes.

The English Football Association (The FA, 2019) Four Corner Model offers a holistic approach, which is often adopted by professional academies to adhere to regulations outlined in the EPPP to support player development. These attributes are characterised by: (a) technical/tactical, (b) physical (c) psychological, and (d) social. This model also formulates the delivery of the national coach education curriculum in England (The FA, 2016) as well as underpins the 'DNA Philosophy' of the England national player-development pathway and performance strategy (The FA, 2014). Academy philosophies are a crucial element in the talent identification and development processes in male youth soccer across England, primarily as their implementation via key stakeholders (i.e., administrators, coaches, practitioners) have a significant impact on individual recruitment, progression, and subsequent achievement in both domestic leagues and the national teams (Cushion et al., 2012). The current professionalised expansion of soccer academies has coincided with a growth in departmental structures, most noticeably with sport science and medicine becoming a key feature (Ryan et al., 2018).

Germany

Soccer is the most popular sport among the German population. This is organised under the auspices of 21 Regional Football Associations and the German Football Association ('Deutscher Fußball-Bund' (DFB) as the main governing body with more than 7 million members (Deutsche Fußball Liga [DFL], 2022a). Talent identification and development are embedded into the pyramid-like educational structure of the DFB (DFB, 2009). The pillar of such pyramid is the so-called *basic development stage* (aged 3–10 years; 'Basisförderung'), which is focused on recruiting as many children as possible in kindergartens, schools, and local clubs.

During this early stage, children's enthusiasm for soccer should be inspired to encourage long-time participation. In addition, this phase is also intended to develop fundamental movement and soccer-specific skills that promote a solid base of children's health and for potential talent development in later years.

Within the *talent development stage* (aged 11–14 years; 'Talentförderung'), players are selected and promoted within youth academies (YAs) or the DFB's Talent Development Program. It is mandatory that all Bundesliga and 2. Bundesliga clubs implement a YA programme (Deutsche Fußball Liga, 2022a). Twenty additional German clubs also fulfil the quality criteria that are assured on a 3-year basis. This regular quality assurance covers structural, infrastructural, and personnel-condition criteria, as well as contractual terms between players and the clubs (see DFL, 2022b for further detail). This has resulted in a total of 56 YAs and approximately 5,600 participating players throughout Germany (DFL, 2022a). Most YAs begin selecting players between the ages of 10 and 12 years yet often run 'soccer schools' or 'prospective teams' for younger kids. Player development in German YAs is mainly based on the clubs' respective philosophies covering, for instance, the creation of supportive talent environments or methodological aspects of practice and coaching.

Talented players who are initially not recruited for a YA can be selected and developed within the DFB's Talent Development Program, which was implemented in the 2002/2003 season, and since then, has undergone only a few structural refinements. This programme consists of approximately 1,300 coaches working at the 357 regional DFB training centres ('DFB-Stützpunkte') across Germany, led by 29 full-time coordinators (Deutsche Fußball Liga, 2022b). All coaches must possess at least the UEFA B License and are paid an honorarium. These practitioners identify and develop around 14,000 talents between the ages of 11 and 15 years. At the core of this programme, players are offered one weekly training session at these training centres in addition to their normal training within local clubs. Individualised player development in small training groups guided by teams of coaches (i.e., approximately one coach for eight players) is ensured by following a nationwide philosophy and learning goals designed on a competency-based approach. The programme's philosophy covers, for example, the creation of appropriate learning conditions, with less competitive pressure, compared to the YA system. The comprehensive nationwide network and complementary work within the talent development stage between YAs, the DFB's Talent Development Program, Regional Associations, and schools (e.g., there are nationwide 37 'elite schools of soccer') are aimed at supporting the process of identification and development of every soccer talent in Germany.

Following the talent development stage, the most talented players move up to the *elite promotion stage* (aged 15–18 years; 'Eliteförderung'). These players aim to prepare for the demands of high-performance soccer within YAs by shifting the focus more on the team performance yet still providing individualised support. An increasing focus on performance and competition is, for instance, achieved through the U17- and U19-Bundesliga that are nationwide leagues organised in three regional conferences. Those competing in these leagues generate the core who are additionally selected for the Youth National Teams and compete internationally against other nations. However, since only a small percentage of players in the elite promotion stage will subsequently participate in one of the three German professional leagues, vital importance is placed on the achievement of school graduations within YAs. As the regional conferences of the German fourth (Regionalliga) and fifth (Oberliga) leagues provide semi-professional conditions, those former youth players who do not attain a professional level are still able to participate in a challenging and competitive league.

Gibraltar

Recognising the journey of any emerging nation in soccer requires a review of the sociocultural norms of the people and their connection to the sport. Although the Gibraltar Football Association (GFA) was formed in 1895, it wasn't until May 2013 that they became a member of the UEFA family and were provided an opportunity to officially compete on an international stage. This is particularly interesting, since the emergence of a new soccer nation at international level offers a wealth of opportunities to design and implement contemporary strategies as well as negate some of the lessons learnt from the more established countries (Bennett et al., 2019). It's also important to emphasise the size of the country. An area spanning 3 miles long and 0.75 miles wide will clearly have its own challenges related to soccer development. This requires Gibraltar (and similar smaller countries) to navigate their way through competition and accept how it can respectfully support the growth of the game within their limitations. Indeed, how this British overseas territory designs talent identification and development systems for a reduced talent pool will be instrumental in optimising players performance, including those based within Gibraltar as well as potential players overseas.

Countries with a greater depth of player participation and historic talent identification and development systems can offer a broader approach towards player recruitment, largely due to the numbers accessible and the selection pool from which it provides. Talent pathways are also unique and relative to their own context, and any association recognising the landscape they are embedded within will be unique to their own soccer story. With a population fewer than 35,000, Gibraltar has an immediate distinction in comparison to many of their counterparts striving to establish talent development programmes. Although recognising there are several talent identification and development models that describe the various stages that athletes may go through to reach an elite level (MacNamara & Collins, 2012), understanding Gibraltar's unique setting and the barriers/challenges it faces (e.g., population and landscape, depth of player participation, industry partnerships, player progression opportunities), highlight that current frameworks that are generally designed for established nations may not be suitable, provide relevance, or support the ecological reality.

In order to support young players' progression, the GFA have established a development programme from U7 to U19, which offers a formal structure of soccer that allows youth to practice and compete regularly. This includes a range of activities, such as fundamentals, a development school, youth development leagues, youth championships, recreational soccer, and an elite youth development programme (Gibraltar Football Association, 2022). As individuals progress towards adulthood, the Gibraltar National League (comprised of eleven teams) is the senior playing level that players aspire towards (UEFA, 2022). The unique challenges faced across talent identification and player progression, however, are not only associated with youth players. For instance, players from outside Gibraltar are being recruited by their domestic league clubs, which could subsequently reduce opportunities for young Gibraltarian players from accessing senior soccer. Additionally, as an emerging soccer culture without any professional soccer team in the country, there could be a disconnect with traditional soccer programmes and pathways associated to a system, such as an English soccer club/academy aligned to the EPPP (The Premier League, 2011).

Although the omission of professional clubs based in Gibraltar may impact upon young players accessing an academy programme, it does not diminish their opportunity to access a national soccer pathway (Ignacio, 2022). Due to the limited depth of potentially talented players, international playing experiences are generally offered earlier in an individual's development compared to many other nations. On one hand, this may support the view that the number of games played at a senior level at an early age is of importance for long-term development (Poli et al., 2015). Whereas, on the other hand, it may also mean that players are being exposed to a level that they are not necessarily ready to compete at. In addition, potentially talented players who are not initially selected into the national pathway may subsequently leave Gibraltar to continue their education, embark on work opportunities, or simply decide to leave their home. As a result, it is important to monitor and track these individuals, as many will continue to play soccer and develop their competencies in a new setting over a prolonged period. Recognising that players can develop over time and individuals may meet the criteria to be selected for national levels later in their careers and without any early identification (Güllich et al., 2022) suggests the need to establish a talent monitoring database where players can be profiled, tracked, and recruited away from Gibraltar. This may help increase the talent available and benefit the levels of performance for both players and teams.

India

India is as diverse as it is large. Each of its 28 states has its own culture, with distinct lifestyles, livelihoods, climate, geography, language, and cuisine. The diversity, while enriching the quality of experiences and perspectives, is a barrier to a centralised structure. With the exception of cricket, sport remains a largely underdeveloped industry in the country, with soccer not a mainstream career option for the majority people (Khasnis et al., 2021). Although India predominantly is not a sporting nation, there are hotspots with a vivacious soccer culture; namely, Kerela, Mizoram, Manipur, Goa, Punjab, and West Bengal. In metropolitan cities like Mumbai and Bangalore, soccer is very popular. With multiple soccer schools and private academies across these cities, soccer is accessible to the middle and upper economic classes. There are many artificial surfaces across these cities that have increased the accessible infrastructure and several grassroots leagues have emerged across these cities as a result. Leagues do not run for an entire season but are supplemented by other short leagues and private tournaments that run throughout the calendar year. Financial support comes predominantly from the community, large corporations, or former athletes. Despite the thriving cultures, soccer as a full-time profession is financially unsustainable. With the exception from the top two tiers of the soccer pyramid (Indian Super League [ISL] and I-League), senior team players will typically have a secondary job to support themselves financially.

Over the last decade, India has made large strides in youth soccer development. In 2012, India launched its Grassroots Development Programme, and in 2017, hosted the men's U17 World Cup. These events have led to subsequent investment and growth in youth development, including leagues and academy accreditation. This has also encouraged clubs to initiate talent identification and development from the U13 age group. In 2017, the All India Football Federation (AIFF) launched an academy accreditation system, wherein youth academies are given ratings on a 5-star scale based on criteria such as number and age of players, licenses of technical staff, curriculum, infrastructure, specialised support staff, and development pathways provided (All India Football Federation, 2022). However, barring a few, most academies do not support the multidimensional development of players, despite many individuals dropping out of school after the age of 16 years to take part. Therefore, if these players do not make it as a professional, their lack of holistic development and education can leave them ill-prepared for adulthood.

India has 83 accredited youth academies (2019/20), 24 senior teams in the ISL and I-league, and over 800 local teams (All India Football Federation, 2022). However, talent development pathways remain disorganised, and while a few academies develop players from youth teams to senior teams, these are a minority. Youth teams are set up through open trials and internal networks before competition and are then disbanded afterwards. With rampant age fraud and a focus on winning, chronologically older players will often continue to play across multiple teams and age groups within the youth system. Some senior teams hold closed trials and have a scouting process, while many other senior teams hold open trials. The top tiers of the soccer pyramid often scout players from lower national leagues and local leagues. Since the supply of players is far more than the demands of the clubs, U18 players are often lost in the maze of older players. The lack of U21/U23 competitions means that U18 players have to make large strides in development to transition into senior sport. While there are players who are able to achieve professional success, the system makes it an exceptionally difficult task, with most players pursuing soccer as a part-time job or only in recreational environments.

Republic of Ireland

The Football Association of Ireland (FAI) is the national governing body for soccer in the Republic of Ireland. Children can begin playing at ages 5 or 6 years in local, volunteer-led clubs. League and cup competitions start at U12, governed by the Schoolboy Football Association of Ireland (SFAI), which is affiliated to its parent organisation, the FAI. The SFAI cater for almost 100,000 players from more than 1,000 clubs across 31 leagues (Football Association of Ireland, 2009). Players participate in local leagues and SFAI national club competitions from U12 to U16. Selected players also represent their leagues in inter-league competitions (and Emerging Talent Programmes) from U12 to U16. Certain inequities exist within this pathway, such as differing opportunities resulting in internal migration patterns towards Dublin-based clubs as well as strong relative age effects (Finnegan, 2019; Finnegan et al., 2016).

The sports of hurling and Gaelic football are traditionally considered to be representative of Irish culture, providing the Irish population with a sense of both place and identity (Cronin, 1994). The 'foreign' status attached to soccer may have hampered its development and it is still used within popular culture (Connaughton, 2018). Despite this history, soccer is now the most popular field sport in the country (Sport Ireland, 2021). Soccer has come to represent a fundamental shift within Irish identity, with the international element allowing for 'measurement' against other nations and the development of a more contemporary sporting identity (Cronin, 1999). The socio-historical influence of religious and cultural differences in Ireland resulted in soccer not being offered in some schools and Gaelic Athletic Association members not being allowed to spectate or play soccer until the removal of 'the ban' in 1971, which has limited the potential talent detection and development pool.

Despite the organisational homogeneity of modern national soccer structures (King, 2017), there are often specific contextual factors that influence stakeholder relations within each setting (e.g., culture, organisational structure). In 2015, the FAI launched a national 'Player Development Plan (PDP) for youth football', which included recommendations regarding small-sided games and non-competitive soccer. Certain aspects have been rejected by some leagues (often due to historical patterns of conflict and antagonism between both governing entities) (Finnegan et al., 2018), resulting in continued incongruous approaches to talent development. The FAI introduced a national U19 league in 2011, expanding down to U13 in 2019. As part of the FAI's licencing programme, senior League of Ireland (LOI) clubs are now obliged to establish a youth squad at U14 (formerly U13), U15, U17, and U19. The aim is to progress youth to their respective senior LOI squad after experiencing a level of youth soccer designed to facilitate 'the best, playing against the best' (FAI, 2013). However, the national league is poorly resourced and structurally weak (Elliott, 2014), despite the demand for top-level soccer remaining strong, with approximately 40,000 people travelling on a regular basis to spectate it in the UK (Malone, 2020).

The potential gap in the pathway from the U19 league to senior soccer threatens to halt the development of youth soccer players. An alternative approach to the development of Irish talent has traditionally depended on migration overseas (generally to the UK) at age 16 years (Bourke, 2003). A recent FIFA (2021) report found that the Republic of Ireland was the country with the most players under 18 years of age who transferred abroad from 2011 to 2020 (although this does include player movement between the Republic of Ireland and Northern Ireland). The proliferation of other overseas players to the English Premier League had an impact on this pathway, with the volume of Irish players declining by 60% between 2009 and 2019 (Malone, 2019). The advent of Brexit has also created a new dynamic, whereby players are prevented from moving to the UK prior to the age of 18 years due to FIFA player movement regulations. This has led to a number of high-profile youth players moving across Europe (e.g., Italy) instead of the traditional UK pathway. This ruling will represent a major cultural change for Irish soccer and will shift the emphasis to the design, management, and funding of player development structures within the Republic of Ireland.

Scotland

Despite high participation rates, an established national federation, and societal similarities to the rest of the United Kingdom, Scotland's soccer success at both club and international levels has been hindered, potentially due to financial and developmental constraints (Adams et al., 2017; Morrow, 2006). Acknowledging these constraints, talent identification and development approaches within Scottish soccer may not be comparable to those reported in England or established nations in Europe, and more in line with those of emerging soccer nations (Bennett et al., 2018; Dugdale et al., 2021).

Although soccer academies in Scotland adopt a similar structure to other nations, with professional parent clubs supporting youth teams from ~U8–U18, the Scottish Football Association (SFA) recently refined their systematic performance strategy. Club Academy Scotland (CAS) is the SFA's structure that defines, operates, and partially funds the academy system in Scotland, alongside coordinating a seasonal games programme. Historically, the CAS structure has provided a standardised pathway for academy players, with the overarching aim of improving performance at both domestic and international levels (SFA, 2017). However, in 2017, the SFA revitalised the CAS framework via an initiative titled 'Project Brave'. Project Brave aimed to improve talent identification and development by evaluating clubs on a criteria-based system and assess measurable performance outcomes that encourage best practice. At the heart of the SFA's performance strategy are seven Performance Schools. These seven schools, located across Scotland, provide talented boys and girls between U12 and U16 the opportunity to train and develop everyday within an education environment. Since their inception in 2012, SFA Performance Schools have been instrumental in the long-term development of male and female players, many of whom successfully transition to professional and international soccer (SFA, 2022).

At aged 18 years, Scottish youth players typically transition to professional soccer or are released. Scotland boasts an impressive youth-to-professional contract success rate (~10%) (Dugdale et al., 2021), which is comparable to reports from other soccer nations. Yet, this may be resultant of a smaller national population and talent pool. Developmental constraints do, however, provide a significant challenge for talent development in Scottish soccer. An absence of a governed development or U21 league invokes a disconnect between those graduating from academy programmes and potential senior first team soccer. The size and structure of the professional leagues in Scotland (ten teams per league) afford little room for error, with many teams often only a few games away from relegation or promotion throughout the season. Accordingly, talent development and the youth-to-senior transition may be impacted due to limited playing opportunities and a potential risk associated with allocating first-team playing time to young players and academy graduates.

Like other emerging soccer nations (Finnegan, 2019), Scotland has observed a migration of top soccer talent seeking opportunities in other nations, most notably in England. Correspondingly, Scotland has explored wider approaches to talent identification for their national teams by identifying players from the rest of the United Kingdom who possess Scottish heritage. These import/export activities are likely to benefit Scotland's national teams but may hinder domestic soccer through an exodus of top talent prospects. This is evidenced by a gradual decrease in home-based players representing and being signed by Scottish Professional Football League (SPFL) clubs over the last few decades. However, Scotland has seized attention in recent years for harvesting several elite talents and progressions in governance related to talent identification and development are apparent. These developments, combined with a rich and passionate national sporting culture, provokes an encouraging time-period for Scottish soccer both presently and in years to come.[1]

The Netherlands

In the Netherlands (Holland), children can start playing soccer from as young as aged 4 years by becoming a member of one of the 2,834 grassroots clubs (The Dutch FA, 2022b). Since every neighbourhood has a club, grassroots soccer is considered the basis for Dutch soccer success. At a national level, talent development processes are mostly maintained by professional soccer clubs in the Dutch Premier League (Eredivisie), second level, and the Dutch FA (KNVB). These professional clubs have organised their developmental programmes in the form of youth soccer academies. From a young age (i.e., > 7 years), potential future elite players can be selected for specialist-training programmes at the academies. However, only 6% sign a professional contract at their own soccer academy (which is permitted from aged 15 years), whilst 3% sign as a player of a top-3 club in the Netherlands, and only 1% become a player in a top competition abroad (i.e., England, France, or Italy) (Jonker et al., 2019). As most of the players who signed a professional contract were selected between the ages of 11 to 15 years (Jonker et al., 2019), several youth soccer academies have decided to select players at a later age, with almost every academy now starting at U12. To accommodate the youth-to-senior transition, academies might choose to have a U21 team that plays in a competition with their respective peers. However, some academies have chosen to be part of the soccer pyramid (i.e., senior teams at third or fourth level) to foster the development of youth players by having stronger/older opponents.

Annually, the KNVB assess the extent to which academies meet the criteria set out in the Kwaliteits & Performance Programma [Quality and Performance Programme] (K&P) (The Dutch FA, 2022a). The objective of this programme is to help academies meet and improve the quality of their training programmes by focusing on: (a) developing and improving (not on controlling), (b) shaping a vision for their academy, (c) a licensing system with choices for clubs, (d) constant advice and monitoring by the KNVB, and (e) number of players attaining professional soccer. As such, academies are assessed based on criteria regarding organisational structure, facilities, quality of staff, education programme, and medical support and receive funding based on meeting these standards. At an academies request, a broader review of the strategy and management (e.g., mission, vision, objectives, contribution of the youth academy, necessary conditions), practice (e.g., execution of training vision), or specific issues (e.g., scouting, performance climate, playing style) takes place. Finally, the K&P provides a basic amount of funding for each academy who are rewarded on the basis of performance and their cooperation with grassroots clubs.

In addition to the academy system, the KNVB has its own talent identification and development programme. This programme consists of Dutch national selection teams (U15–U21) and the Dutch Youth Plan (DYP). Whilst the Dutch national selection teams generally consist of the best players from the youth soccer academies and compete against international opponents, the purpose of DYP is to enable both male and female players, who are not (yet) selected for youth soccer academies but are considered to be talented, to further their development through additional activities to those at their grassroots clubs. As part of the DYP, selected players are introduced to a performance environment, which includes aspects such as playing at a higher level, more (individual) training, physical development, performance training, performance behaviour, nutrition, and combining (top) sport and education.

The United States

Multiple unique pathways can be followed for players to reach professional soccer in the United States (of America). Most, however, begin playing soccer recreationally from early childhood with a local youth association (U4 to U10), followed by competitive competition (U11+), through to talent identification and selection with a United States Youth Soccer (USYS) or United States Club Soccer (USCS) sanctioned club (U11 to U19). This involves Major League Soccer (MLS) academy teams. Once graduated from high school, players' opportunities and options also vary. The majority of players, however, opt to play for a domestic university, with aspirations to be selected in the MLS Super Draft, which involves MLS clubs selecting players from the National Collegiate Athletic Association (NCAA) and National Association of Intercollegiate Athletics (NAIA) participation institutions. Opportunities for other players who played youth soccer with an MLS academy team will come from being offered 'homegrown' contracts, whereby they are promoted to play for the respective first team. In 2008, the MLS began the 'homegrown' player initiative, where clubs set up youth soccer academies with long-term athletic development plans to create a developmental system similar to professional club academies in Europe (Smolianov et al., 2014). This system allowed MLS clubs to sign players who have trained at least 1 year in their respective youth development programme to their first professional contract without being subject to the MLS Super Draft. More recently, MLS introduced the U22 Initiative, which allows clubs to sign up to three players, aged 22 years or younger, to lucrative contracts at reduced budget charge.

Talent development models have advanced over time within soccer in the United States. The US Youth Player Soccer Development Model (2012) implemented player-development stages over time through different age groups, which introduced skills that were age and developmentally appropriate (DiPaolo, 2017). The developmental stages are split into: (a) Zone 1—U6 to U12 (love of the game stage), (b) Zone 2—U13 to U17 (training to train stage), and (c) Zone 3—U18+ (training to win stage). Following Côté et al. (2009) Development Model of Sport

Participation Model (DMSP), each stage is designed to maximise the potential of players within the particular age range. Implementation of this model is evident in the newly formed MLS Next league, where MLS academies and other member clubs compete over an 8-month season from U13 to U19, with the intention to nurture and develop players throughout the age bandings.

Youth soccer in the United States is the number one participatory organised sport for children under aged 12 years and number two (behind basketball) for those under aged 18 years (Kooistra & Kooistra, 2016). Yet, barriers of participation emerge due to the economic requirements of the 'pay-to-play' model (e.g., private academies) that is instilled across the United States. To participate on a club team, costs for registration alone are excessive, thus separating youth participation into wealth classes. Contradictory to other popular soccer nations, the United States' capitalistic economic model of youth soccer creates a divide in which players can financially participate. This has created a notion that soccer in the United States is viewed as an upper-class sport, dissimilar to a large proportion of the world, where soccer is viewed as a sport for the working classes (Allison & Barranco, 2021). This inevitably limits the potential pool of talent in the United States by omitting those who have the long-term potential to achieve expertise but do not have access to the financial resources to support their development.

Considerations for Researchers

Despite only providing a small proportion of international perspectives, it is evident that there are a range of factors that can influence national talent pathways. In an attempt to capture some of the important considerations, Table 16.1 outlines the organisational structures that are embedded into the talent pathways that were presented throughout this chapter, including: (a) population, (b) popularity, (c) sociocultural considerations, (c) formal selection age, (d) activities, (e) trajectories, (f) professional opportunities, and (g) specialist support. Due to the diverse landscape of each country's talent pathway presented, Table 16.2 provides a range of contextual and methodological considerations for researchers (and practitioners) based on national perspectives. Indeed, these could be considered across a range of international settings.

Considerations for Practitioners

A range of contextual and methodological considerations are presented in Table 16.2 to help practitioners (and researchers) better understand how talent identification and development can be optimised in various settings. Practitioners working in countries of a similar ilk to those presented can reflect upon these examples to consider on what may or may not be suitable for their respective settings. In addition to these contextual and methodological factors, practitioners should reflect on the following considerations:

- In some established soccer nations, talent identification is happening younger than ever. However, selecting young groups in this way has enduring consequences, both for the players involved and those who are excluded. As an example, this early specialised approach could lead to inaccurate selections and identity foreclosure. Therefore, (re)consider the ages at which talent identification begins in academy settings.
- Those working with emerging soccer nations should learn from the successful approaches *and* structural flaws in more established soccer nations when designing new policies. This will help

TABLE 16.1 An evaluation of male talent pathways based on country

Country (Population?)	Popularity	Sociocultural Influences	Formal Selection Age	Activities	Trajectories	Professional Opportunities	Specialist Support
Canada (38.01 million)	Soccer is the sport with the most participants in Canada with 1 million registrants across the country. With regards to spectators, an estimated 180,000 people attended games in the new Canadian Premier League in 2021.	Soccer is played by the middle class with very few opportunities to play for free. For those wanting to play at the highest level, it normally requires a higher amount of money, which sees several players excluded from the game. Furthermore, within the Greater Toronto Area, it is common to see teams and even leagues catered to those from one race or country. Canada continues to see a high number of newcomers to the country. Both potential new young players and coaches are likely being missed, however, as the North American model does not mimic the European approach where local youth soccer is typically cheap (if not free).	Opportunities to play soccer begin from U3, although competitive programmes begin at U8. For the few professional teams that do exist in Canada, they have many satellite academies. To develop good relationships with the local clubs, the academies stay away from placing players in their own programmes until U13. The lack of competition nationally also poses a problem and means professional academies find themselves having to travel to the United States for games.	At entry level, children aged four to 6 years are encouraged to develop physical literacy skills, which, in turn, helps develop athletes in the long-term. From a national pathway perspective, Canada Soccer have recently introduced the 'NEX-GEN' programme, whereby integrated youth camps provide an opportunity for national colleagues to work alongside players, coaches, and staff from each of the three Major League Soccer academies (Canada Soccer, 2022b).	In previous years, those attempting to play professionally would look for opportunities in Europe and travel from as young as aged 12 years. More recently, however, there are greater opportunities that exist more locally, such as joining a 'League1' team and then potentially being scouted to either join an MLS team in Canada or join one of the CPL teams. Although, players are more likely to attend university and then seek options to play following their degree.	Professional opportunities are growing within Canada. Founded in 2017, the CPL has allowed players in different regions to gain access to opportunities closer to home. Previously, the only professional options in Canada were that of the three MLS teams.	Within professional clubs and university settings, it is common to have what may be seen as traditional specialist support. This may include athletic therapists, physiotherapists, goalkeeper coaches, and (potentially) a sports science team. Within the children's game; however, these roles rarely exist, where they are generally only equipped with full- and part-time coaching staff. External companies are often used to help provide some specialist services, although this can lead to a lack of club identity. Specifically, the focus can also become on how much these services cost rather than how they may benefit a player.

(*Continued*)

TABLE 16.1 (Continued)

Country (Population)	Popularity	Sociocultural Influences	Formal Selection Age	Activities	Trajectories	Professional Opportunities	Specialist Support
England (55.98 million)	Soccer is the most popular sport played in England, with 6.25 million male adults and 2.49 children aged 5 to 15 participating (The FA, 2015).	Soccer originally derived from a middle-class background, but quickly became a working-class sport at the advent of professionalism. However, it is slowly becoming a middle-class activity again due to the increasing commercialisation and rising costs. From a racial perspective, although black, Asian, and ethnic minority players make up ~25% of the professional playing demographic in England, only 3.4% hold senior coaching positions, whilst less than 1% are represented across all senior governance and senior administration positions at governing bodies and professional clubs (Sports People's think Tank, 2014).	Soccer in England has established systems that encourage *early specialisation*. Specifically, professional soccer academies in England can formally sign players as young as aged 8 years. However, some are selecting players as young as aged 4 years through 'pre-academy' programmes (Austin, 2019).	Hybrid training programmes have become increasingly popular throughout soccer academies in England, whereby they partner with a local school with the purpose of gaining more access to their players. With regards to innovative activities, an emerging grouping approach in England is 'bio-banding' (Malina et al., 2019). This is a strategy to group players based on their maturity status rather than just chronological age, with the purpose of moderating maturity-related differences and create a greater individualised approach.	The majority of players begin soccer during early childhood through playing at a local grassroots club. Between the ages of 8 and 16 years, young players join an academy on schoolboy terms (i.e., part-time attendance), then at aged 16 years, those players who show continued progress are selected to undertake a 2-year, full-time youth training scheme known as an academy scholarship. Upon completion of their scholarship, players either sign a professional contract or are released. Many professional clubs now have an U23 team (rather than a reserve team), with the purpose of helping young players during the youth-to-senior transition.	Soccer in England follows a traditional league system that consists of four professional leagues comprising of 92 teams. However, the fifth tier consists of mainly professional (full-time) teams, whilst the sixth tier (divided into two leagues) also consists of some professional teams. Indeed, there is a comprehensive non-league structure, with tiers seven, eight, and nine also paying their semi-professional players considerable wages.	Sport science support has become common practice throughout soccer academies with a range of full-time employment opportunities. Strength and conditioning and performance analysis are also generally used to support player development. Psychological and nutritional support are becoming increasingly more common. Additionally, research collaborations, often funded through postgraduate studies, are utilised to advance evidence-based practice and facilitate knowledge translation.

Germany (83.13 million)	Soccer is the most popular sport among the male population. Within the 2021/2022 season, the DFB had 7.1 million members. Approximately 1.2 million male children and youths, as well as about 900,000 male adults, were registered as active players (DFB, 2022a).	Soccer clubs in Germany represent the cultural and ethnic diversity of German society. Initial registrations of players of foreign nationality continuously increased between 2013 and 2018 (DFB, 2021). Especially on a grassroots level and in local clubs, volunteering is an essential element and favours a 'community-based' character. In elite youth soccer, semi-professional clubs and YAs mostly include several honorary, part-time, and full-time positions, leading to a more professionalised environment.	Formally, organised soccer starts at U6, though many children start playing earlier in local clubs. The DFB's talent development programmes' initial selection takes place at U11/U12. The talent selection age across German YAs differs, yet most clubs start their selections between the U10 and U12. Players can sign official contracts from the U15 age group.	In childhood, the complementary work of soccer associations, clubs, and schools is considered to allow participation in various soccer-specific activities. These activities aim to get children in touch with the sport and are a building block of initial talent selections. Participation in youth and adult soccer regularly occurs with more than 24,000 clubs throughout Germany (DFB, 2022a).	Due to the nationwide network of complementary working institutions, different 'talent pathways' are possible. Since a large number of players between U11 and U15 can profit from specific talent promotion, a crucial trajectory is considered the step to the 'elite promotion stage', where the focus is on the YA system and youth national teams for the most talented individuals.	In male adult soccer, there are three nationwide professional leagues, including 46 teams (Bundesliga, 2. Bundesliga, and 3. Liga). Yet, there are further professional (full-time) clubs, as well as U21/U23 teams of the YAs, competing in one of the three regional conferences of the German fourth division (Regionalliga).	Additional support through specialist coaches (e.g., goalkeeping or strength and conditioning coaches), medical staff, match analysts, sports scientists, sport psychology consultants, and other experts are established in most YAs and professional teams. Nevertheless, especially in smaller clubs and YAs, full-time employment of such specialists has often still not been attained.
Gibraltar (33,691)	Gibraltar has various national connections and therefore influences from a diverse soccer landscape.	Soccer in Gibraltar is community based, which is evident in the many staff at youth levels who are volunteering.	Soccer can begin at an early age. At the introduction stage (i.e., U7) into the players' journey, there are school competitions and club teams supported and directed from the GFA.	Outside of the league structures, there are various participatory activities, including inter-school soccer whereby players participate in tournaments.	There are no academies that are representative of those across other European countries. Instead, local youth teams provide the practice and competition opportunities.	Professional soccer in Gibraltar is comprised of one league that is split into two separate tables after the new year. This helps to keep the leagues competitive for the teams.	The national league has a level of player support aligned to a semi-professional standard in terms of contact time, due to players not being full-time professionals.

(*Continued*)

TABLE 16.1 (Continued)

Country (Population²)	Popularity	Sociocultural Influences	Formal Selection Age	Activities	Trajectories	Professional Opportunities	Specialist Support
Gibraltar (33,691)	This can be associated to their proximity to Spain as well as its identity as a territory of the United Kingdom. There are few youth clubs with approximately six to eight teams per age group (U7–U19), ten teams at intermediate level, and 11 teams in the men's national league.	There are challenges towards identifying a consistent approach to the way the game is played due to the diversity and reduced population within Gibraltar. Additionally, due to the limited players accessible on Gibraltar, there are constant challenges when talented players leave to pursue their soccer and/or academic journeys.	The school relationships and GFA engagement appears critical to introduce soccer, work to support development, and identify talented individuals as their pool of players achieving advanced levels and international recognition is limited.	These provide additional playing opportunities that can begin to support talent identification and player awareness. Due to the reduced population, there are opportunities for children and in turn young players to play across sports, as well as play-up within age groups to gain broader sporting and social experiences.	Intakes can start at the age of 5/6 years, where youth players can play up to U19. Once a player has progressed through the respective club structure, they can continue into the club's first team squad, which plays within a competitive league within Gibraltar.	It also creates opportunities for both groups to be able to compete and possibly challenge the issues of no relegation within the format of the league. There is also a reserve league and intermediate league, which consists of teams where teams largely play U23 players due to restrictions put on the league. This structure consists of 13 from 18 players being Gibraltarian and only five from the 18 players can be over aged 23 years.	Additional guidance and support continue to be provided through the GFA. As part of the governance, the GFA, in line with UEFA, provide coach education across aspects of the game that supports parents, coaches, officials, and support staff. As players can access international soccer or European club competitions far earlier in their careers in comparison to those from larger countries, additional specialist support can be influenced by the governing bodies for the benefit of the players at an earlier age.
India (1.38 billion)	Though soccer is the second most popular sport in India, in comparison to cricket with	Soccer is mostly a working-class sport in India, except with the pay-to-play models in metropolitan cities.	In the soccer hotspots, such as Goa, Kerela, Mizoram, Manipur, West Bengal, and	In the soccer hotspots, activities consist of inter-school and inter-club tournaments that progress from local to national levels.	Within the U13–U19 AIFF leagues, players are selected into teams at the U13 age category.	India has a three-tier national league with 11, 13, and 16 teams, respectively.	Eight senior teams in the top tier league have specialist support, typically a strength and conditioning coach

766 million fans (IANS, 2019), it only has 1.65 million fans (Mergulhao, 2022) across the country.	Birthplace has a huge impact on access. A few states have a thriving soccer culture, while others have very limited activities.	Punjab, academies start training programmes at the U6 age category. In metropolitan cities like Mumbai and Bangalore, where pay-to-play soccer schools are more common, grassroots soccer starts at the age of 4 years. In other states, academy trials and teams begin at the U13 age category, which is typically the youngest age group for the national league.	The inter-school tournaments are organised predominantly by the central government and sports ministry, while inter-club and community tournaments are run by state soccer associations or local clubs. Some of these regions have annual grassroots leagues and community tournaments. Some academies provide scholarships to players while others are pay-to-play. Soccer schools, with multiple centres, often host inter-centre tournaments. In these hotspots and metropolitan cities, weekend grassroots and amateur soccer leagues are privately run.	Players are typically selected through open trials, while few academies have a scouting network. Few local and residential academies retain players throughout the year. These academies retain players from U12 to U18, with a pathway to the senior team, wherever possible. However, in the absence of U20–U23 teams, the U18s often struggle to make the jump directly to senior teams. As a result, players will often play for senior teams in local leagues. Players are then scouted from these leagues to the national leagues (ISL and I-League).	State leagues have between one- and three-tier leagues and teams are promoted and relegated between these leagues. Apart from these three leagues, player salaries are low and therefore financially unsustainable. Therefore, players must take up secondary jobs to sustain themselves. Moreover, the U18 players have to compete against older players for game time and visibility. This results in a loss of talent, since, combined with rampant age-fraud, the U18s are often lost in the large pool of players who are all fighting to make the breakthrough into the top leagues.	as well as consultant nutritionists and psychologists. The youth national teams have hired psychologists for tournaments; however, it is generally up to the discretion of the coach. Only three academies have expert support, with one academy having full-time specialist support staff. Barring these few organisations, specialised support is inaccessible to clubs and academies. However, as the awareness surrounding specialists increases, players often reach out to consultants for independent support. This is most common during off-season training.

(Continued)

TABLE 16.1 (Continued)

Country (Population)	Popularity	Sociocultural Influences	Formal Selection Age	Activities	Trajectories	Professional Opportunities	Specialist Support
Republic of Ireland (5 million)	Soccer is the most popular team sport played in Ireland (Sport Ireland, 2021). There are approximately 1,000 clubs offering soccer for children. Clubs are generally community-based and volunteer-led.	Soccer in the Republic of Ireland has traditionally been referred to as a 'foreign' game due its representation of Englishness and the threat of a loss of Irish cultural identity (culminating in a ban on spectating and playing soccer that was only lifted in 1971). Despite this, soccer has now come to represent a fundamental shift within Irish identity, with the international element allowing for 'measurement' against other nations and the development of a more contemporary sporting identity (Cronin, 1999).	Children usually begin to play at age 5/6 years. Intra-club games begin at U8, with formal, competitive games beginning at U12 across 31 leagues. Inter-league cup competitions also run from U12–U16. Selected players represent their league in inter-league competitions (and league Emerging Talent Programme centres) from U12 to U16. League of Ireland (LOI) clubs must have U14, U15, U17, and U19 squads as part of their licencing. Due to a lack of resources, this can often entail a merger with a traditionally strong grassroots club.	In 2015, the FAI launched their 'National Player Development Plan (PDP) for youth football', which included recommendations regarding small-sided games, non-competitive soccer, roll-on roll-off subs, and standardised ball weight and size. There has been some resistance to standardisation from some leagues (e.g., leagues retaining a different calendar or game format).	A typical development trajectory would see a 12/13-year-old joining a LOI club at U14 and progressing to U15, U17, or U19's. The potential gap in competitive structure from U19's to senior soccer threatens to halt the development of youth players within the system. The normative pathway saw players be scouted by and join United Kingdom professional clubs from the age of 16 years. However, Brexit will limit this to age 18 years, forcing an urgent focus on the appropriateness of the Irish development pathway.	There are two League of Ireland divisions (Premier and First) with ten and nine teams, respectively. Not all the 19 clubs are fully professional, however. Due to the financial limitations of Irish clubs, youth players do not typically receive payment, although a small number of players in the youth LOI have been put on professional contracts within the past two seasons. Brexit may offer opportunities for more adult players (aged over 18 years) to join British clubs, as Ireland is part of the Common Travel Area with the United Kingdom, and thus Irish players	Access to the highest level of medical and coaching support is impacted by limited resources within Irish club soccer, but the LOI youth regulations include a prerequisite for a UEFA A Licensed coach for each team and a qualified physiotherapist in attendance at all games in the league. There are no such requirements within traditional schoolboy soccer. Access to higher level facilities including strength and conditioning vary from club to club.

Scotland (5.45 million)	In Scotland, soccer is the most popular sport, particularly within the younger population. In a survey conducted between 2007 and 2020, 19% of the 16- to 25-year-old population had participated in soccer within the last four weeks (Statista, 2021). Youth soccer participation levels continue to grow in Scotland, with more than 68,000 registered players across 4,000 teams reported by the Scottish Youth Football Association (SYFA) for the 2021–22 season, which is the highest total in its 22-year history (SYFA, 2021). The Scottish Professional Football League (SPFL) has great economic importance in Scotland, contributing more than £200 million to the economy each year and supporting ~5,700 jobs (SPFL, 2020). Further, attendance figures suggest that almost 5 million fans attend SPFL games annually. Scotland has a rich soccer culture, particularly surrounding its major cities (i.e., Glasgow, Edinburgh, Dundee, and Aberdeen). Notably, the rivalry between Glasgow Rangers and Glasgow Celtic football clubs is considered one of the strongest globally. The foundations of the two Glasgow soccer clubs are built upon the religious	Children usually begin to play soccer at aged ~5 years. The Scottish FA provide a player pathway at participation level, providing organisational guidance for factors such as team size, match rules, officiation, and pitch size (amongst others; SFA, 2022). Club Academy Scotland is the Scottish FA's academy system, which governs the development of players from aged 11 to 18 years. Players typically transition to senior soccer at aged ~18 years.	The grassroots programme within Scotland provides a structured pathway for young players. This includes progression in activities from 4 vs. 4 at aged 5–7 years to 9 vs. 9 at aged 12 years, before progressing to 11 vs. 11 soccer thereafter. The Scottish FA partner with seven 'Performance Schools' to provide players between U12–U16 who are affiliated with a professional club the opportunity to train and develop every day within their education environment. Further, many professional clubs have affiliated community programmes that act as both a community participation initiative, whilst also providing a direct talent pool for recruitment and player transition.	Talented young players with professional aspirations may join an academy programme at U10 for a transition year whilst also continuing to play with their amateur boys or girls club. Young players may also join an academy programme at U11 (the first year captured within the Scottish FA's Club Academy Scotland talent development system). Players may join a professional club at any age group thereafter, with high player turnover reported across the developmental years (Dugdale, Sanders et al., 2021). Comparable to other countries, players may only transition to full-time soccer after aged 16 years, aligning with	The Scottish Professional Football League (SPFL) is Scotland's national men's association football league. As well as operating its league competition, which consists of the top four levels of the Scottish soccer league system, the SPFL also operates two domestic cup competitions: the Scottish League Cup and the Scottish Challenge Cup. There are currently 42 member clubs of the SPFL, 12 within the Scottish Premiership (the top domestic league in Scotland), and ten in each of	Clubs within the Scottish Premier League possess sufficient finances to support their first team and academy with specialist support comparable to elite clubs from other nations. This typically includes sport science and physiotherapy as full-time positions for both first team and academy. However, additional supplementary sciences (such as nutrition and psychology) may be employed in consultancy or part-time roles. Specialist support and provision beyond the Scottish Premier League will vary dependant on the club's financial position.
				are not subject to the same British work permit conditions as other international arrivals.		

(Continued)

TABLE 16.1 (Continued)

Country (Population)	Popularity	Sociocultural Influences	Formal Selection Age	Activities	Trajectories	Professional Opportunities	Specialist Support
		divide between Catholicism (Celtic) and Protestantism (Rangers). At international level, the Scottish national teams have a loyal following. The self-proclaimed 'Tartan Army' who, despite experiencing limited competitive success in recent years, have built a global reputation for their passionate and emotional support.			completion of their schooling requirements. A limitation within Scottish soccer is the lack of formal development or reserve team leagues, presenting a potential barrier for young players attempting to transition from youth-to-professional football.	the Scottish Championship, Scottish League One, and Scottish League Two. Although the 42 teams are listed as 'professional', many teams within the Scottish League One and League Two operate as part-time. Following this, Scotland operates both the Scottish Highland Football League (SHFL) and Scottish Lowland Football League (SLFL). Both leagues sit at level 5 of the Scottish football league system, acting as a feeder to the SPFL.	Resultant of the rapid evolution in the importance of specialist support, many clubs across the Scottish soccer leagues are investing in these staff, even if only on part-time or fixed-hours contracts. In addition, professional clubs have begun partnering with academic institutions to provide further support through academic scholarship programmes.
The Netherlands (17.44 million)	In the Netherlands, soccer is the most popular sport; especially for boys under 18 years of age.	Soccer in the Netherlands is characterised by a community feeling.	Anyone can play soccer anywhere at any time in the Netherlands, regardless of his or her age.	Most soccer academies partner with grassroots clubs to have access to potentially talented players.	There are several trajectories to become a professional player. Players considered to be talented can be selected from an early age of 7 years.	The Eredivisie is the highest level of professional soccer and consists of 18 clubs and is ranked as the	Following the international trends of increasing specialist staff within high performance soccer environments,

The Netherlands (17.44 million)	In total, 1,016,000 males play soccer of which 41.4% are youth players (i.e., < 18 years of age; NOC*NSF, 2021).	There are many grassroots clubs that all have their own identity originating from a period of politico-denominational segregation. Nowadays, clubs are still a central part of family life, with children playing and parents voluntarily participating as parent-coaches or referees.	From U8, the Dutch FA organises competition. This generally means that players at the age of 7 years can be selected for soccer academies. However, this differs largely between soccer academies as several youth soccer academies have decided to select players at a later age, with almost every academy now starting at U12.	The use of data and science in the selection and development of players has become increasingly important. This is often comprised of technical, tactical, psychological, and physical information of players. Recently, the attempts to increase the number of female coaches has been announced by the Dutch FA.	However, this is currently under discussion. Players are allowed to sign a professional contract at aged 15 years. However, based on their educational level, they cannot yet be full-time players. As such, only after aged 16 years can players decide to develop full-time. Since there are ample opportunities for young players to reach professional soccer in the Netherlands, ages 18 to 21 years are regarded as the period where players have to make the step into a first team at professional level if they want to continue playing professionally.	sixth competition in Europe by UEFA in 2022/23. The Eerste divisie (second tier) consists of 16 teams and the winner and runner-up of this division are promoted to the Eredivisie. The club finishing third from the bottom of the Eredivisie goes to separate promotion/relegation play-offs with six high-placed clubs from the Eerste Divisie. The Eerste divisie also includes four U23 teams from soccer academies. These teams are restricted in terms of what players they can field, since the purpose is to develop youth rather than focus on performance. there are growing educational opportunities for performance analysts, sport scientists, and academy managers to support performance and player development.

(Continued)

TABLE 16.1 (Continued)

Country (Population)	Popularity	Sociocultural Influences	Formal Selection Age	Activities	Trajectories	Professional Opportunities	Specialist Support
The United States (329.5 million)	Soccer ranks fourth behind cycling, basketball, and baseball in regularly participated activities for ages 6–12 years, and seventh behind cycling, basketball, baseball, tennis, golf, and tackle football for ages 13–17 years (Aspen Project Play, 2022). Interestingly, from an organised youth sport perspective, soccer is the number one for participation for children under aged 12 years and number two (behind basketball) for those under aged 18 years.	The structure of youth soccer in the United States differs from the rest of the world due to multiple aspects. The culture supporting talent identification and the creation of 'competitive' teams from an early age is prevalent, along with the substantial financial burden to participate. Comparisons of soccer in the United States against the traditional global model of development explain that soccer training centres, developed by the US soccer governing body United States Soccer Federation (USSF), are difficult to access and afford (Smolianov et al., 2015).	The recently formed MLS Next league is comprised of MLS academies and other member clubs who compete during an 8-month season, with selection being from U13 to U19. Players selected for these teams are encouraged to specialise in soccer rather than diversify. Before this entry point age, players typically play for their local club and recreational teams.	Initially at grassroots level, games are formatted at 4 vs. 4 from U6 to U8, 7 vs. 7 at U9/U10, 9 vs. 9 at U11/U12, then move to 11 vs. 11 from U13 onwards. Multiple MLS clubs have affiliations with local grassroots soccer associations, which provides opportunities for players to be recruited to their respective academies. This scouting network has been an initiative for clubs to participate in the recently formed MLS Next league.	Players are selected through a player placement process for MLS Next academies and clubs. Players are scouted from either the MLS Next league or the Olympic Development Program's regional pools for youth national squads.	Professional soccer in the United States consists of one superior league: Major League Soccer. The league consists of franchise clubs whereby there is no promotion or relegation, and the championship is decided through a play-off format. Lower professional leagues consist of the United Soccer League (USL) 1, and USL 2. The MLS Next league will be launched in 2022/23 where reserve teams of the MLS clubs will compete, which will also help the youth-to-senior transition.	Within MLS academies, there are multiple full-time staff including USSF A Licensed coaches, strength and conditioning coaches, sport scientists, and physiotherapists. This group of staff formulate the pathways to professional level through each club's philosophy of development. From U13, players are schooled not only in playing soccer, but how to correctly train physically, by focusing on aspects such as nutrition and injury prevention. Also, for residential players, schooling is provided from certified teachers. These are for players that typically have had to move closer to the area, who sometimes board with another families.

TABLE 16.2 Contextual and methodological considerations for researchers and practitioners based on country

Country	Contextual	Methodological
Canada	Canada has come a long way in the past 10 years, with the men's national team qualifying for its first world cup in over 30 years and only its second time ever. For a country that boasts so many participants, it could be questioned why this has not happened sooner. However, the recent work behind the scenes by the national and provincial governing bodies to bring local clubs together, promote evidence-informed practice and coach education, and follow a long-term player development is starting to pay-off. Provincial governing bodies are also embracing innovation and collaboration, through the creation of offerings such as the 'Games Organisation Guide' (Ontario Soccer, 2018). This offers age-appropriate instructions for coaches and clubs to foster positive developmental environments, including a focus on stages of development, delivering a variety of event types, and competing in various game formats. Embracing these activities and formats will be important for stakeholders moving forward.	The pay-to-play model, much like the United States, clearly hinders access to the game for those who cannot afford the fees. This is the norm for many sports across the country and is a model that works to keep adults employed. However, the start of the new professional league is beginning to provide access to the game for many new people in different regions of the country. Canada has a number of world leading researchers in youth sport, thus regional and national governing bodies are encouraged to work collaboratively with academics to better understand how soccer can widen its participation and pool of potential talent, as well as capture how the professional league has helped engage a new cohort of prospective players. Indeed, Canada Soccer has begun working with universities and researchers (e.g., Jean Côté, Jennifer Turnnidge, Mark Bruner, and Tracy Vallaincourt) to develop a framework for the courses that sees coaches develop their interpersonal skills, such as the 11 behaviours of transformational coaching. As such, it will be worthwhile measuring the effectiveness of such coach education programmes so they can continue to be evolved.
England	Professional soccer academies in England can formally sign players as young as aged 8 years. However, some are identifying possible recruits through 'pre-academy' programmes and subsequently selecting players as young as aged 5 years (e.g., Austin, 2019). This is potentially problematic, since there is no evidence-base to suggest selecting players earlier will result in greater development towards expertise in the long-term.	Talent is not a fixed capacity and evolves dynamically over time. Therefore, despite selection ages becoming increasing younger, many of the qualities that distinguish expert performance at senior levels may not necessarily emerge until later in development (Baker et al., 2019). Moving forward, it is important to capture the experience and trajectories of those who achieve expertise in soccer.

(*Continued*)

TABLE 16.2 (Continued)

Country	Contextual	Methodological
England	In fact, it may indeed exacerbate existing relative age biases, as those who are relative older may be up to 12 months older than their relatively younger peers (Kelly et al., 2020). In the context of an U5 age group, those who are born at the beginning of the selection year would have lived up to 25% longer than their age group-matched equivalents who are born at the end of the cut-off date. This longevity of life is undoubtedly going to have an impact on performance outcomes and thus create selection biases towards relatively older players, which could have enduring consequences for both those involved and those who are excluded. As such, practitioners are encouraged to act with caution when designing high-performance organisational structures for children, as well as consider relative age effects during the initial enrolment into an academy programme.	More specifically, multi-, inter-, and trans-disiplinary research methods are encouraged to understand the longitudinal, holistic journeys of young players towards senior levels, to better understand the factors that contribute to their success and help inform evidence-based practice in academy settings. Moreover, in comparison to the broad range of relative age literature that is available in soccer, there is only a small body of research that has experimented with possible strategies to moderate such effects (Webdale et al., 2020). As such, researchers are encouraged to work collaboratively with practitioners to design, implement, and evaluate a range of potential relative age solutions (Kelly et al., 2021). By doing so, it will help practitioners and policy makers look beyond traditional age group structures, as well as create more appropriate settings for every young player to achieve their potential.
Germany	In the basic development stage, recent initiatives focus on more free-play in small-sided games (SSGs) to provide 'street-soccer' learning conditions. These SSGs will also replace the established seven vs. seven game formats from the U6 to U11 age groups in matches and tournaments from the 2023/24 season (DFB, 2022c; see also Bergmann et al., 2022a, 2022b). These initiatives aim to improve players' technical skills and creativity as well as diminish the focus on winning (e.g., no scores and league tables). Regarding talent identification and development in later stages, relative age-related biases reveal the potential to reduce coincidence through effective yet applicable strategies (Baker et al., 2010).	Throughout the continuous developmental process of talent promotion in Germany, scientific support has been established and already addressed various topics such as the prognostic relevance of talent predictors for adult success (e.g., Höner et al., 2017), their objective and subjective assessment (e.g., Höner et al., 2021), the role of psychological factors (e.g., Höner & Feichtinger, 2016), selection biases (e.g., Leyhr et al., 2021), maturational aspects (Leyhr et al., 2020), coach education (e.g., Wachsmuth et al., 2022), or 'innovative' diagnostic tools (e.g., Beavan et al., 2019). Nonetheless, there are several further topics with the potential to support practical work, some of which are highlighted, as follows: • The long-term impact of structural modifications in the basic development stage, for example, regarding players' skill development and its impact on the member statistics (e.g., drop-out rates).

Country	Contextual	Methodological
Germany	The investigation of players' biological maturity (e.g., Leyhr et al., 2020) allows consideration of developmental characteristics within both selection and training practices (e.g., bio-banding initiatives). As talent development in Germany is under the responsibility of different institutions (e.g., local clubs, DFB talent development program, YAs, Regional Associations, Youth National Teams), a better understanding of individual player pathways (e.g., timepoint for YA participation), as well as the development of supportive and healthy talent environments is crucial objective.	• The combined consideration of a wide range of talent attributes based on multifaceted diagnostics (e.g., motor tests and coach ratings) to increase opportunities for more holistic and individualised player support. • Investigations of maturity-related biases within performance assessments and the applicability of respective diagnostics in applied settings (e.g., bio-banding). • Investigations of conducive practice and coaching methods to promote soccer-specific competencies in the talents.
Gibraltar	Gibraltar experiences many challenges in how it can establish its own playing style, identity, and player identification in comparison to established soccer nations. The growth of the game continues to be supported through the Gibraltar Football Association (GFA), who recognise the impact of player participation, development opportunities, and its commitment to growing the coaching provision. This strategy has been supported through the Football Association of Wales (FAW) but is consistent with UEFA in implementing a detailed coach education provision and in particular the UEFA C certificate, which has become revalidated and will be consistent in level across the soccer landscape. Player pathway opportunities have restrictions once the players transition to senior professional levels and enter consideration towards university and/or career direction. Individuals often leave Gibraltar to continue their academic pursuit and this process can impact the continued development of the player, losing consistent support of the GFA.	Research on talent identification and the areas associated to talent within emerging nations appears to be limited. Recognising there is reduced depth of research around talent identification in this environment prevents establishing validity upon the relevant studies in this field. Understanding the constraints and challenges experienced by an emerging nation in terms of stature, population, resources, and profile can provide research opportunities focused upon a longer-term approach to accessing data in both the early stages and senior stages of the player's journey. Understanding the context of an emerging nation can be framed as areas to support change, accept their unique setting, and establish areas that can become embedded within policies and procedures for the benefit of player participation and performance. Establishing relevant and specific research can align towards supporting and growing both the game and within the journey of a young person provide opportunities, support development, and reduce limitations towards their future. Research directed for the benefit of an emerging nation can be established and applied quicker than many nations due to the reduced processes it must follow and the ability to manage and implement change.

(*Continued*)

TABLE 16.2 (Continued)

Country	Contextual	Methodological
Gibraltar	As such, area of talent identification and player monitoring becomes key for Gibraltar to track the players capable to represent them, whether that is the players they may be aware of but have moved away, or identification of players that although may not have been in the system as a young player are eligible to represent them at international level.	This approach can establish research to practice for the benefit of the Gibraltar and with the country central to how it has been designed, applied, and embedded.
India	Metropolitan cities have a pay-to-play model. This has popularised the sport and made it accessible for certain socioeconomic sections of society. The national interschool tournaments, organised by the central government, are accessible to most, however, the disparity in infrastructure and resources between rural and urban schools also leads to a disparity in development. In the major soccer hotspots; namely, Kerela, Manipur, Mizoram, West Bengal, Goa, and Punjab, grassroots and youth soccer is very active. Players join clubs and academies at the age of U6 and are engaged by the community. Most other regions have youth academies that are only active for a short duration during tournaments. A handful of residential academies have a year-long training programme that exists for multiple years. However, with the implementation of All India Football Federation (AIFF) youth national leagues for U13, U15, and U19 age groups, as well as the academy accreditation programme, has meant academies in regions outside the hotspots have started teams to participate in these leagues. As a result, the number of players being engaged across the country at the U13, U15, and U19 age-groups has increased.	There is a dearth of data and research with respect to Indian soccer, and more specifically youth soccer. Current research on growth, maturation, talent identification, and athlete development are based on studies predominantly from Caucasian populations. The transference, considering different genetics, culture, and lifestyles is unknown (McAuley et al., 2022). As a result, current practice in India is to attempt to replicate pre-existing structures and methodologies from different nations without necessarily adapting it to the specific needs of the country. The next steps forward are to collect and analyse data to identify patterns and trends of a typical Indian soccer player and then create a structure suited to the Indian population (Khasnis et al., 2021). The introduction of multi-layer player development platforms, such as youth leagues, academy accreditation, mandates, and increased funding, have supported the growth of a holistic youth development structure in India. However, the impact is not as tangible. The short duration of the leagues, no clear pathway, and poor scouting and talent development opportunities have resulted in a 'survival of the fittest' environment rather than a player-centred environment. Another serious problem that hinders youth development is age fraud. Many rural areas have poor healthcare facilities, resulting in limited documentation at time of birth.

Country	Contextual	Methodological
		This, coupled with the short-term myopic view around youth development, has created an environment where players frequently lie about their age to stand out amongst younger players. This results in poor development for all involved and is an issue that leads to the loss of talented players who may be younger or later maturing. A mass education around maturation and long-term athletic development is needed to eradicate this problem.
Republic of Ireland	Context-specific research can aid the evaluation of specific programmes aimed at achieving certain outcomes by "filling in the gaps between what policies are intended to do and how people experience them" (Holland et al., 2006, p. 19). Some contextually unique variables in the current landscape include: • Tensions have been identified across Irish soccer's strategic apex landscape that centred on leadership, board composition and political dominance, financial tensions, and a lack of organisational justice (Finnegan et al., 2018). The difficulty in harmonising playing and development structures (via a national player development plan) can be seen in this context as being exceptionally challenging to execute. • The bioecological model of human development (Bronfenbrenner, 2001) suggests that different social settings produce different learning environments, resulting in different experiences from one context to the next. Inequities within the talent development pathway resulted in talented Irish youth traditionally undergoing a 'double drain' (Finnegan, 2019). Talented youth players typically migrated into a Dublin league from neighbouring leagues, due to the enhanced visibility of this league to United Kingdom professional club scouts and international underage coaches.	Future research could explore the developmental processes of male and female youth soccer players and the appropriateness of their environment utilising the following approaches: • Governing bodies/national associations (NAs) are the gatekeepers of a wealth of potentially valuable information regarding talent development pathways (e.g., player numbers, place of birth, relative age at various points along the pathway, typical trajectories). Such entities are encouraged to engage with university sport science departments who can offer relevant academic and research capacities. This can provide additional capacity for the utilisation of such national databases. Along with the publishing and access advantages for the researcher, NAs can then engage in evidence-based decision-making (e.g., on the 'successes' of its talent identification initiatives or where to base talent development hubs based on player populations). • Taking a bioecological perspective to talent development (Bronfenbrenner, 2001), the concept and importance of time should be embedded into all talent development research, in order to assess how legacy issues can impact on current execution of development plans and on future strategic planning. Decision-making from NAs need to be made with the full ecological context in mind; macro-level decisions made with an awareness of the potential

(Continued)

TABLE 16.2 (Continued)

Country	Contextual	Methodological
Republic of Ireland	Placing the Dublin league in a strong position as a dominant, resource-rich organisation while resulting in a deskilling of the neighbouring 'donor' leagues. • With many talented youths playing both codes of football within Ireland (soccer and Gaelic football), and particularly within the context of the strong cultural pull of Gaelic sports, it is incumbent that both codes develop better working relationships both at governing and grassroots level. There can be facilitative benefits to this process. For example, playing Gaelic football was seen as an 'arena of comfort' (Call & Mortimer, 2001) for an Irish youth soccer player engaged in a talent development pathway, providing them with a non-pressurised, social outlet to engage in soccer. • Brexit has meant a shift in the traditional development pathway, which saw young Irish players move to United Kingdom academies. Increased focused must be placed on the appropriateness of Irish academies to support such players. Support must also be increased to aid the acculturalisation of players who transfer to European clubs, seeking out non-traditional development pathways.	knock-on effects at micro-level, and the layers that buffer the macro- to micro-spheres where plans (e.g., development plans) can get rejected or changed so their actual beneficial intent is lost (i.e., subordinate organisations subverting initial NA development plans). • With the emergence of a national league from U14, continued analysis of the migration patterns of youth soccer players will identify whether changing the competition structures in Ireland leads to a lessoning of these internal migratory patterns. • Researchers should explore how best to facilitate the dual functioning of two popular sports within an already narrow playing population (i.e., considerations on the scheduling of each sport, encouraging acceptance), whilst acknowledging the difficulties for youth coaches in terms of the practicalities of scheduling training and setting expectations among youth players.
Scotland	Scotland has adopted several strategies over the past decade to enhance talent identification and development opportunities for young players across the nation: • The introduction of the Performance Schools into the provision of its most talented young players. • The revision of its performance strategy 'Project Brave', imposing a criteria-based system to evaluate academy programmes and introducing measurable performance outcomes that encourage best practice.	Future research should explore the potential constraints identified within Scottish soccer: • Considering the migration of top soccer talent seeking talent development opportunities in other nations, future research should consider comprehensive analyses of talent development systems in Scotland. • Longitudinal analyses should investigate the efficacy of recent initiatives (i.e., Performance Schools, Project Brave) on talent development in young Scottish players.

Country	Contextual	Methodological
Scotland	• Investment into senior international teams and programmes to provide inspiration and national pride to developing and emerging talent. However, financial, organisational, and governance constraints may be limiting the development and progression of Scottish soccer: • The absence of a governed development or U21 league invokes a disconnect between those graduating from academy programmes and potential senior first team soccer. • Top Scottish soccer talent continues to migrate to larger talent development programmes in England and overseas. • Substantial differences are apparent between professional clubs in Scotland presenting a potentially unmanageable void between 'the best' and 'the rest'.	• The benefits, opportunities, potential limitations, and financial implications of the inception of a development or U21 league should be explored with key stakeholders. • Soccer clubs should continue to develop relationships with academic institutions and further expand provision possible through academic scholarship opportunities.
The Netherlands	Several initiatives have been created in the Netherlands to foster the development of players and to diminish a focus on winning at young ages. For example, new rules introduced in grassroots soccer are: • Not keeping scores until the U10 competitions. • Penalty shoot-outs after each match until U12 competitions. • Introduction of small-sided games to foster individual commitment in every match. • Focus on fundamental movement skills to foster motor development of young children. Besides the introduction of new rules, efforts are made to avoid certain phenomena as much as possible, such as: • Research on different grouping approaches to diminish relative age effects. Pilot studies are conducted to assess the effects of a different type of grouping strategy to diminish relative age effects in selection teams. Studies focus on	There are various new initiatives in the Netherlands. Therefore, whilst most of these initiatives have been extensively researched before their introduction, it is important to evaluate their effectiveness on long-term player development. These initiatives include: • Not keeping scores: since the focus should be more on development instead of on winning at young ages, the Dutch FA does not publish match results for U8 to U10 competitions. In addition, for these age groups, there is no season-long league table. Teams play in four group stage-like leagues were at the end of each period they find new opponents better suited at their competitive level. • Penalty shoot-outs: to increase the experience of success for every child, whether they've won or lost the game, each child takes a penalty at the end of each match in U7 to U12 competitions. • Small-sided games: In 2016, the Dutch FA has implemented small-sided games in U6 (4 vs. 4) to U12 (8 vs. 8) competitions. Before that, the only

(Continued)

TABLE 16.2 (Continued)

Country	Contextual	Methodological
The Netherlands	the impact of using a mean age rule instead of using a cut-off date. • Selection becoming younger and younger, which is why cooperation with grassroots organisations and clubs is stimulated in the Quality and Performance Programme by funding.	small-sided game format was a seven vs. seven on half a pitch. • Focus on fundamental movement skills: several programmes are designed for grassroots and professional clubs to foster the development of fundamental movement skills, even when they specialise early. This is executed in cooperation with federations in other sports such as gymnastics and judo.
The United States	Youth soccer in the United States is dominated by the pay-to-play model, whereby fees to participate are (likely) greater compared to the rest of the world, and thus accessibility to the sport is mainly for the middle to upper classes. Scholarships are made available for outstanding players from low-income backgrounds, yet most players playing in MLS academy system come from wealthy backgrounds. Regarding improvements to the sport, US Soccer created initiatives to better aid the development of individual and team players. For example, the 'Build Out Line' for 7 vs. 7 formats (U9/U10), where players are encouraged to maintain possession from the goalkeeper, and the 'Play-Practice-Play' coaching curriculum, where 'deliberate play' has been introduced to allow players to play freely with minimal coach input. Recent research by Malina et al. (2019) into bio-banding with US Soccer has also developed an understanding of having players compete according to maturity level rather than age. This resulted in early-maturing players enjoying the physicality and superior learning experiences of playing with older players, whereas later maturing players were able to perform their technical ability more consistently.	Soccer in the United States has taken criticism from researchers as having 'socialistic' tendencies and devaluing individualism, where valuing team success over individual player development is present in a competitive, capitalistic system (Kooistra & Kooistra, 2016). Previous research into talent identification in United States soccer has stated that for in order for player development guidelines to thrive, improvements in organisation need to occur (Smolianov et al., 2014), suggesting that the pay-to-play model needs to refocus its initiates away from financial gains. Though participation in youth is high across both genders, there is a distinct lack of talent at the professional level, as seen at the United States' inability to qualify for the male World Cup in 2018. The narrow margins for participation regarding finances hinder the openness to play the sport competitively for youth from low-income households. The lack of availability limits participation and thus potential talent at competitive and academy levels; hence, why better athletes tend to play sports with more access (e.g., basketball, American football, or baseball). Areas of the country can also influence participation and levels of play. Typically, densely populated areas have professional clubs who have their own academies and community outreach initiatives that drive interest, whereas rural areas of

Country	Contextual	Methodological
		the country may not have the same structures in place. This limits the development of players due to their geographical location, with lack of popularity due to smaller communities not having access to the same amenities to those who live in highly populated urban areas (Smith & Weir, 2020). Capturing these mechanisms to support player development will be important for future research in youth soccer.

capture innovative practice as well as ensure the same issues are not recreated. Indeed, designing new organisational structures should be seen as an opportunity to create contemporary policies and more appropriate youth soccer settings.
- The migration of talent from smaller and/or emerging nations towards larger and/or established nations appears to 'drain' talent. Thus, practitioners and policy makers should consider legislations to protect their minors, as well as ensure they have a comprehensive tracking and support system for young players who do migrate.
- Priority should be placed on ensuring contemporary, child-centred approaches are utilised to facilitate long-term player development, such as small-sided games, relative age solutions, monitoring growth and maturation, and focus on enjoyment rather than winning.
- Pay-to-play models limit the potential pool of talent to those who can afford fees. In order to create more equitable opportunities and widen the pool of potential talent, practitioners employed in these settings should consider how they can create access to organised youth soccer for those from lower socioeconomic backgrounds.

Conclusion

This chapter offered nine examples of how talent identification and development processes operate across the globe. These international perspectives underscore the diverse sociocultural influences and how developing soccer talent is not a 'one-size-fits-all' approach. For instance, the inconsistent and limited pathways that are offered to players across India, the pay-to-play models that restrict participation opportunities across North America, the early specialised approach that may have unintended consequences in Europe, the implications of player migration on domestic competition in the likes of the Republic of Ireland and Scotland, and the confines of population and emerging nation status on countries such as Gibraltar, are just some of the examples of how sociocultural influences can impact male talent pathways in soccer. Stakeholders should reflect upon the several successful (and unsuccessful) approaches that were illustrated in the chapter and whether the described strategies work within their context. Most importantly, researchers and practitioners are encouraged to evaluate how sociocultural influences could impact their talent pathways before collaboratively designing and implementing policies into their own practice.

Note

1 The authors would like to thank Michael McArdle and Brown Ferguson for their support on the Scotland section contribution.
2 Population data for each country was retrieved from The World Bank: https://datatopics.worldbank.org/world-development-indicators/

References

Adams, A., Morrow, S., & Thomson, I. (2017). Changing boundaries and evolving organizational forms in football: Novelty and variety among Scottish clubs. *Journal of Sport Management*, *31*(2), 161–175. https://doi.org/10.1123/jsm.2016-0286

All India Football Federation. (2022). *Official website of all india football federation* [online]. Retrieved from: www.the-aiff.com/ [accessed 21th January 2022].

Allison, R., & Barranco, R. (2021). 'A rich white kid sport?' Hometown socioeconomic, racial, and geographic composition among U.S. women's professional soccer players. *Soccer & Society*, *22*(5), 457–469. https://doi.org/10.1080/14660970.2020.1827231

Aspen Project Play (2022). *Youth sport facts: Participation rates* [online]. Retrieved from: www.aspenprojectplay.org/youth-sports/facts/participation-rates [accessed 23rd October 2022].

Austin, S. (2019). *Manchester city under-5s Elite squad branded 'absolute madness'* [online]. Retrieved from: https://trainingground.guru/articles/manchester-city-under-5s-elite-squad-described-as-absolute-madness [accessed 4th December 2020].

Baker, J., Schorer, J., & Cobley, S. (2010). Relative age effects. An inevitable consequence of elite sport? *Sportwissenschaft*, *40*, 26–30. https://doi.org/10.1007/s12662-009-0095-2

Baker, J., Wattie, N., & Schorer, J. (2019). A proposed conceptualization of talent in sport: The first step in a long and winding road. *Psychology of Sport and Exercise*, *43*, 27–33. https://doi.org/10.1016/j.psychsport.2018.12.016

Beavan, A., Fransen, J., Spielmann, J., Mayer, J., Skorski, S., & Meyer, T. (2019). The Footbonaut as a new football-specific skills test: Reproducibility and age-related differences in highly trained youth players. *Science and Medicine in Football*, *3*(3), 177–182. https://doi.org/10.1080/24733938.2018.1548772

Bennett, K. J. M., Vaeyens, R., & Fransen, J. (2019). Creating a framework for talent identification and development in emerging football nations. *Science and Medicine in Football*, *3*(1), 36–42. https://doi.org/10.1080/24733938.2018.1489141

Bergmann, F., Braksiek, M., & Meier, C. (2022a). The influence of different game formats on technical actions and playing time parameters—A study with U7 and U9 youth soccer players in a competitive context. *International Journal of Sports Science & Coaching*, *17*(5), 1089–1100. https://doi.org/10.1177/17479541211051654

Bergmann, F., Meier, C., & Braksiek, M. (2022b) Involvement and performance of U9 soccer players in 7v7 and 5v5 matches during competition. *German Journal of Exercise and Sport Research*, *52*, 125–134. https://doi.org/10.1007/s12662-021-00752-4

Bourke, A. (2003). The dream of being a professional soccer player. *Journal of Sport and Social Issues*, *27*(4), 399–419. https://doi.org/10.1177/0193732503255478

Canada Soccer. (2022a). *Long-term player development: A community guide* [online]. Retrieved from: https://canadasoccer.com/wp-content/uploads/resources/Pathway/EN/CanadaSoccerPathway_LTPDCommunityGuide_EN.pdf [accessed 26th October 2022].

Canada Soccer. (2022b). *Canada soccer reintroduces NEX-PRO integration camps at MLS academies* [online]. Retrieved from: https://canadasoccer.com/news/canada-soccer-reintroduces-nex-pro-integration-camps-at-mls-academies/ [accessed 26th October 2022].

Connaughton, G. (2018). *Why the new FAI calendar may force the GAA to clean up its act* [online]. Retrieved from: www.balls.ie/gaa/new-fai-calendar-gaa-to-clean-up-its-act-400543 [accessed 9th November 2021].

Côté, J., Lidor, R., & Hackfort, D. (2009). ISSP position stand: To sample or to specialize? Seven postulates about youth sport activities that lead to continued participation and elite performance. *International Journal of Sport and Exercise Psychology, 7*(1), 7–17. https://doi.org/10.1080/1612197X.2009.9671889

Cronin, M. (1994). Sport and a sense of Irishness. *Irish Studies Review, 3*(9), 13–17. https://doi.org/10.1080/09670889408455460

Cronin, M. (1999). *Sport and nationalism in Ireland: gaelic games, soccer, and irish identity since 1884*. Four Courts Press.

Cushion, C., Ford, P. R., & Williams, M. A. (2012). Coach behaviours and practice structures in youth soccer: Implications for talent development. *Journal of Sports Sciences, 30*(15), 1631–1641. https://doi.org/10.1080/02640414.2012.721930

Deutsche Fußball Liga. (2022a). *Youth academies* [online]. Retrieved from: www.dfl.de/en/topics/youth-academies/ [accessed 30th April 2022].

Deutsche Fußball Liga. (2022b). *Broad range of criteria: Licensing guidelines* [online]. Retrieved from: www.dfl.de/en/topics/youth-academies/a-range-of-criteria-licensing-guidelines/ [accessed 30th April 2022].

DFB. (2009). *Talente Fordern und Fördern. Konzepte und Strukturen vom Kinder- bis zum Spitzenfußball* [Talent identification and development. Concept and organizational structure from grassroots to elite soccer]. Grafische Betriebe E. Holterdorf.

DFB. (2021). *Vielfalt/Anti-Diskriminierung* [Diversity/anti-discrimination] [online]. Retrieved from: www.dfb.de/vielfaltanti-diskriminierung/herkunft/integration/ [accessed 1st May 2022].

DFB. (2022a). *DFB member statistics 2022* [online]. Retrieved from: www.dfb.de/verbandsstruktur/mitglieder/aktuelle-statistik/ [accessed 24th October 2022].

DFB. (2022b). Talentförderung [Talent development]. *DFB Journal, 2*, 67–73.

DFB. (2022c). *Kinderfußball. Leitlinien für die implementierung neuer wettbewerbsformen in den altersklassen U6-U11* [Child soccer. Guidelines for the implementation of new competitive game formats in the U6 to U11 age groups] [online]. Retrieved from: https://assets.dfb.de/uploads/000/259/518/original_Booklet_-_Wettbewerbsformen_im_Kinderfußball__Stand_03_2022.pdf?1650890356 [accessed 30th April 2022].

DiPaolo, D. G. (2017). Leadership education is not enough: Advancing an integrated model of student-athlete development. *Journal of Leadership Education, 16*(1), 216–229. https://doi.org/10.12806/V16/I1/I2

Dugdale, J. H., McRobert, A. P., & Unnithan, V. B. (2021). "He's just a wee laddie": The relative age effect in male Scottish soccer. *Frontiers in Psychology, 12*. https://doi.org/10.3389/fpsyg.2021.633469

Dugdale, J. H., Sanders, D., Myers, T., Williams, A. M., & Hunter, A. M. (2021). Progression from youth to professional soccer: A longitudinal study of successful and unsuccessful academy graduates. *Scandinavian Journal of Medicine and Science in Sports, 31*(S1), 73–84. https://doi.org/10.1111/sms.13701

Elliott, R. (2014). Football's Irish exodus: Examining the factors influencing Irish player migration to English professional leagues. *International Review for the Sociology of Sport, 51*(2), 147–161. https://doi.org/10.1177/1012690213519786

FIFA. (2021). *Ten years of international Transfers: A report on international football transfers worldwide 2011–2020* [online]. Retrieved from: https://digitalhub.fifa.com/m/47c2f0047dd61f3b/original/FIFA-Ten-Years-International-Transfers-Report.pdf [accessed 9th November 2021].

Finnegan, L. (2019). Stepping stones? An exploration of internal football player migration in the Republic of Ireland. *Regional Studies, Regional Science, 6*(1), 596–606. https://doi.org/10.1080/21681376.2019.1685905

Finnegan, L., McArdle, J., Littlewood, M., & Richardson, D. (2018). Somewhat united: Primary stakeholder perspectives of the governance of schoolboy football in Ireland. *Managing Sport and Leisure, 23*(1–2), 48–69. https://doi.org/10.1080/23750472.2018.1513342

Finnegan, L., Richardson, D., Littlewood, M., & McArdle, J. (2016). The influence of date and place of birth on youth player selection to a national football Association elite development programme. *Science and Medicine in Football, 1*(1), 30–39. https://doi.org/10.1080/02640414.2016.1254807

Football Association of Ireland. (2009). *Strategic review of underage football*. pmpGenesis.

Football Association of Ireland. (2013). *Football association of Ireland* [online]. Retrieved from: www.fai.ie/playerdevelopment/player-pathway/training-to-win-phase.html [accessed 9th November 2021].

Gibraltar Football Association. (2022). *Gibraltar football association: Youth football season 2022/23* [online]. Retrieved from: www.gibraltarfa.com/uploads/Youth%20Football/2022/Gibraltar%20FA%20Youth%20 Football%20Season%202022:03%20Strategy_WEB.pdf [accessed 4th November 2022].

Güllich, A., Macnamara, B. N., & Hambrick, D. Z. (2022). What makes a champion? Early multidisciplinary practice, not early specialization, predicts world-class performance. *Perspectives on Psychological Science*, 17(1), 6–29. https://doi.org/10.1177/1745691620974772

Hanley, L. (2022). *How popular is soccer in Canada? A lot more than you might think* [online]. Retrieved from: https://the18.com/soccer-entertainment/how-popular-is-soccer-in-canada [accessed 26th October 2022].

Höner, O., & Feichtinger, P. (2016). Psychological talent predictors in early adolescence and their empirical relationship with current and future performance in soccer. *Psychology of Sport and Exercise*, 25, 17–26. http://doi.org/10.1016/j.psychsport.2016.03.004

Höner, O., Leyhr, D., & Kelava, A. (2017). The influence of speed abilities and technical skills in early adolescence on adult success in soccer: A long-term prospective analysis using ANOVA and SEM approaches. *PLOS One*, 12(8): e0182211. https://doi.org/10.1371/journal.pone.0182211

Höner, O., Murr, D., Schreiner, R., Larkin, P., & Leyhr, D. (2021). Subjective and objective assessment of potential talent predictors in elite youth soccer: Comparing the prognostic validity in a 3-years prospective study. *Frontiers in Sports and Active Living*, 3(115). https://doi.org/10.3389/fspor.2021.638221

IANS. (2019). *Cricket draws 93% of sports viewers in India: BARC* [online]. Retrieved from: www.business-standard.com/article/news-ians/cricket-draws-93-of-sports-viewers-in-india-barc-119060400786_1.html [accessed 11th January 2022].

Ignacio, S. (2022). *Major changes as gibraltar FA looks towards future of youth and learns from past mistakes* [online]. Retrieved from: www.chronicle.gi/major-changes-as-gibraltar-fa-looks-towards-future-of-youth-and-learns-from-past-mistakes/ [accessed 4th November 2022].

Jonker, L., Huijgen, B. C. H., Heuvingh, B., Elferink-Gemser, M. T., & Visscher, C. (2019). How youth football players learn to succeed. In E. Konter, J. Beckmann, & T.M. Loughead (Eds.), *Football psychology. From theory to practice*. Routledge. https://doi.org/10.4324/9781315268248

Kelly, A. L., Côté, J., Jeffreys, M., & Turnnidge, J. (Eds). (2021). *Birth advantages and relative age effects in sport: Exploring organizational structures and creating appropriate settings*. Routledge.

Kelly, A. L., & Williams, C. A. (2020). Physical characteristics and the talent identification and development processes in youth soccer: A narrative review. *Strength and Conditioning Journal*, 42(6), 15–34. https://doi.org/10.1519/SSC.0000000000000576

Kelly, A. L., Wilson, M. R., Gough, L. A., Knapman, H., Morgan, P., Cole, M., Jackson, D. T., & Williams, C. A. (2020). A longitudinal investigation into the relative age effect in an English professional football club: Exploring the 'underdog hypothesis'. *Science and Medicine in Football*, 4(2), 111–118. https://doi.org/10.1080/24733938.2019.1694169

Khasnis, U., Chapman, P., Toering, T., & Collins, D. (2021). Focus on the people: Key stakeholders' perceptions of elite sport in India and its potential for development. *Managing Sport and Leisure* (Advance online publication). https://doi.org/10.1080/23750472.2021.1877568

King, N. (2017). *Sport governance: An introduction*. Routledge.

Kooistra, P., & Kooistra, R. (2016). The ins and outs of US youth soccer: Learning about loyalty and success. *Soccer & Society*, 19(7), 944–965. https://doi.org/10.1080/14660970.2016.1267620

Leyhr, D., Bergmann, F., Schreiner, R., Mann, D. L., Dugandzic, D., & Höner, O. (2021). Relative age-related biases in objective and subjective assessments of performance in talented youth soccer players. *Frontiers in Sports and Active Living*, 3(94). https://doi.org/10.3389/fspor.2021.664231

Leyhr, D., Murr, D., Basten, L., Eichler, K., Hauser, T., Lüdin, D., Romann, M., Sardo, G., & Höner, O. (2020). Biological maturity status in elite youth soccer players: A comparison of pragmatic diagnostics with magnetic resonance imaging. *Frontiers in Sports and Active Living*, 2(195). https://doi.org/10.3389/fspor.2020.587861

MacNamara, Á., & Collins, D. (2012). Building talent development systems on mechanistic principles: Making them better at what makes them good. In J. Baker, S. Cobley, & J. Schorer (Eds.), *Talent identification and development in sport: International perspectives*. Routledge.

Malina, R., Cumming, S., Rogol, A., Coelho e Silva, M., Figueiredo, A., Konarski, J., & Koziel, S. (2019). Bio-banding in youth sports: Background, concept and application, *Sport Medicine*, 49(11), 1671–1685. https://doi.org/10.1007/s40279-019-01166-x

Malone, E. (2019). *Premier class: Irish players struggling to make top grade* [online]. Retrieved from: www.irishtimes.com/sport/soccer/english-soccer/premier-class-irish-players-struggling-to-make-top-grade-1.3980944 [accessed 10th August 2021].

Malone, E. (2020). *Football fan survey: Almost half of Irish adults say they support a club* [online]. Retrieved from: www.irishtimes.com/sport/soccer/english-soccer/football-fan-survey-almost-half-of-irish-adults-say-they-support-a-club-1.4185757 [accessed 29th February 2022].

McAuley, A. B. T., Baker, J., & Kelly, A. L. (2022). Defining "elite" status in sport: From chaos to clarity. *German Journal of Exercise and Sport Research*, 52, 193–197. https://doi.org/10.1007/s12662-021-00737-3

Mergulhao, M. (2022). *Everyone loves FC Goa! 98% football lovers in state support* [online]. Retrieved from: https://timesofindia.indiatimes.com/city/goa/everyone-loves-fc-goa-98-football-lovers-in-state-support-the-club-survey/articleshow/88819173.cms?utm_source=twitter.com [accessed 11th January 2022].

Mills, A., Butt, J., Maynard, I., & Harwood, C. (2012). Identifying factors perceived to influence the development of elite youth football academy players. *Journal of Sports Sciences*, 30(15), 1593–1604. http://doi.org/10.1080/02640414.2012.710753

Morrow, S. (2006). Scottish football: It's a funny old business. *Journal of Sports Economics*, 7(1), 90–95. https://doi.org/10.1177/1527002505282867

NOC*NSF. (2021). *Zo sport Nederland. Trends en ontwikkelingen in sportdeelname in 2020* [This is how Sports is Played in the Netherlands. Trends and Developments in Sports Participation in 2020] [online]. Retrieved from: https://nocnsf.nl/media/4412/zo-sport-nederland-2020_def.pdf [accessed 19th August 2022].

Ontario Soccer. (2018). *Game organization guide* [online]. Retrieved from: https://cdn1.sportngin.com/attachments/document/0112/8106/Game_Organization_Guide.pdf?_gl=1*1h408ys*_ga*MTMwNzQ0NjY2NS4xNjYyNDg2OTEz*_ga_PQ25JN9PJ8*MTY2Njc5NzA0My4xLjEuMTY2Njc5NzA1OC4wLjAuMA..#_ga=2.199681582.1028205279.1666797048-1307446665.1662486913 [accessed 26th October 2022].

Poli, R., Ravenel, L., & Besson, R. (2015). *Talent scouting: An experience capital approach* [online]. Retrieved from: www.footballobservatory.com/IMG/pdf/mr02_eng.pdf [accessed 20th March 2022].

Ryan, D., Lewin, C., Forsythe, S., & McCall, A. (2018). Developing world-class soccer players: An example of the academy physical development program from an English Premier League team. *Strength and Conditioning Journal*, 40(3), 2–11. https://doi.org/10.1519/SSC.0000000000000340

SFA. (2017). *Scottish FA performance strategy* [Online]. Retrieved from: www.scottishfa.co.uk/performance/performance-strategy/ [accessed 1st December 2021].

SFA. (2022). *Scottish FA JD performance schools* [online]. Retrieved from: www.scottishfa.co.uk/performance/jd-performance-schools/ [accessed 1st December 2021].

Smith, K. L., & Weir, P. L. (2020). Female youth soccer participation and continued engagement: Association with community size, community density, and relative age. *Frontiers in Sports and Active Living*, 2(552597), 1–10. https://doi.org/10.3389/fspor.2020.552597

Smolianov, P., Murphy, J., McMahon, S. G., & Naylor, A. H. (2014). Comparing the practices of US Soccer against a global model for integrated development of mass and high-performance sport. *Managing Sport and Leisure*, 20(1), 1–21. https://doi.org/10.1080/13606719.2014.929402

SPFL. (2020). *The economic contribution of the Scottish professional football league* [online]. Retrieved from: https://spfl.co.uk/news [accessed 24th Februaray 2022].

Sport Ireland. (2021). *Irish sports monitor 2021—Mid-year report* [online]. Retrieved from: www.sportireland.ie/sites/default/files/media/document/2021-10/covid-and-sport-mid-year-2021-13-08.pdf [accessed 29th February 2022].

Sports People's Think Tank. (2014). *Ethnic minorities and coaching in elite level football in England: A call to action* [online]. Retrieved from: www.farenet.org/wp-content/uploads/2014/11/We-speak-with-one-voice.pdf [accessed 22nd June 2019].

Statista. (2021). *Share of adults who played football in the past four weeks in Scotland from 2007 to 2020* [online]. Retrieved from: www.statista.com/statistics/535882/football-participation-by-adults-scotland-uk/ [accessed 26th February 2022].

Sullivan, M. O., Vaughan, J., Rumbold, J. L., & Davids, K. (2022). The learning in development research framework for sports organisations. *Sport, Education and Society*, *27*(9), 1100–1114. https://doi.org/10.1080/13573322.2021.1966618

SYFA. (2021). *Youth football: Record numbers now playing in Scotland, says governing body* [online]. Retrieved from: www.scottishyouthfa.co.uk/index.php/members-corner/latest-news [accessed 26th February 2022].

The Dutch FA. (2022a). *Informatie Kwaliteit en Performande Programma Jeugdopleidingen* [Information about the Quality and Performance Porgramme Soccer Academies; online]. Retrieved from: www.knvb.nl/downloads/bestand/24639/knvb-kp-digi-brochure-ls [accessed October 2022].

The Dutch FA. (2022b). *Jaarverslag seizoen 2020/'21* [Annual report season 2020/'21; online]. Retrieved from: https://knvb.h5mag.com/knvb/jaarverslag_2020-2021/ledenaantallen/88177/KNVB_Ledenaantallen_2020__21.pdf [accessed October 2022].

The FA. (2014). *England DNA* [online]. Retrieved from: www.thefa.com/news/2014/dec/04/england-dna-launch [accessed 22nd June 2019].

The FA. (2015). *11 million footballers in England cannot be wrong!* [online]. Retrieved from: www.thefa.com/news/2015/jun/10/11-million-playing-football-in-england [accessed 22nd June 2019].

The FA. (2016). *England coaching pathway* [online]. Retrieved from: www.thefa.com/news/2016/oct/07/discover-the-coaching-pathway [accessed 22nd June 2019].

The FA. (2019). *The playing and coaching philosophy of England teams* [online]. Retrieved from: www.thefa.com/learning/england-dna [accessed 22nd June 2019].

The Premier League. (2011). *Elite player performance plan* [online]. Retrieved from: www.premierleague.com/youth/EPPP [accessed 22nd June 2019].

Toronto Star. (2013). *Ontario youth soccer to stop keeping score, standings* [online]. Retrieved from: www.thestar.com/sports/soccer/2013/02/16/ontario_youth_soccer_to_stop_keeping_score_standings.html [accessed 26th October 2022].

UEFA. (2022). *Gibraltar: A new brand and a new identity* [online]. Retrieved from: www.uefa.com/insideuefa/news/027b-167e5bc9a028-3e5ad1d20d52-1000—gibraltar-a-new-brand-and-a-new-identity/ [accessed 4th November 2022].

US Youth Soccer. (2012). *US youth soccer player development model* [online]. Retrieved from: www.usyouthsoccer.org/us_youth_soccer_debuts_player_development_model/ [accessed 15th May 2021].

Wachsmuth, S., Raabe, J., Readdy, T., & Höner, O. (2022). Evaluating a multiplier approach to coach education within the German Football Association's talent development program: An example of an intervention study targeting need-supportive coaching. *International Sport Coaching Journal*, *9*(3), 305–318. https://doi.org/10.1123/iscj.2021-0027

Webdale, K., Baker, J., Schorer, J., & Wattie, N. (2020). Solving sport's "relative age" problem: A systematic review of proposed solutions. *International Review of Sport and Exercise Psychology*, *13*(1), 187–204. https://doi.org/10.1080/1750984X.2019.1675083

17
GENDER

Disentangling Talent Identification and Development in Women's and Girls' Soccer

Stacey Emmonds, Adam Gledhill, Adam L. Kelly, and Matthew Wright

Introduction

Women's and girls' soccer has seen a substantial rise in participation over the last decade, which has coincided with increased financial support from governing bodies. As an example, financial contributions from the Union of European Football Associations (UEFA) has trebled (UEFA, 2017), whilst participation rates over the last 10 years have grown by a third (Manson et al., 2014). Worldwide, the Fédération Internationale de Football Association (FIFA) has pledged its commitment to increase the number of female[1] soccer players from ~13.3 million (2019) to 60 million by 2026 (FIFA, 2019). This growth and professionalism of female soccer have led to rising investment in talent identification and development of players from a young age. Soccer governing bodies around the world are now investing in talent development environments (e.g., academies, regional talent centres) for girl's that are starting as young as 10-years-old, which often align with similar academy structures that are in place in youth male soccer.

Despite the increased growth and professionalism of female soccer in recent years, there is still a paucity of research exploring talent identification and development in comparison to youth male soccer. As a result, this is an area that continues to require further research, particularly given the acknowledgement that growth and maturation influences the biopsychosocial development of girls and boys differently, which will inevitably have important implications for talent identification and development in youth soccer. The purpose of this chapter is to provide an overview of existing research and recommendations for talent identification and development practices in female soccer. First, the chapter begins by explaining how growth and maturation can impact physical development of youth female soccer players. Secondly, the chapter considers the psychosocial development of female players. Finally, the chapter proposes directions for future research and outlines implications for practice.

The Impact of Growth and Maturation on Physical Development

There is an abundance of research in male youth soccer reporting the influence growth and maturation can have on talent identification and development (Kelly & Williams, 2020; Read et al., 2018; Towlson et al., 2021a). A large body of research has shown that maturation status

DOI: 10.4324/9781032232799-17

has an impact on physical capabilities, and as such, talent identification and development in male youth soccer, with boys of advanced maturity displaying better athleticism that results in a greater likelihood of being identified as 'talented' (Towlson et al., 2021b; Morris et al., 2018). However, findings from male youth studies may not be transferable to females, especially during maturation, given the differences in the timing and tempo of maturation, coupled with differences between the sexes in physical and physiological characteristics from the onset of puberty (Lloyd & Oliver, 2012; see Chapter 4).

In contrast to boys, for whom hormonal and morphological changes associated with maturation are advantageous to athletic development, girls experience different hormonal changes, such as an increase in oestrogen and progesterone, which may also be associated with widening of the hips and an increase in non-functional mass (Bland et al., 2021). Such hormonal and morphological changes may not be advantageous to athletic performance, which may have significant implications for talent identification and development. For example, when compared to boys, a clear plateau in the ability to apply force is observed around the age of PHV circa aged 12 to 14 years (e.g., standing broad jump, 10 x 5 m change of direction speed, and hand grip strength) (Tomkinson et al., 2018). Furthermore, cross-sectional and longitudinal research in girls' soccer players in United Kingdom development pathways has shown progression in sprinting-related physical qualities after PHV (Emmonds et al., 2017; Wright & Atkinson, 2019); however, rapid (100 ms) lower body force application, relative to body weight, showed marked reductions in players after PHV (Emmonds et al., 2017). This may be explained by a potential increase in fat mass associated with peak weight velocity that occurs in females 3.5 to 10.5 months after PHV. These considerations are important for both performance and injury prevention as, for example, serious knee injuries, such as anterior cruciate ligament ruptures, tend to occur within the first 50 ms of ground contact (Krosshaug et al., 2007). Improving the ability to apply force quickly to stabilise the knee is proven to reduce injury incidence and a recommended strategy before PHV (Myer et al., 2013; Petushek et al., 2019). Resistance training has been shown to enhance holistic fundamental movement skills competence, including the product (or outcome) of the movement and the process (how the skill was performed) in children (Collins et al., 2021; Grainger et al., 2020).

Talent Identification and Development

As female participation rates increase, the talent pool from which to draw players from has expanded. This expansion, coinciding with heightened competition, prompts a need for elite-level soccer clubs to develop effective methods of talent identification and development (Randell et al., 2021). These methods should reflect the specific demands of the female game (rather than replicating male provisions) and maximise the recruitment and development of the most talented players (Leyhr et al., 2020; Williams et al., 2020). The quantity and quality of research supporting talent development in youth female soccer is limited, often to either single centre, non-controlled trials and usually analysing observational rather than longitudinal data. However, alongside the increased resources and professionalism of female soccer over recent years, there has been a growing amount of scientific knowledge that underpins talent development (Table 17.1).

High-intensity endurance capacity appears to have some prognostic power in identifying young players that have reached the elite level (national team/first division) of female soccer (Datson et al., 2020). For example, Datson et al. (2020) reported that high-intensity aerobic capacity (assessed via the Yo-Yo IR1) at youth level is a predictor or progression into international squads at U17–U20. However, research has reported that there are limited changes in high-intensity

TABLE 17.1 Physiological and motor determinants of future playing success in elite female youth soccer players (see Randell et al., 2021)

Reference	N	Age	Playing Level	Determinants of Performance	Major Findings
Datson et al. (2020)	228	12.7–15.3	Elite Performance Camps (English FA)	CMJ, 30 m linear sprint, YYIR1	Higher YYIR1 (2040 m) score more likely (47–82%) to be selected into U17–U20 international squad.
Höner et al. (2019)	499	11.4	German Soccer Talent Programme	Sprint time, agility, dribbling, ball control and shooting	Dribbling was the most relevant motor predictor for German Youth National Team Selection.
Vescovi et al. (2011)	414	12–21	High club-level juniors and NCAA, Div 1 US College Players	CMJ, Illinois Agility Test (modified) and 36 m RST	No evidence of mean linear sprint speed (9.1 m) differences across all age groups.
Mujika et al. (2009)	34	17–24	Elite senior female players from the Spanish Super Liga and junior players from the Spanish 2nd Division	CMJ, YYIR1, linear sprint 15 m, ball dribbling 15 m	Elite players (1224 m) superior to Junior (826 m) in YYIR1. No difference in 15 m sprint time between senior and junior players.
Hoare and Warr (2000)	59	15–19	Individual sport and non-soccer team sport players recruited into a soccer training camp	VJ, 20 m PST, 20 m linear sprint, 505 agility test	17 selected players from the 59 demonstrated VJ height in the 80th percentile and maximal aerobic power in the 90th percentile compared to the Australian population values for 15-year-olds. 20 m sprint time faster (3.47 s) than the population average (3.64 s) at 15 years of age.

Note: VJ vertical jump, PST progressive shuttle test, CMJ counter movement jump, YYIR1-Yo-Yo intermittent recovery level 1 test, RST repeated sprint test.

aerobic capacity of youth female soccer players between the ages of U14–U16 (Emmonds et al., 2018) or post-PHV (Emmonds et al., 2020). Therefore, the development of high-intensity running capabilities should be a key component of talent development training strategies.

The slalom dribble test has also been reported to have the capability to differentiate between players that reached youth national team versus regional academy level (Höner et al., 2019). However, sprint duration does not seem to discriminate for talent identification purposes (Höner et al., 2019; Leyhr et al., 2020). These studies are valuable, as they provide some initial insight into primarily physical or motor determinants required for success as an elite, female youth soccer player using a single time-point of analyses. The major limitation of this methodological approach is that cross-sectional studies are limited in their capacity to provide a prediction of future success as adult soccer players (Williams et al., 2020). Talent development is a non-linear, dynamic construct; thus, serial measurements of performance are needed over time to truly understand the trajectory of the elite youth soccer player's development (Randell et al., 2021). Incorporating an array of potential soccer performance determinants into a longitudinal evaluation of the player appears to be the optimal approach to understand talent identification and development in an elite female youth soccer environment.

An attempt to conduct a longitudinal study into talent development has been made by the German Football Federation (Leyhr et al., 2020). The study aimed to explore players' skill level (dribbling, passing, and target shooting) and physical fitness (20 m linear sprints and a slalom agility run without the ball) over a 4-year period in adolescent female players. The study reported that players who were ultimately affiliated with professional clubs were ~1 s faster on the sprint, passing, and agility drills than their peers who played at non-professional levels. Indeed, these differences were apparent from U12 and through to U15. However, findings demonstrated that the rate of improvement for these measures in both groups over time was non-linear. Furthermore, on their own, the metrics (individual assessments) did not have sufficient predictive power to determine success in adult soccer, suggesting there is a need for holistic profiling when exploring talent development. It is noteworthy that all the metrics used in the study were closed skill tests (sprinting, dribbling, and shooting), and therefore, may not be ecologically applicable to soccer. Furthermore, the study did not consider the maturity status of the players, and consequently, it was not possible to differentiate between the influence of growth and maturation from training on the changes on talent development.

The combination of cross-sectional and longitudinal studies currently available in female soccer provides a foundation for talent identification and development in elite youth players, although more work is required. For example, evaluating the influence of the maturation-selection phenomenon across all age groups in elite youth soccer using a longitudinal study design is needed. In addition, exploring other contextually appropriate methods to evaluate talent identification and development, such as modified small-sided games, would be useful (Randell et al., 2021), while the application of constructs that underscore key psychological traits for future success such as resilience and perseverance is warranted.

Relative Age Effects and Talent Development

In male youth soccer, there has been an abundance of research confirming relative age effects (RAEs), whereby boys born in the early part of the year are selected, representing a selection bias which may not be advantageous for long-term talent development (Lupo et al., 2019). However, in female soccer, there have been contrasting findings (see Chapter 10). For example, no significant RAEs have been reported in the United States Soccer Federation (Vincent & Glamser, 2006), French professional championship (Delorme et al., 2010), or the Swiss national teams (Romann & Fuchslocher, 2013). In contrast, however, other studies have found significant RAEs (Götze & Hoppe, 2020; Smith et al., 2018). Currently, research on RAEs in girls' soccer is limited and requires further research to better understand the mechanisms before the influence of RAEs on talent identification and development can be determined. In the meantime, coaches should ensure they consider the birth month of the player when conducting individual performance reviews and designing at talent identification and development strategies.

Talent Development Strategies

Fundamental movement skills are seen as critical building blocks for more advanced training and important prerequisites for complex physical activities like soccer (Logan et al., 2018). Since strength (i.e., the ability to apply force in difference biomechanical conditions) (Carroll, 2001) is associated with improvements in movement skill (Collins et al., 2021), it is important that practitioners (e.g., coaches, sport scientists, strength and conditioning coaches) incorporate strength and movement skill training into their programmes.

It is likely that young players, before experiencing PHV, should be exposed to a variety of fundamental movement skills in a fun and semi-structured environment (Lloyd & Oliver, 2012; Wright & Lass, 2016). The inclusion of resistance or body-weight strength training may also enhance movement skill development (Collins et al., 2019a; Grainger et al., 2020) as well as potential psychological benefits for children (Collins et al., 2019b). With access to appropriate coaching, this can present an opportunity to develop more advanced strength and conditioning movements skills, such as Olympic style weightlifting (Figure 17.1), given the increased neuroplasticity of young children (Schlaug et al., 2009). Furthermore, long-term activities that develop the capacity to apply force eccentrically in short periods of time and promote spring-like landing, such as sensibly progressed plyometric training, should be considered (Pedley et al., 2021). Alternatively, girls could be encouraged to participate in a range of sports providing different physical and psychosocial stimuli, such as gymnastics, rock climbing, martial arts, and racket sports. Although there is currently a lack of strong empirical evidence to support or contradict a multi-sport approach, given the potential drawbacks to early specialisation (Moesch et al., 2011), encouraging girls to pursue a breadth of physical activities from a young age would seem sensible.

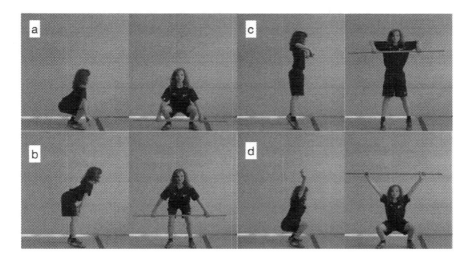

FIGURE 17.1 Example of Olympic-style weightlifting activities in players before the growth spurt. In this example, coaching used analogies to animal shapes at different points in the lift (see Wright & Laas, 2016).

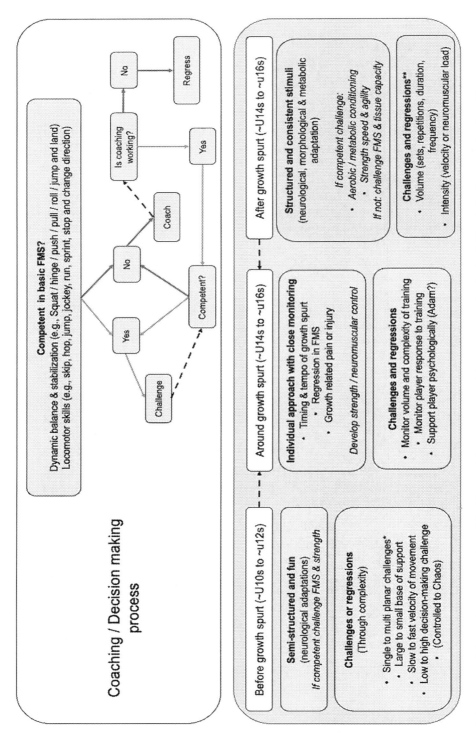

FIGURE 17.2 Schematic representation of decision-making process practitioners can employ in the field to help focus training for girls across maturation groups and based upon fundamental movement skill competence.

When children go through PHV, it is important to consider both the timing and the tempo of growth and how this might affect movement skill. Generally speaking, girls appear to show regressions in neuromuscular control throughout puberty (Quatman-Yates et al., 2012). Stretch-shortening cycle, 'spring-like' performance has also been shown to be poor in girls throughout maturation and, coupled with increases in body mass and absolute peak force on landing, this may contribute to increased ACL injury-risk post-puberty (Pedley et al., 2021). Therefore, when working with players transitioning through and beyond peak height-velocity, incorporating activities that develop force capabilities, such as squatting, lunging, hopping, and landing stabilisation tasks are recommended (Lloyd & Oliver, 2012).

It would be prudent to monitor dynamic movement skill with players circa- or post-PHV. This can be useful information for practitioners planning the training foci for their squad and managing time and resources. Players with poor movement skill and neuromuscular control may be better focusing on strength-related physical qualities, whilst players with excellent movement skill and control may aim to maintain this whilst developing their high-intensity aerobic fitness. Figure 17.2 provides a schematic representation of the decision-making process practitioners can employ in the field to help focus training for girls across maturation groups based upon fundamental movement skill competence.

Psychosocial Considerations

When referring to the notion of psychosocial characteristics, the term 'psychosocial' pertains to the interrelation of individual psychological characteristics with social influences and to the ways in which these shape and guide behaviour (Gledhill et al., 2017). Putting this into context, Gledhill et al. (2017) noted that the definition of the term 'psychosocial' suggests that social influences (such as parents or peers) interact with individual psychological characteristics (such as discipline or commitment) to shape and guide behaviours (such as lifestyle choices or training behaviours), which may then enhance (or debilitate) talent identification and development outcomes in youth soccer. Perhaps unsurprisingly, despite an increase in research focusing on psychosocial factors influencing talent development in women's and girls' soccer (e.g., Gledhill & Harwood, 2014, 2015), there is still an underrepresentation of female soccer players in this body of research when compared to their male counterparts (Gledhill et al., 2017). Undoubtedly, established ideas around the importance of confidence, communication, concentration, commitment, emotional control, and many other aspects are all applicable in female soccer. However, given the recent inroads into this area over the past 7–10 years, the purpose of this section is to draw on research from female soccer specifically to provide an understanding of factors which may influence the developmental trajectory of a female youth soccer player.

Within United Kingdom female soccer, having effective social assets is suggested to contribute to positive talent development outcomes. For example, in their longitudinal study with female youth international soccer players, Gledhill and Harwood (2014) noted the importance of family members and coach-player relationships in the development of female soccer players. Specifically, family members with experience of high level or professional soccer were able to support the technical and tactical development of young female players through effective advice and guidance. Similarly, the experience of family members within soccer was influential in fostering an effective coach-player relationship that subsequently facilitated female players' soccer development. In essence, female players were actively seeking social support from key social assets and, in doing so, were potentially providing themselves with greater resources and coping strategies to navigate their fledgling careers.

In addition to family members, friends inside and outside of soccer both play important roles in the development of elite female soccer players (Gledhill & Harwood, 2014; McGreary et al., 2021). Friends outside soccer fulfil important roles in helping young female soccer players develop important qualities of discipline and self-control, which has increasing importance as players progress through adolescence and can help players to maintain appropriate practice, training, and lifestyle behaviours (Gledhill & Harwood, 2014). The importance of self-control has recently been reinforced in small-scale research from German soccer, with a mixed sample of female and male players (Wolff et al., 2019). Here, it was noted that youth players selected for a talent development programme displayed higher levels of self-control than their non-selected peers, while these self-control differences were evident from a very early age. Intuitively, it is likely that the increased self-control allows young players to take part effectively and volitionally in physical conditioning and injury prevention activities whilst away from soccer, engage with appropriate amounts of deliberate practice, and maintain appropriate general lifestyle behaviours (e.g., nutritional habits, sleep); all of which can influence their talent identification and development outcomes (Gledhill & Harwood, 2015; Wolff et al., 2019).

A female player's ability to reflect and their reflective learning also appear to be important in their development and for successful transitions through different stages of a playing career (Gledhill & Harwood, 2014; McGreary et al., 2021). Whilst early research in this area suggested that a player's ability to reflect may primarily be important for players' technical and tactical development (Gledhill & Harwood, 2014), more recent research (McGreary et al., 2021) suggests the benefits of reflection and reflective learning may extend beyond this. Notably, McGreary et al. (2021) suggest that reflective learning can enable players to appropriately vent frustrations and seek appropriate social support, to learn from their own experiences and understand why they were/were not successful, and it helps players to identify their own development needs; all of which can support players in successfully transitioning from youth to senior female soccer.

A final consideration within female soccer is that of dual-career demands (e.g., Gledhill & Harwood, 2015; McGreary et al., 2021). In their study of unsuccessful, talented female soccer players, for example, Gledhill and Harwood (2015) reported that dual-career demands (e.g., balancing soccer and education or soccer and paid jobs) were deemed a contributing factor in players' unsuccessful attempts to progress their careers, especially in circumstances where key stakeholders (e.g., teachers or parents) were not fully aware of the potential career opportunities in female soccer. Similarly, McGreary et al. (2021) noted that senior female players and transitional female players (i.e., those currently transitioning from youth to senior soccer) experienced dual careers as a salient transitional demand and that players often struggle to find an optimal balance between efforts towards their dual careers. An awareness of these dual-career challenges is important, as they can start in primary school, heighten as a dual-career athlete progresses through school and into university, and are reported to contribute to chronic stress, exhaustion, depression, burnout, and dropout from sporting careers (Sallen et al., 2018). Consequently, female soccer organisations should consider ways in which they can work with education providers to ensure appropriate support is in place for dual-career athletes (Gledhill & Harwood, 2015).

Considerations for Researchers

Despite recent developments in women's and girls' soccer research, many gaps in our understanding of how best to identify and develop young female talented players still exist. High-quality investigations, specific to female soccer, are needed to inform recommendations and improve our understanding of talent identification and development. Previous studies provide a foundation to inform talent identification in female soccer; however, future research should now explore the utility of other contextually relevant methods (e.g., small-sided games) for identifying young talented soccer players. Moreover, further research should aim to adopt a multidimensional approach, including physical, psychosocial, and sport-specific factors, which are recommended to provide the most holistic assessment of talent identification and development.

Future research should aim to identify characteristics that are responsible for both selection and deselection from talent pathways in elite female youth soccer, and this should be conducted using a longitudinal research design that holistically tracks players over a number of years. Lastly, it is evident that female studies remain underrepresented from the talent identification and development literature in youth soccer when compared to their male peers (Curran et al., 2019). This may be due to the professionalisation of female soccer only recently emerging, and thus, their talent pathways are less developed. As such, it is important to recognise the many lessons learnt from the male talent pathways that have been presented throughout this book when designing the evolving female structures to ensure the same issues are not recreated, and instead, use this as an opportunity to create contemporary organisational structures and more appropriate youth female soccer settings (Bennett et al., 2018; Kelly et al., 2022).

Considerations for Practitioners

Based on the research presented throughout this chapter, practitioners should consider the following suggestions when designing, implementing, and evaluating youth soccer programmes when working with young female players:

- Be cognizant that growth and maturation may impact the performance of young female soccer players and consider this when establishing talent identification and development strategies. Specifically, monitor growth rates by measuring stature and body mass every 3 months.
- Review physical performance data of young female players in relation to their maturity status (e.g., biological age) rather than their chronological age during both talent identification and development processes.
- Functional movement screening and strength development should be key components of training at all stages of development for youth female soccer players. Moreover, given the association between career progression and high-intensity running capabilities, practitioners should incorporate high-intensity aerobic conditioning work into training programmes for players PHV.
- Use strategies to help female players develop qualities in self-control, reflection and reflective learning, and self-regulation which may increase their chances of successfully transitioning through their soccer careers.
- Be aware of the possible dual-career demands of female players and provide appropriate support for those who need it.

Conclusion

This chapter has aimed to summarise current research and best practices in talent identification and development in female youth soccer. Findings of this chapter and the recommendations for research and practice can be used to help guide the development of evidence-informed strategies for talent identification development in female soccer. Importantly, researchers and practitioners should be mindful that findings from male literature may not be transferable to their female equivalents, particularly due to the physical and physiological differences between the two genders. As presented in many chapters throughout this book, since the majority of talent identification and development research in youth soccer has focused on youth male samples, researchers should prioritise female studies to capture a greater balanced understanding about both sexes. Meanwhile, practitioners are encouraged to measure physiological and physical data to assist individual player development based on biological maturity (rather than chronological age), as well as create educational tools to help develop important psychosocial skills and help design a range of support systems to facilitate dual-career demands in young female players.

Note

1 In this chapter, 'female' is referred to as the umbrella term for belonging or relating to 'women' (e.g., over aged 18 years) and/or 'girls' (e.g., under aged 18 years).

References

Bennett, K. J. M., Vaeyens, R., & Fransen, J. (2018). Creating a framework for talent identification and development in emerging football nations. *Science and Medicine in Football*, *3*(1), 36–42. https://doi.org/10.1080/24733938.2018.1489141

Bland, V. L., Bea, J. W., Blew, R. M., Roe, D. J., Lee, V. R., Funk, J. L., & Going, S. B. (2021). Influence of changes in soft tissue composition on changes in bone strength in peripubertal girls: The STAR longitudinal study. *Journal of Bone and Mineral Research*, *36*(1), 123–132. https://doi.org/10.1002/jbmr.4168

Carroll, T. J., Riek, S.m & Carson, R. G. (2001). Neural adaptations to resistance training. *Sports Medicine*, *31*(12), 829–840. https://doi.org/10.2165/00007256-200131120-00001

Collins, H., Booth, J. N., Duncan, A., & Fawkner, S. (2019a). The effect of resistance training interventions on fundamental movement skills in youth: A meta-analysis. *Sports Medicine-Open*, *5*(1), 1–16. https://doi.org/10.1186%2Fs40798-019-0188-x

Collins, H., Booth, J. N., Duncan, A., Fawkner, S., & Niven, A. (2019b). The effect of resistance training interventions on 'the self' in youth: A systematic review and meta-analysis. *Sports Medicine-Open*, *5*(1), 1–14. https://doi.org/10.1186%2Fs40798-019-0205-0

Collins, H. M., Fawkner, S., Booth, J. N., & Duncan, A. (2021). The impact of resistance training on strength and correlates of physical activity in youth. *Journal of Sports Sciences*, *40*(1), 40–49. https://doi.org/10.1080/02640414.2021.1976487

Curran, O., MacNamara, A., & Passmore, D. (2019). What about the girls? Exploring the gender data gap in talent development. *Frontiers in Sports and Active Living*, *1*, 3. https://doi.org/10.3389/fspor.2019.00003

Datson, N., Weston, M., Drust, B., Gregson, W., & Lolli, L. (2020). High-intensity endurance capacity assessment as a tool for talent identification in elite youth female soccer. *Journal of Sports Sciences*, *38*(11–12), 1313–1319. https://doi.org/10.1080/02640414.2019.1656323

Delorme, N., Boiché, J., & Raspaud, M. (2010). Relative age effects in female sport: A diachronic examination of soccer players. *Scandinavian Journal of Medicine & Science in Sports*, *20*(3), 509–515. https://doi.org/10.1111/j.1600-0838.2009.00979.x

Emmonds, S., Morris, R., Murray, E., Robinson, C., Turner, L., & Jones, B. (2017). The influence of age and maturity status on the maximum and explosive strength characteristics of elite youth female soccer players. *Science and Medicine in Football*, *1*(3), 209–215. https://doi.org/10.1080/24733938.2017.1363908

Emmonds, S., Scantlebury, S., Murray, E., Turner, L., Robsinon, C., & Jones, B. (2020). Physical characteristics of elite youth female soccer players characterized by maturity status. *The Journal of Strength & Conditioning Research*, *34*(8), 2321–2328. https://doi.org/10.1519/jsc.0000000000002795

Emmonds, S., Till, K., Redgrave, J., Murray, E., Turner, L., Robinson, C., & Jones, B. (2018). Influence of age on the anthropometric and performance characteristics of high-level youth female soccer players. *International Journal of Sports Science & Coaching, 13*(5), 779–786. https://doi.org/10.1177/1747954118757437

Fédération Internationale de Football Association (FIFA). (2019). *Women's football member associations survey report* [online]. Retrieved from: https://digitalhub.fifa.com/m/231330ded0bf3120/original/nq3ensohyxpuxovcovj0-pdf.pdf

Gledhill, A., & Harwood, C. (2014). Developmental experiences of elite female youth soccer players. *International Journal of Sport and Exercise Psychology, 12*, 150–165. https://doi.org/10.1080/1612197X.2014.880259

Gledhill, A., & Harwood, C. (2015). A holistic perspective on career development in UK female soccer player: A negative case analysis. *Psychology of Sport and Exercise, 21*, 65–77. https://doi.org/10.1016/j.psychsport.2015.04.003

Gledhill, A., Harwood, C., & Forsdyke, D. (2017). Psychosocial factors associated with talent development in football: A systematic review. *Psychology of Sport and Exercise, 31*, 93–112. https://doi.org/10.1016/j.psychsport.2017.04.002

Götze, M., & Hoppe, M. W. (2020). Relative age effect in elite German soccer: Influence of gender and competition level. *Frontiers in Psychology, 11*, 587023. https://doi.org/10.3389/fpsyg.2020.587023

Grainger, F., Innerd, A., Graham, M., & Wright, M. (2020). Integrated strength and fundamental movement skill training in children: A pilot study. *Children, 7*(10), 161. https://doi.org/10.3390/children7100161

Hoare, D. G., & Warr, C. R. (2000). Talent identification and women's soccer: An Australian experience. *Journal of Sports Sciences, 18*(9), 751–758. https://doi.org/10.1080/02640410050120122

Höner, O., Raabe, J., Murr, D., & Leyhr, D. (2019). Prognostic relevance of motor tests in elite girls' soccer: A five-year prospective cohort study within the German talent promotion program. *Science and Medicine in Football, 3*(4), 287–296. https://doi.org/10.1080/24733938.2019.1609069

Kelly, A. L., Brown, T., Reed, R., Côté, J., & Turnnidge, J. (2022). Relative age effects in male cricket: A personal assets approach to explain the immediate, short-term, and long-term developmental outcomes. *Sports, 10*(3), 39. https://doi.org/10.3390/sports10030039

Kelly, A. L., & Williams, C. A. (2020). Physical characteristics and the talent identification and development processes in male youth soccer: A narrative review. *Strength & Conditioning Journal, 42*(6), 15–34. https://doi.org/10.1519/SSC.0000000000000576

Krosshaug, T., Nakamae, A., Boden, B. P., Engebretsen, L., Smith, G., Slauterbeck, J. R., Hewett, T. E., & Bahr, R. (2007). Mechanisms of anterior cruciate ligament injury in basketball: Video analysis of 39 cases. *The American Journal of Sports Medicine, 35*(3), 359–367. https://doi.org/10.1177/0363546506293899

Leyhr, D., Raabe, J., Schultz, F., Kelava, A., & Höner, O. (2020). The adolescent motor performance development of elite female soccer players: A study of prognostic relevance for future success in adulthood using multilevel modelling. *Journal of Sports Sciences, 38*(11–12), 1342–1351. https://doi.org/10.1080/02640414.2019.1686940

Lloyd, R. S., & Oliver, J. L. (2012). The youth physical development model: A new approach to long-term athletic development. *Strength & Conditioning Journal, 34*(3), 61–72. https://doi.org/10.1519/SSC.0b013e31825760ea

Logan, S. W., Ross, S. M., Chee, K., Stodden, D. F., & Robinson, L. E. (2018). Fundamental motor skills: A systematic review of terminology. *Journal of Sports Sciences, 36*(7), 781–796. https://doi.org/10.1080/02640414.2017.1340660

Lupo, C., Boccia, G., Ungureanu, A. N., Frati, R., Marocco, R., & Brustio, P. R. (2019). The beginning of senior career in team sport is affected by relative age effect. *Frontiers in Psychology, 10*, 1465. https://doi.org/10.3389%2Ffpsyg.2019.01465

Manson, S. A., Brughelli, M., & Harris, N. K. (2014). Physiological characteristics of international female soccer players. *Journal of Strength and Conditioning Research, 28*(2), 308–318. https://doi.org/10.1519/jsc.0b013e31829b56b1

McGreary, M., Morris, R., & Eubank, M. (2021). Retrospective and concurrent perspectives of the transitions in professional female football within the United Kingdom. *Psychology of Sport and Exercise*, 53, 101855. https://doi.org/10.1016/j.psychsport.2020.101855

Moesch, K., Elbe, A. M., Hauge, M. L., & Wikman, J. M. (2011). Late specialization: The key to success in centimeters, grams, or seconds (cgs) sports. *Scandinavian Journal of Medicine & Science in Sports*, 21(6), e282–e290. https://doi.org/10.1111/j.1600-0838.2010.01280.x

Morris, R., Emmonds, S., Jones, B., Myers, T. D., Clarke, N. D., Lake, J., Ellis, M., Singleton, D., Roe, G., & Till, K. (2018). Seasonal changes in physical qualities of elite youth soccer players according to maturity status: Comparisons with aged matched controls. *Science and Medicine in Football*, 2(4), 272–280. https://doi.org/10.1080/24733938.2018.1454599

Mujika, I., Santisteban, J., Impellizzeri, F. M., & Castagna, C. (2009). Fitness determinants of success in men's and women's football. *Journal of Sports Sciences*, 27(2), 107–114. https://doi.org/10.1080/02640410802428071

Myer, G. D., Sugimoto, D., Thomas, S., & Hewett, T.E. (2013). The influence of age on the effectiveness of neuromuscular training to reduce anterior cruciate ligament injury in female athletes: A meta-analysis. *The American Journal of Sports Medicine*, 41(1), 203–215. https://doi.org/10.1177%2F0363546512460637

Pedley, J. S., DiCesare, C. A., Lloyd, R. S., Oliver, J. L., Ford, K. R., Hewett, T. E., & Myer, G. D. (2021). Maturity alters drop vertical jump landing force-time profiles but not performance outcomes in adolescent females. *Scandinavian Journal of Medicine & Science in Sports*, 31(11), 2055–2063. https://doi.org/10.1111/sms.14025

Petushek, E. J., Sugimoto, D., Stoolmiller, M., Smith, G., & Myer, G. D. (2019). Evidence-based best-practice guidelines for preventing anterior cruciate ligament injuries in young female athletes: A systematic review and meta-analysis. *The American Journal of Sports Medicine*, 47(7), 1744–1753. https://doi.org/10.1177/0363546518782460

Quatman-Yates, C. C., Quatman, C. E., Meszaros, A. J., Paterno, M. V., & Hewett, T. E. (2012). A systematic review of sensorimotor function during adolescence: A developmental stage of increased motor awkwardness? *British Journal of Sports Medicine*, 46(9), 649–655. https://doi.org/10.1136/bjsm.2010.079616

Randell, R. K., Clifford, T., Drust, B., Moss, S. L., Unnithan, V. B., Croix, M. B. D. S., Datson, N., Martin, D., Mayho, H., Carter, J. M., & Rollo, I. (2021). Physiological characteristics of female soccer players and health and performance considerations: A narrative review. *Sports Medicine*, 51(2), 1377–1399. https://doi.org/10.1007/s40279-021-01458-1

Read, P. J., Oliver, J. L., Myer, G. D., Croix, M. B. D. S., Belshaw, A., & Lloyd, R.S. (2018). Altered landing mechanics are shown by male youth soccer players at different stages of maturation. *Physical Therapy in Sport*, 33, 48–53. https://doi.org/10.1016/j.ptsp.2018.07.001

Romann, M., & Fuchslocher, J. (2013). Influences of player nationality, playing position, and height on relative age effects at women's under-17 FIFA World Cup. *Journal of Sports Sciences*, 31(1), 32–40. https://doi.org/10.1080/02640414.2012.718442

Sallen, J., Hemming, K., & Richartz, A. (2018). Facilitating dual careers by improving resistance to chronic stress: Effects of an intervention programme for elite student athletes. *European Journal of Sport Science*, 18(1), 112–122. https://doi.org/10.1080/17461391.2017.1407363

Schlaug, G., Forgeard, M., Zhu, L., Norton, A., Norton, A., & Winner, E. (2009). Training-induced neuroplasticity in young children. *Annals of the New York Academy of Sciences*, 1169, 205–208. https://doi.org/10.1111%2Fj.1749-6632.2009.04842.x

Smith, K. L., Weir, P. L., Till, K., Romann, M., & Cobley, S. (2018). Relative age effects across and within female sport contexts: A systematic review and meta-analysis. *Sports Medicine*, 48(6), 1451–1478. https://doi.org/10.1007/s40279-018-0890-8

Tomkinson, G. R., Carver, K. D., Atkinson, F., Daniell, N. D., Lewis, L. K., Fitzgerald, J. S., Lang, J. J., & Ortega, F. B. (2018). European normative values for physical fitness in children and adolescents aged 9–17 years: Results from 2,779,165 Eurofit performances representing 30 countries. *British Journal of Sports Medicine*, 52(22), 1445–1456. https://doi.org/10.1136/bjsports-2017-098253

Towlson, C., MacMaster, C., Gonçalves, B., Sampaio, J., Toner, J., MacFarlane, N., Barrett, S., Hamilton, A., Jack, R., Hunter, F., & Myers, T., (2021a). The effect of bio-banding on physical and psychological indicators of talent identification in academy soccer players. *Science and Medicine in Football, 5*(4), 280–292. https://doi.org/10.1080/24733938.2020.1862419

Towlson, C., Salter, J., Ade, J. D., Enright, K., Harper, L. D., Page, R. M., & Malone, J. J., (2021b). Maturity-associated considerations for training load, injury risk, and physical performance in youth soccer: One size does not fit all. *Journal of Sport and Health Science, 10*(4), 403–412. https://doi.org/10.1016/j.jshs.2020.09.003

Union of European Football Association (UEFA). (2017). *Women's football across the national associations* [online]. Retrieved from: www.uefa.com/MultimediaFiles/Download/OfficialDocument/uefaorg/Women%27sfootball/02/51/60/57/2516057_DOWNLOAD.pdf

Vescovi, J. D., Rupf, R., Brown, T. D., & Marques, M. C. (2011). Physical performance characteristics of high-level female soccer players 12–21 years of age. *Scandinavian Journal of Medicine & Science in Sports, 21*(5), 670–678. https://doi.org/10.1111/j.1600-0838.2009.01081.x

Vincent, J., & Glamser, F. D. (2006). Gender differences in the relative age effect among U.S. Olympic Development Program youth soccer players. *Journal of Sports Sciences, 24*(4), 405–413. https://doi.org/10.1080/02640410500244655

Williams, A. M., Ford, P. R., & Drust, B. (2020). Talent identification and development in soccer since the millennium. *Journal of Sports Sciences, 38*(11–12), 1199–1210. https://doi.org/10.1080/02640414.2020.1766647

Wolff, W., Bertrams, A., & Schüler, J. (2019). Trait self-control discriminates between youth football players selected and not selected for the German talent program: A Bayesian analysis. *Frontiers in Psychology, 10*, 2203. https://doi.org/10.2289/fpsyg.2019.02203

Wright, M. D., & Atkinson, G. (2019). Changes in sprint-related outcomes during a period of systematic training in a girls' soccer academy. *The Journal of Strength & Conditioning Research, 33*(3), 793–800. https://doi.org/10.1519/jsc.0000000000002055

Wright, M. D., & Laas, M. (2016). Strength training and metabolic conditioning for female youth and adolescent soccer players. *Strength and Conditioning Journal, 38*(2), 96–104. https://doi.org/10.1519/SSC.0000000000000212

18
PARA-SOCCER

Emphasising the Complex and Multidimensional Factors When Identifying and Developing Players with Disabilities

John W. Francis, Dave Sims, Adam Bendall, Adam L. Kelly, and Andrew Wood

Introduction

Throughout this book, concepts associated with talent identification and development in soccer players without disabilities have been examined and build on the well-established body of academic and applied knowledge. In contrast, however, talent identification and development within para-soccer[1] have received limited theoretical and practical attention to date. Para-soccer is a broad term that captures a range of adapted formats of soccer to enable individuals with an impairment[2] to participate. Over the last 20 years in the United Kingdom, for instance, there has been an ever-increasing number of opportunities for individuals with an impairment to participate in soccer due to the establishment of Football Development Programmes and the launch of the English Federation of Disability Sport (2012). Subsequently, three main participation and development pathways for individuals with an impairment have emerged, including: (a) players with an impairment play alongside players without a disability with no adaptions to formats (i.e., mainstream soccer), (b) players with a broad spectrum of impairments (e.g., limited mobility, spatial awareness, and fitness) compete together (i.e., pan-disability soccer), and (c) players with the same impairment compete together in specific formats tailored towards the needs of the players (i.e., impairment-specific soccer for amputee, blind, cerebral palsy, deaf, partially sighted, or powerchair players; see Table 8.1).

It is important to understand that factors related to the individual's impairment (e.g., type of impairment, nature of the impairment, time of impairment, and potential classification) add an additional level of complexity when compared to mainstream talent identification and development in soccer. Although classification systems are designed to level the playing field amongst athletes with impairments, numerous researchers (e.g., Dehghansai et al.,2017b, 2021; Pastor et al., 2019) have synthesised the growing evidence regarding a possible relationship existing between athletes' impairment, their potential classification, and likely performance success in sport. Thus, the variability of development amongst athletes with impairments, coupled with the necessity to understand the complex interactions between various factors, are important aspects for talent identification and development practitioners to consider.

DOI: 10.4324/9781032232799-18

TABLE 18.1 Summary of para-soccer impairment-specific squads

Impairment	Players	Classification	Adaptions
Amputee	7 vs. 7	• Outfield players are either above or below the knee single-leg amputee. • Goalkeepers are single-arm amputees.	• Smaller pitch (60 m x 40 m). • Outfield players play without a prosthesis on and with aluminium wrist crutches. • The goalkeeper is not allowed out of the penalty area.
Blind	Four outfield B1 players and a sighted or partially sighted goalkeeper	• B1 from no perception of light in either eye up to perception of light, but an inability to recognise the shape of a hand at any distance in any direction.	• Solid 42 m x 22 m playing surface. • Touchlines have boards. • Goalkeepers are sighted but restricted to a small area. • The ball has ball bearings. • Players must shout 'voy' before making a tackle.
Cerebral Palsy	7 vs. 7	• FT1 have severe bilateral spasticity affecting the lower limbs (FT1A), or athetosis/dystonia or ataxia involuntary movement and coordination problems (F1B), or unilateral spasticity or hemiplegia (FT1C). • FT2 have moderate bilateral spasticity (FT2A), or athetosis/dystonia or ataxia (FT2B), or unilateral spasticity or hemiplegia (FT2C). • FT3 have mild bilateral spasticity (FT3A), or athetosis/dystonia or ataxia (FT3B), or unilateral spasticity or hemiplegia (FT3C).	• Smaller pitch (75 m x 55 m) and smaller goals (5 m x 2 m). • Shorter games (two halves of 30 minutes). • No offside rule. • Internationally there must be a minimum of 2 x FT1 and maximum of 1 x FT3 on the pitch.
Deaf	11 vs. 11 or Futsal	• Hearing loss of at least 55 dB per tone average in the better ear. • Players must remove any kind of hearing aid(s)/amplification or external cochlear implant parts to compete.	• No adaptions. • The referee uses a flag to draw attention.
Learning Disability	11 vs. 11 or Futsal	• IQ of 75 or below. • Limited 'adaptive behaviour'. • Learning disability must have occurred before the age of 18 years.	• No adaptions.
Partially Sighted	Futsal	• B2 from the ability to recognise the shape of a hand up to a visual acuity of 2/60 and/or field of 5 degrees or less. • B3 from a visual acuity above 2/60 up to 6/60 and/or a visual field of more than 5 degrees and less than 20 degrees.	• Only two B3 players are allowed on the pitch at any time when a team plays with a sighted goalkeeper. • Played according to FIFA futsal rules. • Playing conditions with limited light reflections and intensity. • The colour of the ball is modified.

(*Continued*)

TABLE 18.1 (Continued)

Impairment	Players	Classification	Adaptions
Powerchair	Three outfield and a goalkeeper	• PF1 (higher-level impairment) and PF2 (lower level of impairment) • A player is assessed on postural control, head control, driving skills, and secondary factors. • Impairment types include neurological conditions, orthopaedic involvement, amputees, myopathies/muscle dystrophies, and spinal cord injuries.	• A team must have a minimum of two PF1s on the court at any time. • Indoor 30 m x 18 m hard court surface. • The goals are 6 m wide with no crossbar. • Oversize football (33 cm diameter). • Electric wheelchair with a maximum speed of 10 kph.

Note: Information adapted from Deaf International Football Association (2021), Fédération Internationale de Powerchair Football Association (2021), International Blind Sports Federation (2021), International Federation of CP Football (2021), World Amputee Football (2021), and World Intellectual Impairment Sport (2021).

Dehghansai et al. (2020) applied Newell's (1986) constraint-led approach to explain the *individual* (e.g., stable, malleable, and unstable structural and functional factors), *task* (e.g., general, outcome, sport-specific, and skill-specific factors), and *environmental* (e.g., natural, infrastructure, sociocultural, and interpersonal factors) constraints that are associated with athlete development in para/disability sport. At the forefront of this explanation is the importance of acknowledging how players in para-soccer enter at different ages based on the timing of their impairment. For instance, individuals may be born with an impairment (i.e., congenital) or their impairment arises after birth (i.e., acquired) following an accident (e.g., a brain injury, infection, or disease) or as a side-effect of a medical condition (e.g., amputation or deafness following meningitis). This timing influences how key stakeholders (i.e., coaches, talent identification and development practitioners, and additional support staff) working in para-soccer consider players' readiness to enter into talent programmes, based on both their training and chronological ages (Dehghansai et al., 2017a; Lemez et al., 2020).

To advance our understanding of the key components associated with talent identification and development in para-soccer, this chapter provides a focus on blind soccer to better understand current approaches, challenges, and developments regarding the technical/tactical, physical, psychological, and social demands when identifying and developing blind soccer players. These four attributes, presented in the Football Association's (FA) Four Corner Model (The Football Association, 2019), have been previously utilised in empirical research (e.g., Kelly et al., 2021a; Simmons, 2004; Towlson et al., 2019) and are generally acknowledged as the most appropriate developmental features, since each attribute captures various characteristics and, overall, reflects an element that contributes towards the development of the complete player. However, it is important to note that no attribute operates in isolation (Kelly et al., 2018), and that the four are interconnected and reliant on one another. Whilst these four attributes are initially discussed individually, the connections and overlapping components of the four key attributes are vital (Kelly & Williams, 2020), which reinforces the importance for key stakeholders to facilitate an interdisciplinary approach in existing and new talent identification and development programmes within blind soccer (and wider para-soccer programmes). Since

Blind Soccer

Blind soccer is an adapted version of five-a-side (pitch dimensions of 40 x 20 m), which follows the rules of futsal and is designed for players with a vision impairment who have "reduced or no vision caused by damage to the eye structure, optical nerves or optical pathways, or visual cortex of the brain" (International Blind Sports Federation, 2022) (see Table 18.1). Whilst the developmental roots of the sport go back to the early 1920s in Spain, it was not until 1996 that the sport was internationally recognised by the International Blind Sports Federation (2017) and a further 8 years before the sport made its debut in the 2004 Athens Paralympic Games. Despite the sport being played for over 100 years and in over 36 countries across the world (International Blind Sports Federation, 2018), the existing knowledge and understanding regarding technical/tactical, physical, psychological, and social developmental attributes are limited. The current research largely focuses on technical and tactical features (e.g., Gamonales et al., 2019), physiological demands (e.g., Finocchietti et al., 2019; Souza et al., 2016), injuries (e.g., Magno et al., 2013), and audiological comparisons between blind soccer players and sighted individuals (e.g., Velten et al., 2016). Although these insights are novel, they largely provide reductionist conclusions, focus on players competing at an elite senior level, and do not necessarily shed light on the developmental journeys undertaken to perform on the world stage. As such, there is limited applied transfer from the existing research into practice to inform practitioners regarding how to develop the next generation of blind soccer players.

Within England, children with vision impairment were traditionally identified through their attendance at specialist blind schools or colleges and entered into talent identification programmes located at these sites. More recently, however, 64% of children aged 5–16 years who have a vision impairment now attend mainstream schools or academies (Royal National Institute of Blind People, 2021). As a result of this change, these individuals typically receive limited access to meaningful physical education and signposting to wider sporting opportunities. Subsequently, blind soccer talent identification and development practitioners have been required to think differently when identifying and supporting the development needs of these individuals. Practitioners now face the challenge of supporting eligible individuals at greater geographical distances across the country, rather than residing at specialist educational facilities. This does not only affect the creation of talent environments, but also has implications for broader developmental aspects of team participation, due to minimal player clusters at specific locations.

To help overcome some of these challenges, the English FA and Sport England have launched a small-sided version of blind soccer, named 'Project B1', in an attempt to increase participation rates in the sport alongside their current talent identification and development programme and 5 vs. 5 programmes (e.g., Kent FA, 2021). This has involved creating several Blind Programme Areas in partnership with English Football League clubs and County Football Associations alongside developing a network of blind soccer coaches. Players who are identified from these programmes participate in the National Blind Soccer league and advance into the National Emerging Talent Programme (NETP). Once within the NETP, players are provided with age- and ability-specific programmes to enable them to develop beyond the capacity of the environment that they currently participate and compete in. It is at this point that an individual is likely to transition into the Performance Foundation (PF) team prior to selection into a senior playing squad or continue to develop the required attributes at the NETP level. However, the development and progression of these players are fluid and can follow a non-linear path, due to the timing and type of impairment and the rate of their development. Central to this player-developmental pathway is ensuring a holistic approach is adopted across all four attributes of the FA's Four Corner Model. This chapter will, therefore, apply this model to showcase key considerations for talent identification and development.

Technical/Tactical

The existing research surrounding technical and tactical understanding has been centred around the importance of goal scoring. For example, Gamonales et al. (2018) identified the shooter's situation and their body shape, the shot location, and the opposition affected shooting efficiency during the 2014 Blind Soccer World Championships. Although this is an essential component of the game, Runswick et al. (2021a) highlighted several key technical and tactical skills (i.e., ball controlling, dribbling, passing, shooting, spatial awareness, movement, attacking tactics, and defensive tactics) are needed by blind soccer players, not only to enable them to create goal-scoring opportunities but to also restrict opponents from creating openings. Further work by Runswick et al. (2021b) explored some of these technical and tactical skills, whereby participants who were not blind wore blindfolds rather than participants with existing visual impairments. While some would argue the findings are useful, it is plausible to suggest that individuals wearing a blindfold does not accurately capture a valid insight into a blind soccer player's technical and tactical skill, and thus the findings have little impact on understanding and knowledge transfer.

Acknowledging the strengths and limitations of the previous works, the authors of this chapter have developed the Blind Soccer Technical and Tactical Instrument (B1TTI) for stakeholders working in blind soccer (see Table 18.2). The instrument contains nine components (initial control, dribbling, passing, shooting, battling, off-ball support, creating space to receive, defending individual, and defending in a unit) and outlines five levels of technical effectiveness (Level 0 = Developmental to Level 4 = World Class). Stakeholders can provide a summary of an individual's performance for each component as well as offer an associated level to help identify areas for development within their personal journeys. For example, following the observation of a player's performance in a National Blind League game, a talent identification practitioner might note the player's typical ability to initially control the ball is representative of a Level 1. The instrument can also be used to gather further objective data by quantifying each action an individual undertakes during a game. For instance, during a 30-minute game, a player may have a total of ten attempts, which includes six Level-1 instances and four Level-3 instances. As such, coaches could examine the occasions where the player has picked up the ball quicker and use video or other tools to compare performances, which would subsequently improve feedback and aid their development. Through adopting this more in-depth approach, limitations in a human's ability to recall events and individual bias are removed (Laird & Waters, 2008), and a more meaningful player development plan could be established.

Although the utilisation of the B1TTI is in its initial stages, the authors of this chapter, who are currently implementing and evaluating this tool, are anecdotally recognising differences emerge between the pathway stage and the timing of an individuals impairment. For instance, when players progress from NETP to PF and then towards the senior level, their technical efficiency increases, regardless of the timing of impairment. Moreover, initial analysis has also shown acquired individuals obtain lower scores in their ability to control the ball, in comparison to congenital

TABLE 18.2 The Blind Soccer Technical and Tactical Instrument (B1TTI)

Impairment	Players	Classification	Adaptions
Amputee	7 vs. 7	• Outfield players are either above or below the knee single-leg amputee. • Goalkeepers are single-arm amputees.	• Smaller pitch (60 m x 40 m). • Outfield players play without a prosthesis on and with aluminium wrist crutches. • The goalkeeper is not allowed out of the penalty area.
Blind	Four outfield B1 players and a sighted or partially sighted goalkeeper	• B1 from no perception of light in either eye up to perception of light, but an inability to recognise the shape of a hand at any distance in any direction.	• Solid 42 m x 22 m playing surface. • Touchlines have boards. • Goalkeepers are sighted but restricted to a small area. • The ball has ball bearings. • Players must shout 'voy' before making a tackle.
Cerebral Palsy	7 vs. 7	• FT1 have severe bilateral spasticity affecting the lower limbs (FT1A), or athetosis/dystonia or ataxia involuntary movement and coordination problems (F1B), or unilateral spasticity or hemiplegia (FT1C). • FT2 have moderate bilateral spasticity (FT2A), or athetosis/dystonia or ataxia (FT2B), or unilateral spasticity or hemiplegia (FT2C). • FT3 have mild bilateral spasticity (FT3A), or athetosis/dystonia or ataxia (FT3B), or unilateral spasticity or hemiplegia (FT3C).	• Smaller pitch (75 m x 55 m) and smaller goals (5 m x 2 m). • Shorter games (two halves of 30 minutes). • No offside rule. • Internationally there must be a minimum of 2 x FT1 and maximum of 1 x FT3 on the pitch.
Deaf	11 vs. 11 or Futsal	• Hearing loss of at least 55 dB per tone average in the better ear. • Players must remove any kind of hearing aid(s)/amplification or external cochlear implant parts to compete.	• No adaptions. • The referee uses a flag to draw attention.
Learning Disability	11 vs. 11 or Futsal	• IQ of 75 or below. • Limited 'adaptive behaviour'. • Learning disability must have occurred before the age of 18 years.	• No adaptions.
Partially Sighted	Futsal	• B2 from the ability to recognise the shape of a hand up to a visual acuity of 2/60 and/or field of 5 degrees or less. • B3 from a visual acuity above 2/60 up to 6/60 and/or a visual field of more than 5 degrees and less than 20 degrees.	• Only two B3 players are allowed on the pitch at any time when a team plays with a sighted goalkeeper. • Played according to FIFA futsal rules. • Playing conditions with limited light reflections and intensity. • The colour of the ball is modified.

(*Continued*)

TABLE 18.2 (Continued)

Impairment	Players	Classification	Adaptions
Powerchair	Three outfield and a goalkeeper	• PF1 (higher-level impairment) and PF2 (lower level of impairment). • A player is assessed on postural control, head control, driving skills, and secondary factors. • Impairment types include neurological conditions, orthopaedic involvement, amputees, myopathies/muscle dystrophies, and spinal cord injuries.	• A team must have a minimum of two PF1s on the court at any time. • Indoor 30 m x 18 m hard court surface. • The goals are 6 m wide with no crossbar. • Oversize football (33 cm diameter). • Electric wheelchair with a maximum speed of 10 kph.

individuals who achieved higher scores in their ability to dribble and defend, regardless of stage. As an example, individuals with a congenital visual impairment have been shown to have superior orientational and spatial awareness skills, thus demonstrating a greater ability to pick up on environmental cues and complete tasks (Cattaneo et al., 2007; Houwen et al., 2009). Whilst it is currently unknown if these previous studies actually transfer into sport, the initial experiential differences between acquired and congenital players may provide supporting evidence. Thus, this initial observation highlights the need for talent identification and development programmes to tailor programmes based on the timing of impairment, which aligns with the International Paralympic Committee's views regarding the potential relationship between timing and performance (Runswick et al., 2021a).

Physical

Participants with a visual impairment have been found to have limitations in spatiotemporal relations, impaired balance adjustment, and present a deficit of coordination (Campos et al., 2014). This subsequently reduces the ability to combine movements (Campos et al., 2014; Levtzion-Korach et al., 2000) and creates motor performance impairments that impact on sports training and movements. With regards to physical performance metrics during soccer match-play, Aquino et al. (2017) found blind players who played in the fourth division of the Brazilian Championships covered an average distance of between 8,806 and 9,469 m per game as a team. Moreover, individuals obtained an average velocity of between 4.81 and 5.22 km·h^{-1} and travelled between 40.72 and 63.71 m of high-intensity activities (20.0 km·hr^{-1}) per game, although it is important to acknowledge that this was dependent on match status (i.e., winning, losing, or drawing).

When comparing performance levels across three Brazilian blind soccer divisions, Aquino et al. (2017) found greater physical demands in the lower divisions with higher rates of total distance, average velocity, and high-intensity activities, compared to upper divisions. More recently, Gamonales et al. (2021) examined the most relevant performance variables that influenced the internal and external loads of elite Spanish, Italian, and Czech Republic blind soccer players during four international-friendly games. The researchers found players from the winning team covered 2.64 (2.37) explosive meters per minute (distance with accelerations > 1.12 m·s^{-2}) and had 40.73 (3.91) accelerations (total number of positive speed changes > 1 m·s^{-2}). Together, these findings highlight speed and high-intensity running are not necessarily key physiological aspects for blind soccer talent identification and development programmes to consider. In comparison to 11-a-side soccer, outfield players cover between 9,000 and 12,000 m distance, between 222 and 1,900 m of high-intensity running, and up to 831 m of sprint distance per player (Mallo et al., 2015; Taylor et al., 2017). This could largely be due to blind soccer players being required to decelerate before reaching threshold values of sprints, due to the lack of available space on the pitch, a need to protect themselves from other players and/or the boards, or needing to change direction/accelerate to avoid other players. This potentially highlights the increased importance of reaction time, along with higher importance of running quickly with the ball, once under control, to be successful in the game. However, further research is required to substantiate these suggestions.

Recently, the authors of this chapter have collected speed and repeated speed data over 30 m, static countermovement jump (CMJ) height, reactive strength index (RSI) through repeated CMJs, and anthropometric measures (height, body mass, body-fat percentage, and lean mass). Based on this physical performance data, a fatigue index from repeated sprint data has been generated, whereby the percentage ratio of the averaged first three sprint times and last three sprint times was calculated. The data from these tests allows researchers and practitioners working in talent pathways to replicate game-specific actions that are observable and have been quantified in previous studies. Moreover, this physical performance data shows an increase or decrease in body mass and how percentage body fat that correlates with the increase or decrease of both speed, repeated speed, and fatigue.

From a practical perspective, the data can be applied and interpreted regarding how an individual's distance when closing down the space in a 1 vs. 1 defending situation fluctuates as the onset of fatigue occurs (i.e., the higher the fatigue index, the better the player's ability to effectively close down space repeatedly). Indeed, initial analysis has shown senior blind soccer players generally have a higher fatigue index than PF players (see Figure 18.1). However, it is interesting to note that, as the distance of the sprint increases, the fatigue index for those with an acquired impairment does not reduce as sharply as individuals who were born with a visual impairment, regardless of the playing group. Similarly, the CMJ and RSI tests allow researchers and practitioners to examine an individual's ability to generate (CMJ) and absorb (RSI) leg power, which are key components for generating shooting power and changing direction, with similar trends being observed in soccer players without disabilities. Also, as expected, through the players that the authors of this chapter tested, a negative correlation was found, as percentage body fat was shown to reduce drop off time from the last and first 30 m sprint reduces and RSI increase. These, though, are purely descriptive as the sample size is too small ($n = 8$) to perform robust inferential statistics on the data; thus, further research is warranted to verify these preliminary suggestions.

Other physical performance research from da Silva et al. (2018) has shown how individuals with a visual impairment have worse static balance than sighted individuals and pose a fear of falling while running. Furthermore, Parreira et al. (2017) revealed how postural control is altered during gait to compensate for impaired vision, with these individuals typically having poor control. Whilst no further research has explored whether the timing of impairment influences balance and fear while running in sports settings, it could be argued that the initial data presented previously potentially sheds light on these aspects. For example, players with a congenital impairment have been found to have a greater understanding of distances and superior spatial-awareness skills (Cattaneo et al., 2007; Houwen et al., 2009), and therefore, could be suggested to have less fear when over a shorter distance. However, their gait and running style are less efficient due to "the intensification of the proprioceptive and vestibular systems in an attempt to maintain both static and dynamic stability, linked mainly to head movements" (Parreira et al., 2017, p. 166).

284 John W. Francis et al.

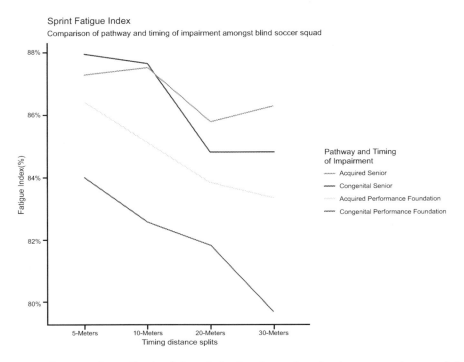

FIGURE 18.1 A comparison of sprint fatigue index based on talent development pathway and timing of visual impairment.

Moreover, congenital individuals have no visual imagery of what an effective running style looks like and rely on specific feedback and coaching from other individuals. In contrast, acquired individuals have better gait patterns and proprioception, as they understand running mechanics from either previously seeing themselves run or the movements of others (Castro et al., 2021). Despite this, blind soccer players have been found to have longer total contact time and initial contact time but a shorter flight phase when sprinting, compared to soccer players without disabilities (Ferro et al., 2002). Taken together, stakeholders working in blind soccer should consider the role of fitness testing to help inform talent identification and development strategies as well as understand how an individual's impairment can have implications on their physical capabilities.

Psychological

Similar to many other sports, not only does blind soccer require a high level of technical/tactical and physical performance, but also mental preparation and psychological skills. In particular, blind soccer players demonstrate extraordinary endeavours of courage, commitment, and skill, and though the impairment does not define an individual's identity, it is, of course, intricately associated with their psychology. In addition to this, the game is volatile, with players having a high risk of physical injury (Fitzpatrick et al., 2021) due to difficulties in foreseeing or bracing physical challenges, coupled with players often adopting lower stances to increase their efforts to hear the ball (Mieda & Kokubu, 2020).

As outlined previously, players are required to perform high-intensity activities, such as repeated sprints, accelerations, decelerations, and changes of directions, which impacts internal and external loads (Gamonales et al., 2021). Players are also unable to ascertain a precise picture of the game, and therefore, rely on the ability to process information communicated to them from the ball, their teammates, the opposition, the two guides, and the sighted goalkeeper. Additionally, psychosocial stressors (in particular, life events or timing of impairment) have been shown to influence performance in several other para-sports (Martin, 2012). Whilst unresearched, blind soccer players appear to be under cognitive load (i.e., the amount of information that can be retained by the working memory at one time) for longer periods than players without a disability. For instance, Cárdenas et al. (2015) suggest team athletes perform in a high-entropy environment that often requires continual exchanges of information between individuals and their surroundings, which causes them to expend mental resources to respond to task demands.

Blind soccer players are required to identify and filter several different auditory noises during a game to control, dribble, pass, and shoot the ball, as well as delaying, denying, and dictating opponents' progress towards the goal. In addition, the pitch dimensions require players to utilise auditory feedback from their environment to help navigate themselves around the pitch. These cognitive demands, combined with the internal and external loads due to the high-intensity activities, can cause a rejection of the suggested load or reduction in cognitive resources, resulting in mental fatigue (Fuster et al., 2021). For example, Gantois et al. (2019) found a significant increase in reaction time concerning increased mental fatigue amongst soccer players, along with impairment in decision-making, and thus, performance. Subsequently, Gabbett et al. (2017) argue that, as cognitive load increases or prolongs, it directly influences whether players are physically and/or psychologically prepared to train or compete.

Research has also highlighted that cognitive load impacts perceptual-cognitive mechanics and skills (Mann et al., 2007). Specifically, experts have been found to be better at picking up perceptual cues and managing cognitive load, resulting in more accurate responses (Kelly et al., 2021b) and a reduction in response times (Klatzky et al., 2006), in comparison to non-experts. These findings are observable within blind soccer, as PF players usually take longer to control the ball and make decisions whether to dribble, pass, or shoot, in comparison to senior players. Thus, it is possible to argue that experienced players can solve more complex tasks and draw on previous experience to reduce the demands on the individual's working memory and subsequent cognitive effort (Scharfen & Memmert, 2019).

As discussed earlier, individuals with a congenital visual impairment have been shown to have superior orientational and spatial awareness skills, thus demonstrating a greater ability to pick up on environmental cues and complete tasks (Cattaneo et al., 2007; Houwen et al., 2009). Therefore, these players could be argued to have a superior ability to regulate cognitive load due to having grown up with a lack of visual feedback and being able to draw on greater experiences. More recently, albeit within youth soccer players without disabilities, Cardoso et al. (2021) illustrated a relationship between cognitive effort and tactical behaviour, as training fosters knowledge acquisition that reduces effortful retrieval of information from the long-term memory, leading to improvements in tactical behaviours and lower cognitive load. In addition, Alarcón et al. (2018) found that cognitive load is related to the emotional state, while Plass and Kalyuga (2019) highlighted emotions are seen as extraneous cognitive load that compete for limited resources of working memory. As such, the ability to regulate these emotions could lead to improvements in performance and should therefore be considered as part of a holistic talent development programme.

To help players regulate their emotions and cognitive load, one of the authors of this chapter (Wood et al., 2018) has recently utilised Rational Emotive Behavior Therapy (Ellis, 1957) and the ABC(DE) framework (Ellis & Dryden, 1997). Through utilising educational sessions, international blind soccer players have been taught that the beliefs surrounding certain critical events determine the emotional and behavioural consequences. These sessions attempted to replace existing irrational beliefs with effective and new alternatives, thus seeking to encourage healthy negative emotions and adaptive behaviours. Consequently, to avoid players disproportionately placing greater irrational beliefs and demands on themselves than the situation warrants, it reduced demands on cognitive load (see Turner & Barker, 2014 for an overview). When utilising this approach to explore penalties, for example, researchers found decreases in total irrational beliefs and an increase in the ability to maintain these decreases in irrational beliefs over time, as well as decreases in pre-performance anxiety and large decreases in systolic blood pressure (Wood et al., 2018). These resulted in a large increase in accuracy (i.e., ball direction after contact), a medium increase in power (i.e., the rate at which the ball travelled after the strike), and a large decrease in ball striking (i.e., contact between the player's foot and the ball on striking), which ultimately resulted in improvements in shooting technique (Wood et al., 2018). These findings elucidate some benefits of using Rational Emotive Behavior Therapy and the ABC(DE) framework and offer some intellectual insight into how players could reduce cognitive load through coping with key events, and therefore, could provide valuable tools to support talent development programmes in blind soccer.

Social

With the exclusion of visual cues, the importance of communication (i.e., listening and speaking) is vital in aiding players' performance. Velten et al. (2014) support this suggestion by highlighting auditory perception and how athletes use, organise, and interpret auditory information is crucial for individuals with visual impairments. As such, there is considerable cross-over between the player's communication skills and their ability to create a mental representation of space, thus reducing cognitive load and improving performance in soccer (Land et al., 2013). More specifically to blind soccer, Velten et al. (2014) found players were better at localising peripheral sound tasks than sighted individuals. They also highlighted that auditory events lead individuals to make turning movements towards the stimulus but also found that these movements were more profound in sighed individuals than in blind soccer players. In addition, Velten et al. (2016) reiterated that auditory spatial information must be quickly and accurately perceived to enhance decision making in blind soccer. These thoughts were shared by Mieda et al. (2019), who showed that blind soccer players had shorter auditory reaction times than sighted soccer players. Whilst similar findings have been discovered, the research completed to date has focused on exploring singular sounds in isolation. However, as mentioned previously, blind soccer players are required to process multiple auditory stimuli during games. Subsequently, individuals might choose to listen and process certain voices over others.

The subtlety of human communication means there is scope for misinterpretation, especially due to the lack of visual feedback. When exploring the role of guides in blind sports, Rector et al. (2018) highlighted that individuals sometimes find it difficult to trust the information. Therfore, stakeholders need to establish and maintain strong, trusting relationships with players (Bateman & Jones, 2019; Rhind & Jowett, 2010). However, it is not just the practitioner-player relationships that are important but also the maintenance of the player-player relationships. Due to the often-low participation numbers in central locations, training is generally individualised rather than team-based. Although this potentially allows players to develop technical skills, training on their own may rely on instructions from practitioners rather than developing strong spatial-awareness skills and player-player relationships. Thus, talent identification and development practitioners need to be wary of these implications when identifying talent and continue to challenge players to develop these key fundamental skills.

As individuals are typically training on their own, they are often not developing important on- and off-field group and teamwork skills to perform as a team in games. Individuals who have acquired blindness often withdraw from social activities and can isolate themselves. This observation is supported by Stevelink et al. (2015), who identified similar coping strategies for ex-service personnel when they have lost vision. However, regardless of the timing of their impairment, those who attend a blind school or college are more confident and independent in their day-to-day activities (Roy & Mackay, 2002), which, arguably, transfers to the playing field. This could be due to receiving more specific support in the early years of visual impairment. For instance, Côté (1999) and Dehghansai et al. (2021) highlight several supportive factors, including home and family life, school, and the community, that can influence an athlete's development in sport. As such, practitioners working in youth blind soccer need to consider each individual's circumstances when identifying and developing talent, as every player will have a different support network that will impact them on a case-by-case basis.

Interdisciplinary Considerations

Although this chapter has examined, reflected on, and highlighted key aspects associated with each attribute of the FA's Four Corner Model, it is important to acknowledge how each corner does not exist in isolation but are woven together and all impact talent identification and development outcomes. Specific to blind soccer (and all other para-soccer activities), it is argued each individual's impairment and classification links to everything. For example, if a player is not comfortable and aware of their surroundings due to an inability to orientate themselves, they will not be able to regulate their cognitive load, understand the required distances between their teammates, and reach the necessary speeds needed to evade defenders and prevent opponents' progress towards their own team's goal. However, it is also important to be aware that, due to the relatively low participatory numbers in blind soccer (and wider para-soccer pathways), players are often accelerated throughout talent pathways. Thus, effective support mechanisms need to be in place through individual development plans that seek to support the player from an interdisciplinary perspective. Whilst the International Paralympic Committee currently believe there is no link between classification and timing of impairment, through the initial data that has been presented in this chapter, trends and patterns have emerged that disagree with this sentiment (International Blind Sports Federation, 2022; International Paralympic Committee, 2022). However, further interdisciplinary evidence is required to help support governing body policies and individual development through monitoring progress and informing how specific interventions affect selection and developmental progress.

Considerations for Researchers

Due to the lack of studies on talent identification and development in para-soccer, there are a range of possible future directions for researchers. First, since the utilisation of the B1TTI is very much in its initial stages (see Table 18.2), researchers should aim to work collaboratively with practitioners to evaluate the effectiveness of such tools and optimise their use, tailoring specific aspects to the impairment team. Moreover, further research focused on designing and implementing the application of performance analysis tools (e.g., video and GPS software) is warranted to help improve feedback and aid talent identification and development procedures in para-soccer. From a physical perspective, the repeated sprint test could help better understand players' fatigue index across impairments and increase knowledge surrounding balance, speed, and fatigue. Moreover, in agreement with da Silva et al. (2018), further work evaluating movement patterns during soccer-specific actions would help describe disability-related movement limitations and aid individual development.

The identification and development of psychological characteristics also offers a variety of possible research avenues. For example, para-soccer players who are both athletic and capable are often accelerated through the various pathways and into their respective senior squads. As a result, these individuals can find themselves catapulted into an extreme environment that is completely unfamiliar and often overwhelming. In this regard, cognitive requirements and coping skills are considered crucial for optimal performance. As such, researchers should capture the mechanisms and psychological implications of selection and progression across a variety of impairment-specific soccer talent pathways as well as examine a range of effective interventions (e.g., Rational Emotive Behavior Therapy) to ensure players are supported and prepared for the level they are entering across different timescales (i.e., immediate, short-term, and long-term). From a social outlook, it is evident that para-soccer players experience different social environments when compared to those without disabilities. Capturing the developmental trajectories and experiences of players based on factors such as school attended and age of acquired impairment could help shed light on how to create positive developmental settings. Lastly, in order for future research to be effectively implemented in applied settings, researchers should be conscious of how they explain their samples and methodologies (e.g., age, competition level, gender, nationality, the impairment-specific soccer activity, and using congenital and acquired perspectives) to the reader or end-user so they can draw valid conclusions and make more accurate judgements based on their personal working environment (McAuley et al., 2022).

Considerations for Practitioners

In light of the current evidence within the context of talent identification and development in para-soccer, and in particular blind soccer, the following considerations are proposed for practitioners employed in para-soccer settings:

- Due to the current lack of learning and educational resources, further sharing of knowledge and work between the International Paralympic Committee and impairment-specific governing bodies is required to reduce the 'trial and error approach' that is often adopted to help inform evidence-based practice (Dehghansai et al., 2021; Mycock & Molnar, 2021). This also includes educating practitioners on how the timing of impairment could potentially influence and inform players' readiness to progress within a talent development pathway, as well as how the school type that para-soccer players are attending can impact their opportunities to access such programmes.
- Currently, decisions by talent identification and development practitioners are largely made based on subjective opinions as to whether players are ready or demonstrating 'key' performance behaviours. Thus, practitioners are encouraged to utilise objective data collection tools and methods, such as those that were outlined in this chapter, to help inform practice in blind soccer (and, more generally, para-soccer).

- It is necessary to introduce load-control strategies that include cognitive load in the monitoring cycles of the player. Since further understanding of the interactions between different loads and tasks are required to aid individual training prescriptions and talent development programmes, practitioners should aim to foster player development through educational interventions and support them during transitions between playing levels.
- Practitioners need to be aware of each player's journey to aid their integration into the team environment. Practitioners should also be cautious of how these social environments may be impacted by the often-low participatory numbers when compared to mainstream youth soccer.
- The FA Four Corner Model offers a practitioner-friendly tool to help capture the interdisciplinary characteristics associated with player identification and development. As such, practitioners should consider all four attributes (i.e., technical/tactical, physical, psychological, and social) when designing developmental plans in para-soccer as well as recognise how they are interlinked and are influencing one another.

Conclusion

Talent identification and development practitioners face additional levels of complexity when identifying and developing players within para-soccer, due to the highly individualised biomechanical, medical, physiological, and psychosocial characteristics. Whilst several of the principles that underpin talent identification and development practices in mainstream soccer can be adopted, practitioners need to understand each individual's impairment. Regarding this, the timing of impairment is a key factor related to a players' readiness to enter into talent development programmes. Through using the FA Four Corner Model and focusing on blind soccer, this chapter has aimed to help the reader develop a better understanding of the technical/tactical, physical, psychological, and social demands associated with this impairment-specific sport. Despite this focus, the key messages and recommendations apply to the other impairment-specific teams. It is also important to acknowledge that each impairment-specific para-soccer team and the players that compete comply with the classification system each activity follows and that there are other impairment-specific factors to be considered (e.g., physical, logistical, and equipment barriers). Whilst various research groups (including the authors of this chapter) have begun collecting objective data and information to inform applied practices, further work is required to strengthen awareness and improve guidance and policies through sharing knowledge and creating resources for others to use.

Notes

1 In this chapter, 'disability' is referred to as "the umbrella term for impairments, activity limitations and participation restrictions, referring to the negative aspects of the interaction between an individual (with a health condition), and that individual's contextual factors (environmental and personal factors)", whereas 'impairment' is referred to as "a loss or abnormality in body structure or physiological function (including mental functions)" (World Health Organization, 2013). The word 'para' is a prefix from the Greek meaning of 'alongside'. More recently, para has been used interchangeably with disability, extending beyond sports solely associated with the Paralympic Games. For the purposes of this chapter, para will be used to define all sports that are competed in by individuals who are unable to participate in general sports due to an impairment.
2 Players must have at least one or more of the following impairments to participate in para-soccer: amputee, cerebral palsy, deaf, emotional behavioural difficulties, hard of hearing, moderate learning disability, partially sighted, physical (not able to run), and/or severe learning disability.

References

Alarcón, F., Castillo-Díaz, A., Madinabeitia, I., Castillo-Rodríguez, A., & Cárdenas, D. (2018). La carga mental deteriora la precisión del pase en jugadores de fútbol [Mental load impairs passing accuracy in soccer players]. *Revista de Psicología Del Deporte/Journal of Sport Psychology*, *27*(2), 155–164.

Aquino, R., Munhoz Martins, G. H., Palucci Vieira, L. H., & Menezes, R. P. (2017). Influence of match location, quality of opponents, and match status on movement patterns in Brazilian professional football players. *Journal of Strength and Conditioning Research*, *31*(8), 2155–2161. https://doi.org/10.1519/JSC.0000000000001674

Aquino, R., Vieira, L. H. P., Carling, C., Martins, G. H. M., Alves, I. S., & Puggina, E. F. (2017). Effects of competitive standard, team formation and playing position on match running performance of Brazilian professional soccer players. *International Journal of Performance Analysis in Sport*, *17*(5), 695–705. https://doi.org/10.1080/24748668.2017.1384976

Bateman, M., & Jones, G. (2019). Strategies for maintaining the coach–analyst relationship within professional football utilizing the COMPASS model: The performance analyst's perspective. *Frontiers in Psychology*, *10*(2064), 1–12. https://doi.org/10.3389/fpsyg.2019.02064

Campos, L. F. C. C., Borin, J. P., Nightingale, T., Costa, A. A., Silva, E., Araújo, P. F., & Gorla, J. I. (2014). Alterations of cardiorespiratory and motor profile of paralympic 5-a-side football athletes during 14-week in-season training. *International Journal of Sports Science*, *2014*(6A), 85–90. https://doi.org/10.5923/s.sports.201401.12

Cárdenas, D., Conde-González, J., & Perales, J. (2015). El papel de la carga mental en la planificación del entrenamiento deportivo. *Revista de Psicología Del Deporte*, *24*(1), 91–100. www.redalyc.org/pdf/2351/235139639011.pdf

Cardoso, F. da S. L., García-Calvo, T., Patrick, T., Afonso, J., & Teoldo, I. (2021). How does cognitive effort influence the tactical behavior of soccer players? *Perceptual and Motor Skills*, *128*(2), 851–864. https://doi.org/10.1177/0031512521991405

Castro, K. J. S., Salomaõ, R. C., Feitosa, N. Q., Henriques, L. D., Kleiner, A. F. R., Belgamo, A., Cabral, A. S., Silva, A. A. C. E., Callegari, B., & Souza, G. S. (2021). Changes in plantar load distribution in legally blind subjects. *PLOS One*, *16*(4), e0249467. https://doi.org/10.1371/JOURNAL.PONE.0249467

Cattaneo, Z., Vecchi, T., Monegato, M., Pece, A., & Cornoldi, C. (2007). Effects of late visual impairment on mental representations activated by visual and tactile stimuli. *Brain Research*, *1148*(1), 170–176. https://doi.org/10.1016/J.BRAINRES.2007.02.033

Côté, J. (1999). The influence of the family in the development of talent in sport. *The Sport Psychologist*, *13*, 395–417. https://doi.org/10.1123/tsp.13.4.395

da Silva, E. S., Fischer, G., da Rosa, R. G., Schons, P., Teixeira, L. B. T., Hoogkamer, W., & Peyré-Tartaruga, L. A. (2018). Gait and functionality of individuals with visual impairment who participate in sports. *Gait and Posture*, *62*, 355–358. https://doi.org/10.1016/j.gaitpost.2018.03.049

Deaf International Football Association. (2021). *Rules*. https://difa.org/documents/rules/

Dehghansai, N., Lemez, S., Wattie, N., & Baker, J. (2017a). Training and development of Canadian wheelchair basketball players. *European Journal of Sport Science* *17*(5), 511–518. https://doi.org/10.1080/17461391.2016.1276636

Dehghansai, N., Lemez, S., Wattie, N., Pinder, R. A., & Baker, J. (2020). Understanding the development of elite parasport athletes using a constraint-led approach: Considerations for coaches and practitioners. *Frontiers in Psychology*, *0*, 2612. https://doi.org/10.3389/FPSYG.2020.502981

Dehghansai, N., Pinder, R. A., & Baker, J. (2021). "Looking for a golden needle in the haystack": Perspectives on talent identification and development in paralympic sport. *Frontiers in Sports and Active Living*, *3*, 635977. https://doi.org/10.3389/FSPOR.2021.635977

Dehghansai, N., Wattie, N., & Baker, J. (2017b). A systematic review of influences on development of athletes with disabilities. *Adapted Physical Activity Quarterly*, *34*, 72–90. https://doi.org/10.1123/APAQ.2016-0030

Ellis, A. (1957). Rational psychotherapy and individual psychology. *Journal of Individual Psychology*, *13*(1), 38–44.

Ellis, A., & Dryden, W. (1997). *The practice of rational emotive behavior therapy*. Springer Publishing Co. https://psycnet.apa.org/record/1997-97445-000

English Federation of Disability Sport. (2012). *Active for life: The English federation of disability sport strategy.* www.efds.co.uk

Fédération Internationale de Powerchair Football Association. (2021). *Classification rulebook.* https://fipfa.org/classification/

Ferro, A., Luis Graupera, J., & Vera, P. (2002). Kinematic and kinetic study of running technique at different high speeds in blind Paralympic athletes. *20 International Symposium on Biomechanics in Sports (2002)*, 523–526.

Finocchietti, S., Gori, M., & Souza Oliveira, A. (2019). Kinematic profile of visually impaired football players during specific sports actions. *Scientific Reports, 9*(1), 1–8. https://doi.org/10.1038/s41598-019-47162-z

Fitzpatrick, D., Thompson, P., Kipps, C., & Webborn, N. (2021). Head impact forces in blind football are greater in competition than training and increased cervical strength may reduce impact magnitude. *International Journal of Injury Control and Safety Promotion, 28*(2), 194–200. https://doi.org/10.1080/17457300.2021.1905667

Fuster, J., Caparrós, T., & Capdevila, L. (2021). Evaluation of cognitive load in team sports: literature review. *The Open Access Journal for Life and Environment Research, 9*(12045). https://doi.org/10.7717/PEERJ.12045

Gabbett, T. J., Nassis, G. P., Oetter, E., Pretorius, J., Johnston, N., Medina, D., Rodas, G., Myslinski, T., Howells, D., Beard, A., & Ryan, A. (2017). The athlete monitoring cycle: A practical guide to interpreting and applying training monitoring data. *British Journal of Sports Medicine, 51*(20), 1451–1452. https://doi.org/10.1136/BJSPORTS-2016-097298

Gamonales, J. M., León, K., Rojas-Valverde, D., Sánchez-Ureña, B., & Muñoz-Jiménez, J. (2021). Data mining to select relevant variables influencing external and internal workload of elite blind 5-a-side soccer. *International Journal of Environmental Research and Public Health, 18*(6), 3155. https://doi.org/10.3390/IJERPH18063155

Gamonales, J. M., Muñoz Jiménez, J., León Guzmán, K., & Ibáñez Godoy, S. J. (2018). Efficacy of shots on goal in football for the visually impaired. *International Journal of Performance Analysis in Sport, 18*(3), 393–409. https://doi.org/10.1080/24748668.2018.1475194

Gamonales, J. M., Muñoz Jiménez, J., León Guzmán, K., & Ibáñez Godoy, S. J. (2019). Shooting effectiveness in football 5-a-side for the blind at the 2016 Paralympic Games. *Revista Internacional de Medicina y Ciencias de La Actividad Física y El Deporte, 19*(76), 745–764.

Gantois, P., Ferreira, M. E. C., de Lima-Junior, D., Nakamura, F. Y., Ricarte Batista, G., Fonseca, F. S., & de Sousa Fortes, L. (2019). Effects of mental fatigue on passing decision-making performance in professional soccer athletes. *European Journal of Sport Science, 20*(4), 534–543. https://doi.org/10.1080/17461391.2019.1656781

Houwen, S., Visscher, C., Lemmink, K. A. P. M., & Hartman, E. (2009). Motor skill performance of children and adolescents with visual impairments: A review. *Exceptional Children, 75*(4), 464–492. https://doi.org/10.1177/001440290907500405

International Blind Sports Federation. (2017). *Blind football rulebook 2017–2021.* www.ibsasport.org/sports/files/960-Rules-IBSA-Blind-Football-(B1)-Rulebook-2017-2021.pdf

International Blind Sports Federation. (2018). *Figures show blind football taking off around the globe.* https://ibsasport.org/figures-show-blind-football-taking-off-around-the-globe/

International Blind Sports Federation. (2021). *Blind football rules.* https://blindfootball.sport/about-football/rules-and-downloads/

International Blind Sports Federation. (2022). *Classification rules.* https://ibsasport.org/wp-content/uploads/2020/07/182-1-IBSA-Classification-rules-2018.pdf

International Federation of CP Football. (2021). *About classification.* www.ifcpf.com/about-classification

International Paralympic Committee. (2022). Classification. *International Paralympic Committee.* www.paralympic.org/classification

Kelly, A. L., & Williams, C. A. (2020). Physical characteristics and the talent identification and development processes in male youth soccer: A narrative review. *Strength and Conditioning Journal, 42*(6), 15–34. https://doi.org/10.1519/SSC.0000000000000576

Kelly, A. L., Wilson, M. R., Jackson, D. T., Goldman, D. E., Turnnidge, J., Côté, J., & Williams, C. A. (2021a). A multidisciplinary investigation into "playing-up" in academy football according to age phase. *Journal of Sports Sciences, 39*(8), 854–864. https://doi.org/10.1080/02640414.2020.1848117

Kelly, A. L., Wilson, M. R., Jackson, D. T., Turnnidge, J., & Williams, C. A. (2021b). Speed of thought and speed of feet: Examining perceptual-cognitive expertise and physical performance in and English football academy. *Journal of Science in Sport and Exercise, 3*, 88–97. https://doi.org/10.1007/s42978-020-00081-2

Kelly, A. L., Wilson, M. R., & Williams, C. A. (2018). Developing a football-specific talent identification and development profiling concept—The Locking Wheel Nut Model. *Applied Coaching Research Journal, 2*(1), 32–41.

Kent, F. A. (2021). *Project B1 CPD session held with university of kent students.* www.kentfa.com/news/2021/oct/19/project-b1-cpd-session-held-with-university-of-kent-students

Klatzky, R. L., Marston, J. R., Giudice, N. A., Golledge, R. G., & Loomis, J. M. (2006). Cognitive load of navigating without vision when guided by virtual sound versus spatial language. *Journal of Experimental Psychology: Applied, 12*(4), 223–232. https://doi.org/10.1037/1076-898X.12.4.223

Laird, P., & Waters, L. (2008). Eyewitness recollection of sport coaches. *International Journal of Performance Analysis in Sport, 8*(1), 76–84. https://doi.org/10.1080/24748668.2008.11868424

Land, W. M., Volchenkov, D., Bläsing, B. E., & Schack, T. (2013). From action representation to action execution: Exploring the links between cognitive and biomechanical levels of motor control. *Frontiers in Computational Neuroscience*, 127. https://doi.org/10.3389/FNCOM.2013.00127/BIBTEX

Lemez, S., Wattie, N., Dehghansai, N., & Baker, J. (2020). Developmental pathways of Para athletes. *Current Issues in Sport Science (CISS), 5*, 2. https://doi.org/10.15203/CISS_2020.002

Levtzion-Korach, O., Tennenbaum, A., Schnitzer, R., & Ornoy, A. (2000). Early motor development of blind children. *Journal of Paediatrics and Child Health, 36*(3), 226–229. https://doi.org/10.1046/J.1440-1754.2000.00501.X

Magno, M., Morato, M., Bilzon, J., & Duarte, E. (2013). Sports injuries in Brazilian blind footballers. *International Journal of Sports Medicine, 34*(3), 239–243. https://doi.org/10.1055/s-0032-1316358

Mallo, J., Mena, E., Nevado, F., & Paredes, V. (2015). Physical demands of top-class soccer friendly matches in relation to a playing position using global positioning system technology. *Journal of Human Kinetics, 47*, 179–188. https://doi.org/10.1515/hukin-2015-0073

Mann, D. T. Y., Williams, A. M., Ward, P., & Janelle, C. (2007). Perceptual-cognitive expertise in sport: A meta-analysis. *Journal of Sport and Exercise Psychology, 29*, 457–478. https://doi.org/10.1123/jsep.29.4.457

Martin, J. (2012). Coping and emotion in disability sport. In J. Thatcher, M. Jones, & D. Lavallee (Eds.), *Coping and Emotion in Sport* (pp. 194–212). Routledge. https://psycnet.apa.org/record/2015-15809-009

McAuley, A. B. T., Baker, J., & Kelly, A. L. (2022). Defining "elite" status in sport: From chaos to clarity. *German Journal of Exercise and Sport Research, 52*, 193–197. https://doi.org/10.1007/s12662-021-00737-3

Mieda, T., & Kokubu, M. (2020). Blind footballers direct their head towards an approaching ball during ball trapping. *Scientific Reports 2020, 10*(1), 1–12. https://doi.org/10.1038/s41598-020-77049-3

Mieda, T., Kokubu, M., & Saito, M. (2019). Rapid identification of sound direction in blind footballers. *Experimental Brain Research, 237*(12), 3221–3231. https://doi.org/10.1007/S00221-019-05670-4/FIGURES/5

Mycock, D., & Molnar, G. (2021). 'The blind leading the blind'—A reflection on coaching blind football. *European Journal of Adapted Physical Activity*, 1–13.

Newell, K. M. (1986). Constraints of the development of coordination. In M. Wade & H. Whiting (Eds.), *Motor development in children: Aspects of coordination and control* (pp. 341–360). Martinus Nijhoff.

Parreira, R. B., Grecco, L. A. C., & Oliveira, C. S. (2017). Postural control in blind individuals: A systematic review. *Gait & Posture, 57*, 161–167. https://doi.org/10.1016/J.GAITPOST.2017.06.008

Pastor, D., Campayo-Piernas, M., Tadeo, J., & Reina, R. (2019). A mathematical model for decision-making in the classification of para-footballers with different severity of coordination impairments. *Journal of Sports Sciences, 37*, 1403–1410. https://doi.org/10.1080/02640414.2018.1560617

Plass, J. L., & Kalyuga, S. (2019). Four ways of considering emotion in cognitive load theory. *Educational Psychology Review, 31*(2), 339–359. https://doi.org/10.1007/S10648-019-09473-5/FIGURES/1

Rector, K., Bartlett, R., & Mullan, S. (2018). Exploring aural and haptic feedback for visually impaired people on a track: A Wizard of Oz study. *ASSETS, 18*, 295–306. https://doi.org/10.1145/3234695.3236345

Rhind, D., & Jowett, S. (2010). Relationship maintenance strategies in the coach-athlete relationship: The development of the COMPASS model. *Journal of Applied Sport Psychology*, *22*(1), 106–121. https://doi.org/10.1080/10413200903474472

Roy, A. W. N., & Mackay, G. F. (2002). Self-perception and locus of control in visually impaired college students with different types of vision loss. *Journal of Visual Impairment and Blindness*, *96*(4), 254–266.

Royal National Institute of Blind People. (2021). *Choosing a school*. www.rnib.org.uk/information-everyday-living-education-and-learning-young-childrens-education/choosing-school

Runswick, O. R., Ravensbergen, R. H. J. C., Allen, P. M., & Mann, D. L. (2021a). Expert opinion on classification for footballers with vision impairment: Towards evidence-based minimum impairment criteria. *Journal of Sports Sciences*, *39*(S1), 30–39. https://doi.org/10.1080/02640414.2021.1881301

Runswick, O. R., Rawlinson, A., Datson, N., & Allen, P. M. (2021b). A valid and reliable test of technical skill for vision impaired football. *Science and Medicine in Football*, *6*(1), 89–97. https://doi.org/10.1080/24733938.2021.1885725

Scharfen, H. E., & Memmert, D. (2019). The relationship between cognitive functions and sport-specific motor skills in elite youth soccer players. *Frontiers in Psychology*, *10*, 817. https://doi.org/10.3389/FPSYG.2019.00817/BIBTEX

Simmons, C. (2004). Fast tracking and player development. *Insight*, *3*(7), 24–25.

Souza, R. P., Alves, J. M. V. M., Gorla, J. I., Novaes, G., Cabral, S. I. C., Neves, E. B., & Nogueira, C. D. (2016). Characterization of the intensity of effort of blind athletes from the Brazilian football 5-a-side national team. *Journal of Health & Biological Sciences*, *4*(4), 218. https://doi.org/10.12662/2317-3076jhbs.v4i4.715.p218-226.2016

Stevelink, S. A. M., Malcolm, E. M., & Fear, N. T. (2015). Visual impairment, coping strategies and impact on daily life: A qualitative study among working-age UK ex-service personnel. *BMC Public Health*, *15*(1), 1–7. https://doi.org/10.1186/S12889-015-2455-1/PEER-REVIEW

Taylor, J., Wright, A. A., Dischiavi, S., & Townsend, A. (2017). Activity demands during multi-directional team sports: A systematic review. *Sports Medicine*, *47*, 2533–2551. https://doi.org/10.1007/s40279-017-0772-5

The Football Association. (2019). *The four corner model*. https://thebootroom.thefa.com/resources/coaching/the-fas-4-corner-model

Towlson, C., Cope, E., Perry, J. L., Court, D., & Levett, N. (2019). Practitioners' multi-disciplinary perspectives of soccer talent according to phase of development and playing position. *International Journal of Sports Science & Coaching*, *14*(4), 528–540. https://doi.org/10.1177/1747954119845061

Turner, M. J., & Barker, J. B. (2014). Using rational emotive behavior therapy with athletes. *The Sport Psychologist*, *28*(1), 75–90. https://doi.org/10.1123/TSP.2013-0012

Velten, M. C. C., Ugrinowitsch, H., Portes, L. L., Hermann, T., & Bläsing, B. (2014). Cognitive representation of auditory space in blind football experts. *Psychology of Sport and Exercise*, *15*, 441–445. https://doi.org/10.1016/j.psychsport.2014.04.010

Velten, M. C. C., Ugrinowitsch, H., Portes, L. L., Hermann, T., & Bläsing, B. (2016). Auditory spatial concepts in blind football experts. *Psychology of Sport and Exercise*, *22*, 218–228. https://doi.org/10.1016/j.psychsport.2015.08.010

Wood, A., Barker, J., Turner, M., & Thomson, P. (2018). Exploring the effects of a single rational emotive behavior therapy workshop in elite blind soccer players. *Sport Psychologist*, *32*(4), 321–332. https://doi.org/10.1123/tsp.2017-0122

World Amputee Football. (2021). *Rules page*. www.worldamputeefootball.org/rules_i.htm

World Health Organization. (2013). *How to use the ICF: A practical manual for using the International Classification of Functioning, Disability and Health (ICF)*. https://cdn.who.int/media/docs/default-source/classification/icf/drafticfpracticalmanual2.pdf?sfvrsn=8a214b01_4

World Intellectual Impairment Sport. (2021). *Football sport specification*. www.virtus.sport/wp-content/uploads/2020/11/7.5-Sport-_-Virtus-Championship-Specification-Football-2020.doc.pdf

19
THE GOALKEEPER

Highlighting the Position Data Gap in Talent Identification and Development

Durva Vahia and Adam L. Kelly

Introduction

Although goalkeepers (GKs) are an integral part of a soccer team, they require a diverse skill set when compared to their outfield teammates. Goalkeepers are involved in low-intensity actions, including walking, jogging, and backpedalling, that are interspersed with high-intensity actions, such as diving, shot stopping, and 1 vs. 1s. Due to the actions that they perform and their position-specific requirements, the profile of a GK needs to be versatile. As such, they are often discarded during talent identification and development research in youth soccer due to the different methodological approaches that are needed to capture their specialist demands.

To help better understand the demands and requirements of the GK, this chapter analyses GKs through three main sub-topics: (a) talent identification, with a specific focus on anthropometric measures and relative age, fitness profiling, match demands, and skills testing, (b) talent development, with a specific focus on training load and training methods, and (c) performance tracking, with a specific focus on contextual factors (i.e., home vs. away, competition level, match outcome, offensive and defensive action, and minute of the match) during senior competitive match-play to help better understand the match demands on GKs, which may potentially inform youth development strategies. Following these three areas, the chapter offers considerations focused on the current research and practices for GKs.

Talent Identification

Talent identification has become central to youth academies procedures, with sport science leading the search to help identify metrics that may predict future success (Roberts et al., 2019). As an example, quarterly measurements of anthropometric (e.g., height, body mass) and physical (e.g., agility, endurance, power, speed) parameters are routine in many youth soccer settings to monitor individual growth and maturation status and support athletic development (Towlson et al., 2017). To combat maturity selection biases (Castillo et al., 2020a), monitoring growth and maturation, often through the prediction of adult height to identify individual's biological age, are becoming more common within academy structures (e.g., Till et al., 2020; see Chapter 4).

DOI: 10.4324/9781032232799-19

Moreover, organisations are becoming increasingly aware of relative age effects (RAEs) (Castillo et al., 2020a), and thus, are observing birthdates and incorporating a range of strategies to try and moderate these during their selection processes (e.g., Mann & van Ginneken, 2017; see Chapter 10). Using this data, age-appropriate training methods have been adopted to encourage long-term athletic development (Llyod & Oliver, 2012; Malina et al., 2005). However, due to the specialist demands for GKs, the transference between outfield player pathways and GKs is limited, and unfortunately, the current talent identification research is predominantly based on outfield players. Indeed, only a few studies have analysed the physical, technical, and tactical requirements of youth GKs and the selection criteria.

Anthropometric Measures and Relative Age

Studies analysing the anthropometric measures of youth male GKs (Gil et al., 2014; Tahara et al., 2006; Wong et al., 2009) and adult male GKs (Ziv & Lidor, 2011; Sporis et al., 2009) found that they were, on average, taller, heavier, and had higher fat percentages than their outfield peers. Specifically, adult GKs were roughly between 180 and 190 cm in height and had a body mass between 77 and 89 kg (Perez-Arroniz et al., 2022; Ziv & Lidor, 2011). For youth GKs between the ages of 16 and 19 years, it was observed that their heights range between 175 and 187 cm and body mass between 69 and 83 kg (Perez-Arroniz et. Al., 2022). This supports the notion that a taller and larger GK will be able to cover more distance across the goal as well as generally being taller and heavier than their outfield peers (Hoxha et al., 2020). As an example, in a study on first and second division leagues in England (Davis et al., 1992), GKs were found to be heavier (86.1 ± 5.5 kg) than forwards (76.4 ± 7.2 kg), full-backs (75.4 ± 4.6 kg), and midfielders (73.2 ± 4.8 kg). This trend was also observed in Croatia, with senior male professional GKs being 3 cm taller and 4 kg heavier than forwards and midfielders (Matković et al., 2003).

Potentially due to the physiological prerequisites of adult GKs, these trends persist in youth soccer. For instance, Gil et al. (2014) found that youth GKs as young as aged 9–10 years were heavier (38.13 ± 3.72 kg) than outfield players (32.96 ± 4.28 kg), taller (143.44 ± 5.35 cm) than outfield players (139.16 ± 5.44 cm), and had higher body fat percentage (11.30 ± 1.35%) than outfield players (9.84 ± 1.25%). This study also found that more mature GKs, with age at peak height velocity (APHV) of 13.51 ± 0.22 years, were selected ahead of their less mature competitors (APHV 13.62 ± 0.25 years). In addition, Gil et al. (2014) showed GKs were more mature (78.34 ± 1.22% of predicted adult height attained [PAHA]) than outfield players (77.5 ± 1.45% PAHA), which has been supported by other studies on youth players (Di Credico et al., 2020; Souza et al., 2020; Ziv & Lidor, 2011). Although evidence suggests that GKs are selected based on their advanced maturity, there is no evidence to show this early advantage results in success at a senior level. As such, it's plausible to suggest that the selection of mature GKs could lead to a potential loss of talent from those who are later maturing. Therefore, it is imperative that stakeholders are aware of this selection bias and create more appropriate environments for GKs of different maturity to be identified and developed.

Studies on senior teams have also shown that relative age effects (RAEs) are a persistent phenomenon among GKs (e.g., Padrón-Cabo et al., 2016; Salinero et al., 2013; Yagüe et al., 2018). For instance, Souza et al. (2020) found that 64.1% of female GKs were born in birth quarter one (BQ1) (i.e., born in the first 3 months of the 12-month selection year) and BQ2, although the findings were not statistically significant. Moreover, Yagüe et al. (2018) found that when comparing BQ1 and BQ2 against BQ3 and BQ4, 58.2% of male GKs in the top-10 European leagues were born in the first half of the year, which was also more than defenders (56.7%), midfielders (58.8%), and forwards (54.8%). However, potentially due to small sample sizes when compared to outfield positions, positional relative age research is limited and remains inconclusive amongst youth level GKs (Jiménez et al., 2008; Souza et al., 202). In a preliminary study on U17–U21 Spanish players, Jiménez et al. (2008) found that, although RAEs were present across all youth age groups, no impact of playing position on RAEs were found in any age group.

Since GKs generally reach peak performance after the age of 20 years (Salinero et al., 2013; Souza et al., 2020), it is vital to consider their long-term potential rather than immediate and/or short-term performance levels during youth competition. As such, the dynamic nature of both maturity status and relative age must be considered when recruiting and developing GKs, as selection based on early maturity and/or relatively older age may lead to identity foreclosure and a loss of potential talent in the long-term (Kelly & Williams, 2020). It is also important to recognise maturation and relative age as two different constructs, since relative age can create differences of up to 1 year within an annual age group, whereas there can be up to 5-to-6 years' difference in biological age in an annual age group (Eisenmann et al., 2020; Malina et al., 2019; Moore et al., 2020). Thus, stakeholders working with GKs should consider relevant strategies to negate these possible biases during talent identification procedures.

Fitness Profiling

Goalkeepers have consistently showed lower VO_2 max values, compared to all other positions, from youth to senior levels (Gil et al., 2014; Slimani et al., 2019; Tahara et al., 2006; Ziv & Lidor, 2011). At senior level, a review from Perez-Arroniz et al. (2022) revealed adult GKs VO_2 max values ranged from 50 and 57 mL $O_2 \cdot kg^{-1} \cdot min^{-1}$ when measured through various different methods (e.g., Yo-Yo tests, repeated sprints, and maximal 1-minute incremental tests). At youth level, a study on male Spanish GKs found that GKs aged 14 to 21 years had VO_2 max values of 48.41 ± 11.10 mL $O_2 \cdot kg^{-1} \cdot min^{-1}$, which was significantly lower than the values for outfield players who ranged from 57.7 to 62.4 mL $O_2 \cdot kg^{-1} \cdot min^{-1}$ (Gil et al., 2007). Tahara et al. (2006) displayed similar findings for GKs aged between 15 and 18 years from a school in Japan, where analysis of percentiles of VO_2 max indicated that 25% of GKs had a VO_2 max lower than that for a soccer player of any other position, whilst 10% showed values lower than that recommended for sedentary men (Gil et al., 2014; Ziv & Lidor, 2011). In contrast, however, Wong et al. (2009) found no difference in youth GKs and outfield players when comparing VO_2 max levels. Although, this is could be due to the fact that the players analysed were under the age of 14 years (13.2 ± 0.95 years), which were younger than those analysed by Gil et al. (2014) (aged 14.5 ± 21.5 years) and Tahara et al. (2006) (aged 16.8 ± 1.1 years). Specifically, the differences in age could have created a high variance of maturity-related physical developments in aerobic capacity, which typically occur between the ages of 11 to 16 years in males and 10 to 15 years in females (Pichardo et al., 2018). Thus, when fitness profiling potential goalkeeping talent in youth soccer, it is important to base results on biological age rather than chronological age as well as consider the implications of gender that may require different approaches (Lloyd & Oliver, 2012; Malina et al., 2019).

Studies on GKs sprint speed, repeated sprint ability (RSA), agility, and power, compared to other positions, have produced mixed results. At senior professional level, for instance, Aziz et al. (2008) found that, although male GKs (aged 24.3 ± 5.6 years) sprint speed was comparable to outfield players, they had a lower RSA, which is potentially due to lower VO_2 max values. However, in contrast, Sporis et al. (2009) found that adult male professional GKS in

Croatia were the slowest in 10 m and 20 m sprints when compared to other positions. Similarly, in a study on amateur players in Turkey (aged 20.95 ± 3.8 years), Kaplan (2010) found that GKs performed the poorest in RSA when compared to other positions. At youth level, Rebelo-González-Víllora et al. (2015) found no difference in RSA in U17 and U19 elite youth GKs in Portugal. Conversely, however, Wong et al. (2009) found that Hong Kong youth GKs (aged 12.2 to 14.1 years) were faster than defenders and forwards in the 10 m sprint but the slowest in the 30 m sprint. With regards to agility, Gil et al. (2014) showed that youth GKs assessed by a 30 m zig-zag test had poorer timings compared to forwards, although they were comparable to other positions. Moreover, in a study on Slovakian youth GKs, Obetko et al. (2019) found that GKs who performed better on agility test had 20% quicker reaction time, though the effect was not statistically significant.

Results on lower body power also show inconclusive findings. Perez-Arroniz et al. (2022) found that professional GKs jumped between 35 and 46 cm in squat jumps (SJ) and between 35 and 48 cm in countermovement jumps (CMJs). They also found lower scores for youth GKs between the ages of 16 and 19 years, with SJ scores ranging between 30 and 41 cm and CMJ scores ranging between 32 and 42 cm. Despite the majority of studies suggesting adult GKs have better vertical jump (VJ) and CMJ compared to outfield players (Sporis et al., 2009; Ziv & Lidor, 2011), Wong et al. (2009) found that youth GKs in Hong Kong had CMJ scores comparable to outfield players. Research has also found that GKs have better leg extensor strength (Ziv & Lidor, 2011) and higher values for eccentric and concentric strength of quadriceps, hamstrings, and hip abductors and adductors (Perez-Arroniz et al., 2022), although the limited transference between leg extensor strength and VJ could be accounted for by the fact that GKs have higher fat mass. Moving forward, it is important that researchers and practitioners capture longitudinal fitness testing data in youth GKs, in order to create benchmarks for potential talent (based on maturity status rather than chronological age). The batch of fitness tests that are used specifically for GKs should also be customised to replicate their position-specific needs and match demands.

Match Demands

Movement patterns of GKs during a match are mostly low-intensity actions, such as walking and jogging. These are interspersed with high-intensity actions, including changes of direction, sprints, dives, and tackles. Hoxha et al. (2020) showed that adult GKs who performed better in explosive actions like acceleration, speed, and reaction time also performed better in matches, as measured by coaches' assessment and goals conceded. Although GKs are required to perform multiple explosive actions in a game, these are generally followed by long periods of recovery, comprised of low-intensity actions. This might reflect why adult GKs can perform at a high level with low VO_2 max values. More specifically, Ziv and Lidor (2011) showed how GKs covered 5,611 ± 613 m during a game, which was mostly completed by walking (4,025 ± 440 m) and jogging (1,223 ± 256 m), with only a small portion covered during running (221 ± 90 m), high-speed running (56 ± 34 m), and sprinting (11 ± 12 m), of which most sprints covered a distance of less than 10 m. Moreover, very few studies consider high-intensity actions, such as clearing, shot stopping, controlling, and saving (Ziv & Lidor, 2011). This supports the need for talent identification processes that appropriately reflect the match demands of the GK. For example, the 10 m sprint test, diving tests, jump and/or explosive power tests, the 505-agility test, and reaction time tests more accurately reflect the match demands of GKs and thus would be suited for talent identification procedures in GKs.

Skills Testing

It is vital to capture a holistic perspective of potential talent during the talent identification process. Thus, the technical and tactical skills of goalkeepers should be considered in addition to their physiological profile. Preliminary research has shown GKs performed poorer than outfield players in dribbling and passing tests (Rebelo-Gonçalves et al., 2015). However, it is important to remember that GKs are selected for different technical skills compared to outfield players (Rebelo-Gonçalves et al., 2015; Ziv & Lidor, 2011). Wong et al. (2009) found that GKs covered less distance (1,293 ± 153 m) than midfielders (2,283 ± 780 m), forwards (1,395 ± 153 m), and defenders (1,393 ± 4 m) in the Hoff dribbling test, although GKs appear to often be omitted from research on skills testing and, therefore, additional research is required to quantify the differences in performance during skills tests between GKs and outfield players. Moreover, researchers are encouraged to design valid and reliable GK-specific skills tests that can be used in talent identification environments to compliment a holistic profile.

As summarised in Table 19.1, talent identification methods for GKs are susceptible to maturation and relative age biases. Moreover, fitness and skills tests are often replicated from outfield players, thereby making it difficult to assess GK-specific physical, technical, and tactical characteristics during talent identification. Overall, improved assessment and selection methods are crucial to better understand the markers of potential and specific match demands for youth GKs.

Talent Development

While there is abundant research on training approaches and its impact on outfield players' output, little is known about GKs training load and training methods. For example, small-sided games have become an increasingly popular training method during talent development due to their versatility and variability on training loads. Whilst it is well understood that the manipulation of time and space during small-sided games can influence the training load in outfield players (Castillo et al., 2020a; Harrison et al., 2015; Jara et al., 2019), the impact is under-analysed in GKs. Without an accurate understanding of the internal and external load of GKs during training and matches, it is difficult to appropriately periodise GK training.

Training Load

Monitoring individual training load has become commonplace in youth and adult soccer to facilitate the periodisation of training programmes. While training load on outfield players and GKs varies significantly due to the variable positional demands, limited evidence exists for normative training load values for GKs. As an example, Babic et al. (2018) found that youth Slovakian GKs (aged 16.5 + 0.6 years) reached a HRavg of 130 ± 5 beats per minute during warm-up and preparatory drills, whilst they reached a HRavg of 156 ± 9 beats per minute during small-sided games. However, the physiological demands of different drills and training sessions are not well understood. Studies of adult professional male GKs found that they cover between 4 to 7 km during training sessions and games (Malone et al., 2018; Perez-Arroniz et al., 2022), whereas outfield players cover between 10 and 14 km (Anderson et al., 2016). Moreover, adult professional GKs complete about 17% of the high-speed distances covered by outfield players (Malone et al., 2018).

For 90-minute matches, adult professional GKs walked for 68–73% of the duration and spent only 0.8–2% of the time engaged in high-intensity actions (Kubayi & Larkin, 2020; Otte et al.,

TABLE 19.1 Summary of talent identification literature for GKs

Reference	Study Design	N	Age	Playing Level	Determinants of Performance	Major Findings
Di Credico et al. (2020)	Observational	42 GKs (male); pre-PHV: 12, circa-PHV: 14, post-PHV: 16	12–16 years	Regional league in Tuscany.	• Anthropometric measures and maturation data (i.e., standing height, sitting height, weight, BMI, body fat percentage, and age at PHV).	• GKs had an unhealthy body composition with the circa-PHV group showing the worst values. • No Relative age effect found in selection of GKs.
Souza et al. (2020)	Observational	107 GKs (68 male, 39 female)	Males: 27.85 ± 5.65 years; Females: 25.9 ± 3.9	A Series, Brazilian Football Championship.	• Date of birth (i.e., birth quarter).	• Relative age effect present in GK selection, although not statistically significant.
Rebelo-Gonçalves et al. (2015)	Mixed longitudinal study	71 GKs (male) and 74 outfield players	11–19 years	Coimbra Youth Soccer Project.	• Anthropometric measures and maturation data (i.e., stature, body mass, fat-free mass, fat mass, biological maturation via Khamis and Roche equation, and chronological age). • Physical performance (i.e., repeated sprint ability, CMJ, aerobic capacity, and agility). • Soccer-specific tests (i.e., ball control, dribbling speed, shooting accuracy, and passing). • Goal orientation (i.e., task orientation and ego orientation).	• Goalkeepers had higher values for fat tissue than outfield players (i.e., U13 and U15: 8.6 ± 5.3 vs. 6.0 ± 4.1; U17 and U19: 12.2 ± 4.8 vs. 9.5 ± 4.9). • No difference in RSA between U17 and U19. • No difference in CMJ for GKs across age groups. • Outfield players have better physiological and skill test performance compared to GKs across all age groups. • The battery of predictor variables was able to correctly predict 100% of GKs and outfield players based on body composition and manipulative skills.

(*Continued*)

TABLE 19.1 (Continued)

Reference	Study Design	N	Age	Playing Level	Determinants of Performance	Major Findings
Gil et al. (2014)	Mixed longitudinal study	10 GKs (male) out of 64 players	9–10 years	County League, Spain.	• Anthropometric measures and maturation data (height, sitting height, body weight, body fat, maturity offset, APHV, PAH, and %PAHA). • Physical performance (i.e., 30 m sprint, slalom agility test, yo-yo IR1, CMJ, and handgrip strength). • Hormones (i.e., testosterone and dehydroepiandrosterone).	• Selected GKs were significantly older, more mature, and had higher predicted adult height than outfield players and non-selected GKs. • Selected GKs were taller, heavier, and had more fat than outfield players and non-selected GKs. • Selected GKs performed better in 30 m sprints and handgrip strength test but poorer in the agility test, CMJ, and yo-yo IR 1 than non-selected players.
Ziv and Lidor (2011)	Literature review	23 studies	20 studies with adults and 3 studies with adolescents (overall age range of 12.2 years to 21.5 years)	Adults: playing in professional leagues across Croatia, Cyprus, Kuwait, England, Turkey, Spain, France, Germany, Iceland, and Italy. Adolescents: highest level of regional youth leagues in Japan, Hong Kong, and Spain.	• Physical characteristics: Anthropometric measures- height, weight, body fat, fat free mass. • Physiological Attributes: Aerobic profile- VO_2 max, Agility and speed- agility, sprint test, and repeated sprint test, Power and strength- CMJ, squat jump, leg extensor, and isokinetic knee extension and flexion). • On-field performance: game metrics- GPS and video analysis.	• Professional adult GKs are usually over 180 cm tall and have a body mass of over 77 kg. • Studies on agility and speed produced mixed results, with some showing similar values between GKs and outfield players and others showing reduced performance in GKs. • Goalkeepers usually have higher vertical jump values when compared with players playing the various field positions. • Goalkeepers cover approximately 5.5 km during a game, mostly by walking and jogging.

| Wong et al. (2009) | Cross-sectional | 70 | 12.2–14.1 years (male) | Highest level (regional) of competition for U14 teams in Hong Kong. | • Anthropometric measures (i.e., height, body mass, fat-free mass, and fat mass).
• Physical performance (i.e., vertical jump, 10 m sprint, 30m sprint, and yo-yo Intermittent Endurance Run).
• Skills tests (i.e., Hoff dribble tests and ball shooting speed). | • Goalkeepers covered less distance than midfielders in the Hoff dribble test.
• Goalkeepers were faster than defenders and forwards in 10 m sprint
• Goalkeepers were slowest in 30 m sprint. |

2020a). This accounts for between 67 to 346 m of high-intensity distance (Perez-Arroniz et. al, 2022) as well as about ten high-speed runs (between 19.9 and 25.2 km/h) and two sprints (>25.2 km/h) of less than 10 m (Kubayi, 2020). White et al. (2020) also found that adult professional male GKs perform more dives (~51 vs. ~10), high-speed changes of direction (~34 vs. ~8), high (~14 vs. ~1) and medium (~19 vs. ~7) jumps, and explosive efforts (~70 vs. ~16) during a ~79-minute goalkeeping-training session when compared to a 90-minute match. These findings suggest that training sessions potentially elicit a higher load on GKs than matches. While these results quantify training load for GKs, only three studies (Babic et al., 2018; Jara et al., 2019; White et al., 2020) have focused on youth GKs. Therefore, further research is needed to understand baselines for youth GKs to support talent development processes.

Micro-cycle periodisation is created relative to the match-day (MD), which is assumed to be the highest training load of the week, and therefore, training weeks are planned to allow players to be at their physical peaking on MD. However, as discussed previously, GKs have a higher load during GK training sessions than MDs; thus, it is important to assess the micro-cycle load on GKs to create better training programmes. When assessing micro-cycle load on GKs during a case study on a professional 21-year-old male GK, Malone et al. (2018) reported increases in the number of high-intensity (> 3 m·s^{-2}) accelerations and decelerations performed on MD-4 when compared with the MD itself. They also found that total wellness scores had minimal variations across the week, with the lowest values on MD+1 and MD-4 (i.e., the day after a match and within 2 days of the next match, respectively). This implies that GKs may not fully recover by the start of the next training week. This also suggests that micro-cycle loading of GKs cannot be the same as outfield players, since days of peak load and recovery vary considerably. Another implication could be the lack of GK-specific methods used to quantify and assess training load. Since GKs are usually confined to the team's defending third, the total distance and other volume metrics covered by them will subsequently be low. Goalkeeper-specific actions, such as dives, recovery saves, 1 vs. 1s, and shot-stopping, should be quantified and monitored to gather a more accurate measure of their load.

Since research on training load on youth GKs is limited, further GK-specific training load assessment is required to identify accurate load of GK-specific actions and GK training sessions. The aforementioned data can be useful as a reference point to plan a micro-cycle attuned to GK load requirements relative to the team.

Training Methods

While the research is limited, there is a clear indication that the impact of training sessions varies between GKs and outfield players. For example, technical sessions like passing, 1 vs. 1s, shooting, and finishing, or tactical sessions like zonal defending, high-press, and build-up play, will have different training outcomes for GKs and outfield players (Jara et al., 2019). While matches elicit the greatest demands of any activity performed by outfield players throughout a competitive week, this was not the case for adult professional GKs when assessed by position-specific performance metrics, such as dives, high-speed distances, explosive efforts, and changes of direction (White et al., 2020). Training sessions elicit higher repetitions of these GK-specific actions and therefore induce a higher training load. While this is not known for youth goalkeepers, this evidence suggests that practitioners working with young GKs should be cautious of their diverse training loads when compared to outfield players and ensure methods are adapted appropriately. As an example, during a case study on U23 GKs playing in the Bundesliga, Otte et al. (2020b) found that 38.8% of training minutes was focused on basic technique, 28.1% on distribution, 15.8% on 1 vs. 1 technique, 9.8% on crosses and interventions, and 7.4% on diving.

Adult professional GKs experience different physical demands compared to outfield players based on training methods across a micro-cycle as well as during a match (Malone et al., 2018; Rowell et al., 2018; White et al., 2020). Training sessions incorporating small-sided games (SSGs) are often used by practitioners to provide a match-specific physical conditioning stimulus for outfield players (Castillo et al., 2020a; Harrison et al., 2015; Martin-Garcia et al., 2019; Rowell et al., 2018). However, due to the positional demands, the stimulus on GKs considerably varies. For example, White et al. (2020) found that adult male professional GKs perform fewer dives (~5 vs. ~10 to ~51) and explosive efforts (~8 vs. ~16 to ~70) during SSGs compared to matches and GK training sessions.

Small-sided games also provide opportunities for GKs to develop technical and tactical skills. For instance, White et al. (2020) found that GK-specific sessions and shooting-based sessions had the highest number of high-intensity actions, including explosive efforts, dives, jumps, and high-speed changes of direction. Jara et al. (2018) showed that in smaller SSGs (size 32 m × 23 m), technical actions and physical involvement of adult male GKs were higher, compared to medium (50 m × 35 m) and larger (62 m × 44 m) SSGs. They also revealed no significant differences in intensities between larger (62 m × 44 m) and medium (50 m × 35 m) SSGs, whilst both showed lower intensities when compared to smaller (32 m × 32 m) SSGs. In addition, the authors highlighted that larger SSGs increased the spatial awareness and pitch exploration in GKs, indicating a higher tactical demand, whilst GKs completed more 1 vs. 1 situations, long passes, and distributions on a larger pitch, whereas they had more block saves and passes with hand or foot on a smaller pitch (Jara et al., 2018). Another study on SSGs found that the reduction in field size, number of players, and goal size resulted in U12 GKs completing more offensive and defensive actions during 5 vs. 5 when compared to 8 vs. 8 (Ortega-Toro et al., 2018). Taken together, these findings suggest that excessive reduction in field size (less than 100 m^2 per player) increases the physical intensity as well as technical and tactical demands for senior GKs; however, a reduction of field size from 314 m^2 per player to 190 m^2 per player has a positive impact in player engagement for youth GKs (Ortega-Toro et al., 2018).

These studies, summarised in Table 19.2, highlight that different training methods, pitch sizes, and number of players per m^2 will impact the training outcome for GKs. Therefore, practitioners can use these findings to design training sessions specific to the developmental needs of the GKs. For instance, the variation in intensity and load between the different training sessions and smaller to larger SSGs can be used to design the micro-cycle for GK training, with smaller games (32 m × 32 m) on higher load days and larger games (62 m × 44 m) on lower load days recommended. As another example, GKs who need to improve their technical skills may benefit from training sessions including 5 vs. 5 SSGs, whereas GKs who need to improve their tactical awareness and game understanding may benefit from larger small-sided games.

Performance Tracking

It is well understood that soccer performance is influenced by a variety of factors, such as home vs. away, competition level, match outcome, offensive and defensive actions, and minute of the match. The purpose of this section is to analyse the impact of these factors on GK performance.

TABLE 19.2 Summary of talent development literature for GKs

Authors	Study Design	N	Age	Playing Level	Determinants of Performance	Major Findings
White et al. (2020)	Experimental	Part A: 8; Part B: 8	Part A: 24 ± 7 years; Part B: 19 ± 2 year	Professionals—English Premier League (male).	• Session type: match, pre-match warm-up, pre-match shooting, GK training, shooting training and small-sided games. • Physical performance: number of dives, number of jumps (high, medium and low), high-speed changes of direction, total distance covered, high speed distance, counter movement jump height.	• GK training elicited most dives (51 ± 11) compared to shooting training, match, pre-match shooting, pre-match warm-up, and SSG (lowest 5 ± 3). • Similar high-speed distances in match and GK training, more than other activities. • Change of Direction (COD) and explosive efforts were max in GK training, exceeding match demands. • Between 1st half and 2nd half of a match: reduced total distance, increased COD and explosive efforts. More dives and explosive efforts between 75–90 compared to 0–15.
Babic et al. (2019)	Cross-sectional	6	16.5 ± 0.6 years	Elite, participating in the highest youth soccer competitions in Slovakia (male).	• Anthropometric measures: Age, height, weight • Physical performance: Heart Rate average (HR_{avg}) and Heart Rate max (HR_{max}) during training and small-sided games (SSGs).	• Difference in HR between training and SSG: • HR_{avg}: 25 ± 9 beats/min. • HR_{max}: 35 ± 12 beats/min. • HR_{avg} in training– 134 ± 8 b/min. • HR_{max}– 159 ± 8 b/min.
Jara et al. (2019)	Experimental	3	24.5 ± 7.2 years	Professional-Bundesliga (male).	• Physical and tactical demands in: • Large SSG (62 m x 44 m) • Medium SSG (50 m x 35 m) • Small SSG (32 m x 32 m)	• Large SSGs: • Lower intensities. • Greater tactical awareness.

Jara et al. (2018)	Experimental	13 (3 GKs)	16.6 ± 0.9 years	Regional division in Spain (male).	• Technical and tactical demands in: • Large SSG (62 m x 44 m) • Medium SSG (50 m x 35m) • Small SSG (32 m x 32 m)	• In larger SSG: 1 vs 1 situations increased, greater variety in offensive actions. • In small SSG: shot stops passes with hand and foot increased in smaller SSG.
Malone et al. (2018)	Case study	1	21	Professional- Eredivisie, Dutch national league (male).	• Physical performance: GPS training load, rate of perceived exertion (RPE), training load, and self-reported wellbeing	• MD had highest value for total wellness score, duration, total distance, average speed, player load and RPE load. • Small to moderate correlations between TL measures and wellness scores.
Ortega-Toro (2018)	Quasi- experimental	4	11.33 ± 0.6 years	Local Spanish youth players (male).	• Technical actions: offensive and defensive technical actions in 8 vs. 8 and 5 vs. 5 tournaments.	• 5 v 5: GKs had more interaction in play and more variability in actions.

Through gaining a greater understanding of performance indicators for senior GKs, practitioners can focus on the specific demands of the game when developing youth GKs as well as support better talent identification procedures.

Home vs. Away

Home team advantages, including better knowledge of the ground and crowd support, often result in home teams playing more offensively and away teams more cautiously with more defensive actions (Castillo et al., 2020b; Pollard & Gómez, 2009; Pollard & Pollard, 2005). For instance, Castillo et al. (2020b) found differences in match performance for adult Spanish professional GKs during home and away games. In away games, GKs conceded more shots on goal, made more saves, and had more goal kicks and restarts than when playing at home. Training sessions that incorporate these patterns of play, during the micro-cycle leading up to an away game, may support greater development of youth GKs. Conversely, this can be a training tool, wherein a GK who needs to improve in specific areas such as restarts and goal-kicks can be selected for away games, thereby ensuring increased repetitions of these specific skills. Preparing young GKs of the demands of home and away fixtures may also be advantageous during their long-term development.

Competition Level

In competitive matches, on average, male professional GKs complete approximately three saves, two clear-outs, and 15–20 successful passes, although these numbers vary depending on the competition level (Castillo et al., 2020b). When playing against higher-level opponents, GKs had a greater number of successful long passes, more interventions, and clear-outs. Against lower-level opponents, GKs had a greater number of passes and fewer ball touches, interceptions, and clearances (Hoxha et al., 2020). However, the technical performance, such as number of saves, goals conceded, and goal attempts, did not differ with the change in the quality of the opponent (Castillo et al., 2020b). This indicates that, against higher-level opponents, GKs had a greater defensive role, whereas against lower-level opponents, GKs are involved in more offensive actions. This is potentially due to the fact that high-level teams were subjected to less attacking play from the opponents, while the reverse happened to GKs of low-level teams (Hoxha et al., 2020). These findings could have a significant impact on GK development. For example, when selecting GKs for matches, those who need to improve their defensive actions can be selected to play against higher-level opponents. This allows a match-related environment with a potentially higher number of repetitions of offensive actions for the GK to develop.

Match Outcome

Match outcomes are a fundamental factor that influence GKs technical and physical performance demands. Match performance metrics vary significantly when comparing wins, losses, and draws in male professional GKs. From a technical perspective, for instance, the GK of a losing team concedes more goals and goal attempts as well as makes fewer clear-outs and less successful short passes (Castillo et al., 2020b). Hoxha et al. (2020) and Kubayi (2020) found that the match outcome also impacts the physical output of GKs. In a study assessing adult professional GKs in Kosovo, Hoxha et al. (2020) showed that GKs of teams that lost covered significantly greater sprint distances, whereas GKs of teams that won completed more ball recoveries and aerial duels. GKs who won also covered longer distances while defending, while those who lost or drew covered greater distances in attack (Hoxha et al., 2020). In a study on GKs participating in the 2019 Copa America soccer championship, Kubayi (2020) found that professional GKs of teams that lost covered more jogging distances (907 ± 314 m vs. 871 ± 302 m) and high-speed distances (33 ± 17 m vs. 27 ± 16 m), although the difference was not statistically significant. This is supports by the finidngs of Szwarc et al. (2019), where professional Polish GKs in teams that lost covered greater running distance than those that won or drew their matches. These results reinforce the need for load monitoring and management strategies explicit to GKs. As an example, GKs of teams that lost will potentially need additional recovery time or strategies. However, due to a lack of quantification of the differences in load, it is unclear if there will be a significant difference in load requiring intervention strategies. Therefore, additional research is required before creating training interventions, particualrly in youth GKs.

Defensive and Offensive Actions

The most frequent defensive technical actions for GKs are saves. Specifically, adult male professional players performed approximately ten saves per game during the 2002 World Cup (Sainz De Baranda et al., 2008), while national leagues report between two and five saves as well as around two clearances per game (Castillo et al., 2020b). An analysis of GKs during the 2002 World Cup found that GKs performed about 6.1 ± 2.7 dives, 3.8 ± 2.3 jumps, and 18.7 ± 6 forward, back, or side displacements per game (Sainz De Baranda et al., 2008). Moreover, GKs at the 2002 World Cup mostly intervened in the penalty area (44.4%), followed by the goal area (17.7%), and outside the penalty area (6.6%) (Sainz De Baranda et al., 2008). The most frequent offensive actions performed were passes, with high-performance GKs completing about 20 successful passes per game (Liu et al., 2015; Serrano et al., 2019). In addition, Villemain and Hauw (2014) found that GKs rated coming off the line as a critical game situation. The high-risk action places a high demand on the psychological and cognitive skills of GKs, and therefore, is rated a significant game moment (Villemain & Hauw, 2014). These findings highlight the importance of training different offensive (e.g., passing and displacements) and defensive (e.g., clearances and interventions) actions performed by GKs to improve the impact of GKs during a game. As a result, training programmes for youth GKs must include adequate, ecological repetitions of these actions to support their development and prepare them for the demands of senior competition.

Minute of the Match

Another variable that impacts physical demands of the GK is the minute of match. In a study on professional adult Polish GKs, Szwarc et al. (2019) found that GKs covered greater distances at walking speed and sprinting in the second half of the game and the last 15 minutes of each half, although this was not statistically significant. Similarly, White et al. (2020) showed that the male professional GKs perform more high-intensity actions in the final 15 minutes of the game when compared to the first 15 minutes during professional matches in England from domestic leagues and cup fixtures, including U18, U21, FA Cup, League Cup, and Southern Premier soccer competitions. Interestingly, they also revealed GKs covered less total distance during the second half (2,663 m) when compared with the first half (2,887 m). Unlike outfield players, however, GKs did not display a significant drop in performance metrics for physical (i.e., high-speed distance, accelerations and decelerations) or technical (i.e., passing speed, pass success) performances during the first and second half (White et al., 2020). Implications of these studies suggest that GKs are not as susceptible to cumulative fatigue during a 90-minute game when compared to outfield players. Additionally, the lack of differences in physical performance in the second half, despite increased physical load, alludes to the possibility that unreliable performance metrics are being used. Thus, GK-specific performance metrics, such as dives, saves, jumps, displacements, and interventions inside the penalty area, would provide a greater understanding of the relationship between load, match time, and performance.

As outlined in Table 19.3, while there is clearly limited research on performance tracking in youth GKs, the foregoing data can be used to develop a greater understanding of the match demands on senior GKs. This can also be used to help inform practitioners when designing talent identification and development strategies to better identify, develop, and prepare young GKs for professional soccer.

Considerations for Researchers

There appears to be a maturation bias and relative age effect during the selection of youth GKs. Researchers must continue to educate practitioners and include GKs in both maturation and relative age research. Despite demands being different, outfield players and GKs are often subject to the same fitness and skills tests. Moreover, GKs are generally excluded from talent identification and development studies, resulting in a limited understanding of the benchmarks and baselines of youth GKs. Future research must focus on appropriate test design and selection to better understand the demands on GKs. Indeed, fitness and skills tests that accurately reflect the demands of GKs will be invaluable for talent identification in youth soccer. In addition, from a multidisciplinary perspective, there appears to be little psychological or social studies that exist for GKs. Since they are often isolated during GK-specific training, and thus, spend less time with their teammates, there may be important implications on psychosocial development opportunities and outcomes in youth that requires further study.

Research assessing training load on GKs often use the same metrics as outfield players too. Through these measures, there appears to be a clear indication that GKs experience different load patterns in a micro-cycle when compared to outfield players. Further research, utilising GK-specific metrics, is required to better understand and adapt periodisation patterns. Moreover, it has been observed that factors that manipulate team performance also influence GKs match demands in senior GKs. Additionally, different scenarios (i.e., home vs. away, competition level, match outcome, offensive and defensive action, and minute of the match) impact the technical and physical demands of senior GKs. However, there is limited understanding of contextual factors and their effect on youth GKs. An improved understanding of match and performance demands in youth GKs will support the development of training plans specific to their positional needs. Lastly, it's important to highlight that the majority of studies that exist are comprised of male participants; thus, priority should be placed on better understanding the female youth GK, particularly since male and female players often require gender-specific approaches and should not be considered as homogenous.

TABLE 19.3 Summary of performance tracking literature for GKs

Reference	Study Design	N	Age	Playing Level	Determinants of Performance	Major Findings
Castillo et al. (2020a)	Observational	48	15.82 ± 1.8 years	Highest competitive level for regional youth in Spain (male).	• Physical performance: 40 m sprints, repeated sprint ability (RSA), change of direction ability. • SSGs: 30m x 20m, 5 vs. 5. • External response: GPS total distance, sprint distance, and accelerations and decelerations.	• U18 and U16 GKs performed better on 40 m sprint, RSA, and COD compared to U14. • U18 GKs performed better than U16 GKs in 40 m sprint and RSA. • No significant difference between U16 and U18s for external load responses in SSGs. • U14 GKs completed lower high intensity acceleration and lower sprint distance compared to U16 and U18 in SSGs.
Hoxha et al. (2020)	Cross-sectional	15	21 ± 6 years	Kosovo first league (male).	• Anthropometric measurements: height, body mass, body mass index • Fitness tests: Illinois Agility Test, 10 m sprint, Side steps, plate tapping, Nelson hand reaction. • Match performance: Success score, Conceded goals.	• Taller GKs had higher motor abilities and fewer goals conceded. • Kosovo GKs were younger than other European leagues. • Performance of GKs was dependent on motor abilities and explosive force factors like acceleration, speed, and reaction time. • GKs of teams that lost covered significantly greater sprint distances. • GKs of high-level teams achieved fewer attacking actions, while low-level teams achieved higher defending actions.
Kubayi (2020)	Observational	30	Adult, age not specified	2016 European Football Championship (male).	• InStat video tracking system: • Physical indicators: Walking, jogging, running, high-speed running and sprinting. • Technical indicators: save, pass, pass accuracy, aerial duels won, tackle, lost ball, ball recovery, foul drawn, and yellow card.	• Mean total distance was 4,819 m, including 68% walking and 0.8% high intensity actions. • GKs that lost covered significantly larger sprint distances than those who won or drew. • GKs that drew had more passes than those that won or lost.

(*Continued*)

TABLE 19.3 (Continued)

Reference	Study Design	N	Age	Playing Level	Determinants of Performance	Major Findings
Sainz De Baranda et al., (2008)	Observational	34	Adult (age not specified)	2002 World cup (male).	• Tactical data: type of opponent attack, area of last pass of attack, zone of shots on goal, body part used for last attack or shot on goal, and zone of GK intervention. • Physical actions of GK intervention.	• Attacks were more from the central zone than wide channels. • GKs intervened more in penalty area than any other zone. • Most frequent GK actions were forward displacement and saves, followed by foot control and clearing. • Most shots at goal were targeted on the ground, while the zone outside the penalty area was the most common shooting zone.

Considerations for Practitioners

Based on the literature presented throughout this chapter, it is evident that GKs are understudied by researchers, and thus, perhaps undervalued by stakeholders during the design, implementation, and evaluation of training programmes in youth soccer. Therefore, practitioners are encouraged to reflect upon the following considerations in order to focus more specifically on their GKs:

- Selection processes for youth GKs must include growth and birthdate data to avoid maturation and relative age biases.
- Fitness and skills tests must be adapted to reflect the position-specific needs of GKs. This may include the 10 m sprints test, diving tests, vertical jump and/or explosive power tests, the 505-agility test, and reaction time tests.
- The training demands of GKs and subsequent recovery patterns vary considerably from outfield players. As such, practitioners must take this into consideration when planning the team's micro-cycle.
- Different SSGs can elicit varied training effects on GKs. These can also be adapted based on the individual developmental requirements of the GK.
- Training sessions for youth GKs must support the technical and tactical development of GKs to prepare them for senior competition, including offensive actions, defensive actions, and GK-specific actions.

Conclusion

It is evident that there is a significant position data gap for soccer GKs in the talent identification and development literature. Where it does exist, a large proportion of the performance metrics applied to GKs are the same as those used for outfield players. With GKs' vastly different training and development demands compared to outfield peers, the use of incorrect metrics during assessments can lead to an unclear understanding of the GK. The variation in training effects between outfield players and GKs for the same session indicates that micro-cycle loading also differs. Thus, fitness and skills tests as well as the periodisation of GKs must be adjusted to suit their specific requirements. Furthermore, while match demands for senior GKs have been assessed, there is limited understanding if there is a linear transference to youth GKs. Moving forward, researchers and practitioners are encouraged to work collaboratively to co-design research and practical implications to focus on creating more appropriate strategies and settings for the identification and development of youth soccer GKs.

References

Anderson, Liam, Orme, P., Di Michele, R., Close, G. L., Milsom, J., Morgans, R., Drust, R., & Morton, J. P. (2016). Quantification of seasonal-long physical load in soccer players with different starting status from the English Premier League: Implications for maintaining squad physical fitness. *International Journal of Sports Physiology and Performance*, 11(8), 1038–1046. https://doi.org/10.1123/ijspp.2015-0672

Aziz, A. R., Mukherjee, S., Chia, M. Y. H., & Teh, K. C. (2008). Validity of the running repeated sprint ability test among playing positions and level of competitiveness in trained soccer players. *International Journal of Sports Medicine*, 29(10), 833–838. https://doi.org/10.1055/s-2008-1038410

Babic, M., Holienka, M., & Mikulič, M. (2018). Internal load of soccer goalkeepers during the improvement of selected game activities. *Journal of Physical Education and Sport*, 18(3), 1731–1737. https://doi.org/10.5817/cz.muni.p210-9631-2020-22

Castillo, D., Escalona, M., Lago-Rodriguez, A., Soto, M., Sanchez-Diaz, S., & Raya-Gonzalez, J. (2020b). Chapter 2: The influence of situational variables on technical performance in elite Spanish goalkeepers during official competition. In D. C. Alvira, & J. Raya- Gonzalez (Ed), *An essential guide to sports performance*. Nova Science Publishers.

Castillo, D., Lago-Rodríguez, A., Domínguez-Díez, M., Sánchez-Díaz, S., Rendo-Urteaga, T., Soto-Célix, M., & Raya-González, J. (2020a). Relationships between players' physical performance and small-sided game external responses in a youth soccer training context. *Sustainability*, *12*(11), 4482. https://doi.org/10.3390/su12114482

Davis, J. A., Brewer, J., & Atkin, D. (1992). Pre-season physiological characteristics of English first and second division soccer players. *Journal of Sports Sciences*, *10*(6), 541–547. https://doi.org/10.1080/02640419208729950

Di Credico, A., Gaggi, G., Ghinassi, B., Mascherini, G., Petri, C., Di Giminiani, R., Di Baldassarre, A., & Izzicupo, P. (2020). The influence of maturity status on anthropometric profile and body composition of youth goalkeepers. *International Journal of Environmental Research and Public Health*, *17*(21), 8247. https://doi.org/10.3390/ijerph17218247

Eisenmann, J. C., Till, K., & Baker, J. (2020). Growth, maturation and youth sports: Issues and practical solutions. *Annals of Human Biology*, *47*(4), 324–327. https://doi.org/10.1080/03014460.2020.1764099

Gil, S. M., Gil, J., Ruiz, F., Irazusta, A., & Irazusta, J. (2007). Physiological and anthropometric characteristics of young soccer players according to their playing position: Relevance for the selection process. *The Journal of Strength & Conditioning Research*, *21*(2), 438–445. https://doi.org/10.1519/00124278-200705000-00026

Gil, S. M., Zabala-Lili, J., Bidaurrazaga-Letona, I., Aduna, B., Lekue, J. A., Santos-Concejero, J., & Granados, C. (2014). Talent identification and selection process of outfield players and goalkeepers in a professional soccer club. *Journal of Sports Sciences*, *32*(20), 1931–1939. https://doi.org/10.1080/02640414.2014.964290

González-Víllora, S., Pastor-Vicedo, J. C., & Cordente, D. (2015). Relative age effect in UEFA championship soccer players. *Journal of Human Kinetics*, *47*(1), 237–248. https://doi.org/10.1515/hukin-2015-0079

Harrison, C. B., Gill, N. D., Kinugasa, T., & Kilding, A. E. (2015). Development of aerobic fitness in young team sport athletes. *Sports Medicine*, *45*(7), 969–983. https://doi.org/10.1007/s40279-015-0330-y

Hoxha, S., Berisha, M., & Thaqi, A. (2020). Analyses of some performance parameters and determination of the norm values in Kosovo First League goalkeepers. *The Journal of Eurasia Sport Sciences and Medicine*, *2*(3), 49–55.

Jara, D., Ortega, E., Gómez-Ruano, M. Á., & de Baranda, P. S. (2018). Effect of pitch size on technical-tactical actions of the goalkeeper in small-sided games. *Journal of Human Kinetics*, *62*(1), 157–166. https://doi.org/10.1515/hukin-2017-0167

Jara, D., Ortega, E., Gómez-Ruano, M. Á., Weigelt, M., Nikolic, B., & Sainz de Baranda, P. (2019). Physical and tactical demands of the goalkeeper in football in different small-sided games. *Sensors*, *19*(16), 3605. https://doi.org/10.3390/s19163605

Jiménez, I. P., & Pain, M. T. (2008). Relative age effect in Spanish association football: Its extent and implications for wasted potential. *Journal of Sports Sciences*, *26*(10), 995–1003. https://doi.org/10.1080/02640410801910285

Kaplan, T. (2010). Examination of repeated sprinting ability and fatigue index of soccer players according to their positions. *The Journal of Strength & Conditioning Research*, *24*(6), 1495–1501. https://doi.org/10.1519/jsc.0b013e3181d8e8ed

Kelly, A. L., & Williams, C. A. (2020). Physical characteristics and the talent identification and development processes in male youth soccer: A narrative review. *Strength and Conditioning Journal*, *42*(6), 15–34. https://doi.org/10.1519/SSC.0000000000000576

Kubayi, A. (2020). Analysis of goalkeepers' game performances at the 2016 European Football Championships. *South African Journal of Sports Medicine*, *32*(1), 1–4. https://doi.org/10.17159/2078-516x/2020/v32i1a8283

Kubayi, A., & Larkin, P. (2020). Match performance profile of goalkeepers during the 2019 COPA America soccer championship. *Medicina Dello Sport*, *73*(3), 453–60. https://doi.org/10.23736/s0025-7826.20.03724-2

Liu, H., Gomez, M. Á., Lago-Peñas, C., & Sampaio, J. (2015). Match statistics related to winning in the group stage of 2014 Brazil FIFA world cup. *Journal of Sports Sciences*, *33*(12), 1205–1213. https://doi.org/10.1080/02640414.2015.1022578

Lloyd, R. S., & Oliver, J. L. (2012). The youth physical development model: A new approach to long-term athletic development. *Strength & Conditioning Journal*, *34*(3), 61–72. https://doi.org/10.1519/ssc.0b013e31825760ea

Malina, R. M., Cumming, S. P., Kontos, A. P., Eisenmann, J. C., Ribeiro, B., & Aroso, J. (2005). Maturity-associated variation in sport-specific skills of youth soccer players aged 13–15 years. *Journal of Sports Sciences*, *23*(5), 515–522. https://doi.org/10.1080/02640410410001729928

Malina, R. M., Cumming, S. P., Rogol, A. D., Coelho-e-Silva, M. J., Figueiredo, A. J., Konarski, J. M., & Kozieł, S. M. (2019). Bio-banding in youth sports: background, concept, and application. *Sports Medicine*, *49*(11), 1671–1685. https://doi.org/10.1007/s40279-019-01166-x

Malone, J. J., Jaspers, A., Helsen, W., Merks, B., Frencken, W. G., & Brink, M. S. (2018). Seasonal training load and wellness monitoring in a professional soccer goalkeeper. *International Journal of Sports Physiology and Performance*, *13*(5), 672–675. https://doi.org/10.1123/ijspp.2017-0472

Mann, D. L., & van Ginneken, P. J. (2017). Age-ordered shirt numbering reduces the selection bias associated with the relative age effect. *Journal of Sports Sciences*, *35*(8), 784–790. https://doi.org/10.1080/02640414.2016.1189588

Martin-Garcia, A., Castellano, J., Diaz, A. G., Cos, F., & Casamichana, D. (2019). Positional demands for various-sided games with goalkeepers according to the most demanding passages of match play in football. *Biology of Sport*, *36*(2), 171. https://doi.org/10.5114/biolsport.2019.83507

Matković, R., Mišigoj-Duraković, B., Matković, M., Janković, B., Ružić, S., Leko, L., & Kondrič, M. (2003). Morphological differences of elite Croatian soccer players according to the team position. *Collegium Antropologicum*, *27*(1), 167–174.

Moore, S. A., Cumming, S. P., Balletta, G., Ramage, K., Eisenmann, J. C., Baxter-Jones, A. D., Jackowski S. A., & Sherar, L. B. (2020). Exploring the relationship between adolescent biological maturation, physical activity, and sedentary behaviour: A systematic review and narrative synthesis. *Annals of Human Biology*, *47*(4), 365–383. https://doi.org/10.1080/03014460.2020.1805006

Obetko, M., Peráček, P., Šagát, P., & Mikulič, M. (2019). Impact of age and agility performance level on the disjunctive reaction time of soccer goalkeepers. *Acta Facultatis Educationis Physicae Universitatis Comenianae*, *59*(2). https://doi.org/10.2478/afepuc-2019-0020

Ortega-Toro, E., García-Angulo, A., Giménez-Egido, J. M., García-Angulo, F. J., & Palao, J. (2018). Effect of modifications in rules in competition on participation of male youth goalkeepers in soccer. *International Journal of Sports Science & Coaching*, *13*(6), 1040–1047. https://doi.org/10.1177/1747954118769423

Otte, F. W., Davids, K., Millar, S. K., & Klatt, S. (2020b). Specialist role coaching and skill training periodisation: a football goalkeeping case study. *International Journal of Sports Science & Coaching*, *15*(4), 562–575. https://doi.org/10.1177/1747954120922548

Otte, F. W., Millar, S. K., & Klatt, S. (2020a). How does the modern football goalkeeper train?—An exploration of expert goalkeeper coaches' skill training approaches. *Journal of Sports Sciences*, *38*(11–12), 1465–473. https://doi.org/10.1080/02640414.2019.1643202

Padrón-Cabo, A., Rey, E., García-Soidán, J. L., & Penedo-Jamardo, E. (2016). Large scale analysis of relative age effect on professional soccer players in FIFA designated zones. *International Journal of Performance Analysis in Sport*, *16*(1), 332–346. https://doi.org/10.1080/24748668.2016.11868890

Perez-Arroniz, M., Calleja-González, J., Zabala-Lili, J., & Zubillaga, A. (2022). The soccer goalkeeper profile: bibliographic review. *The Physician and Sportsmedicine*, 1–10. https://doi.org/10.1080/00913847.2022.2040889

Pichardo, A. W., Oliver, J. L., Harrison, C. B., Maulder, P. S., & Lloyd, R. S. (2018). Integrating models of long-term athletic development to maximize the physical development of youth. *International Journal of Sports Science & Coaching*, *13*(6), 1189–1199. https://doi.org/10.1177/1747954118785503

Pollard, R., & Gómez, M. A. (2009). Home advantage in football in South-West Europe: Long-term trends, regional variation, and team differences. *European Journal of Sport Science*, *9*(6), 341–352. https://doi.org/10.1080/17461390903009133

Pollard, R., & Pollard, G. (2005). Long-term trends in home advantage in professional team sports in North America and England (1876–2003). *Journal of Sports Sciences*, 23(4), 337–350. https://doi.org/10.1080/02640410400021559

Rebelo-Gonçalves, R., Coelho-e-Silva, M. J., Severino, V., Tessitore, A., & Figueiredo, A. J. B. (2015). Anthropometric and physiological profiling of youth soccer goalkeepers. *International Journal of Sports Physiology and Performance*, 10(2), 224–231. https://doi.org/10.1123/ijspp.2014-0181

Roberts, S. J., McRobert, A. P., Lewis, C. J., & Reeves, M. J. (2019). Establishing consensus of position-specific predictors for elite youth soccer in England. *Science and Medicine in Football*, 3(3), 205–213. https://doi.org/10.1080/24733938.2019.1581369

Rowell, A. E., Aughey, R. J., Clubb, J., & Cormack, S. J. (2018). A standardized small-sided game can be used to monitor neuromuscular fatigue in professional A-league football players. *Frontiers in Physiology*, 9, 1011. https://doi.org/10.3389/fphys.2018.01011

Sainz De Baranda, P., Ortega, E., & Palao, J. M. (2008). Analysis of goalkeepers' defence in the World Cup in Korea and Japan in 2002. *European Journal of Sport Science*, 8(3), 127–134. https://doi.org/10.1080/17461390801919045

Salinero, J. J., Pérez, B., Burillo, P., & Lesma, M. L. (2013). Relative age effect in European professional football. Analysis by position. *Journal of Human Sport and Exercise*, 8(4), 966–973. https://doi.org/10.4100/jhse.2013.84.07

Serrano, S, C., Paredes-Hernández, V., Sánchez-Sánchez, J., Gallardo-Pérez, J., Da Silva, R., Porcel, D., Colino, E., García-Unanue, J., & Gallardo, L. (2019). The team's influence on physical and technical demands of elite goalkeepers in LaLiga: A longitudinal study in professional soccer. *Research in Sports Medicine*, 27(4), 424–438. https://doi.org/10.1080/15438627.2018.1555755

Slimani, M., Znazen, H., Miarka, B., & Bragazzi, N. L. (2019). Maximum oxygen uptake of male soccer players according to their competitive level, playing position and age group: Implication from a network meta-analysis. *Journal of Human Kinetics*, 66(1), 233–245. https://doi.org/10.2478/hukin-2018-0060

Sporis, G., Jukic, I., Ostojic, S. M., & Milanovic, D. (2009). Fitness profiling in soccer: physical and physiologic characteristics of elite players. *The Journal of Strength & Conditioning Research*, 23(7), 1947–1953. https://doi.org/10.1519/jsc.0b013e3181b3e141

Souza, I. S. D., Vicentini, L., Morbi, M. D. R., & Marques, R. F. R. (2020). The relative age effect on soccer goalkeeper training in Brazil: Scenarios of the male and female elites. *Journal of Physical Education*, 31(1), 1–13 https://doi.org/10.12800/ccd.v10i30.591

Szwarc, A., Jaszczur-Nowicki, J., Aschenbrenner, P., Zasada, M., Padulo, J., & Lipinska, P. (2019). Motion analysis of elite Polish soccer goalkeepers throughout a season. *Biology of Sport*, 36(4), 357. https://doi.org/10.5114/biolsport.2019.88758

Tahara, Y., Moji, K., Tsunawake, N., Fukuda, R., Nakayama, M., Nakagaichi, M., Komine, T., Kusano, Y. and Aoyagi, K., (2006). Physique, body composition and maximum oxygen consumption of selected soccer players of Kunimi High School, Nagasaki, Japan. *Journal of Physiological Anthropology*, 25(4), 291–297. https://doi.org/10.2114/jpa2.25.291

Till, K., & Baker, J. (2020). Challenges and [possible] solutions to optimizing talent identification and development in sport. *Frontiers in Psychology*, 11, 664. https://doi.org/10.3389/fpsyg.2020.00664

Towlson, C., Cobley, S., Midgley, A. W., Garrett, A., Parkin, G., & Lovell, R. (2017). Relative age, maturation and physical biases on position allocation in elite-youth soccer. *International Journal of Sports Medicine*, 38(3), 201–209. https://doi.org/10.1055/s-0042-119029

Villemain, A., & Hauw, D. (2014). A situated analysis of football goalkeepers' experiences in critical game situations. *Perceptual and Motor Skills*, 119(3), 811–824. https://doi.org/10.2466/25.30.pms.119c30z0

White, A., Hills, S.P., Hobbs, M., Cooke, C.B., Kilduff, L.P., Cook, C., Roberts, C. and Russell, M., (2020). The physical demands of professional soccer goalkeepers throughout a week-long competitive microcycle and transiently throughout match-play. *Journal of Sports Sciences*, 38(8), 848–854. https://doi.org/10.1080/02640414.2020.1736244

Wong, P. L., Chamari, K., Dellal, A., & Wisløff, U. (2009). Relationship between anthropometric and physiological characteristics in youth soccer players. *The Journal of Strength & Conditioning Research*, 23(4), 1204–1210. https://doi.org/10.1519/jsc.0b013e3181fa6eaa

Yagüe, J. M., de la Rubia, A., Sánchez-Molina, J., Maroto-Izquierdo, S., & Molinero, O. (2018). The relative age effect in the 10 best leagues of male professional football of the Union of European Football Associations (UEFA). *Journal of Sports Science & Medicine, 17*(3), 409.

Ziv, G., & Lidor, R. (2011). Physical characteristics, physiological attributes, and on-field performances of soccer goalkeepers. *International Journal of Sports Physiology and Performance, 6*(4), 509–524. https://doi.org/10.1123/ijspp.6.4.509

20
LANGUAGE GAMES

Improving the Words We Use in Soccer Research and Practice

Joseph Baker, Adam L. Kelly, Alexander B. T. McAuley, and Nick Wattie

Introduction

The past two decades have seen a rapid rise in research exploring talent identification and development in youth soccer (e.g., Baker et al., 2020; Gledhill et al., 2017; Johnston et al., 2018). In an ideal world, this increased attention would translate into more helpful and valid evidence for creating 21st century coaching and athlete development policies. Unfortunately, there are important limitations to the evidentiary foundations of research and practice in this area (and for sport generally). A recent scoping review of talent research in sport since 1990 (Baker et al., 2020), for example, found that researchers regularly do not report enough information about their samples for readers to adequately determine who they are reporting on. Relatedly, several research teams (including the authors of this chapter) have recently emphasised the lack of consistency in how key terms are used by researchers, which affects the validity and reliability of evidence (Baker et al., 2015; Johnston et al., 2023; McAuley et al., 2021a; Mosher et al., 2020). At a time when access to evidence is critical, these gaps and inconsistencies inevitably trickle down to practitioners who are often overburdened and/or not capable of evaluating and assessing the quality of scientific research. While the adage 'garbage in, garbage out' usually refers to the link between data collection and results, the same notion applies to the eventual implementation of research findings.

Perhaps more importantly, it should not fall to practitioners to make 'heads or tails' of what researchers are trying to say. In this chapter, there is a focus on the need for clear and consistent language in how current issues in youth development in sport are discussed, particularly within youth soccer. While this focus is on three key areas (i.e., how we define talent, how we consider competition levels, and how we measure early specialisation), the rationale for clarity and standardisation is the same for issues outside the scope of this chapter. The chapter concludes with some recommendations for future work in this area and important considerations for practitioners.

Language Games

> All our work, our whole life is a matter of semantics, because words are the tools with which we work. . . . Everything depends on our understanding of them.
>
> —US Supreme Court Justice Felix Frankfurter

DOI: 10.4324/9781032232799-20

How an individual uses and understands key terms is often determined by that person's experiences and education. Differences between individual perceptions on these factors can cause confusion and contradiction. While the solution seems obvious (e.g., just create clearly interpretable consensus definitions), this task is not as easy as it appears (McAuley et al., 2021a). This is also not a new problem. In 1958, for instance, German philosopher Ludwig Wittgenstein advocated that 'linguistic confusion' (i.e., the misuse and misunderstanding of language) was the root of all philosophical problems. Wittgenstein (1958) further noted that 'language games' (i.e., the use of language and the actions into which it is woven) are an unintentional and inevitable facet of human behaviour. Indeed, Lourenço (2001) argued that the varied use of undefined or vaguely defined words is one of the main limitations of research in psychology. According to philosopher Thomas Kuhn (1962), however, this is *normal science*, and researchers' variations in language can be seen as a type of *puzzle solving* based on a shared perspective on beliefs, language usage, and meaning, which Kuhn referred to as a 'paradigm'. However, this sharing of language can only occur if researchers, practitioners, and other stakeholders have the same paradigm, since paradigms are fundamentally dogmatic and incommensurable (Feyerabend, 1975).

This notion of paradigms is relevant for this discussion of language use in youth soccer. Dohme et al. (2017), for example, found that psychological terms within youth athlete development were only used consistently if an author was involved in more than one paper, and that authors often dismiss their responsibility to clearly explain topic-specific vocabulary. This research may explain, to an extent, why practitioners, the media, and policy makers regularly misconstrue or over-simplify the meanings of terms or use them out of context. Their capacity to interpret and implement research findings is obscured by differing research paradigms (McAuley et al., 2021a). These explanations are not an excuse for inaction, and a necessary step to improvement involves clarifying how words and phrases are defined and described by the researchers using them (i.e., clarifying the paradigm). The lack of coherent understanding of what researchers mean when they use specific terms undermines any conclusions that might be drawn from the evidence. The inconsistencies, for instance, can affect how research studies are conceptualised, how samples are described, and how key terms are operationalised. This chapter explores each of these in the sections that follow.

Putting Concepts of Solid Ground: What Is 'Talent'?

For over a century, 'talent' has been a concept that is inconsistently and/or inadequately defined, but it remains a common element in how coaches, parents, and athletes frame issues of athlete development and performance. Unfortunately, the overwhelming conclusion that can be drawn from prior research is that scholars, coaches, and readers are often not using this term in the same way. For example, in the widely known Differentiated Model of Talent and Giftedness, Gagné (2004) describes talent as "outstanding systematically developed skills" (p. 119). Cobley et al. (2012) describe talent as "the quality (or qualities) identified at an earlier time that promotes (or predicts) exceptionality at a future time" (p. 3). Issurin (2017) defined talent as "a special ability that allows someone to reach excellence in some activity in a given domain" (p. 1994). Davids et al. (2017) grounded their discussion of talent in ecological psychology, suggesting that talent represents the "functional relationship developed between a performer and a specific performance environment" (p. 193). Making things even more confusing, *talent* is often used to refer to 'the thing being developed' (e.g., in 'talent development') as well as 'the individuals who possess the thing being developed' (e.g., when athletes in a development system are referred to as 'talents').

Ultimately, it is important that soccer coaches and other practitioners have clear conceptualisations of the words they use. In a 2019 paper, Baker and colleagues formulated a definition of talent that would differentiate it from related words like skill (i.e., demonstrated ability in a specific area, such as a player's skill at ball handling) and performance (i.e., executing or accomplishing a course of action in a competition setting). While a full exposition of the model is beyond the scope of this chapter, a summary will serve to make this point. In their model, Baker et al. (2019) positioned talent as:

- *Innate:* Prior research in this area, including a very influential discussion in the journal *Behavior and Brain Sciences* (Howe et al., 1998) made the argument that notions of talent needed to be established as innate capacities (i.e., present at birth). This allows them to be more clearly defined and differentiated from related terms like 'skill' and 'capabilities'. Note, this does not mean that talent is fixed and/or incapable of interacting with environmental factors.
- *Multi-disciplinary:* Although few who work in sport would question this component, it is important to clearly establish that talents can come in many forms. This is important to note, since most work in talent and athlete assessment continues to focus on physical and physiological elements of performance. This uni-dimensional focus by researchers may simply reflect prior difficulties in defining and conceptualising talent. Moreover, the term 'talent' is often used in the singular form (which may have also contributed to reductionist approaches) when it more likely that athletes have multiple 'talents'.
- *Emergenic*: Most practitioners under-estimate the complexity of the task of athlete development, seeing talent in an overly simplistic fashion (researchers are also victims of this crime; Simonton, 2001). This is reflected when individuals see talent as reflecting simple, stable characteristics, like how we think about eye colour or whether someone has curly or straight hair. The idea of emergenesis reflects the reality that most complex traits come from patterns of combinations of genes working through multiplicative interactions *in specific environmental contexts.*
- *Dynamic:* As noted earlier, the action and function of innate qualities (i.e., genes) are not fixed but evolve in how they are expressed across developmental time. This process evolves due to interactions between genes and the environments the individual interacts within. This results in unpredictable patterns of development, especially in fields like sport, where many traits related to elite performance are 'polygenic' (i.e., resulting from the interaction of many genes) (McAuley et al., 2021c).
- *Symbiotic:* Why are European soccer players generally more (or differently) skilled than players coming from North America (or vice versa, why do so many baseball players come from North America and not Europe)? Athletes do not develop in a vacuum, and the qualities that a sport values and then tries to instil amongst athletes in the sport are determined by a host of contextual factors, such as cultural importance and relevance to elite sport performance at that specific point in time. There is a symbiotic relationship between the talent-related characteristics of the individual athlete, the value of those characteristics by the developmental environment in which they find themselves, and the task demands of the sport.

This definition of 'talent' is undoubtedly more complicated than the generalisations used by many coaches and researchers, but it has the advantage of being: (a) grounded in research on human development in general and athlete development specifically, (b) more clearly articulated and nuanced than prior definitions, and (c) likely more representative of the complexity researchers and practitioners must deal with when trying to influence and predict athlete development.

Determining Appropriate Groups: Defining 'Elite'

Over the past decade, several frameworks and taxonomies have emerged (e.g., Baker et al., 2015; Swann et al., 2015) to clarify categories and levels of athletic skill. These approaches can be used as a guide when considering how the performance status of cohorts should be described. That said, each approach incorporates auxiliary terms and fails to provide specific recommendations regarding what terms like 'elite' mean (McAuley et al., 2021a). This is particularly important, as the academic literature and practical environments of youth soccer regularly use 'elite' to describe higher-performing players and depict certain settings.

One limitation of labelling youth soccer samples as 'elite' is the presumption that players are homogeneous. However, the context from which each sample is derived (e.g., nationality, region), coupled with the age, competition level, and gender they are participating, can cause a large variation in performance outcomes. This variability in describing the performance levels of 'elite' youth soccer players has made it challenging to draw inferences about inter- and intra-population differences (McAuley et al., 2021a). Researchers in youth soccer may find this extremely problematic, considering their persistent issue with limited sample sizes and reliance on *research synthesis* approaches (e.g., meta-analyses) when making evidence-based decisions (Hecksteden et al., 2022). Indeed, these approaches can be undermined when definitions vary.

The term 'elite' has been applied to a wide range of soccer cohorts, such as players within U9 age groups (see Kirkland & O'Sullivan, 2018 for a critical discussion) and those competing at senior international levels (Baker et al., 2020). Moreover, previous studies have defined sub-cohorts within the same sample (e.g., 'elite' versus 'non-elite') based upon their performance relative only to each other, rather than in the sport as a whole (e.g., Verburgh et al., 2016). Additionally, *professionalism* has been used to infer 'elite' status in soccer (e.g., Morgan et al., 2013), meaning players in professional leagues of varying performance standards (e.g., English Premier League and English Football League Two) could be classified as 'elite'. Ultimately, this makes it difficult to draw valid conclusions, generalise findings, and translate knowledge into practice (McAuley et al., 2021a).

Whilst these measurement-related issues are important, equal deliberation must be given to the potential implications that 'elite' can have in talent identification and development contexts. "Being superior relative to an individual's peer group" is how most dictionaries define 'elite', although, in practical settings, the operationalisation of 'elite' regularly disregards the prospect of a player's position changing over time as part of their individual and peer group's development. For instance, anecdotal evidence suggests an English Premier League soccer academy has an "elite U5 squad", who are "treated like pros" (Austin, 2019). The authors' experience of researching youth soccer contexts suggests there may be major consequences for young players (both included and excluded) who are treated this way (McAuley et al., 2021a).

Even if we were able to develop clear and consistent definitions, labelling young players specifically as 'elite' has many problems. For example, there is no guarantee that a young player's projected outcome will ever be realised to a relative degree of precision. Youth players who are purported to be on different developmental trajectories may actually achieve similar performance standards at adulthood. Conversely, a youth player considered to have low potential may end up outperforming one viewed as having higher potential later in their development. The methods currently used to assess talent and make subsequent predictions are generally inaccurate and unreliable. Specifically, methods that focus on evaluating youth performance end up being poor indicators of performance success at adulthood because early performance success is a weak predictor of later success (Baker et al., 2018). The earlier predictions are made in development, the less accurate they end up being, as time is inversely related to accuracy in prediction models of talent (Till & Baker, 2020). As mentioned previously, talent evolves dynamically over time; many qualities and skills may only emerge later in development (Baker et al., 2019; McAuley et al., 2021b). Thus, early identification and selection procedures are flawed, as they cannot predict these changes. In addition, over time, the encompassing characteristics of optimal performance within soccer could vary considerably. This may result in the present purported prerequisites of high-performance in soccer changing unpredictably in the future (Baker et al., 2018; Till & Baker, 2020).

Improving Measurement Precision: What Do We Mean by 'Early Specialisation'?

Over the past decade, several consensus and position statements have been published, urging coaches against 'early sport specialisation' (e.g., Bergeron et al., 2015; Kliethermes et al., 2021; LaPrade et al., 2016). These statements inevitably emphasise the relationships between early specialisation and deliberate practice, risk of injury, dropout, and compromised athletic development. However, more recently, several research teams (Larson et al., 2019; Mosher et al., 2020) have highlighted the lack of measurement precision in the majority of work in this area. On the surface, these criticisms seem trivial, but a more thoughtful examination highlights how little is actually known about the mechanisms driving the possible negative outcomes associated with early specialisation, which is particularly relevant for coaches trying to mitigate these risks in their athletes.

To be more specific, many studies in this area (see Mosher et al., 2020 for a review) do not distinguish between specialisation (focus on a single sport) and *early* specialisation (focus on a single sport during early development). This distinction is important because researchers in skill acquisition and athlete development agree that future elite athletes will eventually have to specialise, and the questions therefore become ones of 'when is it most appropriate to do this?' and 'what are the risks of doing it at different ages?'. How you define 'early' matters. In youth soccer, early might mean before the age of 12 years, while, in gymnastics, this would be considered on time for specialisation or, perhaps, even late.

Relatedly, what does specialisation mean?[1] In past research, definitions have varied from targeted involvement in a single sport (Leite & Sampaio, 2012), year-round participation in a single sport at the exclusion of other sports (Jayanthi et al., 2015), or participation in a single sport for at least 8 months (Sugimoto et al., 2019). These definitions are troubling, not only because of their inconsistencies but also because they equate specialisation simply with the number of sports an athlete is participating in without capturing measures of the intensity or quality of that participation. For instance, which athlete is at greater risk of injury or dropout: the one who is participating in a single sport they enjoy for a total of 10 hours per week, or the one participating in three sports in the same week for a total of 25 hours of training per week? At present, the answer is unclear because the quality and depth of evidence from prior research has not been detailed enough to inform this question.

While the quality and depth of evidence has undoubtedly been influenced by the conceptual imprecision of past research, the operationalisation of concepts like early specialisation and its counterpart, sampling/diversification, has been equally problematic. Specifically, these concepts have been operationalised as mutually exclusive dichotomies; an either-or way of describing youth sport participation (Côté et al., 2009; Ford & Williams, 2017). While dichotomies such as these are appealing for their simplicity (Dawkins, 2015), it is unlikely that they are capable of accurately describing the reality and nuance of youth sport participation. Indeed, research on concepts such specialised sampling (Sieghartsleitner et al., 2018) and early engagement (Ford et al., 2009) reinforce the notion that this dichotomised operationalisation is probably too simplistic and ecologically invalid. Similarly, data aggregation related to these modes of participation is also important. Are they presented on a year-to-year or season-to-season level, or is an athlete's mode of participation described based on aggregated data (e.g., from 6 to 12 years of age)? The answer greatly influences the fidelity of our understanding of youth sport participation.

Soccer coaches working in youth development can easily manage the 'simple cases' of athletes who are obviously doing too much (e.g., the pure specialiser who may be at increased risk of injury, dropout, etc.) or too little (e.g., the athlete who is not progressing at the same rate as their peers due to lack of training, conditioning, etc.). However, the majority of athletes coaches deal with are not 'simple cases'. Greater clarity on the mechanisms of early specialisation would inform clearer guidelines about what appropriate load looks like across development (e.g., how much is too much?), how different types of training relate to athlete development (e.g., what is the focus of development at this time?), and how these factors might be better managed over the long term to ensure greater retention, satisfaction, and skill development.

With regards to research methodologies, a participation history questionnaire is the most commonly used method to capture the accumulative hours of specific activities that an athlete has previously engaged in. Specifically, this can help researchers identify activities such as coach-led practice, competition, individual practice, peer-led play, and multisport engagement; all of which are all key elements of athlete development. However, it is important to recognise the limitations of this approach. First, the retrospective nature of this questionnaire may limit its accuracy compared to more prospective approaches (i.e., recall of practice activities is limited) (Côté et al., 2005). A second limitation relates to the inefficiencies in how researchers and practitioners consider 'coach-led practice'. Robertson et al. (2019), for instance, highlight the superficial nature of which researchers are reporting youth sport contexts, explaining how current participant reporting practices do not adequately represent the diversity of sports contexts. With this in mind, the common process of simply quantifying the amount of time an athlete spends in coach-led practice hours and subsequently categorising it all as time spent in 'deliberate practice' (which often constitutes towards early specialisation during childhood) is flawed, or at the very least, too crude. For example, the inter- and intra-coefficients of variability that may impact the reliability and validity of age- and club-specific coach-led practice are not considered. As a practical example, coach-led practice within an U9 age group at one club team may look significantly different to another U9 team at a different club. Likewise, coach-led practice within an U9 team may look completely different to an U16 team. Regardless of what the coach-led practice looks like in these different settings, however, the accumulation of these hours (and the subsequent assumptions) is the same within a retrospective questionnaire research context that relates to research outcomes around early specialisation.

Common features of coach-led practice often include the involvement of at least two people—coach and athlete. Coaching is, therefore, a social activity benefiting from interpersonal skills, whilst also being goal-oriented towards improvement in that specific athlete's performance (Cooper & Allen, 2018). However, during this practice, there are many other complex and dynamic coaching processes occurring, many of which involve a range of activities, skills, and social interactions (Cushion, 2007). For instance, one coach may adopt a 'command' style, whilst another coach may adopt a 'guided discovery' approach. Although these are two diverse coaching methods that elicit different outcomes, they fit with the same 'coach-led' practice remit. Similarly, despite both these approaches being considered as 'coach-led' practice, a session designed from an ecological dynamics approach will look different from a series of closed drills (Baker, 2003; Davids & Baker, 2007). All this to say, current understandings of the interpersonal and affective subtleties and nuances of optimal coaching during athlete development, particularly during early stages, is far from complete.

Considerations for Researchers

The concept of 'talent' in high-performance sport generally, or soccer in particular, is unlikely to go anywhere soon. Most approaches to athlete development by coaches, administrators, parents, and athletes are based on the idea that early performance success is an indicator of future potential, despite the gathering mountain of research evidence against this simple conclusion. In order to deconstruct this concept in soccer, researchers need to develop a more thorough understanding of how notions of 'talent' are influencing the system and the long-term implications of this influence on effectiveness and efficiency of approaches to athlete development. Perhaps most importantly, there needs to be greater attention to evaluations of long-term accuracy of talent/athlete development programmes. This type of research will be difficult, given the timeframes involved and the apparent hesitancy of elite and professional clubs to allow access to the data required to adequately evaluate a club's development system, not to mention the limitations of many research designs used in this area (Baker et al., 2022).

The implications of the issues that have been outlined whilst adopting the term 'elite' require a thoughtful response from the research community. Currently, there is no consensus on how the term 'elite' should be applied to distinguish players of different competition levels in soccer (Williams et al., 2017). However, the lack of agreement is not an excuse for inaction, and a necessary first step is clarifying how samples are defined and described. At the very least, researchers should strive for greater *transparency* by providing detailed descriptions of their rationale for categorising their samples as 'elite' (Baker et al., 2020). Specifically, McAuley et al. (2021a) suggest researchers should present information concerning cohort elements, such as: (a) age, (b) competition level and/or league status, (c) gender, (d) nationality and/or province, and (e) sport type. This will allow readers to determine their own classifications for samples more effectively and how findings relate to their respective environments, thus facilitating improved research synthesis and practical interpretations. Also, researchers attempting meta-syntheses should be mindful of the evolution of soccer, as the normative performance metrics of high-level athletes can fluctuate considerably over time. Players previously deemed to be 'elite' or 'talented', may not be currently or in the future due to ever-changing contextual factors. As such, pooling athletes from widespread time-points may introduce significant between-study-heterogeneity and weaken the validity of potentially meaningful findings.

As noted in the previous section, the definitions and designs used in prior work exploring early sport experiences of high-performance athletes have significant limitations. They have been effective for pointing to a certain direction (i.e., greater athletic success is associated with a broader exposure to sport during early development) without spending adequate time on why this might be so. Until there is a more comprehensive understanding of the type of training/coaching that is most effective at different stages of development, and importantly, why/how this leads to superior skill development, we are confusing correlation/association with causation. Greater measurement precision (e.g., what is *early* specialisation?) and more representative categorisation of participation, as well as superior study designs, will go a long way to filling these gaps in our understanding.

An important area of future research will be determining the effect of different words on significant psychological variables, such as locus of control, motivation, perceived competence, and self-efficacy. Popular subjects of discussion at present (e.g., mindset) are underpinned by the belief that the development and long-term engagement of players are subtlety influenced by these messages (Wattie & Baker, 2017). The consequences (immediate, short-term, and long-term) of describing developing young players as 'talented', 'elite' or an 'early specialiser' requires further exploration. Moreover, although this chapter focused specifically on three key terms, there are numerous other variables that require further discussion to better understand their interpretations (e.g., 'the coach's eye', 'character', 'training load'). Investigating these topics is essential to better understand the talent development process, given the limited research in this area.

Considerations for Practitioners

The reality is, language affects all stakeholders in youth soccer—the coach who uses the language, the sport system he/she/they operates within, the player hearing the language, along with parents, other practitioners, and the list goes on (Johnston et al., 2023). Based on the three key areas (and the larger rationale for clarity of terminology) presented throughout this chapter, the following recommendations are offered for practitioners:

- Do not assume coaches, trainers, scouts, parents, and athletes use terms the same way. Be clear of the meaning when using words like 'talent', 'elite', or 'early specialisation'. Also, be clear of what it doesn't mean (e.g., this doesn't mean the player won't have to train hard or make sacrifices).
- It is important to recognise the possible immediate, short-term, and long-term implications of using terms like 'talented', 'elite', and 'early specialiser' to describe developing young athletes. This may send inadvertent messages to stakeholders and build upon pre-existing inequalities and biases throughout organisational structures in youth soccer.
- Internal beliefs regarding the primary sources responsible for athlete capabilities may have enduring consequences on subsequent actions, behaviour, and decisions during identification and development processes. How terms such as 'talent', 'elite', and 'early specialisation' are employed subtlety illustrate these beliefs.
- Be wary of simplistic dichotomies like specialisation *or* sampler. Consider the existence of intermediates and their influence on athlete development.
- Irrespective of one's personal philosophy and opinion on the connotations of particular terms, recognising the athletes' understanding of their meanings is crucial. Misconstrued interpretations could result in the formation of unrealistic expectations, cultivate forms of complacency, or may lead to an undervaluation of potential that results in decreased effort and enjoyment.

Conclusion

A recent systematic review of talent research in sport (Baker et al., 2020) emphasised that soccer was the sport with the greatest wealth of research. However, there are considerable gaps in our understanding of player development specifically in soccer (e.g., what type of coaching/training is most effective at which stages of development, and why?). One step to filling these gaps involves greater clarity and precision in how 'loaded' terms like 'talent', 'elite', and 'specialisation' are used in research and training contexts. Moving forward, researchers and practitioners should consider how such terms are used when designing, implementing, and evaluating research and training environments in order to help advance our understanding of their long-term effects.

Note

1 The same problems plague the contrasting concept of sampling and/or early diversification.

References

Austin, S. (2019). Manchester city under-5s elite squad branded 'absolute madness'. *Training Ground Guru*. https://trainingground.guru/articles/manchester-city-under-5s-elite-squad-described-as-absolute-madness

Baker, J. (2003). Early specialisation in youth sport: A requirement for adult expertise? *High Ability Studies*, *14*(1), 85–94. https://doi.org/10.1080/13598130304091

Baker, J., Johnston, K., & Wattie, N. (2022). Survival versus attraction advantages and talent selection in sport. *Sports Medicine—Open*, *8*, 17. https://doi.org/10.1186/s40798-022-00409-y

Baker, J., Schorer, J., & Wattie, N. (2018). Compromising talent: Issues in identifying and selecting talent in sport. *Quest*, *70*(1), 48–63. https://doi.org/10.1080/00336297.2017.1333438

Baker, J., Wattie, N., & Schorer, J. (2015). Defining expertise: A taxonomy for researchers in skill acquisition and expertise. In J. Baker & D. Farrow (Eds.), *Routledge handbook of sport expertise* (pp. 144–155). Routledge.

Baker, J., Wattie, N., & Schorer, J. (2019). A proposed conceptualization of talent in sport: The first step in a long and winding road. *Psychology of Sport and Exercise*, *43*, 27–33. https://doi.org/10.1016/j.psychsport.2018.12.016

Baker, J., Wilson, S., Johnston, K., Dehghansai, N., Koenigsberg, A., de Vegt, S., & Wattie, N. (2020). Talent research in sport 1990–2018: A scoping review. *Frontiers in Psychology*, *11*, 607710. https://doi.org/10.3389/fpsyg.2020.607710

Bergeron, M. F., Mountjoy, M., Armstrong, N., Chia, M., Côté, J., Emery, C. A., Faigenbaum, A., Hall, G., Kriemler, S., Léglise, M., Malina, R. M., Pensgaard, A. M., Sanchez, A., Soligard, T., Sundgot-Borgen, J., van Mechelen, W., Weissensteiner, J. R., & Engebretsen, L. (2015). International olympic committee consensus statement on youth athletic development. *British Journal of Sports Medicine*, *49*(13), 843–851. https://doi.org/10.1136/bjsports-2015-094962

Cobley, S., Schorer, J., & Baker, J. (Eds.), (2012). Identification and development of sport talent: A brief introduction to a growing field of research and practice, In J. Baker, S. Cobley and J. Schorer (Eds.) *Talent identification and development in sport. International perspectives* (pp. 1–10). Routledge.

Cooper, D., & Allen, J. B. (2018). The coaching process of the expert coach: A coach led approach. *Sports Coaching Review*, *7*(2), 142–170. https://doi.org/10.1080/21640629.2017.1361168

Côté, J., Ericsson, K. A., & Law, M. P. (2005). Tracing the development of elite athletes using retrospective interview methods: A proposed interview and validation procedure for reported information. *Journal of Applied Sport Psychology*, *17*(1), 1–19. https://doi.org/10.1080/10413200590907531

Côté, J., Lidor, R., & Hackfort, D. (2009). ISSP position stand: To sample or to specialize? Seven postulates about youth sport activities that lead to continued participation and elite performance. *International Journal of Sport and Exercise Psychology*, *7*(1), 7–17. https://doi.org/10.1080/1612197X.2009.9671889

Cushion, C. (2007). Modelling the complexity of the coaching process. *International Journal of Sports Science and Coaching*, *2*(4), 345–401.

Davids, K., & Baker, J. (2007). Genes, environment and sport performance. *Sports Medicine*, *37*(11), 961–980. https://doi.org/10.2165/00007256-200737110-00004

Davids, K., Güllich, A., Araújo, D., & Shuttleworth, R. (2017). Understanding Environmental and Task Constraints on Talent Development: Analysis of Microstructure of Practice and Macro-Structure of Development Histories. In J. Baker, S. Cobley, & N. Wattie (Eds.), *Routledge handbook of talent identification and development in sport* (192–206). Routledge.

Dawkins, R. (2015). Essentialism. In J. Brockman (Ed.), *This idea must die* (pp. 84–87). Harper.

Dohme, L.C., Backhouse, S., Piggott, D., & Morgan, G. (2017). Categorising and defining popular psychological terms used within the youth athlete talent development literature: A systematic review. *International Review of Sport and Exercise Psychology*, *10*(1), 134–163. https://doi.org/10.1080/1750984X.2016.1185451

Feyerabend, P. (1975). *Against methods: Outline of an anarchistic theory of knowledge*. New Left Books.

Ford, P. R., Ward, P., Hodges, N. J., & Williams, A. M. (2009). The role of deliberate practice and play in career progression in sport: the early engagement hypothesis. *High Ability Studies*, *20*(1), 65–75. https://doi.org/10.1080/13598130902860721

Ford, P. R., & Williams, A. M. (2017). Sport Activity in childhood: Early specialization and diversification. In *Routledge handbook of talent identification and development in sport* (pp. 116–132). Routledge.

Gagné, F. (2004). Transforming gifts into talents: The DMGT as a developmental theory. *High Ability Studies*, *15*, 119–147. https://doi.org/10.1080/1359813042000314682

Gledhill, A., Harwood, C., & Forsdyke, D. (2017). Psychosocial factors associated with talent development in football: A systematic review. *Psychology of Sport and Exercise*, *31*, 93–112. https://doi.org/10.1016/j.psychsport.2017.04.002

Hecksteden, A., Kellner, R., & Donath, L. (2022). Dealing with small samples in football research. *Science and Medicine in Football*, *6*(3), 389–397. https://doi.org/10.1080/24733938.2021.1978106

Howe, M. J., Davidson, J. W., & Sloboda, J. A. (1998). Innate talents: Reality or myth? *The Behavioral and Brain Sciences*, *21*(3), 399–442. https://doi.org/10.1017/s0140525x9800123x

Issurin V. B. (2017). Evidence-based prerequisites and precursors of athletic talent: A review. *Sports Medicine (Auckland, N.Z.)*, *47*(10), 1993–2010. https://doi.org/10.1007/s40279-017-0740-0

Jayanthi N. A., LaBella C. R., Fischer D., Pasulka J., & Dugas L. R. (2015). Sports specialized intensive training and the risk of injury in young athletes: A clinical case-control study. *American Journal of Sports Medicine*, *43*, 794–801. https://doi.org/10.1177/0363546514567298

Johnston, K., McAuley, A. B. T., Kelly, A. L., & Baker, J. (2023) Language games and blurry terminology: Can clarity enhance athlete development? *Frontiers in Sports and Active Living*, *5*, 1150047. https://doi.org/10.3389/fspor.2023.1150047

Johnston, K., Wattie, N., Schorer, J., & Baker, J. (2018). Talent identification in sport: A systematic review. *Sports Medicine*, *48*(1), 97–109. https://doi.org/10.1007/s40279-017-0803-2

Kirkland, A., & O'Sullivan, M. (2018). There is no such thing as an international elite under-9 soccer player. *Journal of Sports Science & Medicine*, *17*(4), 686–688.

Kliethermes, S. A., Marshall, S. W., LaBella, C. R. et al. (2021). Defining a research agenda for youth sport specialisation in the USA: The AMSSM Youth Early Sport Specialization Summit. *British Journal of Sports Medicine*, *55*, 135–143. http://dx.doi.org/10.1136/bjsports-2020-102699

Kuhn, T. (1962). *The structure of scientific revolutions* (3rd ed.). University of Chicago Press.

LaPrade, R. F., Agel, J., Baker, J., Brenner, J. S., Cordasco, F. A., Côté, J., . . . & Provencher, M. T. (2016). AOSSM early sport specialization consensus statement. *Orthopaedic Journal of Sports Medicine*, *4*(4). https://doi.org/10.1177/2325967116644241

Larson, H. K., Young, B. W., McHugh, T. L. F., & Rodgers, W. M. (2019). Markers of early specialization and their relationships with burnout and dropout in swimming. *Journal of Sport and Exercise Psychology*, *41*(1), 46–54. https://doi.org/10.1123/jsep.2018-0305

Leite, N. M., & Sampaio, J. E. (2012). Long-term athletic development across different age groups and gender from Portuguese basketball players. *International Journal of Sports Science & Coaching*, *7*(2), 285–300. https://doi.org/10.1260/1747-9541.7.2.285

Lourenço, O. (2001). The danger of words: A Wittgensteinian lesson for developmentalists. *New Ideas in Psychology*, *19*(2), 89–115. https://doi.org/10.1016/S0732-118X(01)00002-2

McAuley, A. B. T., Baker, J., & Kelly, A. L. (2021a). Defining "elite" status in sport: from chaos to clarity. *German Journal of Exercise and Sport Research*, *52*, 193–197. https://doi.org/10.1007/s12662-021-00737-3

McAuley, A. B. T., Baker, J., & Kelly, A. L. (2021b). How nature and nurture conspire to influence athletic success. In A. L. Kelly, J. Côté, M. Jeffreys, & J. Turnnidge (Eds.), *Birth advantages and relative age effects in sport: Exploring organizational structures and creating appropriate settings* (pp. 159–183). Routledge.

McAuley, A. B. T., Hughes, D. C., Tsaprouni, L. G., Varley, I., Suraci, B., Roos, T. R., Herbert, A. J., & Kelly, A. L. (2021c). Genetic association research in football: A systematic review. *European Journal of Sport Science*, *21*(5), 714–752. https://doi.org/10.1080/17461391.2020.1776401

Morgan, P. B., Fletcher, D., & Sarkar, M. (2013). Defining and characterizing team resilience in elite sport. *Psychology of Sport and Exercise*, *14*(4), 549–559. https://doi.org/10.1016/j.psychsport.2013.01.004

Mosher, A., Fraser-Thomas, J., & Baker, J. (2020). What defines early specialization: A systematic review of literature. *Frontiers in Sports and Active Living*, *2*. https://doi.org/10.1177/19417381211049773

Robertson, M., Hauge, C., Evans, B. M., & Martin, L. J. (2019). Do participant reporting practices in youth sport research adequately represent the diversity of sport contexts? *Psychology of Sport and Exercise*, *45*, 101559. https://doi.org/10.1016/j.psychsport.2019.101559

Sieghartsleitner, R., Zuber, C., Zibung, M., & Conzelmann, A. (2018). "The early Specialised bird catches the worm!"—A specialised sampling model in the development of football talents. *Frontiers in Psychology*, *9*. https://doi.org/10.3389/fpsyg.2018.00188

Simonton, D. K. (2001). Talent development as a multidimensional, multiplicative, and dynamic process. *Current Directions in Psychological Science*, *10*(2), 39–43. https://doi.org/10.1111/1467-8721.00110

Sugimoto, D., Jackson, S. S., Howell, D. R., Meehan III, W. P., & Stracciolini, A. (2019). Association between training volume and lower extremity overuse injuries in young female athletes: implications for early sports specialization. *The Physician and Sportsmedicine*, *47*(2), 199–204. https://doi.org/10.1080/00913847.2018.1546107

Swann, C., Moran, A., & Piggott, D. (2015). Defining elite athletes: Issues in the study of expert performance in sport psychology. *Psychology of Sport and Exercise*, *16*, 3–14. https://doi.org/10.1016/j.psychsport.2014.07.004

Till, K., & Baker, J. (2020). Challenges and [possible] solutions to optimizing talent identification and development in sport. *Frontiers in Psychology*, *11*, 664. https://doi.org/10.3389/fpsyg.2020.00664

Verburgh, L., Scherder, E. J. A., van Lange, P. A. M., & Oosterlaan, J. (2016). The key to success in elite athletes? Explicit and implicit motor learning in youth elite and non-elite soccer players. *Journal of Sports Sciences*, *34*(18), 1782–1790. https://doi.org/10.1080/02640414.2015.1137344

Wattie, N., & Baker, J. (2017). Why conceptualizations of talent matter: Implications for skill acquisition and talent identification and development. In J. Baker, S. Cobley, J. Schorer, & N. Wattie (Eds.), *Routledge handbook of talent identification and development in sport* (pp. 69–79). Routledge.

Williams, D. A., Day, S., & Stebbings, G. (2017). What does 'elite' mean in sport and why does it matter? *The Sport and Exercise Scientist*, *51*, 6.

Wittgenstein, L. (1958). *Philosophical investigations*. Basil Blackwell.

21
THE COVID-19 PANDEMIC

Rethinking Directions for Talent Development in Youth Soccer

Alysha D. Matthews, Meredith M. Wekesser, Karl Erickson, Scott Pierce, and Adam L. Kelly

Introduction

On March 11, 2020, the World Health Organization (WHO, 2022) declared COVID-19 as a global pandemic. The pandemic has impacted billions of people across the globe, with over 494 million confirmed cases and 6 million deaths as of April 2022. Many countries implemented mandates that prohibited individuals from gathering in large numbers to mitigate spread of the virus (Hammami et al., 2020). To adhere to these health guidelines, nearly all in-person activities ceased (Parnell et al., 2020). In the wake of these responses, youth sport was suddenly interrupted, leaving athletes and coaches without the opportunity to properly conclude their seasons (Kelly et al., 2020).

Amid COVID-19 restrictions, children engaged in less physical activity and more sedentary behaviour, with early evidence showing girls and older children were more vulnerable to these effects (Dunton et al., 2020). Specific to youth soccer, a decrease in players' cardiorespiratory endurance levels was exhibited from changes in training during the lockdown period (Kalinowski et al., 2021). Not only has physical health been impacted, but athletes' mental health has been as well. For example, a study examining 13,000 adolescent athletes surveyed during the pandemic found that they reported worse mental health (i.e., anxiety and depression) and quality-of-life scores, compared to scores in pre-pandemic samples (McGuine et al., 2021). In addition, highly trained English adolescent swimmers (Newbury et al., 2022) and English academy soccer players (Carter et al., 2021) displayed signs of sub-optimal nutrition behaviour during lockdown, which was not corrected once they returned, and thus, could have immediate, short-term, and long-term implications on performance. These noteworthy changes in athletes' health and behaviours should be concerning to youth sport stakeholders and prompt them to consider how to minimise negative effects while promoting health and positive youth development through sport.

The unparalleled pause to sport programming propelled this current research team to study this once-in-a-lifetime phenomenon and consider what changes could emerge from this interruption of normalcy. More specifically, it sought to explore how parents, coaches, and administrators were reflecting upon the current youth sport landscape and how they might (re)imagine youth sport upon its return. These efforts allowed the research team to reach over 500 youth sport parents, coaches, and administrators across 21 countries. Specific to soccer, a total of 200 individuals from seven countries (majority United States) shared their visions, including 115 parents, 59 coaches, and 26 administrators. This chapter provides an overview of the Personal Assets Framework (PAF) (Côté et al., 2014, 2016) and presents important findings from these key stakeholders in youth soccer based on the PAF's dynamic elements, personal assets (i.e., 4Cs), and long-term outcomes (i.e., 3Ps). Moreover, this chapter synthesises stakeholder perspectives and addresses tensions among parents, coaches, and administrators. Finally, this chapter challenges youth soccer stakeholders to (re)imagine the landscape of talent development while providing practical recommendations for researchers and practitioners.

Personal Assets Framework

Participation in youth sport has been shown to foster several positive benefits and developmental outcomes for athletes, such as increased physical fitness and health promotion, positive social relationships, and interpersonal skills amongst many more (Côté & Fraser-Thomas, 2007; Fraser-Thomas et al., 2005). Further, research has shown that these long-term outcomes are heavily influenced by social agents in the sport environment (Erikstad et al., 2021). While there are many positive outcomes associated with youth sport participation, improvements can be made to advance youth athletes' development and sport experience. During the COVID-19 pandemic, a qualitative, open-ended survey was employed by the authors of this chapter to explore different stakeholder perspectives regarding the youth sport experience. Not only was it hoped to better understand youth sport parent, coach, and administrator perspectives, but it also aimed to examine the alignment or contention between stakeholders. Finally, the main goal was to disseminate findings back to stakeholders and provide practical recommendations and actions that could contribute to positive change for youth sports. To achieve this, the PAF was utilised to understand the unique process of athlete development in youth soccer during the COVID-19 pandemic.

The PAF posits that individuals develop through their immediate sport experience as they interact with three 'dynamic elements', including: (a) personal engagement in activities, (b) quality social dynamics, and (c) appropriate settings and organisational structures (Côté et al., 2014, 2016). These three dynamic elements create an immediate sport experience where a holistic range of personal assets, or 'the 4Cs', (i.e., competence, confidence, connection, and character) develop. As the elements change throughout the course of individuals' development, long-term outcomes, or the '3Ps' (i.e., participation, performance, and personal development), are attained. For an in-depth account of the PAF and the implications of the COVID-19 pandemic on youth sport, see Kelly et al. (2022) commentary. Since parents, coaches, and administrators play a key role in influencing long-term player outcomes, the PAF offers a strong framework to guide the interpretation of stakeholder perspectives in youth soccer. Further, the PAF provides a clear picture as to what aspects are emphasised or might need extra attention across each stakeholder group to facilitate optimal talent development environments, with consideration to the potentially lasting changes induced by the COVID-19 pandemic.

(Re)Imagining Youth Soccer Findings

This section presents each stakeholder group's perspectives on the influence of the COVID-19 pandemic on youth soccer and their talent development systems. This includes integration of the 4Cs (i.e., young athletes' personal assets to be developed) and 3Ps (i.e., long-term outcomes), and uses the dynamic elements of the PAF as a guiding interpretive framework. To ensure continued participation of youth in soccer, it is critical for researchers and practitioners to understand whether stakeholders have similar or differing viewpoints regarding the athlete development process. The PAF offers a framework to highlight how stakeholders view each of these elements and suggest future directions to enhance the concurrent processes of athlete development. Analysing the perspectives of three differing youth soccer stakeholders will highlight any gaps in the common pursuit of athlete development.

Parent Perspectives

Dynamic Elements

Prior to the pandemic, most parents rated youth soccer as moderately to extremely important for their families. A critical difference to other stakeholders was the importance parents placed on the quality relationships element during the pandemic. Aligned with the increase in anxiety and depression symptoms of adolescent athletes during the COVID-19 lockdown (McGuine et al., 2021), parents noted a decline in their children's social well-being and expressed the importance of youth soccer providing opportunities for players to build connections with their peers and coaches. On the other hand, parents enjoyed having more family time during the pandemic. This realisation led to desired changes in activities, whereby parents wanted a balance of youth soccer with family time and to decrease travelling time (which is also reflected in the *Administrator Perspectives* section). This is particularly relevant for professional soccer academies, who often ask their players from as young as aged 8 years to travel several hours just for an away fixture.

Parents also discussed how changes in the required or expected activities of youth soccer would make the setting more appropriate. Parents desired that youth soccer would be an activity that complimented their family rather than dominated, especially allowing their children to play multiple sports. This seems logical, particularly for those players who are competing at younger age groups, since sampling various activities can contribute to the development of expertise in soccer (Hornig et al., 2016). However, parents felt that this culture shift was outside of their control, implying the role administrators could play in bettering the context of youth soccer.

The 4Cs and the 3Ps

Parents discussed the goals they had for their children's involvement in youth soccer prior to and after the pandemic. Aligning with the PAF, long-term developmental outcomes addressed were *participation* and *personal development*, with little change in views between pre- and during-lockdown perspectives. The outcome of *performance* was not stressed by parents as a goal for their children, which highlights the idea that youth soccer should be prioritising participation and personal development over performance outcomes. This perception held by parents may come from youth soccer coaches over-focusing on skill development (Galatti et al., 2016) and defining talent with technical skills over psychological and social factors (Miller et al., 2015).

Parents also discussed the 4Cs they wanted their children to develop through soccer, specifically *confidence*, *competence*, and *character*. As these short-term changes in individual players are desired by parents, it would be fruitful for youth soccer to prioritise asset-building, which may also support the long-term talent development process. The importance parents placed on talent development decreased when imagining returning to soccer, and instead, parents emphasised the physical, psychological, and social benefits that soccer allowed for their children to experience. Therefore, talent development should be a goal for players, as long as youth soccer organisations aim to incorporate the development of personal assets as part of their programmes to support the holistic development of individuals.

Coach Perspectives

Dynamic Elements

Coaches also showed concern for the activities and settings designed by youth soccer organisations. However, they discussed these dynamic elements from their own perspective, rather than from that of the players. Coaches believed that, prior to the pandemic, organisational standards were often not set for coaches. This contributed to inappropriate coaching behaviours (e.g., supporting ego orientations through emphasising winning, inability to instruct technical skill development) and a misalignment between the values of coaches and those of the organisation. Coaches should be emphasising fun and effort rather than winning and competition to keep players in sport (Bailey et al., 2013). Providing a solution, coaches expressed the desire for their organisations to govern a more professional setting by creating standards for coach behaviour.

Another concern surrounded the activities and support provided by their organisations. Coaches stressed not receiving enough organisational support during the pandemic, except for a few online activities. During the pandemic, they expressed a need for systematic support from their administrators, while hoping for more open communication between the administrators and coaches when returning to play.

The 4Cs and the 3Ps

Coaches grounded their need for professionalisation in developing the individual asset of *competence*. Specifically, parent volunteer coaches were seen as a threat to the competence of their profession. Through the reflective pause the pandemic provided, coaches wanted to see changes by administrators to make youth soccer coaches more qualified, set clearer standards, support volunteers at building their own competence, as well as coordinate strengths of coaching staffs to better reach all players and their unique needs. Coaches of youth players need to make developmental considerations. However, professional youth soccer coaches were found to not consider age when deciding how to act as a coach (Partington et al., 2014). This gap alludes to a need for refined training (e.g., child development information) for youth soccer coaches to effectively engage with any age group.

Overall, coaches were looking to their administrators for more help and support in building their own assets. Youth soccer coaches felt strongly about the effectiveness of their coaching strategies and that they were supporting players towards the 3Ps of the PAF prior to the pandemic. Coaches not only emphasized their role in developing talent, but the *character* of their players as well. This perspective is particularly enlightening, as coach development programmes have been shown to often focus more specifically on technical and tactical development rather than fostering psychological and social outcomes (Lefebvre et al., 2016). Realising that the pandemic was a period of adversity for players, coaches lowered the importance of talent development in their practice, as youth soccer during this time needed to support the physical, psychological, and social well-being of their players.

Administrator Perspectives

Dynamic Elements

When reflecting on the activities that organisations offered, administrators believed they needed to better align with the 3Ps. Specifically, administrators discussed players' engagement in activities while recognising the importance of providing a balance for families within youth soccer. Suggestions included adapting season length to allow for multiple-sport participation and limiting the amount of travel in the hope that youth soccer would become a more balanced participation setting for families. Coincidingly, Côté and Hancock (2016) underscore ten policies that administrators could consider integrating into their programmes (e.g., 3–4-month seasons, limit lengthy travel, provide healthy competitive opportunities).

Another important discussion was the cost of youth soccer programmes. Although administrators viewed their programming cost as appropriate or inexpensive, the parent perspectives did not align with this idea. Previous research has shown those who are from higher socioeconomic status have greater access to youth sport (e.g., Allison & Barranco, 2021; Brown et al., 2022), which may be exacerbated once we return from the COVID-19 pandemic (Kelly et al., 2022). Some administrators discussed the feasibility of lowering the cost of programmes to ensure all children were able to engage in activities after the pandemic, although the ease of this sentiment was not shared by all. However, it is critical, especially after the attrition caused by the COVID-19 pandemic, to provide opportunities for soccer that are accessible for all (Watson & Koontz, 2021).

The 4Cs and the 3Ps

Administrators were asked to discuss the mission of the organisation where they worked during the pandemic. Most administrators presented missions that aligned with *performance*, *participation*, and *personal development* (i.e., the 3Ps). Moreover, the goals they set for players reflected the outcomes of the PAF yet needed to be clearer about *how* individuals would develop the 3Ps. Interestingly, however, administrators did not discuss the 4Cs of the PAF, which is an important gap in understanding and ameliorating the developmental infrastructure of youth soccer. Assessing organisations' emphasis and ability to build individual assets may help administrators align the pathway for players to develop through elements to the desired long-term outcomes. For instance, a study on developmental assets of adolescent soccer players found that team success did not have any relationship to asset building; it was instead transformational leadership that was positively related (Vella et al., 2013). Thus, administrators should offer coach development programmes that support coaches' ability to implement transformational leadership strategies (Turnnidge & Côté, 2017).

Through the focus on the developmental process, the importance administrators placed on talent development decreased when imagining returning to youth soccer after the pandemic. This shift stemmed from the increased importance placed on fun and life-skill development that players should experience in youth soccer. Moving forward, youth soccer administrators working in talent pathways (e.g., academies) should consider how to implement activities to promote fun and life-skill development alongside developing soccer-specific competence.

Integration of Findings

The PAF is a useful model to integrate findings from stakeholder perspectives across different timescales. The main takeaways across each aspect of the PAF are presented in Figure 21.1, which offer key strategies for stakeholders to incorporate while supporting players' development. The

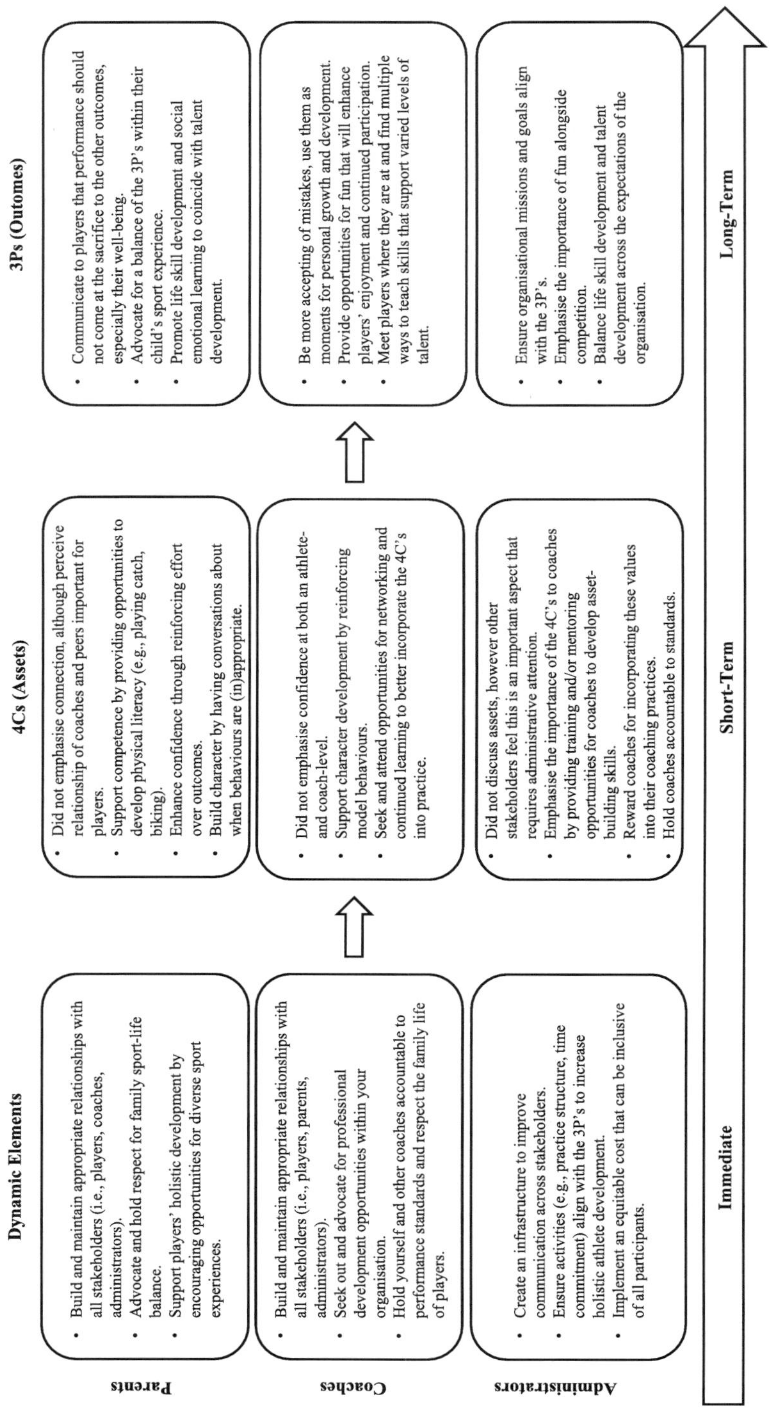

Dynamic Elements

Parents
- Build and maintain appropriate relationships with all stakeholders (i.e., players, coaches, administrators).
- Advocate and hold respect for family sport-life balance.
- Support players' holistic development by encouraging opportunities for diverse sport experiences.

Coaches
- Build and maintain appropriate relationships with all stakeholders (i.e., players, parents, administrators).
- Seek out and advocate for professional development opportunities within your organisation.
- Hold yourself and other coaches accountable to performance standards and respect the family life of players.

Administrators
- Create an infrastructure to improve communication across stakeholders.
- Ensure activities (e.g., practice structure, time commitment) align with the 3P's to increase holistic athlete development.
- Implement an equitable cost that can be inclusive of all participants.

4Cs (Assets)

- Did not emphasise connection, although perceive relationship of coaches and peers important for players.
- Support competence by providing opportunities to develop physical literacy (e.g., playing catch, biking).
- Enhance confidence through reinforcing effort over outcomes.
- Build character by having conversations about when behaviours are (in)appropriate.

- Did not emphasise confidence at both an athlete- and coach-level.
- Support character development by reinforcing model behaviours.
- Seek and attend opportunities for networking and continued learning to better incorporate the 4C's into practice.

- Did not discuss assets, however other stakeholders feel this is an important aspect that requires administrative attention.
- Emphasise the importance of the 4C's to coaches by providing training and/or mentoring opportunities for coaches to develop asset-building skills.
- Reward coaches for incorporating these values into their coaching practices.
- Hold coaches accountable to standards.

3Ps (Outcomes)

- Communicate to players that performance should not come at the sacrifice to the other outcomes, especially their well-being.
- Advocate for a balance of the 3P's within their child's sport experience.
- Promote life skill development and social emotional learning to coincide with talent development.

- Be more accepting of mistakes, use them as moments for personal growth and development.
- Provide opportunities for fun that will enhance players' enjoyment and continued participation.
- Meet players where they are at and find multiple ways to teach skills that support varied levels of talent.

- Ensure organisational missions and goals align with the 3P's.
- Emphasise the importance of fun alongside competition.
- Balance life skill development and talent development across the expectations of the organisation.

Immediate → Short-Term → Long-Term

FIGURE 21.1 Key strategies for stakeholders to incorporate while supporting youth soccer players' development.

broader picture highlights an important gap in youth soccer, which is developing the 4Cs. Even though the assets were not emphasised by administrators, the parent and coach perspectives were that the 4Cs are important tools to support athlete development. This section shares a summary of the dynamic elements, 4Cs, and 3Ps of the PAF across each stakeholder (i.e., parents, coaches, and administrators). Through a further integration of findings, key areas for improvement when considering the context of youth soccer and talent development are suggested.

Dynamic Elements

The dynamic elements were discussed across all stakeholders. Specifically, activities and settings were reflected on by all, yet quality relationships were only considered by parents. Parents presented their desire for children to develop relationships with their peers and asked for a balance between family and soccer. Although not explicitly stating relationships, coaches expressed a desire to be more connected to the administrators and other coaches within their organisations, suggesting the need for relational support. Stakeholders held similar opinions when discussing the importance of activities and settings within the youth soccer context. The current context of youth soccer highlighted concerns from these coaches about the lack of professionalisation for coaching and from these parents about the presence of relative age effects. Through reflection of typical participation of players within youth soccer, stakeholders suggested the need for activities to be better aligned with the desired outcomes (i.e., 3Ps). Moreover, as proposed by Côté and Hancock (2016), suggestions for appropriate settings surrounded a lesser time commitment (whether weekly or across a season) required by soccer players and their families also seems to be an important consideration moving forward.

The 4Cs

The 4Cs were discussed by parents and coaches as ways to reach the desired long-term outcomes (i.e., 3Ps) of youth soccer participation, although administrators did not mention these. Administrators spoke more specifically about the goals of the programme, activities provided to players, and organisational missions. These long-term organisational-level targets are necessary for administrators to be thinking about, yet the short-term, individual-level targets (i.e., 4Cs) are critical to achieving the 3Ps. This gap suggests a need for stakeholders to focus on the 4Cs when creating activities in order to align players with the outcomes of youth soccer.

Each of these three stakeholder groups have important roles when developing young soccer players. For example, administrators can set expectations for coaches to incorporate free play instead of structured play or competition, coaches can create life-skill development activities alongside technical drills, and parents can offer positive reinforcement and external support. Consequently, it is imperative for stakeholder values across the youth soccer system to align to ensure congruence with all individuals and that everyone is striving towards the same goals (Dorsch et al., 2022; Maurice et al., 2021). Being on the same page can afford the youth soccer system the opportunity to systematically implement talent development strategies and balance talent development alongside other key areas of player development.

The 3Ps

The 3Ps were also mentioned across all stakeholders, who encouraged the continued support of these outcomes for youth who participate in soccer. Stakeholders believed these outcomes were important, yet emphasised the difference between focusing solely on talent development and taking

TABLE 21.1 Sample quotes from each stakeholder when reflecting on the aspects of the PAF

Stakeholder	Dynamic Elements	Assets (4Cs)	Outcomes (3Ps)
Parent	"[I have] more desire to change the current culture which is overly demanding and pushing early specialisation and too much time and travel."	"I want my kids to learn the importance of maintaining a healthy lifestyle and staying active. I want them to have fun and to learn how to be a good teammate and a leader on the court or field. I want strong, confident kids who are healthy in body and mind."	"[I want my kids] to have fun playing a game and play with and against athletes at a similar competitive level. To spend a long time developing them as athletes by making them play multiple sports to develop their overall athleticism over time."
Coach	"I would like to see all adults, including parents, make a concerted effort to refocus on the players. Currently, decisions in youth soccer have become driven by money and business reasons. If you look at how far teams travel to play and how often players move clubs/teams when they don't get what they want, it's not a culture that really supports youth development."	"You're in a leadership role to mould the youth. It [a coach] should be competent and serious about moulding them to have good morals and values while helping them develop in the sport. However, coaching and child psychology education should be required; but it should not have to cost an arm and a leg to acquire. It should be free or very low cost and mandated by the national governing agency of soccer."	"I would like to have a little more shared values with opponent coaches and parents that see the big picture instead of a quick win. Stacking teams with the best talent from all over is detrimental to developing local talent and supporting families and a community. I enjoy watching girls develop and grow in the sport [of soccer]."
Administrator	"I think we require a large time commitment from our players, and we need to do a better job at offering a better sport-life balance."	"[I think we need] more emphasis on being a team, service, growth, and character development. I think they will improve as players if this is added."	"[We intend to put] a spotlight on the reasons we play: the philosophy, goals, and our overall mission."

a holistic approach to personal development. Using a quantitative ranking measure, stakeholders ranked their desired emphasis on talent development and other key aspects of soccer (e.g., exercising, making friends, being part of a team). Interestingly, findings showed that stakeholders ranked talent development as less important when imagining a return to sport, compared to their initial rankings prior to the pandemic. Instead, stakeholders increased the rankings for physical and social health benefits of soccer participation. In particular, one issue that was presented by coaches and parents was the idea of relative age effects. Meaning, adult leaders in youth sport support the development of relatively older athletes who show signs of advanced physiological and psychosocial skills, compared to their relatively younger peers when they are grouped based on chronological age (Kelly & Williams, 2020). This concept can cause a disparity in players' experiences of development;

thus, stakeholders should consider how they group young players and possible strategies to moderate relative age effects in youth soccer (Kelly et al., 2021; see Chapter 10). Overall, the stakeholders perceived talent development as a valued aspect and outcome of youth soccer participation. However, this finding highlights stakeholders' collective desire for soccer organisations to balance talent development with other aspects of development (i.e., life skills, social-emotional learning, fitness, motor development). See Table 21.1 for sample quotes from each stakeholder group when reflecting on the dynamic elements, 4Cs, and 3Ps.

Tensions Between Stakeholders

It is imperative to the function of development in youth soccer for stakeholders to have a coherent mission and efficient communication to appropriately support children that participate (Martindale et al., 2005). However, it appears tensions lay between coaches and administrators. For instance, coaches relayed their needs from their organisations, asking for more open communication and asset-building opportunities. Parents and coaches also discussed similar tensions and requested change from administrators to better support the 3Ps. Both parents and coaches discussed talent development, especially the presence of relative age effects in youth soccer. Coaches further shared concerns that talent development had too much emphasis and, due to the organisational structure, coaches were stacking their teams with talented players that increased the talent gap across teams. Parents presented the economic concerns behind talent development, such as needing to spend an increasing amount of money each season, which leaves out some talented players that are unable to afford programming.

Parents and coaches seem to be sacrificing more to benefit the youth who participate in soccer, especially their own time and health. Yet, why is there a demand to sacrifice themselves for soccer players? This problem may be trickling down from the system and out of their control. Parents and coaches looked to administrators to make changes in the activities provided to players and shift the settings in which youth soccer takes place. As such, it seems logical for administrators to develop an infrastructure for talent development that does not require even more effort from parents or coaches, which can allow for these specific stakeholders to place less emphasis on talent development and focus on other aspects of athlete development (e.g., life skills and social-emotional development).

Considerations for Researchers

COVID-19 presented a unique opportunity to reflect upon existing organisational structures and stakeholder perspectives as well as consider how the impact of the pandemic can shape the future of organised youth soccer. Researchers working in talent development are encouraged to examine how COVID-19 altered youth soccer, since it holds various avenues for future research (see Kelly et al., 2020 for an overview). The PAF provides a useful framework for researchers to illustrate the possible mechanisms and outcomes of youth soccer as a result of COVID-19. By evaluating the engagement in activities, social dynamics, and appropriate settings, it will allow stakeholders to better understand the potential implications on immediate (i.e., dynamic elements), short-term (i.e., 4Cs), and long-term (i.e., 3Ps) developmental outcomes. Moreover, the opportunity to evaluate existing youth soccer structures, alongside carrying forward the impactful strategies that have been forcefully developed during lockdown, may facilitate a greater emphasis on positive youth development in the future.

Given the current uncertainty regarding these effects, it would be worthwhile for future research to examine how participation in soccer activities (e.g., coach-led practice, youth-led practice, youth-led play, competition) during the time of COVID-19 has/will influence youths' developmental trajectories. Moreover, even beyond the recent COVID-19 restrictions, since the dynamics of technological advancements and their rapid integration into different social spheres such as youth soccer (i.e., the 4th Industrial Revolution; Smith et al., 2019) were already beginning to outpace traditional predictions, it will also be important to explore how these virtual methods of delivery may continue or evolve in youth soccer. Lastly, this crisis may have exacerbated inequities between youths due to their geographic location and socioeconomic status. As such, it is important for researchers to capture who may be at greater risk of youth soccer dropout and mental health issues due to the COVID-19 pandemic to ensure this effect is minimised.

Considerations for Practitioners

This chapter allowed the authors to capture how key stakeholders would (re)imagine youth soccer during a time of COVID-19. As such, it has provided a useful opportunity to design considerations for practitioners upon their return from COVID-19 and face a 'new normal'. Based on the perspectives of each stakeholder group and the extant literature presented throughout this chapter, five postulates are provided for practitioners as important future directions for development in youth soccer:

- Consider the logistics for players and parents when designing programmes to ensure they add to the players' and parents' lifestyles rather than take away from them. Focus should be placed on how players and parents can spend more quality time with their families and less time on travelling to organised youth soccer.
- Mental health and well-being may be affected by both participating (e.g., fear, stress) and abstaining (e.g., social isolation) from youth soccer activities during the COVID-19 pandemic. These risks extend beyond the youth players themselves, as there are also concerns for parents, coaches, administrators, and soccer organisations. Thus, education and support should be provided for *all* those involved in youth soccer programmes.
- Philosophies should be designed around developing players as well-rounded young people (i.e., personal development) rather than solely focusing on creating future professional soccer players (i.e., performance). This could be achieved through additional coach education concentrating on enhancing transformational leadership skills, which could subsequently help transform players' values and motivate them to achieve performance outcomes beyond their normal expectations or limits (see Chapter 13).
- Consider the costs associated with organised youth soccer. The continued access to structured activities may come at a financial cost, and as a result of the COVID-19 pandemic, monetary outlay for organised youth soccer may not be a financial priority for some families. Therefore, young players may be withdrawing from soccer programmes or moving even further away from being able to access them due to not being able to afford the associated fees and resources.
- Ensure that stakeholder values align and consider the 3Ps *and* the 4Cs when designing youth soccer programmes. Indeed, by placing less emphasis on talent development, stakeholders may provide a context where the 4Cs are developed. It seems that asset building may be a suggested avenue to increase talent and engagement while guiding athletes to reach the 3Ps. It is important that stakeholders of youth soccer emphasise talent development, but not at the sacrifice of continued participation and personal development.

Conclusion

Talent development is an important piece in the athlete development process that can support soccer players' performance. However, a narrow focus on performance outcomes can limit individuals' scope of personal development and participation in soccer. As all 3Ps need to be considered when supporting the holistic development of players, there needs to be a balance between them. Throughout this chapter, each stakeholder has acknowledged this need for balance (e.g., sport-life balance, talent vs. life-skill development). A clear alignment of perspectives was found, yet the challenge remains on integrating these stakeholders together in their pursuit of supporting young soccer players. Therefore, strategies have been suggested for each role of the stakeholder to support the long-term outcomes of soccer participation. It is proposed these practical suggestions will shift the context of soccer to a more balanced perspective of athlete development, which may support players efforts toward talent development. Moving forward, it will be critical to monitor and evaluate how the COVID-19 pandemic has impacted stakeholders across the immediate, short-term, and long-term to ensure the potential impact is minimised.

References

Allison, R., & Barranco, R. (2021). 'A rich white kid sport?' Hometown socioeconomic, racial, and geographic composition among U.S. women's professional soccer players. *Soccer & Society*, 22(5), 457–469. https://doi.org/10.1080/14660970.2020.1827231

Bailey, R., Cope, E. J., & Pearce, G. (2013). Why do children take part in, and remain involved in sport? A literature review and discussion of implications for sports coaches. *International Journal of Coaching Science*, 7(1).

Brown, T. W., Greetham, P., Powell, A., Gough, L., Khawaja, I., & Kelly, A. L. (2022). The sociodemographic profile of the England and Wales Cricket Board (ECB) talent pathways and first-class counties. *Managing Sport and Leisure*. https://doi.org/10.1080/23750472.2021.1949382

Carter, J. L., Kelly, A. L., Williams, R. A., Ford, T. J., & Cole, M. (2021). Exploring sports nutritionists' and players' perspectives of nutrition practice within English professional football during the COVID-19 pandemic. *Science and Medicine in Football*, 5(S1), 32–37. https://doi.org/10.1080/24733938.2021.1984559

Côté, J., & Fraser-Thomas, J. (2007). Youth involvement in sport. In P. R. E. Crocker (Ed.), *Sport psychology: A Canadian perspective* (266–294). Pearson Prentice Hall.

Côté, J., & Hancock, D. J. (2016). Evidence-based policies for youth sport programmes. *International Journal of Sport Policy and Politics*, 8(1), 51–65. https://doi.org/10.1080/19406940.2014.919338

Côté, J., Turnnidge, J., & Evans, M. B. (2014). The dynamic process of development through sport. *Kinesiologica Slovenica: Scientific Journal on Sport*, 20, 14–26.

Côté, J., Turnnidge, J., & Vierimaa, M. (2016). A personal assets approach to youth sport. In A. Smith & K. Green (Eds.), *Handbook of youth sport* (pp. 243–256). Routledge.

Dorsch, T. E., Smith, A. L., Blazo, J. A., Coakley, J., Côté, J., Wagstaff, C. R., Warner, S., & King, M. Q. (2022). Toward an integrated understanding of the youth sport system. *Research Quarterly for Exercise and Sport*, 93(1), 105–119. https://doi.org/10.1080/02701367.2020.1810847

Dunton, G. F., Do, B., & Wang, S. D. (2020). Early effects of the COVID-19 pandemic on physical activity and sedentary behavior in children living in the U.S. *BMC Public Health*, 20(1351). https://doi.org/10.1186/s12889-020-09429-3

Erikstad, M. K., Johansen, B. T., Johnsen, M., Haugen, T., & Côté, J. (2021). "As many as possible for as long as possible"—A case study of a soccer team that fosters multiple outcomes. *The Sport Psychologist*, 35(2), 131–141. https://doi.org/10.1123/tsp.2020-0107

Fraser-Thomas, J. L., Côté, J., & Deakin, J. (2005). Youth sport programs: An avenue to foster positive youth development. *Physical Education and Sport Pedagogy*, 10, 19–40. https://doi.org/10.1080/1740898042000334890

Galatti, L. R., Scaglia, A. J., Bettega, O. B., & Paes, R. R. (2016). Coaches' perceptions of youth players' development in a professional soccer club in Brazil: Paradoxes between the game and those who play. *Sports Coaching Review*, 5(2), 174–185. https://doi.org/10.1080/21640629.2016.1201359

Hammami, A., Harrabi, B., Mohr, M., & Krustrup, P. (2020). Physical activity and coronavirus disease 2019 (COVID-19): Specific recommendations for home-based physical training. *Managing Sport and Leisure*, 27(1–2), 26–31. https://doi.org/10.1080/23750472.2020.1757494

Hornig, M., Aust, F., & Güllich, A. (2016). Practice and play in the development of German top-level professional football players. *European Journal of Sport Science*, 16(1), 96–105. https://doi.org/10.1080/17461391.2014.982204

Kalinowski, P., Myszkowski, J., & Marynowicz, J. (2021). Effect of online training during the COVID-19 quarantine on the aerobic capacity of youth soccer players. *International Journal of Environmental Research and Public Health*, *18*(12), 6195. https://doi.org/10.3390/ijerph18126195

Kelly, A. L., Côté, J., Turnnidge, J., & Hancock, D. (2021). Editorial: Birth advantages and relative age effects. *Frontiers in Sports and Active Living*, *3*(721704), 1–3. https://doi.org/10.3389/fspor.2021.721704

Kelly, A. L., Erickson, K., Pierce, S., & Turnnidge, J. (2020). Youth sport and COVID-19: Contextual, methodological, and practical considerations. *Frontiers in Sports and Active Living*, *2*(584252), 1–4. https://doi.org/10.3389/fspor.2020.584252

Kelly, A. L., Erickson, K., & Turnnidge, J. (2022). Youth sport in the time of COVID-19: Considerations for researchers and practitioners. *Managing Sport & Leisure*, *27*(1–2), 62–72. https://doi.org/10.1080/23750472.2020.1788975

Kelly, A. L., & Williams, C. A. (2020). Physical characteristics and the talent identification and development processes in youth soccer: A narrative review. *Strength and Conditioning Journal*, *42*(6), 15–34. https://doi.org/10.1519/SSC.0000000000000576

Lefebvre, J. S., Evans, M. B., Turnnidge, J., Gainforth, H. L., & Côté, J. (2016). Describing and classifying coach development programmes: A synthesis of empirical research and applied practice. *International Journal of Sports Science & Coaching*, *11*(6), 887–899. https://doi.org/10.1177/1747954116676116

Martindale, R. J. J., Collins, D., & Daubney, J. (2005). Talent development: A guide for practice and research within sport. *Quest*, *57*, 353–375. https://doi.org/10.1080/00336297.2005.10491862

Maurice, J., Devonport, T. J., & Knight, C. J. (2021). Toward improved triadic functioning: Exploring the interactions and adaptations of coaches, parents, and athletes in professional academy soccer through the adversity of COVID-19. *Frontiers in Psychology*, *12*, 609631. https://doi.org/10.3389/fpsyg.2021.609631

McGuine, T. A., Biese, K., Petrovska, L., Hetzel, S. J., Schwarz, A., Reardon, C., Kliethermes, S., Bell, D. R., Brooks, A., & Watson, A. M. (2021). Mental health, physical activity, and quality of life of US adolescent athletes during COVID-19-related school closures and sport cancellations: A study of 13,000 athletes. *Journal of Athletic Training*, *56*(1), 11–19. https://doi.org/10.4085/1062-6050-0478.20

Miller, P. K., Cronin, C., & Baker, G. (2015). Nurture, nature and some very dubious social skills: An interpretative phenomenological analysis of talent identification practices in elite English youth soccer. *Qualitative Research in Sport, Exercise and Health*, *7*(5), 642–662. https://doi.org/10.1080/2159676X.2015.1012544

Newbury, J. W., Foo, W. L., Cole, M., Kelly, A. L., Chessor, R. J., Sparks, S. A., Faghy, M. A., Gough, H. C., & Gough, L. A. (2022). Nutritional intakes of highly trained adolescent swimmers before, during, and after a national lockdown in the COVID-19 pandemic. *PloS One*, *17*(4), e0266238. https://doi.org/10.1371/journal.pone.0266238

Parnell, D., Widdop, P., Bond, A., & Wilson, R. (2020). COVID-19, networks and sport. *Managing Sport and Leisure*, *27*(1–2), 78–84. https://doi.org/10.1080/23750472.2020.1750100

Partington, M., Cushion, C., & Harvey, S. (2014). An investigation of the effect of athletes' age on the coaching behaviours of professional top-level youth soccer coaches. *Journal of Sports Sciences*, *32*(5), 403–414. https://doi.org/10.1080/02640414.2013.835063

Smith, A. L., Erickson, K., & Malete, L. (2019). Advancing youth sport scholarship: Selected directions and considerations. *Kinesiology Review*, *8*, 269–277. https://doi.org/10.1123/kr.2019-0046

Turnnidge, J., & Côté, J. (2017). Transformational coaching workshop: Applying a person-centred approach to coach development programs. *International Sport Coaching Journal*, *4*(3), 314–325. https://doi.org/10.1123/iscj.2017-0046

Vella, S. A., Oades, L. G., & Crowe, T. P. (2013). The relationship between coach leadership, the coach–athlete relationship, team success, and the positive developmental experiences of adolescent soccer players. *Physical Education and Sport Pedagogy*, *18*(5), 549–561. https://doi.org/10.1080/17408989.2012.726976

Watson, A., & Koontz, J. S. (2021). Youth sports in the wake of COVID-19: A call for change. *British Journal of Sports Medicine*, *55*(14), 764–764. http://doi.org/10.1136/bjsports-2020-103288

World Health Organization (2022, April 8). Coronavirus disease (COVID-19) pandemic. Retrieved from: www.who.int

22

FROM KNOWLEDGE TO ACTION

Bridging the Gap Between Research and Practice in Youth Soccer

Adam L. Kelly and Jennifer Turnnidge

Introduction

One of the central aims of this book was to offer a range of considerations for researchers and practitioners working in youth soccer. Now that the *what* (i.e., specific information) and *why* (i.e., cause or rationale) have been explored, a logical closing chapter should be to focus on *how* (i.e., by what means) to translate some of these considerations into future research and practice. As such, the purpose of this chapter is to encourage researchers and practitioners to work alongside each other to co-design, implement, and evaluate evidence-informed practice to create more appropriate settings in youth soccer.

Many approaches have been discussed within this book to help understand talent identification and development through both a researcher and practitioner lens. It is evident that these processes are complex, dynamic, and multidimensional and thus require a broad range of knowledge and actions from stakeholders (Kelly & Williams, 2020). Whilst there are various take-home messages throughout each individual chapter that will enable researchers and practitioners to create more appropriate settings in their respective environments, there are two key 'calls to action' for stakeholders to consider that were consistent across numerous chapters: (a) engage in meaningful collaborations in all phases of the knowledge creation and implementation processes, and (b) focus on mobilising knowledge that fosters inclusive and equitable soccer environments. By addressing these calls to action, it is hoped that we can create positive experiences for all of those invested in youth soccer.

Calls to Action

So, how can these calls to action be achieved? First, we need to focus on fostering meaningful collaborations when designing, implementing, and evaluating research and soccer programmes. This includes ensuring that all partners are involved in decision-making processes and are provided opportunities to share their expertise and experiential knowledge in safe and supportive environments. Meaningful collaborations should be grounded in the principles of mutual respect and inclusion. By engaging in meaningful collaborations, we can improve the relevance of research and soccer programmes, and hopefully, enhance their contribution to talent identification and development processes.

The second call to action builds on using meaningful collaborations to create inclusive soccer environments. This collaborative approach in which the lived experiences of particular communities and stakeholders is considered essential to achieve equitable outcomes. A first step to foster inclusion is for all partners to reflect on the ways in which talent identification and development are entrenched in historical inequities and continue to perpetuate inequity in current soccer contexts. For instance, organisational policies related to talent identification and development have influenced who can access quality soccer experiences. More specifically, Chapter 10 illustrated how relatively younger players are not merely 'underrepresented' in soccer talent pathways. Rather, they are systematically excluded through the design and implementation of organisational policies (i.e., age-group structures). As such, researchers and practitioners should reflect upon and adapt their policies to ensure that they are creating accessible and inclusive soccer pathways. Stakeholders are also encouraged to reflect on ways they can foster more accessible and inclusive sport experiences. Not only will this create more equitable opportunities, but it will also widen the pool of potential talent through supporting as many as possible, for as long as possible, in the best environment possible (Erikstad et al., 2021).

Another way we can address these calls to action is by recognising that talent identification and development processes need to be person-centred and context specific. These processes should be dynamic so that they reflect diverse stakeholder needs that evolve over the course of their developmental trajectories. Moreover, talent identification and development should be focused on creating inclusive soccer pathways in which all individuals can thrive. Most notably, the lack of literature focused on the experiences of women and girls that was available to present throughout the book (see Curran et al., 2019 for a review) emphasises the need for more equitable approaches. Lastly, transformational change of talent identification and development may require a cultural shift. By taking a strength-based approach (Eccles & Gootman, 2002; Rubin et al., 2012) that values the richness of diverse experiences, perspectives, and voices, we can create talent pathways in youth soccer that support everyone's development and well-being. In order to achieve this, it is important to consider an integrated knowledge translation approach to guide the delivery of sustainable, evidence-informed interventions.

The Knowledge to Action Framework

Knowledge mobilisation involves using high-quality knowledge during decision-making processes. The aim of knowledge mobilisation is to encourage researchers and key stakeholders (e.g., practitioners and policymakers) to work collaboratively to support research-informed policies and practices (Straus et al., 2013). Personal contact and co-production between researchers, practitioners, and policymakers is vital for research uptake and creating evidence-informed practice. This involves moving research from the study (e.g., article, book, conference, laboratory) into the hands of people and organisations who can put it to practical use.

There are several knowledge mobilisation frameworks (see Esmail et al., 2020 for a review) that each provide valuable insight into bridging the gap between research and practice. For the purposes of this chapter, attention will be focused on using the 'Knowledge to Action' (KTA) conceptual framework (Graham et al., 2006). The KTA guides the implementation of sustainable, evidence-informed interventions in sport. This approach emphasises involvement of all stakeholders in the research process, the critical importance of contextual factors, and tailoring knowledge to the needs of people who are going to use it (Field et al., 2014). The KTA framework includes two processes: (a) evidence-informed *knowledge creation*, which involves the refinement of primary studies into knowledge tools or products through the process of synthesising existing knowledge, and (b) the *action cycle*, which is the process that leads to the application of knowledge and skills previously created through informing future policy and systemic change.

The first part of the KTA, knowledge creation, is a funnelled approach that begins with knowledge inquiry into primary studies that is then synthesised to help make sense of all the relevant information on a subject (e.g., talent identification and development in youth soccer). Based on this knowledge, tools and/or products are designed to present information in a user-friendly way, with the purpose of influencing stakeholders' proceeding actions (i.e., the narrow end of the funnel) (Graham et al., 2006). It is important to emphasise that each phase of knowledge creation should be tailored to the needs of knowledge users with the purpose of positively impacting real-word settings (Holt et al., 2018).

The second part of the KTA, the action cycle, is a step-by-step process that leads to the implementation or application of the knowledge tools and/or products formerly created. This cycle is represented by the following phases: (a) identify problem then identify, review, and select knowledge, (b) adapt knowledge to the local context, (c) assess barriers to knowledge use, (d) select, tailor, and implement interventions, (e) monitor knowledge use, (f) evaluate outcomes, and (g) sustain knowledge use (Graham et al., 2006). The action cycle is linked to knowledge creation by the phase of identifying the problem then identifying, reviewing, and selecting knowledge (Holt et al., 2018).

Although the KTA was originally designed for healthcare professions (e.g., medicine, nursing, pharmaceuticals, rehabilitation, public health), sport and exercise disciplines have begun to realise the benefits of a KTA approach (e.g., Tomasone et al., 2020). Particularly relevant examples from the sports literature include positive youth development (Holt et al., 2018) and para-sport (Allan et al., 2021). For instance, Holt et al. (2018) created 'PYDSportNET', a knowledge translation project designed to enhance the use of research evidence promoting positive youth development (PYD) through sport. More specifically, Holt et al. (2018, p. 135) explained how they utilised the KTA when designing PYDSportNET to achieve the following objectives: "(a) consolidate the evidence base by systematically reviewing PYD through sport research (knowledge creation), (b) create knowledge products for PYD through sport (knowledge creation), and (c) examine stakeholders' perceptions of research problems, along with barriers, challenges, and opportunities associated with using research findings (action cycle)". Likewise, Allan et al. (2021) used the KTA to develop a narrative learning tool for coaches of athletes with a disability. Together, these studies demonstrate the usefulness of applying the KTA to sport settings, which are adaptable to the context of youth soccer.

From Knowledge to Action in Youth Soccer

Based on our current knowledge and the literature presented throughout this book, it is evident that research in youth soccer is not always being translated into applied practice (Turnnidge & Kelly, 2021). As an example, the limited adoption of proposed relative age solutions is perhaps due to the lack of collaboration between researchers and practitioners leading to issues surrounding integrated knowledge translation (Verbeek et al., 2021). This book also shines a light on under-researched populations during knowledge inquiry based on factors such as gender (i.e., women and girls), abilities (i.e., para-soccer), and position (i.e., goalkeepers). For instance, Chapter 2 (male = 89.3%, female = 1.3%, no gender reported = 9.4%; McCalman et al., 2021) and Chapter 3 (male samples = 79.2%; Rechenchosky et al., 2021) illustrated the disparities in technical testing and tactical knowledge/performance research, respectively, between males and females. Therefore, focus should be placed on better understanding talent identification and development across diverse groups, particularly since the ecological and external validity of the many outfield male populated studies are likely not applicable to other contexts. To be specific, girls and boys mature differently (Chapter 17), players with disabilities may benefit from adapted techniques (Chapter 18), and goalkeepers have unique positional demands (Chapter 19). The likely causes of the disparity in research is the lack of funding available coupled with the smaller pool of participants. As such, in the context of the KTA, funders and knowledge creators should prioritise working with groups who are largely absent in the current literature.

Designing new tools and products must be seen as an opportunity to create contemporary policies and more appropriate youth soccer settings. Those working with underrepresented groups and emerging soccer nations should learn from the successful approaches *and* structural flaws from the available evidence (e.g., Chapter 16). This will help practitioners tailor innovative practice for their respective environments as well as ensure similar issues are not recreated. Both researchers and practitioners should be engaged in the co-creation of tools and products to ensure they are meaningful and relevant. While this chapter has, so far, underscored opportunities for future research and practice, this book has also outlined numerous successful examples of how research can be situated within the funnel knowledge creation. Specifically, various chapters reviewed studies (e.g., systematic reviews, narrative reviews, Delphi studies, editorials, commentaries) that align with the KTA stages of knowledge inquiry, knowledge synthesis, and development of products/tools that could be replicated in the future.

It is also important to highlight how some chapters also explored some successful examples of work that aligns with the action cycle. For instance, Chapter 4 showed that, due to the large variation in the timing of maturation and the overrepresentation of early maturers in talent development programmes (e.g., identifying problem, adapting knowledge to the local context, assessing barriers to knowledge use), 'bio-banding' (Cumming et al., 2017) is becoming a common practice in academy soccer to negate against these maturity-related biases and help create more appropriate settings (e.g., select, tailor, and implement interventions, monitor knowledge use, evaluate outcomes). Moving forward, it will be important to continue evaluating the impact of bio-banding on long-term player development, since the current studies that exist have often evaluated tournament formats (e.g., sustain knowledge use).

Some national governing bodies and professional soccer clubs have also seen the benefit of looking beyond the technical and tactical development of coaches, through implementing interpersonal skills into their philosophy. For example, in line with the KTA, Turnnidge et al. (2017) suggested that coach development programmes could improve by: (a) placing a greater emphasis on facilitating coaches' interpersonal behaviours, (b) using appropriate and systematic evaluation frameworks to guide the evaluation of interpersonally focused coach development programmes, and (c) incorporating behaviour change theories into the design and implementation of these coach development programmes. By doing so, organisations could use transformational coaching as a component of an educational programme to facilitate coaches' development of leadership behaviours (e.g., Chapter 13).

These examples may be adaptable for other talent identification and development disciplines that are evolving in youth soccer, such as social influences (i.e., Chapter 6), sociocultural background (i.e., Chapter 7), career transitions (i.e., Chapter 9), a flexible chronological approach (i.e., Chapter 11), creativity (i.e., Chapter 12), genetics (i.e., Chapter 14), and nutrition (i.e., Chapter 15). Most notably, the immediate, short-term, and long-term impact of COVID-19 on youth player development remains relatively unknown (i.e., Chapter 21). In an attempt to mitigate against the possible impact of the recent global pandemic across all timescales, researchers and practitioners should work together to create knowledge and design, implement, and evaluate relevant interventions (see Kelly et al., 2021 for a review).

Lastly, in order to make sure researchers and practitioners are all moving in the same direction to achieve their intended outcomes (Johnston et al., 2023), the language used in research and practice needs to be consistent and have clarity (i.e., Chapter 20; see McAuley et al., 2021 for an example). Interestingly, however, Bruner et al. (2022) recently presented how there were 243 unique operational definitions to represent 'positive youth development through sport' when reviewing the academic literature, which could cause confusion and contradiction in applied practice. As such, employing the KTA through knowledge synthesis approaches and engaging in the co-creation of consensus could help achieve greater consistency and clarity in terms and their definitions. Figure 22.1 presents an example of how to apply the KTA framework to youth soccer.

Considerations for Researchers and Practitioners

Throughout this book, each chapter has separately outlined considerations to guide researchers' and practitioners' future study and practice, respectively. In this section, however, to promote collaboration between all stakeholders, some ways in which both researchers and practitioners can engage in all phases of the KTA in their current and future initiatives are explored together (see Table 22.1). Overall, these considerations encourage stakeholders to reflect on whose experiences are being prioritised in research and practice as well as to embrace innovative approaches to explore and share the stories of those whose experiences have gone untold.

These considerations also emphasise the importance of capacity building (United Nations, n.d.), which is a key component of knowledge translation. This involves enhancing the knowledge and competencies of all stakeholders to ensure that meaningful knowledge mobilisation is achieved. Accordingly, it is important to ensure that all stakeholders are provided opportunities to develop their skills. For instance, researchers may offer programme evaluation training sessions that include trainees, coaches, and decision-makers. This can also involve leveraging each stakeholder's expertise and social networks to support one another in the design, implementation, and evaluation of evidence-informed interventions. Researchers and practitioners are encouraged to reflect upon the considerations provided in Table 22.1 to help inform their KTA processes.

Conclusion

Knowledge mobilisation approaches offer a salient avenue for creating evidence-informed and inclusive talent identification and development. By engaging in meaningful collaborations and co-production across each phase of the knowledge mobilisation process, we can work together to create positive soccer experiences for all. It is important to recognise that knowledge mobilisation

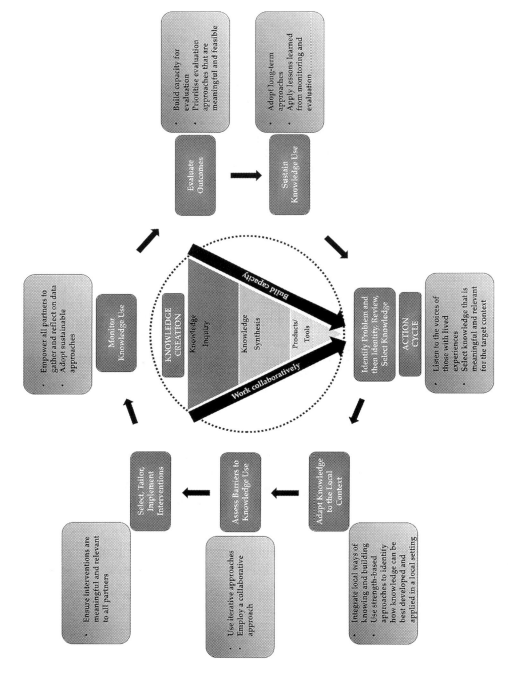

FIGURE 22.1 Applying the KTA framework to youth soccer.

Adapted from Graham et al. 2006

TABLE 22.1 Considerations for researchers and practitioners when using the KTA framework

KTA Process	Considerations
Knowledge inquiry	• Focus on building capacity to enable partners to actively engage in knowledge inquiry (e.g., planning research design, developing data collection tools, conducting data analysis) • Emphasise studies that include diverse experiences (e.g., women and girls, players with disabilities, goalkeepers)
Knowledge synthesis	• Focus on synthesising knowledge that answers meaningful and relevant questions • Explore novel ways to synthesise different forms of knowledge (e.g., document analysis, policy analysis, artefact analysis) • Build capacity for all partners to engage in knowledge synthesis (e.g., reviewing study quality) • Employ knowledge synthesis approaches to explore gaps and limitations in the current knowledge base
Developing knowledge products/tools	• Start with partners' needs to ensure products and tools are meaningful and relevant • Engage in the co-creation of products and tools • Consider how tools may need to be tailored for diverse populations
Identify problems	• Listen to diverse voices (e.g., be generous with your time and attention) • Be curious (e.g., ask questions to find out what is most meaningful and relevant for your partners)
Adapt knowledge to the local context	• Employ strength-based approaches to identify how knowledge can be best developed and applied in a local setting • Integrate and prioritise local ways of knowing and being
Assess barriers to knowledge use	• Listen to those with lived experiences • Employ an iterative approach that enables reflection and learning from past experiences
Select, tailor, and implement interventions	• Ensure interventions are meaningful and relevant • Use a collaborative approach to decision-making
Monitor knowledge use	• Build capacity for all partners to gather and reflect on data • Use on-going, integrated approaches
Evaluate outcomes	• Build capacity for evaluation processes (e.g., designing evaluation tools, reviewing evaluation data) • Prioritise evaluation approaches that are meaningful and feasible
Sustain knowledge use	• Focus on building long-term partnerships grounded in mutual respect • Adopt iterative approaches that can evolve as partners' needs change

is not a one-time process. Rather, it is a lifelong, iterative process that requires reflection, adaptation, and humility. By embracing innovative approaches to knowledge design, implementation, and evaluation, we can enhance the quality of young players' experiences and the subsequent outcomes associated with talent identification and development in youth soccer.

References

Allan, V., Gainforth, H., Turnnidge, J., Konoval, T., Côté, J., & Latimer-Cheung, A. (2021). Narrative as a learning tool for coaches of athletes with a disability: Using stories to translate research into practice. *Physical Education and Sport Pedagogy*. https://doi.org/10.1080/17408989.2021.2006619

Bruner, M. W., McLaren, C. D., Sutcliffe, J. T., Gardner, L. A., & Vella, S. A. (2022). Conceptualizing and measuring positive youth development in sport: A scoping review. *International Review of Sport and Exercise Psychology*. https://doi.org/10.1080/1750984X.2022.2070861

Cumming, S. P., Lloyd, R. S., Oliver, J. L., Eisenmann, J. C., & Malina, R. M. (2017). Bio-banding in sport: Applications to competition, talent identification, and strength and conditioning of youth athletes. *Strength & Conditioning Journal*, *39*(2), 34–47. https://doi.org/10.1519/SSC.0000000000000281

Curran, O., MacNamara, Á., & Passmore, D. (2019). What about the girls? Exploring the gender data gap in talent development. *Frontiers in Sports and Active Living*, *1*, 3. https://doi.org/10.3389/fspor.2019.00003

Eccles, J. S., & Gootman, J. A. (2002). *Community programs to promote youth development*. National Academy Press.

Erikstad, M. K., Tore Johansen, B., Johnsen, M., Haugen, T., & Côté, J. (2021). "As many as possible for as long as possible"—A case study of a soccer team that fosters multiple outcomes. *The Sport Psychologist*, *35*(2), 131–141. https://doi.org/10.1123/tsp.2020-0107

Esmail, R., Hanson, H., Holroyd-Leduc, J., Brown, S., Strifler, L., Straus, S. E., Niven, D. J., & Clement, F. M. (2020). A scoping review of full-spectrum knowledge translation theories, models, and frameworks. *Implementation Science*, *15*, 11. https://doi.org/10.1186/s13012-020-0964-5

Field, B., Booth, A., Ilott, I., & Gerrish, K. (2014). Using the knowledge to action framework in practice: A citation analysis and systematic review. *Implementation Science*, *9*, 172. https://doi.org/10.1186/s13012-014-0172-2

Graham, I. D., Logan, J., Harrison, M. B., Straus, S. E., Tetroe, J., Caswell, W., & Robinson, N. (2006). Lost in knowledge translation: time for a map? *The Journal of Continuing Education in the Health Professions*, *26*(1), 13–24. https://doi.org/10.1002/chp.47

Holt, N. L., Camiré, M., Tamminen, K. A., Pankow, K., Pynn, S. R., Strachan, L., MacDonald, D. J., & Fraser-Thomas, J. (2018). PYDSportNET: A knowledge translation project bridging gaps between research and practice in youth sport. *Journal of Sport Psychology in Action*, *9*(2), 132–146. https://doi.org/10.1080/21520704.2017.1388893

Johnston, K., McAuley, A. B. T., Kelly, A. L., & Baker, J. (2023) Language games and blurry terminology: Can clarity enhance athlete development? *Frontiers in Sports and Active Living*, *5*, 1150047. https://doi.org/10.3389/fspor.2023.1150047

Kelly, A. L., Erickson, K., & Turnnidge, J. (2021). Youth sport in the time of COVID-19: Considerations for researchers and practitioners. *Managing Sport & Leisure*, *27*(1-2), 62–72. https://doi.org/10.1080/23750472.2020.1788975

Kelly, A. L., & Williams, C. A. (2020). Physical characteristics and the talent identification and development processes in youth soccer: A narrative review. *Strength and Conditioning Journal*, *42*(6), 15–34. https://doi.org/10.1519/SSC.0000000000000576

McAuley, A. B. T., Baker, J., & Kelly, A. L. (2021a). Defining "elite" status in sport: From chaos to clarity. *German Journal of Exercise and Sport Research*, *52*, 193–197. https://doi.org/10.1007/s12662-021-00737-3

McCalman, W., Crowley-McHattan, Z. J., Fransen, J., & Bennett, K. J. M. (2022). Skill assessments in youth soccer: A scoping review. *Journal of Sports Sciences*, *40*(6), 667–695. https://doi.org/10.1080/02640414.2021.2013617

Rechenchosky, L., Menezes Menegassi, V., de Oliveira Jaime, M., Borges, P. H., Sarmento, H., Mancha-Triguero, D., Serra-Olivares, J., & Rinaldi, W. (2021). Scoping review of tests to assess tactical knowledge and tactical performance of young soccer players. *Journal of Sports Sciences*, *39*(18), 2051–2067. https://doi.org/10.1080/02640414.2021.1916262

Rubin, C. L., Martinez, L. S., Chu, J., Hacker, K., Brugge, D., Pirie, A., Allukian, N., Rodday, A. M., & Leslie, L. K. (2012). Community-engaged pedagogy: A strengths-based approach to involving diverse stakeholders in research partnerships. *Progress in Community Health Partnerships: Research, Education, and Action*, *6*(4), 481–490. https://doi.org/10.1353/cpr.2012.0057

Straus, S., Tetroe, J., & Graham, I. D. (Eds.). (2013). *Knowledge translation in health care: Moving from evidence to practice* (2nd ed.). Wiley.

Tomasone, J. R., Flood, S. M., Latimer-Cheung, A. E., Faulkner, G., Duggan, M., Jones, R., Lane, K. N. Bevington, F., Carrier, J., Dolf, M., Doucette, K., Faught, E., Gierc, M., Giouridis, N., Gruber, R., Johnston, N., Kauffeldt, K. D., Kennedy, W., Lorbergs, A., Maclaren, K., Ross, R., Tytler, K., Walters,

A. J., Welsh, F., & Brouwers, M. C. (2020). Knowledge translation of the Canadian 24-Hour Movement Guidelines for Adults aged 18–64 years and Adults aged 65 years or older: A collaborative movement guideline knowledge translation process. *Applied Physiology, Nutrition, and Metabolism*, *45*(10), S103–S124. https://doi.org/10.1139/apnm-2020-0601

Turnnidge, J., & Côté, J. (2017). Transformational coaching workshop: Applying a person-centered approach to coach development programs. *International Sport Coaching Journal*, *4*, 314–325. https://doi.org/10.1123/iscj.2017-0046

Turnnidge, J., & Kelly, A. L. (2021). Organizational structures: Looking back and looking ahead. In A. L. Kelly, J. Côté, M. Jeffreys, & J. Turnnidge (Eds.), *Birth advantages and relative age effects in sport: Exploring organizational structures and creating appropriate settings* (pp. 239–246). Routledge.

United Nations. (n.d.). *Capacity-building* [online] Retrieved from: www.un.org/en/academic-impact/capacity-building [accessed 25th November 2022].

Verbeek, J., Lawrence, S., van der Breggen, J., Kelly, A. L., & Jonker, L. (2021). The average team age method and its potential to reduce relative age effects. In A. L. Kelly, J. Côté, M. Jeffreys, & J. Turnnidge (Eds.), *Birth advantages and relative age effects in sport: Exploring organizational structures and creating appropriate settings* (pp. 107–124). Routledge.

INDEX

Note: Page numbers in *italics* indicate a figure and page numbers in **bold** indicate a table.

3Ps and 4Cs *see* Personal Asset Framework
5Cs coaching model 69, *70*, 71; considerations for practitioners 77

ABC(DE) framework 286
achievement goal theory 189
ACTN3 R577X polymorphism 200
Africa 101, 135, 200
age at peak height velocity (APHV) 295; *see also* PHV
Aina, O. 159
Alarcón, F. 285
Allan, V. 341
American football 142
amputee 276, **277**, **281**, 287n2
Aquino, R. 282
Arab States 101
Arthur, C. 165, 185
Asia 101
average team age (ATA) 142; competitions, optimum age profile (mean + range) during *142*
ATA *see* average team age

B1TTI *see* Blind Soccer Technical and Tactical Instrument
Baker, Joseph 318; *see also* genetics in soccer; language and words used in soccer research and practice
Balish, S. 103
Barnes, C. 17
Barnsley FC Academy 158
Barnsley, R. H. 133

baseball and baseball players 132, 318
basketball and basketball players 38, 132, 238
Bass, B. 72, 185
Becker, M. 153
Bell, D. 114
Belling, P. 35
Bendall, Adam *see* para-soccer
Bennett, K. 35
Bergkamp, T. 23
Bergmann, Fynn *see* male talent pathways in soccer
bio-banded tournament 157–158; responses to six specific questions by players of contrasting maturity status to participation in *57*
bio-banding 5, 47, 55–58, 342; conclusions 61; EI and EE based on 222; focus on male participants 60; future studies needed on growing concept of 214; maturation classification **56**; RAEs and 143; technical performance measures of an U14 chronological age group competition compared to 85–90% bio-banded competition **58**
birth month distribution of U14 players selected into a male youth soccer development programme in Ireland *134*
birth quarters (BQ): female players 135, 137; male players 133–135; percentage of players selected onto a male youth soccer development programme within each BQ, compared to the expected national BQ distribution *134*; percentage of professional contracts awarded based on the total number of academy players within

each BQ, compared with the expected BQ distribution based on national norms *139*; optimum age profile (mean + range) during ATA competitions *142*; potential relative age solutions 141–143; senior soccer and transition 137–141
birth quartile distribution based on gender, age group, and qualification status in European U17, U19, and senior tournaments **138**
birth quartile distribution for competitive female soccer players in Ontario, Canada, aged 10–16 years (longitudinal, 1-year cohort) *136*
birth quartile distribution for recreational female soccer players in Ontario, Canada, aged 10–16 years (longitudinal, 1-year cohort) *137*
birth quartile distribution of the ten best male European professional soccer leagues *141*; percentage of professional contracts awarded based on the total number of academy players within each BQ, compared with the expected BQ distribution based on national norms *139*
blindness, inattentional 37, 42
blind soccer 11, 276, **277**, 278–289, 290n2; International Blind Sports Federation 279; Project B1 279
Blind Soccer Technical and Tactical Instrument (B1TTI) 280, **281**, 288
body fat 50, 51, 264; percentages 283
body mass index (BMI) and body mass 60, 199, 213, 215, 221–222
Boucher, J. 142
boundary conditions that coaches can manipulate to emphasise different creative components *173*
BQ *see* birth quarters
Braybrook, Kevin *see* male talent pathways in soccer
Brazil 18, 99, 104, 113, 140, 200; blind players in Brazil Championship 282; study of hydration in U18 male youth soccer players 220
Briggs, M. 213
Bruner, M. W. 85, 343; *see also* social influences on talent development in soccer
Bryson, A. 26

Calvo, Alberto Lorenzo *see* creativity in soccer
candidate gene association study (CGAS) 199–200, *204*
Cárdenas, D. 285
Cardoso, F. da S. L. 285
career transitions from youth team to first team 121–129; deselection and exit from academy system 123–124; loan transition 126–128; non-normative transitions 121; quasi-normative transitions 121; selected and deselected players, characteristics of 121–123; youth-to-senior transition 124–126
Carter, Jennie 220, 221; *see also* nutrition in soccer
CAS *see* Club Academy Scotland
CDF *see* Creativity Developmental Framework
cerebral palsy 276, **277**, **281**, 287n2
CGAS *see* candidate gene association study
China 101, 135, 200
Chinese male soccer players 137
Chinese Super League 17, 20
CLAS *see* Coach Leadership Assessment System
CLAS-GRS *see* Coach Leadership Assessment System—Global Rating Scale
Club Academy Scotland (CAS) 235
Coach Leadership Assessment System (CLAS) 9, 183, 186–189
Coach Leadership Assessment System—Global Rating Scale (CLAS-GRS) 9, 183, 189–192
coaching *see* transformational coaching
Cole, Matthew *see* nutrition in soccer
COM-B model 221
constraints *see* developmental constraints; personal constraints
constraints-based coaching 168
constraints-based developmental systems model 132
constraints-led approach 3
Cook, C. 122
cooking skills 221, 222
Côté, Jean 71, 112, 237, 331–333; *see also* DMSP; playing up and playing down; transformational coaching
countermovement jump (CMJ) **59**, **265**, 283, 297, **299–300**
Coutinho, Diogo *see* creativity in soccer
COVID-19 pandemic, impact on talent development in youth soccer 327–337; Personal Assets Framework (PAF) and 11–12, 328–335; re-imagining youth soccer talent development systems 328–331; tensions between stakeholders 333–335
Creative Soccer Platform, The *see* The Creative Soccer Platform (TCSP)
creativity in soccer 167–180; creativity comprehensive frameworks 168–170; creativity-supportive learning environments 174–178; small-sided games (SSG) and 171–176; using *variability* to spark 172–174; *see also* CDF; Skills4Genius; SSG; TCSP
Creativity Developmental Framework (CDF) 168, 175, 179; structure *168*
Crisis Resource Management global rating scale 189
Cumming, S. 56

Da Silva, E. S. 283, 288
Datson, N. 264, **265**

Davids, K. 3, 317
deaf 276, **277**, **281**, 287n2
defenders 38, 140–141, 160, 387, 296–298
Dehghansai, N. 278, 287
Demands, Resources, and Individual Effects (DRIVE) model 126–127, *127*
Deprez, D. 50–51
deselection 2, 6; avoiding early deselection 141; career transitions involving 73, 74, 121; elite female youth soccer, further research needed into 271; exit from academy system and 123–124; four phases of 74; high- and low-order themes describing coach perceptions of the deselection process in girls' competitive youth sport **75**; how and why RAEs evolve over process of 143; 'reselected' and 'deselected' players for coach subjective ratings of 'skill' attributes **25**; *see also* selection, deselection and dropout
Deutscher Fußball-Bund (DFB) 98, 230; Talent Development Program 231
developmental constraints 235–236
Developmental Model of Sport Participation (DMSP) 112, 237–238; soccer trajectories within *112*
DFB *see* Deutscher Fußball-Bund
Dickson, Alban C. S. *see* psychosocial growth, development, and potential challenges in youth soccer
DMSP *see* Developmental Model of Sport Participation
DRIVE model *see* Demands, Resources, and Individual Effects (DRIVE) model
dropout (youth soccer) 6, 132, 143, 154; 'early specialisation' and 320; grade retention and 157; playing down and 158; playing up and 160, 162; women and girls 270; *see also* selection, deselection and dropout
Dugdale, James H. *see* male talent pathways in soccer; psychosocial growth, development, and potential challenges in youth soccer; technical issues in developmental outcomes and career progression, subjective and objective performance parameters contributing to
Dunn, J. 68, 70, 122

early sampling 6; athlete development and **111**, 111–114, **115**
early specialisation 6; advantage 110–111; pros and cons of **115**; as term, defining defining 320–322, 323
e-Delphi poll: agreed player attributes resulting from **23**; agreed position-specific attributes resulting from **24**
EE *see* energy expenditure

EI *see* energy intake
'Elite Player Performance Plan' (EPPP) 98, 230, 232
Emmonds, Stacey 51; *see also* gender in soccer
energy expenditure (EE) 212–213, **215–216;** bio-banding and assessing 222; strategies to assess and address 223
energy intake (EI) 212–213, **215–216;** bio-banding and assessing 222; strategies to assess and address 223
England 10, 26; 2018 World Cup 160; first and second division leagues, study on 295; male youth academy soccer players, dietary research studies on 221; male talent pathways in soccer in 128, 229–230, **240**, **250**; Kelly's study of socioeconomic status of academy soccer players from 99; national coach education curriculum 230; playing-up in youth soccer, findings regarding 153–154; RAEs in 133–134, 139–140; Sport England 279; U9–U16 academy 21, 160; U10 male academy 20; White's study on goalkeepers in professional matches in 307
English Football Association (FA) 230, 278–280
English Football League academy 58, **59**
English Premier Academy League 101
English Premier League 17, 35, 97–98, 122; 'Elite Player Performance Plan' (EPPP) 98, 230, 232
EPPP *see* 'Elite Player Performance Plan'
Erickson, Karl *see* COVID-19
Erikstad, M. K. 113
Eveleigh, Chris *see* male talent pathways in soccer

'family observation schedule' 189
FDP *see* Foundation Development Phase
Fédération Française de Football (FFF) 98
Fédération Internationale de Football Association (FIFA) 235, 263
feet exchange, concept of 101
female soccer players: ACL injury rates 55; bio-banding, influence on 60; birth quartile distribution for competitive female soccer players in Ontario, Canada, aged 10–16 years (longitudinal, 1-year cohort) *136*; birth quartile distribution for recreational female soccer players in Ontario, Canada, aged 10–16 years (longitudinal, 1-year cohort) *137*; Bruner's research findings on 85; Canada 102, 154; coach and social influences on 73; female youth soccer, RAEs and 133, 135–138; FIFA's pledged support of 263; genetics 199, 203; Germany 113; goalkeepers 295, 296, 308; Güllich's research findings 113; ingroup effect on 85; maturation,

assessing 48; Netherlands 237; nutrition 10, 212, 221–222; physiological and motor determinants of future playing success, elite level 18, **265**; prosocial and antisocial behaviors in 85; RAEs 7, 133, 135–138, 140–144; schematic representation of decision-making process practitioners can employ in the field to help focus training for *268*; sprints and CODS, assessing 52; Scotland 235; strength and power, assessing 51; Täuber and Sassenberg's research findings on 85; underrepresentation and underreporting of, in research literature 1, 28, 140, 143, 269, 221, 223, 342; US professional players, demographics of 99; Van Maarseveen's research findings on 36; Youth Physical Development model 53, *54*; *see also* gender

Fenner, J. 20

Ferguson, Matthew *see* male talent pathways in soccer; pathways of athlete development in youth soccer

FFF *see* Fédération Française de Football

field theory 6, 84, 92

FIFA *see* Fédération Internationale de Football Association

Finnegan, Laura 102, 133; *see also* male talent pathways in soccer; relative age effects (RAE)

Finn, J. 125

Finn, Stephen *see* male talent pathways in soccer

flexible chronological approach (FCA) 142; conceptualizing 159–161

footedness in soccer 25–27

Ford, P. R. 111, 113

Forsman, H. 111, 122

forwards (soccer position) 86, 141, 295–298

Foundation Development Phase (FDP) (U9–U11) 19, 154, 161, 230; age group mean values and *z*-scores across PCE 'during' and 'post' tests *36*; 'lower potentials' within 21; match analysis statistics, including *z*-scores and *t*-tests based on age phase (i.e., FDP and YDP) and non-standardised means based on age group (i.e., U9–U16) **22**; technical test results, including *z*-scores and *t*-tests based on age phase (i.e., FDP and YDP) and non-standardised means based on age group (i.e., U9–U16) **19**

Four Corner Model (FCM) 3, 152–155, *156*, 230, 278, 280; interdisciplinary considerations 287, 289; para-soccer and 280, 287, 289; YDP and 161–162

France: Charte du Football Professionnel 98; Fédération Française de Football (FFF) 98; Ford's research findings on specialization of players from 113; Ligue 1 *141*; Ligue de Football Professionnel (LPF) 98; RAE in 133, 140

Francis, John W. *see* para-soccer

Full-Range Leadership Model 9, 183–184, *184*, 186, 189–191

Gabbett, T. J. 285

game-based: rules 170; scenarios 5; situations 34, 37–38, 41, 171, 172; simulation tests 42

Gamonales, J. 280, 282

Gantois, P. 285

García-Calvo, T. 90

gender in soccer (women and girls' soccer) 263–271; growth and physical maturation 263–266; psychosocial considerations 269–270; RAE and talent development 266–268; talent identification 264–266

genetics in soccer 3, 9, 197–205; candidate gene association study (CGAS) 199–200, *204*; genome-wide association study (GWAS) 200, 204, 204; heritability of soccer characteristics 198–199; molecular genetics and 198–203; practical applications of 203–204; principle concepts in 197–198; progress of genetic research in soccer *202*; prominent characteristics of genetic research in soccer *204*

genome-wide association study (GWAS) 200, 204, 205

Germany 10, 18–19, 228, 230–231, **241**, **250–251**; Bundesliga team 140, *141*; Deutscher Fußball-Bund (DFB) 98; relative age effects in male youth soccer 133

Gibraltar 10, 228, 232–231, **241–242**, **251–252**, 257

Gibraltar Football Association (GFA) 232, **251**

Giusti, N. 114

Gledhill, Adam *see* gender in soccer

goalkeepers (GKs) 11, 20, 111; 4 x 4 with 171; German 140; RAEs and 141; position data gap in talent development of 294–311; talent development of 298–308; summary of talent development literature for GKs **304**; summary of talent identification literature for GKs **299**; summary of performance tracking literature for GKs **309**

talent identification of 294–298; underrepresentation in technical literature 28

goal scoring opportunities in soccer 51; variables related to **58**

Goldman, Daniel E. 153–156; *see also* playing up and playing down

Gough, Lewis *see* nutrition in soccer

grade retention 157

growth and maturation 48–50

growth spurt: in boys compared to girls 61; example of Olympic-style weightlifting

activities in players prior to *266*; injury risk 42, 55, 60; PHV and 49–50; pre-pubertal 52
Güllich, A. 113
GWAS *see* genome-wide association study

Halliwell, W. 142
Hancock, D. 132, 331–333
Hannon, M. 212–213, **219**
Harwood, C. G. 76, 267–269; *see also* 5Cs
heavy training 213–214, **219**
Helsen, W. 142–143
Holt, N. 68, 70, 122, 341
Höner, Olivier **265**; *see also* male talent pathways in soccer
Huijgen, B. 18, 122

identification, selection, and development process in soccer, key elements 2
India 10, 228, 233–234, **252–253**
ingroup effect 85
injury risk, influence of maturation on 55
Ireland, Republic of 10, 228, 234–235, **244**, **253–254**; birth month distribution of U14 players selected into a male youth soccer development programme in *134*
Italy 18, 86, 103, 235, 236; map of regions of *103*; Serie A *141*

Jiménez Sáiz, Sergio L. *see* creativity in soccer
Jonker, Laura *see* male talent pathways in soccer

Kalyuga, S. 285
Kannekens, R. 37
Keegan, R. 89
Keller, B. 18, 35
Kelly, Adam L. 18–20, 36, 133–134, 139, 153–155, 159; *see also* career transitions from youth team to first team; COVID-19 pandemic; creativity in soccer; gender in soccer; genetics in soccer; goalkeeper; para-soccer; knowledge to action; language and words used in soccer research and practice; male talent pathways in soccer; maturity status, influence on physical performance; nutrition in soccer; pathways of athlete development in youth soccer; playing up and playing down; psychosocial growth, development, and potential challenges in youth soccer; relative age effects; social influences on talent development in soccer; sociocultural influences on talent development in soccer; tactical knowledge and performance in youth soccer players; talent identification and development in youth soccer; technical issues in developmental outcomes and career progression, subjective and objective performance parameters contributing to; transformational coaching
Kent, Sofie *see* career transitions from youth team to first team
Kim, J. 189
Khamis, H. 49
Klopp, Jürgen 174
knowledge to action: on moving from research to action in youth soccer 339–343
Knowledge to Action (KTA) framework 339–343; considerations for practitioners **345**
KTA *see* Knowledge to Action (KTA) framework
Kulik C. L. C. 153
Kulik, J. A. 153

language and words used in soccer research and practice 316–324; 'early specialisation', defining 320–322, 323; 'elite', defining 319–320, 322; language games in 316–316; 'talent', concept of and defining 317–219, 322
Larkin, P. 22–23, 37
laterality 25–27
Lawrason, S. 188
Lee, T. D. 110
Lefebvre, Jordan S. 188; *see also* transformational coaching
LEGO Serious Play methodology 174–175, *177*
Lewin, K. 6, 84, 92
Ligue de Football Professionnel (LPF) 98
Lingard, Jesse 158
Lloyd, R. S. 53; *see also* YPD model
Loughborough Short Passing Test 18
LPF *see* Ligue de Football Professionnel
Lupo, C. 140

Maguire, Harry 156–157
Major League Soccer (MLS)(United States) 237; Next league 238; Super Draft 237
male talent pathways in soccer 228–258; Canada 228–229; contextual and methodological considerations for researchers and practitioners based on country, summary table **249–257**; England 229–230, **240**, **250**; evaluation of male talent pathways based on country, summary table **239–248**; Germany 230–231, **241**, **250–251**; Gibraltar 232–233, **241–242**, **251–252**, 257; India 228, 233–234, **252–253**; Ireland 228, 234–235, **244**, **253–254**; Netherlands 236–237, **246–247**, **255–256**; Scotland 226, 235–236, **245–246**, **254–255**, 257; United States 237–237, **248**, **256–257**
Manchester City FC 98
Manchester United FC 156–157
Martínez-Moreno, A. 186

Martin, Luc 86; *see also* social influences on talent development in soccer
Matthews, Alysha *see* COVID-19
maturity status, influence on physical performance 47–61; bio-banding and 55–58; growth and maturation 48–50; injury risk, influence of maturation on 55; influence of maturation on physical performance 50–53; trainability of physical qualities 53–54
McAuley, Alexander B. T. 322; *see also* genetics in soccer; pathways of athlete development in youth soccer
McCalman, W. 19
McClaren, Colin D. 111, 114; *see also* social influences on talent development in soccer
McGucken, M. 188
Memmert, Daniel 37–41
Messi, Lionel *170*
midfielders **24**, 38, 141, 295–296, 298; central **24**, 26
Mills, A. 122
MLS *see* Major League Soccer (United States)
Moon, S. 153
moral behaviour 85, 86
Morawska, A. 189
Morganti, G. 103
Morris, Robert 128; *see also* career transitions from youth team to first team
Mujika, I. **265**
Murata, Alex 112, 115; *see also* pathways of athlete development in youth soccer; psychosocial growth, development, and potential challenges in youth soccer
Myer, G. D. 110

National Emerging Talent Programme (NETP) 279–280
National Women's Super League (NWSL) 99
Neely, Kacey C. 74; *see also* psychosocial growth, development, and potential challenges in youth soccer
Netherlands 236–237, **246–247**, **255–256**
NETP *see* National Emerging Talent Programme
Newell, K. 278
North America: baseball players 318; female youth soccer statistics 135; ice hockey 132; pay to play models in 257
Northern Ireland 235
North, Matthew *see* nutrition in soccer
novem system 142
nutrition in soccer 212–223; barriers and enablers in 220–221; carbohydrate intake 215; dietary intake 212–214; female players 221–222; hydration needs 215–220; nutrition support for soccer players, key practical decisions in *222*; protein intake 214–220

OASSIS *see* Online Assessment of Strategic Skill in Soccer
occlusion displays for PCE tests *36*
Oliver, Jon L.: YPD model 53, *54*; *see also* maturity status, influence on physical performance
Online Assessment of Strategic Skill in Soccer (OASSIS) 35
overinvolved parents 76

PAF *see* Personal Assets Framework
PAH *see* predicted adult height
PAHA *see* predicted adult height attained
para-soccer 1, 3 10–11, 276–290; impairment-specific squads **277–278**
Parreira, R. 283
partially sighted 276, **277**, **281**, 287n2
pathways of athlete development in youth soccer 109–117; contemporary issues and concerns 114–115; early sampling and athlete development **111**, 111–114; early specialisation advantage 110–111; pros and cons of early specialision and early sampling **115**
PCDEQ *see* Psychological Characteristics for Developing Excellence Questionnaire
PCE tests *see* perceptual-cognitive expertise (PCE) tests, occlusion displays for *36*
peak-height velocity (PHV) 48–56, 60; age at peak height velocity (APHV) 295; girls and women 264–269, 272; goalkeepers 295; post- 60, 265; pre- 56, 60
perceptual-cognitive expertise (PCE) tests 34–37, 41; age group mean values and *z*-scores across PCE 'during' and 'post' tests *36*; occlusion displays for *36*
Performance Management Application (PMA) 230
performer constraints 203, 204, 205
Personal Assets Framework (PAF) 11–12, 328–335; 3Ps 161, 328–333, **334**, 335–335; 4Cs 161, 328–333, **334**, 335–336; sample quotes from each stakeholder when reflecting on the aspects of the PAF **334**; three dynamic elements of 12
PHV *see* peak-height velocity
physical considerations *see* maturity status, influence on physical performance
Pierce, Scott *see* COVID-19
Plass, J. 285
playing up and playing down 8, 56, 58, 152–162; flexible chronological approach (FCA), conceptualizing 159–161; playing down 157–159; playing down case study 158–159; playing up 153–157; playing up case study 156–157
PMA *see* Performance Management Application
Portugal 18–19; Primeira Liga *141*; soccer players from 35, 113, 212, 297

Powerchair 276, **278**, **282**
predicted adult height (PAH) 50, **59**
predicted adult height attained (PAHA) 56, **59**, 241
Primeira Liga *141*
professional career: 'leg drain' 101
professional contract: Deprez's study of Belgian youth players 50–51; endurance as distinguishing factor in receiving 51; England 230; English youth soccer, percentages of 98; four general dimensions of mental toughness linked to 122–123; Netherlands 237; percentage awarded based on the total number of academy players within each BQ, compared with the expected BQ distribution based on national norms *139*; relatively younger athletes achieving 137, 139–140; Scotland 235–236; sprint as distinguishing factor in receiving 51; summary of non-zero coefficients for the likelihood of signing **123**
psychological support *see* psychosocial growth, development, and potential challenges in youth soccer
Psychological Characteristics for Developing Excellence Questionnaire (PCDEQ) 99
psychosocial growth, development, and potential challenges in youth soccer 67–77; influence of external stakeholders on 71–73; psychosocial development *68*, 68–71; selection, deselection and dropout in 73–76
psychosocial competencies associated with soccer success during adolescence, overview of concepts, sub-categories, and categories pertaining to *68*
psychosocial skills in youth soccer using the '5Cs', examples of how to promote the development of *70*
'PYDSportNET' 341
Pygmalion effect 132

Radnor, John M. *see* maturity status, influence on physical performance
RAEs *see* relative age effects (RAE)
Rasmussen, L. 177, 178
reactive strength index (RSI) 283
Rational Emotive Behavior Therapy 286
Read, P. J. 114
Rebelo-González-Víllora, R. 297, **299**
Rechenchosky, L. 34, 41
Rector, K. 286–287
redshirting 157
Reeves, Matthew J. *see* sociocultural influences on talent development in soccer; technical issues in developmental outcomes and career progression, subjective and objective performance parameters contributing to

relative age effects (RAE) 7, 132–144, 152; goalkeepers and 296; increasing awareness of 295; moderating 158–160; talent development and 266
relative age fair cycle system 142
'reselected' and 'deselected' players for coach subjective ratings of 'skill' attributes **25**
resting metabolic rate (RMR) 214
RMR *see* resting metabolic rate
Robertson, M. 321
Roberts, Simon J. 23; *see also* sociocultural influences on talent development in soccer
Roche, A. 49
rugby 132, 172
Runswick, O. 280

Sampaio, Jaime *see* creativity in soccer
Santos, Sara 171–172, 174; *see also* creativity in soccer
Sassenberg, K. 85
Sayler, M. 153
Schmidt, R. 110
Scotland 19, 226, 235–236, **245–246**, **254–255**, 257; Club Academy Scotland (CAS) 235; RAE in 133
selection, deselection and dropout in youth soccer 73–76
self-determination theory 189
sexual age and maturation 48; delayed 213
Shanmugaratnam, Achuthan *see* social influences on talent development in soccer
Sieghartsleitner, E. 111
Simard, Mathieu *see* social influences on talent development in soccer
Sims, Dave *see* para-soccer
Singapore Sports Academy 185
skeletal age 48
skeletal muscle fibres 202
skeletal muscle mass 199
Skills4Genius 8, 167, 168, 174–176, 180; practice design *175*; practice design applied in soccer *177*
small-sided games (SSG) 171–176, 250; 4 vs 4 20–21, 171, 172; 6 vs 6 172; 7 vs 4 171; Germany **248**; goalkeeper training using 303, **304–305**, **309**, 311; Skills4Genius 174, *175*, 176, *177*; as training approach, use of 168
Smith, A. L. 73
Smith, Kristy L. 102, 135–136, 140; *see also* relative age effects (RAE)
Smith, N. 189
soccer trajectories within the Developmental Model of Sport Participation *112*
social agents 6, 61, 73, 84, 89, 132, 328
Social Agents model 132

social and cultural influences on soccer *see* sociocultural influences on talent development in soccer
social identity 85–86, 92
Social Identity Theory (SIT) 85
social influences on talent development in soccer 6, 20, 27, 84–92; group cohesion 87–89; identity leadership 86–87; implications for talent development 91; motivational climate 89–90; social identity 85–86
social psychology 86
sociocultural influences on talent development in soccer 6, 97–105; birthplace effects 102–104; contextual overview 97–98; cultural backgrounds 100–101; gender as 10; sociodemographic influences 98–100
sociodemographic influences 98–100
social support 67
somatic age 48
somatic maturity 49
'Southern question' *see* Italy
sprint fatigue index, based on talent development pathway and timing of visual impairment *284*
SSG *see* small-sided games (SSG)
Stones, John 158–160
Steenbergen-Hu, S. 153
street soccer 175, 248
student-designed games 174, *175*
Suraci, Bruce *see* genetics in soccer

Tactical Creativity Approach (TCA) 168
tactical knowledge and performance in youth soccer players, developing 34–42; tactical knowledge 35–37; tactical performance 37–38; virtual reality in 38–41
talent identification and development in youth soccer: disciplinary approaches that can be applied to *4*; introduction to and overview of 1–12
Tanner staging 48
task and social cohesion among recreational soccer athletes of coaches trained to promote a task-related motivational climate (MAC) and controls (AC and Control) *90*
task cohesion, psychological need satisfaction, and positive youth development outcomes in youth soccer *88*
Täuber 85
TCSP *see* The Creative Soccer Platform
Teaching Games for Understanding (TGfU) 168, 175
technical issues in developmental outcomes and career progression, subjective and objective performance parameters contributing to 17–29; indicators of potential and recruiter perspectives 22–25; laterality 25–27; laterality case study 27; performance analysis 20–22; technical testing 18–20
TGfU *see* Teaching Games for Understanding
The Creative Soccer Platform (TCSP) 8, 167, 174, 177–179; description of TCSP assumptions applied in youth soccer teams **178**
Thomas, Chris 56
Toms, Martin R. *see* pathways of athlete development in youth soccer
Till, Kevin *see* relative age effects
Towlson, C. 3
transformational coaching 183–192; Coach Leadership Assessment System (CLAS) 9, 183, 186–189; Coach Leadership Assessment System—Global Rating Scale (CLAS-GRS) 9, 183, 189–192; Full-Range Leadership Model *184*; global rating 189
Tsai, W. 38
Tuchel, Thomas 174
Turnnidge, Jennifer 186, 188; *see also* knowledge to action; playing up and playing down; transformation coaching

U9–U16 21, 27, 133, 139; age group mean values and z-scores across PCE 'during' and 'post' tests **36**; Canada 229; FDP phase 19, 36, 154, 230; match analysis statistics, including z-scores and t-tests based on age phase (i.e., FDP and YDP) and non-standardised means based on age group (i.e., U9–U16) **22**; technical test results, including z-scores and t-tests based on age phase (i.e., FDP and YDP) and non-standardised means based on age group (i.e., U9–U16) **19**; YDP phase 154
U9: coach-led practice 321; 'elite' 319
U10: Fenner's evaluation of 20
U14: birth month distribution of U14 players selected into a male youth soccer development programme in Ireland 133, *134*; Ireland 234; Norway 113; protein intake 214; technical performance measures of an U14 chronological age group competition compared to 85–90% bio-banded competition **58**
U16 213, 229, 234, 235
U16–U20 training to compete 229
U17: birth quartile distribution based on gender, age group, and qualification status in European U17, U19, and senior tournaments **138**
underdog hypothesis 7, 56, 58, 139–140, 144
United States 99, 237–238, **256–257**; *see also* Major League Soccer (MLS)

Vaeyens, R. 18
Vahia, Durva *see* goalkeeper; male talent pathways in soccer
Van Maarseveen, M. 36
variability: creativity sparked by 172–174
Vella, S. 185
Velten, M. 286
Verbeek, Jan *see* male talent pathways in soccer; technical issues in developmental outcomes and career progression, subjective and objective performance parameters contributing to
Vescovi, J. **265**
virtual environments *39, 40*
virtual reality and tactical knowledge 38–41

Ward, P. 35
Wattie, Nick 28, 132; *see also* language and words used in soccer research and practice
Wekesser, Meredith M. *see* COVID-19
Welbeck, Danny 158
Williams, A. M. 98
Williams, Craig A. 2; *see also* maturity status, influence on physical performance
Williams, M. A. 35, 118
Wilson, Mark R. *see* tactical knowledge and performance in youth soccer players

wingers 26
Wood, Andrew *see* para-soccer
Wood, Greg 39; *see also* tactical knowledge and performance in youth soccer players
words used in soccer *see* language and words used in soccer research and practice
Wright, Matthew *see* gender in soccer

YDP *see* Youth Development Phase
Youth Development Phase (YDP) (U12–U16) 19, 21, 230; age group mean values across PCE **36**; Four Corner Model and 161; match analysis statistics **22**; technical test results, including *z*-scores and *t*-tests based on age phase (i.e., FDP and YDP) and non-standardised means based on age group (i.e., U9–U16) **19**
Youth Physical Development model: females 54; males *53*
youth-to-senior transition 98, 122, 124–127, 236, 270; individual, external, culture model of *126*

Zhou, C. 17
Zuber, C. 122
Zucchermaglio, C. 86

Printed in the United States
by Baker & Taylor Publisher Services